Financial Accounting

Financial Accounting: Practice and Principles

Third Edition

**By Jan Bebbington, Rob Gray
and Richard Laughlin**

THOMSON

Australia • Canada • Mexico • Singapore • Spain • United Kingdom • United States

THOMSON

Financial Accounting: Practice and Principles – 3ʳᵈ Edition

For more information, contact Thomson Learning, High Holborn House, 50-51 Bedford Row, London WC1R 4LR or visit us on the World Wide Web at: http://www.thomsonlearning.co.uk

British Library Cataloguing-in-Publication Data
A catalogue record for this book is available from the British Library

ISBN 1-86152-771-3

First edition published by Van Nostrand Reinhold (International) Co. Ltd 1988
Reprinted 1989, 1994
Second edition by International Thomson Business Press 1996
Third edition 2001
Reprinted 2004 by Thomson Learning

Typeset by Saxon Graphics Ltd, Derby
Printed in Singapore by Seng Lee Press

Contents

Preface   xi

Part I   Background and Introductory Ideas   1

1   What is accounting? And why study it anyway?   **3**

   1.1   Introduction   3

   1.2   What is accounting?   6

   1.3   Accounting and financial accounting   12

   1.4   Studying to be a professional?   16

   Summary   20

   Key terms and concepts   20

   Further reading   21

   Notes   21

2   Cash, cashbooks and units of account   **22**

   2.1   Introduction   22

   2.2   The case of Mr Brain – a student   23

   2.3   Analysis of Mr Brain's cashbook   31

   2.4   Some lessons from Mr Brain   35

   Summary   37

   Key terms and concepts   38

   Further reading   38

   Notes   39

**3   Organizations, organizational subsystems and the flows of double-entry
   bookkeeping**   **40**

   3.1   Introduction   40

   3.2   Types of organizations   42

   3.3   Characteristics of organizational types   44

   3.4   Organizations, systems and accounting   47

   3.5   Mr Brain and this systems view   54

   Summary   58

   Key terms and concepts   59

Further reading   60

Notes   60

Part II   Bookkeeping and Accounting Records   61

**4 Organizational flows: a categorization of basic transactions, accounting
   records and double-entry bookkeeping**   **63**

4.1 Introduction   63

4.2 Eight types of accounting transactions   72

4.3 Some further points about commercial and non-commercial
     organizations   78

Summary   81

Key terms and concepts   82

Further reading   82

Notes   82

**5 Putting the eight basic transactions to work, producing the accounting
   records and an initial trial balance**   **83**

5.1 Introduction   83

5.2 A detailed worked example: Bird Industries Ltd   84

5.3 The initial trial balance   99

Summary   102

Key terms and concepts   103

Further reading   104

Notes   104

Appendix 5: Single-entry bookkeeping and the spreadsheet   104

**6 The accounting information system: organizing and controlling the
   accounting records**   **107**

6.1 Introduction   107

6.2 Capturing the accounting data   112

6.3 Organizing the accounting records   114

6.4 Controlling the accounting records   119

Summary   126

Key terms and concepts   126

Further reading   126

Notes   127

**7 The trial balance and categorization: the accounting conventions,
   assets, liabilities, revenues, expenses, provisions and reserves**   **128**

7.1 Introduction   128

7.2   Categorizing the trial balance entries   132

7.3   The accounting conventions   137

7.4   The accounting conventions and the basic categories   143

7.5   So what are end-of-period adjustments?   149

Summary   150

Key terms and concepts   151

Further reading   151

Notes   151

Part III   End-of-period Adjustments and the Financial Statements   153

**8   Accruals, prepayments and general provisions and an introduction
to the production and format of the profit and loss account
and balance sheet   153**

8.1   Introduction   153

8.2   What are accruals, prepayments, income in advance and general
provisions?   157

8.3   A worked example with accruals, prepayments and provisions   161

8.4   Laying out the profit and loss account and balance sheet   169

Summary   171

Key terms and concepts   172

Further reading   172

Notes   172

Appendix 8A: The basic T-accounts for Yothu Yindi Ltd, 2001   174

Appendix 8B: End-of-period adjustments for Yothu Yindi Ltd without
using the extended trial balance – using only T-accounts   176

9   Depreciation of fixed assets and profits and losses on disposal   179

9.1   Introduction   179

9.2   Calculating depreciation   181

9.3   The bookkeeping for depreciation   187

9.4   Yothu Yindi Ltd: fixed assets and depreciation   193

9.5   The disposal of fixed assets   197

9.6   A worked example on depreciation and disposals of fixed assets   199

9.7   Issues arising with depreciation   199

Summary   202

Further reading   202

Key terms and concepts   203

Notes   203

Appendix 9: The new financial statement for Yothu Yindi Ltd, 2001   203

10   Stock allocation, valuation and the cost of sales   **207**

10.1   Introduction   207

10.2   The valuation of stock and inventory: the simple case   212

10.3   The valuation of stock and inventory: the more complex cases   220

10.4   An illustration of stock end-of-period adjustments   224

Summary   234

Key terms and concepts   235

Further reading   235

Notes   235

11   Bad and doubtful debts (and another look at provisions)   **237**

11.1   Introduction   237

11.2   Accounting for bad and doubtful debts   238

11.3   Provisions revisited and the 'accounting decisions'   246

Summary   249

Further reading   249

Key terms and concepts   250

Notes   250

12   From the trial balance to the financial statements: ownership claims, profit, appropriations and social reality   **251**

12.1   Introduction   251

12.2   Ownership claims   254

12.3   The published profit and loss account and balance sheet   266

12.4   Starting to think about financial statements   267

Summary   271

Key terms and concepts   272

Further reading   272

Notes   273

13   Partnerships   **275**

13.1   Introduction   275

13.2   Partnership capital and current accounts   277

13.3   Further partnership issues   286

13.4   Thinking about financial accounting – again   290

Summary   292

Key terms and concepts   292

Further reading 292

Notes 293

Appendix 13: Full T-accounts and financial statements for the
Jeopardy Partnership 294

14 Accounting regulation and company accounts 297

14.1 Introduction 297

14.2 An overview of the regulation of financial accounting 300

14.3 Introduction to company law and the format of company accounts 305

14.4 Pronouncements by the professional accountancy bodies 316

14.5 Other regulations and the regulation of non-company organizations 322

Summary 323

Key terms and concepts 324

Further reading 325

Notes 325

Part IV Beyond the Profit and Loss Account and Balance Sheet 327

**15 Reading the financial statements and annual report: cash flow
analysis and interpreting financial numbers 329**

15.1 Introduction 329

15.2 Company liquidity and cash flow 331

15.3 The cash flow statement 334

15.4 Reading the financial statements 346

15.5 Ratio analysis 350

Summary 363

Key terms and concepts 364

Further reading 364

Notes 364

16 Accounting for changing prices: an introduction 366

16.1 Introduction 366

16.2 The effect of changing prices on financial statements:
a worked example 370

16.3 Methods of asset valuation (and expense determination) 375

16.4 Concepts of capital maintenance 379

16.5 Accounting for changing prices and the accounting profession 383

16.6 Some further refinements 384

16.7 A review, summary and some concluding remarks on accounting
for changing prices 387

	Key terms and concepts	390
	Further reading	390
	Notes	390
17	**Expanding the reporting function: social and environmental accounting and reporting**	**391**
	17.1 Introduction	391
	17.2 Disclosures in company annual reports	393
	17.3 Social accounting and reporting	398
	17.4 Environmental accounting and reporting	403
	17.5 The pros and contras of SEAR	406
	Summary	406
	Key terms and concepts	408
	Further reading	408
	Notes	408
18	**Thinking about accounting: theoretical perspectives on financial accounting and reporting**	**410**
	18.1 Introduction	410
	18.2 Data-oriented approach	414
	18.3 Decision usefulness approach	418
	18.4 Organizational resource approach	424
	18.5 An evaluation of the alternatives	426
	Summary	430
	Key terms and concepts	430
	Further reading	431
	Notes	431
Part V	**Where Have We Been? Where Do We Go Next?**	433
19	**Where have we been? Where do we go next?**	**435**
	19.1 Looking back over the course	435
	19.2 Looking forward	438
	19.3 Education and the accounting profession	439
	Notes	440
	References	441
	Index	445

Preface

This is the third edition of what was formerly *Financial Accounting: Method and Meaning*. Given the 'method and meaning' series has been discontinued the text has been renamed as *Financial Accounting: Practice and Principles*. The new title, we believe, accurately identifies the key elements of the text. That is, at the core of this text is the dual aim of communicating both how to **do** accounting and how one may **think about the doing** of accounting. In addition, we have sought to weave throughout the text (as well as the students' workbook and teachers' manual) teaching development ideas which aim to prompt both teachers and students to **think about how one goes about the teaching and learning** activity.

The essence of our approach to introductory financial accounting involves three elements. First, an organizational flow model is introduced to local financial accounting activities in its organizational context. Second, this model is used to derive a system-based (and systematic and logical) approach to bookkeeping and the construction of financial statements. Third, whilst in no way playing down the importance of the techniques of financial accounting and bookkeeping, the text makes an explicit attempt to forge a link between a traditional techniques-oriented approach to introductory financial accounting and the wider issues of accounting theory.

Our aim has always been to ensure that students can do the accounting expected of them but also start to gain an appreciation of the wider issues they will eventually consider in their study of accounting. We firmly believe that if the uncertainties of accounting are not introduced at the introductory stage then students are likely be more resistant to thinking about accounting at later stages of their education. In addition, and on a more positive note, we also believe that introducing the uncertainties and controversies surrounding accounting at an early stage enhances students' enjoyment of accounting and makes it a more interesting topic to study. Indeed, between publishing the second edition of this text and the current one, our approach to introductory financial accounting won Dundee University's award for innovative teaching (apologies for the self-promotion – but we do think it is telling that the judges were impressed that we managed to make accounting interesting and thereby encouraged 'deep' learning in our students).

This edition of the text is firmly embedded on the format of the second. We have modified some elements of the chapters in light of the feedback received from students and from those who have used the text over the last five years and we believe that the text runs a little more 'smoothly' as a result. We have updated worked examples where it seemed appropriate and have sought to provide more contemporary examples of financial accounting and reporting practice within the text. In addition, we have substantially rewritten Chapter 17 (on social and environmental accounting and reporting) to reflect the massive growth in practice and research in that area while ensuring that the chapter remains a concise introduction to what is now a very complex field in its own right.

We would like to thank in advance all those who use the text and we hope you enjoy it. As authors, we should be only too pleased to hear comments, queries and suggestions from you. Our principal objective in writing this text is to offer a way of teaching introductory financial accounting that is interesting for the lecturer and which is interesting, stimulating and productive for the students. We wish you a happy and productive educational experience.

Acknowledgements

In addition to those people who we thanked in the first and second editions of this text we wish to express our sincere gratitude to those who continue to use this text and who have provided feedback to us over the years. We would like to acknowledge the encouragement and patience of Jennifer Pegg of Thomson Learning as well as Michael Fitch (the copy editor on this edition). In addition, we would like to thank those who, at various times, listened to us obsessing about bookkeeping, accounting and deadlines.

Jan Bebbington (University of Aberdeen)
Rob Gray (University of Glasgow)
Richard Laughlin (Kings College, London)
February 2001

Part I
Background and Introductory Ideas

What is accounting? And why study it anyway?   1

Learning objectives

After studying this chapter you should be able to:

- give a general definition of accounting;

- recognize accounting's historical background;

- explain the difference between bookkeeping, financial accounting, financial reporting, management accounting and financial management and begin to understand their interrelationship;

- define the four characteristics of accounting, explain why they are important and how they apply to organizations;

- explain how and why accounting is more than a set of procedural techniques;

- recognise the implications of accounting being a 'profession';

- argue a case with non-accountants as to why accounting is, perhaps surprisingly, anything but 'dull and boring' and therefore why an intelligent person like you is willing to spend a significant proportion of their life studying it.

1.1 INTRODUCTION

1.1.1 Background

It seem that many people (including accounting students) find it astonishing that anyone would choose to study accounting. The idea that the study of accounting might be 'fun' or 'fascinating' is usually met with gales of laughter (see Figure 1.1). Perhaps this wouldn't matter so much if the people rolling in the aisles at the ridiculous idea that accounting might be interesting were not those who had chosen to study accounting. What is strange, to us, is that people who plan to study for anything up to 6 or 7 years (the time in the UK necessary to acquire an accounting degree and become a qualified accountant) would be entertained by such a notion. It seems, at best, tragic that students have consciously chosen to be bored out of their skulls for 6 years in order to…? Well, why? To be rich? To have a safe and secure job? Because it came immediately after 'Aardvark training' in the careers guide? This is very puzzling.

So, the first lesson in studying accounting is to recognize that accounting need not be anything other than fascinating. Oh, it *can* be a sort of financial plumbing for the terminally tedious if you let it – but it need not be. Now, of course, it is highly unlikely that your study of accounting is going to involve you in wrestling person-eating tigers, slaying

```
Accounting is ... (delete as appropriate)
1.    My life
2.    A barrel of laughs
3.    Extremely interesting
4.    The only school subject I could do
5.    What my Mum/Dad/careers teacher/girlfriend/boyfriend/horoscope recommended
6.    A way of getting rich
7.    Safe and secure
8.    Don't know
9.    Don't care
```

Figure 1.1 Describe accounting

dragons, kayaking waterfalls, leaping off tall buildings or playing the definitive lead-guitar solo – it's not *that* interesting. It *is* true that you are going to have to learn a lot of detailed skills (some of which skills are listed in Figure 1.2). Indeed, Figure 1.2 could be considered as a fairly uncontentious description of what accounting is about.

```
•    Tax calculation and planning
•    Keeping the books for business
•    Saving money
•    Budgeting
•    Working out the cost of things
•    Preparing accounts
•    Helping run a business
•    Receivership
•    Consultancy
•    Auditing
```

Figure 1.2 Accounting is about ...

These skills need to be learnt and, far more importantly, understood. There is a frightening tendency for accounting students to want to know only the finer detail of accounting techniques and to resist the deeper questions about why these techniques are important. Try and remember that if your major ambition is to be great at bookkeeping and following rules without any ability to discuss, theorize and argue about those rules you are likely to find yourself facing a career as a street-sweeper. This book is being typed on a personal computer that has some bookkeeping software on its hard disc.[1] The lot, together with a printer, costs less than £1,500. It can do bookkeeping and basic financial accounting a great deal better, quicker and more reliably than we can – or than you will be able to. What distinguishes you from the computer and the software is: (a) the computer is a great deal cheaper and more reliable than you are – so nobody in their right mind will employ you to do bookkeeping in favour of the computer; and (b) the computer is completely stupid, cannot think and obeys rules slavishly. You will be employed because you are *not* a computer. So the second lesson to learn about accounting is that it must be something a great deal more than rule-following and techniques – however difficult these rules and techniques may be.

Figure 1.3 is also a description of what accounting is about and it is this together with the deep understanding of the tools, rules and procedures that ensures that accounting is as fascinating a study as you could hope to find.

- Unemployment
- Production of medical breakthroughs
- Democracy
- Enhancing social welfare
- Environmental crises
- Exploitation of labour
- Social conflict and the dominance of capital
- Witchcraft
- Language
- Economic efficiency
- Poverty

Figure 1.3 Accounting is also about …

It may not be immediately obvious that accounting is also about the issues listed in Figure 1.3. But accounting is about constructing information, and information creates images of the world about us. Accounting is one of the – if not the – most powerful image creators. These images then influence how people think about their world and how they react to it. This, in turn, influences what people see as important and – by default – unimportant. That influences the decisions they take as a result. Accounting is extremely important here and one thing that accounting is *not*, is a precise science. As we shall see, there are many, many ways in which a figure like *'profit'* can be calculated. In fact, all *'accounting numbers'* are based in part on 'facts' and in part on guesswork and estimation. Therefore, the information that accountants present is *never* 'right'. At best, it is only ever more or less right or more or less wrong. Thus, the information that accountants present may lead to better or worse images and, thus, better or worse decisions. Similarly, accounting is only a *partial* image. It leaves (important) things (such as human well-being and the natural environment) out of its image. This encourages decision-makers to ignore these things. The result of all this is that accounting may well, for example, encourage short-term decision-making by business. A short-term emphasis in accounting will then encourage businesses not to undertake long-term research and development or perhaps encourage businesses to leave people unemployed. Similarly, accounting can, and does, encourage some businesses to grow and others to contract, it influences how managers' performance is assessed and it encourages businesses to ignore environmental degradation and the dislocation of local (and international) communities.

We will touch upon these issues throughout the book (see, especially, Chapters 17 and 18 and the further reading), but for now it is necessary to note that accounting is a highly influential and integral part of most economic, social and political decisions. Accounting may well be 'technical' on the surface, but 'dull' and 'boring'? Never! Studying accounting therefore involves a unique blend of sophisticated and highly useful techniques and procedures with a requirement to understand the social, economic and political world in which these techniques are placed – and to understand the considerable (but often hidden) effects of our accounting practices. We genuinely hope that you enjoy your study of accounting as much as we do. We've been studying accounting for more than 55 years (horrors!) between us and once we realized that accounting was not the dry, tedious, moronic regurgitation of rules that many books might encourage you to think it is, we haven't had a dull moment since. We hope that this book will help you start to see just how important and fascinating accounting can be.

1.1.2 Design of the chapter

This chapter is intended to give an overview of accounting. That is, it tries to help you start thinking about accounting – both as a series of techniques and as a profession with extensive social and political implications. To this end the chapter is organized as follows. The next subsection provides a very brief historical background to accounting. Section 1.2 will examine the definition of accounting and in particular the four characteristics of conventional accounting:

- accounting entities;
- economic events;
- financial description;
- the 'users' of accounting information.

This overview of accounting then provides a basis for section 1.3 where we look at the elements that make up **financial accounting** and show how the book is organized to reflect these different elements. Section 1.4 then introduces you to the idea of accounting as a *profession* and what that means for us as accountants. Some of these implications – including the implications for your education – are briefly examined. The chapter concludes with a summary of the main points, the identification of key words and some suggested further reading. (At that point you are in a position to turn to the workbook exercises for Chapter 1.)

1.1.3 A brief history of accounting and its conventions

The history of accounting dates back to, at least, the early civilizations of Egypt, Greece and Rome. For the majority of its history, the accounting activity has been concerned with simple record-keeping and the discharge of stewardship. This latter role refers to the requirement that a steward, entrusted with the master's resources, provide an 'account' of the management (stewardship) of these resources. These 'accounts' were common practice throughout medieval times in both secular and religious estates.

'Accounting textbooks' also have a long history. In 1494, Lucia Pacioli, a Franciscan monk, published the first known treatise on double-entry bookkeeping. Bookkeeping was far from new even then and had played an important role in the systematic financial control of trading enterprises from the late thirteenth century in Italy, as it does now the world over.

The more recent history of accounting tends to date from the Industrial Revolution in Britain. This period not only brought about an increase in the size and complexity of organizations but also saw the beginnings of modern company law. These two aspects of the Industrial Revolution are normally assumed to herald the growth in importance and status of the accounting function. The rise in complexity and size of organizations brought with it a need for more sophisticated methods of financial control, particularly the improved control of costs. The UK's 1844 Joint Stock Companies Act explicitly identified the need for the maintenance of 'books of account' and established the principle of companies presenting formal financial accounts (which had to be audited) to their owners (shareholders) and to those to whom they owed money (creditors).

It is from this basis that most 'traditional' accounting has developed. That is, the basic elements of a 'traditional' view of accounting are usually taken as:

- bookkeeping;
- financial reporting (the presentation of a formal financial account of the organization);
- cost accounting (see section 1.3.3).

The continued increase in the number, size and complexity of organizations, particularly companies, from 1844 to the present day has brought with it the range of challenges and issues that now constitute the staple diet of academic and professional students of accounting.

These challenges and issues will form the basis of this book. However, one preliminary observation should be made at this stage. The development of 'traditional' accounting, as we normally consider it, has been driven by developments in the commercial sector (in particular, those relating to companies) and especially by the interest of the holders of capital in that sector (e.g. shareholders). 'Traditional' accounting thus tends to take the most lop-sided view of the world, ignoring, as it does, most of the public sector and the needs of (for example) employees and the rest of society. It is only very recently that such concerns have manifested themselves in any serious way in the study and practice of accounting. We will certainly not be ignoring this 'traditional' view, but on the grounds that accounting is concerned with rather more than helping the shareholders of companies get rich, we will introduce and integrate these wider questions as we go along (see, particularly, Chapters 17 and 18).

The conventions which underpin both the study and practice of accounting are therefore based upon commercial organizations and the needs of capital. This shows itself particularly in our concentration on financial description and in accounting's central concern with the measurement of periodic income or profit attributable to the owners. These central conventions will be elaborated upon (and challenged) in the remaining chapters of the book.

1.2 WHAT IS ACCOUNTING?

1.2.1 A definition of accounting

It perhaps comes as something of a surprise to learn that it is not easy to define 'accounting'. The usual assumption is that accounting is what accountants do, but this is neither accurate nor helpful. It neither identifies the phenomena and activities we shall be studying nor does it help understand *why* the accountant does what he or she does. More importantly still, just looking at the current activities of accountants and the techniques that are employed does not necessarily encourage us to examine the *functions* that accounting serves in society. We need to be able to *evaluate* current accounting practices and to consider whether accountants *should* be doing what they do. Just because accountants are traditionally involved in, say, company reporting to shareholders does not *necessarily* mean that they are reporting in the best ways, or that an emphasis on reporting to shareholders is *necessarily* right. Accounting is not something which is set in tablets of stone. Current accounting practice is a result of habit, history, law and expedience, as well as social, political and economic choice. We need to be able to evaluate whether those choices are the best ones and whether other possibilities exist to do accounting in different ways. Further, we need to look behind current accounting practices in order to assess their ethical, social, political, economic and environmental foundations so that, as a profession, we can evaluate whether or not current accounting is really the best that can be currently achieved. Do remember that accounting is a socially constructed artefact – we, the accounting profession, invent or create accounting. In theory at least, therefore, accounting can be anything that we want it to be. To accept current accounting practice as necessarily 'right' is not only foolish and historically idiotic but is also an abdication of our professional responsibility (see section 1.4.1).

In order to get us started, a typical definition is provided by the American Accounting Association (AAA). This is summarized in Figure 1.4. You should study this definition and, although it is far from perfect, you should be sufficiently familiar with it to be able to recall it and discuss it throughout your study of accounting.

Throughout the chapters that follow, we shall be explaining how accountants go about identifying, collecting, describing, recording, processing and communicating information and we will be asking about who has a need or right to this information and, indeed, whether it does support economic decision-making. We shall also be questioning whether we can simply assume that current accounting actually does contribute to the enhancement of social welfare. *There is little question that accounting should contribute to social welfare; there is, however, very little reliable evidence that it actually does so. This deserves our attention as our studies develop.*

In 1966 the American Accounting Association defined accounting as:

'... the process of identifying, measuring and communicating economic information to permit informed judgments and decisions by the users of that information'.

In 1975 they added that the *purpose* of this process was:

'... to provide information which is potentially useful for making economic decisions and which, if provided, will enhance social welfare'.

Thus we might deduce that accounting involves:

- Identifying
- Collecting
- Describing
- Recording
- Processing
- Communicating

... INFORMATION ABOUT WHAT HAS HAPPENED TO SELECTED PEOPLE (WHO HAVE A NEED FOR IT?)

... TO SUPPORT ECONOMIC DECISIONS

... IN ORDER TO ENHANCE SOCIAL WELFARE

Figure 1.4 Accounting defined

1.2.2 The characteristics of accounting

The AAA definition of accounting is useful as far as it goes. It does not, however, allow us to distinguish between accounting and (say) what journalists and newscasters do. There is clearly some major difference between accountants and journalists – but what is it? Whilst we will look at 'non-conventional' areas of accounting later in the book, the majority of our attention will be focused upon 'conventional' or 'traditional' perspectives of financial accounting. Conventional accounting is distinguished by **four characteristics** which, between them, permit us to distinguish conventional accounting from other activities. These are shown in Figure 1.5. We shall consider these characteristics in a little more detail.

(a) Accounting entities

It is convenient (and often practically essential) to treat those different units in a society for which we wish to account as (relatively) discrete and separate. An accounting entity is any unit, of any size or composition, in society, in whose account of activities we are interested. (We will call this the **focal organization**.)

Thus you are an accounting entity if someone is interested in accounting for you as an individual. If you owned a shop, that would be another separate accounting entity. (By convention we would only treat you and your shop as a single accounting entity if you went bankrupt.) If you owned a series of shops, each would be a separate accounting entity and we might also choose to identify a large entity – 'You Enterprises' – if we wanted to see how the group of shops was performing overall.

What we identify as 'entities' is largely a matter of expedience (depending upon what we want to know), although the legal system of a country may define certain types of entities – for example, through the taxation system, or via the law relating to companies. So, whether we are concerned with an individual, a household, a club, a charity, a company, a group of companies, a hospital, a church, a local authority, or whatever is, in the first place, irrelevant as each can be treated as an accounting entity and many of the aims and objectives, skills and methods of accounting can be applied equally to each.

(b) Economic events

'Economic events' are those which involve, in some way or another, the natural physical, human, capital and financial resources of a community. This, however, does not help us

Accounting is to be distinguished from (e.g.) journalism because of its focus upon (limitation by):	
(a) The DISCRETE INDIVIDUAL UNITS OF SOCIETY upon which accounting focuses and with whose events accounting is concerned	ACCOUNTING ENTITIES
(b) The TYPE OF EVENTS with which accounting is concerned (the 'identifying' activities)	ECONOMIC EVENTS
(c) The WAY IN WHICH THESE EVENTS ARE DESCRIBED (the 'collecting', 'describing' and 'recording' activities)	FINANCIAL DESCRIPTION
(d) The PEOPLE FOR WHOM THIS INFORMATION IS PREPARED (the 'processing' and 'communicating' activities)	USERS

Figure 1.5 The four characteristics of conventional accounting

greatly as most events have some economic implications. It is therefore necessary to be more specific and say that accounting is concerned with those events which have *direct economic implication for the entity* under specific consideration at that time (i.e. the accounting entity or focal organization as we shall call it). As we shall see, 'direct economic events' can be identified as those which have direct cash implications for the focal organization – the cash implications might be actual or potential and might occur in the past, in the present or at some time in the future.

Thus for most organizations, events such as purchasing supplies and services, negotiating loans and dealing with changes in the tax system or a new source of demand are relevant economic events. Whereas the state of the weather, the latest fashions, what was on TV last night and who won the Cup Final are relevant economic events only for certain particular entities (e.g. water authorities, fashion houses, TV critics, two football clubs and so on).

(c) Financial description

While accounting is concerned with more than just simple cash transactions, the conventional accounting process concentrates a large proportion of its effort on the *financial characteristics* of the relevant economic events. Thus, for example, the arrival of a van-load of groceries at the local shop is of accounting interest to the shop only insofar as a specific financial indebtedness has now occurred (the shop owes some cash to the supplier) and the shop now has a particular value of goods available for resale. The colour of the van, the time it arrived, the driver's preferences in music and whether or not the van was booked for illegal parking, although part and parcel of the relevant economic event, do not have *direct* financial implications for the shop. They are characteristics of the event which cannot be described relevantly by the conventional financial accounting process and as a result are not of direct economic and financial interest to the shop.

(d) The users of information

A critical point about information is that it serves no possible purpose unless it is needed, wanted (and perhaps used) by someone, somewhere, for something. That is, the accounting process has absolutely no intrinsic value. Any value derives from the use to which the output of the process (the information) is put.

However, identifying just who the 'users' are and what rights, wants or needs with respect to information they really have, is one of accounting's most difficult problems. We will return to this problem in a little more detail later in this chapter and there is much more detail later in the book (see, particularly, Chapters 15, 17 and 18). For the time being, we will make do with a general statement that:

> The accounting activity operates to satisfy the information requirements of individuals and groups who have some reasonable right to and need for accounting information.

Thus, the committee of a canoe club need to know whether they can afford, for example, to buy a new canoe for club use; shopkeepers need to know who owes them money; shareholders need to know whether they are able to receive a dividend; the government needs to know how much local authorities are spending on education; and so on. These, amongst others, are the groups and individuals that our society acknowledges as needing and having a right to accounting information. The accounting process serves them by identifying, collecting, describing, recording and processing data about the financial aspects of relevant economic events and communicating the results to them. Further, it is worth emphasizing that conventional accounting tends to place much greater emphasis on the *financial participants* of the focal organisation than on other participants or potential users. That is, those who have a direct financial interest in the focal organization (typically shareholders, lenders, creditors and tax authorities, for example,) are generally deemed to have a greater right to accounting information than those with a social, environmental or human interest in the organization (for example, employees, society, communities and environmentalists). We will re-examine this assumption, and particularly what this means for *accountability*, as the book progresses (see especially Chapters 17 and 18).

These four characteristics are summarized in Figure 1.6. We must emphasize, though, that there is theoretically no limit to the ways in which 'accounts' can be prepared, the groups or entities which they describe or the groups for whom they are prepared. 'Conventional' or 'traditional' accounting refers to what accountants generally do. We will be looking later at other accounts such as 'value-added', 'social accounts' and accounts for the performance of non-commercial organizations which challenge 'conventional' views on what accountants should be doing. For example, as an appetizer, we can say there is no absolute reason why accounts, in general, must be in financial terms.

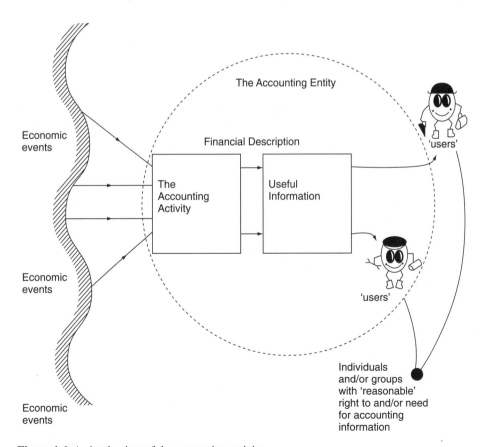

Figure 1.6 A simple view of the accounting activity

1.2.3 Identifying the accounting transactions

There are two major reasons for dwelling on how we delineate conventional accounting. First, it permits us to be clearer about what accounting is not. This becomes very important later on as we attempt to interpret accounting information and to examine its limitations. The second, and more pressing, reason is that it gives us a guide as to how accounting identifies the events or transactions in which it is interested. These are the transactions which flow into our bookkeeping and then into our financial statements. It is obviously essential that we can determine which transactions to 'capture' and which to ignore. The practicalities of this will emerge as we progress and we will spend some time on this activity in Chapter 5. However, we also need to be clear about the conventions and assumptions which have guided our 'capture' of events because once the transactions are 'identified', 'described' and 'recorded' then financial accounting's own peculiar logic takes over and we will tend to forget the assumptions and (more usually) simply take them for granted. We want to be as clear as possible about our taken-for-granted assumptions (and we will discuss these below). Only in this way can we begin to really try and understand this amazing thing called 'accounting'.

1.3 ACCOUNTING AND FINANCIAL ACCOUNTING

Accounting is typically thought of as consisting of three major areas:

- financial accounting;
- management accounting; and
- financial management.

These, plus other areas (such as auditing and taxation) need some explanation before we start getting into the detail of financial accounting. The next two subsections look at financial accounting and, in subsection 1.3.3, we briefly review management accounting and financial management.

1.3.1 Financial accounting

The central focus of financial accounting is the production of a flow of information, from the focal organization to those external to the organization, about its actions and activities. In 'traditional' or 'conventional' financial accounting this flow of information is presented in the financial statements. The central elements in these financial statements for the majority of entities are the **balance sheet** and the **profit and loss account** (although these are by no means the only, or necessarily the best, statements that an organization can produce) and these are typically produced annually.[2]

As a result, the study of financial accounting involves:

- examining how the data and records for these statements are collected and organized – bookkeeping (which is dealt with in Chapters 2–10);
- examining the conventions and practices of preparing these statements – financial accounting and accounting policy (Chapters 11–13);
- considering what one can (and cannot) learn from these statements – financial statement analysis (Chapters 14 and 15);
- investigating the questions of what information organizations should be producing – external reporting and accounting theory (Chapters 16, 17 and 18).

The purpose of providing this overall financial picture is to provide information to groups external to the organization. We have already met a number of these – bankers, shareholders, charity donors and the government, for example. A general term for these is **external participants** or **recipient organizations**, as we will come to call them in Chapters 3 and 4, but you will also see the phrase **users of accounts** to mean much the same sort of thing. This external focus means that a full study of financial accounting also involves an examination of who constitute these external groups; what information they need and why; and how (and if) we respond to their needs.

In addition, it falls to this area of the subject to consider other ways in which accounting information might pass between the entity and the 'outside world' – for example, recording flows of cash, controlling the payment of wages and the purchase of materials and services, keeping a check on what we owe and what is owed to us.

In Chapter 2 we meet the case of Mr Brain, a student, and see that his financial accounting involves:

- the information that he provides to his parents;
- the information that he might supply to the bank manager for a loan or to other external participants for other purposes;
- the analysis of Mr Brain's financial situation;
- his financial record-keeping of, for example, what he owns, what he owes and what he is owed.

1.3.2 The structure of financial accounting

There are many different ways in which we can approach the study of financial accounting, bookkeeping and external reporting. There are three basic approaches:

i   One can start with the financial statements. These are the outputs of the financial accounting system and the law and conventions which govern them are demanding – so much so that it is often the logic of the financial statements which determines what has to go into the bookkeeping and financial accounting systems. That is, the **outputs** (the financial statements) determine both the **inputs** (identifying accounting transactions and recording them in the bookkeeping system) and the **processes** (the adjustment of the accounting numbers) of the financial accounting system. (Look back to Figure 1.6 for reference.) This approach involves working backwards from the financial statements to the accounting information system. It has much to recommend it but effectively denies that bookkeeping and accounting might have a logic separate from the financial statements. So we prefer to work forwards from the beginning of the system. We think this is more logical. We will, however, take retrospective views of the process – looking back from the financial statements – later in the book.

ii Alternatively, one can start with a mass of rules and procedures and simply wade through them until some sort of daylight emerges. This approach is based upon – and encourages – learning by rote. This is something we are opposed to, think is a lot less interesting than other approaches and believe insults your intelligence and we are pretty well convinced that it tends to restrict our ability to think about accounting – which is, after all, the object of the exercise!

iii The third approach is the one we take here. We start with some basic ideas, place them in an organizational context and then build up the bookkeeping and accounting from that. This has the advantage of being chronologically sensible and allows us to identify the logic of bookkeeping and financial accounting and where that logic starts to break down. It also helps you, the student, to build up your understanding of financial accounting in systematic chunks. Experience shows that this helps avoid you getting swamped by confusion or from disappearing in a morass of procedures and rules.

The basic outline of the approach we are taking is shown in Figure 1.7.

Figure 1.7 shows five basic stages to the study of financial accounting. We have started with the background in this chapter. The idea is to give you some of the basic conceptual and technical building blocks necessary to begin to construct the financial accounting process. This will include an examination of cash (in Chapter 2) and an introduction to the nature of organizations (in Chapter 3). In Part II, we use these building blocks to construct the logic of double-entry bookkeeping, to explain the accounting information system and to produce the 'initial trial balance' (this and other terms will be explained later). It is essential that you can do this basic bookkeeping in your sleep. This is the basic mechanical 'stuff' of accounting and although it is fairly moronic and follows a pretty weird way of looking at the world, it is logical. Once you have conquered bookkeeping, you are then ready to move on to Part III. This is where we start to adjust the basic accounting and bookkeeping numbers so that they can be used to build the financial statements. Any logic here is both sketchy and accidental. To produce a set of conventional financial statements we simply have to put our intelligence on one side and follow the rules. Where there is a logic we will pull it out and also highlight why this stage in the accounting process is so bizarre. This is the stage where we make the **accounting decisions** and it is largely here that the guesswork, judgement and political and social dimensions of accounting most obviously rear their heads. It is here that we need to spend time looking at the law and

Structure of the book						
Part 1	Part 2		Part 3		Part 4	Part 5
Background	Bookkeeping & the accounting information system	The initial trial balance	Trial balance adjustments	The financial statements	Developments, alternatives & interpretation	Summary, developing your study of accounting and future possibilities
• Starting to think about accounting • Cash as the basis of accounting	• What distinguished accounting & bookkeeping transactions? • How are transactions categorized? • What are double-entry & accounting record-keeping?		• How do we present the financial picture of an organization? • Accounting conventions, rules & regulations • Decisions about the treatment of accounting information • Concerns about the disclosure and reporting of financial information		• How can we use the financial statements? • What other possibilities are there? • How can we (& should we) think (theorize) about accounting?	• What have we learnt? • What have we still to learn? • What is the future for accounting & the accounting profession?
Chapter 1 Chapter 2 Chapter 3	Chapter 4 Chapter 5 Chapter 6	Chapter 7	Chapter 8 Chapter 9 Chapter 10 Chapter 11	Chapter 12 Chapter 13 Chapter 14	Chapter 15 Chapter 16 Chapter 17 Chapter 18	Chapter 19

Figure 1.7 A simple structure for financial accounting

other regulation of accounting – and ask some fairly hard questions about the resultant current accounting practice. Part IV moves beyond the conventional financial statements, looks at ways of reading the story provided by company accounts and considers alternative 'accounts' and ways of presenting 'accounts'. So here, we will also look at accounting for inflation and changing prices as well as social and environmental accounting. This will also provide the jumping-off point for a brief introduction to 'thinking about accounting' – better known as 'accounting theory' – although accounting students (and qualified accountants) would sometimes appear to think of 'theory' as a dirty word – the sort of thing that civilized folk do not do in polite company. Without 'theory', however, accounting has no real basis for claiming to be a profession (see section 1.4). Part V provides an overview of the paths we have travelled throughout the book and then looks forward to where your future studies of financial accounting will take you.

It is also traditional to consider matters such as tax and auditing within the ambit of financial accounting. Whilst these are better studied in depth later in one's courses, we will touch upon taxation and some of its important elements within financial accounting and we will provide a broad introduction to auditing. As we shall see, auditing depends totally upon the quality of financial accounting and, it can be argued, the quality of financial accounting depends totally upon the auditor. This mutual relationship means that if we are to understand the practice of financial accounting we also need to know something of the practice of auditing. This is especially emphasized in Chapter 14.

1.3.3 Management accounting and financial management

Accounting is, however, a great deal more than just bookkeeping, financial accounting and reporting. The basic raw materials that we shall be dealing with in this book – financial data – are also used by the organization in a number of other connections. The most obvious of these is to supply management with information on which they can make decisions, assess performance and attempt to exercise control over the organization. This is the area we tend to call **management accounting**. Management accounting tends to emphasize the perspective of those inside the organization – the internal participants. As such, your study of management accounting will influence – and be influenced by – your study of management information systems, management studies, business policy, and so on. The other major area of accounting is called variously **financial management**, **finance** or **business finance**. The main themes explored in this area are the different ways in which businesses can be financed and the relative merits and demerits of each way. This extends to examining organizational investment decisions, the management of funds within organizations (treasury) and, especially, the behaviour of stock markets and stock prices. Financial management will also be the area where your study of economics, econometrics and, perhaps, business mathematics will be most obviously employed.

There are considerable interplays between the three main branches of accounting – although the interplay is often very complex. For illustration though, the basic data which are picked and recorded in the bookkeeping system will often form a large part of the data with which management accountants may attempt to establish product costs or construct simple budgets. Also, it is certainly the case that many of the financial accounting techniques which we will meet later do find themselves being used in the management accounting system as well – but often in a way which is suboptimal for the organization. Senior management in major companies will often have difficulty in deciding which area of measurement on which to concentrate – the management accounting information or the financial accounting information which emerges in the financial statements. These will often conflict and, with the increasing power of the stock markets (as we shall study in financial management), it is often the financial accounting information that is (frequently incorrectly) seen as being the more important measure of corporate success.

The interactions between financial accounting, management accounting and financial management are more extensive and complex than this. Your future studies will explore many of these interplays. For now it is sufficient to simply flag up that the three areas do not sit in separate, tidy little boxes and you, if you are be an effective accountant, should try and remember this as your studies develop.

1.4 STUDYING TO BE A PROFESSIONAL?

1.4.1 Is accounting a profession – and so what?

Most students who study accounting seem to expect that, in return for 6 or more years of grafting away learning esoteric techniques, society will accord them a status, a value and a decent salary. Why should we expect this? Part of the reason is that during your 6 years you will have acquired a very useful set of talents and part of the reason is supply of and demand for accountants. But this is only part of the reason. Why does society appear to think our skills are that important? It doesn't appear to value carpenters, plumbers and electricians (who also have extensive skills which are in short supply) in the same way. In part the reason lies in the Companies Acts. Most countries have legislation which regulates corporate behaviour and in that legislation accountants feature in a unique way. The regulation of companies is seen as so important that a special profession must oversee that regulation. That profession is accountancy. So our status derives primarily (though not entirely) from society's desire to regulate the powerful economic forces of companies.[3] Society (as reflected in the Acts) goes further and permits the accounting profession to govern the rules for regulating companies (via the financial statements and auditing) and also to govern who shall be considered fit to act as an accountant. That is, accountants are allowed to regulate themselves. This **self-regulation** is one of the features that defines us as a profession. The other two are:

- that the profession serves **the public interest** (and when there is a conflict between an accountant's private interest and the public interest then the public interest should dominate);
- that the profession has **a theoretical basis** for its actions and procedures.[4]

Thus, if we are to fulfil society's expectations that we act as a profession we must ensure that our self-regulation is effective, in the public interest and grounded in a sound theoretical understanding of what we do. If we fail to achieve this (and there is much suggestion that we do currently fail) then we may cease to be a profession if society reclaims its previously granted authority and autonomy. In such circumstances, we are being dishonest if we continue to pretend that we are a profession and continue to hide behind the Companies Acts. Without the Companies Acts, there is less demand for accountants and auditors and accounting matters a whole lot less in society. Even at a selfish level, that has obvious implications for our continued employment and well-being. So it does matter whether or not accounting is a profession.

1.4.2 What is education – and so what?

Whilst it may be possible to inculcate the values of a professional through training, it is education that can provide a theoretical foundation and help develop the intellectual abilities of the putative professional. Education is, therefore, more than just a training. A training can teach you – very successfully and importantly – what to do and how to do it. A training will not teach you *why* you do it and neither will it provide you with a way of thinking about what you do. Training, by itself, can turn you into a 'skilled robot', as Cheryl Lehman notes in Figure 1.8. Being able to think about what you do is crucial when, for example, something new comes along, or when an old way of doing starts to cause problems, or when you want to try and evaluate what you do. Accounting is changing all the time. For illustration, during the 1990s accountants around the world had to cope with many new issues – accounting for brands and other 'intangibles', accounting for the environment, accounting for new financial instruments, new criticisms of auditing and so on. (We shall explain these and have a closer look at many of them as we go through this book.) A 'well-educated' accountant should be able to think about these, identify a theoretical basis for change and assess whether or not a change seems likely to be in the public interest. Education should, therefore, stretch and challenge you. Accounting education can be especially challenging – and a great deal more interesting as a result.

Figure 1.9 provides you with a way of thinking about the educational process you are embarking upon. It shows the different levels of reasoning and intellectual maturity that a student exhibits as the educational process develops. To simply let oneself passively accept what happens in lectures – and, indeed, what we say in this book – is not only boring but ensures that you do not develop your 'thinking muscle'. 'Learning and churning' *may* get you through but it won't be interesting and it won't help you either do particularly well or become a particularly effective accountant. For that you need to seek to understand ('comprehension') what is happening and how to apply it. Then you need to learn how to think systematically about what you know, understand and can apply ('analysis'). Then you will be in a position to synthesize different ideas and evaluate good and bad ideas in a systematic and reasoned manner. (As we shall see, there are many different ways of doing bits of accounting. An educated professional will be able to come to a conclusion on which is the best way and why that is a preferred way of handling a particular transaction or problem.)

A bored – and boring – student will adopt what is usually called a 'shallow learning strategy'. What a 'real' education involves is a 'deep learning strategy' (see Figure 1.10).

Study Figures 1.9 and 1.10 carefully. It should be fairly obvious that whilst deep learning may well involve a little more work, it will certainly be a great deal more interesting. We will certainly be trying to encourage you to adopt a deep learning strategy

---

Accounting students are trained in how to do ... [W]hy [is] either unarticulated or not scrutinised. This is tantamount to establishing that the first task of teachers is to serve the economy by turning out 'skilled robots and uncritical consumers for the hi-tech age' rather than regarding the classroom as a place to question rules and standards, a place to direct, formulate and cultivate character and the ethos of life.

Education should, by definition, be a human advance, something we can morally approve of, denoting an increase in human achievement. Can we say that the emphasis in accounting education ... entail[s] a qualitative human advance?

(*Lehman 1988*)

Figure 1.8 Accounting education

1. **Knowledge:** This is the lowest level of learning. It includes recall and memory.

2. **Comprehension:** This is the lowest level of understanding. The student uses facts or ideas without relating them.

3. **Application:** This is the intellectual skill that entails the use of information in specific situations. Information may be in the form of general ideas, concepts, principles or theories which must be remembered and applied.

4. **Analysis:** This skill involves taking apart information and making relationships in order to discover hidden meaning and the basic structure of an idea or fact. The student is able to distinguish between fact and opinion and to assess consistency.

5. **Synthesis:** The student is able to reassemble the component parts of an idea in order to develop new or creative ideas.

6. **Evaluation:** This is the highest level of cognition. It involves making judgements on materials, information or method. In problem-solving, it involves selecting from amongst competing alternative solutions by systematic evaluation of the alternatives

Figure 1.9 Bloom's taxonomy of learning/cognitive objectives

Surface approach/Shallow-reiterative/ Reproducing/Concrete-operational

- Intention simply to reproduce parts of the content;
- Accepting ideas and information passively;
- Concentrating only on assessment requirements;
- Not reflecting on purpose or strategies in learning;
- Memorizing facts and procedures routinely;
- Failing to recognize guiding principles or patterns.

Deep approach/Deep-elaborative/ Transforming/Formal-operational

- Intention to understand material for oneself;
- Interacting vigorously and critically with content;
- Relating ideas to previous knowledge and experience;
- Using organizing principles to integrate ideas;
- Relating evidence to conclusions;
- Examining the logic of the argument.

Figure 1.10 Defining feature of approaches to learning

and that involves *you* – in challenging what we and your lecturers tell you. Education makes your brain hurt but, eventually, makes it work better. That seems a worthwhile pursuit, doesn't it?

1.4.3 Learning accounting? Or understanding accounting?

The foregoing has two purposes. First, it is to encourage you to want to study accounting in depth – to really try and dig beneath its apparently controversy-free surface. The second purpose is to try and break down any tendency you might have to want to just learn the techniques without asking the 'why' and 'so what' questions. Perhaps it helps if you can begin to see accounting as consisting of a series of 'layers' – each of which depends on the others. These are summarized in Figure 1.11.

The first, inner, 'layer' is the traditional core techniques of accounting. These are the absolute basics that you must be able to apply – and understand. This book will provide you with a firm grasp of many of these – and other courses in, for example, management accounting and costing, will provide others. Then follow the more advanced techniques. We will look at some of these, but they are generally the core of later courses of study. The point about this second 'layer' is that the debatable nature of accounting becomes much

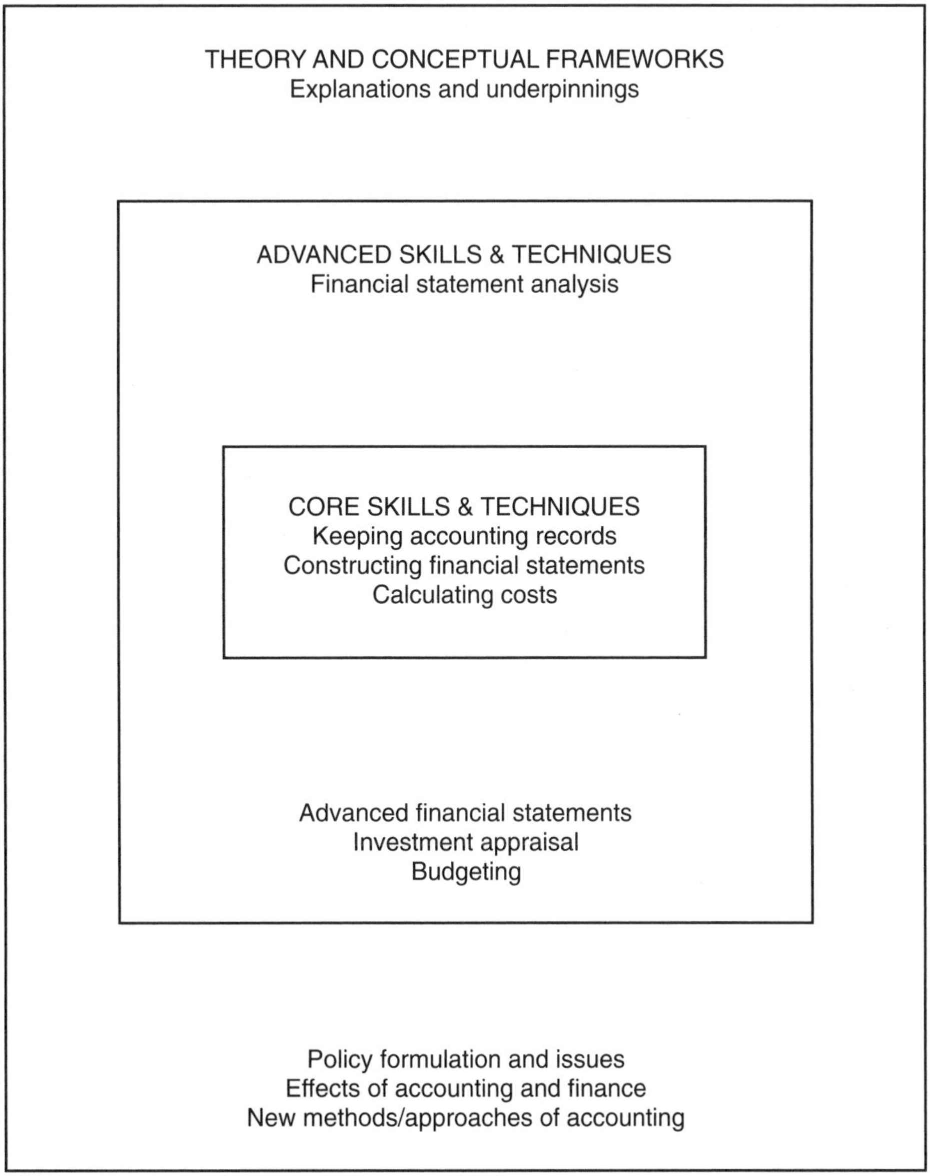

THEORY AND CONCEPTUAL FRAMEWORKS
Explanations and underpinnings

ADVANCED SKILLS & TECHNIQUES
Financial statement analysis

CORE SKILLS & TECHNIQUES
Keeping accounting records
Constructing financial statements
Calculating costs

Advanced financial statements
Investment appraisal
Budgeting

Policy formulation and issues
Effects of accounting and finance
New methods/approaches of accounting

Figure 1.11 The 'layers' of accounting teaching

more apparent. Not only do these advanced techniques become more difficult to master but they also highlight that no accounting method can ever be absolutely 'correct' – each is just the result of debate and political, economic and social decisions. The outer 'layer' is the theoretical foundations of traditional accounting practice. This includes the assumptions, assertions, choices and preferences that go to make up current accounting practice. Whilst these tend to be introduced in later stages of your course, we shall be introducing some of them from the beginning – not only because this makes the accounting more interesting but also because it seems inappropriate to get into 'bad habits' early on in one's studies. Traditional accounting education would erect the edifice of conventional accounting techniques in an unproblematic way and, towards the end of a course, start to identify the problems. It is much more productive to try and identify the assumptions and problems as we actually construct the edifice. In that way we can be more explicit about the limitations we are building in as we go along. But, perhaps most importantly of all, this more 'theoretically based' approach – which does not in any way discount the importance of the techniques – should encourage a more educational and less regurgitative approach to your studies. Shallow learning does not 'a good accountant make'.

SUMMARY

Accounting is an activity which (conventionally) involves identifying, collecting, describing, recording, processing and communicating information in financial terms about the economic events of an entity to groups and individuals that have a need or right to the information. This is usually assumed to be for decision-making purposes and is also assumed to contribute to the social welfare of the nation.

Financial accounting is primarily concerned with producing financial statements for external participants. But to do this, there must be an accounting and bookkeeping system that will produce reliable information and which will provide a basis for informed accounting decisions about the contents of those financial statements.

Despite appearances, this is not a technical, rule-following process. There are rules and techniques which must be mastered – but accounting is also a social, economic and political activity that is intended to serve the public interest of society. How does this work? This will be explored as the book develops but it is not achieved by passive, non-thinking accountants – or by passive non-thinking students. Accounting lays claim to being one of society's most respected and valued professions and fulfilment of this responsibility requires an educated profession with a lively, questioning intellect and a good grasp of the theoretical underpinnings of the accounting activity.

Key terms and concepts

Here is a list of the key terms and concepts which have featured in this chapter. You should make sure that you understand and can define each one of them. Page references to definitions in the text appear in the index in bold type.

- Accountants
- Accounting
- Accounting education and training
- Accounting entity
- Accounting history
- Bookkeeping
- Deep/shallow learning
- Economic events

- Financial accounting
- Financial description
- Financial management
- Financial participants
- Financial statements
- Learning
- Management accounting
- Profession
- Users of information

FURTHER READING

Further reading at this stage falls into roughly three parts:

(i)   You should start reading financial statements. Start to build up a personal library of company and non-company annual reports, keep them to hand and consult them as we go along. They will become more intelligible and useful from about Chapter 7 onwards but if you start now you will find them useful – and most interesting;

(ii)   You should start reading the financial pages of a good newspaper and should regularly read one of the professional accountancy magazines. Your university may be able to do a deal for you on either of these or you may be able to persuade some rich relative to buy you a subscription for Christmas (ooh, that'll be worth waiting for!).

(iii)   You should start trying to read around the subject of accounting. You will, from time to time, wish to consult other textbooks. That is not a problem, but do be aware that most will take a different – and frequently atheoretical – approach to accounting. (How a professional discipline like accounting can be studied at university in an atheoretical way defeats us, however.) But there are also many interesting sources of different insights on accounting. We will refer to these in the Further Reading sections as we go along. Some that you should enjoy at this stage (and which will be useful throughout this course) are Carsberg and Hope (1984), which is a nice series of simply written articles for introductory studies, Hird (1983), which gives a more radical view and the opening chapters of Tinker (1985) are entertaining. Tinker (1992) has a few rude things to say about accountants and accounting lecturers.

NOTES

1.   Just the sort of thing you will be meeting in the computer laboratories during this course. On these machines you will do your computer-based training, your accounting records exercises and your introductions to databases and spreadsheets.

2.   It is increasingly common to find organizations producing something called a *cash flow statement* as a third basic financial statement. We will look at this statement in some detail in Chapter 15.

3.   It is worth noting that without a Companies Act of the form which we find in most 'developed' and 'developing' countries, the demand for accountants – and thus their status and salaries – would be a great deal lower.

4.   This is widely debated, but these basic characteristics are derived from Millerson (1964) and Greenwood (1957). A further characteristic offered by some commentators is that a profession is an organization that protects its members, to keep out 'undesirables' and to maintain a mystique about itself – which in turn leads to the maintenance of a high salary level for that profession. If you find this characteristic more descriptive you will be interested to know that you are in agreement with Karl Marx. It is funny how many accounting students who see themselves as 'right-wing' actually agree with so much of what Karl Marx had to say! For more ideas on professions see, for example, Allen (1991), Armstrong and Vincent (1988), Sikka *et al.* (1989), Willmott (1990), Zeff (1987).

2 Cash, cashbooks and units of account

Learning objectives

After studying this chapter you should be able to:

- define cash;

- draw up a simple cashbook;

- draw up a columnar cashbook;

- draw up a cashbook which distinguishes cash-in-hand from bank transactions;

- identify how the cashbook illustrates the four characteristics of traditional accounting;

- identify the limitations of the cashbook and explain that is does not show 'well-offness' or levels of consumption and earning in a period.

2.1 INTRODUCTION

2.1.1 Chapter design and links to previous chapter

Chapter 1 introduced some of the basic building blocks of traditional or conventional accounting and provided some ideas as to why we might be interested in studying accounting. More particularly, Chapter 1 identified the four basic characteristics which define the traditional accounting activity. These were:

- the concept of the accounting entity;
- the concentration on economic events;
- the restriction to financial description of those events;
- that information produced by the accounting activity should be useful to those who have a reasonable right to it.

Although we will have cause to question each of these as the book progresses they nevertheless provide the basis for the traditional accounting activity. The most basic element of that activity is **cash**. It is on cash – and the accounting records which we need to maintain for cash – that this chapter will concentrate.

In the next subsection we will look at the nature of cash. Then section 2.2 introduces Mr Brain, a student in his first term at college, and explains how to construct a simple cashbook for him. The section then goes on to show how we can develop this simple cashbook to produce a columnar, analysed cashbook and one which distinguishes between cash-in-hand and cash at the bank. The section concludes with a brief introduction to the petty cashbook. Section 2.3 pulls out some of the lessons we can draw from the cashbook and briefly introduces the income statement and balance sheet. The section concludes with an introduction to the concept of 'unit of account' and the issues raised by foreign currencies. Section 2.4 looks at why information is demanded and supplied. There then follows a summary to the chapter.

2.1.2 The nature of cash

Cash is funny stuff. Although we all tend to take it for granted it is probably the most important part of the accountant's traditional job to keep track of it. There are two major reasons why you should have a really good grasp of cash and how to account for it. First, it is probably the case that more businesses collapse and more organizations get into trouble because they have not looked after their cash than for any other reason. Second, cash records are the backbone of traditional accounting **record-keeping** and if you can get these right then an awful lot else that follows will seem more straightforward. There is also a third reason, which is worth just signposting at this stage. You will come to see that cash is just about the only part of accounting that is uncontentious and can really be relied upon. (Unfortunately, even this is only true in certain circumstances!) So, in keeping with our intention of building up the accounting process piece by piece, we will start with the safest, most reliable, least contentious piece of accounting and go on from there.

What is cash? Well, that is not as obvious as it might seem. For our purposes, **cash** will be that **unit of account** which we can use immediately to either buy goods or pay people to whom we owe money. It therefore includes the coins you have in your pocket, the notes you have in your wallet, the roll of used $100 bills you have stuffed under your mattress and the money you have in bank or building society current accounts and deposit accounts that can be readily accessible. So note, as far as our basic accounting is concerned, there is no necessity to distinguish between cash in your pocket and payments by cheque – the accountant will treat both as cash. However, as we shall see, it might actually be convenient (as opposed to essential) to distinguish between 'cash-in-hand' and 'cash at the bank'.

There is then a lot of stuff which is **near-cash**. This might include money in a deposit account which requires you to give 10 days' notice for its withdrawal, or government bonds which will take a few days to turn into actual cash, or shares in a reliable company or even things which are nearly as good as (or better than) cash, like gold. As we shall see later in this chapter (when we touch upon currencies) and, especially, in Chapter 14, it can be very important to be clear on what is cash or near-cash (often referred to as '**funds**' in accounting). The accountancy profession has had difficulty with deciding what definition of 'funds' is most appropriate and this suggests that cash and near-cash are not as straightforward as we might want them to be. However, for our purposes we will keep things simple for the time being and just stick to stuff which is obviously 'cash'.

We will now turn to an example and look at a practical illustration of cash and a record of cash – a 'cashbook' or 'cash account'.

2.2 THE CASE OF MR BRAIN – A STUDENT

2.2.1 The simple cashbook

We will move on from the general points we have made so far and have a look at a simple practical example of **financial record-keeping**. We can then use this simple example to illustrate the points that we have made up to now and use it as a basis for introducing some of the more interesting, challenging and complicated ideas that we will be using later in the book. Now to the example.

Please read carefully through Figure 2.1. One's first reaction might be to try an 'unpick' the story of Mr Brain – is he overspent or what? If this was a record of your first term at college you might do a few quick calculations to find out how bad the news was. You might produce something like Figure 2.2.

This outline produced in Figure 2.2 is fine as far as it goes (and indeed will prove useful later on), but it is only a summary and can only be produced at the end of the term. To give us a more detailed record and one which can be constructed as the term progresses, we need to '**draw up**' a **simple cashbook**. ('Draw up' is a piece of inevitable accounting jargon. It means lay out a page in a book – or construct a computer file – in a traditional

---

A. Brain, the child of somewhat meticulous parents, has come to college for the first time. His parent have insisted that he provide a full account of his financial activities at the end of term. He records the following transactions.

		£
2 Oct.	Receive cash from parents	200
2 Oct.	Pay rent to landlord for October	20
2 Oct.	Go to local store and stock up on food	10
5 Oct.	Buy bus pass	5
5 Oct.	Buy textbooks	3
30 Oct.	Pay turf accountants	16
30 Oct.	Pay bar bill for October	62
2 Nov.	Receive cash present from Aunty Gertrude	10
3 Nov.	Buy dartboard	8
3 Nov.	Pay rent to landlord for November	20
6 Nov.	Lend Jack cash to pay police fine	20
20 Nov.	Go to post office and draw out savings from summer employment	50
30 Nov.	Pay bar bill for November	57
6 Dec.	Borrow some cash from Fred	2
7 Dec.	Buy in a crate or two of Guinness	20
10 Dec.	Buy train ticket home	5
12 Dec.	Leave landlord something towards the rent	10

Wishing to impress his parents, he wants to present the above as a 'proper' set of 'books and accounts', but having only studied accounting for one term he has not got a clue where to begin.

The following points are also relevant:

i He still owes the landlord £10 for December's rent, plus a £5 retainer for the Christmas vacation.

ii He only drank half of the Guinness he bought on 7 December.

iii He has not paid his bar bill for December: this amounts to £34.

iv Term started on 2 October and finished on 12 December.

Figure 2.1 Mr Brain's first term at college

way and fill in the appropriate and useful details and information.) A **cashbook** is a simple statement of cash received and cash paid out during a particular period – in Mr Brain's case, one term. An accountant would draw up a simple cashbook to look something like Figure 2.3.

Before anybody starts worrying, although the cashbook looks like a clutter of numbers, words and lines, it is very straightforward and just takes a few moments to get used to. There are a few simple conventions operating here:

- The first is that in a cashbook the cash receipts are always shown on the left-hand side and the cash payments are always shown on the right-hand side. LEARN THIS! You must get this right.

Cash at start of term	0
Cash received during term: (Parents, Aunty, Post Office, Fred)	262
Cash paid out during term: (Payments plus loan to Jack)	256
Cash left at end of term	6
(Other stuff: Mr Brain owes some money, is owed some money and has some bits and pieces at the end of the term which he didn't have at the beginning. **NB** These are not directly cash items and we will return to them later.)	

Figure 2.2 Mr Brain's financial situation – term 1

Simple cashbook for Mr Brain – Term 1			
Receipts *Date*		Payments *Date*	
2/10 Parents	200	2/10 Landlord	20
2/11 Aunty Gertrude	10	2/10 Grocers	10
20/11 Post Office	50	5/10 Bus pass	5
6/12 Fred	2	5/10 Textbooks	3
		30/10 Turf accountants	16
		30/10 Pay bill at the bar	62
		3/11 Dartboard	8
		3/11 Landlord	20
		6/11 Loan to Jack	20
		30/11 Pay bill at the bar	57
		7/12 Guinness	20
		10/12 Train ticket	5
		12/12 Landlord	10
			256
		12/12 BALANCE CARRIED DOWN	6
	262		262

Figure 2.3 Simple cashbook for Mr Brain – term 1

- The second convention is the custom of dividing the page down the (approximate) middle. The heavier lines form a T-shape and most classroom bookkeeping is done with these 'T-accounts' (as they are called). The convention is most easily accepted if you think of the vertical dividing line being the spine of a conventional book. If you were keeping a cashbook you might buy yourself a basic school exercise book and use the left-hand page for receipts and the right-hand for payments. Mr Brain's cashbook is just like this.
- Third, we label everything. If you were keeping a cash record you would label the record with dates, to whom it related, etc., in order to avoid confusion. Also your 'labels' tell you what the document is a record of. (This is a simple cash record.) Very few accounting activities are small enough to be able to manage with just a cashbook and so it helps to know exactly which accounting record you are looking at.
- Fourth, if you look at the total columns, you will see that the last numbers on both the receipts and the payments sides are the same. This is another rigidly held convention in keeping books. It is simply a matter of tidiness to show the accounting for that particular period is completed. It does not, of course mean, that Mr Brain's receipts and payments were exactly the same in the period. The two sides are made the same by introducing a **balancing figure** – in this case the '**balance carried down**'. (We will explain this term later. For the moment in this cashbook it just means what is left over. All accounts are made to balance by inserting either 'balancing' figures – as in this case – or some 'amount of usage' figure. We shall see in Part II of the book how to do this.) The balancing figure in Mr Brain's cashbook says how much cash he has left over on 12 December (£6) and should, of course, equal what he has in his bank account plus the cash he has in his pocket.
- Fifth, you will notice that we have used double underlining in places. This indicates that the column stops there. We will meet single underlining from time to time and this will usually imply a subtotal will follow it.
- Finally, we have called this a 'cashbook' in order to give you the idea of the simple record that we might keep for ourselves, for a club we were involved in or for a major international company for which we were cashier. We could also have called it a 'cash account'. We will tend to use the terms 'cashbook' and 'cash account' interchangeably although in large organizations there might well be a small but practical difference between them. That is, the cashbook might well be summarized, say on a monthly basis, into a cash account. We will consider how we organize the books of account in Chapter 6. For the time being continue to think of the two as interchangeable.

We now have our first basic piece of bookkeeping. We have a T-account, appropriately labelled, with – in the case of our cashbook – our cash receipts on the left and our cash payments on the right. We have balanced off the account and the 'balancing figure' tells us something – in this case how much cash Brain has left over. Virtually all the basic bookkeeping we will be doing over the next few chapters will follow this format (with a few adjustments for what goes on either side of the T-account).

This simple cashbook is quite a useful little record but we might well want it to provide more information – especially if our organization had a more complicated economic life than Mr Brain. To achieve this we might want to produce a **columnar cashbook**, or to separate out transactions that involved coins and notes from those that involved cheques – i.e. we might want separate **cash-in-hand** and **bank records** and, finally, our activities may be such that we might also want to keep a **petty cashbook**. We shall briefly look at each of these in turn in the next few sections.

2.2.2 The columnar cashbook

If instead of wanting just a simple record of Mr Brain's cash transactions we had wanted to know what sort of receipts came his way and what sorts of payments he made, we could do this with a **columnar cashbook**. An example of how Mr Brain's columnar cashbook might look is shown in Figure 2.4.

First check that you can see where the elements of Figure 2.3 (the simple cashbook) are in Figure 2.4. We still have the dates, the labels, the descriptions and, in the 'total column', we have the amounts of receipts and payments. The only difference is that we have added a series of columns which describe the types of receipts and the types of payments. You can have as many (or as few) columns as you choose. The determining factor is what information you want to be able to glean easily from the account. We can see at a glance, for example, that Brain paid out £139 on drink and £50 on rent. The description/narrative column tells the reader a little more about the specific items that went to make up the totals. To repeat – it is up to the accountant what columns s/he uses (there are really very few rigid conventions here) and that should be wholly determined by what the accountant thinks the user of the information wants and/or needs to know. (For illustration, we might have chosen to categorize the payments into 'Basic sustenance and travel', 'Work', 'Play' and 'Other' columns. This might have produced totals of £70, £3, £163 and £20.) Notice also that the totals of the specific columns should add to the total or subtotal in the totals column. That is, in the jargon, accounts should **cross-cast**.

Virtually any organization will keep a cashbook along these lines. This approach is especially important when there are many transactions but the organization does not keep a complete set of accounting records[1] You must, therefore understand the principles – which are fairly straightforward – and be able to produce such a columnar cashbook. However, this is the sort of thing that is very much easier to learn in practice than in the classroom. Therefore:

RECEIPTS											PAYMENTS	
Date	Savings	Loan	Gift	Total	Date	Drink	Food	Travel	Gambling	Rent	Sundry	Total
2/10 Parents			200	200	2/10 Landlord					20		20
2/11 Aunty G			10	10	2/10 Shop		10					10
20/11 P.Office	50			50	5/10 Bus pass			5				5
6/12 Fred		2		2	5/10 Texts						3	3
					30/10 Turf accountants				16			16
					30/10 Bar	62						62
					3/11 Dart B.						8	8
					3.11 Landlord					20		20
					6/11 Loan						20	20
					30/11 Bar	57						57
					7/12 Drink	20						20
					10/12 Train			5				5
					12/12 Landlord					10		10
	50	2	210	262		139	10	5	16	50	31	256
					Balance							6
				262								262

Figure 2.4 Columnar cashbook for A. Brain 1 October – 12 December 200X

- you should try to become treasurer of a club or society or even help a small organization with its bookkeeping;
- try for (at least a limited period of time) to keep a cashbook of your own economic activities.

We will not place overmuch emphasis on this sort of detail (i.e. columnar) throughout the book. For most of our purposes, the simple cashbook will suffice.

But the columnar cashbook, on its own, may not be enough. For one thing, we have not distinguished between Mr Brain's coin and notes transactions and those for which he wrote cheques. This may be important and so deserves a brief examination.

2.2.3 Distinguishing between cash-in-hand and bank transactions

There are a number of reasons for perhaps wanting to distinguish cash transactions which involve notes and coins (what we shall call **cash-in-hand**) from those which involve cheques. For the larger organization, the main reason will be to help control the amount of cash that is sloshing around the place (we will briefly look at this in Chapter 6 but this is also the sort of topic you will cover in financial management). This is less important for Mr Brain but, whatever one's economic complexity, one will, at least, need to check one's own accounting records with those of the bank and this is another major reason for keeping 'cash' and 'bank' separate (see Chapter 6).

To illustrate how this is done we will return to Mr Brain's simple cashbook. (We could have used the columnar cashbook, but why make things more complicated than they already are?) We now need to know a bit more information. Let us assume that the receipts from the Post Office and Fred were in cash and the payments for the groceries, for the textbooks, for the dartboard, to Jack and for the train ticket were also in cash, whilst all other transactions were via cheques. Then we can produce a cash–bank book as in Figure 2.5.

Figure 2.5 simply splits up Mr Brain's receipts and payments into those which have passed through the bank and those which have been dealt with through cash-in-hand. So far, so good. But there is a major problem with Figure 2.5. If you look carefully, you will see that Mr Brain made a number of payments in cash in October and early November when, in fact, he didn't have any cash! This means that Mr Brain, having opened his bank account, must have drawn some of it out in cash in order to pay the grocers, to buy the textbooks and dartboard and to make the loan to Jack. Our cash–bank book must show this. Furthermore, if you think about it for a moment, if he drew some cash out of the bank, then there would not be enough in the bank for him to write the cheques at the end of December. He must either have paid some cash back into the bank or gone overdrawn. Let us assume, therefore, that Mr Brain drew £50 out of his bank account on 2 October and, realizing that he would be unable to cover all his cheques, when he drew his savings out of the Post Office, paid £40 back into the bank on 20 November. If he does this and we reflect it in his cash–bank book, his accounting record will look something like Figure 2.6.

The new entries are shown in italics simply to highlight them for you. (In practice such 'internal' bookkeeping entries might be marked in the record as *contras* to show that they are, indeed internal to this record.) We have first of all shown Mr Brain 'spending' £50 of his bank money to 'buy' £50 of cash. This £50 is then shown as a receipt by his cash column. Exactly the opposite happens when he pays cash into the bank. He 'pays' £40 of his cash in order to get a £40 receipt in the bank. We now have a record of Mr Brain's cash position and how he arrived at it.

Cash–bank book for Mr Brain – Term 1					
RECEIPTS	**Cash**	**Bank**	**PAYMENTS**	**Cash**	**Bank**
Date			Date		
2/10 Parents		200	2/10 Landlord		20
2/11 Aunty Gertrude		10	2/10 Grocers	10	
20/11 Post Office	50		5/10 Bus pass		5
6/12 Fred	2		5/10 Textbooks	3	
	52	210	30/10 Turf accountants		16
			30/10 Pay bill at the bar		62
			3/11 Dartboard	8	
			3/11 Landlord		20
			6/11 Loan to Jack	20	
			30/11 Pay bill at the bar		57
			7/12 Guinness		20
			10/12 Train ticket	5	
			12/12 Landlord		10
				46	210
			12/12 Balance carried down	6	0
	52	210		52	210

Figure 2.5 Cash–bank book for Mr Brain – term 1

Cash–bank book for Mr Brain – Term 1					
RECEIPTS	**Cash**	**Bank**	**PAYMENTS**	**Cash**	**Bank**
Date			Date		
2/10 Grant cheque		200	2/10 *Withdraw cash*		50
2/10 *Cash from bank*	50		2/10 Landlord		20
2/11 Aunty Gertrude		10	2/10 Grocers	10	
20/11 Post Office	50		5/10 Bus pass		5
30/11 *Pay in cash*		40	5/10 Textbooks	3	
6/12 Fred	2		30/10 Turf accountants		16
			30/10 Pay bill at the bar		62
			3/11 Dartboard	8	
			3/11 Landlord		20
			6/11 Loan to Jack	20	
			30/11 *Pay in cash*	40	
			30/11 Pay bill at the bar		57
			7/12 Guinness		20
			10/12 Train ticket	5	
			12/12 Landlord		10
	102	250		86	260
12/12 Balance carried down		10	12/12 Balance carried down	16	
	102	260		102	260

Figure 2.6 Cash–bank book for Mr Brain – term 1

However, to make the individual columns balance we have had to put in two balancing figures. This is important. Before getting mesmerized by the figures, think about what has happened. Mr Brain has cash receipts of £102 and cash payments of £86. In cash, therefore, he has £16 in his pocket. However, his bank has bank receipts of £250 and bank payments of £260. His bank has therefore paid out £10 more than he has – he is overdrawn by £10. His overall cash situation is still the same as it was though. He has £6 left over at the end (his cash less his overdraft). The two balancing figures thus represent his (positive) left-over cash (£16) and his (negative) left-over overdraft (£10). Balancing figures can thus occur on either or both sides of an account. They need to be interpreted with care – we will learn how to do this more fully as we go on.

Now, of course, a big organization may have many different bank accounts and so this sort of moving around between accounts and between accounts and cash can be a fairly significant exercise in its own right. However, once again to keep things as simple as we can at this stage, we will not bother with these complexities. (Although, did you notice that, to be fully accurate, we should have included an extra 'bank column' for Mr Brain's Post Office account?)

So, we have seen how to draw up a simple cashbook and then how we can increase the information contained in that accounting record by, first, producing a columnar cashbook which itemizes types of receipts and payments and, second, producing a cash–bank record that shows transfers between our cash-in-hand and our bank account. There is one final type of cashbook which we should mention here for completeness – the **petty cashbook**.

2.2.4 The petty cashbook

Your college will have a cashbook (probably held on a computer) and will record receipts and payments as they occur. The cash receipts and payments of the college will include many massive receipts from student fees or major research grants (for example) and enormous payments for (for example) new buildings or (not so enormous payments for) wages and salaries. Such transactions will run into many thousands of pounds or dollars. However, there will also be tiny little cash transactions. When you pay a few pence/cents for a bit of photocopying or the department urgently needs a first-class stamp, the departmental secretary does not go dashing across to central administration (which might be miles away) to get/pay in the cash and to get the transaction immediately recorded. They will have a cash float of some sort probably run on what is called an *imprest system*.[2] This will be known as the **petty cash** – because 'petty' means small from the obvious French roots. The secretary will keep a record of all receipts and payments which go through the petty cash and this will be the **petty cashbook**. It will be identical in every way to our simple cashbook except that the amounts and items involved are usually very small, day-to-day items. So, for example, Mr Brain might keep a petty cashbook instead of recording all the cash-in-hand details in the cash column of his cashbook. His cashbook would then just show movements between petty cash and the bank.

You must realize that there are no hard and fast rules about how cashbooks must be kept – just so long as they are accurate and helpful and do not count things twice or miss things altogether.

Now that we have managed to produce a basic financial accounting record – with variations – it will be useful if we stop for a moment and try and pull out some of the issues that are involved in the cashbook.

2.3 ANALYSIS OF MR BRAIN'S CASHBOOK

2.3.1 Some developments from the cashbook

The most obvious thing we learn from the cashbook is that Mr Brain's spending patterns do not seem particularly out of the ordinary (for students of our acquaintance) and that he has £6 left at the end of term. However, there is additional financial information that either Mr Brain or his parents might wish to know but which is not immediately apparent from the cashbook. This additional financial information might include:

- what his 'true' financial situation is;
- whether he is better or worse off at the end of the period;
- what resources he actually consumed (rather than spent) during the term.

The provision of this additional financial information is what the **financial statements** are intended to achieve. The financial statements – traditionally dominated by the **income statement** (or **profit and loss account**) and the **position statement** (or **balance sheet**) are complex creatures and it will take most of this book simply to show how they are constructed. However, it is the case that the basic idea behind these statements is relatively straightforward. And it will certainly be useful if you have at least some idea of what we are trying to achieve with our bookkeeping, trial balances and adjustments and so forth. Returning to Mr Brain's situation at college we can actually learn quite a lot about the principal notions that underlie the balance sheet (which is designed to tell us a number of things including his financial position at a point in time) and the income statement (which is also designed to tell us a number of things including what he has consumed and earned during the period and whether he is better or worse off at the end of the period).

If you look back to Figures 2.1 and 2.2 you will remember that there were a number of pieces of information that we didn't use. Even though they were shown as being 'relevant' they ended up at the bottom of Figure 2.2 as 'other stuff'. It is this 'other stuff' together with the information in the cashbook that will help us construct a very basic sort of balance sheet and income statement. We will approach it by trying to answer the question 'Is Mr Brain better off or worse off at the end of the term than he was at the beginning of the term?'. One way of answering this question is shown in Figure 2.7.[3]

The question has assumed that Mr Brain, student, started the term with nothing at all except, as we learn later, savings of £50 which he 'invests' in himself and his education during the term. At the end of the term, however, he has £6 (as we found out from the cashbook) and he also has some other things – see Figure 2.7. He also has a bit of 'negative ownership' – that is, he owes some money. If we compare what he started off with (what he owes to himself), what he owns, owes and is owed,[4] we find that he is £54 worse off at the end of the term than at the beginning – not £6 better off as we might have been tempted to infer from his cashbook. This summary of what is owed and owned is a sort of *balance sheet*. As we will come to see, a balance sheet is little more than a sophisticated restatement of ownership and owing-ness.

Oddly enough, we can come to the same conclusion if we ask a different sort of question: 'Did Mr Brain consume more or less than he earned during the term?'. This is not simply what he received and what he spent but what he 'earned' (which is, in this case, what he received less what he may have to pay back) and what he 'consumed' (which is what he spent less what he has left over plus what he consumed – drank, ate, lived in – but did not pay for). As Figure 2.7 shows, this also produces a 'worse-off-by' figure of £54. If

(a) He has:
Owned by him:
- Cash (£6); Dartboard (£8); Textbook (£3) plus half his Guinness (£10)
Owed to him:
- Jack owes (£20)

(b) But he 'has not':
Owed by him:
- Landlord (£15); Fred (£2) plus Bar (£34)
Owed to his 'owners' (himself):
- Savings (£50)

These figures are the basis for his position statement or **balance sheet**.

(c) He 'earned':
- Parents (£200) plus Aunty (£10)
(d) He 'used up':
- Booze (£163); Rent (£65); Food (£10); Travel (£10) plus Gambling (£16)

These figures are the basis for his income statement or **profit and loss account**.

Note:
(a) − (b) = £47 − £101 = £−54
(c) − (d) = £210 − £264 = £−54
Is this magic, or what?????????

Figure 2.7 Is Mr Brain better off or worse off at the end of the term than he was at the beginning?

Mr Brain were a commercial organization such as a company (see Chapter 3), this would be his loss for the period.

If this does not seem crystal-clear at this stage, there is no need to get anxious. We will be spending a long time over the following chapters leading up to these points. However, you should think hard about why these two separate calculations produce the same answer. If you can work this out and, indeed, say why it must be the case and then explain it to a non-accountant, you have understood one of the most important features of basic bookkeeping and financial accounting. This is a most useful yardstick by which to judge your progress.

So, to summarize, the cashbook provides a basic record of actual cash transactions during a defined period. It does show us what an entity has spent and received. It does not show whether Mr Brain is better or worse off, what he has actually consumed and earned or either what he has 'left over' or what his financial situation is. To achieve this we need additional information which is not contained in the cashbook. Then we have to do some additional calculations to produce what we will learn to call a balance sheet and an income statement or profit and loss account. The simple cashbook can be developed to show transfers between cash-in-hand and the bank and/or to show categories of receipts and payments. The cashbook is the most basic, and perhaps the most important, financial record that any organization can keep.

With the cashbook tucked firmly under our belts, we can now use this financial record to illustrate some of the points we made in Chapter 1.

2.3.2 Mr Brain and the characteristics of accounting

Thinking back to the way we defined accounting and the four characteristics of conventional accounting we can see how they operated in Mr Brain as an accounting entity; that is, we separated him from the rest of the world and looked at the transactions that he made with his immediate environment, as illustrated in Figure 2.8.

We did not include the detailed financial actions of the household, the college or any other group of which Brain was a part because it was Brain alone in whom we were interested. Of course, somebody (presumably an accountant) was somewhere treating the individual shops, bars, landlord, etc., as other accounting entities and writing up books for them. Those books would include their transactions with Brain.

Furthermore, in order to account for our accounting entity, we not only had to define very carefully 'what was Mr Brain and what was not Mr Brain' but also we had to define the exact period of time for which we were accounting. In Mr Brain's case, the accounting period was one term. So an accounting entity is defined in both space and time.

Second, we concentrated on *relevant economic events*. We did not, in this exercise, consider Brain's performance during his course at the college, whether he was homesick or how good he was at darts, as these are events which do not have immediate and direct economic consequences on A. Brain, the student.

Third, all the events were described in *financial terms*. Although it may be of interest, we did not describe what beer Brain drank (other than Guinness) or what textbook he bought. We simply identified the financial attributes of these event. (We will learn that economic events are largely determined by whether or not we can provide a financial description for them – and the financial description will, in most cases, be determined by whether an event can be represented by a flow of cash into or out of the accounting entity (focal organization) in past, in present or in future accounting periods.)

Finally, the whole process was undertaken for a purpose – namely, the requirement by the Brain elders that their son provide a financial explanation of his activities to them. The

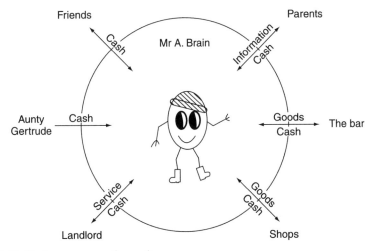

Figure 2.8 Mr Brain – an accounting entity

parents were the eventual users of the information and their wants and needs had to be, in this case, partly anticipated.

Thus the exercise succeeded in identifying, collecting, describing, recording, processing financial information about economic things that have happened to Mr Brain which could then be communicated to the people who (apparently) had a need of such information.

2.3.3 Currencies and the unit of account

Before leaving our initial analysis of cash for the time being, we can use the example of Mr Brain to make a general point about currencies and the unit of account. The above analysis has recorded everything in the UK currency – pounds sterling. It would be a simple matter to rewrite all the above analysis into a different currency by, for example, replacing all the £s with $s (whether US, Australian, New Zealand, Canadian or Singaporean, for example) or Dutch guilders, Deutschmarks, francs, pesetas, or whatever. That is, in order to do our accounting we need a specified **unit of account**. We could, should we so wish, account entirely in bottles of Guinness, loaves of bread or CDs. We could make a specified 'thing' our unit of account.[5] However, it is traditional in the (so-called) developed economies to account using a specified unit of money. This is generally considered to be more convenient – although, as we shall see in Chapter 16, it can raise some serious problems in times of inflation and changing prices.

So, as long as we stick to a single specified unit of account, conventional accounting can proceed fairly well. But what happens when we mix up currencies? What would we have done if Mr Brain's Aunty Gertrude lived in Australia and had sent Brain $10 instead of £10? What would we have done if the landlord lived overseas and demanded payment entirely in Dutch guilders so that Brain had paid 50 NFl for rent during the period? If this were the situation how much cash would Mr Brain have at the end of the term? Work it out for yourself but Mr Brain would have (£46 + A$10 − 50 NFl). How much is that? It depends, obviously, on the exchange rate at the time. Now the solution to a problem of this sort is very simple (at least in the classroom). All we do is turn all transactions into the same currency: £, A$, NFl, or perhaps a fourth currency, say, NZ$. Then we can account for all transactions in the same unit of account. (Try looking up today's currency rates and working out Mr Brain's cash situation at the end of term.)

However, in practice, this is a far from simple matter – and one which many organizations face day by day. Currencies fluctuate all over the place and, just to make matters awkward, banks charge significant fees for turning one currency into another one. To illustrate, say that £1 = A$2 and the bank charge £3 for currency translation. Aunty Gertrude's $10 will only produce £2 in Mr Brain's cashbook. When you consider the numbers of transactions that General Motors, Exxon, Yamaha and the World Bank must have, you can perhaps see that the 'unit of account' problem can be a major challenge to our bookkeeping and accounting.

The specification of a unit of account is clearly central to accounting and to the 'financial description' characteristic. The currency problem is one of which you need to be aware and if you can handle it at this level then cash issues need not cause you any problems. We will return to this issue, very briefly, in Chapter 14.

2.4 SOME LESSONS FROM MR BRAIN

At the beginning of this chapter we said we would be trying, throughout the book, to look at both the *how* and the *why* of accounting. So now that we know *how* to prepare a cashbook for Mr Brain's parents let us step back and have a more general look at the role that accounting information played in the relationship between Brain and his parents. Four questions spring to mind:

i   Why did Brain supply information?
ii   Why did his parents ask for the information?
iii Why did they ask for financial information?
iv   Why did he supply it in a cashbook format?

2.4.1 Why do entities supply information?

Taking the first question, we know that Brain, like any sensible person, will provide information to three groups of people:

- those whom we wish to have the information, i.e. it is volunteered information (e.g. 'Darling, I love you'; 'Sorry, George, you'll have to buy the tea tonight – I'm broke'; 'I really enjoyed that lecture, Dr Jekyll');
- those whom we believe it is in our interest to inform (e.g. 'Oops, sorry, officer, I hit some black ice'; 'Certainly, Mr Bank Manager, my grant cheque will be in on the 30th without fail'; 'I have seven children and a sick grandmother to support, M'lud');
- those who have a right to the information – most realistically, an enforceable right, but in an ideal world a simple moral right would do. (The Inland Revenue and Brain's parents are particularly appropriate examples.)

Of course, these groups are not necessarily discrete. Brain may want his parents to know his spending habits, he may also think he may get a more favourable treatment from them if he gives the information (i.e. it is in his interest) and, third, they may be able to enforce what they see as a right to the information.

2.4.2 Why do people request information?

In effect what is happening in Mr Brain's case is that he is being held *accountable* by his parents. At its simplest his parents are holding him responsible for:

- certain (as yet specified) behaviour and/or activity while at college;
- accounting for that behaviour or action.

That is, he is responsible for his actions and responsible to account for those actions (i.e. accountable).

Now, this is a very general perspective that applies to most accounting entities (e.g. charities and donors, companies and shareholders, local authorities and their electorates). It naturally follows that we need to know for what actions our company, a charity, Mr Brain or any other focal organization is being held responsible and then prepare an account that *relates to those actions*. Thus if the Brain elders are imposing a responsibility on their son to manage his cash sensibly, then a cashbook is the right form of account to discharge that accountability. They can assess his behaviour with respect to cash from it. If, however, they are imposing a responsibility to work hard and 'do well' academically, then a cashbook is of very little use because it does not relate to the academic actions for which he is accountable.

This brings us to probably the key point in accounting. Remember that our purpose is to provide information to those who have a right to it. But why might they want such information? Curiosity? An affection for reports? No, these are trivial reasons. In traditional accounting it is normally assumed that our aim is to provide information that will be helpful to users and, usually (without being too specific at this stage), upon which they can base decisions. One purpose might be to enable the entity to be controlled. For either the entity (company, charity, health authority or individual) to control itself or be controlled, it is necessary to know its **objective(s)** (that which it seeks to achieve and that for which it will be held responsible), how well it achieved its objective(s) (its **effectiveness**), and its **efficiency** in pursuing its objective(s). Accounting is a major mechanism by which the entity may discharge its accountability for its efficiency and effectiveness with respect to its held objective(s).

Now, of course, this all seems rather over the top for a student – objectives? responsibility? efficiency? But remember we chose the simplest of all cases – the individual. As soon as we move to organizations, in the next chapter, control of efficiency and effectiveness become prerequisites for organizational success, not to say survival. Even in Brain's case it does not seem too preposterous to imagine that the parents might try and achieve some measure of control over their offspring. To achieve this control they must take decisions about what actions are open to them – in this case not paying a parental contribution for his education or simple moral pressure may be the choice. So the information must also be suitable input to the controller's decision model.

It is quite likely that Brain and his parents may hold different objectives and so would need different information. This again is frequently the case in the more complex entities. This all goes to show that a lot is expected of the accountant and their information. Thus it comes as no surprise to learn that the accountant has a problem identifying and reconciling all these different requirements and their sources (the 'users').

2.4.3 What sort of information?

It becomes apparent that if accountants stick with financial information only ('conventional' or 'traditional' accounting as we have called this) then much of the information necessary to discharge accountability cannot be provided. Financial information alone cannot tell you how effective or efficient a charity, university or health authority has been because their objectives are primarily non-financial. Where any entity has non-financial objectives (and all do) then accounting in financial terms has a limited usefulness. Nevertheless, accounting in financial terms does have many applications and it is upon these that we will concentrate for most of the book, returning to 'non-financial' accounting as seems appropriate. There is little question that accounting for non-financial objectives is a particularly difficult and exciting challenge for accountants at the present time.

2.4.4 Why do accountants supply information?

Finally, then, why do we as accountants respond to requests for information? The simple answer is: because we are employed to do so. We are a service industry. This is not the whole story, though. As we discussed in Chapter 1, we accountants claim to be professionals and, as a result, our activities must serve the 'public interest'. Our accounting information must, in some way or other, be good for society. That involves difficult **ethical choices** and depends upon our social, economic and political beliefs about society. There is, therefore, no easy way to decide how we (and the accounting entity) should decide who shall have information and the form in which our (financial) information should be presented. To produce information simply because we are paid to do it – although important – is to suggest that accountants will do anything if they are paid enough. There is a rude word for this and it is not one that a real professional will feel happy with. Furthermore, to simply produce information because we mindlessly follow a set of rules is the mark of a robot and an abnegation of our professional duty. Ask yourself, would society pay so much and ascribe such status to a profession that slavishly followed rules and could be bought off easily by anybody with a bit of cash? Accounting is much more important than that and the accountancy profession owes society and the public interest a much better deal. Only if the accountancy profession can meet the highest professional standards and the highest ethical values will it fulfil such expectations.

Amongst the principal questions which this book will begin to answer is how accountants decide on what information should be disclosed by organizations, what form that information should take and who has a right to receive the information. As we shall see, these are difficult questions and, although we can only scratch the surface of them in an introductory text like this, you must not allow yourself to slip into thinking that accounting is straightforwardly technical, mechanical and arithmetical. It is a great deal more than this.

SUMMARY

Cash is probably the most important of the 'raw materials' that accountants work with. It is also one of the most important elements of an organization – if that organization is to survive. Therefore a record of cash is a crucial part of the accounting records and a very important element in the information that any organization needs to run its day-to-day affairs. The basic accounting record we use for this is the **cashbook**. The main points about the cashbook are summarized in Figure 2.9.

Whilst the cashbook is very important, there is a lot that it does not tell us. Cash – and increases and decreases therein – is not the same as 'well-offness' and whilst we have introduced some of this difference, we will spend a fair amount of time in later chapters exploring how those differences arise. We say, in fact, that the cashbook needs to be supplemented by, at a minimum, an income statement or profit and loss account and a balance sheet. How we set about keeping more detailed accounting records that will enable us to put together these statements is the work of Parts II and III of the book.

But we discovered that, even when we were considering the cashbook – the most basic of the accounting records – there was a lot about the nature of accounting that we could learn from it. We saw how it reflected the **definition of accounting,** how it reflected and illustrated the **four characteristics of accounting** and how it raised important questions about the nature of accounting information and why we produce it at all. Thus, we see one of the really fascinating things about accounting – both its theory and its practice. That is, accounting involves both (a) neat and tidy accounting records and accounting procedures which produce interesting and useful information and (b) those simple records embody within them a whole range of important assumptions about the world we live in and can be used to tell us an enormous amount about our world. So accounting is both technical

1. The cashbook is the record, usually daily or weekly, of the cash transactions made by the organization.

2. The cashbook may be a simple record (as we have just seen for Mr Brain) or it may be analysed or columnar.

3. The analysis in a cashbook could be:

   (a) separating out cash (actual movements in actual coins and notes) and bank (movements of 'cash' via cheques, standing orders, pay-ins or withdrawals) and/or

   (b) separately identifying categories of receipts and payments (as we shall see for Mr Brain).

4. The detail in a cashbook may be summarized into a cash account. This would record the weekly, monthly or yearly totals (for example). In this textbook we use the terms 'cashbook' and 'cash account' interchangeably as seems appropriate at the time and analyse (or not) the cashbook/cash account as seems appropriate to the issue/question we are examining. The determining factor is the information needed.

5. There is also something called the *petty cashbook*. 'Petty' means small in this context and it would record, for example, the movements in actual cash from a cash float kept in the office for stamps, milk, window cleaning and other sundry small cash expenses. We will generally put such items through the cashbook/cash account itself and not concentrate overmuch on the petty cashbook.

Figure 2.9 A summary of the cashbook

and algorithmic and social, economic and political. This is why accounting is worth studying and why it takes so many years of intense effort by intelligent people like you to produce good, professional accountants.

Key terms and concepts

The following key terms and concepts have featured in this chapter. You should ensure that you understand and can explain each one. Page references to definitions appear in the index in bold type.

- Accountability
- Accountancy profession
- Accountants
- Accounting period
- Balance carried down
- Balance sheet
- Balancing figure
- Cash
- Cashbook
- Cash-in-hand
- Columnar cashbook
- Cross-cast
- Currencies
- Income statement/profit and loss account
- Information
- Near-cash
- Payments
- Petty cashbook
- Receipts
- T-account
- Unit of account

FURTHER READING

The readings we suggested for Chapter 1 are still useful here. In addition, you should by now be reading annual reports, a good newspaper and a professional accountancy magazine. Items concerned with cash (especially when business failure is being discussed) should appear in these. Further, most professional accountancy bodies have, in recent years, been worrying about cash, 'funds' and 'near-cash'. (See Chapter 15 for more detail on this area.) In the UK, some of this discussion centred around the Accounting Standards Board's (ASB) Statement on Cash Flow Statements (Financial Reporting Standard (FRS) No.1, issued in 1990 and revised in 1996). (See Chapter 14 for more detail on the regulation of accounting.) This makes interesting and relevant reading. (Other countries will have a similar standard – you should look for this in your own country.) Finally, as mentioned in the text, the best way to get a grip on cash and cashbooks is to actually do one – either for yourself or for some organization with which you are involved – a club, a charity or perhaps a small business venture you are considering.

NOTES

1. The principal reasons why many organizations – especially smaller organizations – do not keep full accounting records are related to available personnel time and expertise. In turn this affects whether, indeed, it is worth all the time and effort to keep detailed financial records – whether the benefits to the organization exceed the considerable costs they would incur. Does your folk group or rock band, your sports team or your social club – or whatever – keep very detailed accounting records? We should think not. The same goes for businesses.
2. The imprest system roughly works as follows. A figure for the size of the float is decided – say, £10. The expenditure from that float is calculated every now and then – daily, weekly, monthly or whatever – and, if approved, the expenditure is reimbursed to the float, bringing it back to its imprest level of, in this case, £10.
3. You will be able to trace all the numbers in Figure 2.7 with the possible exception of the 'used-up' figures for booze and rent. The booze figure comprises the £139 cash spent on booze *plus* the £34 he has spent at the bar but still owes (he has consumed this even if he hasn't paid for it yet) *less* the £10 of Guinness he has left over. The rent figure comprises the £50 he has spent (from his cashbook) *plus* the £15 he still owes the landlord.
4. The more usual accounting terminology for these things are capital (what is owed to the owners), assets (what is owned), creditors (what is owed by us) and debtors (what is owed to us). These terms will be defined again as the book progresses. Figure 2.7 uses something we will meet later called the 'accounting equations' which say that [Assets = Capital + Profit – Loss + Liabilities] and [Profit = Income – Expenditure].
5. Indeed some very interesting new local economic trading schemes (LETS) account entirely in terms of such things as 'obligations', 'hours of work' or an invented, fictitious currency called a 'green dollar' or a 'time dollar'.

3 Organizations, organizational subsystems and the flows of double-entry bookkeeping

---

Learning objectives

After studying this chapter you should be able to:

- demonstrate the link between an accounting entity and an organization;
- give a general definition of an organization;
- explain the difference between commercial and non-commercial organizations;
- define several different types of organization;
- describe and understand a systems model of organizations;
- describe the systems and subsystems of this model;
- demonstrate the flows into and out of the organization;
- demonstrate how these flows provide an organizational basis for accounting record-keeping;
- produce three basic T-accounts and show how the double-entry bookkeeping system enters data to these accounts;
- explain debits and credits;
- feel comfortable with an organizational model of the bookkeeping process.

3.1 INTRODUCTION

3.1.1 Chapter design and links to previous chapters

Chapter 1 introduced a definition of accounting, talked about the work of accountants and explored why studying accounting – and thinking about it – was so important. In particular, Chapter 1 gave us the **four characteristics of traditional accounting**. Chapter 2 then put these four characteristics to work. We identified a very simple **accounting entity** – Mr Brain, the student – and we identified a number of the **economic events** that affected him.

We then provided a **financial description** of those economic events. This description in our particular instance was in terms of **cash**. With this we produced an **accounting record** that we called Brain's **cashbook** and discussed why he should have this. The basic reasons for producing this (as with most accounting records) was because there were people and organizations who wanted to – and had a right to – use that information. These **users** of accounting information could be either 'internal' to the accounting entity (Mr Brain himself in our simple example) or 'external' to the organization (such as Mr Brain's parents). They might use this information for a variety of purposes but chief amongst them would be the desire to control the accounting entity, to develop its accountability and, perhaps, to take decisions based on that information.

Cash transactions were, we saw, the most basic of the ways in which we could financially describe economic events for an accounting entity. The cashbook was the most basic of the accounting records and a single individual was the simplest form of accounting entity. Unfortunately, life is rarely this simple. Much of what follows in this book will be attempting to account in more sophisticated ways for more complicated organizations. This chapter begins this process.

It should be obvious by now that the starting point for accounting is the existence of an accounting entity. We cannot provide an account until we know what it is we are accounting for. Now, as we have seen, how we define the accounting entity in which we are interested is governed by many factors – sometimes it is just the judgement of the accountant, sometimes a large organization like a transnational corporation or a central government department will define accounting entities for administrative and control convenience and sometimes the accounting entity will be governed by law – as in the case of a company (see also Chapter 14). Whatever our accounting entity, they all have in common that they are – or they can be viewed as being – **organizations**.[1] By looking carefully at organizations – and how accountants traditionally view them – we can start to see how accounting practice and organizational life are closely interrelated.

The objective of this chapter, therefore, is to provide a general way of thinking about organizations and then to show how the bookkeeping system reflects the organization it is accounting for. Put more generally, we will define an organizational view of traditional accounting and demonstrate how the concept of organization helps define the accounting entity and provides a basis for the bookkeeping and accounting system.

The chapter is organized as follows. The next subsection provides a definition of an 'organization'. Section 3.2 introduces some of the differences between commercial and non-commercial organizations. Section 3.3 provides some definitions of different types of organizations. Section 3.4 provides a systems model of (way of thinking about) an organization, demonstrates the flows of information, cash and goods and services which occur in any organization and then links this to accounting record-keeping – bookkeeping. This section finishes with an introduction to debits, credits and double-entry bookkeeping. Section 3.5 revisits Mr Brain and applies what we have learnt in this chapter to his situation – producing a basic set of accounting records in the process.

Finally, *a note to the reader*. Considerable experience with teaching the following approach to thinking about accounting shows us that it works extremely well for students who have not studied accounting before – if they carefully follow the steps outlined below. For those who *have* studied it before, be patient. If you can work through what must seem like a long-winded way of doing things you will never need to get confused about bookkeeping again. If, of course, you always get your bookkeeping and accounting 100 per cent correct all the time then there is nothing that our 55 years of experience can teach you.

3.1.2 What is an organization?

If all accounting entities were as simple and uncomplicated as Mr Brain, accounting would be a relatively straightforward process. Of course, this is not the case. Most accounting activity focuses upon organizations which can vary from the relatively simple (e.g. clubs or one-person businesses) to the very complex (e.g. central government or multinational corporations). Whilst the very basic principles of accounting do not change from organization to organization, the issues raised, the sophistication required and the detailed structure of the accounting activity vary enormously.

The *Oxford English Dictionary* defines **organization** as:

> a body, system or society, given orderly structure; brought into working order; furnished with vitality.

Thus, the critical elements of an organization are:

- that it is ordered (i.e. organized) – however well or badly;
- that it is purposive – it is directed towards some aim(s) or objective(s);
- that it has an existence separate from those individuals who operate it, own it and/or work in it – a business can always be sold or transferred and although its character might change that business still exists; a charity can change its directors and trustees but the charity still exists, and so on;
- that it is dynamic – it is a changing organism, interacting with, responding to and influencing its host society.

Each organization is a separate accounting entity and may itself contain smaller accounting entities. Groups of companies (like the Ford Motor Company or Shell) are usually organized like this and frequently have smaller divisions and operating units which are, themselves, treated as separate entities for accounting purposes. The same is true for a local or federal government, for Greenpeace or a national health service.

As with Mr Brain in Chapter 1, the accounting process attempts to provide information that will discharge the entity's accountability and, in so doing, supply information that allows users of that information to take formal decisions about the planning and/or control of the entities under consideration. To do this the information must reflect and relate to the objectives held for the entity by that user of the information and must be in a form useful to him/her for that purpose.

The accounting activity, in reflecting the different purposes of entities, will therefore vary across different types of organization. The accounting activity in local government will be very dissimilar in many ways from that of a church or an insurance company. (We shall look at some of these differences as we go along.)

3.2 TYPES OF ORGANIZATIONS

There are many ways in which we might categorize organizations: large/small, manufacturing/service, successful/failed and so on. Although we will encounter and use many such distinctions, the principal characteristics which we tend to focus upon are the organization's ownership, objectives and structure. In Figure 3.1 you will see the major categorizations that will serve our purposes in this book.

There is a lot of detail contained in Figure 3.1 and so some words of explanation are in order. The term 'public sector' refers specifically to ultimate control and/or ownership by the current government on behalf of the state. On the other hand, the 'private sector' is owned and/or controlled by individuals, groups, companies (especially insurance companies), trust funds, pension funds, charities and such like. The distinction blurs in many places where, for example, a local government pension fund owns a large number of

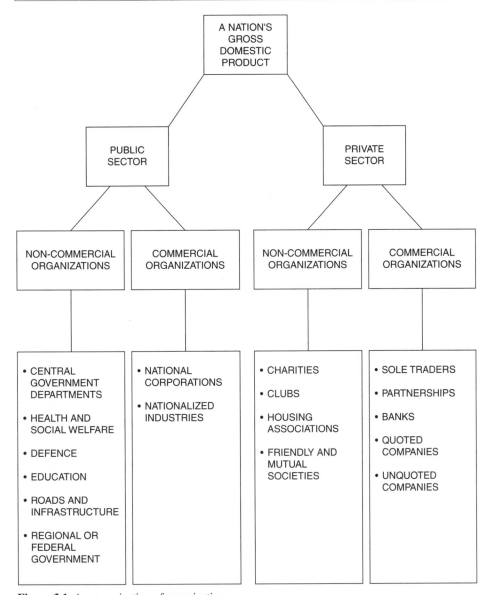

Figure 3.1 A categorization of organizations

company shares or the government has a large holding of shares in a company or in the case of many organizations (like charities) which are subject to and dependent upon government policy, directive and grants.

Our key distinction is between commercial and non-commercial organizations. (A common alternative choice of terms is 'for-profit' and 'not-for-profit'.) **Commercial organizations** are (usually) established with commercial objectives in mind. These include the minimum requirement to break even and presumably one or more of: making a profit, growth, long-term survival, maximizing their share of the market, improving the quality of product or service, securing greater economic power and/or achieving independence and so on. At its simplest, commercial organizations should generate funds from their principal activities.

Non-commercial organizations are the polar opposite: they try and generate funds through, for example, donations, grants or budget allocations rather than through trading, to the extent that funds are necessary for them to carry on their principal activities. In public-sector non-commercial organizations the generation of funds is a political process dependent upon the policies of the government of the day. It is normally assumed that a commercial (say) health-care organization generates funds *by* delivering health care whereas a national health service generates funds *in order* to deliver health care. (For more detail see Anthony and Young 1984, Chapter 2.)

Non-commercial organizations cover a very wide range of activities and objectives but they have a number of factors in common:

- they generally deliver services (rather than products);
- they are generally labour-intensive;
- their output (the amount of service) is generally determined by their inputs (e.g. cash/labour available);

and, perhaps most significantly with respect to the traditional accounting model:

- their quality of output (i.e. their success) is not related to financial success; and so the conventional financial accounting activity cannot *link* or *relate* input to output as it can in commercial organizations. (We will return to this crucial point in later chapters).

Having said all this, we are perhaps in danger of making too great a distinction between commercial and non-commercial organizations. Both groups fit our earlier definitions, are directed towards goals, are (as we shall learn to see them) dynamic systems interacting with their host society and both groups require information for the discharge of accountability, for planning and for control. The need for accounting exists in both types. The tendency to emphasize the difference is largely historic in that the major emphasis in conventional accounting – in terms of practice, theory and recruitment – has been on commercial organizations. How this arose, how it changed and whether or not this emphasis is a 'good thing' are complex questions which we will touch upon as the book progresses. The detail is, however, a little beyond our introductory studies of financial accounting.[2]

The final tier of Figure 3.1 gives examples of the different categories of organizations and we shall provide just a little basic information about some of these in the following section.

3.3 CHARACTERISTICS OF ORGANIZATIONAL TYPES

You will need to have at least a rudimentary knowledge of organizational characteristics for your introductory studies in accounting. Much of this knowledge will be gathered as your study of financial accounting develops and from other subjects in your course (e.g. law), but the following outline will serve for the time being. You are reminded, though, that these outlines *are* rudimentary and additional information can be gained from the further reading listed at the end of this chapter.

3.3.1 Commercial organizations

(a) Sole trader

A sole trader is literally a one-person business.[3] If you start a small business on your own – say, buying and selling second-hand CDs – you would be a sole trader. There is no formal mechanism for starting up a sole-trader business – one just gets on with it. The business and the proprietor are treated as separate accounting entities and the business's assets and liabilities (i.e. what the business owns – has 'left over' – plus what it owes to others) are kept separate from those of the individual who runs the business. The business is subject to ordinary (personal) taxation and should the business go bankrupt the sole trader's personal assets (e.g. the house and car) are liable to be called upon to pay any outstanding business debts. This is known as **unlimited liability** and the business and the owner are not treated as separate legal (as opposed to accounting) entities.

(b) Partnership

When two or more people join together in business then a partnership exists. It is slightly more formal (governed, in the UK for example, by the Partnership Act of 1890) than the sole trader in that, at a minimum, the partners need to agree amongst themselves about how much they each put into and take out of the business. The business is, again, a separate accounting entity but not a separate *legal* entity in that unlimited liability exists (in most cases). Most firms of accountants and lawyers are organized as partnerships. (For more detail see Chapter 13.)

(c) Company

A company is a completely separate legal and accounting entity from those who own it (the shareholders). It is a very formal organization governed in most countries by a series of Companies Acts (see Chapter 14). Most companies enjoy **limited liability**, meaning that the debts of the business cannot be passed on to the owners. In return for this privilege, companies must comply with a great deal of law which governs such things as publishing detailed financial accounts and having these independently attested (i.e. audited, see Chapters 6 and 14). There are also separate taxation laws for these organizations. Companies may be public (meaning listed on the Stock Exchange where their shares may be bought and sold – these are referred to by the letters 'plc' in the UK) or private (meaning their shares are not publicly traded – referred to by the letters 'Ltd' in the UK). More detail on companies is provided in Chapter 14.

(d) Nationalized industry

Generally speaking, a nationalized industry is a series of separate, independently owned companies that have been bought by the government and brought together as a large unit, usually for reasons of political and economic stability. They are closely controlled by government and used as a tool for economic and political policy. As a result these organizations are not free to pursue the straightforward commercial goals that one expects of (say) companies, but must also pursue *social*, politically determined goals, which normally cover such things as providing employment and a continual and reliable service, even when these goals are not economically viable by ordinary financial criteria.

(e) Other commercial organizations

There can be many variations on the basic commercial organizational types given here. The variations may arise through different forms of ownership, for example, and will usually be governed by particular parts of the law. Banks would be an obvious illustration of this. Each country will have its own specific examples – like the building societies in the UK – but we leave this detail for later in your studies.

3.3.2 Non-commercial organizations

(a) Local (or state) government

These organizations, funded principally by government grants (from taxation) and, perhaps by various local taxation systems, provide a range of services that are either deemed more socially desirable to be controlled by government or which the open market would not supply. They tend to cover, for example, education, health, the police force, the fire brigade, social services, housing, refuse, highways, etc. Each local or state government is normally controlled by elected representatives who are free to direct the policy of the authority within the constraints set by the law and central (or federal) government policy. Their objectives are principally politically determined and social rather than economic in nature and are directed towards the maintenance and improvement of society's welfare rather than society's wealth (as traditionally defined).

(b) Charities

In the UK, for example, there are approximately 130,000 charities. Charity status will be granted by the central government in some form or other (in the UK this is done by the Charity Commissioners) who also exercise a degree of control over their operation. It is normal for charities (e.g. Oxfam) to have trustees who act as personal guarantors to the debts of the organization. Charities are exempt from most taxation and are required to pursue their chosen social goals.

(c) National/central (or federal) government

Each nation state has its organs of government which will involve various departments which oversee such issues as education, health, law, defence, national infrastructure, trade and industry, environmental protection and so on. Each will be an accounting entity within the larger central government accounting entity. Although the volume of financial transactions that pass through central government tends to be enormous it is traditionally the case that the accounting tends to be both relatively 'unsophisticated' (although this is changing over time) and varies from country to country. Accounts for central governments have historically tended to be shrouded in secrecy and therefore less readily studied.

(d) Other non-commercial organizations

The diversity of non-commercial organizations is considerable and varies considerably from country to country and time to time. Your own college or university may very well be a non-commercial organization. You may belong to clubs, societies, pressure groups or religious organizations that are non-commercial but which do not have charitable status.

Each will have its own culture and organization and, as a result, its own accounting and financial systems.

We can now turn to developing a generalized model of organizations which will serve as the basis for our development of accounting throughout the rest of the book.

3.4 ORGANIZATION, SYSTEMS AND ACCOUNTING

3.4.1 An organization is a system

We can understand organizations and the role of accounting in a much clearer way if we employ the concept of **systems**. A system is defined as:

> [A]n organised unitary whole, composed of two or more components or subsystems and delineated by identifiable boundaries from its environmental suprasystem.
>
> *(Kast and Rosenweig 1974: 101)*

We should add that a system may often be 'living' and have purpose, pattern and coherence. Clearly, what we have defined as an organization fits this definition of a system. By employing the concept of systems we can capture the complexities and interactions between organizations (i.e. between systems) and between an organization and its own **subsystems**. The accounting information system plays a major role in these interactions.

A system is a dynamic thing, ever-changing and designed with some purpose in mind. As with accounting entities so systems can be as small or as large as suits our purpose. The universe is a system; the earth is a system; each nation and society is a system; each organization within society is a system. Every organization contains further systems right down to (say) the circulation or antibody system in each individual. Now, what is important is that each of these systems interacts with, responds to and influences other systems. That is, the vast majority of systems are *open* systems. Thus, for example, if we are to understand an individual's physiological system and why and how it does what it does, we need to know how his/her system is influenced by the larger system within which it sits – the environment. To just take a view of an individual as a totally separate and independent entity – a *closed* system – would be to fail ever to understand that individual ('no man is an island' and all that) and would be a wholly inaccurate view of what really happens. We are all dependent on our physical, social and economic environment in many, many ways. So it is with organizations. Unless we look at the environment of the organization we will not properly understand the way in which accounting systems have developed and the role they play in the organization and in linking an organization to its environment.

Figure 3.2 identifies a number of the major interactions between a manufacturing organization and (what we shall come to call) its **substantial environment**. A similar diagram could be drawn for a university, a charity or any other type of organization. Although perhaps a little whimsical, the figure illustrates a number of the influences between the organization (the **focal organization**, as we have been calling the accounting entity) and some of the other systems with which it interacts. The organization is subject to laws with which it must take steps to comply. The organization pays taxes which influence what the government can spend. The type, ability, militancy, motivation, etc., of the employees have crucial effects on the organization and in return the local community has spending power. Cut-backs at the organization – as a result of perhaps low-quality

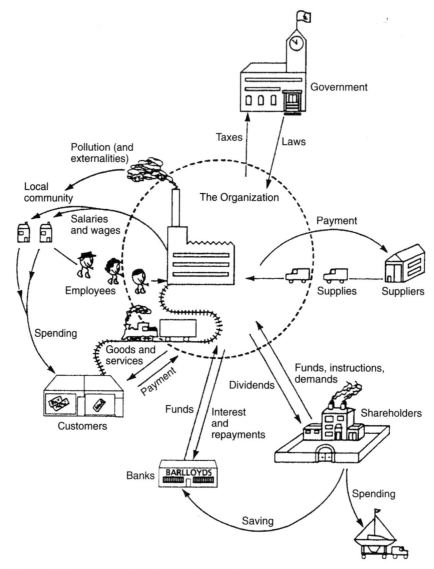

Figure 3.2 Some interactions between the organizational system and its substantial environment

supplies, competitors' actions or lack of available funds – would significantly influence the local community, customers, suppliers and perhaps even the government. And so on. (And many of the influences are much more complex and more subtle than this, for example the organization's influence on government policy or the air quality in the local community. See for example, Gray *et al.* 1996, Chapter 1.)

3.4.2 An organization and its major systems

We can generalize Figure 3.2 and include the organization's subsystems. This is done in Figure 3.3. This figure show the four main levels of systems with which we will be concerned:

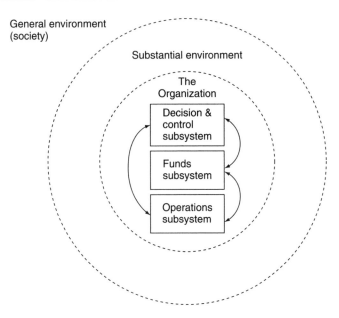

Figure 3.3 A systems view of organization and accounting (adapted from Lowe and McInnes 1971)

- the general environment;
- the substantial environment;
- the focal organization; and
- the organizational subsystems.

(a) The general environment

The first level of system is the **general environment** or society as a whole. This rather general term includes not only all the individuals and organizations that constitute the society in question, but also all the institutions, laws, mores, history, conventions and shared cultures which are as much the society as the people in it. Because of the complexities of the relationships in modern society, virtually all the elements of 'society as a whole' will influence and/or be influenced by all the other elements in some way. However, in order to keep our analysis from becoming far too complex we may distinguish a second level (of 'resolution')[4] of system – the **substantial environment**.

(b) The substantial environment

This is a subset of the general environment. It contains all those elements which have direct or relatively immediate influence or effect upon, or can be directly influenced or affected by, the organization in question (the 'focal organization'). The most obvious elements of this second level of system will be the owners/controllers of the focal organization, the suppliers and customers, the competitors, the labour force and the unions, perhaps the local community and all the relevant laws on such matters as taxation, the environment and the right of the parties involved (i.e. what are called the **participants**). We saw some of these in Figure 3.2. As we shall see, the accounting system only recognizes certain portions of the substantial environment – those relating to the financial description of economic events.

(c) The focal organization

This brings us to the **focal organization**. This is simply a useful piece of terminology to indicate the 'organization in which we are interested' – the accounting entity for which we are accounting. We have already given some indication of the variety of different organizational types. Each of these will be continually influencing and being influenced by (i.e. interacting with) the substantial environment.

(d) Organizational subsystems

Each organization will consist of a number of **organizational subsystems**. These are the constituent systems within the organization which are designed to enable the organization to function efficiently and effectively and to be controlled. There are many such subsystems, e.g. production, delivery of service, quality control, cash control, personnel, safety and so on. We can consider all of these under three main groups of subsystems:

- the operation subsystem;
- the funds subsystem;
- the decision and control subsystem (including the accounting system).

3.4.3 The organizational subsystems

The **operation subsystem** in an organization is that which governs its principal physical activities. In a manufacturing company, for example, it is this system that governs the acquisition of inputs such as materials, machines, labour, etc., and ensures the orderly organization of these to produce goods (the outputs) and eventually get them to the customers. In a hospital, on the other hand, this subsystem would cover the admission of patients and the scheduling of operations as well as the acquisition of materials and the employment and use of staff.

The **funds subsystem** governs the acquisition and receipt (input) of (primarily) cash for the organization (from loans, from grants, from the owners via share capital, payments from customers, and the like) and the payment of cash (output) to, for example, suppliers, employees and bankers (i.e. interest and loan repayments). As far as we are concerned for purposes of our bookkeeping, the funds system is simply concerned with cash. Thus the cashbook or cash account (which we met in Chapter 2) provides a complete picture of the inputs to and outputs from the funds subsystem.

The **decision and control subsystem** as its name suggests, governs the planning and direction of the organization. This includes the organization of the other subsystems (funds and operations) as well as controlling and directing the different subsystems dealing with the 'outside world' (e.g. sales system, procurement system, public relations, advertising, negotiations with those lending money, etc.). Its principal activity concerns the inputs and outputs of **information** to and from the organization. (The accounting system is an especially crucial element here and we will look at this in more detail in Chapter 6.)[5]

This enables us to develop Figure 3.3 further to show how the **inputs and outputs to the organizational subsystems** operate. This is shown in Figure 3.4. This figure shows more clearly the essence of the organization system: namely the inputs to the organization (from systems in the substantial environment), outputs from the organization (to systems in the substantial environment) and the internal subsystems which enable the inputs and outputs to be properly utilized and controlled.

This organizational model can be developed further and it can be most usefully used to think about organizations from a wider perspective than the accounting system adopts. Certainly, in your more advanced studies – particularly of management, management information systems, organization behaviour and so on – you will be looking at organizations from a broad point of view. However, we know that the traditional accounting system takes a restricted view on the world, concerned as it is with only financial description of economic events. Therefore there are many inputs to and outputs from these three subsystems which accounting ignores. (We shall see, especially in Chapter 17, that this has some worrying consequences.) Accounting only recognizes those inputs to and outputs from the organization and its organizational subsystems which represent economic events which can be financially described. Thus:

- the decision and control subsystem as employed by the accounting system only recognizes **information inflows and outflows** which relate directly to financial transactions (these are principally to do with who owes cash to or is owed cash by the focal organization);
- the funds subsystem as employed by the accounting system recognizes the **cash inputs and outputs** (of the cashbook);
- the operations subsystem as employed by the accounting system only recognizes those **inflows and outflows of goods and services** which have been paid for or which will be paid for (mainly purchases and sales).

3.4.4 The organizational systems and accounting record-keeping

With this model in mind we start to build up the accounting record system – the **bookkeeping** or **double-entry bookkeeping system** – of the focal organization. We will be developing the bookkeeping throughout the next few chapters and discussing the bookkeeping and accounting system in broad terms in Chapter 6. However, we can move towards the basic bookkeeping system by looking back at Figure 3.4, thinking about the restricted view that the accounting system takes (remembering the four characteristics) and recalling the definition of accounting we looked at in Chapter 1.

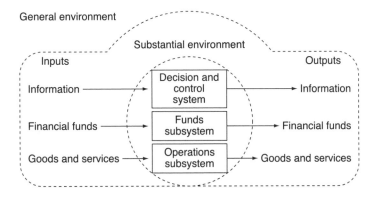

Figure 3.4 The organizational system, its substantial environment and its input and output flows

In Figure 3.4, we have identified three types of things that organizations deal with: **information, funds, and goods and services**. We have seen that the traditional accounting system only recognizes the information, funds, and goods and services insofar as they have direct financial implications. We also recall from our definition of accounting that accounting is concerned with **identifying, collecting, describing, recording, processing and communicating** information. We have just identified the characteristics of that information in which we and the accounting system are interested, we now want to collect, describe and record it. (Processing and communication come later.) This is what Figure 3.5 does.

All Figure 3.5 is doing is collecting together the inputs of information and the outputs of information, the inputs of funds and the outputs of funds, the inputs of goods and services and the outputs of goods and services and keeping each of them in their own place. What we have are three T-accounts.

The middle, funds, subsystem T-account is the most obvious. This is the **cashbook** which we met in Chapter 2. It records the inflows/inputs of cash on the left-hand side and the outputs/outflows of cash on the right-hand side. (Look back to the cashbooks in Chapter 2 and see that this is exactly the same.)

But, if the accounting system is to reflect the whole organization – or at least reflect it all from the accounting point of view – we still have to record the information flows and the flows of goods and services. So we have to have some sort of *information account* and some sort of *goods and services account*. This is what we have in Figure 3.5.

Now, we shall see in section 3.5, when we have another look at Mr Brain's accounting, that putting all our 'information' into a single *information account* and all our 'goods and services' into a single *goods and services account* is going to cause confusion. And we will start to solve that problem in Chapter 4. However, for the moment let's stick with this simple model and see what else we can glean from it.

There should be two questions which leap immediately to mind. First, where on earth did the terms 'debit' and 'credit' in Figure 3.5 spring from? Second, and much more importantly, where does the accounting system get these information and goods and services inputs and outputs from?

Decision and control subsystem account ('INFORMATION ACCOUNT')	
INFORMATION ——> (Input or Debit)	INFORMATION ——> (Output or Credit)

Funds subsystem account ('CASH ACCOUNT')	
CASH ——> (Input or Debit)	CASH ——> (Output or Credit)

Operations subsystem account ('GOODS and SERVICES ACCOUNT')	
GOODS and SERVICES ——> (Input or Debit)	GOODS and SERVICES ——> (Output or Credit)

Figure 3.5 Bookkeeping for the organizational flows

3.4.5 Debits, credits and double-entry

We have seen that the bookkeeping activity is basically concerned with identifying and capturing selected inflows and outflows of information, goods and services and funds as they enter or leave the focal organization. Traditionally, accounting refers to these inflows as **debits** and the outflows as **credits**. Life for the accountant would be a great deal simpler if we could just stick with the terms 'inflows' (or inputs) and 'outflows' (or outputs) because at least these terms have a meaning in the organizational context we have outlined above. Life, it seems, is never simple and we must be able to use the more common terms 'debits' and 'credits' which mean exactly the same as inflow and outflow.

In fact, one of the biggest single problems that students of accounting and bookkeeping have is trying to make some sense of the two terms 'debit' and 'credit'. *They do not mean anything* except the left-hand side of a T-account and the right-hand side of a T-account. They are meaningless in today's English language and it might be better if we could call them 'bananas' and 'oranges' or some other words which illustrated that the words have no sensible meaning. Some of the major points relating to debits and credits are summarised in Figure 3.6 which you should study carefully.

We cannot over-emphasize the following:

- do not try and make the terms 'debit' and 'credit' mean anything other than left and right or inflow and outflow;
- do not confuse the terms 'debits' and 'credits' as used by the bank on your bank statement (look at Figure 3.6 again where this is explained).

Bearing these points in mind we will use both terms for the next few chapters until you feel comfortable with them.

So, where do these other inflows/debits and outflows/credits come from? The answer is they come from the **double-entry** nature of the bookkeeping system.

The bookkeeping and accounting system recognises a **duality** to every transaction. In a sense it is like that law from physics: every action has an equal and opposite reaction. When you buy a loaf of bread, two things happen: (i) you pay over some cash and (ii) you receive a loaf of bread. When you sell your prize collection of Batman comics two things

---

- 'Debits' means bookkeeping entries recorded on the left-hand side of a T-account.

- 'Credits' means bookkeeping entries recorded on the right-hand side of a T-account.

- Debits are what we have called 'inflows/inputs' to our organizational flows diagram. Credits are what we have called 'outflows/outputs'.

- **Debits and credits do not mean, and cannot mean, anything else like 'good for the business' and 'bad for business'. DO NOT TRY AND MAKE THEM MEAN SOMETHING.** The best way to remember them is: debits = inflows, credits = outflows.

- Debits and credits **DO NOT mean the same as on your bank statement**. The bank statement is the bank's accounting record of its relationship with you (that is, the debits and credits are taken from its perspective). As a result, the bank statement provides a mirror image of your relationship with the bank. Therefore the debits and credits on the bank statement are the bank's debits and credits, NOT your (cashbook) debits and credits. A 'credit' on your bank statement means to you that you have increased your cash: this would be an inflow to your cash subsystem – a debit – in your books. Remember that we have emphasized that you should be clear as to which focal organization you are preparing accounts for – as you can see from the above example, knowing whose accounts you are preparing is absolutely vital to ensure you have your debits and credits correct.

Figure 3.6 Debits and credits

happen: (i) you receive some cash and (ii) your Batman comics disappear. This is what **double-entry** is about. When you buy the loaf of bread: there is (i) outflow/credit from your funds subsystem (cashbook), you have spent some money, and (ii) an input/debit to your operations subsystem (goods and services account), you have received some stuff. When you sell your Batman comics: there is (i) an inflow/debit to your funds subsystem (cashbook), you have received some cash, and (ii) an outflow/credit from your operations subsystem (goods and services account), you haven't got the comics any more. If you paid £1 (or $1 or whatever) for the bread and received £10 (or whatever) for your Batman comics, you could record the double-entry as in Figure 3.7.

Spend a few moments making sure you can see what we have done. (Note that we have not needed to use the decision and control subsystem (information) account on this occasion.) This is the essence of double-entry bookkeeping. It really is as simple as this but, to make sure you are happy with it, we will revisit Mr Brain and see what we can do with his double-entry bookkeeping and then spend all of Chapter 4 refining, developing and practising this arcane art.

3.5 MR BRAIN AND THIS SYSTEMS VIEW

Although it might at first seem a little strange, we can consider Mr Brain as an organization and, from the example in Chapter 2, illustrate Brain's substantial environment and his organizational subsystems.

3.5.1 Brain's substantial environment and organizational system

The elements of Brain's substantial environment that we consider (either explicitly or implicitly) in the example included:

- his parents (who provided money, support, instructions and guidance);
- other 'organizations' which have provided funds (Aunty Gertrude, Fred for the loan);
- goods-and-services-supplying organizations to which Brain paid money (the landlord, the bookies, the Spar shop, etc.);

Decision and control subsystem account ('INFORMATION ACCOUNT')	
INFORMATION ———-———-> (Input or Debit)	INFORMATION ———-———-> (Output or Credit)

Funds subsystem account ('CASH ACCOUNT')	
CASH Sell Batman comics £10 ———-———-> (Input or Debit)	Buy loaf of bread £1 CASH ———-———-> (Output or Credit)

Operations subsystem account ('GOODS and SERVICES ACCOUNT')	
GOODS and SERVICES ———-———-> Receive loaf of bread £1 (Input or Debit)	GOODS and SERVICES Sell Batman comics £10 ———-———-> (Output or Credit)

Figure 3.7 Buying bread and selling Batman comics

- the law (which, for example, governed his contract with the landlord);
- the college (which provided his 'social environment' and his 'service-delivery environment' – i.e. his study and education);

and so on. This substantial environment effectively provided:

- the options available to him;
- indications of what was expected of him;
- the rules within the focal organization (Brain) acted and pursued his objectives.

Brain, in turn, influenced and affected each of these other organizational systems in his substantial environment in some way, to a greater or lesser degree.

In effect, it was the elements of the substantial environment (together with Brain's own desire, presumably, to survive and satisfy his personal aims) that required that Brain:

1. seek to control his organizational system; and
2. establish an accounting system.

He sought (perhaps ineffectually) to control his organizational system via his decision and control subsystem. This subsystem attempted to ensure that he achieved his aims whilst remaining within the constraints imposed upon his activities by other elements of the environmental system. To achieve this, it was necessary for Brain to control his funds subsystem in order to finance the inputs to his operations subsystem whilst remaining solvent and alive (i.e. he had to eat). He then had to control all the inputs to his operations subsystem (his effort, goods, services, textbooks, lectures, etc.,) in order to produce the output from his operations subsystem that he sought – enjoyment, good exam marks, a permanent hangover or whatever.

We saw that the traditional financial accounting system helped him do *some* of this, but it did not cover what were, in many respects, the most important elements of the operations subsystem – the inputs and outputs related to his social and educational success. As we have said, for *non-commercial* organizations (of which Brain is one), traditional financial accounting *cannot* successfully relate the inputs and outputs of the operations subsystem because whilst the inputs can be measured in financial terms, the outputs cannot, and we are thus unable to compare like with like.

Finally, the substantial environment, in the form of his parents, required that the organizational system – 'A. Brain, student' – provide an account of itself. Brain's decision and control subsystem (through his accounting system) prepared a cashbook for the parents and (hopefully) discharged this accountability.

3.5.2 Brain's organizational subsystems and double-entry bookkeeping

If you look back to Figure 2.1 you will note that Mr Brain had 19 events which meet the four characteristics of accounting. These are his financial transactions for which we must account. Twelve of these transactions are straightforward – and we already have enough information to do the double-entry. These are his purchases of goods and services. In each case there is an outflow/credit from his funds subsystem (cashbook) and an inflow/debit to his operations subsystem (goods and services account) – he paid out cash and received either stuff or services. These are shown in Figure 3.8.

Check Figure 3.8 and ensure that you can see that (a) the cash account contains part of his cashbook and (b) all those transactions are shown in his goods and services account.

Inflow/Debit	Information Account		Outflow/Credit

Inflow/Debit	Cash Account		Outflow/Credit
	Landlord		20
	Grocers		10
	Bus pass		5
	Textbooks		3
	Turf accountants		16
	Bar bill		62
	Dartboard		8
	Landlord		20
	Bar bill		57
	Guinness		20
	Train ticket		5
	Rent		10

Inflow/Debit		Goods and Services Account	Outflow/Credit
Landlord	20		
Grocers	10		
Bus pass	5		
Textbooks	3		
Turf accountants	16		
Bar bill	62		
Dartboard	8		
Landlord	20		
Bar bill	57		
Guinness	20		
Train ticket	5		
Rent	10		

Figure 3.8 Brain's bookkeeping for his simple transactions

The goods and services account now shows all the inputs to the operations subsystem for which Mr Brain has paid cash. It is a record of the stuff and services he has paid for. Every transaction which we have accounted for, we have accounted for twice – we have employed double-entry. As a result, in Figure 3.8, the total of outflows/credits equals the total of inflows/debits. This must always be so.

However, we are still missing a series of transactions, some of which involved cash and which we entered in our cashbook in Chapter 2 (money from parents, Aunty Gertrude, Jack, savings, Fred) and two transactions which did not involve cash but involved 'owing' (the outstanding rent and the outstanding bar bill). All of these transactions involve the 'information account'. That is, whilst we know one half of the bookkeeping for the transactions involving the cash receipts (they go as inflows/debits in the cashbook) and one half of the bookkeeping for the last rent and bar bill transactions (they are part of the goods and services that Brain has acquired even though he hasn't paid for them), where does the other half of the bookkeeping go? How do we complete the double-entry? The answer is that the other entries go into the information account – for reasons that we will explain in detail in Chapter 4 and beyond. For completeness, Figure 3.9 shows how Brain's basic bookkeeping should look (with all these 'new' transactions shown in italics).

We will spend much more time on this bookkeeping in the next chapter but, for the time being there a few points to note. First, every transaction is in the accounts twice: once as an inflow/debit and once as an outflow/credit. This is the golden rule of **double-entry**: you must find both an inflow/debit and an outflow/credit for each transaction. Second, as a result, if you add up all the inflows/debits and all the outflows/credits you must get the same total. This is an essential consequence of the arithmetic. And it is crucial to what follows. Third, we have not explained why some things ended up in the 'information account'. The

Inflow/Debit		**Information account**	Outflow/Credit
Loan to Jack	*20*	*Money from parents*	*200*
		Aunty Gertrude	*10*
		Post Office savings	*50*
		Loan from Fred	*2*
		Owed to the landlord	*15*
		Owed to the bar	*34*

Inflow/Debit		**Cash account**	Outflow/Credit
Money from parents	*200*	Landlord	20
Aunty Gertrude	*10*	Grocers	10
Post Office savings	*50*	Bus pass	5
Loan from Fred	*2*	Textbooks	3
		Turf accountants	16
		Bar bill	62
		Dartboard	8
		Landlord	20
		Loan to Jack	*20*
		Bar bill	57
		Guinness	20
		Train ticket	5
		Rent	10

Inflow/Debit		**Goods and services account**	Outflow/Credit
Landlord	20		
Grocers	10		
Bus pass	5		
Textbooks	3		
Turf accountants	16		
Bar bill	62		
Dartboard	8		
Landlord	20		
Bar bill	57		
Guinness	20		
Train ticket	5		
Rent	10		
Owed to the landlord	*15*		
Owed to the bar	*34*		

Figure 3.9 Brain's basic bookkeeping for all his transactions

cash and the goods and services accounts are fairly easy to see. The rest has ended up in the information account at this stage because there was nowhere else to go. We will explain this in Chapter 4. Fourth, we have not balanced off the accounts – although we could have done so and, in a formal bookkeeping exercise would do so. You already know how to balance off the cashbook (we saw this in Chapter 2). However, if we balanced off the other accounts – in the form we currently have them – we would be adding up apples and pears. What would the balances mean? Actually, they would not mean very much at all because we have too many different sorts of things in each account. The balancing figures would just tell us about 'stuff' – and 'stuff' is not normally considered to be a useful category in accounting. For this reason, we will have to break down the accounts by categorizing the various types of transactions. This, again, we will do in Chapter 4.

SUMMARY

This chapter represents the end of Part I of the book. You have come a very long way in these three chapters. We have met definitions of accounting and seen these definitions at work in the simple case of a student. But the important thing has been, rather than just ploughing on with doing bookkeeping by following rules, we have been trying to think about accounting and to give you some mental pictures with which to undertake this thinking. An unthinking accountant is a dangerous accountant! This chapter has, especially, attempted to provide you with a mental model with which to think about accounting and, in particular, about basic bookkeeping. If you can adopt this way of thinking, you need never find difficulty with basic bookkeeping procedures.

This chapter concentrated upon organizations. We did this for two reasons. The first, and immediately practical reason, was that you do need to know a little about the different sorts of organizations that exist because the accounting process for each can vary. (This is most dramatically obvious in your introductory studies for sole traders, partnerships and companies as we shall see. The differences are, in fact, greater between commercial and non-commercial organizations but these, for reasons of history and convention, will claim less of our time.) The second (and more important) reason, was to give you a conception (a picture in your head) of the accounting entity in such a way that it could be related to the bookkeeping process.

To achieve this, we examined a simple 'systems model' of organizations – this was a way of thinking about all organizations. We saw that all organizations deal with basically three things: **information**, **cash** and **goods and services.** And these three things flow into and out of the organization from the substantial environment. We can further envisage them as flowing into and out of three subsystems within the organization: the decision and control subsystem (information), the funds subsystem (cash) and the operations subsystem (goods and services). The accounting system recognizes these three types of things as long as they relate to **economic events** which have **financial description**. The accounting system then records these flows in T-accounts (or a computer-constructed equivalent), recording the inflows/debits and the outflows/credits separately. These inflows/debits and outflows/credits are equal and for every inflow/debit there must be an outflow/credit. This **duality** is an essential part of the accountant's view of the world and provides the basis for the **double-entry bookkeeping**. By this process, the accounting system identifies, collects, describes, records and (as we shall see) processes and communicates this information to 'users'. This is summarized in Figure 3.10.

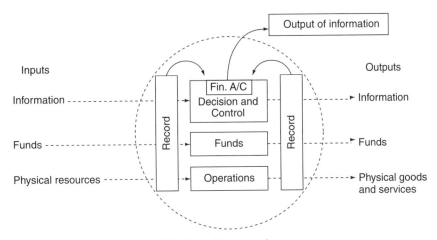

Figure 3.10 A simple systems view of the financial accounting process

We can now see that the accounting system in general – but particularly the bookkeeping process – is concerned with 'logging' (recording) inflows and outflows of information, funds and goods and services as they pass into and out of the organization. This information is used to produce records (we have now seen the information account, the cashbook and the goods and services account). These records, as we shall see in due course, are then used to process the information in such a way that financial accounting information can be communicated to the external participants – the 'users'.

Part II, which starts with the next chapter, Chapter 4, gives some flesh to these basic bookkeeping bones in order to produce more sophisticated accounting records which will provide a sufficient basis for the financial statements.

Key terms and concepts

The following key terms and concepts have featured in this chapter. You should make sure that you understand and can explain each one. Page references to definitions appear in the index in bold.

- Cash account, information account, goods and services account
- Commercial organization:
  - Sole trader
  - Partnership
  - Company
- Credits
- Debits
- Double-entry bookkeeping
- Duality
- Focal organization
- General environment
- Inputs/inflows to and outputs/outflows from the organizational subsystems
- Non-commercial organization:
  - Local government
  - Charity
  - Central government
- Organization
- Organizational subsystems:
  - Operations subsystem
  - Funds subsystem
  - Decision and control subsystem
- Substantial environment
- Systems

FURTHER READING

Additional reading has been mentioned in the chapter. Most textbooks on accounting do not use the organizational systems model on which this chapter is based and therefore we do not recommend that you turn to these for further general information at this stage. The organizational systems model is based on Lowe and McInnes (1971) and Lowe (1972) and these are well worth reading. Kast and Rosenweig (1974) and Donald (1979) provide very useful introductions to systems thinking – an approach which is developed for accounting by Gray *et al.* (1996). For detail in the organizational types, you could look at any accounting textbook and this would give you a further introduction to companies and probably sole traders and partnerships. For the non-commercial organizations you could usefully have a look at Wallis (1970, Chapter 10) or Anthony and Young (1984, Chapter 2). To start you on the bookkeeping, a computer-based training package may help – there are several around and some of them are sponsored by the professional accountancy bodies themselves.

NOTES

1. However, do be careful. 'Accounting entity' and 'organization' may not always be synonymous terms. An accounting entity is something we are accounting for, an organization is anything we define as an organization. One may include the other, be synonymous with the other or be a subset of the other.
2. But for more detail see, for example, Broadbent *et al.* (1991).
3. Do note that a one-person business may very well have employees. It is the *ownership* that resides in the single individual.
4. The 'level of resolution' in this context is a visual, analogy which one might use with, for example, a telescope. A lower *level* of resolution widens one's field of vision, allowing one to see more – but in less detail. A *higher* level of resolution focuses the telescope on a smaller part of the picture (in this case a complex system), thus permitting the viewer to study it in greater detail. So, in the present context we are lowering the level of resolution to look at more of the system(s) – e.g. society – and raising the level of resolution to study smaller parts – e.g. the accounting entity – in more detail.
5. In case it is bothering you, the model can be extended to take account of *internal* movements/flows of information which the accounting system might also be required to record. This degree of sophistication is not essential for our studies here but we will touch upon it in Chapter 4.

Part II
Bookkeeping and Accounting Records

Organizational flows: a categorization of basic transactions, accounting records and double-entry bookkeeping

4

Learning objectives

After studying this chapter you should be able to:

- distinguish accounting transactions from non-accounting transactions;

- identify the organizational inflows and outflows as they pass into and out of the focal organization;

- specify whether the inflow and the outflow relate to information, funds or goods and services;

- produce the three basic T-accounts for information, cash and goods and services from basic bookkeeping transactions;

- identify and define the eight basic bookkeeping transactions;

- specify the inflow/debit and outflow/credit for each type of the eight basic transactions;

- produce basic accounting records (bookkeeping) for a simple accounting entity with simple transactions;

- explain, using the language of inflows and outflows, the differences between commercial and non-commercial organizations.

4.1 INTRODUCTION

4.1.1 Chapter design and links to previous chapters

Part I of the text provided the background to thinking about basic financial accounting and bookkeeping. Part II will now develop this background and add a lot of detail so that we can produce a set of basic accounting records – the bookkeeping – that will be recognizable to a practising accountant.

We saw that the first task of the accounting system was to **identify, collect, describe** and **record** certain of the transactions of an **accounting entity**. The accounting system only recognized those transactions which could be defined as **economic events** which could be **financially described**. There are many ways in which we might go about trying to distinguish and identify the accounting transactions. We are saying to you that the easiest (and most reliable) way is to start by **identifying your accounting entity** and then thinking of that entity as an **organization** with **inflows and outflows of information, funds** and **goods and services**. We then identify which of these inflows and outflows should be described financially. This we do by identifying which flows have direct **cash** implications: that is, transactions which have resulted in cash changing hands in the past, now or in the future. These are then the accounting transactions for which we must account – keep accounting records.

But which accounting records? In Chapter 3 we also saw two further, very important, things. First, when an accountant looks at one of the accounting transactions, they see a **duality**. That is, the accounting system recognizes that each transaction has two aspects: one of them an inflow to the focal organization and one of them an outflow from the focal organization. These two aspects give us the name of **double-entry bookkeeping**. So, whatever records we keep, we must find two aspects for each transaction and record both of them. Where do we record them? We saw that the inflows to and outflows from the funds subsystem could be collected within an account we now know as the **cashbook**. The rest of the flows could be collected together as inflows or outflows of information in (what we called for convenience) an **information account**, whilst the inflows and outflows of goods and services could be collected together in an account which we called (again for convenience) a **goods and services account**. This gave us three basic T-accounts which are repeated in Figure 4.1.

These three T-accounts represented the three organizational subsystems. We saw how we can collect the inflows of information, cash and goods and services in their respective accounts and call them **debits** and collect together the outflows of information, cash and goods and services in their respective accounts and call them **credits**. These three T-accounts form the basis of double-entry bookkeeping.

What we have seen so far is very useful as far as it goes but, like all models of the world, it tends to oversimplify things a little too much. So, in order to make this model work for us we have to extend it a bit further. The reason for this is that three accounts are really not enough to provide the sort of bookkeeping system most organizations need. The 'information account' and the 'goods and services account' end up collecting too many different sorts of information and goods and services to be really *useful* to us. So, to make these records useful we need to:

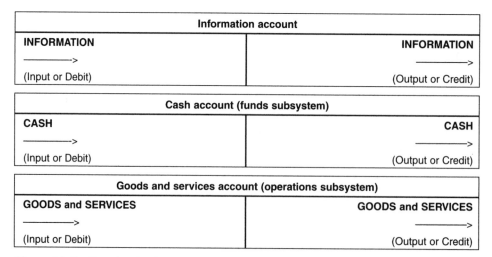

Figure 4.1 Bookkeeping for the organizational flows

i categorize our transactions with a little more care;
ii break down the information account and the goods and services account into smaller accounts that collect 'like things' with 'like things' (so that the accounts do not just have a lot of 'stuff' in them);
iii then process those records to produce our financial statements.

This chapter and Chapter 5 will spend time developing and explaining (i) and (ii), Chapter 6 will then explain some of the practical mechanics with which accountants go about this process and Chapter 7 and Part III will explain point (iii).

This chapter is organized as follows. The next subsection is largely revision – but important revision that tidies up and formalizes what you already know. In it we work through another simple example, identifying which transactions the bookkeeping system recognizes, identifying the appropriate inflows to and outflows from the three subsystems and collecting these in the three T-accounts for information, funds and goods and services. The section rounds off with providing a general organization flow diagram that can be used to identify all the basic bookkeeping entries. Section 4.2 introduces and explains the **eight basic bookkeeping transactions**. These are the 'raw materials' with which any bookkeeping system works. Each of these eight types of transactions is defined and the inflows/debits and outflows/credits identified and explained. In the process, we expand the number of T-accounts with which we want to work and explain why we may, and indeed do, have a very large number of T-accounts – although they all follow the basic rules we enumerate in the chapter. The section rounds off with asking you to produce a more conventional-looking set of T-accounts for Mr Brain (from Chapter 2) and Ms Able (who is introduced in this chapter). The chapter finishes with the usual summary, key terms and further reading.

4.1.2 Reinforcing the organizational flows

The best way to start this process of developing our accounting records is to make sure that the basic bits and pieces are making sense. We shall do this by looking at another simple example and then developing our organizational systems model. Then we can go on to look at a more complex illustration that will show a full set of basic accounting records working. Please read through Figure 4.2.

We are now thinking of Ms Able as our **focal organization** – she is our accounting entity – and it is her flows in which we are interested. So the first thing to do is envisage an organizational systems model for Ms Able. Figure 4.3 is how this might look (and it is just a minor variation on Figure 3.4).

The second thing to do is work through the information contained in Figure 4.2 and work out what is actually happening.

Ms Able, a student friend of Mr Brain, decides to make some money at college during her first week back. She has the good fortune to be the daughter of parents who run a successful grocery store. She buys from them some basic groceries, coffee, bread, etc., for £10 (or $10 or whatever) cash paid immediately.

Taking them back to college she sells half of them to Mr Brain who pays her immediately £6 in cash. She sells the rest to a fellow student, Ms Ouri, for £7 payable next week.

What would the accounting records of Ms Able look like if they were to reflect these transactions?

Figure 4.2 The example of Ms Able and her bookkeeping

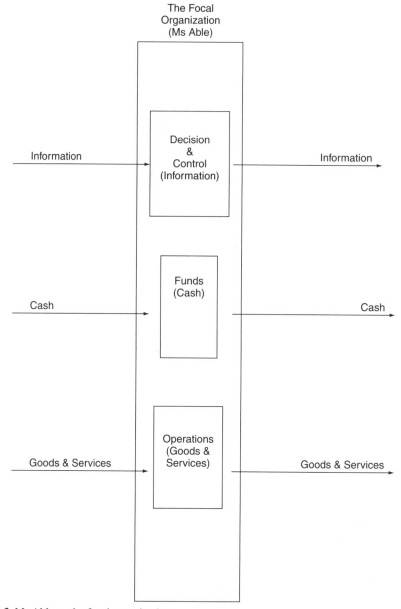

Figure 4.3 Ms Able as the focal organization

> **Hint**
>
> When working through a bookkeeping or accounting question, do not be put off by the language and terminology. Work out in your own words what is actually happening. There is nothing sophisticated about these questions. If you can't put the question into your own little words – *ask someone*. You must try to have a clear mental picture of the actual events you want to record.

The process for Ms Able must go something like this:

i   'Excuse me, Mum, can I buy some coffee and stuff from you to sell at college? I can afford about £10.'
    (This is a flow of information. An outflow of information from the focal organization's (Ms Able) decision and control subsystem to the decision and control subsystem of another organization in Ms Able's substantial environment – her Mum. The accounting system ignores it because it does not lead directly to a transfer of cash in the past, present or future.)

ii 'Yes, dear, I can let you have this lot and, because it's you, you can have it at cost price.'
    (This is more information. It is an outflow from Mum's decision and control subsystem and an inflow of information to Ms Able's decision and control subsystem. Again, the accounting system ignores it because it does not lead directly to the transfer of cash.)

iii 'Hmm', says Ms Able, 'that looks like a good deal. I'll accept it. I'll pay Mum £10.'
    (This is still more information. This time it is internal to the focal organization (Ms Able) and involves a decision to accept the deal and a decision to pay the cash. The accounting system still ignores it.)

iv 'Here you are, Mum. Here's £10 for the stuff. Thanks a bunch!'
    (The cash is paid over. Now the accounting system recognizes it. Before this point there was no commitment to exchange cash. Now there is and the accounting system goes to work. We are talking about cash and so we have an outflow/credit from the funds subsystem – a credit entry in the cashbook of the focal organization. Mum would also record it in her cashbook as an inflow to her funds subsystem but we are not accounting for Mum – she is not our focal organization. But we have only one entry for our focal organization: we have an outflow/credit. We need an inflow/debit.)

v   'Here you are, dear, here's the coffee and stuff you wanted. Thanks for the cash.'
    (Here is a flow of goods and services – actually a flow of goods consisting of coffee and other groceries. It is an outflow from Mum's operations subsystem – but we are not accounting for her – and an inflow to Ms Able's operations subsystem: an inflow/debit to her goods and services account.)

These transactions are shown in Figure 4.4.

Each of the steps we have enumerated above is numbered and shown on Figure 4.4. Go through it carefully and make sure you are happy with each step. When you are, you should be able to do the associated double-entry. Try it yourself and then check it against Figure 4.5.

You will see we have only recorded one transaction – that which actually involved the commitment to move cash around. So, why did we need to go through the *five* stages above just to get one piece of double-entry? This was to emphasize what we have been saying: the bookkeeping reflects a particular view of organizational activity. We need to know what is happening and then identify those parts of what is happening that fall within the ambit of the accounting system. This is what we have done.

The next stage is to find out what Ms Able did when she got to college. We can now skip all the detailed comings and goings and concentrate upon the accounting events of interest. From the accounting point of view, Ms Able does the following:

i   Sells Mr Brain half her coffee and other groceries for which Mr Brain gives her £6 in cash immediately.

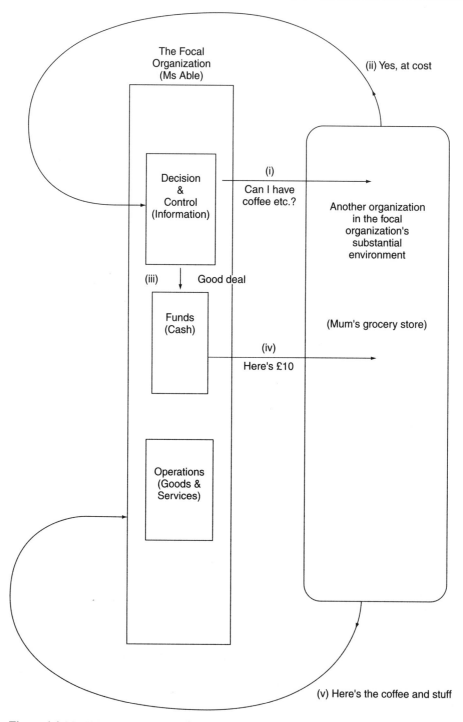

Figure 4.4 Ms Able's purchase of coffee etc.

Inflow/Debit	Information account	Outflow/Credit

Inflow/Debit	Cash account	Outflow/Credit
	Pay Mum for coffee etc.	£10

Inflow/Debit	Goods and services account	Outflow/Credit
Receive coffee and stuff from Mum £10		

Figure 4.5 Able's bookkeeping for her grocery purchases

> *(Cutting a long story short, Ms Able passes half her groceries to Mr Brain from her operations subsystem. She has an outflow/credit from her goods and services account – a sale. She receives £6 from Mr Brain as an inflow/debit to her cashbook. **Have you spotted the potential problem? See the 'hint' box.**)*

ii   Sells the other half of her coffee and stuff to Ms Ouri who accepts the groceries and promises to pay £7 for them next week.

> *(Half of this transaction is the same as that involving Mr Brain. We have an outflow/credit from Ms Able's goods and services account. But where is the inflow/debit? It certainly isn't cash – at least not yet. It certainly isn't goods and services because Ms Ouri is promising to pay cash. It is a promise. This is information and goes into the information account.)*

Once again we can show these transactions on the organizational flow diagram for Ms Able, and then complete our double-entry bookkeeping. The flows are shown in Figure 4.6.

Again, check through the flows, ensure that you can see why only these flows are of concern to the accounting system and then check to make sure that you can see why the flows are doing what they are doing. (If you can't, go back and check them again.) When you are happy about these flows, do the double-entry bookkeeping and check your answer with Figure 4.7.

This might seem a somewhat long-winded way of getting a few entries into three T-accounts, but be patient. First, we will speed up: by the end of the chapter we will be roaring along and we just want to be sure that you can crawl well before we start running and jumping. Second, if you have managed to get this far and understand what we have

---

Hint

Here we have an accounting transaction which is fairly straightforward except that it involves two different amounts of money. Half of Ms Able's coffee etc. cost £5 and she is selling it for £6. We have emphasized that the two elements of a double-entry transaction must be the same. So, do we put the thing in the accounting records as £5, £6 or something different? Well, we enter it as £6 because this was the financial description of the *sale* transaction. The difference (which we might be tempted to think of as 'profit') we will deal with later.

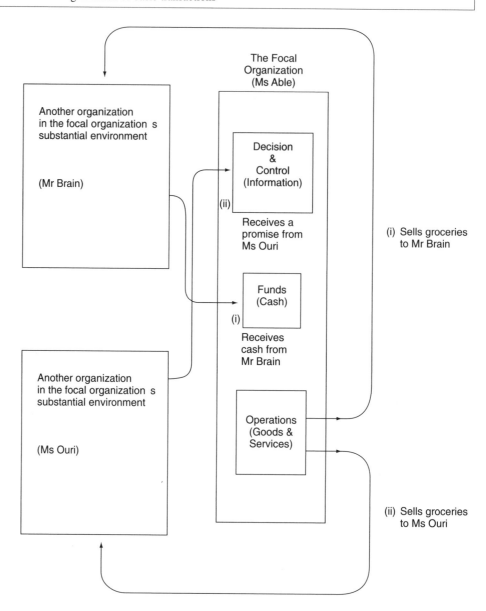

Figure 4.6 Ms Able's sale of groceries

done so far, you have come a very long way indeed and are very close to having a solid grasp of bookkeeping. You have identified events and decided which the accounting system recognizes and which it does not. You have identified the appropriate flows related to those accounting events and determined an inflow/debit and an outflow/credit for each one. You have then entered each of these into one of three T-accounts. In terms of keeping basic bookkeeping records, that is all there is! The rest (and there is a lot of 'rest' we are afraid) is just about adding detail. The next subsection will tidy up what we have learnt so far and then get on with sorting out this detail.

Inflow/Debit	Information account		Outflow/Credit
Ms Ouri thanks you for the coffee and promises to pay you	£7		

Inflow/Debit	Cash account		Outflow/Credit
Cash from sale to Mr Brain	£6	Pay Mum for coffee etc.	£10

Inflow/Debit	Goods and services account		Outflow/Credit
Receive coffee and stuff from Mum	£10	Sell half of groceries to Mr Brain	£6
		Sell half of groceries to Ms Ouri	£7

Figure 4.7 Ms Able's bookkeeping for her grocery purchases and sales

4.1.3 A model for all the basic bookkeeping system's organizational flows

So we have a focal organization and we have inflows/debits and outflows/credits of three sorts of things: information, cash and goods and services. These flows were collected into three T-accounts for each of information, cash and goods and services. These flows go to and come from other organizations in the focal organization's substantial environment. We saw Ms Able dealing with three which we labelled 'another organization in the focal organization's substantial environment'. This is not a very snappy phrase, is it? So, for convenience (and only for convenience because we won't worry about them too much), we will categorise them as 'cash-providing organizations' and 'cash-receiving organizations'. In Ms Able's case, her Mum was a cash-receiving organization (because Ms Able, our focal organization paid cash to that organization). And Mr Brain and Ms Ouri were cash-providing organizations because they either did provide – as in the case of Mr Brain – or were going to provide – as in the case of Ms Ouri – cash to the focal organization.

These two types of organization and the focal organization are shown in Figure 4.8. All of the basic bookkeeping transactions for the focal organization can be traced using this diagram. With practice, using this diagram can ensure that you never get your debits and credits mixed up – and believe us, this is a godsend for anybody doing bookkeeping! There are just a few points to make about this to make it all a bit clearer. First, we are only concerned with the focal organization. The other organizations are there for completeness only. Second, an organization which is a cash-providing organization for one transaction might be a cash-receiving organization for another transaction. For example, a focal organization might buy from and sell to the same organization. This doesn't matter, we are only trying to model the flows. Third, we haven't put all the possible lines in Figure 4.8. There is no need to make it totally cluttered. From time to time you may need to add a line/flow yourself. However, the diagram does show most of the major ones. Fourth, we won't be repeating this diagram time and time again. So you may want to be able to turn back to it to trace out the flows as questions and examples develop. Eventually, you will be able to hold it – or at least the important bits – in your head and will be able to ignore the diagram itself. But, fifth, do make sure you have this diagram firmly in mind. You will find from time to time that you cannot remember which bit of a particular transaction is a debit or a credit; you then need to be able to recall this diagram and it will provide the answer.

Well, with that tidied up we can move on and think about what sorts of transactions our basic bookkeeping system is faced with.

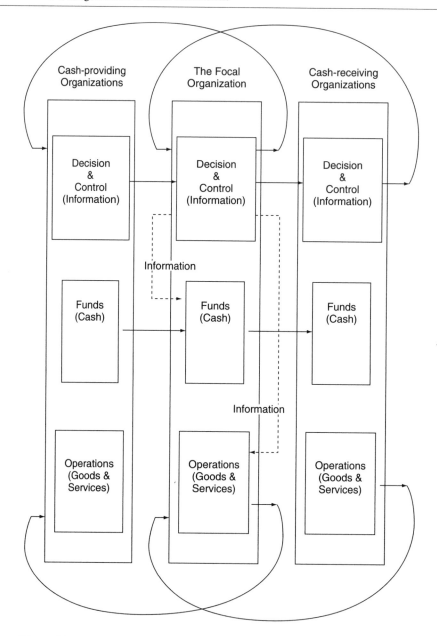

Figure 4.8 A general model of the focal organizations's bookkeeping flows

4.2 EIGHT TYPES OF ACCOUNTING TRANSACTIONS

4.2.1 Identifying the transactions

There are eight basic transactions which are recognized and recorded by the bookkeeping system. These are shown in Figure 4.9. Study this figure carefully as it will help a great deal in the next few chapters.

---

1. CASH PURCHASES: The focal organization receives goods and/or services (e.g. buildings, materials, labour, accommodation) in exchange for a cash payment made at approximately the same time.

2. CASH SALES: The focal organization dispatches/sells goods and/or services in exchange for a cash receipt at approximately the same time.

3. CREDITORS: The focal organization purchases goods and/or services but does not pay for them immediately. It therefore owes money to the supplier.

4. INVESTMENTS AND LOANS BY THE FOCAL ORGANIZATION: The focal organization makes a cash payment in anticipation of receiving a cash return at a future date (in interest or dividends plus repayment of the initial sum).

5. GRANTS AND TAXES PAID BY THE FOCAL ORGANIZATION: The focal organization makes a cash payment but receives nothing directly and obviously in return.

6. DEBTORS: The focal organization dispatches/sells goods and/or services in return for a promise of a cash receipt sometime in the future. It is therefore owed money by its customer.

7. CAPITAL FOR AND LOANS TO THE FOCAL ORGANIZATION: Cash is paid to the focal organization in the expectation that the focal organization will provide a cash return at some time in the future (in interest or dividends plus repayment of the original sum).

8. GRANTS TO THE FOCAL ORGANIZATION: Cash is received by the focal organization in recognition of or in expectation of certain aspects of its activity. No direct, obvious output is made by the focal organization.

Figure 4.9 The eight basic transactions

Each of these eight transactions must have two elements (remember the golden rule that every debit must have a credit) and we know that each of these debits and credits must be information, cash or goods and services. What is happening is that we are recognizing that the three types of things (information, cash and goods and services) which we have worked with so far need further refining. Basically, we need more than three T-accounts if each account is to mean anything. One way to start is to collect together all the different types of transactions into different accounts. This will be a start but, as we shall see, we shall have to break these accounts down even further when we end up with different sorts of things in the same account which have important accounting differences even though they arose from the same sort of transaction.

4.2.2 The bookkeeping for the eight basic transactions

The organizational flows and the bookkeeping for these transactions are summarized in Figure 4.10. Study this figure as we slowly go through the details of it – element by element.

Please note: The actual names given to the accounts in Figure 4.10 are driven by a combination of convenience and convention. They are discussed in the following sections.

(a) Cash purchases

We have already seen a number of these. Ms Able made some cash purchases of groceries and Mr Brain made several cash purchases of different things. The cash purchases result

TRANSACTION	INPUT SYSTEM	Debit account title	OUTPUT SYSTEM	Credit account title
1. CASH PURCHASES	Goods and Services	**Purchases** (noting different types of things purchased)	Funds	**Cashbook**
2. CASH SALES	Funds	**Cashbook**	Goods and Services	**Sales** (noting different categories of sales)
3a. CREDITORS (The set-up transaction)	Goods and Services	**Purchases** (noting as above)	Information	**Creditors** (noting different creditors)
3b. CREDITORS (The discharge transaction)	Information	**Creditors**	Funds	**Cashbook**
4a. INVESTMENTS/LOANS BY FO (The set-up transaction)	Information	**Investments or Loans Made Account**	Funds	**Cashbook**
4b. INVESTMENTS/LOANS BY FO (The discharge transaction)	Funds	**Cashbook**	Information	**Principal, Interest or Dividends**
5. GRANTS/TAXES PAID BY FO	Information	**Grants or Taxes Account**	Funds	**Cashbook**
6a. DEBTORS (The set-up transaction)	Information	**Debtors** (noting different debtors)	Goods and Services	**Sales** (noting as above)
6b. DEBTORS (The discharge transaction)	Funds	**Cashbook**	Information	**Debtors**
7a. CAPITAL FOR/LOANS TO FO (The set-up transaction)	Funds	**Cashbook**	Information	**Capital or Loans Received Account**
7b. CAPITAL FOR/LOANS TO FO (The discharge transaction)	Information	**Principal, Dividends or Interest**	Funds	**Cashbook**
8. GRANTS TO THE FO	Funds	**Cashbook**	Information	**Grants Received**

Figure 4.10 A schedule of the basic bookkeeping for the eight basic transactions

in an outflow/credit of cash and an inflow/debit of goods and services. We can keep these inflows/debits in a goods and services account or, more typically, we can separate out the different sorts of goods and services that we have purchased. You will recall that Mr Brain purchased accommodation, travel, food, drink, the services of a turf accountant, a dartboard and a textbook. In Chapter 2 we said it might be useful to distinguish the different sorts of things he purchased and we did this with different columns of the (analysed/columnar) cashbook. Similarly, we will find that putting all our purchases into a single account – we can call it a goods and services account or a *purchases account* (both are acceptable) – will end up with too many different 'things' in the one place. We will want to separate them out into different sorts of purchases and goods and services. How we do this is partly a matter of convenience, partly a matter of usefulness, partly a matter of convention, but also, as we shall see, partly a matter of accounting regulations as well. We will come to this.

(b) Cash sales

We have also seen some of these. Ms Able made a cash sale to Mr Brain. An outflow/credit was recorded in the goods and services account as she gave the groceries to Mr Brain and this was matched by an inflow/debit to her cashbook as Mr Brain paid her. Cash sales tend to be fairly straightforward with an inflow/debit to the cashbook and an outflow/credit from the goods and services/*sales account*. But, from time to time a focal organization will make cash sales of different types of things. These might be different product or service lines which it wishes to identify separately or it may wish to identify in which geographical region or country its sales were made. Then it might keep different sales accounts. Of most importance to us, when an organization sells one of its larger, structural things – like a building, a vehicle or a machine (things we shall come to call 'fixed assets') – we will have to treat these quite differently. So it matters what is sold in the cash sale. (We deal with this more in Chapters 7, 9 and 10.)

(c) Creditors

Now things start to get a little more awkward. The focal organization buys something and we record an inflow/debit in a goods and services or *purchases* (or whatever) *account*, as we discussed above. But the focal organization does not pay for this purchase straight away. What we make in exchange is a promise – information that we will pay. Thus the matching bookkeeping entry is an outflow/credit from an information account. There are many different possible types of information accounts where we would keep similar types of information together. One of the most important is the information flows about people the focal organization owes money (or goods and services) to – the creditors. We therefore open a *creditors account* and, if we are a big organization we might want to open a separate account for each creditor – simply so that we didn't end up getting them all jumbled together and muddled. It is very useful to know to whom we owe money!

But you will notice in Figure 4.10 that there are two creditor transactions. Well, eventually, the focal organization is going to pay off its debt. What happens then? There is an outflow/credit from the cashbook – the focal organization makes a payment to its creditor. What about the inflow? This will be to the information accounts and, in particular, to the same creditors account in which we first put the indebtedness. The inflow/debit of information is saying 'you have paid me and you do not owe me any more', so we put in a debit entry which cancels the original credit entry. Do note: we are constructing accounting records and we wish, therefore, to keep a detailed record of what has gone on. Tempting though it might be to just rub out the original entry in the creditors account, this is bad practice and should be avoided – even though the accounting effect is the same in the end.

(d) Investments and loans made by the focal organization

In your introductory studies these will not be especially common transactions but we do need to know a bit about them. This is a shame because they are a bit of a nuisance. What happens is that the focal organization (FO) decides to (perhaps) buy some shares in another company (see Chapters 12 and 14), puts some money by other means into a business or decides to lend someone or something some money. There is clearly an outflow/credit from the cashbook as the cash leaves the focal organization to the place where it is to be lent or invested. The inflow/debit must be of information. The information is that the focal organization either (i) now owns part of an organization (this is usually the case in investments) or (ii) owns a debt in another organization (in the case of a loan). The inflow/debit of information will be recorded in an *investments account* or in a *loans made account*.

So far, so good. But the focal organization will expect two things to occur in future accounting periods. First, the focal organization will expect (i) to receive repayments of (what is known as the 'principal' of) the loan in due course (depending upon the loan agreement) and (ii) either repayment of (the principal of) the investment or the ability to sell it to someone else (as one does with shares and the like). In either of these cases there is clearly an inflow/debit to the cashbook as the cash to repay the loan or investment arrives in the focal organization. The outflow/credit is an outflow of information which is set against the original entry to show the reduction in indebtedness or ownership – we credit the account containing the original or principal of the loan or investment. Second, the focal organization will expect to receive some regular cash payments from the organization it has invested in/lent to as the 'price' for investing or lending the money. These will be probably in the form of either dividends (in the case of an investment) or interest (in the case of a loan). This will result in an inflow/debit to the cashbook as the cash arrives. But where will the outflow go? It will not go against the investment/loan! This is because (i) outflows are not reductions in the principal and (ii) they represent some sort of 'earning' from 'putting money to work'. They are therefore kept separately and the outflow/credit goes to an 'interest received' or a 'dividends received' account.

There, we said they were a bit of a nuisance, didn't we? Now don't nod off, we know this is on the wrong side of thrilling but we have to get through it – and we are about halfway. So make yourself a nice cup of tea and let's carry on.

(e) Grants and taxes paid

These are quite easy. What happens is that (i) the focal organization is given a bill for taxation and pays it or else (ii) the focal organization pays out a grant (or a donation) to some other organization (such as a charity). There is no directly observable return to the organization for doing either of these things although it has little choice about the taxes and may be paying out donations for the positive publicity it brings. What we have, in terms of the bookkeeping, is clearly an outflow/credit from the cashbook as the cash goes zooming off to buy the government another nuclear submarine or disappears into Greenpeace's bottomless demand for small rubber boats.[1] The inflow/debit is a sort of information – a sort of 'thank you' account – which we record in a *taxation* or a *donations/grants paid account*.

(f) Debtors

Debtors are very important and, indeed, we saw Ms Able involved in a debtor transaction with Ms Ouri. What is happening in a debtor transaction is that the focal organization is (usually) making a sale and the customer is allowed 'credit' whereby they can pay in a few days, a few weeks or maybe even a few months. Most large organizations work like this. So, in the initial transaction there is an outflow/credit from the operations subsystem as the good or the service leaves the focal organization. We call this a sale and credit it to the *sales account*. (See the other points above under cash sales.) The inflow/debit must be information and, in order to distinguish it from other forms of information, we will debit it to a *debtors account*. We may have many debtors accounts for much the same reason as we may have many creditors accounts.

Also, rather like the creditors example, we have to recognise that the customer will (we hope) eventually pay the focal organization what they owe it – the discharge transaction. So there must be an inflow/debit to the cashbook as the debtor pays off their debt. The outflow/credit will be of information saying 'thanks for the cash, you don't owe us anymore'. So it will be a credit set against the debit which is already sitting in the debtors account from the original (the set-up) transaction.

(g) Capital for and loans to the focal organization

These will be slightly more common in your introductory studies than the investments and loans going the other way which we saw in (d) above. They are, however, no less difficult and we will in fact come back to them and spend a lot of time on these issues in Chapters 12, 13 and 14. For the time being, we do need to know how to do the basic bookkeeping. First, there is the obvious inflow/debit to the cashbook as the first injection of capital or the amount of the loan is received by the focal organization. This inflow/debit must be matched by an outflow/credit and this will, again, be of information. Effectively, this information is saying either 'you now own part of me' or 'I owe you this loan'. We will therefore enter an outflow/credit to the *capital* or the *loans received account* as appropriate.

This is, however, only the set-up transaction. That is, ownership and loans tend to last for more than one accounting period and tend to involve (i) the repayment of principal (in the case of a loan) or (ii) the possibility of repaying the capital or the selling of the capital (the shares) to someone else. The repayment of the principal or the repayment of the capital will simply reverse the set-up transaction. There will be an outflow/credit from the cashbook and this will be matched by an inflow/debit of information saying 'you have reduced your indebtedness' – a credit to the loan account or to the capital account.

But these transactions also involve the payment of dividends (or other ownership payments – see Chapters 12 and 13) or interest as charges for the use of the money. Each of these will involve an outflow/credit from the cashbook as the cash for the dividends or the interest is paid to the owner or lender. The inflow/debit will not be put to the 'principal of the loan account' or the 'capital account' – for the same reasons as we gave under (d) above. The inflow/debit will be shown against a **dividends paid account** or an **interest paid account** and the dividends and interest will not only be kept separate from each other but will also be kept separate from the principals.

Once again, we said these were hard to account for – and they are. We will return and examine them in a great deal more detail later on in the book.

(h) Grants to the focal organization

It is nice to be able to finish on a relatively uncommon and, as far as our introductory studies are concerned, relatively simple transaction. A grant may be paid to the focal organization for many reasons. The most common might be a government grant to help the company (for example) relocate or employ handicapped people. There is clearly an inflow/debit of cash as the grant is received by the focal organization. This then is matched by an outflow/credit of information. Of what, is not particularly clear (in effect a 'thank you'), so don't worry about it. *Open a grants received account and credit that.*

4.2.3 Looking back at the eight transactions

Hopefully, as you have worked through Figure 4.10 and each of the eight transactions above, patterns have emerged. Perhaps the most obvious thing is that each of them involves cash and the cashbook at some stage – if not in the set-up transaction then in the discharge transaction which follows at some later stage. When thinking about the flows and the resultant double-entry, *it is often easiest to work out where the cashbook will fit in first and then work out the matching flow*. This is perhaps not so easy for debtors and creditors, but even here you could work it back if you needed to. Perhaps it has also struck you that not only are accounting transactions rather more complicated than we might at first have thought, but, also, the descriptions given above clearly miss out bits and pieces. For example, how do we treat (say) interest which we owe but haven't yet paid? Well, don't worry about it yet, but you can work it out from the above descriptions.

One of the most obvious things to emerge from the above descriptions is that they are tedious. They are the building blocks that you just have to know. If you can (as you should) relate them to the organizational flows then they should become rather less uninteresting. But, you will be pleased to know, if you can really grasp this, then the bulk of the real tedium is now behind you. If you haven't grasped this then you must go back and work at it until you do. If you haven't got each building block in place, what follows will be unintelligible, tedious and, it has to be said, embarrassing as you continually make a fool of yourself in class.

In Chapter 5 we will look at a new and much more detailed example and construct the accounting records (do the bookkeeping) for that. However, before we do this you really should go back to Mr Brain and Ms Able and rework their data into a series of T-accounts working from the information contained in Figure 4.10 and the descriptions of the last few pages. When you have done that (and no cheating) check your answers with Figures 4.11 and 4.12. If you have any mistakes, go back and find out why and re-do it until you get it right! Good luck. (You might find it useful to compare your answers with Figures 3.9 and 4.5.)

When you have done this, then you can safely assume that you have grasped the basics of double-entry bookkeeping.

Now is an appropriate moment to have another look at where non-commercial organizations fit into the picture. This is the task of the next section.

4.3 SOME FURTHER POINTS ABOUT COMMERCIAL AND NON-COMMERCIAL ORGANIZATIONS

Organizations are complex things and our ways of thinking about them (our 'theories of organizations') change over time. As a result, the model of an organization that we are employing in this book (see Figure 3.4) represents only one of a number of possible ways of portraying complex organizational systems. It is a very (perhaps over-) simple model but it has been chosen because it allows us to clarify some of the underlying organizational

Inflow/Debit	Money from parents' account (Grants/Donations to FO)		Outflow/Credit
	Parents		200

Inflow/Debit	Aunty Gertrude account (Grants/Donations to FO)		Outflow/Credit
	Aunty Gertrude		10

Inflow/Debit	Savings account (Capital/Loans to FO)		Outflow/Credit
	Post Office savings		50

Inflow/Debit	Debtors account		Outflow/Credit
Loan to Jack	20		

Inflow/Debit	Creditors account		Outflow/Credit
	Loan from Fred		2
	Owed to the landlord		15
	Owed to the bar		34

Inflow/Debit	Cash account		Outflow/Credit
Parents	200	Landlord	20
Aunty Gertrude	10	Grocers	10
Post Office savings	50	Bus pass	5
Loan from Fred	2	Textbooks	3
		Turf accountants	16
		Bar bill	62
		Dartboard	8
		Landlord	20
		Loan to Jack	20
		Bar bill	57
		Guinness	20
		Train ticket	5
		Rent	10

Inflow/Debit	Goods and services/Purchases account (Rent)		Outflow/Credit
Landlord	20		
Landlord	20		
Rent	10		
Owed to the landlord	15		

Inflow/Debit	Goods and services/Purchases account (Food and Drink)		Outflow/Credit
Grocers	10		
Bar bill	62		
Bar bill	57		
Guinness	20		
Owed to the bar	34		

Inflow/Debit	Goods and services/Purchases account (travel and other services)		Outflow/Credit
Bus pass	5		
Turf accountants	16		
Train ticket	5		

Inflow/Debit	Goods and services/Purchases account (fixed assets – that is, 'things' which we shall keep for a longish period of time)		Outflow/Credit
Textbooks	3		
Dartboard	8		

Figure 4.11 Mr Brain's T-accounts for all his transactions

Inflow/Debit	Debtors account		Outflow/Credit
Ms Ouri	£7		

Inflow/Debit	Cash account		Outflow/Credit
Cash from sale to Mr Brain	£6	Pay Mum for coffee etc.	£10

Inflow/Debit	Goods and services/Purchases account (groceries for resale)		Outflow/Credit
Coffee and other groceries from Mum	£10		

Inflow/Debit	Goods and services/Sales account (cash and credit sales)		Outflow/Credit
		Groceries to Mr Brain	£6
		Groceries to Ms Ouri	£7

Figure 4.12 Ms Able's T-accounts for her grocery purchases and sales

relationships which find their expression in accounting records. Despite the inevitable reservations that one should always have about simple models, our organizational flow model can be used to good effect to clarify the important distinctions between commercial and non-commercial organizations and, in the process, extend and formalize the points that have already been made in Chapter 3.

In general, all organizations buy goods and services whether for cash or on credit. They all need finance, whether it comes through capital, loans, grants or sales of goods and services; they all purchase goods and services which are transformed into further goods and services which sometimes are sold in exchange for funds. In fact, it is these relationships themselves which, in large measure, define the essence of an accountant's view of an organization. This seems to suggest that accountants might see all focal organizations as being the same. However, as Chapter 3 highlighted, this is not so. The differences are important but, for the accounting system, the discriminating factors are the actual organizational flows and the way in which the accounting system recognizes them.

One of the key differences which allows us to separate focal organizations into commercial and non-commercial categories centres around the different types of inputs into the organizations' funds subsystems. Basically, commercial organizations are financed more through capital, loans and sales whereas non-commercial organizations derive their funding largely through grants.

Thus, a commercial organization typically sells a particular product or service in return for receiving a specific financial amount in return. For instance, a company may sell cars, boats or planes, with a clearly defined price per unit. Similarly, firms of accountants or lawyers will offer their technical expertise to individuals and organizations at so much per hour or per day. Thus, in the commercial organization, all activities are reduced to a common denominator – cash. In other words, there is an equivalence between the flows that pass through the funds and the operations subsystems – each producing an equivalent cash flow at some stage.

On the other hand, a non-commercial organization may offer a service to individuals and organizations and not expect direct payment in return. Thus, for instance, a hospital or a school may offer a service to patients or pupils for what appears to be no fee at all. The actual finance of the hospital or school comes from a grant from the government and this grant, in turn, comes from the taxes on the individuals and organizations. The taxes and their allocation are determined partly by money available, partly by politics and partly by the services offered by the hospital or school. The funding of charities and local authorities and the services that they offer follow the same principles.

These distinctions can also be expressed in terms of the objectives of the two types of organization. Despite the inherent complexity of organizational objectives we can capture the essence as follows. The objectives of commercial organizations are primarily to sell goods and services in exchange for a financial reward above the costs incurred in producing these products. The objectives, therefore, can be expressed, from a certain perspective, through the cash received and paid. On the other hand, the objectives of non-commercial organizations, expressed largely through the services rendered, are more complex and have little clear relationship to the financial grants received. Thus the services rendered by non-commercial organizations (which expresses something about their objectives) cannot be measured solely in terms of these grants received whereas in commercial organizations the cash receipts do have a more meaningful relationship to their economic objectives.

Undoubtedly there is a large grey area between what we are calling 'commercial' and 'non-commercial' and thus it seems helpful to envisage this distinction as a type of continuum. Many organizations are clearly in either the commercial or non-commercial grouping but there are many which are some hybrid of the two. Thus, for instance, government-owned industries and mutual societies can often exhibit characteristics of both receiving direct grants from government and offering services to the public which are not totally related to the charges made.

Despite these uncertainties we believe that the distinction is meaningful and that these defining characteristics of commercial and non-commercial organizations provide a clue as to why accountants and accounting texts have concentrated in the main on the commercial organizations. The reason, quite simply, is the necessity in traditional financial accounting to express the basic records in terms of the double-entry recording system. As we indicated above, the traditional records of accounting concentrate on the flows into and out of the focal organization with the requirement that all requisite transactions are recorded in dual terms and measured in a common money unit. These restrictions on recording fit well with commercial organizations since the primary medium for interpreting cash sales and debtors transactions is, in fact, funds. Put another way, even though the operations subsystem flow is made up of some tangible goods and services, it is exchanged for a defined amount of funds and hence it is possible to describe this flow in cash equivalent terms without creating a marked information loss. On the other hand, to capture adequately the essence of these flows in non-commercial organizations and record matters in duality terms becomes an immense and incompatible measurement problem. As a result much more attention in the accounting literature is given to the organizations where the double-entry recording system provides more meaningful results – the commercial organizations in other words.

SUMMARY

This chapter has brought our material about the cashbook (in Chapter 2) and the organizational flows and three basic T-accounts (of Chapter 3) to the point where we can start producing something that starts to look like conventional accounting records. We have worked over the process of imagining the accounting entity as an organization consisting of a series of flows into and out of three subsystems and then identifying those flows as inputs or outputs of information, cash or goods and services. We found that we could accept the inflows/debits and outflows/credits of cash as they stood because this produced our basic cashbook for us. We did discover, however, that the information and the goods and services flows contained too many different things. We, therefore, had to break these categories down into smaller, more useful types of things. We started this by identifying and defining **eight basic bookkeeping transactions.** These are the raw materials of bookkeeping and you really must know them. With these eight basic transactions, together with our organizational flows diagram, we can do all the basic bookkeeping we need to get us moving on the road to knowing about, understanding and thinking about financial accounting.

Chapter 5 will take these basic raw materials and put them to work in a more detailed and 'realistic' example. At the end of that, you will know the rudiments of bookkeeping!

Key terms and concepts

The following key terms and concepts have featured in this chapter. You should make sure that you understand and can explain each one. Page references to definitions appear in the index in bold type.

- Accounts for grants or taxes
- Capital
- Capital accounts
- Commercial and non-commercial organizations
- Creditors accounts
- Debtors accounts
- Dividend accounts
- Dividends
- Eight types of bookkeeping transactions:
  - cash purchases
  - cash sales
  - creditors
  - investments/loans by FO
  - grants/taxes paid by FO
  - debtors
  - capital/loans to FO
  - grants to FO
- Interest accounts
- Loan accounts
- Loan interest
- Loan principal
- Purchases
- Purchases accounts
- Sales
- Sales accounts

FURTHER READING

Because we are approaching the bookkeeping process in a somewhat different way than you will find in a traditional accounting textbook it is not easy to recommend further reading at this stage. Indeed, experience shows that if you start looking at other textbooks at this stage you may get confused and that would be fatal. Only when you can work with comfort and confidence in the method we have outlined above should you spend time with other introductory accounting textbooks. We hope that you will reach this point at the end of Chapter 5 – when you will gain greatly from consulting as wide an array of other approaches as possible. For the time being, concentrate on this text and practising the approach.

NOTES

1. Which largely arises because of the government's purchase of nuclear submarines!

Putting the eight basic transactions to work, producing the accounting records and an initial trial balance

5

Learning objectives

After studying this chapter you should be able to:

- analyse a list of events in the life of an accounting entity and identify the basic accounting transaction;

- identify the accounting records (the T-accounts) to be used;

- analyse the basic accounting transactions in terms of inflows/debits and outflows/credits;

- draw up a set of accounting records/books of account;

- close off those accounts with a balancing entry;

- construct an initial trial balance;

- recognize some of the limitations of the initial trial balance (TB).

5.1 INTRODUCTION

5.1.1 Chapter design and links to previous chapters

Chapter 4 gave us the **eight basic bookkeeping transactions** and showed us what they mean in terms of both the organizational flows and in terms of the bookkeeping necessary to produce the accounting records in T-account format. In the process we learnt that the initial three T-accounts for information, cash, and goods and services were insufficient for our purposes. We began to see that we can, actually, open as many T-accounts as we want. Too many T-accounts can obviously be a nuisance in practice but a useful hint is 'if in doubt, open a T-account!'. Whilst we shall see that the demands of the financial statements effectively guide many of our decisions about what T-accounts should be opened and what should go in each one, in general we will not go far wrong if we keep each T-account for 'similar sorts of things'. Now, this idea of 'similar sorts of things' is highly contentious. However, we are talking, as you will remember, from a conventional accounting point of view and the accounting system is interested in similar accounting things. So, whilst one of our debtors may be a sumo wrestler and another an Icelandic poet, the accounting system sees them as similar – they are both debtors. Many of these categories of 'similar things' will emerge as we progress and we will start formalizing the process in Chapter 7.

This chapter is designed to reinforce what happened in Chapter 4. It consists principally of a detailed worked example in which we explore, explain and account for a series of transactions of a new company. This should leave you with a very firm grasp of the rudiments of bookkeeping. Then, having reinforced the bookkeeping, we move on to balance off the accounts and then explain and produce an **initial trial balance** for the company. The initial trial balance represents a most important milestone in your studies – it both signals that you have reached the end of the rudimentary bookkeeping and provides the basis upon which we will start to build the accounting that is necessary to bring us to the financial statements.

The chapter is organized as follows. The next subsection is only short and is intended as a bit of an aside to keep you thinking. The main section of the chapter is the worked example of Bird Industries. Section 5.3 explains the process of balancing off the accounts and then proceeds to do it for Bird Industries. This is followed by a discussion of the trial balance and we discover how to produce one again for Bird Industries. The chapter also contains an appendix which shows you how to conduct double-entry bookkeeping by single entry(!) in a matrix format. This would allow you to keep basic accounting records in a very simple way in a computer spreadsheet.

5.1.2 Not losing the wood for too many trees?

We are now at the stage when all our attention is focused on trying to get to grips with this most peculiar way of looking at the world known as bookkeeping. It is worth just looking up for a minute or so in order to remember why we are doing this. Bookkeeping is not an intellectually demanding activity – computers can do it. There is nothing here that demands a brain the size of a planet. It just requires hard work until you get the idea. Then it will be like riding a bicycle – you will never completely forget it. But, remember, the world doesn't really need bookkeepers – it needs people who understand bookkeeping so that they can undertake sensible and intelligent accounting. We know it is difficult to remember that you are supposed to be draining the swamp (understanding accounting) when you are up to your armpits in alligators (detailed bookkeeping), but you have to try. The best way of doing this is partly intellectual and partly habit. Hold the organizational model in your mind whenever you are trying to work out some bookkeeping. This way you can always link back what you are doing to the bigger picture. (Indeed, it is very easy, when you are used to this approach, to link bookkeeping entries back to environmental degradation and social dislocation, for example. Using the diagram it is possible to show that accounting has a major responsibility for the environmental crisis! We shall look at this again in Chapter 17.) The other part of not losing sight of the wood for the trees is to continue regular reading of the professional accountancy press and regular reviewing of organisational annual reports. If you get into the habit of these two you will find your studies a great deal more interesting and, as a result, a great deal more successful and pleasurable.

Homily over. Let's continue with the bookkeeping.

5.2 A DETAILED WORKED EXAMPLE: BIRD INDUSTRIES LTD

5.2.1 Understanding the transactions

In this section we are going to look in detail at one month's transactions of a new company. (Companies are explained in detail in Chapter 14.) We will go through each of the transactions, slowly, so that you can get into the habit of thinking through transactions and can see where everything goes – and why.

We will:

- first, present the information for which we are going to account;
- second, go through, transaction by transaction, identifying the flows and the accounts;
- and then, present the T-accounts in double-entry format.

This is a slow way of doing it and, in time, you will short-circuit this process. But, for the time being, let us just be certain that each step along the way is safe and sure.

Now please read through the Bird Industries (BI) example in Figure 5.1.

Bird Industries Limited (BI Ltd hereafter) is a company set up on 1.1. 200X by A. Tweet, A. Wing and A. Feather to manage a business to sell special bird food and bird houses.

Tweet, Wing and Feather believed that the market was buoyant enough to allow them to make a living out of the company. After careful thought the company was formed with the three individuals as worker directors. *[Directors are the managers, as distinct from the owners, of any commercial organizations. They can, as in the case of BI Ltd, also be shareholders, but they are technically and legally in a different role in this capacity – see Chapters 12 and 14 for more details about these arrangements.]*

Some selected transactions from the company's first month are given below.

1. *1 January.* Tweet, Wing & Feather put £27,000 of their own money into the business in terms of:

   (a) £21,000 as ordinary share capital (shared equally between each owner)

   (b) Ms Tweet put an additional £6,000 as a short-term loan to be repaid within the next six years on the condition that a 2% interest on the balance of the loan outstanding is paid at the end of each month.

2. *1 January.* BI Ltd purchased a small warehouse from Wareco Ltd for £20,000. Payment was made by cheque.

3. *2 January.* BI ordered the following items and paid immediately by cheque:

   (a) Grain mixing equipment from Grainco Ltd £1,000

   (b) Machinery to make bird houses from Machco Ltd £1,500

   (c) Second-hand mini-van (for purposes of delivering goods) from Carco Ltd £2,500.

4. *3 January.* BI Ltd placed orders for the following all on 30 days' credit (i.e. must be paid by 3 February):

   (a) Sundry seed from Seedco Ltd £1,000

   (b) Sundry wood from Woodco Ltd £1,000

   (c) Sundry bags and packaging from Bagco Ltd £300.

5. *3 January.* BI Ltd received goods from Grainco, Machco and Carco.

6. *4 January.* BI Ltd received goods from Seedco, Woodco and Bagco.

7. *4 January.* BI Ltd advertised its products employing Adverto Ltd at a cost of £300 cash to handle this advertising project.

8. *7 January.* Tweet, Wing and Feather start work on the mixing and packaging of seed and the making of bird houses.

9. *8 January.* Some tentative enquiries are received from Bird Supplies Ltd (a retail outlet).

10. *9 January.* Terms are offered to Bird Supplies.

11. *12 January.* Firm orders are received from Bird Supplies Ltd for:

    (a) Mixed seed at a price of £500 (cost of seed £250)

    (b) Bird houses at a price of £400 (cost of materials £200).

    It was agreed that Bird Supplies Ltd should be allowed 2 weeks' credit.   ➜

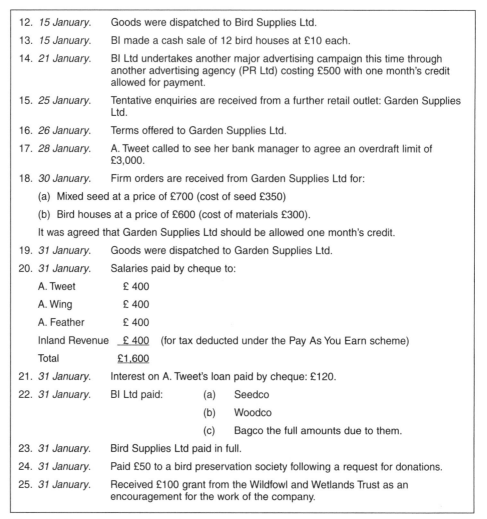

12. *15 January.*	Goods were dispatched to Bird Supplies Ltd.	
13. *15 January.*	BI made a cash sale of 12 bird houses at £10 each.	
14. *21 January.*	BI Ltd undertakes another major advertising campaign this time through another advertising agency (PR Ltd) costing £500 with one month's credit allowed for payment.	
15. *25 January.*	Tentative enquiries are received from a further retail outlet: Garden Supplies Ltd.	
16. *26 January.*	Terms offered to Garden Supplies Ltd.	
17. *28 January.*	A. Tweet called to see her bank manager to agree an overdraft limit of £3,000.	
18. *30 January.*	Firm orders are received from Garden Supplies Ltd for:	
	(a) Mixed seed at a price of £700 (cost of seed £350)	
	(b) Bird houses at a price of £600 (cost of materials £300).	
	It was agreed that Garden Supplies Ltd should be allowed one month's credit.	
19. *31 January.*	Goods were dispatched to Garden Supplies Ltd.	
20. *31 January.*	Salaries paid by cheque to:	
	A. Tweet	£ 400
	A. Wing	£ 400
	A. Feather	£ 400
	Inland Revenue	£ 400 (for tax deducted under the Pay As You Earn scheme)
	Total	£1,600
21. *31 January.*	Interest on A. Tweet's loan paid by cheque: £120.	
22. *31 January.*	BI Ltd paid:	(a) Seedco
		(b) Woodco
		(c) Bagco the full amounts due to them.
23. *31 January.*	Bird Supplies Ltd paid in full.	
24. *31 January.*	Paid £50 to a bird preservation society following a request for donations.	
25. *31 January.*	Received £100 grant from the Wildfowl and Wetlands Trust as an encouragement for the work of the company.	

Figure 5.1 Financial transactions of Bird Industries Ltd

You will note (we hope) that the details in Figure 5.1 are very much a selection of all the things that will have happened to Bird Industries in their first month. The accounting system (which we will describe in Chapter 6) has selected all those events that fit our **four characteristics**. We have then just listed them in chronological order. With these accounting events we can produce the bookkeeping in the T-accounts (and later go on and produce financial statements for Bird Industries). Let's now go through each accounting event carefully.

Hint

You will notice that we have distinguished between Tweet, Wing and Feather and the *accounting entity* Bird Industries. We are accounting for Bird Industries as our focal organization, not Tweet, Wing or Feather. The owners and the organization are separate *accounting entities* and, as we shall learn in more detail later in the book, also separate legal entities.

Event 1a

Tweet, Wing and Feather have put £21,000 of their own money into the organization as share capital. (Share capital is explained in more detail in Chapter 14; we do not need to worry too much about the detail at this stage.) This is a 'capital for FO' transaction. There is an inflow/debit to the funds subsystem (which, for simplicity, we will keep in a single-column cashbook and not worry about either the bank/cash-in-hand distinction or analysing the cashbook). In return, there is a outflow/credit of information out of the focal organization saying 'thanks for the cash, you are an owner of Bird Industries'. The bookkeeping will involve (a) opening a cashbook, and (b) opening a share capital account. We can summarize these entries as follows. (*Please note* that this is just a *summary* of the entries. We open the actual T-Accounts in the next subsection.)

EVENT NUMBER 1a			
INFLOW/DEBIT		OUTFLOW/CREDIT	
Account title	*Amount*	*Account title*	*Amount*
Cashbook	£21,000	Share capital	£21,000

Our accounting entity is thus created. But, we must remember that a 'capital/loan' transaction has at least two elements: the 'set-up' transaction (which we have just seen) and the 'discharge' transaction. In the present case this might mean the payment of a dividend at some later stage. We have no information on this and so ignore it – for the time being (but try not to forget it as it may be important later on).

Event 1b

Now Tweet puts in some more money to the focal organization, but this time as a loan (again the distinction will be pulled out in more detail later but the essential differences are that the share capital confers *ownership* and the right to *dividends* if the company makes a profit (and chooses to pay the dividend) whereas a loan only confers *indebtedness* and the right to *interest* whether or not the company makes a profit). It is the same sort of transaction as above and so the inflow/debit and the outflow/credit look much the same.

EVENT NUMBER 1b			
INFLOW/DEBIT		OUTFLOW/CREDIT	
Account title	*Amount*	*Account title*	*Amount*
Cashbook	£6,000	Loans received	£6,000

However, this time we are given some information about the 'discharge' transaction. At the end of every month, Bird Industries must pay to Ms Tweet a sum of 2% interest per month. (The 2% is calculated on the amount outstanding of the *principal* sum unless we are told otherwise.) This monthly interest will be [2 per cent × £6,000] = £120. We are not yet told about this, but, at the end of the *accounting period* the focal organization will either have to pay the amount or show the amount as owing. Either way we will have to do some bookkeeping for it – at the end of the month. So, make a note of this too.

Event 2

Now the focal organization gets down to business. BI buys a warehouse and pays for it immediately. There must obviously be an outflow/credit from the funds subsystem as BI pays for the warehouse and a corresponding inflow/debit to the operations subsystem. This is a cash purchase transaction (see Figure 4.10). For a variety of reasons, not least our desire to keep different sorts of things separate, we will put this warehouse in a warehouse account. The transaction looks like this:

EVENT NUMBER 2			
INFLOW/DEBIT		OUTFLOW/CREDIT	
Account title	*Amount*	*Account title*	*Amount*
Warehouse	£20,000	Cashbook	£20,000

So BI's cash has gone down, but it owns something – a warehouse.

Event 3 (and 5)

BI orders some materials and a van. The focal organization pays for the items on 2 January (by writing a cheque) but doesn't receive them immediately. (If you look through the question, you will see it all arrives the next day.) This could cause us a bit of a problem. Clearly, there are three outflows/credits from the funds subsystem as the three cheques are paid out. What should we do about the inflow/debit? Strictly speaking, we should recognize that we have an effective inflow/debit of information from the other three (cash-receiving organizations – remember these from Chapter 4?) by which they promise to deliver these items to BI. That is, it is, strictly speaking, a debtor transaction (see Figure 4.10), except that the debtor owes us goods and services, not cash. We could certainly do this and then, when we get to Event 5, go through the rigmarole of putting through the discharge transaction. However, for simplicity, given that the events are so close together,[1] we can treat this as a cash purchase transaction and, in practice – in a real company – this is what would happen. The flows and entries would look like this.

EVENT NUMBER 3 (and 5)			
INFLOW/DEBIT		OUTFLOW/CREDIT	
Account title	*Amount*	*Account title*	*Amount*
(a) Equipment and machinery	£1,000	(a) Cashbook	£1,000
(b) Equipment and machinery	£1,500	(b) Cashbook	£1,500
(c) Motor vehicle	£2,500	(c) Cashbook	£2,500

So, we have paid out some more cash and received a series of inflows to our operations subsystem. You will note that, for convenience and convention only, we have put the equipment and the machinery in the same account. They could have been put into different accounts – and, depending on the practical issues in the business, this might be advisable. However, machinery and equipment are similar sorts of things and for this question no great harm is done by putting them together.

Event 4 (and 6)

Now this is a bit different. We, once again, have this slight lag in time between the order and the goods arriving (see Event 6). Once again we can ignore this time lag.[2] However, the lag between the receipt of the goods and the payment of the cash is anything up to 30 days. This is a credit purchase or creditor transaction. There is an inflow/debit to our operations subsystem as the goods arrive and, in return, there is an outflow/credit of information from the decision and control subsystem. We will show these events as follows.

EVENT NUMBER 4 (and 6)			
INFLOW/DEBIT		**OUTFLOW/CREDIT**	
Account title	*Amount*	*Account title*	*Amount*
(a) Seeds	£1,000	(a) Creditors (Seedco)	£1,000
(b) Wood	£1,000	(b) Creditors (Woodco)	£1,000
(c) Bags and packaging	£300	(c) Creditors (Bagco)	£300

We have opened a series of goods and services/purchases accounts for seed, wood and bags. We have kept them separate because we are not sure at this stage whether or not they are similar things from the accounting point of view. (This will make more sense later – see especially Chapter 10.) We have then opened a creditors account. A large organization would open a separate account for each creditor (see Chapter 6) but BI is a small focal organization and we can keep things simple by putting them together for the time being.

Events 5 and 6

We have already dealt with these above – see Events 3 and 4.

Event 7

Now the focal organization is purchasing some advertising services for which it will pay cash. This is a cash purchase transaction just like Events 2, 3 and 5 above. The transactions look like this.

EVENT NUMBER 7			
INFLOW/DEBIT		**OUTFLOW/CREDIT**	
Account title	*Amount*	*Account title*	*Amount*
Advertising	£300	Cashbook	£300

That the focal organization bought services or goods makes no difference to the basic bookkeeping but because advertising is a different sort of thing from seeds, vehicles, warehouses and machinery we have opened a separate account.

Event 8

This is an interesting event in the life of the organization and clearly important from the point of view of controlling it. On the face of it, though, it is not an accounting transaction as it does not have direct cash implications, although it might do if we were to pay Tweet, Wing and Feather some wages. We do not know anything about this in the question so far. So the bookkeeping system ignores it.[3]

Events 9 and 10

Just like Event 8, these are important events in the life of the organization but they do not have direct cash effects and so the bookkeeping ignores them.

Events 11 and 12

We again have a lag between the order and the dispatch but because no cash or things have changed hands we simply ignore Event 11 as a bookkeeping event and wait until 15 January before doing anything. BI has received a promise to pay cash at some future date – an inflow/debit of information. This has been matched by the despatch of goods to Bird Supplies of *sales* value £500 and £400 – an outflow/credit to the operations subsystems accounts. The focal organization has a 'debtors' transaction. [**NB** As we discussed earlier – see Chapter 4 – this transaction is at the sales value]. The additional information in the question (about the cost of what is sold) is very important both in our later calculations – in the **processing** stage of the financial accounting activity and for the management accounting activity (see Chapter 10). We haven't reached the processing stage yet and so the bookkeeping system simply notices these cost figures (and then ignores them) and works on the sales amounts. The flows and double entry look like this.

EVENTS NUMBER 11 and 12			
INFLOW/DEBIT		**OUTFLOW/CREDIT**	
Account title	*Amount*	*Account title*	*Amount*
Debtors (Bird Supplies)	£500	Sales (Mixed seed)	£500
Debtors (Bird Supplies)	£400	Sales (Bird houses)	£400

Event 13

This is a simple transaction. Someone has heard about the bird houses that BI makes and walked into the BI warehouse and bought 12 at £10 each. There is clearly an inflow/debit of cash into the funds subsystem and must be matched by an outflow of bird houses – an outflow/credit of goods and services to the sales account. This is a 'cash sales' transaction and looks like this.

EVENT NUMBER 13			
INFLOW/DEBIT		**OUTFLOW/CREDIT**	
Account title	*Amount*	*Account title*	*Amount*
Cashbook	£120	Sales (Cash: bird houses)	£120

Event 14

This is just the same as the previous advertising campaign except that the focal organization will not pay for it immediately. There is an inflow/debit of services (the advertising) and an outflow/credit of information in the form of a promise to pay. This is thus a 'creditor' transaction and looks like this.

EVENT NUMBER 14			
INFLOW/DEBIT		**OUTFLOW/CREDIT**	
Account title	*Amount*	*Account title*	*Amount*
Advertising	£500	Creditors (PR Ltd)	£500

Events 15 and 16

We met this situation above. Although important to the focal organization the bookkeeping system ignores these until they have direct cash implications.

Event 17

The arranging of a bank overdraft facility is one which often trips up students. Has there been an actual economic event which can be financially described? Well, no, there hasn't. BI now has the ability to undertake future cash transactions (which obviously are economic events with financial description) but has not actually undertaken any such transaction. The bookkeeping system ignores it!

Events 18 and 19

How we are back in the realm that we recognize. We treat these transactions exactly the same as the earlier transactions involving Bird Supplies. These are debtor transactions and look like this.

EVENTS NUMBER 18 and 19			
INFLOW/DEBIT		**OUTFLOW/CREDIT**	
Account title	*Amount*	*Account title*	*Amount*
Debtors (Garden Supplies)	£700	Sales (Mixed seeds)	£700
Debtors (Garden Supplies)	£600	Sales (Bird houses)	£600

Event 20

Now, here is a new one! What is all this about? Wages, salary and taxation are complicated matters but, at least at our stage, the basic bookkeeping is quite simple. Take this in stages – the salaries and then the taxation.

First, the focal organization has paid out £1,200 (3 × £400) as salaries. There is thus an outflow/credit from the cashbook. This has to be matched by something. Well, the salaries are paid in return for the services rendered by Tweet, Wing and Feather – their labour. So the corresponding inflow/debit must be to the operations subsystem as a purchase of a service – as a payment for labour.

Second, the focal organization has an outflow/credit of cash to pay the taxation due on the payroll. There is obviously an outflow/credit from the cashbook. The corresponding inflow/debit isn't actually for anything (unless we wanted to count a very small amount of highway, a bit of a school or a part of a bomber). It is an inflow/debit of information saying that the organization has fulfilled its duty as a responsible citizen and complied with the taxation laws – in effect a release of indebtedness. Alternatively we may wish to add this amount to the wages account as it is in effect a necessary payment which is related to the wages and the taxation paid on the wages is tax due by the employees of the organization rather than by the organization itself.

The four events look like this.

EVENT NUMBER 20			
INFLOW/DEBIT		**OUTFLOW/CREDIT**	
Account title	*Amount*	*Account title*	*Amount*
Salaries (Tweet)	£400	Cashbook (Salaries)	£400
Salaries (Wing)	£400	Cashbook (Salaries)	£400
Salaries (Feather)	£400	Cashbook (Salaries)	£400
Taxation (Payroll)	£400	Cashbook (Taxation)	£400

Event 21

Here is what we called the 'discharge transaction' in Event 1b above. The focal organization now pays the interest which is due on the loan. There is an outflow/credit from the funds subsystem and a corresponding inflow/debit to the decision and control subsystem (effectively discharging this month's indebtedness) which we will put in an 'interest' account. It will look like this.

EVENT NUMBER 21			
INFLOW/DEBIT		*OUTFLOW/CREDIT*	
Account title	*Amount*	*Account title*	*Amount*
Interest	£120	Cashbook (interest)	£120

Event 22

Here we have the discharge transactions for Events 4 and 6 above. The focal organization pays off its debt (an outflow/credit from the cashbook) and has a corresponding inflow/debit of information which cancels out the indebtedness. This we show as a debit to the creditors account.

EVENT NUMBER 22			
INFLOW/DEBIT		**OUTFLOW/CREDIT**	
Account title	*Amount*	*Account title*	*Amount*
(a) Creditors (Seedco)	£1,000	(a) Cashbook (Creditors)	£1,000
(b) Creditors (Woodco)	£1,000	(b) Cashbook (Creditors)	£1,000
(c) Creditors (Bagco)	£300	(c) Cashbook (Creditors)	£300

Event 23

In this transaction, Bird Supplies pays its debt. It is therefore the discharge transaction of Events 18 and 19 and is the reverse of Event 22 above. The focal organization receives some cash and so has an inflow/debit to its cashbook. It matches this with an effective outflow/credit of information from the decision and control subsystem, cancelling the indebtedness. This flow of information goes to the existing debtors account like this.

EVENT NUMBER 23			
INFLOW/DEBIT		**OUTFLOW/CREDIT**	
Account title	*Amount*	*Account title*	*Amount*
Cashbook (Debtors)	£500	Debtors (Bird Supplies)	£500
Cashbook (Debtors)	£400	Debtors (Bird Supplies)	£400

Events 24 and 25

These are both grant/donation transactions – one of them to the focal organization and the other from or by the focal organization. The donation paid by BI is clearly an outflow/credit from its cashbook and an inflow of information (perhaps of a 'thank you') to its decision and control subsystem which it will record in a grants and donations made account. The grant from the Wildfowl and Wetlands Trust (WWT) is just the opposite: the inflow/debit to the cashbook is matched by an outflow/credit of information recorded in a 'grants and donations received account'. The two transactions will look like this.

EVENTS NUMBER 24 and 25			
INFLOW/DEBIT		**OUTFLOW/CREDIT**	
Account title	*Amount*	*Account title*	*Amount*
(24) Grants/donations made	£50	Cashbook (donations)	£50
(25) Cashbook	£100	Grants/donations received	£100

And, with that, we have completed our analysis of the transactions of the first month of the life of Bird Industries Ltd.

5.2.2 Producing the T-accounts for Bird Industries

Analysing the transactions is the difficult part of the basic bookkeeping process. Having done this, it is a simple matter to produce the T-accounts themselves. As you become more confident you will find that you can skip this formal analysis stage and go directly to the T-accounts. However, in the early stages of your bookkeeping experience, time spent going through each transaction and trying to understand it – as we have done above – will be time well spent. Furthermore, if, at a later stage in your studies, you find yourself struggling with some transactions, it makes a lot of sense to go through them stage by stage as we have done, rather than dashing straight off to the T-accounts and then wondering where to put things.

Figure 5.2 shows the detail of Bird Industries' T-accounts. Each event has been entered into a T-account exactly as we analysed it above. Go through Figure 5.2, item by item, making reference to the above analysis, Figure 5.1 (which itemized Bird Industries' accounting events) and Figure 4.10 (which itemized the eight basic transactions). Make absolutely sure that you can see where every entry came from *and* ensure that you could have produced these T-accounts yourself. This is a critical point in your bookkeeping studies and you *must* get it right.

INFORMATION SUBSYSTEM ACCOUNTS

Inflow/Debit	Share capital	Outflow/Credit
	1a Cashbook	21,000

Inflow/Debit	Loans received	Outflow/Credit
	1b Cashbook	6,000

Inflow/Debit		Loan interest	Outflow/Credit
21 Cashbook	120		

Inflow/Debit		Debtors		Outflow/Credit
11a Sales (Bird Supplies)	500	23a Cashbook (Bird Supplies)		500
11b Sales (Bird Supplies)	400	23b Cashbook (Bird Supplies)		400
18a Sales (Garden Supplies)	700			
18b Sales (Garden Supplies)	600			

Inflow/Debit		Creditors		Outflow/Credit
22a Cashbook (Seedco)	1,000	4a Seeds (Seedco)		1,000
22b Cashbook (Woodco)	1,000	4b Wood (Woodco)		1,000
22c Cashbook (Bagco)	300	4c Bags and pack (Bagco)		300
		14 Advertising (PR Co)		500

Inflow/Debit		Taxation	Outflow/Credit
20d Cash (Salaries)	400		

Inflow/Debit		Grants/Donations made	Outflow/Credit
24 Cashbook (BPS)	50		

Inflow/Debit	Grants/Donations received	Outflow/Credit
	25 Cashbook (WWT)	100

FUNDS SUBSYSTEM ACCOUNTS

Inflow/Debit		Cashbook	Outflow/Credit
1a Share capital	21,000	2 Warehouse	20,000
1b Loan	6,000	3a Equip and machinery	1,000
13 Sales	120	3b Equip and machinery	1,500
23a Debtors	500	3c Motor vehicle	2,500
23b Debtors	400	7 Advertising	300
25 Grants/Donations	100	20a Salaries	400
		20b Salaries	400
		20c Salaries	400
		20d Taxation	400
		21 Interest	120
		22a Creditors	1,000
		22b Creditors	1,000
		22c Creditors	300
		24 Grants/Donations	50

OPERATIONS SUBSYSTEMS ACCOUNTS

Inflow/Debit	Warehouse		Outflow/Credit
2 Cashbook	20,000		

Inflow/Debit	Motor vehicle		Outflow/Credit
3c Cashbook	2,500		

Inflow/Debit	Equipment and machinery		Outflow/Credit
3a Cashbook	1,000		
3b Cashbook	1,500		

Inflow/Debit	Seeds		Outflow/Credit
4a Creditors	1,000		

Inflow/Debit	Wood		Outflow/Credit
4b Creditors	1,000		

Inflow/Debit	Bags		Outflow/Credit
4c Creditors	300		

Inflow/Debit	Advertising		Outflow/Credit
7 Cashbook	300		
14 Creditors	500		

Inflow/Debit	Sales		Outflow/Credit
		11a Debtors	500
		11b Debtors	400
		13 Cashbook	120
		18a Debtors	700
		18b Debtors	600

Inflow/Debit	Salaries		Outflow/Credit
20a Cash (Tweet)	400		
20b Cash (Wing)	400		
20c Cash (Feather)	400		

Figure 5.2 The basic T-accounts for Bird Industries

Figure 5.2 itemizes each accounting transaction by reference to the event number. It would be normal, in practice, to give each accounting entry a unique identifying label (see Chapter 6 for more detail) and to give the date against each transaction. We have not done this – but only for reasons of simplicity and clarity.

You will also notice that each entry in a T-account has a bit of narrative against it – a word or two about that transaction. This is *very* important because it tells you, when you come to look back at the transaction, what it is you are looking at. In general, the simplest way of doing this is to write against the entry where the other entry (of the double-entry) will appear. So the 'Share capital' account shows 'Cashbook – £21,000'. This tells us that there has been an outflow/credit from the share capital account and this has been matched by an inflow of cash to the cashbook. That is, the share capital was paid for in cash. Each of the bookkeeping entries was like this.

So what does all this tell us?

Well, first of all, the T-accounts are simply a *record of transactions*. They are maintained so we know what has happened. You can well imagine that from day to day, questions and queries emerge, such as 'Has Bird Supplies paid us yet?', 'How much cash have we got?', 'What did we pay for those bags?', 'How much do we currently owe to our creditors?', etc. The bookkeeping records should be able to answer these questions.

Second, the T-accounts, when read like a story, tell us quite a lot about Bird Industries' first month – what they bought, what they sold, where the cash went to and came from and so on. We might actually be content to leave the accounts as they are in Figure 5.2 but this would be a bad move for three reasons:

i   some of the accounts have a lot of entries in them and having to add them up every time we want to know something will eventually prove inefficient – imagine what General Motors' cashbook must look like after a few months;

ii we cannot be certain that we have entered everything correctly – some check is needed;

iii the T-accounts do not tell us what we have earned/used up or what we have left over. These are things which (do you remember?) we said the profit and loss account and the balance sheet would tell us. We have to do quite a lot of work to get from these T-accounts to the financial statements.

It is to start to deal with these issues that we always 'balance off' an account at the end of the accounting period (you will remember that we talked about this in Chapter 2). This we now do.

5.2.3 Double-entry and balancing off the T-accounts for Bird Industries

Before we go any further, you should try adding up all of the inflows/debits and all of the outflows/credits that are shown in Figure 5.2. You should find that they both come to £62,490. The figure of £62,490 is likely to be totally meaningless in most organizations but the fact that all the debits and all the credits amount to the same figure is not meaningless. This shows that you did do double-entry and, whenever you put in an inflow/debit you also entered an outflow/credit. That is (your debits = your credits). As you know by now, this must always be the case. It is this characteristic that we will be exploiting in this and the following section.

At the end of every **accounting period** (every week, month, quarter or year), the accounts must be **closed off** or **balanced off**. That is they must be made to balance by the addition of a **balancing item**. This has the effect of 'closing' that T-account to show that we have finished with it and leaves us with the balancing figure which will be an important part of the financial accounting process. We then take these balancing figures to something which is called an **initial trial balance** (which we look at in more detail in the next section).

> **Hint (especially for students who have studied bookkeeping before)**
>
> Remember that there are three basic stages to the bookkeeping and financial accounting process: putting together the accounting records (the bookkeeping), adjusting the accounting records for the 'end-of-period' adjustments and then producing the financial statements. We have, so far, only concentrated on the first of these and we are making our way slowly to the other two. There are a number of ways of making these 'end-of-period' adjustments, but they all have the same effect. Basically, the difference lies in either (a) adjusting the T-accounts to allow for things like depreciation, cost of sales, etc. and then taking the balances to the trial balance or (b) taking the basic balances direct to the initial trial balance and then doing these adjustments through the extended trial balance. We will concentrate upon this second approach because it allows students to build up their accounting knowledge in smaller, bite-sized chunks. If you do not like this method and *always get your own way right* then stick to what you know.

What we are doing is, in effect, tidying up our bookkeeping so that we can get on with the business of producing financial statements. The process is very simple and really only a matter of arithmetic.

At the end of every accounting period: (i) go through *each and every* T-account, (ii) add up all the debits and the credits in each T-account, (iii) rule off the account and (iv) insert a balancing figure so the total on each side is the same.

In some accounts (like the share capital account for Bird Industries) this is very simple, in others (like the cashbook) this is a little more complicated. Look back at Figure 5.2.

Let us start with the share capital account. This has only one entry – a credit entry for £21,000. To make this account balance we must put in a debit balancing entry for £21,000 and rule off the account. Now look at the cashbook. Here, the total debits equals £28,130 and the total credits equals £29,370. Rule off the account and, as the total of credit entries is bigger than the total of debit entries, make the credit total the total for the account. In order to make the debit total equal the credit total we need a **balancing figure** of £1,250 on the debit side. (*NB As a test, what does this figure of £1,250 represent?*[4])

We do this for every account and the result is shown in Figure 5.3.

Inflow/Debit	Share capital		Outflow/Credit
Bal c/d to Trial Bal.	21,000	1a Cashbook	21,000

Inflow/Debit	Loans received		Outflow/Credit
Bal c/d to Trial Bal.	6,000	1b Cashbook	6,000

Inflow/Debit	Loan interest		Outflow/Credit
21 Cashbook	120	Bal c/d to Trial Bal.	120

Inflow/Debit	Debtors		Outflow/Credit
11a Sales (Bird Supplies)	500	23a Cashbook (Bird Supplies)	500
11b Sales (Bird Supplies)	400	23b Cashbook (Bird Supplies)	400
18a Sales (Garden Supplies)	700		
18b Sales (Garden Supplies)	600	Bal c/d to Trial Bal.	1,300
	2,200		2,200

Inflow/Debit		Creditors	Outflow/Credit	
22a Cashbook (Seedco)	1,000	4a Seeds(Seedco)		1,000
22b Cashbook (Woodco)	1,000	4b Wood (Woodco)		1,000
22c Cashbook (Bagco)	300	4c Bags and pack (Bagco)		300
Bal c/d to Trial Bal.	500	14 Advertising (PR Co)		500
	2,800			2,800

Inflow/Debit		Taxation	Outflow/Credit	
20d Cash (Salaries)	400	Bal c/d to Trial Bal.		400

Inflow/Debit		Grants/Donations made	Outflow/Credit	
24 Cashbook (BPS	50	Bal c/d to Trial Bal.		50

Inflow/Debit		Grants/Donations received	Outflow/Credit	
Bal c/d to Trial Bal.	100	25 Cashbook (Wildfowl and Wetlands Trust)		100

Inflow/Debit		Cashbook	Outflow/Credit	
1a Share capital	21,000	2 Warehouse		20,000
1b Loan	6,000	3a Equip and machinery		1,000
13 Sales	120	3b Equip and machinery		1,500
23a Debtors	500	3c Motor Vehicle		2,500
23b Debtors	400	7 Advertising		300
25 Grants/Donations	100	20a Salaries		400
		20b Salaries		400
		20c Salaries		400
		20d Taxation		400
		21 Interest		120
		22a Creditors		1,000
		22b Creditors		1,000
		22c Creditors		300
Bal c/d to Trial Bal.	1,250	24 Grants/Donations		50
	29,370			29,370

Inflow/Debit		Warehouse	Outflow/Credit	
2 Cashbook	20,000	Bal c/d to Trial Bal.		20,000

Inflow/Debit		Motor vehicle	Outflow/Credit	
3c Cashbook	2,500	Bal c/d to Trial Bal.		2,500

Inflow/Debit		Equipment and machinery	Outflow/Credit	
3a Cashbook	1,000			
3b Cashbook	1,500	Bal c/d to Trial Bal.		2,500
	2,500			2,500

Inflow/Debit		Seeds	Outflow/Credit	
4a Creditors	1,000	Bal c/d to Trial Bal.		1,000

Inflow/Debit	Wood		Outflow/Credit
4b Creditors	1,000	Bal c/d to Trial Bal.	1,000

Inflow/Debit	Bags and Packaging		Outflow/Credit
4c Creditors	300	Bal c/d to Trial Bal.	300

Inflow/Debit	Advertising		Outflow/Credit
7 Cashbook	300		
14 Creditors	500	Bal c/d to Trial Bal.800	800
	800		800

Inflow/Debit	Sales		Outflow/Credit
		11a Debtors	500
		11b Debtors	400
		13 Cashbook	120
		18a Debtors	700
Bal c/d to Trial Bal.	2,320	18b Debtors	600
	2,320		2,320

Inflow/Debit	Salaries		Outflow/Credit
20a Cash (Tweet)	400		
20b Cash (Wing)	400		
20c Cash (Feather)	400	Bal c/d to Trial Bal.	1,200
	1,200		1,200

Figure 5.3 Balancing off the basic T-accounts for Bird Industries

BUT where do these 'balances' go? They *must* go somewhere. This is, after all, double-entry bookkeeping and every debit must have a credit. We take them all to a **trial balance**. And, where we had to put in a debit amount to make an account balance we put a credit entry (a credit balance) in the trial balance. Where we had to put in a credit amount to make the account balance, we put in a debit entry (a debit balance) in the trial balance. We don't yet know enough about trial balances to really see how to do this, but it explains why each balancing item says 'Balance carried down to the Trial Balance' (or 'Bal c/d to Trial Bal').

This tidies up each and every one of our T-accounts and gives a series of balancing figures. What do we do with these? We turn to the trial balance and worry about that next. But just before we do that, please go back to Figure 5.3 and make sure you could replicate all those balancing figures.

5.3 THE INITIAL TRIAL BALANCE

5.3.1 Putting the initial trial balance together

A trial balance's principal function is, as its name suggests, to try out the balances and see if they do, in fact, balance. That is, it is a place where we see if [*all the debits = all the credits*]. It thus checks whether for every debit you have entered a credit and vice versa and thus gives you some comfort about the arithmetic accuracy of your bookkeeping. *But, please note*, it does not check whether you have entered the debits and credits in the right accounts. You have to follow through the logic of the last two chapters to do that.

So, to produce an end-of-period trial balance (TB), we simply bring all the balancing figures which we have entered in the T-accounts to the trial balance and list them. A list of all the debit balances and a list of all the credit balances must, if we've done our work properly, balance. It is as simple as that.

The trial balance is produced by listing all the names of the accounts down the left-hand side of the page and providing two columns down the right-hand side of the page, one for debits and one for credits. The Bird Industries trial balance at the end of January 200X will look like Figure 5.4.

In this figure you can see that the balance from each account has been brought to the trial balance and listed there. For every debit which was used to balance an account we show a credit in the trial balance and vice versa – and thus our double entry is preserved. *Before going any further, make quite sure that you can trace each balance from the T-accounts to the trial balance AND put it on the correct (debit or credit) side.*

The initial trial balance is a very important point in your studies. It means we have reached the end of the basic bookkeeping. You must be able to do everything we have covered so far in your sleep and standing on your head. You must practise and revise this material until it is second nature. What follows in financial accounting relies upon a very sound knowledge of this material and if what follows is to make sense, you must know this stuff.

There is another good reason why you should know this. From here onwards financial accounting becomes highly contentious and debatable. At least up until this point we have been able to use a sort of logic to derive the T-accounts and the trial balance based upon

TRIAL BALANCE FOR BIRD INDUSTRIES: 31 January 200X		
Account	**Debit**	**Credit**
Share capital		21,000
Loans received		6,000
Loan interest	120	
Debtors	1,300	
Creditors		500
Grants/Donations made	50	
Grants/Donations received		100
Taxation	400	
Cash		1,250
Warehouse	20,000	
Motor vehicle	2,500	
Equipment and machinery	2,500	
Seeds	1,000	
Wood	1,000	
Bags and packaging	300	
Advertising	800	
Sales		2,320
Salaries	1,200	
	31,170	31,170

Figure 5.4 Initial trial balance for Bird Industries at 31.1.200X

the accountants' **four characteristics**, the **organizational flow model** and the assumptions of **duality**. These, via the **eight basic transactions** gave us a basis upon which to build the accounting records. From here on, financial accounting builds upon the initial trial balance but in a far from theoretically or practically consistent manner. From here onwards we are into guesswork, rules and *ad hoc* bits of theory. From our point of view, it therefore makes sense to have a really firm foundation from which to build the financial statements even if the building process itself may leave a lot to be desired.

So, revision and practice and practice and revision of the foregoing will pay ample dividends. You must have a very firm grip on this basic material.

5.3.2 Some arithmetic hints and tips

As you construct trial balances as your studies progress, you will sometimes find that your trial balance doesn't balance. Later on, when we meet balance sheets, you will sometimes find that your balance sheet doesn't balance. This means that you have made a mistake. Except in an examination (when you may well not have enough time to look for mistakes) you should try and find where your mistake (or mistakes) has occurred. The following, are a few hints to help you.

i   Always be neat when you are doing bookkeeping by hand. Lay out your T-accounts carefully so that (a) you can read all the numbers and (b) the numbers sit tidily one under another. Thus, your additions should be easier. Far, far too often we see students answers that are so scruffy as to be unintelligible and virtually impossible to add up, with numbers all over the place. If you use a ruler and rule out your T-accounts before entering the transactions, you will often save yourself a lot of time and trouble.

ii When a trial balance (TB) doesn't balance, first check your additions and then find out by how much you are out. Look back through your numbers for that amount and for half that amount. You are looking for that amount in case you have only entered it once instead of twice. You are looking for half that amount in case you have put it on the wrong side by either entering two debits (credits) instead of one debit (credit) and one credit (debit) or in case you have brought a balance to the TB on the wrong side. So, for example, if (say) we had put loan interest in Bird Industries' TB in as a credit balance instead of as a debit balance, then the credit total would have been £120 too high and the debit total would have been £120 too low. The difference would have been £240, so we have to look for half of this.

iii Next check that you have brought all the account balances to the TB and that you have brought them to the right side.

After that, chasing mistakes gets more complicated. It is likely that you have made more than one mistake or else you may have transposed numbers (e.g. written $213,000 instead of $312,000). It is difficult to find these sorts of mistakes and so you may often have to go back to the beginning and trace all your entries through. (However, there is a way of tracing some errors – see the short article by Cowton (1989) which shows how to use the 'rule of nine' to get you out of trouble.)

It is obviously better not to make mistakes in the first place, so take care and think through what you do, as you do it. With the foregoing guides and the organizational systems flows you need never make a basic bookkeeping error.

5.3.3 Interpreting and developing the trial balance

Having gone to all this trouble to produce an initial TB it might be rather nice if we could make use of it. The problem is that, really, we cannot use the numbers in the TB as they stand. They are just a summary of the T-accounts and, as such, mean very little. Whilst we maybe can make some sense of Bird Industries' TB this is only because it is a very simple organization and this is its first accounting period. Once we get into future accounting periods and more complex organizations, interpreting the TB becomes virtually impossible. So don't try!

What we have to do is now examine each of the figures in the TB and undertake the **end-of-period adjustments** and the *categorization* **process** in order to produce **financial statements** that (hopefully) will be capable of interpretation. What we find that we need to do is:

- identify **assets** and **liabilities**;
- identify **expenses** and **revenues**;
- consider the **ownership claims**;
- consider **provisions** and **reserves**;
- undertake other **end-of-period** adjustments that will permit us to calculate the profit/loss of the organization and 'left-over' portion of what is owned, owed and owing to produce a balance sheet that might perhaps tell us something about the accounting entity's wealth.

It is this, and not the foregoing, that constitutes **accounting** rather than **bookkeeping** and we will examine this in a lot of detail from Chapter 7 onwards. The initial TB then becomes the basis from which we adjust the accounting numbers to produce our basic financial statements through what we will come to call the **extended trial balance**. So, at the risk of repetition, the initial TB is a pivotal point between the (relatively logical) bookkeeping and the (frequently confusing and always judgemental) accounting decisions that build upon the bookkeeping to produce the financial statements. Now, in order to round off this area of bookkeeping, it is advisable to know rather more about where all these accounting transactions come from, how they are identified and captured and how the accounting records are organized in practice. This is the job of Chapter 6.

SUMMARY

This chapter has concentrated on putting the eight basic accounting transactions to work in a specific example, showing how to close off accounts and then take the balancing figures to produce an initial trial balance. The stages we undertook to do this are shown in Figure 5.5.

You now need practice to make sure you can do these basic bookkeeping entries in your sleep – they have to become almost automatic. But, much more importantly, you should try and understand each of the ways in which we did the bookkeeping. As we have said earlier, you almost certainly have access to computers and computer software that can do this basic bookkeeping better than you can. Your relative advantage lies in trying to understand these transactions. In Chapters 4 and 5 we have provided a sort of logic that can articulate the bookkeeping process. If, however, you find yourself asking questions which we have not answered in this book, do not be dismayed. Indeed, you should be pleased because the rules of bookkeeping are not iron laws and even the structure we have

1. Identify the accounting entity and the period for which we are to account (the 'accounting period').

2. Identify the accounting transactions – those which satisfy the four characteristics and thus have in the past, do in the present or will in the future lead to flows of cash into or out of the focal organization.

3. Analyse each accounting transaction in terms of the inflows/debits and outflows/credits which best represent the event of interest (for the basic bookkeeping process, each transaction will be of one of the eight basic transaction types which are summarized in Figure 4.10).

4. Determine which T-accounts to open in order to keep 'similar things' together. If in doubt, open a T-account.

5. Do the double-entry for each and every transaction, remembering that every debit must have a credit and vice versa.

6. Close off each and every account with a balancing figure.

7. Take that balancing figure to an initial trial balance – remembering to keep the double-entry going so you debit an account (to close it) and credit the TB, or credit an account (to close it) and debit the TB.

8. The TB should balance. If it doesn't, look for the difference.

9. The TB is only the starting point of the accounting process and, as a result, the TB – in itself – means little other than arithmetic accuracy in your bookkeeping.

10. The TB will be the basis upon which we will do the end-of-period adjustments in order to produce the profit and loss account and the balance sheet.

Figure 5.5 Stages in the basic bookkeeping process

given here begs a lot of questions. You should learn to ask those questions and look for answers. In this way you will enjoy your study of accounting.

You now have a sound basic knowledge of the bookkeeping process. We now have to build on that. In the next chapter we will introduce accounting information systems and look at how the accounting records are organized and controlled – not least so that the data we use to produce our accounting are not complete garbage. And then Chapter 7 will examine the trial balance in more detail, looking at the sorts of things we will have to do to develop it far enough to produce financial statements for us. This will involve a bit more 'theory', but without this theory you would just become rule-followers and we don't have to spell out the dangers of that – or at least we hope we don't!

Key terms and concepts

The following key terms and concepts have featured in this chapter. You should make sure that you understand and can explain each one. Page references to definitions appear in the index in bold type.

- Account titles
- Accounting period
- Balancing figure
- Balancing off accounts
- Closing off accounts
- Double-entry bookkeeping
- End-of-period adjustments
- Extended TB
- Inflows/debits and outflows/credits
- Initial trial balance
- Labelling transactions
- Loan principal and interest
- A record of transactions
- Salaries and taxation
- When the TB doesn't balance

FURTHER READING

What you need most at this stage is practice with the methods shown here. Most of your reading should be re-reading this chapter and Chapter 4 until the ideas are clear in your mind. The Workbook that accompanies this text provides examples for you to work through to reinforce the material. For further definitions and examples you can look at almost any basic bookkeeping and accounting text – although be aware that each will approach the subject in a slightly different way and introduce ideas in a slightly different order.

NOTES

1. There are no hard and fast rules on how close together the two elements of a transaction must be for us to treat it as a 'cash' transaction rather than as a 'debtors/creditors' transaction. In practice it is simply a matter of expedience. That is, any organization will not process its paperwork (invoices, orders, cheques, etc. – see Chapter 6) instantaneously. If by the time the clerk processes the transaction the other part of the transaction has occurred, then, to all intents and purposes that was a cash transaction. The question will usually make it clear. As a general rule if the receipt/despatch of goods and the cash payment/receipt are more than two or three days apart you might be well advised to treat it as a debtor/creditor transaction.
2. In this case, the lag is between the order and the economic event occurring. Orders are tricky in a legal sense but, for bookkeeping purposes, we will normally only focus on the movement of goods or the movement of cash. The bookkeeping system is trying to reflect a form of 'organizational reality' and so we must try and understand what is happening in the organization and then let the bookkeeping reflect that as far as seems practicable.
3. At least for the time being. The management accounting system will capture this information because it will want to know what is happening in the organization and what costs are associated with which products.
4. The figure of £1,250 represents the balance of cash-in-hand and the amount of cash at the bank at the end of the month. The figure is *negative* because there have been more funds outflows (credits) than funds inflows (debits). Now you know why Tweet arranged a bank overdraft. If you didn't get this, you *must* go back and do some revision.

APPENDIX 5 SINGLE-ENTRY MATRIX BOOKKEEPING AND THE SPREADSHEET

A particularly useful way of testing your bookkeeping understanding and improving your basic computer skills is doing bookkeeping using a single-entry matrix format. This is such

		OUTFLOW/CREDITS		
		Decision and Control Subsystem	Funds Subsystem	Operations Subsystem
INFLOW/ DEBITS	Decision and Control Subsystem	Null	Investments by the FO	Trade debtors
	Funds Subsystem	Share capital	Null	Cash sales
	Operations Subsystem	Trade creditors	Cash purchases	Null

Figure 5A.1 Simple matrix of organizational flows

a good test that if what follows seems perfectly straightforward then your basic bookkeeping is fine. If it doesn't, you should go back and revise it carefully.

The essence of the idea can be illustrated by Figure 5A.1. The matrix, for illustration only, takes us back to the simple three-account, organizational flows of earlier chapters. We can use this matrix to capture double-entry with a single entry. For example, a cash sale involves an inflow to the funds subsystem (as the cash is paid to the focal organization for the goods) and an outflow from the operations subsystem (as the goods leave the premises). With the inflows shown by the left hand of the matrix and the outflows shown by the top of the matrix a single entry (as in Figure 5A.1) can capture both sides of the transaction. Inflow from the left, outflow to the top. It is as simple as that.

Six of the eight basic accounting transaction types have been shown in Figure 5A.1 and the rest could easily be placed there also (but would clutter up the diagram).

Now, as we saw earlier, having three basic accounts is not really helpful so all we have to do is 'open' categories along the left and along the top for debit and credit entries. As most organizations get very complicated very quickly we could end up with a lot of cells in the matrix. This is where the computer spreadsheet comes in. It is a simple matter to identify the blocks along the top and along the left, then freeze the titles and then do the double entry by single entry. The totals of the accounts require a little thinking about but it becomes the total of the credit column less the total of the debit row for any particular account – spreadsheets are especially happy handling this sort of thing if you can think it through first.

The results for Bird Industries would look a bit like Figure 5A.2 – but, please note, it makes life simpler if the titles down the left and those along the top are symmetrical. Figure 5A.2 contains only the active cells for reasons of space and clarity.

Each transaction (with its 'event number' from earlier in the chapter shown in brackets) is shown in the matrix. Try and follow each transaction and see why each ends up where it does. The total columns are the totals of debits (along the right-hand side) and the totals of credits (along the bottom). The two totals must, by definition, be equal if the programs/your additions are correct. The balance on each account can then be found by using the spreadsheet to merge the debit and credit totals for each account.

The approach can be used in many ways and can be developed to include financial statements. Its major value lies in encouraging you to think about bookkeeping record-keeping in a different way and not get locked into one set of procedures without thinking about them.

OUTFLOW /CRS INFLOW /DRS	Cash	Drs	Crs	Share Capital	Loans Received	Sales	Grants /Donation	inflow/debit totals
Cash		(23) 500 (23) 400		(1) 21,000	(1) 6,000	(13) 120	(25) 100	£28,120
Drs						(11) 500 (11) 400 (18) 700 (18) 600		£2,200
Crs	(22) 1,0000 1,000 300							£2,300
Warehouse	(2) 20,000							£20,000
Equip and mach	(3) 1,000 (3) 1,500							£2,500
Motor vehicle	(3) 2,500							£2,500
Seeds			(4) 1,000					£1,000
Wood			(4) 1,000					£1,000
Bags			(4) 300					£300
Adverts	(7) 300		(14) 500					£800
Salaries	(20) 400 (20) 400 (20) 400							£1,200
Taxation	(20) 400							£400
Interest	(21) 120							£120
Grants- Donations	(24) 50							£50
OUTFLOW /CREDITS								£62,490
TOTALS	£29,370	£900	£2,800	£21,000	£6,000	£2,320	£100	£62,490

Figure 5A.2 A matrix representation of Bird Industries' bookkeeping transactions

The accounting information system: organizing and controlling the accounting records

6

Learning objectives

After studying this chapter you should be able to:

- define the elements of an accounting information system (AIS);
- visualize and recreate the elements of the AIS;
- describe in broad terms how data are captured for the bookkeeping system;
- outline the functions of various source documents;
- describe the role of the daybook/journal and complete a sales daybook and purchases daybook for a simple example;
- define what is meant by a chart (or index) of accounts and demonstrate how it would be used in the bookkeeping process;
- describe the organization of the books of account into ledgers;
- show the role of the general ledger and complete one for a simple example;
- explain why accounting records need to be accurate and illustrate various ways of controlling accounting data including the use of control accounts, suspense accounts, audit, the system on internal control and various reconciliations;
- perform a simple bank reconciliation.

6.1 INTRODUCTION

6.1.1 Chapter design and links to previous chapters

So far, we have learnt quite a lot about the mechanics of bookkeeping. We first saw how to identify accounting transactions by reference to the four characteristics. We then saw how to identify the inputs/debits and outflows/credits which relate to each of the basic accounting transactions and, as result, we could perform the double-entry bookkeeping for those transactions. Finally, we looked at how each of the accounting records (the T-accounts) could be balanced off and the balances brought to the initial trial balance. Learning about this is crucial to your development as an accountant – but it is certainly not enough. As we have already discussed, computers can do this – and computers do not get to be partners in accountancy firms. There are a number of elements to accounting which distinguish the accountant from the bookkeeper. Two of these elements we have met already (the ability to understand the bookkeeping process – and recognize its limitations

– and the professional dimensions of accountancy practice). Some of these elements which differentiate accountants from bookkeepers will be developed in later parts of the book (the making of the accounting decisions in order to produce the financial statements, the ability to theorize about accounting and to understand accounting policy and the ability to interpret accounting numbers and to suggest other ways of doing the accounting). This chapter will concentrate on one of the other elements which will help you become a useful accountant as opposed to a competent bookkeeper – the **accounting information system**.

How the flows into and out of the organization subsystems are captured, recorded, organized and controlled is a matter covered by the design of the **accounting information system**. So far we have considered the accounting system as consisting of:

- a list of accounting transactions;
- the categorization of each of those transactions in order to identify the subsystem into which flowed the **input/debit** and from which flowed the **output/credit**;
- a breakdown and further classification of these transactions into the **eight basic accounting types of transactions**;
- this enabled us to identify (crudely) the type of T-account into which the transaction was to be entered as an **input/debit** and the type of T-account into which the transaction was to be entered as an **output/credit**;
- each transaction had two effects and this meant that each had to be entered into the **bookkeeping system** twice – **double-entry**;
- at the **end of the accounting period** the T-accounts were balanced off and the total (simple arithmetic) balance taken directly to the **initial trial balance** (where the **end-of-period adjustments** could be performed) (or the end-of-period adjustments were put into the T-accounts and then those balances taken to the trial balance);
- the end-of-period adjustments (as we shall see) are designed to adjust the bookkeeping numbers so that they more realistically reflected the aims of the ultimate statements – the **profit and loss account** and the **balance sheet**.

So far so good, but three important things are missing from this process.

First, how do we (or the bookkeeper) know that the accounting transactions have actually taken place? How, for example, did we know that Bird Industries had made those sales? How could we be sure, for example, that Ms Tweet had not undertaken many more accounting transactions that we didn't know about? How does Exxon or General Motors know what accounting transactions have occurred? That is, we need to know *how the accounting data are captured*.

Second, how are we going to record all these accounting transactions? Yes, we will put them into T-accounts. But how will we do this? When will we do this? (Every hour? every day? every year?) Will the T-accounts be on the backs of envelopes? What rules (if any) will we have so that, for example, we always put the same sorts of transactions in the same sort of account. And so on. That is, we need to know *how the books of account will be organized*.

Third, how can we be sure that our accounting records are accurate? Having done our best to capture the data and to carefully organize the accounting records, wouldn't it make sense to check them from time to time? For this, we need to know something about *how to control the accounting records*.

This chapter is about these three things: capture, organization and control of the accounting transactions and records. It is this, plus the bookkeeping (which we have already met) and the accounting (that we will meet later), that goes to make up the

accounting information systems. These elements are summarized in Figure 6.1 – which can perhaps act as a 'map' of where we are in the book at the moment.

In the next subsection, we will provide a brief overview of the accounting information system and the place of bookkeeping within the system. Section 6.2 will concentrate on 'capturing the data', section 6.3 will concentrate on 'organizing the accounting records' and section 6.4 will introduce some of the issues involved in 'controlling the accounting data'.

6.1.2 An overview of the accounting information system and bookkeeping

Figure 6.2 is a repeat of Figure 3.10. It shows the way in which we have been thinking about the accounting entity (the organization) and the flows which form the basis of the

- Identifying data/flows
  - (the four characteristics)
- Capturing the data/flows
  - (source documents)
- Recording the data/flows
  - (journals, ledgers, [the T-accounts])
- Organizing the records/books of account
  - (chart of accounts)
- Controlling the accounting system
  - (internal control, reconciliations, other checks)
- Constructing the financial statements
  - (TB and accounting policy)
- Controlling the financial statements
  - (internal audit, internal control and the statutory audit)
- Financial reporting

Figure 6.1 Accounting information systems

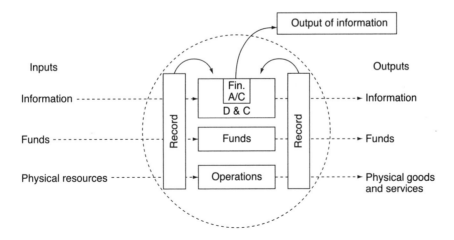

Figure 6.2 A simple systems view of the financial accounting process

accounting and bookkeeping processes. The essence of this approach was that we could see a series of flows into (debits) and out of (credits) the organization and the task of the bookkeeping system was to record these. How does this happen? Well, some of the answer is shown in Figure 6.3.

Figure 6.3 shows that the first stage is to record the flows (shown as 1 on the diagram). Then (stage 2) we entered these flows in the accounting records. These were summarized in the initial trial balance (stage 3). This trial balance (as we shall be discovering as the book advances) will form the basis of the end-of-period adjustments (stage 4) which help us construct the financial statements (stage 5). So we need some way in which to record the flows, to organize them and to make sure that they are entered in the accounting records in a systematic way – so we do not lose any transactions and so that we do not end up putting the same transaction through the books more than once (although, of course, each time we put a transaction through the books we do it by double-entry).

A different way of seeing this process is shown in Figure 6.4. This shows a systems view of the accounting information system, concentrating on the financial accounting side of the story. Looking first at the unbroken arrows which link the boxes in Figure 6.4 we can go through the accounting system step by step.

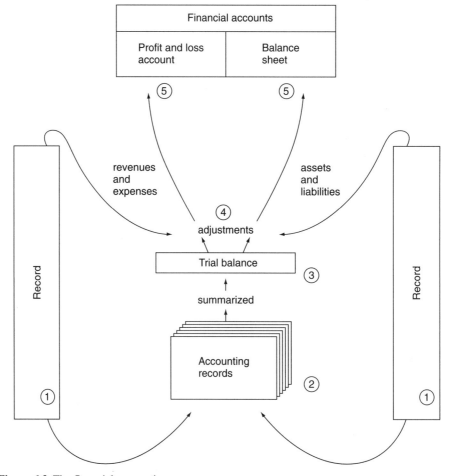

Figure 6.3 The financial accounting process

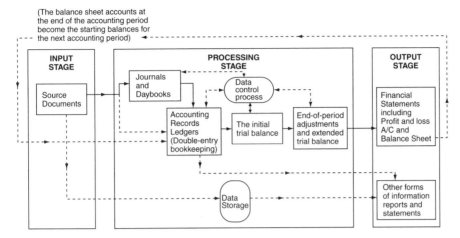

Figure 6.4 Stages in the accounting information system cycle

The flows into and out of the organization are captured by something called **source documents**. (These are explained in section 6.2 below.) The source documents are sorted out into the different types of documents and then entered directly into the accounting records (an approach suitable for smaller organizations) or else are recorded in detail in something called **journals** or **daybooks** (explained in section 6.3 below). The accounting records are then completed and, as we have seen, balanced off at the end of the accounting period to form the initial trial balance. The initial trial balance plus the end-of-period adjustments forms the basis for the financial statements. This, as we now know, is the basic financial accounting and bookkeeping process.

There are, however, a number of other factors at work in Figure 6.4. First, you may notice a dashed line from the balance sheet (in the financial statements) showing as a source document to the accounting records. We haven't dealt with this yet (see Chapter 12 in particular) but, when an organization has been in operation for more than one accounting period, it does not start off each new accounting period with a 'blank sheet'. It has all the 'left-over' things – creditor, debtors, other assets and liabilities – which must re-enter the bookkeeping system in the next accounting period in order to keep the accounting picture of the organization as complete as possible. These figures from the balance sheet become what are known as the **opening balances** (or sometimes 'balances brought forward').

The second thing to notice about Figure 6.4 is that there are arrows showing data flows to 'other forms of information'. This is to recognize that the data which are collected by the financial accounting system are also used in other ways by other parts of the accounting information and management information systems. One of the most obvious of these is the **management accounting system** which (if you are not already studying) you will be studying shortly.

The third and final point we wish to make about Figure 6.4 is the **data control process**. This refers to the procedures that organizations install to make sure that the accounting data are reliable and not subject to error and fraud. This will be explained in section 6.4 below.

With the overview shown in Figure 6.4 held firmly in mind, we can now move on to the detail of the system.

6.2 CAPTURING THE ACCOUNTING DATA

Think first about the problem that is faced by a bookkeeping system. It is essentially the same problem, whatever the size of the focal organization. For example, do you know all your accounting transactions for the last month? Do you know all your cash outflows (the credits) and what you received for them (the debits)? Do you know all your cash inflows (debits)? Do you know exactly who you owe and how much? And so on. The answer is 'probably not' because you have not kept a detailed record of every accounting transaction you have made. Now, you could sit down and try to recreate your transactions using your memory, your bank statements, bits of paper like till receipts and invoices and, perhaps, your diary. This would give you a rough guide to what had happened and you could recreate a reasonable set of books for the last month but it would (almost certainly) be partial. That is, you would have an *incomplete record* of your accounting transactions. (We will look at incomplete records again later.)

Now imagine if ICI or Renault tried to do this! The sheer enormity of the number and complexity of transactions would produce chaos. So, what the accounting information system (AIS) tries to do is ensure that every accounting transaction creates a record or document at the time of the transaction. These are the **source documents**. The bookkeeper does not rush around from the loading bay (to record deliveries and sales) to the warehouse (to record receipts of materials) to the clocking-in system (to record who came to work – labour costs) – this is simply not possible. So, procedures are set up to ensure that when (for example) goods and services are despatched, they cannot leave the premises without a piece of paper or a formal electronic entry in the computer system (a source document). Similarly, goods and services cannot be provided to the focal organization without a piece of paper or an electronic entry (source document being received) and so on. This is broadly summarized in Figure 6.5.

So, it is the piece of paper created by the event (the source document) *not* the event itself which is the basis of the bookkeeping. Each source document is collected for a period – a day, a week, a month perhaps – and then sent over to the bookkeeping section of the focal organization where the data entry begins.

If you were keeping 'complete records' for your own personal accounting transactions, you would have to walk around with a whole series of blank documents (say, a book of receipts, a book of vouchers for each expenditure, a blank set of invoices and a means of recording all other transactions) and fill these in as you undertook accounting transactions.

---

1. The basic bookkeeping system records all the defined flows which pass across the systems boundary (the inputs and outputs of the organizational system).

2. In order to be systematic and ensure that the bookkeeping system does record all the appropriate flows there must be some system for capturing the flows.

3. This function is performed by the AIS and the system of internal control (SIC) working together, which ensures all flows are represented by source documents.

4. The source documents will generally consist of:

   - documents received by the FO from other organizational systems with which it deals;
   - copies of documents which the FO provides to outside organizational systems;
   - documents generated internally by the FO.

5. It is the *documents,* not the events themselves, which form the basis of the bookkeeping system.

Figure 6.5 Accounting information systems: source documents

Hint

It is perhaps easier in your initial studies to think of this rather primitive manual system. As integrated computer networks and systems become the norm, however, mechanisms are developed to record in the computer and electronic bookkeeping system the event as it happens. For example, think of a supermarket checkout where the credit (outflow of sales) is recorded by the checkout operator swiping the barcode on each product and the cash till automatically records the debit (the cash received). The bookkeeping is then done automatically but additional control problems do arise (but we leave these for later in your studies).

This would clearly be difficult, time-consuming and a great way of losing friends (although there would be no difficulty recognizing accounting students!). So, we tend not to find the more systematic and sophisticated AIS existing in smaller focal organizations. These small organizations might have a drawer into which go all the invoices, scraps of paper, notes on the back of envelopes and bank statements and so on and then, periodically, the bookkeeping is recreated from the **incomplete records** of the organization's accounting transactions.

For the more complex organizations there will be a whole set of procedures and documentation by which to capture each and every accounting transaction. Some examples of these source documents are given in Figure 6.6.

There are few hard and fast rules about how a data capture system should operate or the source documents that will be employed. Designing (and understanding) the data capture system is both very important and very difficult. We have been able to give only the briefest of outlines here but, perhaps, you can see that the bookkeeping transactions do not just come out of thin air. The process that produces the paperwork that describes the accounting transactions is clearly crucial. If this process is flawed then the bookkeeping

FUNDS SUBSYSTEM (CASH) SOURCE DOCUMENTS			
INPUT/DEBITS	**EXAMPLE OF SOURCE DOCUMENT**	**OUTPUT/CREDITS**	**EXAMPLE OF SOURCE DOCUMENT**
Cash	Receipt	Cash	Expense claim form
Cheques	Remittance advice	Cheques	Cheque stubs
Direct debits	Bank advice	Standing order	Bank statement
OPERATIONS SUBSYSTEM (GOODS AND SERVICES) SOURCE DOCUMENTS			
INPUT/DEBITS	**EXAMPLE OF SOURCE DOCUMENT**	**OUTPUTS/CREDITS**	**EXAMPLE OF SOURCE DOCUMENT**
Materials and machines	Delivery note & goods received note	Sales	Despatch note & sales invoice
Labour	Time sheets	Disposal of a fixed asset (see Chapter 9)	Written authority to dispose of asset
DECISION AND CONTROL SUBSYSTEM (INFORMATION) SOURCE DOCUMENTS			
INPUTS/DEBITS	**EXAMPLE OF SOURCE DOCUMENT**	**OUTPUTS/CREDITS**	**EXAMPLE OF SOURCE DOCUMENT**
Owed from trade debtors	Sales invoice	Liabilities to trade creditors	Purchase invoice
Commitment to buy	Contract	Liability to the owners	Share certificate

Figure 6.6 Examples of source documents used in an accounting information system

becomes largely meaningless. Being able to think through how reliable (or unreliable) our accounting data are must be one of the hallmarks of a useful accountant.

6.3 ORGANIZING THE ACCOUNTING RECORDS

6.3.1 The daybooks and journals

So, our focal organization has captured the data relating to its accounting transactions (probably in very physically diverse areas of the organization) – what does it do with them now? These source documents will be collected together for a period (perhaps a day, a week or a month) by the individuals concerned (the cashier, the goods inwards clerk, the dispatch clerk and so on) and then sent over to the bookkeeper(s) – either physically (put in an envelope and taken/posted to the appropriate department) or electronically (entered into remote computer terminals which are linked by a network which can be accessed by the bookkeeper). Each batch of source documents can either be entered directly into the double-entry bookkeeping system or can be entered into an intermediate accounting document – the **daybook** or **journal**.

The daybooks/journals[1] are known as the **books of prime entry** because this is the first time they enter the accounting system, but the term is intended to distinguish these entries from those which actually go directly to the double-entry bookkeeping system (the 'T-accounts' as we called them). There are no hard and fast rules governing these records of prime entry. Generally speaking, any sizeable organization will find it convenient to keep a few of these records. The most common are the **sales daybook** and the **purchases daybook**. Some organizations also keep such records for, for example, all cash receipts, all cash payments, all equipment bought and sold, all movements of stock and so on. It is simply a matter of convenience and control (see below). If daybooks are kept, then it is these documents, and not the source documents, which become the source of the bookkeeping process, the place from which the events which go into the double-entry bookkeeping system are drawn.

Figure 6.7 gives some data about an organization that uses a daybook. Please read through them.

As we said above, the most common daybooks would be for sales and purchases. As each sale is made, the evidence of the sale – the sales invoice – is given to the clerk who looks after the sales daybook and it is entered there. Periodically the totals from this are entered into the double-entry system. In practice, any sizeable organization would have very many of these accounting transactions each day. Rather than entering each one into the bookkeeping system individually – the clerk will enter them into the **daybooks/journals**. One way of doing this is shown in Figure 6.8.

There are a number of things worth noting about Figure 6.8. First, the daybooks can be maintained in any form convenient to the organization. They may simply be sheets of paper or books – such as an exercise book. They might be a specially designed form from an accounting stationers or, increasingly, they will be held in specially designed computer files. Next, notice that the date is entered. Then, comes the description (which may be much more detailed than we have shown here) of each side of the transaction. This description will also show the accounts to which the entry will be posted in due course. Next comes something we have called 'folio'. This can be very important. This 'folio' can serve two crucial functions. First, it might be used to give a unique identifier to the source document (so that the focal organization can go back to it later if need be to learn more

On Monday 36th December 2042, the daybook clerk of the Unseen University received bits of paper (known as 'sales' invoices and purchase invoices) which informed her/him that:

● 400 students in Weatherwax Hall of residence had individually been sent invoices for their term in hall – £100 each.

● Messrs Rincewind Ltd had delivered and invoiced the university for six filing cabinets at £50 each and three bookcases at £20 each.

● The Accountancy Department has just completed a one-day course on 'ED 99 – Accounting for Good Taste' on which there were 20 participants each paying £2,000. Four had already paid, eight paid by cash, and the rest (names and addresses attached) have been invoiced.

● Wotenvironment Ltd have delivered and now invoiced the University for 60 reams of photocopying paper – total with discounts £200.

Figure 6.7 An example of the daybook/journal

PURCHASES DAYBOOK/JOURNAL

Date	Description and name of account	Folio	Debit	Credit
36/12/2042	Office equipment a/c Rincewind Ltd	AE12 CA01	 360.00	360.00
36/12/2042	Consumables (paper) a/c Wotenvironment Ltd	EP73 CW29	200.00	 200.00
	TOTALS		560.00	560.00

SALES DAYBOOK/JOURNAL

Date	Description and name of account	Folio	Debit	Credit
36/12/2042	A.A. Aardvark (student) a/c A.B. Aardvark (student) a/c A. Abdul-Ahm (student) a/c etc. etc. (for all 400 students) Weatherwax Hall sales a/c	DA01 DA02 DA03 etc. SW07	100.00 100.00 100.00 etc.	 40,000.00
36/12/2042	KPMG (advance) a/c PW (advance) a/c TR (advance) a/c EY (advance) a/c [being the matching of the cash advances already received from these firms] Cash receipts (on day) a/c C and LD (debtors) a/c AA (debtors) a/c etc. etc. [being those who still owe for the course] Accountancy Department (sales) a/c	SK90 SP91 ST92 SE93 CB04 DC75 DA71 etc. SA111	2,000.00 2,000.00 2,000.00 2,000.00 16,000.00 2,000.00 2,000.00 etc.	 40,000.00
	TOTALS		80,000.00	80,000.00

Figure 6.8 Extracts from the Unseen University's sales and purchases daybooks

about the transaction – see the discussion of controlling the data below). Another purpose is to identify which account the item is to go to – the **accounts code**. This is discussed in the section on the **chart of accounts**, below. Finally, we have the actual amounts which have to be debited and credited to the different accounts. (**NB** it may well be that a daybook might have separate columns for different identifiers for the source document and the accounts code.)

The daybooks are then used, typically every month, to enter the debits and credits in the bookkeeping system. In the case of a computerized accounting system, this might be done automatically by the machine (thus making the accounts code doubly important) or via the bookkeepers who exercise some control over the data before allowing them to be transferred into the ledger system (see below).

The next stage is to work out where each of the entries should go in the bookkeeping system.

6.3.2 The chart or index of accounts

The chart or index of accounts is a rather grand title for a very simple – though very important – document. Its purpose is to provide a detailed list of all the accounts ('T-accounts') that the organization keeps in its bookkeeping system with a description of the account and (usually) detailed guidance on what sorts of things should go into which account. Each account will be given an **accounts code** and this will be used to guide each bookkeeping entry to the right place. (An important, though boring, job for the accountant is the 'coding of source documents'.) The accounts codes will be linked with the organization's **accounting procedures manual** which will lay down the detail of how each and every accounting transaction should be dealt with (as well as guiding how the trial balance, end-of-period adjustments and financial statements are to be treated).

The **chart of accounts** will be drawn up at the same time as the accounting information system is being designed. It will be done by a senior member of the accounting staff because it will reflect the whole organization, its structure and the uses to which the organization wishes to put its accounting information. Little illustrates the importance of the chart of accounts better than the experience of those countries which have typically been influenced by the French, German and Russian approaches to financial accounting. In these countries, the chart of accounts is a national chart of accounts which all organizations follow in their bookkeeping and financial accounting. It leads, when employed in a national context, to a very different approach to accounting and financial reporting.

An example of how an extract from an outline chart of accounts might look for a manufacturing organization is shown in Figure 6.9. This outline might, especially for the more complex organizations, be subdivided into many other sub-accounts detailing, for example, different types of debtors and individual debtors accounts.

In your introductory studies, you are unlikely to have a great deal to do with the chart of accounts except in your exercises with a computer accounting system. As a result you will have to make your own judgements as to the account in which to place any particular accounting transaction. This does make life a bit more difficult for you but it does ensure that you can grasp the logic – or at least conventions – behind the way accounts are split up in practice. This is something we will spend more time on in Chapter 7.

You will have noticed that in Figure 6.9 we did not just list the accounts haphazardly. There was a degree of organization to them; they clustered around different types of things

Revenue (100–199)

101 Sales: Product A, Country 1

102 Sales: Product A, Country 2

103 Sales: Product B, Country 1

etc.

108 Other revenue

Expenditure (200–399)

210 Direct materials

220 Consumables

230 Other materials

240 Salaries

250 Energy

260 Repairs

270 Contracting out

280 Rent etc.

390 Other expenditure

Current assets (400–499)

410 Trade debtors

420 Other debtors

430 Inventory: Group a

440 Inventory: Group b

450 Cash in bank

460 Petty cash

470 Prepayments

etc.

Liabilities and equity (500–599)

510 Trade creditors

520 Sundry creditors

530 Loan creditors

540 Share capital

550 Accruals

etc.

Fixed assets (600–699)

610 Buildings

620 Land

630 Machinery

640 Equipment

650 Road vehicles

660 Non-road vehicles

etc.

and so on.

Figure 6.9 An extract from a possible outline chart of accounts

– assets, liabilities, expenditure and revenue. You may be beginning to see what is intended by these terms (we will spend a lot of time on them in the next few chapters), but do not worry if they do not make a lot of sense just yet. We need to use them a little in the next section so, please, just take them for read at the moment and hold your rabid enthusiasm in check for just a little while longer.

6.3.3 The ledgers

Through convention and convenience, the 'T-Accounts' of an organization tend to be organized into groups known as **ledgers** which are large books or computer files in which the 'T-accounts' are kept. The organization of the books will be shown by the chart (or index) of accounts. A simple though typical organization of these ledgers would be:

- **Cashbook** – exactly as we have seen it, perhaps distinguishing between bank and cash and/or 'petty cash';
- **Debtors (or sales) ledger** – where all the debtors accounts (or at least the trade debtors accounts) are kept together;
- **Creditors (or purchases) ledger** - where all the creditors (or at least the trade creditors accounts) are kept together;
- **Nominal ledger** – where all the other accounts are held. So here will be purchases accounts, sales accounts, all the different types of expenses accounts including wages, the loan accounts, the amounts owed to the owners (because they are different sorts of creditors as we shall see), asset accounts, etc. The nominal ledger may easily be split up into more manageable sub-ledgers to keep like things together – typically private ledger (where the owners transactions and directors' matters would go), asset ledger, expenses ledger and revenues ledger. The split is for *convenience and habit*.[2]

6.3.4 The general journal

Earlier we met the term 'journal' as synonymous with 'daybook', but as we mentioned in note 1, there is another use of the term 'journal. This is the reference to a separate book used for *correcting entries and making end-of-period adjustments* – usually known as the **general journal**.

Throughout the accounting period it is quite possible to make a mistake and enter a transaction incorrectly – an incorrect amount, or entry in the wrong T-account, for example. Whilst these may be corrected simply through deletion this seems to make folk nervous and so a record of the alteration may be kept in the general journal. Let us, for example, imagine that the Unseen University in the example above (Figures 6.7 and 6.8) had made a couple of bookkeeping mistakes and had (i) incorrectly charged A.B. Aardvark for accommodation in Weatherwax Hall when it should have been B.A. Aardvark – her cousin; and (ii) mistakenly posted the invoice for the office equipment to Rincewind Ltd when it should have been to Librarian plc. The general journal would be used to record the necessary correcting entries and might look something like Figure 6.10.

Similarly there are other occasions when a piece of double-entry must be performed but there are no documents of prime entry available. The principal examples of this would be:

- **end-of-period adjustments:** the adjustments to (e.g.) the initial trial balance for all the matters we must put through in order to make the profit and loss account and the balance sheet more 'realistic' (this is dealt with in detail in the following chapters);

CORRECTING ENTRIES FOR DECEMBER 2042				
Date	Description and name of account	Folio	Debit	Credit
36/12/2042	Rincewind Ltd Librarian plc [Being the correction of a credit arising from the purchase of office equipment mistakenly posted to Rincewind Ltd instead of Librarian plc]	CA01 CL03	360.00	360.00
36/12/2042	A.B. Aardvark (student) a/c B.A. Aardvark (student) a/c [Being the correction of a debit arising from the charging of residence fees for Weatherwax Hall incorrectly to A.B. Aardvark instead of B.A. Aardvark]	DA03 DA07	100.00	100.00
Approved for posting, signed (Chief Accountant)				
	TOTALS		460.00	460.00

Figure 6.10 Extract from the Unseen University's general journal

- **opening/closing balances of the accounting period:** as we have already mentioned (and will study in some detail) we will have a set of bits and pieces with which we finish one accounting period which will be used to start up the next (these will be the balances on the balance sheet). These may be put through the general journal. Also, the transfer of the simple arithmetic balances from the T-accounts to the initial trial balance could be done through the general journal.

So, the general journal is used to record a bookkeeping adjustment for which there would otherwise be no written record. This has the advantages of (a) making the process more formal, (b) ensuring that a record of important adjustments is made so they can be followed through later and (c) providing a mechanism for the system to be controlled (see below) so that folk do not make foolish mistakes and/or are not tempted to start popping journal entries through to (say) increase their wages or increase the indebtedness of the focal organization to their sister-in-law's window-cleaning business. The general journal looks just the same as the daybook/journals and each adjustment (say) is shown, as we have seen, with both its debit and its credit entries.

6.4 CONTROLLING THE ACCOUNTING RECORDS

6.4.1 Why control accounting data and the system of internal control

Having now seen how a formal bookkeeping system captures the data and organizes the accounting records we need, at least briefly, to look at the way the focal organization can try and control the accounting data. A major purpose of the AIS is to ensure that all data are quickly, accurately and completely recorded and that no erroneous entries creep into the system. No matter how good the system, a few errors may occur and so some sort of control needs to be exercised. How this control is set in place is a massive area of study in itself so we can only scrape the surface here.

Whilst, as we shall see, accuracy is something of a mythical quality when talking about financial statements, it is possible to achieve a high degree of accuracy in the bookkeeping records. It is also very desirable to do so for many reasons, including:

- assessing who owes us and how much;
- assessing who we owe and how much;
- knowing what we own and how long we have owned it;
- knowing how well we are managing our cash flow;
- knowing how much cash is tied up in the business;
- bookkeeping provides a lot of basic data which are the platform for the financial statements and many other performance appraisal, investment appraisal and management decisions. It makes sense if these are as accurate as possible (where that is possible).

So the AIS needs to be designed to ensure that (a) everything that should be recorded, is recorded and recorded correctly, and (b) nothing that shouldn't be recorded slips into the system.

To achieve this, each organization will have some form of **system of internal control** (SIC) which will cover everything from physical security to the authorization of expense claims. It will also cover aspects of the bookkeeping system and, in particular, it will cover who can enter transactions in the books and what can be entered and where. The SIC will also operate a number of checks on the data. We have already met one of these – the initial trial balance. Although perhaps not the most penetrating of controls, the TB must balance and this gives at least some control over the double-entry system. There will be many others. These may include **control accounts**, **suspense or error accounts**, **various reconciliations** and other **self-checking systems**. A word about each of these might be useful at this stage.

A **control account** is usually maintained to check on the accuracy of the ledger to which it relates. A typical example is the **debtors** (or sales) **control account** which acts as a check on the debtors ledger. You will recall that a debtors ledger may have many different accounts for each of the different debtors. In a large company this may run to thousands of accounts. The debtors control account is simply an account into which the totals of all the debtors ledger accounts are placed: the total debtors brought forward, the sales in the period, the cash received from debtors, plus any other details related to debtors. (This might include such things as discounts and carriage costs – things which we will not be bothering too much about in our introductory studies you will be pleased to learn.)[3] If the total (the balance) on the debtors control account is the same as the totals from the debtors ledger then we can be fairly satisfied that the bookkeeping system has, to a degree at least, been accurate. *Please note* that, as far as this book is concerned, we will not be worrying about this too much. We will use a debtors ledger only when we have a lot of accounts. In the examples we have met so far (look back to Bird Industries, Figure 5.2, for example) we have put all the debtors and their cash into the same account and called this the 'debtors account'. In these circumstances, the 'debtors account' is a collective of the debtors ledger – a summary of the individual debtors accounts. So, in effect, our 'debtors accounts' have acted as a debtors control account. For small organizations the debtors (or the creditors) control account is not necessary. It is only when the bookkeeping becomes extensive and complicated that it becomes necessary.

A **suspense or error account** might more accurately be known as an 'I-do-not-know-what-to-with-this account' account. It can be used for all sorts of things but its most common purposes are: (a) as a place to put items that we are wondering about (for example, a cheque received from someone but we do not know what it is for – put it in the suspense account until we find out whether it should be sent back or where it should go); and (b) as a place to put errors that crop up from time to time (for example, if we cannot get our TB to balance or our debtors control account is different from our debtors ledger, the difference would go into the suspense account until we found where the difference(s) came from).

Various reconciliations are used to cross-check different parts of the accounting system. The use of the debtors control account is one such reconciliation. We shall meet another – the bank reconciliation – below. But others can be helpful. A common one is to reconcile the daybook with the appropriate ledger to make sure we have missed nothing. Indeed, as we shall see briefly in the next section, auditors may often use reconciliations to check on the accuracy of the record keeping.

Finally, most large organizations will use an array of **self-checking systems** to ensure the accuracy of figures. For example, suppose a company maintains a purchases daybook which lists all the trade purchases and distinguishes between cash purchases and purchases on credit. These will be entered from the daybook into a purchases account (inflow to the operations subsystem, debit purchases), the cash purchases will be entered in the cashbook (outflow from the funds subsystem, credit cash) and the credit purchases will be recorded in the creditors ledger (outflow of information, credit creditors). The creditors ledger will have been entered from the daybook. The purchase ledger clerk may find it helpful to add up the total of the trade creditors entered in the month and check that this equals the total of the trade credit purchases invoices for the same period. They ought to be the same, and if they are not, something is wrong somewhere. (This process may be conducted – as here – as a reconciliation exercise or may be conducted through the control account.)

These are just some of the ways in which the bookkeeping and accounting information system sets about trying to ensure the accuracy of the basic accounting records. There are many more, but most of these can wait till later in your studies. For now, there are two specific areas of control that you need to know a little about – audit and bank reconciliations.

6.4.2 Internal and external audit

'Audit' is an increasingly abused word. For example, the 1970s saw the rise of the 'social audit', the 1980s saw the discovery of the 'plant closure audit' and the 'ethical audit, whilst the 1990s was the decade of the 'environmental audit'. We shall discuss these briefly in Chapter 17. For conventional accounting, audit has two separate meanings. The first is the **statutory audit** of a company's financial statements under the Companies Acts in which a suitably qualified accountant, who is supposed to be independent of the focal organization, investigates the financial numbers contained in the financial statements and expresses a public opinion as to whether or not these statements give what is known as a 'true and fair' view of the organization's operations. This is also known as **independent attestation**. It is an important part of your accounting studies and will be considered in more detail in Chapter 14. The other meaning relates to **internal audit**. This use of the term has a much wider remit than the statutory audit. At its most basic it means that a designated group of people in the focal organization (usually, but not always, accountants) are assigned the duty to check on the accounting and management information systems of the focal organization in order to ensure that they are accurate, reliable, efficient and not subject to error and fraud. How they go about this process is a course in itself but you can assume that they would follow the sorts of patterns we have discussed in this chapter and look at control accounts, suspense accounts and so on and would also take samples of accounting transactions and follow them through the process we have described in this chapter – ensuring that all procedures, codings and entries have been complied with. Internal audit is, thus, an important part of the focal organization's system of internal control over the AIS. It acts as a sort of overall check on what is happening – and what can happen – in the accounting transaction processing of which bookkeeping is such a crucial part.

6.4.3 Bank reconciliations

As we touched upon above, reconciliations can be a very important part of the way in which the focal organization keeps a check on the accuracy of the bookkeeping system. One important source of reconciliation arises when the focal organization gets the opportunity to reconcile its records with those of an outside organization. This may arise in a number of ways. One of the most common arises when a (finance-receiving) organization sends the focal organization a statement of account which is, in effect, a printout of that company's debtors ledger as it relates to the focal organization. (Note that the (finance-receiving) organization will be treating the focal organization as a debtor whilst the focal organization will be treating the finance-receiving organization as a creditor. If this isn't clear, think it through – and perhaps refer back to Figure 4.8.) This gives the focal organization the opportunity to reconcile its records with that of the other company and investigate any differences.

A similar opportunity arises with a bank statement. A bank statement is a bank's record of its financial dealings with the focal organization. As such, it should be a mirror image of the focal organization's cash book – excluding, of course, the cash-in-hand transactions. (Look back to Figure 3.6 if you cannot recall – or are confused about – why the bank statement shows a 'credit' for when you have got a cash inflow and your cashbook shows a 'debit' for the same thing.) Therefore, all things being equal, the focal organization's cashbook and the bank statement should agree. However, they rarely do.

> **Hint**
>
> If you do not do so already, you should do a regular bank reconciliation on your own bank account. Apart from helping you cope with the penury of student life, it will be very helpful practice for you. If you do not keep a cashbook for yourself (shame on you!) you can at least reconcile the bank's balance with your cheque stubs or cheque record which you really do need to keep up to date.

As a control and check on the cash book (and on the bank itself) it is considered good practice to try and reconcile – at the end of the accounting period – the balance shown by the focal organization's bank statement with the balance shown by the focal organization's cashbook. Differences between the two will arise for a number of reasons. These will include:

- *incorrect entries in the cashbook* (e.g. mistakes, perhaps a direct debit whose amount was incorrectly estimated by the focal organization);
- *incorrect entries in the bank statements* (e.g. items put to the wrong account, bank charges at too high a rate);
- *deposits to the bank appearing in the cashbook which have not appeared in the bank statement* (e.g. items paid in but not yet cleared and cheques received by the focal organization and entered in the cashbook but not yet taken to the bank);
- *payments made by the focal organization from the cashbook which have not yet been presented and cleared by the bank* (e.g. cheques which have been raised and despatched (for goods, services, wages, etc.) which have either not yet been presented to the bank or which have not yet been cleared);
- *receipts shown in the bank statement not yet entered in the cashbook* (e.g. amounts paid directly into the bank by customers or, for example, dividend cheques);
- *payments shown in the bank statement not yet entered in the cashbook* (e.g. bank charges, interest, standing orders).

Thus, differences can arise between the cashbook and the bank statement for three main reasons – (a) errors by either the bank or the focal organization; (b) differences in the timing of the bookkeeping entries being made; and (c) transactions of which one or other party is not aware. Whilst performing a bank reconciliation can seem confusing at first, you should take it slowly, thinking through what is actually happening and therefore likely to cause a difference. The best way to approach it is in stages. The stages are summarized in Figure 6.11.

The stages shown in Figure 6.11 are what you should do if you were reconciling your own bank statement. You start by finding out exactly how much cash you (the focal organization) actually have (the true position) and bringing your records up to date. Then you identify the timing difference and errors (if any) arising in the bank's statement. And then the two (your cashbook and the bank's statement) should agree.

Whether they agree or not, this is not the end of the process. It is essential – and one of the purposes of the exercise – to try and discover why these differences arose. They may have done so for very simple reasons that will always arise – simply, for example, as a

---

1. BRING THE CASHBOOK UP TO DATE:

- Check additions and brought forward figures;
- Correct any incorrect entries in the cashbook;
- Debit the cashbook with any (correct) receipts not entered;
- Credit the cashbook with any (correct) payments not yet entered.

2. THE CASHBOOK SHOULD NOW SHOW THE CORRECT BALANCE.

3. CORRECT THE BANK STATEMENT FOR DIFFERENCES:

- Correct any incorrect entries;
- Add/subtract (depending on whether one has a positive balance or is overdrawn) receipts that have not been processed by the bank;
- Subtract/add (depending on whether one has a positive balance or is overdrawn) payments made by the focal organization but which have not been presented to/cleared by the bank.

4. THE TWO SHOULD NOW AGREE.

Figure 6.11 Stages in a bank reconciliation

result of the time it takes for an organization to take a cheque to the bank and for the bank to clear that cheque.[4] Other differences may have arisen through, for example, failures in the focal organization's AIS to record or note actual or potential receipts and payments – most typically, standing orders, direct debits and bank charges.[5] These failures must be investigated and identified in order to assess whether the AIS can be amended to make the bookkeeping records more reliable. Finally, differences which are either errors or mis-understandings may arise and these must be identified and discussed with the bank. The bank reconciliation is only a means to an end – checking on the reliability of the AIS – not an end in itself.

To show how this all works, let us consider an example. Figure 6.12 shows the cashbook of Bird Industries for February 200X and the bank statement received at the end of February. Our task is to reconcile them. Now please read through Figure 6.12.

We will follow the stages outlined in Figure 6.12. We will be asking you to undertake the reconciliation as we go along. The answers to each part of the reconciliation are given

BIRD INDUSTRIES CASHBOOK

Date	ACCOUNT	REF	£	Date	Cheque	ACCOUNT	REF	£
Feb.				Feb.				
9	Sales (Garden Supplies)	RA06	700	1	TB	Balance b/fwd	CB01	2,250
17	Sales (Garden Supplies)	RA06	600	1	201	Ardsell Ltd (advert)	CA06	500
17	Cash sale	RAC1	200	1	202	Petty cash	PCV1	100
26	Sales (The Hopeful Kakadu Ltd)	RA09	1,500	7	203	Sunflower Ltd (seeds)	CS07	1,000
				7	204	International Receptacle Inc (bags etc)	CS02	300
				7	205	Circularity Ltd (wood)	CS09	1,000
				26	206	Salaries	WS02	1,200
				26	207	Taxation	WS03	400
				26	S.O.	Loan interest	LI45	120
			3,000					8,670
	Balance c/d		5,670					
			8,670					8,670

LOANS R US BANK: BIRD INDUSTRIES BANK STATEMENT

Date	Details	Debit	Credit	Balance
Feb.				
1	Balance b/fwd			1,250
6	202	100		1,350
7	201	500		
7	SO 16/AE462	100		1,950
9	Lodged		700	1,250
15	205	1,000		2,250
17	Lodged		800	1,450
20	204	300		1,750
26	SO 469/IK731	120		1,870

Figure 6.12 Bank reconciliation for Bird Industries, February 200X

in the notes to this chapter (notes 6–9 give answers to the questions as we go through the example).

First, the bank statement and the cashbook should be checked for basic arithmetic, copying or other simple mistakes. Do this now. You should find two mistakes – in the cashbook.[6] Mistakes of this sort should not arise in a simple case like Bird Industries and really should not be possible in a good computerized accounting system. However, it pays to take nothing for granted. Also, identify whether the cash balance at the end of the month is a positive balance or an overdraft.[7]

Second, cross-check as many of the bank and the cashbook items as possible, ticking them off when you are sure that an entry in the cashbook has an entry in the bank statement and that they are the same in size and direction. This will leave you with the items on which you need to concentrate.[8]

Third, write up the cashbook for any (correct) receipts and payments that are missing from the cashbook – are there any?[9]

Fourth, identify any entries in the cashbook which are not included in the bank statement. The result of all this would produce you a bank reconciliation which looked like Figure 6.13.

Work this example through until it is clear. A bank reconciliation is a basically simple exercise as long as you are systematic about it and keep a clear head. For many large organizations bank reconciliations may run into hundreds of adjustments but the principles are just the same.

You only need practice with these; do not let them become an irritant and, whilst they are far from exciting(!) bank reconciliations are very useful devices.

Hint

Sometimes, students get a bit confused as to whether they should be adding on or taking away and in which 'direction' they are trying to go. If this causes you confusion, a slightly simpler way is to do the first part of the reconciliation to the 'true cash figure' and then adjust the bank statement figure for the things which are in the cashbook but not in the bank statement. That is, in our example, you make the cashbook and the bank statement come to an overdraft balance of £2,970.

DESCRIPTION	AMOUNT (£)
Balance brought down per cashbook	(o/d)2,870
ADD Standing order not recorded in the cashbook	100
Correct balance per cashbook (This should be the actual amount of cash the focal organization actually has)	2,970
ADD Cashbook receipts not in the bank statement (the sales to The Hopeful Kakadu Ltd)	1,500
	4,470
LESS Cashbook payments not yet recorded in the bank statement (£1000 to Sunflower; £1,200 to salaries; £400 to taxation)	2,600
BALANCE PER BANK STATEMENT (You hope!)	1,870

Figure 6.13 Bank reconciliation statement for Bird Industries, February 200X

SUMMARY

Rather than accepting without question the figures which are presented to the bookkeeping system, an important part of the accountant's task is to understand and design the processes to make sure that the bookkeeping process is part of a well-functioning accounting information system (AIS). We examined three elements of this system in this chapter: data capture, organizing the accounting records and controlling the accounting data. It is important that you have a basic understanding of where the bookkeeping process fits within the AIS and understand what has gone on before the data arrive, ready to be entered into the double-entry system. In addition, you should have some idea about the potential reliability of the basic accounting data and how we might undertake various exercises to improve that reliability. Without some appreciation of this and some understanding of how we can be assured of the reliability of the bookkeeping data it is pretty stupid to go blithely ahead debiting and crediting what could be absolute garbage. Your later studies, most notably in information systems and in auditing, will develop these ideas to a considerable degree. Hopefully, this chapter has provided you with some appreciation of what is happening 'out there' in the big organizational world in which bookkeeping operates.

Key terms and concepts

The following key terms and concepts have featured in this chapter. You should ensure that you understand and can explain each one. Page references to definitions appear in the index in bold type.

- Accounting information system (AIS)
- Accounting procedures manual
- Accounts code
- Balance carried forward (c/fwd)
- Bank and other reconciliations
- Books of prime entry
- Chart (or index) of accounts
- Control accounts
- Controlling the accounting data
- Correcting entries
- Data capture
- Daybooks and journals
- End-of-period adjustments
- The general journal
- Incomplete records
- Independent attestation
- Internal and external audit
- Ledgers
- Nominal ledger
- Opening and closing balances
- Organizing the accounting records
- Purchases ledger
- Reconciliations and self-checking systems
- Sales ledger
- Source documents
- Suspense (or error) account
- System of internal control
- Transposition errors

FURTHER READING

There is a considerable amount of excellent additional material on the issues covered in this chapter. Browse the shelves and catalogue of your library for textbooks with a title like accounting information systems. These texts are likely to be helpful and, on the strict accounting issues, most introductory accounting textbooks will have something which will give you a different perspective on what we have discussed here. In addition, you should find any good auditing textbook will give you a useful introduction to the system of internal control.

NOTES

1. When we are talking about books of prime entry the terms 'daybook' and 'journal' can be used interchangeably. (The term 'journal' coming from the French for 'day'.) The term 'journal' is, however, also sometimes used for a very specific type of prime-entry record which involves the correction of mistakes and the end-of-period adjustments. We will meet this use of the term below.

2. We should point out, if you haven't already noticed, that, conventionally, accounting records are not organized around the three organizational subsystems (decision and control, funds and operations) with which we began the book. Those three subsystems were simply a way of thinking about the accounting entity and the accounting information flows. It will continue to be useful and any other configuration of accounting systems can always be brought back or related to the three subsystems in our organizational model. Conventionally, however, accounting and bookkeeping do not use these terms. Rather, conventional accounting is driven by a combination of convenience, habit, past practice and the requirements of the Companies Acts governing financial reporting (which we shall meet in due course). Do not, please, let these different ways of looking at the same thing confuse you. They are intended to help you develop your appreciation of the intellectual dimensions of your putative profession.

3. You may very well, however, meet practical examples of control accounts in the computer accounting ledger packages you use in your laboratory accounting studies.

4. It will usually take several working days (i.e. not Saturdays and Sundays) for a bank to clear a cheque. Instantaneous funds transfer, for ordinary folk anyway, is largely an advertising myth.

5. For processing cheques, opening accounts, transferring money, operating standing orders, letting you queue for a teller and for the privilege of them having the use of your money, etc.

6. The first mistake is that the brought forward figure is incorrect (look back to Figures 5.3 and 5.4 where the books for the first month of Bird Industries were reproduced). The second mistake is one of transposition – the addition of the cashbook payments was correct but then written as £8,670 instead of £6,870. Thus the cash balance per the cashbook should be £2,870 instead of £5,670.

7. It is an overdraft which has increased during the month.

8. The receipts from Garden Supplies and the cash sale are presumably lodged together as the £800. If you were sitting in a company doing this bank reconciliation you would find out if this were so. After cross-checking you should have unmatched: one cashbook receipt (The Hopeful Kakadu), three cashbook payments (Sunflower, Salaries and Taxation), and one bank payment (the standing order for £100).

9. There is one, the standing order that the bank has paid but of which there is no record in the cashbook. Having checked that this is a bona fide transaction we would add this £100 on to the overdraft.

7

The trial balance and categorization: the accounting conventions, assets, liabilities, revenues, expenses, provisions and reserves

Learning objectives

After studying this chapter you should be able to:

- give a simple explanation of the profit and loss account and the balance sheet;
- explain what end-of-period adjustments are and why we need them;
- give a simple definition of revenues, expenses, assets and liabilities;
- explain the accounting equations and how they work;
- explain what an extended trial balance is;
- define the accounting conventions, explain why we need them and indicate some of the problems that arise with them;
- give illustrations of revenues, expenses, assets and liabilities;
- describe and illustrate the main categories of assets;
- describe and illustrate the main categories of liabilities and claims;
- explain what a provision is and show how the extended trial balance is used to account for it;
- identify the main types of end-of-period adjustments which will be put through an extended trial balance.

7.1 INTRODUCTION

7.1.1 Chapter design and links to previous chapters

So far we have seen how we can identify an *accounting entity* and how the *four basic characteristics* enable us to identify the things with which the conventional accounting system is concerned. We have seen how the *accounting information system* captures, organizes and controls the data which are needed for our bookkeeping activities. We then saw how we can identify the *double-entry procedures* for each type of transaction, open a set of T-accounts and enter the events into our bookkeeping system. Finally, we summarized the T-accounts by *balancing off* each account at the end of each *accounting period* and took each *balance* to the *initial trial balance* – maintaining the double-entry through debiting an account to close it off and crediting the initial trial balance – or crediting an account to close it off and debiting the initial trial balance. This produced an initial trial balance which serves three functions: (a) it allowed us to check the arithmetic accuracy of the bookkeeping and ensure that **[Total debits = Total credits]**; (b) it signalled the completion of the *basic bookkeeping process*; (c) it serves as the basis for our *accounting* and, in particular for the *accounting decisions* which, via a series of *end-of-period adjustments*, will enable us to produce the *financial statements*.

In this chapter we will introduce the **end-of-period adjustments** and the **extended trial balance**. To do this it is necessary to introduce you to a variety of new material. This will include the **accounting equations**, the **accounting conventions** and some useful detail on the main categories of things with which accounting is concerned – **revenues**, **expenses**, **assets** and **liabilities** – in order to produce the financial statements.

The chapter is organized as follows. The following subsection will provide a brief introduction to the **profit and loss account** (or income statement) and the **balance sheet** (or position statement). This is to provide a 'signpost' so that you can keep an eye on where we are headed. Section 7.2 then introduces the main categories of **revenues**, **expenses**, **assets** and **liabilities** and shows the relationship between these and the profit or loss figure in what are known as the **accounting equations**. The end of this section will introduce the concept of the **extended trial balance**. Section 7.3 explains, in some detail, the traditional **accounting conventions** which we need in order to organize our accounting activity so that we can produce the financial statements. Section 7.4 provides more detail on the four basic account categories (revenues, expenses, assets and liabilities) and provides illustrations of the most usual elements that fall into each category. This section rounds off with an introduction to the idea of a **provision** and shows how the extended trial balance can be used to account for it. Section 7.5 summarizes the major end-of-period adjustments which we will examine in detail in the following chapters. The chapter finishes with the usual summary, key words and concepts and guidance on further reading.

7.1.2 Introducing the basic financial statements

One of the principal purposes of the bookkeeping process is to provide a basis for the financial statements of the focal organization. Our job in this chapter – and the next few chapters – is to get from the (relatively straightforward) initial trial balance to the basic financial statements via a series of end-of-period adjustments. We will do this via the **extended trial balance**. However, to help you orient yourself and to give you a chance to understand why we are going to put ourselves to all this trouble, we need to know a little bit about the financial statements at this stage. It is easier to get somewhere if we know our destination.

Financial statements are complex things, usually contained within the annual report of an accounting entity – a company, a charity, a local government organization or whatever.

Hint

We have said before and we will say again, you should be taking steps to collect a set of actual financial statements from various accounting entities. If you have followed this advice, you are now in a position to pull off your shelf the annual reports of two or three companies (for example) and have a look at their financial statements. What follows will make more sense if you can see the actual output that this process is designed to achieve.

Later on in this book we will touch upon many of the elements of the financial statements – and much of your future study in accounting will be concerned with the detail of these statements. However, the financial statements are virtually always dominated by two crucial statements – the **profit and loss account** (or **income statement**) and the **balance sheet** (or **position statement**). It is these which are of principal concern to us at this stage in your studies. So, what are they?

Well, it is very important that you know that there is considerable dispute about what a profit and loss account and a balance sheet are for. How can that be? Surely the purpose of the profit and loss account is to show the profit or the loss, isn't it? And the purpose of the balance sheet is to show, well, to show the balances, isn't it? The answer to these questions is 'Yes, sort of'. It is, however, a lot more complex than that and much of your future studies in accounting will be concerned with trying to understand what these statements are for and what they should be for – not necessarily the same thing. Suffice it to say at this stage that the term 'profit' – which is crucial to the design of both statements – is an almost impossible thing to define in a way that everybody agrees with. In fact **profit** is a fiction – an abstract creation with little or no concrete meaning. We will see some of this as the book advances. But, for the time being, just bear in mind that what follows is a very simple version of what actually happens in practice and the old remark that the answer to the question 'What is this year's profit?' is 'What would you like it to be?' is a lot closer to reality than many accounting students would like it to be!

Well, we have to start somewhere. And the simplest way to think of these two statements is to:

i   think of the profit and loss account as a statement of what has been earned and consumed/used up in the accounting period. More formally (and, again, somewhat simply), the profit and loss account is a statement of the revenues earned in the accounting period *less* what was expended during that accounting period to earn those revenues in order to arrive at a conclusion as to how much better off or worse off the focal organization is at the end of the accounting period (whether it made a profit or a loss).

ii Think of the balance sheet as a statement of what is left over at the end of the accounting period in terms of what is owed, owing and owned. More formally (and, again, somewhat simply), the balance sheet is a financial statement of the focal organization at a single point in time which itemizes the useful economic things the organization owns at that point in time, identifies the debts owing to and from the focal organization and shows how the organization is financed and what monies have accrued to those who have financed the organization.

We will refine these definitions somewhat as we progress, but they will serve well as basic definitions. The point to hold firmly in your mind is that the **profit and loss account** (or income statement) relates to what has happened in the last accounting period. It is a summarized description of what happened in a particular period of time – it relates to the past and past events which, once the accounting period has passed, you can, on the whole, forget about. On the other hand, the **balance sheet** (or position statement) is a statement at one particular point in time – the accounting date. It relates to what the focal organization has at that point in time and, thus, may relate to what the organization will do – or can do, or must do – in the future.

Now, it should be possible for you to see that our initial trial balance doesn't let us simply or completely identify what has been earned/used up or what is owed, owing and owned. It contains bits of both. Let us have a look. Referring back to Bird Industries we could see, for example:

- The debtors owe money to the focal organization. This is important information because we want them to pay the focal organization in future accounting periods. So this leads us to recognize that debtors relate to some period after the accounting date – they will pay us in the future. And, note that this is despite the fact that the events which created the debtors (e.g. sales) have occurred in the past. The sales will appear in the profit and loss account as events relating to the past.
- The creditors represent money the focal organization owes. The focal organization will have to pay this in the future. So the creditors appear on the balance sheet as they relate to what will happen after the accounting date – despite the fact that the events which created them (e.g. purchases) occurred in the past. The purchases will – to an extent anyway (see below) – appear in the profit and loss account as a series of past events.
- The warehouse and other things are owned by the focal organization and can be used in future periods and so we would expect them to appear in the balance sheet. But we have 'used up' some of them – they are not necessarily in as good shape as when we bought them. So there will be some amount of 'used-upness' to be taken from the balance sheet figures and put into the profit and loss account as relating to past periods.
- Similarly, we have bought many things – raw materials, labour, etc., and some of these are used up (i.e. used in production and/or to make things which have been sold), but some will be left over – that is, some of our raw materials, for example, will still be sitting around in the factory.

Do not get confused by this. Some things do not categorize easily. That is what we have to try and sort out here.

We need some systematic way for sorting out the entries in the initial trial balance into 'profit and loss account things' (earned, consumed and used up) and 'balance sheet things' (left over, owing, owed and owned). This is what we do in the **extended trial balance.** The initial trial balance entries are systematically examined to determine whether they are (a) profit and loss account items, (b) balance sheet items or (c) a bit of both. And then, we go and check to see if there is anything we have missed which should be in (a), (b) or (c) but which the bookkeeping system has missed. So the **extended trial balance** involves four stages and these stages are collectively known as the **end-of-period adjustments.** (We have met these before and used the general journal in Chapter 6, Figure 6.10, to operate them.) Taken as a whole, they are so awkward that this and the next four chapters will concentrate upon the most important – but simplest – of them.

So, to summarize, we need to:

i   take the initial trial balance;
ii categorize the entries according to 'profit and loss account type' and 'balance sheet type';
iii adjust the entries – via the end-of-period adjustments – so that we have two discrete sets relating to the two basic financial statements;
iv produce a basic set of financial statements.

The extended trial balance will be our workplace to do all this.

But, before we get stuck into this, we need to introduce you to some accounting language – some terms which relate to important accounting concepts with which we will work in this chapter and all subsequent chapters. That is, you won't find the annual reports from organizations such as ICI, Nissan and IBM employing terms like 'used up' and 'left over' and so on. They will use formal accounting language, so we had better get that sorted out first.

7.2 CATEGORIZING THE TRIAL BALANCE ENTRIES

7.2.1 What categories do we use?

Actually, we have met the terms we shall be using before. Chapter 5 (section 5.3.3) and the chart of accounts in Figure 6.9 both listed the main categories of things we need. They are summarized in Figure 7.1.

Although it is far from simple to really define these terms in wholly satisfactory ways, we can give some basic definitions:

- **revenues** – inflows earned during the current accounting period that will be (or have been) received/honoured during this and/or future accounting periods;
- **expenses** – the cost of those resources consumed or used up in the present accounting period in generating operations subsystems outputs;
- **assets** – resources owned and available for use by the focal organization for this and future accounting periods;
- **liabilities and claims** – obligations that are legally required to be met by the focal organisation in future accounting periods.

A major part of our task in this chapter is to be able to allocate balances from the trial balance to these different categories – and indeed to refine these categories further. In order to do this, we must have a better understanding of the categories themselves and how they relate to each other. This we will do by first having a look at the **accounting equations** and then proceeding to examine the basic **accounting conventions** before returning to examine our four basic categories – of assets, liabilities and claims, revenues and expenses – in more detail.

7.2.2 The accounting equations

The relationships we are seeking to exploit can be summarized in what are known as the **accounting equations**. We now know from Figure 7.1 that the profit and loss account

Informal description	Formal name	Where does it go?
Earned by the focal organization	REVENUES (or income)	Profit and Loss Account (or income statement)
Consumed/Used up by the focal organization	EXPENSES (including provisions)	
Owed by the focal organization	LIABILITIES AND CLAIMS (including creditors, accruals provisions and ownership claims)	Balance Sheet (or position statement)
Owing to the focal organization	ASSETS (including debtors, stock, land, buildings, machines etc.)	
Owned by the focal organization		

Figure 7.1 Categorization of initial trial balance entries

consists of revenues and expenses and the balance sheet consists of assets and liabilities and claims. But we also know that revenues and expenses are very unlikely to be identical. The difference between the two will be the profit or the loss. So:

Equation A:
[REVENUES] – [EXPENSES] = [PROFIT/LOSS]

We also know (because we made it so) that:

Equation B:
[TOTAL DEBITS] = [TOTAL CREDITS]or
[TOTAL INPUTS/INFLOWS] = [TOTAL OUTPUTS/OUTFLOWS]

Now, by looking back over the last few chapters you could probably work out – if you haven't already – that in the initial trial balance:

Equation C:
[TOTAL DEBITS] = [EXPENSES] + [ASSETS]
Equation D:
[TOTAL CREDITS] = [REVENUES] + [LIABILITIES AND CLAIMS]

That is, the debit balances are related to the assets and expenses accounts (as you might expect as the majority of the entries to these accounts were debit entries) whilst the credit balances are generally on the liabilities and claims accounts (again, as you might expect). So, it must be the case from Equations C and D that, in the initial trial balance at any rate:

Equation E:
[EXPENSES] + [ASSETS] = [REVENUES] + [LIABILITIES AND CLAIMS]

But what about the balance sheet? And what about the profit/loss shown in the profit and loss account (Equation A)? Well, if we add profit/loss to each side of Equation E, something interesting happens:

Equation F:
[EXPENSES] + [ASSETS] + [PROFIT/LOSS] =
[REVENUES] + [LIABILITIES AND CLAIMS] + [PROFIT/LOSS]

Now take away the profit and loss account equation (Equation A) from Equation F and you are left with:

Equation G:
[ASSETS] = [LIABILITIES AND CLAIMS] + [PROFIT/LOSS]

And this is the balance sheet equation.

You must understand this. The foregoing is a combination of simple arithmetic and algebraic manipulation based on a series of definitionally true statements. Play with this until it feels really comfortable – let the penny drop about why some things are debits or credits and why profit/loss must appear on both statements if they are to balance. If this clicks for you, much of what follows will be so much easier. It is summarized in Figure 7.2.

It makes sense to dwell on these equations for a few minutes to make sure you can actually see how they work. This we do in the following subsection.

The Trial Balance:

Assets + Expenses = Revenues + Liabilities and claims

[Total debits] = [Total credits]

So:

Revenues – Expenses = Assets – Liabilities and claims

The Profit and Loss Account:

Revenues – Expenses = Profit/Loss

The Balance Sheet:

Assets – Liabilities and claims = Profit/Loss

or:

Assets = Liabilities and claims + Profit/Loss

Figure 7.2 A summary of the accounting equations

7.3.2 Working with the accounting equations

The essential point about the accounting equations is not that they simply confirm what we know already – that [Total debits/inflows] = [Total credits/outflows] – but rather that they illustrate the way in which the two major accounting financial statements – the profit and loss account and the balance sheet – work together or 'articulate'.

Consider a very simple example. Let us imagine that you establish a little business at university buying and selling computer game discs. The business only runs for a month – November – and you have only a few transactions. These are shown in Figure 7.3.

Let us start with the basic trial balance equation shown in Figure 7.2. This equation plus each stage of the changes in the equations are summarized in Figure 7.4.

Before we start up our new enterprise, we have nothing 'in the accounting entity' – no revenues, no expenses, no assets and no liabilities. Then we take out the loan from our parents. In bookkeeping terms we would [Debit/inflow Cash $50] and [Credit/outflow Loans $50]. We now have an asset (cash) and a liability (the loan). The resulting equation for 1 November balances – as shown in Figure 7.4.

Next, on 6 November, we buy the games. In bookkeeping terms this would be [Debit/inflow Purchases $50] - but we are going to put them into stock (see below) and [Credit/outflow Creditors $50]. What has happened is that we now hold $50 worth of games (asset) which we will treat as our stock at this stage. (This is one of the difficult issues in end-of-period adjustments and we will examine it in detail in Chapter 10.) In return, we now owe $50 (liability). The accounting equation for 6 November in Figure 7.4 balances again.

Then, on 10 November we sell our stock. At this point they become expenses of the business ('used up'), so they are moved from assets (what we own) to expenses (what we have consumed). That is, we [Debit/inflow Purchases $50] and [Credit/outflow Stock $50]. But we have also to show the sale. We receive $70 for the games and make a sale of $70. The bookkeeping for this would be [Debit/inflow Cash $70] and [Credit/outflow Sales $70]. Thus, we increase our asset of cash and simultaneously increase the revenue item by way of sales. The accounting equation for 10 November also balances in Figure 7.4.

1. On 1 November, you borrow $50 from your parents.

2. On 6 November you buy 10 games for $50 and promise to pay for them on 20 November.

3. On 10 November you sell all 10 games for $70, receiving the cash immediately.

4. On 20 November you pay for the games.

5. On 30 November you repay your parents.

(Ignore issues like interest and whether it is legal to buy and sell such games.)

Figure 7.3 The accounting equations: Game Girl Ages Enterprises

THE ACCOUNTING EQUATIONS								
Date	Assets	+	Expenses	=	Revenues	+	Liabilities and claims	
31 October	$0	+	$0	=	$0	+	$0	
1 November	$50 (cash)	+	$0	=	$0	+	$50 (loan)	
6 November	$50 (cash) $50 (stock)	+	$0	=	$0	+	$50 (loan) $50 (debt)	
10 November	$50 (cash) $70 (cash)	+	$50 (exp)	=	$70 (sale)	+	$50 (loan) $50 (debt)	
20 November	$70 (cash)	+	$50 (exp)	=	$70 (sale)	+	$50 (loan)	
30 November	$20 (cash)	+	$50 (exp)	=	$70 (sale)	+	$0	

Figure 7.4 An illustration of the accounting equations for Game Girl Ages Enterprises

On 20 November we pay for the games. In bookkeeping terms this would be [Debit/inflow Creditors $50] to cancel the debt and [Credit/outflow Cash $50] to show the flow of cash out of the focal organization to pay for the debt. In terms of the equations, we have decreased our assets (cash) and decreased our liabilities (creditors). The equation for 20 November in Figure 7.4 still balances.

Finally, on 30 November, we pay back our parents' loan. In bookkeeping terms this would involve [Debit/inflow Loan $50] to discharge the loan and [Credit/outflow Cash $50] to reflect the outflow of cash to pay off the loan. In terms of the equations we have reduced our assets (cash) and simultaneously reduced our liabilities (loans). The equation for 30 November in Figure 7.4 still balances.

Now, if you look back at Figure 7.2 where the different equations were summarized, you will see that, perhaps, it might have been more interesting to put all of these accounting transactions directly through the profit and loss account and balance sheet equations. We could have done that but, if you look closely, you will see that as each new transaction went through we would have had to calculate the profit/loss at that point. That is tricky, and so, in keeping with traditional accounting systems, we wait until the end of the accounting period to produce the profit and loss account and the balance sheet. So what do the profit and loss account and the balance sheet equations look like? These are summarized in Figure 7.5.

Well, at the end of the accounting period – in this case the month of November – the final trial balance equation can be reworked to produce the profit and loss account and the balance sheet equations. This is done in Figure 7.5. So now the debit and credit balances are split up into those relating to the past (the profit and loss account items) and those relating to the future (the balance sheet items). The profit and loss account shows that during November a revenue of $70 was (past tense) achieved with an expenditure of $50

THE ACCOUNTING EQUATIONS							
Trial balance equation	Assets	+	Expenses	=	Revenues	+	Liabilities and claims
	$20 (cash)	+	$50 (exp)	=	$70 (sale)	+	$0
Profit/loss account equation	Revenues	–	Expenses	=	P/L		
	$70 (sale)	–	$50 (exp)	=	$20 (P/L)		
Balance sheet equation	Assets	=	Liabilities and claims	+	P/L		
	$20 (cash)	=	$0	+	$20 (P/L)		

Figure 7.5 The accounting equations: Game Girl Ages Enterprises

leaving a profit of $20. The balance sheet equation shows that on 30 November, we have (present tense) an asset of $20 (cash) and this is balanced by a profit of $20. Do not worry yourself about the idea of a profit balancing an asset – if this seems counter to common sense. It will be explained in more detail later on.

This illustrates a number of important points. First, the trial balance can be split into the profit and loss account items and the balance sheet items. Second, to do so requires the addition of this item 'profit and loss' to both financial statements. Third, it is apparent that any movement in one of the statements arising from a transaction (a debit) produces an equal and opposite movement (a credit) in one of the two financial statements. The two statements are thus very closely linked. So, for example, a change in a balance sheet item will produce a change in either another balance sheet item or a change in a profit and loss account item. Thus, it is theoretically possible to do all one's double-entry directly into the financial statements (e.g. a cash sale: debit cash (balance sheet), credit sales (profit and loss account); or purchase a warehouse for cash: credit cash (balance sheet), debit warehouse (balance sheet) and so on). For the sake of maintaining proper accounting records (the T-accounts or equivalent) and in order to keep life more straightforward, we will not be exploring this possibility in any depth.

7.2.4 A simple extended trial balance

In the above example of Game Girl Ages Enterprises we used the accounting equations to get from the initial trial balance to the financial statements. Because the example is so simple, it is an appropriate point to show you what an **extended trial balance** for this business at the end of November would look like. The data from Figure 7.5 have been rearranged in Figure 7.6 to produce a very basic extended trial balance.

The extended trial balance in Figure 7.6 will take just a minute or two to get used to. First, note that the first three columns are identical to the initial trial balance we have worked with already. The first column lists all the account names and then the next two columns list the debit (Dr for short) and the credit (Cr for short) balances. Because our accounting entity in this case is so simple there are very few entries in the trial balance at the end of November. Spend some time to convince yourself you can see why the trial balance columns are like they are.

Then, the extended trial balance has three further pairs of columns. The adjustments column is where the end-of-period adjustments will go. Fortunately, in this example there aren't any – Chapters 8, 9, 10 and 11 will concentrate upon these.

EXTENDED TRIAL BALANCE at 30 NOVEMBER								
Account	Trial balance		Adjustments		Profit and loss		Balance sheet	
	Dr	Cr	Dr	Cr	Dr	Cr	Dr	Cr
Cash	$20						$20	
Loan								
Stock								
Expenses	$50				$50			
Creditors								
Sales		$70				$70		
P and L					$20			$20
TOTALS	$70	$70			$70	$70	$20	$20

Figure 7.6 A simple extended trial balance for Game Girl Ages Enterprises at end of November

So, the next two pairs of columns then itemize the profit and loss account and the balance sheet – maintaining the debits (Drs) and credits (Crs). You can check back to the accounting equations in Figure 7.5 to confirm that the figures are in the correct places.

Now, instead of looking back to the equations, simply look along the rows of Figure 7.6. You will see that each item in the trial balance has been taken and placed in its appropriate place within the final pairs of columns. Cash has been taken to the balance sheet, expenses and sales have been taken to the profit and loss account. And they maintain their character as debits or credits in the process. Next, the balancing figure in the profit and loss account is calculated – this is the profit or loss. In our case it is $20. But to retain the double-entry system this profit or loss must be balanced somewhere. In our case we have a profit – a debit entry in the profit and loss account. This must be balanced with a credit entry in the balance sheet. And all our columns now balance.

What has been happening here is a sort of arithmetic elegance. When we see more complex extended trial balances we will learn that arithmetically each row must satisfy the requirement that [Debits less credits in the trial balance and adjustment columns] = [Debits less credits in the profit and loss account and balance sheet columns]. Check that you can see this in our simple example.[1] It proves to be a useful rule-of-thumb in more complex extended trial balances.

This exposition provides you with the simplest of all extended trial balances – so simple it was hardly worth the effort. However, the extended trial balance will become especially helpful as we progress.

So let us now return to our examination of the categorization process from the initial trial balance. We have not forgotten that during our accounting equations we had cause to move the $50 purchase of games first to stock and then from stock to purchases (expenses). Why we do that relates to 'used-upness' and 'left-overness'. To get a better grip on these ideas we need to look at the **traditional accounting conventions** which attempt to codify what we have been doing here. We turn to these in the next section.

7.3 THE ACCOUNTING CONVENTIONS

Accounting, in its recording of the inputs and outputs of the focal organization, employs a number of basic *conventions* or *concepts*. They underlie all traditional accounting in commercial organizations and are generally employed in non-commercial organizations as well. These **accounting conventions** are:

- the money measurement convention;
- the entity convention;
- the going concern convention;
- the accrual or matching convention;
- the prudence or conservatism convention (including the conventions of 'cost' and 'realization');
- the consistency convention;
- the periodicity convention.

You have already met all of these in one form or another. For example, the first two conventions formed two of the four characteristics which we have been working with. And the 'periodicity' convention we have used to relate our accounting to specific accounting periods. We now need to examine these traditional **accounting conventions** a little more formally.

7.3.1 Money measurement

As a result of the money measurement convention, traditional financial accounting (a) recognizes only those flows into and out of the organizational subsystems which can be expressed in monetary terms and (b) records those flows in monetary terms. At a very broad level, we can say that traditional accounting is only concerned with items and/or events which have in the past, do in the present or will in the future involve a movement of cash.

7.3.2 Entity convention

The entity convention means that accountants see the world as a series of interacting systems (entities) and *account* for each of these systems individually. Frequently, though, we also have occasion to account collectively for a group of systems (for example, a group of companies) by **consolidating** the accounts of each of the smaller systems. That is, we account for each entity (say each company or local health authority) and then bring together (consolidate) all these accounts in order to account for the supra-entity – the group of companies or a national health service, for example.

The principal significance of the entity convention is that the organization and the participants of that organization are treated as *separate* accounting entities (i.e. as separate organizational systems). Thus, for example, in Chapter 5 we accounted for Bird Industries but learned nothing about the activities of the three main internal participants – Tweet, Wing and Feather – beyond their operations within Bird Industries. We would account separately for the organizational system of Tweet, Wing and Feather, treating each as an accounting entity which interacted with, *inter alia*, Bird Industries. Hence the results, sometimes puzzling to students, that owners' claims (e.g. shares) are a *liability* – owed by the focal organization to other organizational systems, the owners.

7.3.3 Going concern convention

Under the going concern convention we account for an organization on the assumption that it will continue in operation, substantially in its present form, for the foreseeable future. The importance of this convention lies in the fact that although financial statements traditionally contain the cost of assets and expenses (known as the *historic cost convention*, but see Chapter 16), the statements implicitly suggest some (albeit dubious) concept of *value*. That is, the balance sheet implicitly suggests a value for the organization, whilst the profit and loss account implicitly indicates the increase or decrease in this value (the profit or loss) in the last accounting period. This implicit suggestion is not a problem as long as the cost of the asset, for example, is a good indicator of its worth. This is often not the case (see Chapter 16), especially if the organization is about to cease through, for example, liquidation or bankruptcy. Notably, the cost of the machines, the inventory and especially the intangible assets which have been recorded in the financial statements are very likely to be higher than the organization could sell them for if it were to close down. However, if the financial statements were prepared on the basis that the organization was to cease at the accounting date, the assets would all be shown at their 'closing-down sale' value (known as **realizable value**), which is usually much less than their historical cost figures.

7.3.4 Accrual and matching convention

These two terms are sometimes used to mean two slightly different things although their effect is much the same. That is, both terms refer to the process of ensuring that the financial attributes of an event which *fall* in a particular accounting period are *recorded* in that period.

The **accrual convention** refers, basically, to the accountant's distinction between the receipt or payment of cash and the legal right or duty to receive or pay cash. Thus, we saw in Bird Industries, for example, that the receipt of materials in January (input to the operations subsystem) was treated as an *expense* in January because that was when the legal duty to pay the cash arose, even though the cash for the materials (output from the funds subsystem) may not have been paid to the supplier until February or later. Similarly, sales of goods in January (outputs from the operations subsystem) were counted as revenues in January because the legal right to receive the cash arose then, even though the cash from those sales (input to the funds subsystem) might not be received until a later accounting period.

The **matching convention** refers to the process of ensuring that costs are allocated to the accounting period in which the revenue they help generate is recorded. Thus, for example, the cost of fixed assets is spread, via depreciation, over the life of the asset in order to *match* the cost with the periodic revenues it help generate (see Chapter 9).

We have treated, and will continue to treat, the terms 'accrual' and 'matching' as synonymous, as they both have the effect of ensuring that the financial accounts of the period reflect what was 'earned' and 'consumed' in that period. However, because of the importance of the accrual or matching convention, it is worth dwelling on it for a moment. Consider the example given in Figures. 7.7 and 7.8 which, although a rather extreme case, illustrates the 'distortion' in the picture given by the financial accounts when the accrual concept is not employed.

If we assume that Figure 7.7 gives all the transactions of Alder Ltd, that all purchases and sales were paid for when they were made, then the accounts on a *cash basis* (i.e. non-accrual, receipts and payments accounts) would look as shown in the first part of Figure 7.8.

These cash-basis profit/loss figures make Alder Ltd look like a most up-and-down sort of business and it is very difficult to evaluate its profitability. In addition, Alder's balance sheet would show only the owners' claims (initial equity plus profit and loss account) and

---

Mr and Mrs Catkin started business as Alder Limited in 2003 with £25,000 of their own money (this makes them shareholders of this business). The following transactions relate to the first four years of Alder Ltd.

(i)   At the start of 2003, Alder Ltd bought:

- the leasehold for 20 years on a small industrial unit on a government-sponsored industrial estate for £10,000;

- a machine with a life of three years for £9,000; and

- enough raw materials for £30,000 worth of sales, for £6,000.

(ii) In 2003 sales of £15,000 were made.

(iii) In 2004 sales of £15,000 were made.

(iv) In 2005 another £12,000 of raw material was bought and sales of £15,000 were made.

(v)   In 2006 another machine was purchased to replace the original machine. The new machine cost £9,000. In addition, sales of £15,000 were made.

Figure 7.7 Alder Limited

cash (£15,000 in 2003, £30,000 in 2004, £33,000 in 2005 and £39,000 in 2006), as all the other things have been shown as consumed. The problem is, of course, that by preparing accounts on a cash basis we have failed to *match* the expenses with the revenues they helped to earn. That is, we have not allocated either the stock of raw materials or the leasehold or machine to the different accounting periods in which they were consumed.

If we prepare accounts on the *accrual* basis then the situation looks a lot different (see the second part of Figure 7.8). Now we have a more realistic description. Alder's level of activity has been constant and the organization's profit shows this. The balance sheet would now show, not just the owners' claims and cash, but the changes in the amount of the assets (which arises from the matching process) for the leasehold, the machine and the stock. This, hopefully, is a better indication of the value of the business. (How we actually calculate these figures on an accrual basis is covered in detail in the next few chapters.)

We have now spent rather a long time on the accrual or matching convention but not only is it crucial to the accounting activity, it also often causes problems for students. In addition (as we will see with, for example, bad debts, in Chapter 11) it frequently conflicts with what is called the 'prudence or conservatism convention' (see below).

7.3.5 Prudence or conservatism convention

The **prudence** or **conservatism convention** refers to the accountant's tendency to be cautious – cautious almost to the point of pessimism. This caution shows itself in the following 'unwritten rules'. In traditional financial accounting the accountant:

- *should not* record income until it is certain and/or realized ('realized' may be taken as meaning having received the cash);
- *should* anticipate all possible losses and record them as soon as she or he knows of their existence;
- when faced with a choice of asset or revenue valuations should choose the lowest; and
- when faced with different estimates of costs should choose the highest.

The effect of this is to try and ensure that profit and the value of the organization shown on the balance sheet are never overstated – to be cautious, prudent and conservative in one's accounting. Some of the practical demonstrations of the prudence convention include:

Alder Ltd – Profit and Loss Accounts (cash basis (receipts and payments))

	2003 £	2004 £	2005 £	2006 £
Receipts:				
Sales	15,000	15,000	15,000	15,000
Payments:				
Leasehold	10,000	–	–	–
Machine	9,000	–	–	9,000
Raw materials	6,000	–	12,000	–
	25,000	–	12,000	9,000
'Profit/(Loss)'	£(10,000)	£15,000	£3,000	£6,000

Alder Ltd – Profit and Loss Accounts (accruals basis)

	2003 £	2004 £	2005 £	2006 £
Income				
Sales	15,000	15,000	15,000	15,000
Expenditure:				
depreciation of leasehold	500	500	500	500
Depreciation of machine	3,000	3,000	3,000	3,000
Stock used	3,000	3,000	3,000	3,000
	6,500	6,500	6,500	6,500
Profit	£8,500	£8,500	£8,500	£8,500

Alder Ltd – Balance Sheets

	2003 £	2004 £	2005 £	2006 £
Liabilities				
Capital	25,000	25,000	25,000	25,000
Profit ad loss a/c	8,500	17,000	25,500	34,000
	£33,500	£42,000	£50,500	£59,000
Assets				
Leasehold	9,500	9,000	8,500	8,000
Machine	6,000	3,000	–	6,000
Stock	3,000	–	9,000	6,000
Cash	15,000	30,000	33,000	39,000
	£33,500	£42,000	£50,500	£59,000

Figure 7.8 Cash versus accrual accounts for Alder Limited

- do not record profit on a contract (e.g. building a new road) until the contract is finished and all expenses and revenue known for certain;
- value stock at the lower of either its costs or its net realizable value (i.e. the net proceeds of selling it);
- treat your intangible assets as expenses – you cannot be sure that your goodwill is *really* valuable or that your research and development will produce a new profitable product;
- if you think your product may be unsafe (e.g. you need to recall a motor car to replace a faulty part), account for it straight away.

You will see that if we allow the prudence convention to dominate, it will make a nonsense of much of the accounting we have so far considered. In particular, *prudence* frequently conflicts with *accrual*. If you look back at Alder Ltd, you will see that the preparation of a profit and loss account on the cash basis was far more prudent than the later accounts on the accrual basis. Again, if you think back to the going concern convention you will see that prudence would suggest we should always account at the value for which we could sell things – at the valuation that assumes that the worst (cessation of the business) will occur. This conflicts with the going concern convention. (In fact the prudence convention is worse than this, because in times of even moderate inflation, a valuation on a closing-down sale basis would possibly overstate buildings and land whose resale value would probably be greater than their cost. Prudence would suggest that the asset should be entered in the accounts at less than this, i.e. at the net book value if this was lower than the resale value.)

Therefore, to make any sense of our accounting, the accrual and going concern conventions dominate over the prudence convention. The prudence convention is then used to *temper* some of the effects of applying the accrual and going concern concepts. This conflict, and the lack of clarity about how the conflict should be resolved, is one of the main reasons given for considering accounting standards to be essential for the orderly practice of traditional financial accounting (see Chapter 14). For the time being, you should simply note that the 'practical demonstrations of the prudence convention' listed above are rarely, if ever, applied in quite such a thoroughly pessimistic way.

7.3.6 Consistency convention

The consistency convention concerns the accountant's attempt to ensure, as far as possible, that the financial statements of the focal organization are prepared on the same basis every year and are thus comparable through time so that sensible evaluation may be made by the participants about the focal organization's economic and financial performance. If the consistency convention were not applied then participants would be unable to assess whether changes in, for example, the reported profit figure or the value of net assets were the result of changes in economic circumstances or of changes in accounting practice. Thus, for example, as we shall see in the following chapters, different bases of stock valuation or depreciation lead to different figures in the profit and loss account and thus to different profit figures. Without the consistency convention (it is argued) an unscrupulous manager could use different accounting bases over time in order to manipulate the figures. (Perish the thought!)

7.3.7 Periodicity convention

The periodicity convention requires that financial accounts be drawn up for a specific, stated period (known in company law as the **accounting reference period**), usually one year. There may arise reasons why a focal organization may account for a period other than 12 months (e.g. following a merger between two companies with different accounting reference dates or a new business which starts up during the course of a year but wishes to have its accounting reference date or *year-end* as (say) the end of December each year for administrative convenience), but whatever the accounting reference period and the accounting reference date or year-end, the period to which the financial statements relate must be clearly stated.

The only real practical problems that occur with the periodicity convention are those which arise from its artificiality. That is, if a focal organization draws up its accounts to 31 December and an event occurs three minutes after midnight on 1 January, this event will not, strictly speaking, be included in that period's accounts. Had the event occurred four minutes earlier it would have been. This problem (of '*cut-off*') is overcome to some extent by the reporting of what are called *post-balance-sheet events* (these are touched upon in Chapter 14).

The other problem with periodicity is that it requires that the progress of the focal organization be considered in discrete 12-month chunks. It can be argued that the importance attached to the yearly financial statements has encouraged managers to think in yearly chunks to the potential detriment of the long-term welfare of the organization (and society!). This is widely argued and the possibility should always be borne in mind as a potential consequence of the accountant's conventions.

These seven accounting conventions together provide the basic framework within which traditional financial accounting takes place. They are not of themselves, however, sufficient to ensure a firm foundation for the production of financial statements. Simply because they are conventions will not ensure that all accountants will apply them, and the conflict between the conventions means that accountants might legitimately prepare financial accounts for similar organizations according to widely different bases. In addition, the conventions do not provide sufficient guidance on what information financial statements should disclose or on who has a right to these financial statements.

To attempt to overcome these problems governments lay down detailed rules in the form of law and the professional bodies of accountants seek to refine the law and reduce the conflict through such things as *accounting standards*. These are dealt with in Chapter 14.

7.4 THE ACCOUNTING CONVENTIONS AND THE BASIC CATEGORIES

Whilst a great deal of your future studies in accounting will be concerned with problems of defining, understanding and accounting for the basic categories of revenues, expenses, assets and liabilities, and claims, we need to say just a little more about them at this stage. Indeed, the fundamental level of moving from the trial balance to the basic financial statements is essentially a problem of operationalizing the accrual/matching and the prudence conventions within the periodicity convention. So, in this section, we will briefly review the main categories in the light of the accounting conventions. This will be brief – just enough to get us through the end-of-period adjustments in Chapters 8, 9, 10 and 11. We will then return and examine them in a little more detail in Chapters 12, 13 and 14.

7.4.1 What are revenues?

> **Hint**
>
> Turn to your library of annual reports and identify the revenues mentioned by your organizations. To what degree are they separated into different sorts of revenues? Do you think you understand what they are talking about? If not, ask your tutor in the next seminar.

Revenues, at least in your introductory studies, are generally fairly straightforward. For a company, revenues generally arise from **trade sales** (although these must be distinguished from sales of major assets – see Chapter 9). For a local government, revenues might include taxation receipts and grants from central government. For a charity, revenues might include donations. For a university, revenues will include students' fees and grants. But each will be treated in broadly the same way. They will be identified as revenues in the accounting period (periodicity convention) if they have been earned in that period (accrual or matching convention). The accounting period when the monies are actually received does not matter for the identification of the revenues – although it will be identified in the cashbook or debtors ledger, thus reflecting the other side of the accounting equation in the assets (cash or debtors).

The only real problems that arise with revenues at this stage concern the following:

- In some cases it becomes difficult to say when the revenues are actually earned. This is especially true on long-term contracts – for example, when the focal organization is building a factory or a railway for someone else. This will be spread over a number of accounting periods and so how do we establish which revenues should actually be recorded in which accounting periods? This will not detain us here. There is guidance from the accounting profession on this subject and we will touch upon it briefly in Chapters 12 and 14. It is a matter for your further studies.
- In some cases, although the focal organization has earned the revenues, we cannot be sure that the focal organization will actually be paid for them. Then we have to exercise the *prudence convention* by estimating *bad and doubtful debts*. This is examined in Chapter 11.

7.4.2 What are expenses?

Expenses raise many more problems – again arising principally from the need for matching. The first step in this is to determine whether an expenditure is a **capital expenditure** – in which case it is treated as an asset (see section 7.4.3 below) – or a **revenue expenditure** – in which case it will probably be treated as an expense in this accounting period. Assets are dealt with more carefully below and so we will just dwell upon **revenue expenditure** here.

There are a whole range of economic transactions that any focal organization may have which look like ordinary expenses (revenue expenditures). These might include such things as purchases of raw materials, wages and salaries, electricity and other energy costs, rent, advertising, accountants' fees, distribution costs and so on. They can, however, all cause us trouble! This is because of the matching convention. We only want our profit and loss account to show those things which have been consumed in the production of the revenues recorded for that accounting period. So purchases of raw materials, for example, are quite likely to include some materials that have left the factory as part of finished goods for sale (these we will call *cost of sales* – see Chapter 10) and some, at the accounting date, will be left over still to be used (these we will call *stock* or *inventory* – see Chapter 10). Similarly, the focal organization's recorded expenditure on energy, rent, wages and so on is very likely to consist of some payments in advance and some amounts still owing. These we refer to respectively as *prepayments* and *accruals* and they are covered in Chapter 8.

Furthermore, there will be expenses which the double-entry bookkeeping has missed altogether. These will be broadly of two sorts. First, there will be other expenditures which we seriously suspect that the focal organization will have to pay or has otherwise incurred but we cannot be too certain about them at the accounting date. These are known as **provisions**. These are dealt with below, along with something called 'reserves'. Second, where we have used a major asset but have not recorded its 'used-upness' we have a special case of the **provision**. This we call *depreciation*. Depreciation has a separate chapter to itself and is examined in detail in Chapter 9.

So, now you know. Treat 'expenses' with considerable respect. A significant amount of the end-of-period adjustment problem (the 'accounting decisions') is tied up with identifying and classifying expenditures and so much of what follows is concerned with just this issue.

7.4.3 What are assets?

If you look at any set of financial statements (we do not have to remind you to do so again, do we?) you will see three classes of **assets** referred to:

- fixed assets;
- current assets

(these two are sometimes referred to collectively as 'tangible assets'); and, less common, but at least as important:

- intangible assets.

You will recall from section 7.2 above that assets can be thought of as resources owned by the focal organization and available for economic use in this and/or future accounting periods. They are things which are owned by and useful to the focal organization.

Fixed and current assets are distinguished by the accounting system because it is thought that there is an essential difference in their natures. That is, they tend to differ in terms of (a) their expected lifespan, and (b) how they are used – the role they play – in the organisation. **Fixed assets** are:

- expected to last for more than one accounting period;
- provide the infrastructure for the operations subsystem – rather than being themselves converted into outputs from the operations subsystem (sales in a business) they provide the wherewithal for the current assets to be so converted;
- they contribute to the operations subsystem as a whole rather than in discrete 'bits';
- they exhibit more stability over time.

By contrast, **current assets** are shorter-term assets whose individual components (for example, the pieces of stock, the elements of cash, the individual debtors) can generally be expected to change over time and whose individual elements are directly concerned with (amongst other things) the process of the operations subsystems' conversion of inputs (e.g. purchases) into outputs (e.g. sales). They are not stable over time.

Figure 7.9 summarizes the main elements you can expect to find within the categories of fixed and current assets – we will meet them again in subsequent chapters.

Intangible assets seem to cause the worldwide accounting profession all kinds of trouble. They comprise resources which fit the basic definition of an asset but they are intangible – you cannot touch them or feel them. Every organization has intangible assets and they will consist of things like knowledge, skill, reputation, synergy, and other special advantages of the organization. No organization can operate unless it has some skilled employees, some knowledge about its products and markets, some ideas, some reputation for its products or services and so on. If your university were to privatize and become a company, its buildings and equipment would be a relatively small part of its value. The value would depend upon its reputation, the talent of its staff, where it was located, its

Fixed assets	Current assets
• Land	• Inventory (stock)
• Buildings (freehold and leasehold)	• Work-in-progress
• Machinery	• Debtors
• Equipment	• Prepayments
• Vehicles	• Bank accounts
• Furniture and fittings	• Cash

Figure 7.9 Different types of fixed and current assets

major breakthroughs, the quality of its students and so on. However, accountants seem reluctant to account for these intangible things – in part due to the prudence convention. And so only some of all the possible intangible assets are generally accounted for. The main ones you will find in company accounts are:

- Goodwill (At its simplest, this is the difference between the value of the business as a whole and the sum of the values of its component parts. It thus includes the company's reputation, experience, customer base, special experience and so on. It is usually only accounted for when one company buys another.)
- Research and development expenditure (The costs incurred in exploring new ideas and products. The knowledge so gained may be the most important economic resource of the company.)
- Brands (A company's brand name can be crucial to its success. Whilst Bloggs trainers may be every bit as good as Nike trainers people buy Nike for the name (the brand), which is not the case for Bloggs. The name 'Nike' is a major asset, the name 'Bloggs' is not.)[2]
- Software development costs (The physical asset of a piece of software is trivial – a few floppy disks perhaps; the real asset is what is on the disk and this can be the company's major asset.)
- Exploration costs (e.g. for energy or mining companies) (Costs incurred in discovering and exploiting new reserves of energy or resources – very similar in nature to research and development expenditure.)
- Patents, trademarks, licences and copyright (These arise when an organization buys or sells 'know-how'. These things become important assets of the organization.)

Intangible assets raise many problems for the accountant. In essence, the accountant will often be unsure whether there really is an asset – and so follow the matching convention – or whether the knowledge, or whatever, does or does not really exist – and so treat it as an expense, following the prudence convention. As a result, the accounting profession gives guidance on these things and we will return to this subject in Chapters 12 and 14.

7.4.4 What is a liability or claim?

Liabilities and claims can usefully be thought of as falling into three broad categories:
i   short-term (or 'current') liabilities;
ii   long-term (usually 'financing') liabilities;
ii   ownership claims.

Current liabilities relate to legal liabilities of the focal organization to either pay monies or deliver goods at some future time (usually within the next financial year). They are thus future-related and appear in the balance sheet. The most frequently seen element of current liabilities is creditors or trade creditors relating to the supply, to the focal organization, of various goods and services. In addition, however, there will be other current liabilities which may include: a bank overdraft (which is effectively a short-term loan from the bank), amounts owing to the taxation authorities for tax not yet paid, wages and salaries still owing at the accounting date, and amounts owing to those who finance the organization – these liabilities may be owed either in terms of interest or in terms of dividends. (Financing is dealt with below and in Chapter 12.) These liabilities arise from the application of the periodicity convention. Finally, we might also expect current liabilities to contain accruals which are estimated liabilities (and are covered in detail in Chapter 8) and provisions, which we have already met briefly and which we re-examine in the next subsection.

Long-term liabilities are usually financing liabilities: that is, money lent to the organization for provision of long-term infrastructure. Such financing usually takes the form of long-term loans and debentures which the focal organization has to service through annual payments of interest and longer-term repayments of principal. These are re-examined in Chapter 12.

Ownership claims relate to what the focal organization owes to those who actually own the organization. We saw in Chapter 3 how different forms of organization involved different forms of ownership claims. In the business sector, such claims will usually take the form of ownership capital and drawings (for the sole trader) and the form of share capital and dividends (for companies). These issues are complex and are examined in detail in Chapters 12, 13 and 14.

The broad classes of liabilities and claims that we will meet are summarized in Figure 7.10.

7.4.5 What is a provision?

The calculation of provisions is one of the major elements of the end-of-period adjustments. A **provision** is:

> the estimated financial amount of an expense relating to the present accounting period, the incidence of which is certain (or virtually certain) but the magnitude of

Current liabilities	Long-term liabilities	Ownership claims
• Trade creditors	• Bank loan	• Share capital (companies)
• Other creditors	• Debentures	• Partners' capital (partnerships)
• Bank overdraft	• Other loan stock	• Proprietor's capital (sole traders)
• Taxation		• Other amounts owned to the owners (e.g. accumulated profits and losses)
• Interest		
• Dividends		
• Other accruals (e.g. wages and salaries)		
• Other provisions		

Figure 7.10 Different types of liabilities and claims

which cannot be determined with certainty until some time in the future (e.g. when an invoice is received).

It is, therefore, something which will not emerge directly from the bookkeeping process or be apparent in the initial trial balance. An end-of-period adjustment will have to be made to identify and estimate the level of the expense we think has been incurred [Debit the appropriate expense account in the adjustment column of the extended trial balance] and establish this as a provision in the balance sheet to recognize the potential diminution in the value of an asset or the increase in a potential liability.

We will examine specific types of provisions for *depreciation*, *stock obsolescence* and *doubtful debts* in Chapters 9, 10 and 11 (respectively). But we can usefully introduce a general type of provision at this stage and, as a taster for the next four chapters, show how it works through the extended trial balance.

Let us go back to our nice simple example in section 7.2.3 – Game Girl Ages Enterprises. Turn back to Figure 7.3 to remind yourself of the basic transactions and Figure 7.6 to remind yourself of the trial balance and financial statements. Let us now imagine that we had offered a warranty or guarantee on the products we sold – 'Full refund if not 100% satisfied' was our motto. (Most companies and a considerable amount of sale of goods law operate such a system.) By the end of November, we had received no complaints, but can we be sure? That is, are we sure that we shall receive no complaints in the future relating to the sales which we have just made? No, we aren't, and so, following the prudence convention, we make a provision for the potential warranty costs. Let us assume that we know it is almost certain that one in ten games is duff. That is, we are nearly certain that one customer will want their money back and, because we didn't check too carefully where the games came from, we rather fear that one other game might be a bit dodgy. So, following prudence, let us imagine that we decide to make a warranty provision of $14 – an estimate (a guess) of our likely liability. How do we do this? Consider Figure 7.11.

The trial balance is exactly the same (except that an extra line for provisions now appears. But note that it has nothing against it in the trial balance columns). The first difference is in the adjustment columns. This is where we undertake the end-of-period adjustments and, in this case, **create a provision**. Think what we want to happen. We are

EXTENDED TRIAL BALANCE at 30 NOVEMBER								
Account	Trial balance		Adjustments		Profit and loss		Balance sheet	
	Dr	Cr	Dr	Cr	Dr	Cr	Dr	Cr
Cash	$20						$20	
Loan								
Stock								
Expenses	$50		$14		$64			
Creditors								
Sales		$70				$70		
Provisions				$14				$14
P and L (loss)						$6		$6
TOTALS	$70	$70	$14	$14	$70	$70	$20	$20

Figure 7.11 Extended trial balance for Game Girl Ages Enterprises at the end of November with a warranty provision

saying that we think we will have to pay out a further $14 in future accounting periods but we are not certain. So, to be cautious, we recognize that our expenses for the accounting period may be understated by the $14 we will have to pay to discharge our liability to our customer(s). So we need to increase our expenses by $14 and increase our liabilities by $14. This requires two entries in the adjustments column – to maintain the double-entry logic. Thus we [Debit expenses] and [Credit provisions]. The double-entry is maintained, the expenses are increased and a provision now exists. Most importantly, the two columns in the adjustment columns balance – this must be the case.

We now do our horizontal, row arithmetic (as we did in section 7.2.4 above) to see what effect this has on the financial statements. Cash stays the same, the rows for loans, stock and creditors stay blank. The expenses row has changed and so the amount shown in the profit and loss account must change. Following our earlier arithmetic this must be $64 (the debits less the credits in the trial balance and adjustment columns must equal the debits less the credits in the financial statements columns). If we now calculate our profit and loss account we find that $70 less $64 gives us a profit of $6. Our columns still total the same. To keep the double-entry intact, this new profit figure must be taken across to the balance sheet. And, following the row arithmetic logic, provisions must go into the balance sheet at $14. So the balance sheet now balances again.

So the rule with the extended trial balance is that each pair of columns – particularly the adjustment columns – must balance at all times and any item in the adjustment column must affect the financial statements. The rule with the provisions is that they increase expenses incurred in the accounting period and because they are not yet paid they are added to liabilities and shown as provisions[3] (i.e. they are a lot like creditors and, as we shall see, accruals).

7.5 SO WHAT ARE THESE END-OF-PERIOD ADJUSTMENTS?

Throughout this chapter we have (a) talked about categorizing the initial trial balance entries as a preparation for producing the basic financial statements and (b) continually raised little worries about many of the items that we want to categorize. So what is going on?

Well, we could simply go ahead and produce a set of financial statements based exclusively on our initial trial balance entries; but to do so would run counter to the accounting conventions. Why? Because very few of the items we have identified in our bookkeeping and initial trial balance will accurately reflect the periodicity and matching conventions. How can this happen after all the trouble we have taken with our bookkeeping? Broadly this problem arises because:

- There are some things which have changed over time but the accounting information system (AIS) has not prompted an equivalent bookkeeping entry. The most obvious of these relates to the use made of fixed assets during the accounting period.
- There are some things which have changed their nature during the accounting period but our AIS may not have picked them up. The most obvious relates to movements into and out of stock to represent 'cost of sales'.
- There are some things for which the AIS has not yet produced bits of paper and so our bookkeeping system does not yet know about them. The most obvious of these are sundry creditors and accruals and provisions. Some of these, also, can only be calculated at the end of the year. These might include amounts owing for taxation, electricity, dividends and interest.

● There are some things which the focal organization will have paid for in advance – what are known as *prepayments*. The amount (usually of a service) which is still owed to the focal organization at the end of the accounting period must be calculated. These prepayments often include things like rents and rates (where applicable).

So, to more closely approximate the 'true and fair' picture which a set of financial statements is supposed to provide, we must undertake a series of end-of-period adjustments. The difficulty, especially at this stage in your studies, is trying to remember which ones need such adjustments. Figure 7.12 summarizes the main ones on which we will concentrate and shows you where, in the next few chapters, we will deal with them.

SUMMARY

Working with the accounting information system to produce accounting records (the T-accounts) and, eventually, an initial trial balance involved much, usually implicit, use of accounting conventions. When we begin the process of moving from the initial trial balance to the financial statements we have to make these conventions much more explicit. This chapter was principally concerned with introducing new language and refining some ideas you have already met in order to prepare the way for the end-of-period adjustments through the extended trial balance.

We began by having a brief look at the basic financial statements – the profit and loss account and the balance sheet – so that we had some idea where we were trying to get to. Then we talked a little about some of the categories of 'things' that conventional accounting works with: the revenues and expenses, the assets and the liabilities. With these we were able to develop the accounting equations and to see how the trial balance, profit and loss account and balance sheet interact. With this information, we were then able to have our first look at a (very simple) extended trial balance.

ADJUSTMENTS	EXAMPLES	WHERE COVERED?
Accruals	Electricity, wages, sundry creditors, telephone	CHAPTER 8
Prepayments	Rent, rates, telephone	
General provisions	Warranties	
Depreciation	Fixed assets, machines, etc.	CHAPTER 9
Disposal of fixed assets	Fixed assets, vehicles, etc.	
Stock allocation	Inventory and cost of sales	CHAPTER 10
Stock valuation	How to determine cost of stock	
Stock provisions	Slow moving, obsolete	
Bad debts	Bankrupt customers	CHAPTER 11
Doubtful debts	Unreliable payers	
Reserves	Fixed asset replacement	CHAPTERS 12, 13, 14
Financing arrangements	Interest, dividends, movement on long-term stock and/or in owner's capital	
Ownership claims	Dividends, share issues, proprietor's drawings, partners' shares of profits, etc.	

Figure 7.12 A summary of end-of-period adjustments

But, even here, some potential difficulties were presenting themselves. So we then examined the accounting conventions in some detail and then revisited the basic financial statement categories in the light of these conventions. This now paves the way for the next few chapters wherein we will examine the end-of-period adjustments in some detail.

Key terms and concepts

The following key terms and concepts have featured in this chapter. You should ensure that you understand and can explain each one. Page references to definitions appear in the index in bold type.

- Accounting conventions
- Accounting equations
- Accrual and matching convention
- Assets
- Balance sheet
- Capital and revenue expenditure
- Consistency convention
- Current assets
- Current liabilities
- End-of-period adjustments
- Entity convention
- Expenses
- Extended trial balance
- Fixed assets
- Going concern convention

- Income statement
- Intangible assets
- Liabilities and claims
- Long-term liabilities
- Money measurement convention
- Ownership claims
- Periodicity convention
- Position statement
- Profit
- Profit and loss account
- Provisions
- Prudence convention
- Revenues
- Warranty provision

FURTHER READING

If you are continuing to follow the advice we gave earlier and are both collecting and studying annual reports as well as regularly monitoring one of the professional accountancy magazines then much of what has happened in this chapter will be fairly familiar to you. This is probably the best use of your time at this stage. Should you wish to reinforce any of this material, most good introductory textbooks will contain definitions and illustrations of these key terms. Should you wish to go a little further, then an introductory accounting theory textbook is your best choice. Something like Perks (1993) should provide you with entertainment and food for thought.

NOTES

1. So, for example, Cash: [$20 – $0 + $0 – $0] = [$0 – $0 + $20 – $0]
   or P and L: [$0 – $0 + $0 – $0] = [$20 – $0 + $0 – $20]
2. Of course, this also depends on whether you are concerned about the social policy of the organizations that own the brands. Nike has received a great deal of negative press coverage for their labour practices while Bloggs may not have. Indeed, if Bloggs provides a fair deal for its workers you may prefer them to Nike and this may be reflected in the subsequent value of their brand. See also Chapter 17 which starts to investigate these issues.

3. Those of you who have been following the logic closely may wonder why prudence does not encourage us to show the sales as lower rather than show expenses as higher. This would certainly be more logical and we have to say that we can think of no good reason why accounting convention tells us to do things this way. The same problem arises with bad and doubtful debts in Chapter 11. There is no logic to it that we can see.

Part III
End-of-period Adjustments and the Financial Statements

Accruals, prepayments and general provisions and an introduction to the production and format of the profit and loss account and balance sheet

8

Learning objectives

After studying this chapter you should be able to:

- understand how the periodicity convention gives rise to the need to make adjustments to accounting records in order to prepare financial statements;

- explain what is meant by accruals and prepayments;

- identify the more common accruals and prepayments;

- calculate the end-of-period adjustment for accruals and prepayments;

- explain and execute the bookkeeping necessary for accruals and prepayments;

- explain the meanings of opening balances and brought-forward figures;

- execute the bookkeeping necessary to account for opening balances;

- have an improved appreciation of provisions;

- define profit and loss account and balance sheet;

- use an extended trial balance to produce end-of-period adjustments and produce an initial set of financial statements;

- produce a simple set of financial statements in an accepted format;

- have some idea about the uses of the profit and loss account and balance sheet as well as a recognition of some of their limitations.

And from the appendices:

- explain and execute the bookkeeping for accruals, prepayments and general provisions entirely through T-accounts without using a trial balance.

8.1 INTRODUCTION

8.1.1 Chapter design and links to previous chapters

This chapter builds on the understanding you should have to date from the first two parts of the book. You should now be able to perform basic bookkeeping (the debits/inflows and the credits/outflows) so that you can produce T-accounts. In addition you should be able to balance these accounts off and produce a basic (initial) *trial balance*. And you know what an extended trial balance looks like and (basically) why we need one. (At least, you should know all this by now!) Later in this chapter (and in subsequent chapters) we will be working through further simple examples to give you practice in this basic bookkeeping. You also should have by now some idea about the basic *end-of-period adjustments*. These were summarized in the last chapter in Figure 7.12 and are rehearsed for you in Figure 8.1.

In order to find end-of-period adjustments easy to do there are several bits of information which you should keep in your mind. We have covered all this material in prior chapters, so thinking about and making sense of these elements is good revision. First, you should have a very clear picture in your mind of how various transactions are captured by the accounting information system (AIS) and entered in the T-accounts. Further, given the volume of transactions going through the accounts you should also have appreciated that an effective AIS will treat all similar transactions in a similar manner. Second, you should have a fairly clear idea of what information the financial statements should convey. If you recall, we would want the profit and loss account to show all revenue for a particular period (regardless of whether or not that revenue has had a cash transaction associated with it) less all expenses incurred (which may or may not be paid in cash) in that accounting period. In addition, the balance sheet should show a 'snapshot' of the financial position of the focal organization at a point in time (and should therefore include all things owed by and owing to the focal organization). You should also have realized that the need to prepare accounts arises from the periodicity convention and in applying this convention we are artificially splitting continuous business activity into segments of time.

The above elements of accounting (the bookkeeping, how the accounting data are recorded, the financial statements and applying the periodicity convention) would not cause any problems if you had the kind of business which you could halt at a point in time and let all the relevant accounting transactions 'catch up' with the underlying movements in cash, goods and services, and information. For the vast majority of businesses, however,

---

End-of-period adjustments are designed to:

1. Amend the accounting records for flows (events) which have taken place but have not yet been recorded (or fully recorded):

- e.g. goods and services received but not yet charged for (ACCRUALS);

2. Amend the accounting records for flows (events) which have not yet taken place (or not yet taken place fully) which we have recorded:

- e.g. services and goods paid for in advance (PREPAYMENTS, INCOME IN ADVANCE);

3. Amend accounting records for flows which we have recorded and which relate to things that have happened – but the recording is 'inaccurate':

- e.g. goods and services we have received and have recorded but which is partly used up (e.g. STOCK/INVENTORY, DEPRECIATION AND PROFIT OR LOSS ON DISPOSAL);

4. Amend the accounting records for flows which have occurred and which we have recorded but for which 'it is believed' a 'better' accounting treatment (recording or valuation) could be achieved:

- e.g. adjusting the 'picture' (e.g. STOCK VALUATION, PROVISIONS, ITEMS COVERED BY ACCOUNTING POLICY);

5. Amend the accounting records for reasons of the future or for caution (prudence):

- e.g. PROVISIONS AND RESERVES.

Figure 8.1 End-of-period adjustments – a recapitulation

at any particular end-of-year date (which may or may not be the end of the calendar year) there will be various events 'sloshing about' which are only half-recorded, not recorded or recorded in what is (with hindsight) an inappropriate way. End-of-period adjustments are designed to 'correct' the initial trial balance for these events, keeping in mind how the AIS has dealt with the events (or not) in the past and how it will (or will not) deal with these events in the future. In summary, what you need to have a clear idea of (in order to find end-of-period adjustments easy) is: how the AIS would have recorded a particular transaction, a clear picture of what has happened to the focal organization (that is, returning to our input/output model, what physical flows have taken place) and an idea of what the financial statements should look like in order to reflect the 'reality' of these organizational flows.

In this chapter we will be examining *accruals*, *prepayments* and, in a superficial way, *general provisions* as examples of end-of-period adjustments. In addition, we shall very briefly consider *income in advance* as another, less common, end-of-period adjustment.

This chapter is organized as follows. In the next section we will introduce and define the terms. It will also provide a summary of how the different items need to be treated. Section 8.3 will provide an example for you to work through to refine your bookkeeping skills and then will work with you to show how each of the relevant items from the example should be treated in an extended trial balance. Section 8.4 will provide an introduction to the format of a simple profit and loss account and balance sheet. The final section provides a summary of the chapter.

The chapter also has two short appendices. These are intended to help clarify things if you are struggling at all and the second appendix provides a different way of looking at the example from the chapter. The first appendix provides the bookkeeping for the worked example in the chapter. Appendix 8B rehearses the adjustments covered in this chapter but puts them directly through the T-accounts rather than using an extended trial balance. (Some people are taught this way and some folk find it easier.)

8.2 WHAT ARE ACCRUALS, PREPAYMENTS, INCOME IN ADVANCE AND GENERAL PROVISIONS?

You will recall from Chapter 7 that many (if not most) of the problems we face in accounting arise from the *periodicity* convention. That is, we divide the flow of time up into artificial accounting periods of, typically, one year. We then set about allocating the accounting events into those artificial periods of time. Unfortunately, most events do not neatly relate to yearly (or monthly or quarterly) periods of time. But because of the *accrual* or *matching* convention (which we met in Chapter 7) we do have to try and match events (and parts of events) to the time periods to which they relate and try and match the accounting events which involve costs to the periods in which the associated revenues were generated. Finally, you will recall that the *prudence* or *conservativism* convention encouraged the accountant to be (usually) pessimistic in his or her recognition of costs and revenues. We will see all of these at work in this chapter.

8.2.1 Accruals

Accruals[1] are a form of *creditor transaction* (look back to Figure 4.10). They arise when the focal organization has received and/or used some goods or services but not yet paid for them and has not yet been charged for them. If the focal organization receives some goods and services, and is charged for them, then we have a **normal creditor transaction**. The charge – via an invoice – is used to [Debit the purchases account] and [Credit the creditor account]. However, the accrual is slightly different and usually arises when:

- There is a lag between the supply of the goods or services and the receipt of an invoice and this lag spans the end of an accounting period. That is, for example, we account to 31 December each year, receive goods in December, but do not receive the invoice until January. These are known as **invoice accruals** or **sundry creditors**.
- The focal organization is charged in arrears for the use of a good or service. The most common example of this is heat and power for which a focal organization is charged (invoiced) retrospectively for what it has used. These are known more generally as **accruals** or **sundry accruals**.

What is distinctive about both of these accruals is that, at the balance sheet or accounting date, the bookkeeping system knows nothing about them. There has been no entry relating to the particular transaction in the T-accounts. We therefore rely upon the *accounting information system* (AIS) to 'capture' things like this. Part of the function of the AIS is to capture events – say the delivery of goods or services – so that the accounting system can record them appropriately. The practical effect of this is that, immediately after the balance sheet date (say 31 December), the accountant must be able to assess *all* the economic events which have occurred but about which they have no information. The AIS *should* have recorded all receipts/usage of goods and services, as they occurred, so that an estimate can be made of the bills which the focal organization will receive in the future – and the amount that would be due if the bills had been received on the balance sheet date.

The range of potential accruals is enormous. For our purposes we can concentrate on just a few of the most common ones. These, together with how we should treat them, are summarized in Figure 8.2.

The details of Figure 8.2 will become clearer as we work through an example later. However, at this stage, the principles should be fairly clear. Just one point deserves especial attention. You will note that we have not been overly fussy about terminology. That is, you may wish to have a series of individual accounts for individual accruals, or they may all go into an account called (say) sundry accruals, creditors and provisions. Or you may choose anywhere in between these extremes. It doesn't matter much – as long as you are clear that each relates to an expense of the period, which has not been fully recognized by the accounting system and is not, therefore, represented in the T-accounts. The confusion with 'provisions' will be somewhat clarified below and in the next few chapters.

8.2.2 Prepayments

Prepayments are simply *payments in advance*. They are *a form of the debtors transaction* (see Figure 4.10) except that, whereas in a normal debtors transaction the debtor still owes the focal organization money for goods already despatched, the **prepayment** transaction occurs when the debtor owes the focal organization the goods or services, having received the money in advance. Prepayments generally arise in one of two ways:

- Money is sent with the order for the goods or services before the balance sheet date but the goods or services are received after the balance sheet date. (You may have experienced this sort of transaction when you are ordering from a catalogue for mail order, for example.)

Transaction	How it arises	What to do about it	The bookkeeping	
			Debit (inflow)	Credit (outflow)
WAGES	Employees are paid in arrears. Payment is not immediate. Wages have not been paid for period before balance sheet date	The amount owing will be known at balance sheet date or very soon thereafter. Put through wages accrual for actual amount	Wages (goods and services account)	Accruals and sundry creditors (for example)
SUNDRY CREDITORS	Goods and services delivered and/or used but not invoiced by balance sheet date	Wait for invoice for actual amount or estimate likely amount. (An estimate would make it a provision – see below)	Appropriate goods and service account	Sundry creditors (or provisions)
ELECTRICITY, GAS AND OTHER UTILITIES (SUCH AS WATER)	The utility company normally charges for actual usage in arrears. It is unlikely that bills will relate exactly to the accounting period	Wait for invoice or estimate the likely amount. (An estimate would be a provision)	Electricity (or power or heat and light)	Accruals and sundry creditors (or provisions) for example
TELEPHONE	Many telephone companies charge in advance (see below) for the rental of the line and in arrears for the actual calls made. It is unlikely that bills will relate exactly to the accounting period	Wait for invoice or estimate the likely amount. (An estimate would be a provision)	Telephone	Accruals and sundry creditors (or provisions) for example

Figure 8.2 Examples of simple accruals and their treatment

- Money is paid in advance for goods or services which then are delivered in regular instalments but not all of the outstanding goods or services have been delivered by the balance sheet date. The most common example you will have met is the payment in advance for your accommodation – your rent – when the service – the delivery of your accommodation – then occurs regularly after the payment.

The distinctive feature of both of these transactions is that although the bookkeeping system will have recorded the initial transaction involving the movement of cash (so in this way prepayments are quite different from accruals), the accountant has to rely upon the AIS to remind them that all the goods and services relating to that transaction have not been received. As a result, some end-of-period adjustment will have to be made to more accurately reflect the situation. In brief (and the example later in this chapter will reinforce this point), the original entry in the books of account would be [Debit the expense account] and [Credit the cash account]. In order to 'correct' this entry so that the financial statements tell the correct 'story' it is necessary to [Debit the prepayments account] and [Credit the expense account] (see also Figure 8.3). The end result of these entries is that the expense account will only show expenses incurred in the current period and that there will be an additional asset account in the balance sheet (the prepayments account) which represents the fact that in the next accounting period the focal organization is entitled to receive goods and services without having to pay for them.

There are potentially many prepayments that a focal organization may be involved in. For our purposes, we can concentrate upon the more common ones. Some of these are summarized in Figure 8.3.

Transaction	How it arises	What to do about it	The bookkeeping	
			Debit (inflow)	Credit (outflow)
RENT	Landlords invariably want rent in advance. Period covered by the rent is unlikely to match exactly to the balance sheet date	Calculate the amount of service still due to the focal organization. This is a 'debtor' – the prepayment of rent	Prepayments (or sundry debtors)	Rent (to reduce the rent 'usage')
RATES (AND OTHER LOCAL CHARGES FOR SERVICES IN ADVANCE)	Local government may require payment in advance on a monthly, quarterly or yearly basis. The service is then assumed to be delivered regularly thereafter	Calculate the amount of service (on a time basis) still owing to the focal organization	Prepayment	Rates (or whatever) to reduce 'usage'
TELEPHONE	Many telephone companies charge in advance for the rental of the line (but see Figure 8.2 for actual calls made). It is unlikely that bills will relate exactly to the accounting period	Look at last telephone bill and allocate line rental on a time basis. Calculate line rental still owing to the focal organization	Prepayments	Telephone (to reduce line rental charge)
INSURANCE etc.	Payment for the year ahead	Calculate on time basis amount still owing to focal organization	Prepayments	Insurance etc.
SERVICE CONTRACTS	It is common to pay a maintenance contract for the coming year on equipment (e.g. so that one can call out a service engineer to fix the photocopier)	Allocate on a time basis the outstanding period of the contract and calculate the value of the service owing	Prepayments	Service contracts

Figure 8.3 Examples of simple prepayments and their treatment .

Much of the detail of these prepayments will become clearer when we do an example to illustrate them. All you need to concentrate upon at this stage is that we are trying to allocate payments and goods and services to the accounting periods to which they relate. With prepayments, we have payments which relate to future accounting periods and so, at the balance sheet date, the accountant has to calculate how much relates to the current accounting period and how much relates to future accounting periods.

8.2.3 Income in advance

End-of-period adjustments involving income in advance are much less common than accruals and prepayments. Income in advance is important, however, for particular industries. Basically, income in advance arises where a focal organization receives cash prior to delivering goods and services. At any year end, therefore, there will be monies held by the organization which relate to goods and services to be delivered in the next accounting period. Industries where income in advance is likely to arise are the airline industry (airline tickets are usually prepaid), theatres (where people will have prepaid to see a particular show) and other situations where deposits are taken (for example, in hotels and conference centres). The principles are the same for income in advance as for the other end-of-period adjustments. Given that the accounting information systems will have recorded all income in the same way, [Debit the cash account] and [Credit the sales account], it is necessary to take out of the sales account those sales which relate to a future accounting period. That is, for the income-in-advance transactions the delivery of goods and services will take place in a future accounting period so the income associated with these transactions should properly be recognized in the future accounting period. The accounting required to ensure that the T-accounts show this 'reality' is [Debit the sales account] and [Credit the income in advance account]. The income-in-advance account ends up on the balance sheet and is a liability account. You could think of it as the obligation to provide goods and services in the future for which you will not receive a cash payment (because the cash was received in the current accounting period).

8.2.4 General provisions

General provisions seem to be popping up all over the place don't they? We introduced them in some detail in the last chapter (in section 7.4.5). We are only reintroducing them here for completeness. You will have noticed already that when we are calculating accruals, we are sometimes not sure what the exact amount of the accrual should be. We therefore make an estimate of the amount involved. At that point, the accrual becomes, strictly speaking, a provision. So the whole issue of accruals and provisions begins to blur somewhat. Do not worry, because the principles are still the same – even if the terminology gets rather random at times.

The practical problem is that in any organization it is highly unlikely that the AIS will have spotted every potential accrual and sundry creditor or that the accountant can be bothered calculating everything to the nearest few pounds. So, to be on the safe side, the accountant will throw in a few provisions to cover the stuff they are not too sure about – for warranties, for goods which might be returned to the focal organization, for the upgrading of our machines that will be necessary when the health and safety inspectors catch up with the focal organization's lax standards, for the employees' wage rise for the last three months which is still being negotiated – all the things we have forgotten to include.[2] More formally, these are situations which are not yet accounting transactions but will be, or might be, in the near future *but* for which the liability will relate to this accounting period – not the one into which the transaction actually falls.

We will see these again, briefly in the worked example below and in more detail in the next few chapters. You will (hopefully) come to notice that, in terms of how we treat them and their effect on the financial statements, accruals and provisions have a lot in common.

Well, that is quite enough chat for the time being! Let's get on with some bookkeeping and accounting and see how these things work in practice.

8.3 A WORKED EXAMPLE WITH ACCRUALS, PREPAYMENTS AND PROVISIONS

8.3.1 A word before we start

The example below is designed to do four things:

i   reinforce your bookkeeping ability;
ii reinforce your ability to construct an initial trial balance;

iii develop your ability with an extended trial balance; and

iv introduce the new material on accruals, prepayments and provisions and illustrate how it works.

It is therefore very important that you *do* work through the example as requested to make absolutely sure you can handle this material.

However, we are also going to take this opportunity to hit you with another piece of new information. So far, the examples we have considered have been related to *new* organizations which are just setting up and getting started. What is different about these situations? Well, there are no 'brought-forward figures'. That is, each example has started with a 'clean sheet of paper'. What happens when we are accounting for a *continuing* organization? Well, each accounting period starts with the things 'left over' from the previous accounting period. Where do we find the 'things left over from the previous accounting period'? *If you cannot answer this question with confidence then you had better start working a bit harder and go back to the start of the book and begin again. This is very basic!* (If you need to check your answer it is in the endnotes).[3]

So, what does this all mean? It means that a continuing focal organization *does have* some 'opening balances'. That is, the T-accounts begin on the first day of the new accounting period with a **balance brought down**. These balances obviously come from the balance sheet at the end of the previous accounting period. So, the very first thing to do when accounting for a continuing organization is to take each and every item from the last balance sheet and bring them into the T-accounts of the new accounting period as 'opening balances'. (If this is still a problem, look back to Figure 6.4 which shows this in diagrammatic form.)

This is the new information we want to demonstrate in the following worked example.

8.3.2 Yothu Yindi Ltd: the information

Yothu Yindi Ltd have traded for a number of years as consultants on Aboriginal land rights and they have asked you to prepare their financial statements for the year ended 31 December 2001. They operate from offices which they rent. Their balance sheet for 2000 is given in Figure 8.4.

Hint

We have discussed balance sheets but this is the first you have seen in the book. You should, however, have seen several by looking through the library of annual reports which you are building up. Figure 8.4 is a very simple balance sheet. It lists the current assets (you know what those are) and the current liabilities (you also know those). It then shows 'net assets', which are the assets (including the fixed assets if there were any) less the current liabilities. These are shown as balancing against 'owners' or shareholders' funds' in the second part of the balance sheet. If you are not yet comfortable with these we will be examining them in more detail in Chapters 12 and 13.

You discover that Yothu Yindi Ltd do not keep regular accounting records but they provide you with the following information:

Yothu Yindi Ltd: Balance Sheet at 31 December 2000 (all figures are in dollars)			
FIXED ASSETS	There are no fixed assets		0
CURRENT ASSETS:			
Trade debtors		50,000	
Prepayments:	Rent	20,000	
	Goods	10,000	
	Rates	6,000	
	Telephone	1,000	
Cash		30,000	
		117,000	
CURRENT LIABILITIES:			
Trade creditors		60,000	
Sundry creditors		10,000	
Accruals and provisions	Wages	2,000	
	Electricity	400	
	Gas	200	
	Telephone	500	
		73,100	43,900
NET ASSETS			$43,900
REPRESENTED BY:			
Share capital			40,000
Profit and loss account			3,900
SHAREHOLDERS'/OWNERS' FUNDS			$43,900

Figure 8.4 Yothu Yindi Ltd balance sheet as at 31 December 2000

1. *Sales and trade debtors:* The company has been paid by all the debtors owing at 31 December 2000. The company made sales during the year of $500,000. They have been paid for $470,000 worth of these (this year's) sales.
2. *Purchases and trade creditors:* The company has paid all the trade creditors owing at the end of the last financial year. They have made trade purchases during the year of $200,000 and have paid for $165,000 of these. The company use up all their purchases during the year and have no closing stock. (This is a matter considered in more detail in Chapter 10.)
3. *Rent:* The offices are rented and the rent of $120,000 per annum is paid for the year in advance in March each year.
4. *Goods from sundry payments in advance:* All the goods for which the company paid in advance were received during 2001. (They had previously been paid for but had not been recorded as a purchase.) There are goods paid for in advance but not yet delivered of $1,000 at the end of 2001.
5. *Rates and utilities:* The figure for 'rates' relates to the charge for using local water and sewerage systems. The charge is $24,000 per annum charged in advance and due on 1 April each year.
6. *Telephone:* Rental of the telephone line is charged quarterly in advance at $6,000 per annum on 1 March, 1 June, 1 September and 1 December. Telephone calls are charged in arrears on the same dates. It is estimated that the company makes $6,000 worth of phone calls a year. The company pays the telephone bills immediately they are received.
7. *Sundry creditors:* In addition to the trade creditors, all the previous year's sundry creditors invoiced the company and were paid. All invoices were correctly estimated

by the company. At 31 December 2001, the company estimate that they have received goods on credit to the value of $2,000 which have not yet been invoiced.

8. *Wages:* Wages are paid to employees one month in arrears (i.e. wages for work in June is paid at the end of July). The annual wage bill is $24,000.

9. *Electricity and gas:* These are charged quarterly in arrears on the same dates as the telephone charges. The bills are paid immediately they are received. The bills for 2001 are $4,800 for electricity and $2,400 for gas.

You are required to produce the T-accounts and initial trial balance for Yothu Yindi Ltd for 2001. Do it now and then check you answer against that shown in Appendix 8A at the end of this chapter. Do not try and calculate the end-of-period adjustments for the end of 2001 just yet.

Hints

a   Bring your opening balances down into trade debtors, rent, goods (payments in advance), rates, etc. accounts.

b   Put through all the transactions you are told about – remembering the double-entry. (If in doubt think about what is really happening and think about the inflows and outflows.)

c   Just take what is in the accounts off to the initial trial balance. The adjustments will be done there.

Well, that wasn't too bad, was it? Was it? If it was, then check back through the answer given in Appendix 8A. If this still causes problems then you really should (i) work back through the book, (ii) go and work through any computer-assisted learning (CAL) packages your college has on this and (iii) ask your tutor for some help. You should be able to do this by now.

You should have ended up with an *initial trial balance* which looked something like Figure 8.5. Now, we can turn to the end-of-period adjustments and see how we treat these accruals and prepayments in the question.

8.3.3 Yothu Yindi Ltd – the end-of-period adjustments

We might as well follow the order of the items given in the question itself:

1 and 2. Sales, purchases, debtors and creditors: There are no end-of-period adjustments that affect these in this question (but see Chapters 10 and 11).

3. Rent: The initial trial balance is showing an amount of $140,000 for rent for the year. The annual charge is $120,000 as given in the question and this is the amount that must be shown in the profit and loss account. What has happened? There was a prepayment of $20,000 in the opening accounts. This was cash paid last year but which related to 2001 usage. In March, $120,000 is paid but this relates to a whole 12 months – including two months of the next accounting period. So the charge for 2001 is the opening $20,000 plus the paid $120,000 less the amount that relates to next year, $20,000 (two-twelfths of $120,000). This leaves a prepayment of $20,000. The TB must be adjusted. The amount shown against the rent figure needs to be reduced to $120,000 and a *prepayment* must be created. So, the adjustment column of the extended TB in Figure 8.5 must show a credit

INITIAL TRIAL BALANCE at 31 DECEMBER 2001								
Account	Trial balance		Adjustments		Profit and loss		Balance sheet	
	Dr	Cr	Dr	Cr	Dr	Cr	Dr	Cr
Debtors	30,000							
Rent	140,000							
Pay in advance	1,000							
Rates	30,000							
Telephone	12,500							
Creditors		35,000						
Sundry creditors		2,000						
Wages	22,000							
Electricity	4,400							
Gas	2,200							
Share capital		40,000						
Profit and loss a/c		3,900						
Sales		500,000						
Purchases	212,000							
Cash	126,800							
TOTALS	580,900	580,900						

Figure 8.5 An initial trial balance for Yothu Yindi Ltd at the end of December 2001

of $20,000 against the rent figure and a debit of $20,000 against (a newly created row called) Prepayments.[4] (We will call this *Adjustment i.*)

4. Goods from sundry payments in advance: You will recall from Figure 8.3 that usually no adjustments are necessary for this item. Think this through. It is the case here.

5. Rates and utilities: The opening balance sheet showed a prepayment of $6,000 for rates. This, the question tells us, relates to the first three months of the accounting year (i.e. $2,000 per month). In April, the company pays its rates bill of $24,000 for the coming 12 months – three months of which relate to the next accounting period. The charge for the year is therefore the initial $6,000 plus $24,000 paid in April less the $6,000 that relates to 2002. This gives us a charge to be shown against the rates for $24,000 and a prepayment of $6,000. To achieve this, in the adjustment column we credit rates ($6,000) and debit prepayments ($6,000). (*Adjustment ii.*)

6. Telephone: The telephone is tricky because there is a prepayment (for the rental) and an accrual (for the calls) in the same figure. It is not necessary to go through all the detail above. Let's keep it simple now. The company pays a bill for (approximately) $3,000 on 1 December 2001. Of this, $1,500 is a payment in advance for one quarter's rental of the line ($6,000 ÷ 4), and thus, whilst $500 is for December, $1,000 is a prepayment for 2002. A prepayment needs to be created being credit telephone, debit prepayments (*Adjustment iii*). The other half of the December payment is for telephone calls in the quarter before 1 December. So, at the balance sheet date, the company owes the telephone company for all the calls it has made during December 2001. How much is this? We do not know! So we make an estimate of $500 because that seems to be the monthly call level in the rest of the year ($6,000 ÷ 12). So we create an accrual/provision by debiting telephone ($500) and crediting accruals and provisions ($500). (*Adjustment iv.*)

7. Sundry creditors: The information in the question was sufficient for the bookkeeping on this issue to be done at the time. So this already *is* an accrual and so no more needs to be done.

8. Wages: We know that the wage bill for the year should be $24,000. We know that wages are paid monthly in arrears ($24,000 ÷ 12 = $2,000) so we can surmise that we still owe our employees their wages for December of $2,000. (We can confirm this because we started the year with a wages accrual of $2,000. We will ignore the fact that the employees do not seem to have a rise this year!) So the accrual is created by debiting wages with $2,000 and crediting accruals with $2,000. *(Adjustment v.)*

9. Electricity and gas: The question tells us that we have not been charged for the electricity and gas we have used in December. Therefore we have to make an estimate. Our best estimate is electricity $400 ($4,800 ÷ 12) *(Adjustment vi)* and gas $200 ($2,400 ÷ 12) *(Adjustment vii)*. We debit the expense accounts and credit accruals.

When all this is done, the extended trial balance looks like Figure 8.6. Check carefully and make sure you can see where every entry has come from and goes to. Check and make sure you know why each item has been treated as it has. Confirm that you know why the adjustment columns balance.

Initial trial balance at 31 December 2001								
Account	Trial balance		Adjustments		Profit and loss		Balance sheet	
	Dr	Cr	Dr	Cr	Dr	Cr	Dr	Cr
Debtors	30,000							
Rent	140,000			(i) 20,000				
Pay in advance	1,000							
Rates	30,000			(ii) 6,000				
Telephone	12,500		(iv) 500	(iii) 1,000				
Creditors		35,000						
Sundry creditors		2,000						
Wages	22,000		(v) 2,000					
Electricity	4,400		(vi) 400					
Gas	2,200		(vii) 200					
Share capital		40,000						
Profit and loss a/c		3,900						
Sales		500,000						
Purchases	212,000							
Cash	126,800							
Prepayments: Rent			(i) 20,000					
Prepayments: Rates			(ii) 6,000					
Prepayments: Tel.			(iii) 1,000					
Accruals: Tel.				(iv) 500				
Accruals: Wages				(v) 2,000				
Accruals: Elec.				(vi) 400				
Accruals: Gas				(vii) 200				
TOTALS	580,900	580,900	30,100	30,100				

Figure 8.6 An extended trial balance with adjustments for Yothu Yindi Ltd as at end of December 2001

8.3.4 Yothu Yindi Ltd: the financial statements

Having done all this, it is a relatively easy matter to produce the profit and loss account and the balance sheet. There are really only two things to remember:

(i) what goes into which statement (and you really should be clear on this by now. If not – yet again – go back and rework the earlier material until it is second nature);

(ii) that each row of the extended trial balance must work arithmetically taking (a) the initial trial balance columns and the adjustments columns and (b) the financial statements columns and remembering that debits and credits are arithmetically opposite (if this is not clear, look back to Chapter 7, section 7.2.4 and read through it again).

If you are clear on this, then Figure 8.7 should hold no surprises.

All that we have done in Figure 8.7 is sum the rows across, taking the profit and loss account items (the used-up things) to the profit and loss account and the balance sheet (left-over) items to the balance sheet.

Spend a little time familiarizing yourself with Figure 8.7. We can probably summarize the main elements that you must take from this exercise as follows:

Extended trial balance at 31 December 2001								
Account	Trial balance		Adjustments		Profit and loss		Balance sheet	
	Dr	Cr	Dr	Cr	Dr	Cr	Dr	Cr
Debtors	30,000						30,000	
Rent	140,000			20,000	120,000			
Pay in advance	1,000						1,000	
Rates	30,000			6,000	24,000			
Telephone	12,500		500	1,000	12,000			
Creditors		35,000						35,000
Sundry creditors		2,000						2,000
Wages	22,000		2,000		24,000			
Electricity	4,400		400		4,800			
Gas	2,200		200		2,400			
Share capital		40,000						40,000
Profit and loss a/c		3,900						3,900
Sales		500,000				500,000		
Purchases	212,000				212,000			
Cash	126,800						126,800	
Prepayments: Rent			20,000					
Prepayments: Rates			6,000					
Prepayments: Tel.			1,000				27,000	
Accruals: Tel.				500				
Accruals: Wages				2,000				
Accruals: Elec.				400				
Accruals: Gas				200				3,100
Profit/loss for year					100,800			100,800
TOTALS	580,900	580,900	30,100	30,100	500,000	500,000	184,800	184,800

Figure 8.7 A full extended trial balance with adjustments for Yothu Yindi Ltd at end of December 2001

- The accounts down the left-hand side represent the T-accounts that you used for the question *plus* the new 'accounts' – or headings if you prefer – that we had to open to capture the new categories of things created by the end-of-period adjustments. These were prepayments accounts, accrual accounts and the profit and loss for the year. Do note that the initial trial balance columns only have figures against those accounts which represented T-accounts. (We *know* this is obvious but it as well to be sure!)
- Go down the trial balance row by row and see what happened:
  - Debtors: nothing happened to these so there are no adjustments and the same figure appears (as an *asset*) in the balance sheet.
  - Rent: this was an inflow of $140,000 – from which has been taken an outflow of $20,000 (which has been put into the debit column of the adjustments to form the prepayment) – and the result is a total *expense* of $120,000 in the profit and loss account.
  - Payments in advance: nothing has happened to these and so they have gone directly to the balance sheet because they are an *asset*.

  And so on. You should try and learn to *read* a trial balance in this way, following slowly and carefully what has happened to the numbers.
- Next we can look at the profit and loss account and balance sheet and see what is happening here. In the profit and loss account we have one credit/outflow (sales) and against it we have a whole bunch of inflows/debits which are the expenses for the period. The sales (revenue) less the expenses in the accounting period produces the profit or loss for the period. *The profit and loss account contains the revenues and expenses for the accounting period and shows the resultant profit or loss for that period.* In the balance sheet we have some debits, which are different kinds of assets (different types of current assets in this case) and some credits which are going to be types of liabilities, plus the profit and loss account.[5] Thus we have a balance sheet which shows the assets owned by the focal organization – including amounts owed to the focal organization and the liabilities and owners' claims owing by the focal organization. (See the first few pages of Chapter 7 if you need a revision of the definitions of the profit and loss account and balance sheet.)

The actual effect of these additional calculations in order to take account of the accruals and prepayments is relatively small (although they need not be). The purpose of the calculations is, however, a sort of combination of (a) our attempts to satisfy the matching or accrual concept and (b) our attempts to ensure that the balance will show us – as nearly as possible – what the focal organization owes (the additional accruals and provisions) and what it is owed (the additional prepayments). Although accruals and prepayments may get larger and a little more complicated, the principles we have met in the foregoing example will not really change.

The basic ideas behind provisions will, also, not change much. However, the provision will not always look as simple and straightforward as we may have suggested here. We will dwell on such matters in the following chapters.

Before doing that, however, let us return to Yothu Yindi Ltd and finish off their financial accounts. (Finish off? You thought we had finished, didn't you? Well, not quite.)

8.4 LAYING OUT THE PROFIT AND LOSS ACCOUNT AND BALANCE SHEET

In Figure 8.7 we saw a profit and loss account and balance sheet for Yothu Yindi Ltd. This was not the first time we had seen some sort of profit and loss account and/or balance sheet (look back to Figures 7.5, 7.6, 7.8 and 8.4). But this is the first time we have put together fairly complicated versions of these statements more or less from scratch. The form of the profit and loss account and balance sheet in Figure 8.7 is really rather random. That is, the order in which things appear is largely haphazard and dependent upon the order in which we constructed the initial trial balance. Furthermore, we did not, in Figure 8.7, bring together the different categories of things (revenues, expenses, assets, liabilities and claims) on which we have lavished so much attention in recent pages.

So, to round it all off, we can put the Yothu Yindi figures into something that an accountant would find more recognizable as a profit and loss account and balance sheet. That is, we can rearrange the figures to produce a *basic* set of **financial statements**. One way of showing these is presented in Figure 8.8.

YOTHU YINDI LTD: PROFIT and LOSS ACCOUNT FOR THE YEAR ENDING 31 DECEMBER 2001
(all figures are in dollars)

SALES		500,000
less **PURCHASES (or cost of goods sold)**		(212,000)
GROSS OR TRADING PROFIT		288,000
EXPENSES:		
Rent	120,000	
Rates	24,000	
Telephone	12,000	
Wages	24,000	
Electricity	4,800	
Gas	2,400	
		(187,200)
NET PROFIT FOR THE PERIOD		$ 100,800

Yothu Yindi Ltd: Balance sheet at 31 December 2001
(all figure are in dollars)

FIXED ASSETS	There are no fixed assets		0
CURRENT ASSETS:			
Trade debtors		30,000	
Prepayments:	Rent	20,000	
	Goods	1,000	
	Rates	6,000	
	Telephone	1,000	
Cash		126,800	
		184,800	
CURRENT LIABILITIES:			
Trade creditors		35,000	
Sundry creditors	Wages	2,000	
Accruals and provisions	Electricity	2,000	
	Gas	400	
	Telephone	200	
		500	
		40,100	
			144,700
NET ASSETS			**$144,700**
REPRESENTED BY:			
Share capital			40,000
Profit and loss account			104,700
SHAREHOLDERS'/OWNERS' FUNDS			**$144,700**

Figure 8.8 Basic set of financial statements

8.4.1 A simple profit and loss account

Figure 8.8 shows the simplest way of laying out a profit and loss account. It starts with revenues (in this case sales), pulls together most of the expenses of the accounting period (after calculating accruals and prepayments and, later, we shall see, other provisions) and then shows a profit (or loss) for the period. The only really odd thing in Figure 8.8 is the separation of purchases (or, more accurately, **cost of goods sold**) from other expenses in order to show a **gross** or **trading profit**. Strictly speaking, a profit and loss account for a business is supposed to show two separate sections (in fact we will learn later on that it actually ends up having three separate sections). These two sections are the **trading account** in which the **gross profit** is calculated, and the **profit and loss account** where the **net profit** is calculated. Strictly speaking, therefore, the first statement in Figure 8.8 should be called the *trading and profit and loss account*. The gross profit – which is calculated in the trading account – is the profit (it should rarely, if ever, be a loss) is the revenue earned from trading, less the actual **direct costs** of selling those goods or services. The resultant **cost of goods** (or **services**) **sold** includes the cost of the materials, any manufacturing costs the focal organization has undertaken plus other direct costs such as packaging each product and transporting it to the place of sale. The remaining expenses therefore become what are often called the **indirect costs** or **overheads** of the business for that period.

The reasons for going to this trouble to separate out these different bits of the trading and profit and loss account are primarily a result of historic habit – but there is a useful reason behind it. By making this distinction between gross and net profit one can easily see where the expenses of the business are located. If the business is making a gross loss it is doing something very wrong – its selling price is too low or it has a silly level of direct costs. If a business is making a trading profit but a net loss, then perhaps its overheads are too high. This distinction helps tell us something about the financial success of the business. This is useful to investors and bankers (whom will shall meet in more detail later on in Chapters 14 onwards) and it is also useful to the management of the focal organization for purposes of **control**. So, we learn something here. Financial accounting has *at least* two uses – one for external parties and one for internal parties. (In earlier chapters we met other possible uses for the financial accounts we are preparing. Can you remember any of them?[6])

Having said all this, the important thing to learn, for the time being, is the basic layout of the profit and loss account as given in Figure 8.8. This is the format we will stick with from now on. (Do note, however, that this format of the profit and loss account does not require that we go back and restructure the way in which we put together the profit and loss account columns in the extended trial balance (as shown in Figure 8.7). The layout in the extended trial balance is simply an arithmetic convenience. The layout shown in Figure 8.8 is the format of an *actual* profit and loss account. This is the sort of thing you will see in any set of published financial statements *when* you consult them.)

The other point to make at this stage is that although we will continue to show *cost of goods sold* and *gross profit* in the profit and loss accounts we use in the forthcoming chapters, we will not make too much fuss about the *trading account* itself. A trading account *can* be shown in enormous detail but this concern with detail is a matter best left to your practical experience and professional training. So, for now, when we say 'profit and loss account' we mean 'trading and profit and loss account but in a simplified format just showing sales, cost of goods sold and gross profit'. We will look at this matter again in Chapter 10 when we look at *stock* and *inventory*.

8.4.2 A simple balance sheet

The balance sheet in Figure 8.8 is very similar to that shown in Figure 8.4. It shows the assets collected by type – fixed assets and current assets – and then it shows current liabilities to produce a net assets figure. This last number (net assets) is sometimes referred to as *net capital employed in the business* and while this is a useful way to think of this figure, do be careful – there are many difficult issues which arise in trying to calculate capital employed. (But see Chapter 15.)

You will also see on Figure 8.8 a subtotal of $144,700 which is arrived at by deducting current liabilities from current assets. This figure ($144,700 in our case) is often referred to as 'net current assets'. Apart from convention (and, we should say, the Companies Acts – see Chapter 14) these figures can be helpful when we are interpreting (reading the story of) the financial statements. This we will consider in Chapter 15.

Finally, a balance sheet shows the shareholders' or owners' funds – conventionally shown under the heading of 'represented by'.[7] This way of laying out a balance sheet seeks to reinforce the impression that the central purpose of financial accounting is to provide a picture, a story, perhaps even information, for those who own the business – the shareholders. This should emphasize to you that accounting (or at least conventional accounting – see Chapters 17 and 18) is primarily concerned with helping the wealthy owners. Conventional accounting is thus an essentially capitalist activity in which shareholders are considered to be much more important than employees, communities, the environment or whatever. If you are, by political persuasion, a right-wing capitalist then this causes no problems at all. We only mention it at this stage because, on average, less than half the people reading this book will be committed to right-wing, capitalist politics. For the rest, there is an essential tension. Thus one may just like to think at this stage about why a socialist or an environmentalist should consider it to be in the public interest (remember this from Chapter 1?) to help rich investors get richer. We will return to this towards the end of the book.

A final word about the balance sheet will not go amiss at this stage. Whilst the profit and loss account shows profit or loss (or at least a measure which we can think of as profit/loss – see Chapter 15), what does the balance sheet show us? This is *not* an easy question. Strictly speaking, it shows the *unexpired balances of the business*. That is, the amount of 'stuff' which is still available to be transferred to the profit and loss account as expenses and revenues in future accounting periods. It is the 'bits left over' at the end of a period of accounting. But do these numbers *mean* anything? The answer is 'possibly' but only if treated with great care. That is, only under the most restricted circumstances does the balance sheet show the *value* of the business. It *may* give a *guide* to the value but it is highly unlikely to be the *actual* value. Think about this and bear it in mind in what follows. Chapters 15, 16 and 18 will re-examine this question.

So that brings us to the end of this chapter. What have we learnt?

SUMMARY

This chapter started the process of calculating *end-of-period adjustments* and putting (posting) these figures through the extended trial balance in order to produce a profit and loss account and balance sheet. We started with **accruals** and **prepayments** and also had another very brief look at **provisions**. We learnt how to recognize the more common forms of accruals and what accounting treatment they need (see Figure 8.2). We then repeated this for prepayments (see Figure 8.3). We then worked through a simple example in order to see how they worked. This was done in stages:

i   we identified and calculated the accrual or prepayment;

ii   we then identified the bookkeeping necessary to reflect this;

iii   the bookkeeping was done by putting *two* entries (to maintain the double-entry) in the adjustment columns of the extended trial balance. These two columns must, by definition, always balance;

iv   each item in the extended trial balance was then categorized as being a *profit and loss account item* (a revenue or an expense) or a *balance sheet item* (an asset, a liability or a claim);

v   each row of the extended trial was then summed across to get a total for that row in either the profit and loss account or the balance sheet columns of the extended trial balance;

vi   the profit and loss account columns of the extended trial balance were then summed and the balancing figure entered. This was the profit or the loss for the accounting period. This, in order to preserve the double-entry, must also be entered – on the opposite side, of course! – in the balance sheet as the amount owed to the owners for this accounting period's activities;

vii   finally, these numbers were taken to a profit and loss account and balance sheet in the more traditional format. This format is summarized in Figure 8.9.

For the sake of refining your practical abilities in these aspects of bookkeeping, you might now go on and work through the appendices of this chapter.

Key terms and concepts

The following key terms have featured in this chapter. You should make sure you understand and can explain each one. Page references to definitions appear in the index in bold.

- Accruals
- Balance sheet
- Balances carried forward
- End-of-period adjustments
- Extended trial balance

- Opening balances
- Prepayments
- Profit and loss account
- Provisions

FURTHER READING

The most useful things you can be doing are working carefully through these examples *and* spending time reading the professional press and studying annual reports from various organizations. If you need further reading specifically on the topics of this chapter consult any introductory textbook on accounting in the library.

NOTES

1.   *Accruals* (the plural) is a noun referring to a particular type of accounting transaction. *Accrual* (the singular) is an adjective referring to the convention which governs the matching process. *Accruals* arise, in part, as a result of the *accrual* convention. By now you should be getting used to the confusions inherent in accounting terminology!

XYZ LTD: PROFIT AND LOSS ACCOUNT FOR THE YEAR ENDING 200X (figures in £/$/¥)		
SALES		XXX,XXX
less Cost of Goods Sold		(XXX,XXX)
GROSS OR TRADING PROFIT		XXX,XXX
EXPENSES:		
Listed by category	X,XXX	
......	X,XXX	
......	X,XXX	
......	XX,XXX	
Sub-total of Expenses		(XXX,XXX)
NET PROFIT FOR THE PERIOD		*XXX,XXX*

XYZ LTD: BALANCE SHEET AT 200X (figures in $/£/¥)		
FIXED ASSETS		XXX,XXX
CURRENT ASSETS:		
Trade Debtors	XX,XXX	
Prepayments:	XX,XXX	
Cash	XX,XXX	
	XXX,XXX	
CURRENT LIABILITIES:		
Trade Creditors	XX,XXX	
Sundry Creditors	XX,XXX	
Accruals and Provisions	XX,XXX	
	XX,XXX	
NET CURRENT ASSETS		XXX,XXX
NET ASSETS		**XXX,XXX**
REPRESENTED BY:		
Share Capital		XX,XX
Profit and Loss Account		XXX,XXX
SHAREHOLDERS'/OWNERS' FUNDS		**XXX,XXX**

Figure 8.9 Very simple pro-forma profit and loss account and balance sheet

2. This might seem outrageous but it is eminently practical and serves to remind you that accounting and bookkeeping are not accurate sciences but estimating arts. Just to prove the point, one of the authors, on one of his first jobs during his training had been tasked with checking the calculations for the trade creditors figure which was to go into the company's financial statements. Having laboriously checked the figure and made adjustments to get the figure 'totally accurate' the financial director then said 'thanks, but we need a provision of, say, 4 million to be added to that figure'. This was on a creditors figure of about 12 million. All the effort for accuracy was largely a waste of time!! A true story, folks!

3. The answer is the balance sheet where all the things left over, the things owed, owing and owned – the assets, liabilities and claims – are stored.

4. Note that the double-entry must be maintained in the adjustments column of the extended trial balance. That is, the adjustment column's debits and credits must always be identical.

5. Do not get confused by this. Remember that the financial statements show the amount owing to the owners – the shares and the profits. These are owed *by* the company *to* the owners. They are just the same as other liabilities in this regard. They are owed by the business to someone else.

6. The most obvious uses relate to controlling cash – how much have we got? what was it spent on? etc. The next most obvious thing we can learn from our financial accounts is how much we

owe and how much we are owed – and by and to whom? These are obviously helpful things for the owner and/or the manager of an organization.

7, The amount of the profit and loss account shown in Figure 8.8 comprises the profit for the period ($100,800) plus the brought-forward profit from previous periods ($3,900 – see Figure 8.4).

APPENDIX 8A: THE BASIC T-ACCOUNTS FOR YOTHU YINDI LTD 2001

As with all bookkeeping exercises, the trick is to approach it slowly and systematically.

- First: bring down all the balance sheet balances. We have marked these below with '*'. You then have all the things left over from the previous accounting period ready to start this accounting period;
- Second: enter all the transactions given in the question. They are numbered below with the same numbers as used in the question. Each transaction must be entered twice. If in difficulty, think whether the transaction directly involves cash and then trace it back from that. If not, think about the inflows and outflows and try and imagine what is *actually* happening;
- Third: balance off the accounts and take the balances to the initial trial balance – maintaining the double-entry.

Inflow/Debit	TRADE DEBTORS		Outflow/Credit
*Balance brought forward	50,000	1.Cash	50,000
1.Sales during the year	500,000	1.Cash	470,000
		Balance to TB	30,000
	$550,000		$550,00

Inflow/Debit	RENT		Outflow/Credit
*Prepayment b/fwd	20,000		
3.Cash	120,000	Balance to TB	140,000
	$140,000		$140,000

Inflow/Debit	PAYMENTS IN ADVANCE		Outflow/Credit
*Payments in advance b/fwd	10,000	4.Purchases (goods received)	10,000
4.Cash	1,000	Balance to TB	1,000
	$11,000		$11,000

Inflow/Debit	RATES & UTILITIES		Outflow/Credit
*Prepayment b/fwd	6,000		
5.Cash	24,000	Balance to TB	30,000
	$30,000		$30,000

Inflow/Debit	TELEPHONE		Outflow/Credit
*Prepayment (Rental) b/fwd	1,000	*Accrual b/fwd (calls)	500
6.Cash (Rental)	6,000		
6.Cash (Calls)	6,000	Balance to TB	12,500
	$13,000		$13,000

Inflow/Debit	TRADE CREDITORS		Outflow/Credit
2.Cash	60,000	*Brought forward	60,000
2.Cash	165,000	2.Purchases	200,000
Balance to TB	35,000		
	$260,000		$260,000

Inflow/Debit	SUNDRY CREDITORS		Outflow/Credit
7.Cash	10,000	*Invoice Accruals b/fwd	10,000
Balance to TB	2,000	7.Purchases 2,000	
	$12,000		$12,000

Inflow/Debit	WAGES		Outflow/Credit
8.Cash	24,000	*Accrued wages b/fwd	2,000
		Balance to TB	22,000
$24,000	$24,000		$24,000

Inflow/Debit	ELECTRICITY		Outflow/Credit
9.Cash	4,800	*Accrued electricity b/fwd	400
		Balance to TB	4,400
	$4,800		$4,800

Inflow/Debit	GAS		Outflow/Credit
9.Cash	2,400	*Accrued gas b/fwd	200
		Balance to TB	2,200
	$2,400		$2,400

Inflow/Debit	SHARE CAPITAL		Outflow/Credit
Balance to TB	$40,000	*Balance b/fwd	$40,000

Inflow/Debit	PROFIT & LOSS ACCOUNT		Outflow/Credit
Balance to TB	$3,900	*Balance b/fwd	$3,900

Inflow/Debit	SALES		Outflow/Credit
Balance to TB	$500,000	1.Debtors	$500,000

Inflow/Debit	TRADE PURCHASES		Outflow/Credit
2.Creditors	200,000		
4.Paid in advance	10,000		
7.Sundry creditors	2,000	Balance to TB	212,000
	$212,000		$212,000

Inflow/Debit	CASHBOOK		Outflow/Credit
*Balance brought forward	30,000	2.Creditors	60,000
1.Debtors	50,000	2.Creditors	165,000
1.Debtors	470,000	3.Rent	120,000
		4.Goods in advance	1,000
		5.Rates	24,000
		6.Telephone (rental)	6,000
		6.Telephone (calls)	6,000
		7.Sundry creditors	10,000
		8.Wages	24,000
		9.Electricity	4,800
		9.Gas	2,400
		Balance to TB	126,800
	$550,000		$550,000

APPENDIX 8B: END-OF-PERIOD ADJUSTMENTS FOR YOTHU YINDI LTD
WITHOUT USING THE EXTENDED TRIAL BALANCE – USING ONLY T-
ACCOUNTS

Many students learn to do their end-of-period adjustments without using an extended trial balance but rather put all the end-of-period adjustments directly through the T-accounts. Ideally all students should be able to use either method with equal facility (although we still maintain that your learning process will be enhanced if you do use the extended trial balance approach).

Look back to Appendix 8A as this will form the basis of the T-accounts approach. In Appendix 8A you will find all the double-entry for the company for the year. At the end of each T-account, a balance is taken to the (initial) trial balance and there we did the adjustments. The only difference *there can be* between the T-account and extended trial balance approaches lie in where those adjustments are performed. *Do note* that the adjustments themselves must be the same – it is only the bookkeeping that can change.

The following T-accounts therefore shows you the figures and accounts from Appendix 8A with the new entries for prepayments and accruals and the new totals and balancing figures. These new figures are shown in bold and marked with a '#' sign.

Study the T-accounts carefully. The changes that have been made are really quite simple but it will help clarify your thinking if you can follow them through.

First, the prepayments we calculated in the original question have been entered directly into the appropriate T-accounts. The prepayments for rent, rates and telephone are now shown as credits in those accounts and the debits are now shown in a new T-account for prepayments. The accruals for telephone wages, electricity and gas are now shown as debits in those accounts and as credits in the new accruals account.

Second, the balances have been recalculated. This is necessary because there is no longer an adjustment column in the trial balance and therefore the numbers we are showing as balances will be the numbers which will appear in the financial statements themselves.

Note, also, that we have now given you a set of choices about what to do with the balancing figures in each T-account.

Choice 1: You could take the balance directly to a trial balance ('Bal to TB') and then proceed as we have previously through an extended trial balance but without an adjustment column. That is, just use a trial balance to check for arithmetic accuracy and then take all the revenues and expenditures to the profit and loss account and all the assets and liabilities to the balance sheet.

Choice 2: You could take the numbers *directly* from the T-accounts to the financial statements. That is, you would be (for example) debiting trade creditors and crediting the balance sheet, or crediting rent and debiting the profit and loss account. This is certainly simple but loses the control over the numbers and so must be used only with great care.

Choice 3: This is a peculiar but common choice. That is, you will read in some textbooks that the balance sheet is not part of the double-entry system. (We, obviously, beg to differ.) What these books argue is that you take off all the 'balances' shown as profit and loss account items to the profit and loss account. Then you *bring down* the remaining balances and these are used to start the books for the next accounting period – these are your opening balances. You then go back through your brought-down figures and construct your balance sheet from these. We think this is silly. It is much more straightforward – in our view anyway – to treat the trial balance and balance sheet as part of the double-entry system and then use the balance sheet to provide your opening balances.

The only real advantages to putting the end-of-period adjustments through the T-accounts are its undoubted simplicity and, as we shall see in later chapters, it is often a great deal less messy when dealing with certain complicated end-of-period adjustments.

Our recommendations to you are:

i   Stick to the extended trial balance approach as much as you can – at least until you are 100% certain about bookkeeping and end-of-period adjustments. (100% certain means you regularly get 100% – or thereabouts – in *all* your bookkeeping exercises!)

ii   You use the T-account adjustment method only for those more messy adjustments. We will look at some of these in the next three chapters – certain aspects of depreciation, stock and bad and doubtful debts can get messy. These can be a real nuisance – partly due to the very practical problem of the amount of paper needed. If you try and do the more messy adjustments entirely through the extended trial balance you can get lost. And we wouldn't want that now, would we?

Inflow/Debit	TRADE DEBTORS		Outflow/Credit
*Balance brought forward	50,000	1.Cash	50,000
1.Sales during the year	500,000	1.Cash	470,000
		Bal to TB/Bsheet/bal c/d	30,000
	$550,000		$550,00

Inflow/Debit	RENT		Outflow/Credit
*Prepayment b/fwd	20,000	# Prepayment	20,000
3.Cash	120,000	Balance to TB/P andL a/c	140,000
	$140,000		$120,000

Inflow/Debit	PAYMENTS IN ADVANCE		Outflow/Credit
*Payments in advance b/fwd	10,000	4.Purchases (goods received)	10,000
4.Cash	1,000	Bal to TB/Bsheet/bal c/d	1,000
	$11,000		$11,000

Inflow/Debit	RATES & UTILITIES		Outflow/Credit
*Prepayment b/fwd	6,000	# Prepayment	6,000
5.Cash	24,000	Bal to TB/P andL a/c	24,000
	$30,000		$30,000

Inflow/Debit	TELEPHONE		Outflow/Credit
*Prepayment (Rental) b/fwd	1,000	*Accrual b/fwd (calls)	500
6.Cash (Rental)	6,000	# Prepayment	1,000
6.Cash (Calls)	6,000	Bal to TB/P andL a/c	12,500
	500		
Accrual	$13,000		$13,000

Inflow/Debit	TRADE CREDITORS		Outflow/Credit
2.Cash	60,000	*Brought forward	60,000
2.Cash	165,000	2.Purchases	200,000
Bal to TB/Bsheet/bal c/d	35,000		
	$260,000		$260,000

Inflow/Debit	SUNDRY CREDITORS		Outflow/Credit
7.Cash		10,000	*Invoice Accruals b/fwd	10,000
Bal to TB/Bsheet/bal c/d		2,000	7.Purchases	2,000
		$12,000		$12,000

Inflow/Debit	WAGES		Outflow/Credit
8.Cash		24,000	*Accrued wages b/fwd	2,000
#Accrual		2,000	Balance to TB P and L a/c	24,000
$24,000		$26,000		26,000

Inflow/Debit	ELECTRICITY		Outflow/Credit
9.Cash		4,800	*Accrued electricity b/fwd	400
#Accrual		400	Balance to TB P and L a/c	4,400
		$5,200		$5,200

Inflow/Debit	GAS		Outflow/Credit
9.Cash		2,400	*Accrued gas b/fwd	200
#Accrual		200	Balance to TB P and L a/c	2,200
		$2,600		$2,600

Inflow/Debit	SHARE CAPITAL		Outflow/Credit
Bal to TB/Bsheet/bal c/d		$40,000	*Balance b/fwd	$40,000

Inflow/Debit	PROFIT & LOSS ACCOUNT		Outflow/Credit
Balance to TB sheet/bal c/d		$3,900	*Balance b/fwd	$3,900

Inflow/Debit	SALES		Outflow/Credit
Bal to TB/B P and L a/c		$500,000	1.Debtors	$500,000

Inflow/Debit	TRADE PURCHASES		Outflow/Credit
2.Creditors		200,000		
4.Paid in advance		10,000		
7.Sundry creditors		2,000	Balance to TB P and L a/c	212,000
		$212,000		$212,000

Inflow/Debit	CASHBOOK		Outflow/Credit
*Balance brought forward		30,000	2.Creditors	60,000
1.Debtors		50,000	2.Creditors	165,000
1.Debtors		470,000	3.Rent	120,000
			4.Goods in advance	1,000
			5.Rates	24,000
			6.Telephone (rental)	6,000
			6.Telephone (calls)	6,000
			7.Sundry creditors	10,000
			8.Wages	24,000
			9.Electricity	4,800
			9.Gas	2,400
			Bal to TB/Bsheet/bal c/d	126,800
		$550,000		$550,000

Inflow/Debit	PREPAYMENTS		Outflow/Credit
Rent		20,000		
Rates		6,000		
Telephone		1,000	Bal to TB/Bsheet/bal c/d	27,000
		$27,000		$27,000

Inflow/Debit	ACCRUALS		Outflow/Credit
			Telephone	500
			Wages	2,000
			Electricity	400
Bal to TB/Bsheet/bal c/d		3,100	Gas	200
		$3,100		$3,100

Depreciation of fixed assets and profits and losses on disposal

9

Learning objectives

After studying this chapter you should be able to:

- give a general definition of depreciation;
- briefly explain the purpose of depreciation;
- define the elements needed to calculate depreciation;
- describe different methods of calculating depreciation;
- explain what is meant by net book value;
- demonstrate how to calculate straight-line depreciation;
- demonstrate how to calculate reducing-balance depreciation;
- describe how depreciation is shown in the profit and loss account and balance sheet;
- do the bookkeeping for depreciation end-of-period adjustments in an extended trial balance;
- do the bookkeeping for depreciation end-of-period adjustments through T-accounts;
- calculate the profit or loss on disposal of a fixed asset;
- do the bookkeeping and financial accounting for the disposal;
- discuss some of the broader accounting issues which arise with depreciation.

9.1 INTRODUCTION

9.1.1 Chapter design and links to previous chapters

Chapters 1 to 7 brought us through the bookkeeping process and helped us produce an initial trial balance. Chapter 8 started us on the process of adjusting that initial trial balance in order to produce a profit and loss account and balance sheet – the basic financial statements. In this chapter we continue that process by looking at the issues arising from the **depreciation of fixed assets** and any subsequent sale of a fixed asset which produces a **profit or loss on disposal**. In many regards, the material in this chapter will represent the most difficult part of your basic bookkeeping and accounting studies. In much of this subject of accounting, there are so many things which need to be held in the mind at one time. This is especially true of this chapter.

As a result, we will talk you through this material slowly and systematically. Stop the moment something doesn't make sense to you and see if you can sort it out. If you can deal with this material there is nothing in basic accounting that need bother you. If you cannot deal with this material than there are some parts of your basic bookkeeping and accounting on which you are shaky and you need to go back and study them again. If the things do not seem to be flowing for you, then something is wrong and needs to be checked out.

The chapter is organized as follows. The next subsection will explain a little about depreciation, what it is and why we need to bother with it. Section 9.2 will look at the elements that we need in order to calculate depreciation and then look at the different methods for calculating it. Section 9.3 will then walk you through the bookkeeping for depreciation and how it appears in the T-accounts, the extended trial balance and in the profit and loss account and balance sheet. Section 9.4 provides an example to work through to ensure that you have grasped everything so far. Section 9.5 then turns to examine what happens when the focal organization sells a fixed asset. And we look at how to calculate (what is called) the *profit and loss on disposal* – and where we put the resultant numbers. Section 9.6 provides another example to reinforce this material. Section 9.7 discusses a few of the accounting issues that have arisen throughout the chapter. We conclude with the usual summary of the chapter. Have fun!

9.1.2 What is depreciation?

Depreciation can be thought of as (a) an attempt to allocate the cost of a fixed asset over its estimated useful life where that life is estimated to be more than one accounting period and (b) a method of recognizing the diminution in a fixed asset's value as a result of use over time.

To all intents and purposes at this stage in your studies, depreciation is something which only happens to *fixed assets*. (Just to make sure you are happy about what fixed assets are, refer back to section 7.4.3 and Figure 7.9.) In fact, you have already met depreciation in a basic sort of way when we looked at Alder's accounts on cash and accrual bases in Figure 7.7. There, we looked at the difference between matching and prudence in relation to the way in which expenses and fixed assets were treated. It made a big difference to reported profits. We will now provide an illustration that we will work with throughout this chapter.

Let us go back to Yothu Yindi (from Chapter 8) and imagine that the company had bought a fixed asset in 2000 – say a wind-powered generator for $20,000 cash. And let us assume that the generator is expected to last for 10 years and then to be worthless. The bookkeeping is simple [debit fixed assets, credit cash]. The company, clearly, expects to gain benefit from this asset for the next 10 years. But to show this in the 2000 financial statements as a simple purchase would be to ignore the *matching* or *accrual* convention. That is, to treat it as a simple purchase in 2000 would be to show a large expense against profit in 2000 but a zero expense against profit for the next 9 years – although the asset would still be contributing towards profit. So the accountant attempts to show how the benefit from this generator will be **matched** with the revenues it generates (ahem!) over the whole of its **estimated useful life** – in this case, 10 years. In this way the profit and loss account will show *part* of the cost of this asset in each of the 10 years. This allocation of the cost over its useful life is **depreciation** – also more commonly known in North America as **amortization**.

Now, just to confuse you, depreciation is actually many different things at once. However, to get us started we will just approach it as being the allocation of a fixed asset's cost over its useful life and then, later, come back and look at what else depreciation is.

So, let us start simply and have a look at what we need to work out a depreciation calculation and then look at how we might calculate it. Only then will we worry about where all the numbers go in the bookkeeping and what it all means.

9.2 CALCULATING DEPRECIATION

9.2.1 The raw materials for a depreciation calculation

Rule one is that when the focal organization has a fixed asset, then the accountant can expect to depreciate that fixed asset in each accounting period for which the asset is in use. Rule two is that rule one is often incorrect! Rule three is we will ignore rule two for now. (We will explain this typical accounting confusion later in the chapter.)

So, if we have a fixed asset we will depreciate it. Therefore what we need for a depreciation calculation is – yes, you've guessed it – a fixed asset. But we also need some other pieces of information:

- We need to know, not just that the focal organization has a fixed asset, but *when it was purchased* and *its cost when purchased*.
- We need to know the **estimated useful life of the fixed asset**: for how long is the asset expected to be owned by the focal organization and to generate revenues/reduce costs for us?
- At the end of the fixed asset's estimated useful life, will the asset be useless? Will it be sold? Repaired? Scrapped? That is, at the end of its estimated useful life, do we *estimate that the fixed asset will have a scrap or terminal value*, usually known as the **estimated scrap value** or ESV?
- Finally (for now at least), we also need to know the focal organization's **depreciation policy**. The depreciation policy will cover many things but there are two things we need to know from the beginning:

i   How does the organization *assume* that the fixed asset wears out over time. That is, does the organization assume that the asset will wear out evenly over its life (what is called **straight-line depreciation**) or does the organization assume that it wears out more quickly in the early years of its life (usually called **reducing-balance depreciation**). We will meet these methods (plus others) in subsection 9.2.2 below.

ii We need to know when the depreciation is to be charged. That is, an organization is unlikely to acquire and dispose of its fixed assets at the exact beginning or end of an accounting period. Do we therefore depreciate monthly for example – in the interests of accuracy? Some companies do, but we will keep it simple and assume that every fixed asset is depreciated on a yearly basis and only depreciated if it is in the books at the end of the accounting period. That means that an asset is depreciated for a full year in the year of purchase and not depreciated at all in the year of sale.

These basic pieces of information allow us to identify the parameters for the calculation of depreciation. That is, [Cost] less [Estimated scrap/terminal value] = [Cost to be depreciated].

Or, in other words, these figures let us calculate the 'net cost' of the fixed asset to the focal organization. This is the amount of expenditure we must then spread (depreciate) over the estimated useful life of the asset. So, if we look back at the example of our wind-powered generator, this had a net cost of $20,000 (cost of $20,000 – estimated terminal value of 0). This $20,000 then needs to be spread (depreciated) over the 10 years which the company estimated as the useful life of this asset.

How we spread that cost depends on the depreciation policy of the company – on the **method of calculating depreciation**.

9.2.2 Methods of calculating depreciation

Methods of calculating depreciation can be thought of as falling into three broad categories:

(a) straight-line depreciation;
(b) reducing-balance depreciation;
(c) other (usually more complicated) methods of calculating depreciation.

(a) Straight-line depreciation

This method of calculating depreciation works on the *assumption* that the asset will wear out evenly throughout its estimated useful life. Thus the (what we called) 'net cost' of the fixed asset will be spread evenly over its estimated useful life. *Thus*, each year (accounting period) for the number of years for which the asset is estimated to have a useful life, the profit and loss account will show an identical annual charge (expense or *provision*) for this fixed asset.

The general way of calculating this is:

STRAIGHT-LINE DEPRECIATION CALCULATION	
Annual straight-line depreciation charge for asset X =	$\dfrac{\text{[Cost of Asset X]} - \text{[Estimated scrap value]}}{\text{Estimated useful life (years) of asset X}}$

So, let's look back to the wind-powered generator. Its straight-line depreciation annual charge would be $2,000 – being the $20,000 (the net cost) divided by 10 (the estimated useful life). So, for this fixed asset, $2,000 will be charged to the profit and loss account in each of the 10 years of the asset's useful life. Thus, over the 10 years of the asset's estimated useful life, the profit and loss account will bear charges totalling the full original cost of the fixed asset (10 × $2,000 = $20,000).

But, as we mentioned in the definition of depreciation (in section 9.1.2 above), depreciation is not *just* a means of charging the cost of an asset to the profit and loss account in accordance with the accrual/matching concept, it is also a means of recognizing the diminution in the asset's value over time. This brings us to the concept of a fixed asset's **net book value (NBV)**. The NBV of an asset is its original cost, less the *total* annual charges for depreciation recorded to date (what is called *accumulated depreciation* – see below). On day one of the asset's life, NBV is equal to the cost of the asset (no depreciation has been charged). At the end of its first year of use, we have charged one year's depreciation to the profit and loss account and the NBV is the cost less that one year's charge. In the second year of the asset's life, we again charge the same amount to the profit and loss account for that year's depreciation. The NBV of that asset is now the cost less *two* years' depreciation charge. This can be summarized as:

STRAIGHT-LINE NET BOOK VALUE CALCULATION	
The net book value of asset X in the *n*th year of its estimated useful life =	[Cost of asset X] −*n* × [Annual depreciation charge]

So, if we look again at our wind-powered generator, we can now estimate what the annual charge *and* the NBV will be for the whole of the asset's life. This is shown in Figure 9.1.

Work through Figure 9.1 and make sure you can see where every number came from. If you have difficulty, keep at it until the penny drops. It is really very straightforward – if a little bizarre!

(b) Reducing-balance depreciation

Alternatively, an organization *might assume* that a fixed asset will wear out more quickly in the earlier years of its estimated useful life (and/or that repair costs necessary to maintain the asset will increase as the asset moves towards the end of its life). In this case, the organization will want a method which allocates a larger depreciation charge in the earlier years of the asset's life and a diminishing charge as the asset grows older. This is the **reducing balance** method.

The general rule for calculating reducing-balance depreciation is that each year a *percentage* of the remaining *net book value* is charged as that year's asset depreciation. This general rule is as follows:

REDUCING-BALANCE DEPRECIATION CALCULATION	
Annual reducing-balance depreciation charge for asset X =	× $\dfrac{\text{[Net book value of asset X]}}{\text{[Estimated/chosen percentage for asset X]}}$

So, to begin with, the reducing balance method starts from the same place as the straight line method with a calculation of the asset's '*net cost*'. Then comes the tricky bit – we have

For a fixed asset with an original cost of $20,000, as estimated scrap value of $0 and an estimated useful life of 10 years			
Year	Annual depreciation charge to the profit and loss account	Total depreciation charged to date 'ACCUMULATED DEPRECIATON'	Net book value of the asset in each year
0 (Start of asset's life)	$0	$0	$20,000
1	$2,000	$2,000	$18,000
2	$2,000	$4,000	$16,000
3	$2,000	$6,000	$14,000
4	$2,000	$8,000	$12,000
5	$2,000	$10,000	$10,000
6	$2,000	$12,000	$8,000
7	$2,000	$14,000	$6,000
8	$2,000	$16,000	$4,000
9	$2,000	$18,000	$2,000
10	$2,000	$20,000	$0

Figure 9.1 A calculation of annual depreciation charge and net book value on the straight line method

to estimate a percentage charge which, when taken over the asset's estimated useful life, will reduce the NBV to the estimated scrap value – or very close to it. So, how do we estimate this percentage? There are two methods – guessing and using algebra. Guessing is OK but can take a surprisingly long time to work out a useful percentage figure. The algebraic method is considered more 'scientific' (it isn't of course – it just *looks* more accurate!) and is derived from a formula:

REDUCING-BALANCE CALCULATION OF THE REDUCING PERCENTAGE	
The reducing-balance depreciation percentage for asset X =	$100[1 - \sqrt[n]{(\text{Est'd scrap value} \div \text{Cost})}]$ where n = estimated life of asset X

This percentage is then applied to the NBV of the asset at the end of the *previous* accounting period to produce the depreciation charge for that accounting period and the new NBV.

Let us return to the case of the wind-powered generator. What would be the depreciation pattern for that asset using the reducing balance method? First, we need to calculate the reducing-balance percentage. *But,* we immediately hit a problem. Our wind-powered generator has a zero estimated scrap value. This would give us a 100 per cent reducing-balance percentage.[1] That is, we would depreciate the whole asset in one year. This is not the point of the exercise at all! So, to make the arithmetic work, we will assume a scrap value of $1 just for the sake of arithmetic convenience. This gives us a reducing balance percentage of 63 per cent:

$$100[1 - \sqrt[10]{(1 \div 20,000)}] = 100[1 - 0.37] = 63\%$$

(Check that you can get this figure. Your calculator should be able to do 10th roots.)

Now, armed with our reducing-balance percentage, we can calculate the depreciation charges and NBV for the asset's life. This is shown in Figure 9.2.

For a fixed asset with an original cost of $20,000, as estimated scrap value of $1 and an estimated useful life of 10 years			
Year	Annual depreciation charge to the profit and loss account	Total depreciation charged to date 'ACCUMULATED DEPRECIATON'	Net book value of the asset in each year
0	0	0	20,000
1	12,600	12,600	7,400
2	4,662	17,262	2,738
3	1,725	18,987	1,013
4	638	19,625	375
5	236	19,861	139
6	87	19,949	51
7	32	19,981	19
8	12	19,993	7
9	4	19,997	3
10	2	19,999	1

Figure 9.2 A calculation of annual depreciation charge and net book value on the reducing balance method

In Figure 9.2, each year the reducing-balance percentage has been applied to the previous NBV. In Year 1, this means we took 63 per cent of $20,000. This produced a charge for the year of $12,600 and an NBV at the end of Year 1 of $7,400. In Year 2, we took 63 per cent of $7,400 to produce a charge for Year 2 of $4,662 and an NBV at the end of Year 2 of $2,738, and so on.

You will notice how very different is the stream of depreciation numbers produced each year by the reducing balance method from those produced by the straight line method. This has important implications to which we will return later. However, you will also notice that the total depreciation charged for the asset over its life is identical under each method (let's not quibble about $1). This *must* be the case as the same asset has the same cost and the same estimated useful life and the whole net cost must be depreciated over that life. This may seem obvious, but it is easy to forget it!

These two methods – the straight line and reducing balance methods – are the most widely used methods (at least in the English-speaking world) but they are, by no means, the only methods that are used.

(c) Other methods of calculating depreciation

Generally speaking, an organization can choose any method at all that seems appropriate to allocate the cost of a fixed asset over its estimated useful life. In practice, however, the methods used are restricted by: (i) the accounting rules and regulations of the country (we will return to this at the end of this chapter and look at accounting rules and regulations in more detail in Chapter 14), (ii) the type of organization we are considering and (iii) general conventions – in that organization or for that type of asset, for example.

Examination of the ways in which depreciation should be calculated can, in fact, become very complicated indeed. First of all there are several further ways of calculating the depreciation charge. One method, which is known as the 'sum of digits' method, allocates the total cost of the asset by means of a formula that broadly approximates to the reducing balance method of calculating the depreciation charge.

Then, there are other conceptions of what it is we should actually depreciate. For example, suppose we had taken out a loan to buy our wind-powered generator. Then, is the cost of the asset the $20,000 purchase price or the cost of the loan (the $20,000 plus the interest we have to pay to the bank for borrowing that money)? In many government departments around the world, the 'depreciation' charge is actually what it costs to borrow the money to buy the asset. And this approach has been suggested as a more useful way of considering company depreciation.

To really examine these sorts of issues would take us a long way from our current path of examining basic bookkeeping and financial accounting and so we will not take this further here. Simply, try and remember that there are *many* possible ways in which we can approach the issue of how to depreciate a fixed asset. And whilst a nice straight-line calculation has all the advantages of straightforward simplicity – and is to be commended for this reason alone – this does not, *in any sense,* mean it is the *right* way to depreciate fixed assets.

Our coverage so far is summarized in Figures 9.3, 9.4 and 9.5.

So, now we can begin to calculate the figures involved in depreciating a fixed asset, what do we do with the numbers when we have them? That is the purpose of the next section.

An attempt to allocate the cost of an asset over its estimated useful life where that life is estimated to be more than one accounting period.

i. This follows the accrual or matching concept.

ii. This process creates:

   a   a charge for the year which is shown in the P & L; and

   b   a provision which consists of all the previous year's charges added together plus this year's charge (which goes to the balance sheet).

iii. The cost of the asset less the total provision for depreciation built up so far leaves the net book value (NBV).

iv. The NBV is the amount of the asset's cost which has not yet been 'used up'.

v. There is an implicit (but dodgy) assumption that the total depreciation provision should, at the time the asset needs replacing, be sufficient to replace the asset.

Figure 9.3 Depreciation revision –1

STRAIGHT-LINE DEPRECIATION

a $$\frac{(Cost\ of\ asset) - (Estimated\ scrap\ value)}{(Estimated\ useful\ life\ of\ asset)}$$

= Estimated annual depreciation charge to P & L

b   The estimated depreciation charge to the P & L is the same each year.

c   The total depreciation provision shown in the balance sheet is the sum of the depreciation charges on that asset to date (or [annual depreciation charge] × [years in use so far]).

d   (Cost) – (Total depreciation provision) = NBV

e   NBV at the end of estimated useful life = (Estimated scrap value)

Figure 9.4 Depreciation revision – 2

REDUCING BALANCE

a   1st Year:

(Cost) – (ESV) × (% Estimated/chosen) = Depreciation charge for the period.

b   Subsequent years: (Reducing balance NBV) × (% Estimated) = Depreciation charge for the period.

c   The yearly charge for depreciation on any one asset is never the same from one year to the next – each year is lower than the previous year's charge.

d   The NBV never quite gets to zero (although the amount involved is trivial).

e   The total provision for the depreciation taken over the whole life of the asset must be virtually identical to that under the straight line method because both methods are allocating the same cost over the same life. The difference is to do with which periods bear which charges.

Figure 9.5 Depreciation revision – 3

9.3 THE BOOKKEEPING FOR DEPRECIATION

9.3.1 The basic elements

So far, our coverage of depreciation has been fairly straightforward. The difficult bit – or rather the bit that tends to cause confusion in students' minds – starts here.

In the previous section we did two things:

i   We calculated the amount of depreciation which was to be charged to the profit and loss account for the accounting period in question. This is the *depreciation charge for the year*.
ii   This depreciation charge for the year was then added to previous charges for previous years in order to reduce the reported cost of the fixed-assets value – to produce the *net book value*. This amount – of the total charges to date – is called the *accumulated depreciation*.

Both of these amounts are *provisions* because the amounts are *estimated*. There is the estimated charge (or provision) for the year (or accounting period) and the accumulated estimated provision. The charge for the year is an *expense* to be shown in the profit and loss account. The accumulated depreciation provision is an *accumulated provision* to be shown in the balance sheet.

The depreciation charge for the year is shown in the profit and loss account just like any other expense of the accounting period.

The accumulated depreciation provision, whilst shown in the balance sheet, is *not* shown with other provisions but shown as a *deduction from fixed assets* in order to show on the balance sheet the *net book value*.

9.3.2 Bookkeeping through an extended trial balance

Once the depreciation charge has been calculated we can put through the appropriate end-of-period adjustments. The basic double entry is straightforward:

[Debit: Depreciation charge for the year]

[Credit: Accumulated depreciation provision]

So, in an extended trial balance, we need two extra lines *for each fixed asset for which we will calculate depreciation*. One line will be 'depreciation charge for the year' which will take the debit and the other will be 'accumulated depreciation provision' which will take the credit. *Note:* if the asset has been owned for more than one year, there will be an accumulated depreciation provision brought forward already – being the accumulation of the previous charges from earlier accounting periods.

Look back to Figures 9.1 and 9.2 which summarized the depreciation on the wind-powered generator. Under the straight-line depreciation method (Figure 9.1), the column marked 'annual depreciation charge to profit and loss account' is the amount debited against the profit and loss account in that accounting period (remembering that, under the straight-line depreciation method, the amount charged each year is identical). So this debit goes into the adjustment column of the extended trial balance against 'depreciation charge for the year'. This same amount, the $2,000, must also be then credited to the accumulated depreciation provision. The effect of this is summarized in Figure 9.6 which shows an extract from Yothu Yindi Ltd's extended trial balance for the first three years of the fixed asset's useful life with the company. (Work through Figure 9.6 and ensure that you can see where each number comes from. As a hint, do recall that your closing balance sheet for one accounting period becomes the opening balance for the next accounting period.)

The effect is just the same with the reducing balance method – except, of course, the charge is not the same for each year. So Figure 9.7 just rehearses Figure 9.6, but with reducing-balance depreciation figures.

The only other point to note at this stage is that in neither Figure 9.6 nor Figure 9.7 did we 'net off' the cost of the fixed asset and the accumulated depreciation. *This is important.* The only place we actually ever net the two off is in the final balance sheet itself. This is also true when we undertake these bookkeeping transactions through the T-accounts. (Why we keep them separate involves a combination of tradition, regulation and the resultant

SHOWING THE BOOKKEEPING FOR THE DEPRECIATION OF A WIND-POWERED GENERATOR (STRAIGHT-LINE DEPRECIATION METHOD)

EXTENDED TRIAL BALANCE at 31 DECEMBER 2000 (Extract)

Account	Trial balance		Adjustments		Profit and loss		Balance sheet	
	Dr	Cr	Dr	Cr	Dr	Cr	Dr	Cr
Sales								
Debtors								
......etc.								
Fixed asset at cost	20,000						20,000	
Dep'n for the year			2,000		2,000			
Accum depreciation		0		2,000				2,000
TOTALS	XXXXX	XXXXX	XXXXX	XXXXX	XXXXX	XXXXX	XXXXX	XXXXX

EXTENDED TRIAL BALANCE at 31 DECEMBER 2001 (Extract)

Account	Trial balance		Adjustments		Profit and loss		Balance sheet	
	Dr	Cr	Dr	Cr	Dr	Cr	Dr	Cr
Sales								
Debtors								
......etc.								
Fixed asset at cost	20,000						20,000	
Dep'n for the year			2,000		2,000			
Accum depreciation		2,000		2,000				4,000
TOTALS	XXXXX	XXXXX	XXXXX	XXXXX	XXXXX	XXXXX	XXXXX	XXXXX

EXTENDED TRIAL BALANCE at 31 DECEMBER 2002 (Extract)

Account	Trial balance		Adjustments		Profit and loss		Balance sheet	
	Dr	Cr	Dr	Cr	Dr	Cr	Dr	Cr
Sales								
Debtors								
......etc.								
Fixed asset at cost	20,000						20,000	
Dep'n for the year			2,000		2,000			
Accum depreciation		4,000		2,000				6,000
TOTALS	XXXXX	XXXXX	XXXXX	XXXXX	XXXXX	XXXXX	XXXXX	XXXXX

Figure 9.6 An extract from the extended trial balance for Yothu Yindi Ltd

SHOWING THE BOOKKEEPING FOR THE DEPRECIATION OF A WIND-POWERED GENERATOR (REDUCING-BALANCE DEPRECIATION METHOD)								
EXTENDED TRIAL BALANCE at 31 DECEMBER 2000 (Extract)								
Account	Trial balance		Adjustments		Profit and loss		Balance sheet	
	Dr	Cr	Dr	Cr	Dr	Cr	Dr	Cr
Sales								
Debtors								
......etc.								
Fixed Asset at cost	20,000						20,000	
Dep'n for the year			12,600		12,600			
Accum depreciation		0		12,600				12,600
TOTALS	XXXXX	XXXXX	XXXXX	XXXXX	XXXXX	XXXXX	XXXXX	XXXXX

EXTENDED TRIAL BALANCE at 31 DECEMBER 2001 (Extract)								
Account	Trial balance		Adjustments		Profit and loss		Balance sheet	
	Dr	Cr	Dr	Cr	Dr	Cr	Dr	Cr
Sales								
Debtors								
......etc.								
Fixed asset at cost	20,000						20,000	
Dep'n for the year			4,958		4,958			
Accum depreciation		12,600		4,958				17,558
TOTALS	XXXXX	XXXXX	XXXXX	XXXXX	XXXXX	XXXXX	XXXXX	XXXXX

EXTENDED TRIAL BALANCE at 31 DECEMBER 2002 (Extract)								
Account	Trial balance		Adjustments		Profit and loss		Balance sheet	
	Dr	Cr	Dr	Cr	Dr	Cr	Dr	Cr
Sales								
Debtors								
......etc.								
Fixed asset at cost	20,000						20,000	
Dep'n for the year			1,538		1,538			
Accum depreciation		17,558		1,538				19,096
TOTALS	XXXXX	XXXXX	XXXXX	XXXXX	XXXXX	XXXXX	XXXXX	XXXXX

Figure 9.7 An extract from the extended trial balance for Yothu Yindi Ltd

ease of calculating both the charge for the year and any profit or loss on disposal – see later.) For now, just *get into the habit of keeping all fixed assets (or groups of fixed assets) separately and keeping the cost of an asset and the accumulated depreciation for that asset separate*. NOW, reread the last sentence and commit it to memory!

9.3.3 Bookkeeping through the T-accounts

The process is, as you would expect, virtually identical to performing the double-entry through the extended trial balance.

We open a T-account for each fixed asset (or group of fixed assets)[2] and a T-account for depreciation charge for the year and a T-account for accumulated depreciation provision. *Keep them all separate.*

Then, when we have calculated the depreciation charge for the accounting period we debit the depreciation charge account and credit the accumulated depreciation provision account. The depreciation provision account will have a brought-forward amount of previous depreciation charges *if* the fixed asset is not in its first year of useful life.

These points can be summarized by looking at the T-accounts for Yothu Yindi Ltd and their wind-powered generator. This is shown, for the first three years, in Figure 9.9 (for the straight line method) and Figure 9.10 (for the reducing balance method). In addition, Figure 9.8 summarizes this approach and is a useful figure to use for revision.

BOOKKEEPING FOR DEPRECIATION

IN YEAR 1:

Extended Trial Balance Method:

i   Add two extra lines to the TB:

- Depreciation charge for Year;
- Depreciation Provision;

ii   In the adjustments column:

- Dr. Depreciation Charge;
- Cr. Depreciation Provision;

iii   In the formal P & L the depreciation charge will show as an expense of the period;

iv   In the formal balance sheet the depreciation provision will be shown as a separate deduction from the cost of the asset.

Through the T-Accounts Method

i   Open separate T-accounts for:

- Depreciation charge for Year;
- Depreciation Provision;

ii   In the T-accounts:

- Dr. Depreciation Charge;
- Cr. Depreciation Provision;

iii   In the formal profit and loss account and balance sheet depreciation is treated as above.

IN SUBSEQUENT YEARS:

… continue exactly as in year 1 except:

- You already will have a provision for depreciation brought forward from previous year(s).
- This will consist of previous year's charges to the profit and loss account built up over the years.
- It will show as an existing line in the TB and/or a T-account opened at the beginning of the accounting period.
- The debit/inflow side of the double-entry is identical (for the depreciation charge for the period).
- The credit/outflow side of the double-entry is added to the brought forward provision so that the carried forward provision is equal to the (b/fwd + depreciation charge for period).

NB KEEP EACH ACCOUNT FOR EACH CATEGORY OF FIXED ASSET, EACH ACCOUNT FOR THE PROVISION FOR DEPRECIATION AND THE ACCOUNT FOR THE DEP. CHARGE FOR THE YEAR SEPARATE.**

Figure 9.8 Depreciation revision – 4

2000

Inflow/Debit	FIXED ASSET: WIND-POWERED GENERATOR		Outflow/Credit
2000 Cash	20,000	31.12.00 Bal c/d	20,000

Inflow/Debit	DEPRECIATION CHARGE: WIND-POWERED GENERATOR		Outflow/Credit
31.12.00 Accum Depn: Charge for year	2,000	31.12.00 Profit and loss account	2,000

Inflow/Debit	ACCUMULATED DEPRECIATION: WIND-POWERED GENERATOR		Outflow/Credit
31.12.00 Bal c/d	2,000	31.12.00 Charge for year	2,000

2001

Inflow/Debit	FIXED ASSET: WIND-POWERED GENERATOR		Outflow/Credit
1.1.2001 Bal b/d	20,000	31.12.01 Bal c/d	20,000

Inflow/Debit	DEPRECIATION CHARGE: WIND-POWERED GENERATOR		Outflow/Credit
31.12.01 Accum Depn: Charge for year	2,000	31.12.01 Profit and loss account	2,000

Inflow/Debit	ACCUMULATED DEPRECIATION: WIND-POWERED GENERATOR		Outflow/Credit
		1.1.01 Bal b/d	2,000
31.12.01 Bal c/d	4,000	31.12.01 Charge for year	2,000
	4,000		4,000

2002

Inflow/Debit	FIXED ASSET: WIND-POWERED GENERATOR		Outflow/Credit
1.1.2002 Bal b/d	20,000	31.12.02 Bal c/d	20,000

Inflow/Debit	DEPRECIATION CHARGE: WIND-POWERED GENERATOR		Outflow/Credit
31.12.02 Accum Depn: Charge for year	2,000	31.12.02 Profit and loss account	2,000

Inflow/Debit	ACCUMULATED DEPRECIATION: WIND-POWERED GENERATOR		Outflow/Credit
		1.1.02 Bal b/d	4,000
31.12.02 Bal c/d	6,000	31.12.02 Charge for year	2,000
	6,000		6,000

Figure 9.9 T-accounts for Yothu Yindi Ltd for the depreciation of a wind-powered generator (straight line method)

Study these two figures and make sure you can follow them through. Notice that, once again, the original cost of the fixed asset, the depreciation charge for the year and the accumulated depreciation provision are all kept separate.

It only now remains to show how this will look in the financial statements.

9.3.4 Depreciation in the profit and loss account and balance sheet

The way in which the depreciation charge for the year enters the profit and loss account is straightforward. It simply appears as one of the *expenses*. The balance sheet is, as you

2000

Inflow/Debit	FIXED ASSET: WIND-POWERED GENERATOR		Outflow/Credit
2000 Cash		20,000	31.12.00 Bal c/d	20,000

Inflow/Debit	DEPRECIATION CHARGE: WIND-POWERED GENERATOR		Outflow/Credit
31.12.00 Accum Depn: Charge for year		12,600	31.12.00 Profit and loss account	12,600

Inflow/Debit	ACCUMULATED DEPRECIATION: WIND-POWERED GENERATOR		Outflow/Credit
31.12.00 Bal c/d		12,600	31.12.00 Charge for year	12,600

2001

Inflow/Debit	FIXED ASSET: WIND-POWERED GENERATOR		Outflow/Credit
1.1.2001 Bal b/d		20,000	31.12.01 Bal c/d	20,000

Inflow/Debit	DEPRECIATION CHARGE: WIND-POWERED GENERATOR		Outflow/Credit
31.12.01 Accum Depn: Charge for year		4,958	31.12.01 Profit and loss account	4,958

Inflow/Debit	ACCUMULATED DEPRECIATION: WIND-POWERED GENERATOR		Outflow/Credit
			1.1.01 Bal b/d	12,600
31.12.01 Bal c/d		17,558	31.12.01 Charge for year	4,958
		17,558		17,558

2002

Inflow/Debit	FIXED ASSET: WIND-POWERED GENERATOR		Outflow/Credit
1.1.2002 Bal b/d		20,000	31.12.02 Bal c/d	20,000

Inflow/Debit	DEPRECIATION CHARGE: WIND-POWERED GENERATOR		Outflow/Credit
31.12.02 Accum Depn: Charge for year		1,538	31.12.02 Profit and loss account	1,538

Inflow/Debit	ACCUMULATED DEPRECIATION: WIND-POWERED GENERATOR		Outflow/Credit
			1.1.02 Bal b/d	17,558
31.12.02 Bal c/d		19,096	31.12.02 Charge for year	1,538
		19,096		19,096

Figure 9.10 T-accounts for Yothu Yindi Ltd for the depreciation of a wind-powered generator (reducing balance method)

might have guessed, slightly more involved. You will notice that we kept the cost of the asset and the accumulated depreciation separate. The only time we bring them together is in the balance sheet. If we consider the case of Yothu Yindi Ltd who bought the wind-powered generator, then their 2000 balance sheet – using only the straight-line depreciation – will include the extract shown in Figure 9.11.

And that's all there is to it. To reinforce what we have done so far, we will now rework Yothu Yindi's 2001 bookkeeping and financial statements assuming that they now have a few fixed assets.

Fixed Assets	Cost	Accum Dep'n	NBV	
Wind-powered generator	20,000	2,000	18,000	18,000
Current Assets				
etc......				

Figure 9.11 'A company' balance sheet as at 31 December 2000

9.4 YOTHU YINDI LTD – FIXED ASSETS AND DEPRECIATION

Let us begin by assuming that when we first examined Yothu Yindi Ltd in Chapter 8, we somehow missed the fixed assets! We have seen the wind-powered generator they bought in 2000 so, sticking with the assumption that the company operates a straight-line depreciation policy, the company's 2000 balance should have looked like Figure 9.12.

Let us briefly check through Figure 9.12. First, we now have a fixed asset (as previously shown in Figure 9.11). The double entry for that asset [Debit fixed assets: Credit cash] requires that the cash is reduced by $20,000. Second, the asset was depreciated and the double entry for that [Debit profit and loss account: Credit accumulated depreciation] resulted in the reduction of the asset to its NBV of $18,000 and requires that we reduce the profit and loss account by $2,000. So the balance sheet still balances.

Let us further assume that we also missed the fixed assets of Yothu Yindi Ltd in 2001 in which year they also bought a four-wheel drive vehicle for $16,000 cash. Let us assume that Yothu Yindi Ltd estimate that the vehicle will have a useful life of 5 years with an

YOTHU YINDI LTD: BALANCE SHEET AT 31 DECEMBER 2000 (all figure are in dollars)				
FIXED ASSETS	**Cost**	**Acc Depn**	**NBV**	
Wind-powered generator	20,000	2,000	18,000	18,000
CURRENT ASSETS:				
Trade Debtors			50,000	
Prepayments:	Rent		20,000	
	Goods		10,000	
	Rates		6,000	
	Telephone		1,000	
Cash			10,000	
			97,000	
CURRENT LIABILITIES:				
Trade Creditors			60,000	
Sundry Creditors			10,000	
Accruals and Provisions	Wages		2,000	
	Electricity		400	
	Gas		200	
	Telephone		500	
			73,100	23,900
NET ASSETS				**$41,900**
REPRESENTED BY:				
Share Capital				40,000
Profit and Loss Account				1,900
SHAREHOLDERS'/OWNERS' FUNDS				**$41,900**

Figure 9.12 Yothu Yindi Ltd: balance sheet at 31 December 2000

estimated scrap value of $1,000. We will maintain the assumption that Yothu Yindi Ltd's depreciation policy is to depreciate all assets on a straight line method and that they allow a full year's depreciation in the year of purchase and no depreciation in the year of disposal.

What this additional information requires us to do now is to rework the T-accounts for 2001 (which we previously considered in Appendix 8A) and to rework and complete the extended trial balance for the company for 2001 (which we previously produced in Figure 8.7). All the T-accounts which we produced for 2001 will remain exactly the same as they are in Appendix 8A with the exception of cash and the profit and loss account; also we will need additional T-accounts for our fixed assets and accumulated depreciation. Figure 9.13 shows these accounts for 2001 – *after the addition of the new wind-powered generator but before we have considered the purchase of the new vehicle.* (This simplification at this stage is only for clarity of exposition.)

Take a few moments to orient yourself to Figure 9.13. We are looking at the T-accounts for the company for 2001. (We can ignore all the other accounts because they are unaffected by these changes to fixed assets.) The opening balances for cash and for the profit and loss account have been adjusted and we have opened two new accounts for the cost of the fixed asset and for the accumulated depreciation brought forward.

Now, we can see what happens when the new vehicle is introduced. The new vehicle requires some double-entry bookkeeping – [Debit fixed assets: Credit cash]. If, as we have recommended, we leave our end-of-period adjustments until the extended trial balance, this is the only bookkeeping we need to do. This bookkeeping is then reflected in Figure 9.14. In the figure, we have also closed off the accounts in readiness to take them all to the extended trial balance at the end of the 2001 accounting period.

With the addition of fixed assets
(showing only those accounts which are affected by the generator brought forward)

Inflow/Debit	PROFIT AND LOSS ACCOUNT		Outflow/Credit
		*Balance b/fwd	$1,900

Inflow/Debit	CASHBOOK		Outflow/Credit
*Balance brought forward	10,000	2.Creditors	60,000
1.Debtors	50,000	2.Creditors	165,000
1.Debtors	470,000	3.Rent	120,000
		4.Goods in advance	1,000
		5.Rates	24,000
		6.Telephone (rental)	6,000
		6.Telephone (calls)	6,000
		7.Sundry creditors	10,000
		8.Wages	24,000
		9.Electricity	4,800
		9.Gas	2,400

Inflow/Debit	FIXED ASSET: WIND-POWERED GENERATOR		Outflow/Credit
1.1.01 Bal b/d	20,000		

Inflow/Debit	ACCUMULATED DEPRECIATION: WIND-POWERED GENERATOR		Outflow/Credit
		1.1.01 Bal b/d	2,000

Figure 9.13 Extract from the T-accounts for Yothu Yindi Ltd, 2001

With the addition of fixed assets
AND THE PURCHASE OF A NEW VEHICLE

2001

Inflow/Debit	PROFIT AND LOSS ACCOUNT	Outflow/Credit
Balance to TB	$1,900	*Balance b/fwd $1,900

Inflow/Debit	CASHBOOK	Outflow/Credit
*Balance brought forward	10,000	2.Creditors 60,000
1.Debtors	50,000	2.Creditors 165,000
1.Debtors	470,000	3.Rent 120,000
		4.Goods in advance 1,000
		5.Rates 24,000
		6.Telephone (rental) 6,000
		6.Telephone (calls) 6,000
		7.Sundry creditors 10,000
		8.Wages 24,000
		9.Electricity 4,800
		9.Gas 2,400
		PURCHASE OF VEHICLE 16,000
		Balance to TB 90,800
	$530,000	$530,000

Inflow/Debit	FIXED ASSET: WIND-POWERED GENERATOR	Outflow/Credit
1.1.01 Bal b/d	20,000	31.12.01 Bal to TB 20,000

Inflow/Debit	ACCUMULATED DEPRECIATION: WIND-POWERED GENERATOR	Outflow/Credit
31.12.01 Bal to TB	2,000	1.1.01 Bal b/d 2,000

Inflow/Debit	FIXED ASSET: 4-WHEEL DRIVE VEHICLE	Outflow/Credit
2001 CASH	16,000	31.12.01 Bal to TB 16,000

Figure 9.14 Extract from the T-accounts for Yothu Yindi Ltd, 2001

Once again, check that the new entries in Figure 9.14 make sense to you. (Note that the new entry – for the purchase of the new vehicle, is shown in upper-case letters.) This information can now all be transferred to the extended trial balance where we can undertake the end-of-period adjustments – in this case the calculation of depreciation.

We already know the annual depreciation charge for the wind-powered generator – $2,000 – so now no more needs to be done at this stage. In the extended trial balance we will simply debit depreciation charge for the year and credit accumulated depreciation provision as we have done previously. We do, however, need to consider the vehicle.

Look back to section 9.2 if you have any problems with what follows. The vehicle cost $16,000 and it has an estimated scrap value of $1,000. Its net cost is therefore $15,000. Its estimated useful life is 5 years and therefore the straight-line depreciation charge will be $3,000 per year ($15,000 ÷ 5). Armed with this information we can put through the end-of-period adjustments for Yothu Yindi's depreciation. These are shown in Figure 9.15. This is simply Figure 8.8 but with the fixed assets and depreciation added. The accounts that have been affected by our adjustments are all shown in bold.

Account	Trial balance Dr	Cr	Adjustments Dr	Cr	Profit and loss Dr	Cr	Balance sheet Dr	Cr
EXTENDED TRIAL BALANCE at 31 DECEMBER 2001								
Debtors	30,000						30,000	
Rent	140,000			20,000	120,000			
Pay in advance	1,000						1,000	
Rates	30,000			6,000	24,000			
Telephone	12,500		500	1,000	12,000			
Creditors		35,000						35,000
Sundry creditors		2,000						2,000
Wages	22,000		2,000		24,000			
Electricity	4,400		400		4,800			
Gas	2,200		200		2,400			
Share capital		40,000						40,000
Profit and loss a/c		1,900						1,900
Sales		500,000				500,000		
Purchases	212,000				212,000			
Cash	90,800						90,800	
Prepayments: Rent			20,000					
Prepayments: Rates			6,000					
Prepayments: Tel.			1,000				27,000	
Accruals: Tel.				500				
Accruals: Wages				2,000				
Accruals: Elec.				400				
Accruals: Gas				200				3,100
Fixed assets cost:								
– Generator	20,000						20,000	
– Vehicle	16,000						16,000	
Dep'n charge:								
– Generator			2,000		2,000			
– Vehicle			3,000		3,000			
Accum dep'n:								
– Generator		2,000		2,000				4,000
– Vehicle				3,000				3,000
Profit/loss for year					95,800			95,800
TOTALS	580,900	580,900	35,100	35,100	500,000	500,000	184,800	184,800

Figure 9.15 A full extended trial balance with adjustments for Yothu Yindi Ltd at end of December 2001

Yet again, please take the time to go through these adjustments carefully and to ensure that they all seem natural and straightforward. Yet again, if they do *not* seem so, please go back and rework them. If you can handle these adjustments, you are well on the way to being able to handle any end-of-period adjustments that you will face in your introductory studies. If you are confident about Figure 9.15, then it will be a matter of moments for you to produce the new financial statements for Yothu Yindi Ltd. Just to confirm that you can do them, produce a formal set of financial statements from Figure 9.15 and then check your answer with Appendix 9A.

This exercise brings this part of the example to a close and permits us to go on to the last new technical material for this chapter – the disposal of fixed assets.

9.5 THE DISPOSAL OF FIXED ASSETS

We have now seen how to bring fixed assets into the bookkeeping and financial accounting system and how to depreciate them. We have kept things fairly simple by concentrating on straight-line depreciation and on depreciating assets which are in the books of the organization at the accounting date for a full year. So we have seen how to depreciate fixed assets in the year in which they are acquired and how to open accounts for depreciation charges for the year and accounts for accumulated depreciation provisions. We then also saw how to depreciate existing assets for subsequent years of their useful life within the accounting entity. So far, so good. But what happens when either the asset comes to the end of its useful life or the focal organization decides to get rid of an existing fixed asset? That is the purpose of this section.

When a focal organization disposes of a fixed asset it is necessary to do a number of things and - *most importantly, for your sanity* - to do these things in a very systematic way to avoid confusion. The steps we must take are as follows:

i The focal organization sells or otherwise disposes of the asset. This will result in either a figure for **sales proceeds** or a **cost of disposal**. That is, did the organization succeed in selling the asset or did it have to pay for someone to come and take it away? We will concentrate, for the moment, on selling an asset and actually receiving some cash for it. The 'costs of disposal' involves very little additional difficulty. So, first, there will be a cash or credit sale of the fixed asset with the appropriate bookkeeping. (We will see what this is in a moment.)

ii Next, the focal organization has to get the fixed asset out of its books. The fixed asset is represented in the books of the focal organization by two accounts – the **cost of the fixed asset account** and **the accumulated depreciation provision for that asset**. We must remove the contents of these accounts as they apply to the asset which is being disposed of. (Note, it should be apparent that there is no 'depreciation charge for the year' to remove because that is an end-of-period adjustment. The last depreciation charge will have been in the accounting period preceding the one in which the asset is disposed of. For simplicity, as we said earlier, many organizations do not depreciate a fixed asset in the year in which it is disposed of. We are continuing with that convention.)

iii Finally, the focal organization needs a systematic way to perform this bookkeeping. The key to this is to open a new account called 'Disposal of asset account'. All the items mentioned above go into this account.

Before we look at an asset disposal and an asset disposal account, there is one further piece of information you need. When a fixed asset is disposed of, if the world was exactly the way accountants would like it to be, then the sale proceeds would exactly equal the NBV of the asset. That is, if the asset is sold at the end of its estimated useful life, then the accountant expects the asset to be sold for the estimated scrap value which was assessed at the start of the asset's life. If the asset is disposed of at any other time – either before or after the end of the asset's estimated useful life – then the accountant might expect the asset proceeds to equal the estimated scrap value plus the portion of the asset which has not yet been depreciated – that is, the asset's NBV. (Think about this if it is not immediately clear.) However, it rarely (if ever) happens like this. So, there will be a difference between the sale proceeds of the asset and the asset's existing NBV. The difference between these two figures is known (inaccurately, we should say) as **the profit**

or loss on disposal of the fixed asset. This figure will also be calculated in the asset disposal account and will, in fact, be its balancing figure.

The steps outlined above are summarized in Figure 9.16. If you always follow these steps, in this order – for each asset separately – you should never have any difficulty. The moment you try and work with NBV or try and keep all assets in the same account or keep assets along with their depreciation in the same account or try and dispose of several assets through the same account, you are very likely to come seriously unstuck. If you follow Figure 9.16 you should end up with a disposal account which looks like Figure 9.17.

There is only one thing to especially note about Figure 9.17 at this stage. For each asset disposal you will only record either a 'profit on disposal' (PPP in Figure 9.17) *or* a 'loss on disposal' (LLL in Figure 9.17). You cannot have both.

The effect of Figure 9.17 is to remove the fixed asset entirely from the books of the focal organization. The only thing that remains is the profit or loss on disposal and this goes off to the trial balance and, from there, to the profit and loss account. The reason it goes to the profit and loss account is not, strictly speaking, because it is called a 'profit' or a 'loss' – these are really misnomers in this case – but because this figure is a recognition that the depreciation charged in previous years was actually higher or lower than it should have been. The original depreciation went through the profit and loss account – the adjustment to that depreciation should go through there as well for (at least a degree of) consistency.

The only thing to do now is to work through an example and see if you can put all you know about depreciation into practice.

THE DOUBLE ENTRY

1. Open an Asset Disposal Account

2. Move the original cost of the asset to the disposal a/c

   Cr. Asset a/c

   Dr. Disposal a/c

3. Move the accumulated dep. on the asset to disposal a/c

   Dr. Accumulated depreciation a/c

   Cr. Disposal a/c

4. Enter the sale proceeds to the disposal a/c

   Dr. Cash Cr. Disposal a/c

5. The difference is the 'profit' or the 'loss' on disposal. This goes to the Trial Balance and/or the Profit and Loss a/c

---

Figure 9.16 Profit or loss on disposal of fixed assets – summary

Inflow/Debit		DISPOSAL OF X ASSET ACCOUNT	Outflow/Credit
X Asset a/c: (Cost)	YYYY	X Asset Dep. a/c: (Accum. Dep.)	DDD
		Sale Proceeds: (Cash)	SSS
Profit on Disposal	PPP	Loss on Disposal	LLL
	AAAA		AAAA

Figure 9.17 A pro-forma asset disposal account

9.6 A WORKED EXAMPLE ON DEPRECIATION AND DISPOSALS OF FIXED ASSETS

In 2002, Yothu Yindi Ltd had the following transactions in its fixed assets. You are required to show these transactions in the books of Yothu Yindi Ltd and produce an extract from the formal profit and loss account and balance sheet of the company for the year ended 31 December 2002. *The company continues to adopt a policy of depreciating assets purchased during the year for a full year and not depreciating assets in their year of disposal.*

- In March 2002 the company sold its wind-powered generator for $18,000 cash.
- In April 2002 the company bought a small wind-farm for $100,000, paying $50,000 in cash and promising to pay the rest of the sale price in 2003. The company expects the wind-farm to have a useful life of 20 years and expects the costs of disposing of the machinery to be covered by the sale proceeds from the scrap machines.
- In May 2002 the company sold the four-wheel drive vehicle for $10,000 and bought two vehicles for $13,000 and $17,000 in cash. These vehicles are expected to last for 5 years and to have disposal values of, respectively, $3,000 and $2,000.

Approach the question systematically:

i   open the appropriate T-accounts;
ii   bring down the opening values;
iii open the disposal accounts;
iv   empty the asset accounts;
v   empty the accumulated deprecation accounts;
vi   account for the proceeds of the sale;
vii close off the accounts;
viii take the figures to the extended trial balance;
ix   complete the depreciation calculations for the year;
x   enter the depreciation end-of-period adjustments in the adjustments column;
xi   keeping the double entry intact, take the figures to the profit and loss account and balance sheet.

Now try it yourself and then check your answer with Appendix 9B. The trick is to go through the question slowly and systematically, ticking off items as you deal with them and taking the stages one at a time. With care, you should have no problems with this. Only one further point is worth noting here. In the profit and loss account, there is a question as to where to place the profits and losses on disposal. Ideally, such gains and losses should be shown separately from trading expenses and revenues. Exactly where the gains and losses end up is not a big issue, but we will touch upon this again in Chapter 14.

This just leaves us with the promised section that looks a bit more carefully at the nature of depreciation.

9.7 ISSUES ARISING WITH DEPRECIATION

There are a number of issues that have arisen in this chapter – either explicitly or implicitly – which we believe we can usefully spend a little time on. This is not in order to improve your technical abilities with bookkeeping and financial accounting but rather to help you continue to think about what it is you are doing. The issues, however, are ones on which you will spend more time in later years of your study of accounting.

9.7.1 Are fixed assets always depreciated?

Do you remember that at the beginning of section 9.2 we suggested that not all fixed assets are always depreciated? Well, whilst you can assume that, to all intents and purposes, plant, machinery, vehicles, fixtures and fittings and so on *are* depreciated, it is not always the case that *land and buildings* are always depreciated. The reason usually given for not depreciating land and buildings is that they actually may *rise* in value whilst they are held by the focal organization and so to record a diminution in their value may be inappropriate. So, the argument goes, to show a declining NBV which is significantly lower than the amount the asset could be sold for, could be seriously misleading to those reading the financial statements. Well, this is probably true. But, goes the counter-argument, not to depreciate land and buildings is, in effect, to say that, on a matching basis, the revenues generated by the focal organization (partly as a result of using that land and buildings) are not being matched with the costs of owning them – we are treating land and buildings as if they were free!

This strikes right at the heart of the accounting problem. There is no consistent theory underlying accounting practice and so, no matter how much disdain you might feel for theory, it is inevitable that conundrums like this cannot be resolved in a simple way. What we have here is a conflict between the idea that financial statements are, on the one hand, supposed to reflect a *matching* process (i.e. should be dominated by the profit and loss account), whilst, on the other hand, it is often suggested that financial statements are supposed to reflect the value of the organization – that they should be based on a *valuation* principle (i.e. they should be dominated by the balance sheet). This problem is just the tip of a much bigger accounting problem which we will touch upon again in Chapters 14, 16 and 18.

For now, try and accept that land and buildings owned by a focal organization may not be depreciated. Try not to confuse this with land or buildings which are held on a *leasehold* by the focal organization. When we talk about owning land and buildings we are typically talking about a *freehold* – that is, the land and buildings are entirely the owners'. A leasehold means that the person owns, not the land and/or buildings, but the *lease* for that land and buildings. This lease might be for a very large amount of money and for a very long time, but, eventually, the land and buildings will return to their owner. If a lease has a fairly short life, then it is normal to depreciate it in the normal way. In fact, this is more typically called **amortization** – a word which is of North American origin and which means exactly the same as 'depreciation'. Indeed, if you are more familiar with North American texts, as we said earlier in the chapter, you will be more used to using 'amortization' than 'depreciation'. So, land and buildings are rarely amortized if they are freehold and may be amortized if they are leasehold. The confusion this may cause need not keep you awake at nights – at least not until later in your career as an accountant.

9.7.2 Depreciation for replacement

We mentioned earlier that there is often an assumption that the depreciation which an organization is 'stashing away' is, in effect, an internal fund with which to replace the asset when its useful life ends. We also noted at the time (with very little explanation) that this was a 'dodgy' assumption. This is a good time to explain the point further. The first thing you should remember is that depreciation has absolutely nothing to do with cash. When an asset is depreciated there is no cash impact on the accounts. Rather, all that happens is that a charge is made to the profit and loss account and a contra asset account is built up in the guise of accumulated depreciation. While it is obvious that there is no cash fund created by depreciation it is less obvious whether or not the act of providing for depreciation may lead to the organization having resources with which to replace the asset when it is sold. In theory, and sometimes in practice, this does arise because the organization (in recognizing the depreciation expense) has kept some of what would otherwise be profit in the organization which may lead to its having a capacity to replace an asset as it wears out. If this is the case then it is unlikely that the organization has consciously planned to 'keep' profits aside to acquire the asset. That depreciating assets will place the organization in a position to purchase another asset is a pure coincidence. It is dubious to assume that an organization will be able to replace an asset merely by recognizing depreciation. This assumption is inaccurate because technology changes, inflation and strategic and legislative changes mean that replacement of the asset will not be as straightforward as all that. Generally speaking, we advise you to ignore this assumption – except in the special case we shall review in Chapter 16.

9.7.3 Some implications arising from depreciation

We could spend a long time discussing depreciation and, indeed, some eminent accounting scholars have spent much of their lives examining just this problem. However, we will be more modest here and restrict ourselves to a further series of conundrums that have arisen in this chapter and which you might have spotted. When we set about depreciating our assets we did three important things. First, we *estimated* the useful life of the asset, then we *estimated* the scrap value and then we *chose* the depreciation method. This process of estimation and choice goes on every day in accounting. How one makes that choice has an enormous impact on the financial statements. Look back over the chapter and you will see that:

i   We identified at least three methods of depreciation and whilst each of them will produce the same *total* depreciation over the life of the asset, they produce startlingly different figures for each year. (Look back at Figures 9.1 and 9.2. Here is the same simple asset depreciated under two different methods and in, for example, Year 1, there is a six-fold difference in the depreciation charge. That is, the profit reported in that year could be altered by $10,000 without any difficulty at all.) If depreciation is a large item in a profit and loss account, this could be important.

ii   The estimated scrap value will make a difference to how much annual depreciation one charges. This is especially true under the reducing balance method. If you look back at Figure 9.2, we used a depreciation percentage of 63% with an estimated scrap value of $1. Had the estimated scrap value been $100, hardly a massive amount, the depreciation percentage would have been 41% – an enormous difference.

iii The estimated life of an asset is clearly difficult to guess reliably. A machine can be made obsolete in only a year or two by a change in technology, the strategy of the firm or, for example, environmental legislation. An estimated life of 10 years might be shrunk to 2 years. Alternatively, some assets may keep on going and going, way beyond their expected useful life.

The point to remember is that the depreciation charge to the profit and loss account is a very significant figure in many organizations' financial statements – and *there is no way on earth that any accountant can ever get it 'right' other than by sheer chance.* As a result, the profit cannot *ever* be 'right' in the sense of strictly accurate. It just isn't possible.

9.7.4 Depreciation, taxation and national differences

A final point to ponder is that not every country in the world approaches depreciation as we have done here. There are many important differences in the ways that different countries do their accounting. One of the most significant centres around how the depreciation is calculated. Throughout the world, it is usually the case that there are very strict rules about how depreciation must be calculated when a business is being assessed for its taxation liability. Given that most business taxation relates to profits and that depreciation has a big impact on profits, this is not surprising. However, in the English-speaking countries (and a number of others) it is usual that the rules used by the taxation authorities and those used to prepare the published financial statements (see Chapter 14) are quite different. There is therefore a major difference between the profit reported to shareholders and the profit reported to the taxation authorities! This situation does not obtain in other countries – most notably Germany and German-influenced countries, where the taxation accounts and the published accounts will be the same.

Depreciation, therefore, is a useful guide to the differences between countries and it is a useful juncture at which to point out to you that profits reported in different countries and for different groups of people will *not* be the same – or sometimes, even similar. There is no such thing as a single profit figure. Do not forget this!

SUMMARY

Depreciation is a potentially complex subject. It is an attempt by the accountant to allocate the cost of a fixed asset over the useful life of that asset in accordance with the matching principle. To do this, however, involves a series of assumptions (about the life of the asset, its pattern of usage and its final value) and choices (about the method to use to make this allocation). These assumptions and choices lead to very different charges to the profit and loss account in each accounting period. The 'accuracy' of the accountant's decisions is effectively tested when the asset is disposed of and the size of the profit or loss on disposal gives an indication of the extent to which the asset was under- or over-depreciated in previous accounting periods. The bookkeeping for depreciation is complex but, if approached in a systematic way, should not cause you too many problems. The keys are: first, to ensure that you are completely clear about the distinction between the *depreciation charge for the year* and the *accumulated depreciation provision*; and, second, to ensure that all elements of the fixed assets, their depreciation charges and their accumulated depreciation provision are kept separate from each other. If each is dealt with separately, the confusion that often results should be kept to a minimum.

FURTHER READING

Once again you will find material on depreciation in any introductory accounting textbook. From our point of view, however, we think it is important that you recognise the arbitrary nature of depreciation but without getting too sucked in to the theoretical complexities of the academic and professional debates about depreciation. In this sense, reading through

Key terms and concepts

The following key terms and concepts have featured in this chapter. You should ensure that you understand and can explain each one. Page references to definitions appear in the index in bold type.

- Accumulated depreciation provision
- Amortization
- The arbitrariness of depreciation
- The arbitrariness of the profit figure
- Depreciation
- Depreciation for taxation
- Depreciation charge for the year
- Depreciation policy
- Disposal of fixed assets

- Estimated scrap value
- Estimated useful life
- Fixed assets
- Net book value
- Non-depreciation of assets
- Profit or loss on disposal
- Reducing balance method
- Sale proceeds
- Straight line method

annual reports, looking at their depreciation policies and practices will be as useful as anything.

NOTES

1. The reasons for this are arithmetic. It should be fairly obvious to you why this is the case. If it is not, you might like to brush up your arithmetic skills and just accept this as an arithmetic quirk for the time being.
2. The phrase 'a group of fixed assets' should not concern you. For many organizations, it will be impracticable to depreciate every single fixed asset separately so they will be held in groups which, in general, will be determined by the depreciation policy relating to those assets. So all manufacturing machines might be held together and all packing machines held together. Similarly, the staff cars may be held together but plant vehicles treated separately.

APPENDIX 9A THE NEW FINANCIAL STATEMENTS FOR YOTHU YINDI LTD 2001

Including the depreciation of fixed assets

YOTHU YINDI LTD: PROFIT and LOSS ACCOUNT FOR THE YEAR ENDING 31 DECEMBER 2001 (all figures are in dollars)		
SALES		500,000
less PURCHASES (or cost of goods sold)		(212,000)
GROSS OR TRADING PROFIT		288,000
EXPENSES:		
Depreciation for the year	5,000	
Rent	120,000	
Rates	24,000	
Telephone	12,000	
Wages	24,000	
Electricity	4,800	
Gas	2,400	(192,200)
NET PROFIT FOR THE PERIOD		95,800

YOTHU YINDI LTD BALANCE SHEET				
AS AT 31 DECEMBER 2001 (all figures are in dollars)				

FIXED ASSETS	Cost	Acc Dep'n	NBV	
Wind-powered Generator	20,000	4,000	16,000	
4-wheel drive vehicle	16,000	3,000	13,000	29,000
CURRENT ASSETS:				
Trade Debtors			30,000	
Prepayments:		Rent	20,000	
		Goods	1,000	
		Rates	6,000	
		Telephone	1,000	
Cash			90,800	
			148,800	
CURRENT LIABILITIES:				
Trade Creditors			35,000	
Sundry Creditors			2,000	
Accruals and Provisions		Wages	2,000	
		Electricity	400	
		Gas	200	
		Telephone	500	
			40,100	108,700
NET ASSETS				**$137,700**
REPRESENTED BY:				
Share Capital				40,000
Profit and Loss Account:		brought forward	1,900	
		for the year	95,800	97,700
SHAREHOLDERS'/OWNERS' FUNDS				**$137,700**

APPENDIX 9B THE FIXED ASSET T-ACCOUNTS FOR YOTHU YINDI LTD 2002

Inflow/Debit	FIXED ASSET (Cost): GENERATOR		Outflow/Credit
1.1.02 Bal b/d	20,000	3.02 Disposal Account	20,000

Inflow/Debit	FIXED ASSET (Cost): 4WD VEHICLE		Outflow/Credit
1.1.02 Bal b/d	16,000	5.02 Disposal Account	16,000

Inflow/Debit	ACCUM DEPRECIATION: GENERATOR		Outflow/Credit
3.02 Disposal Account	4,000	1.1.02 Bal b/d	4,000

Inflow/Debit	ACCUM DEPRECIATION: 4WD VEHICLE		Outflow/Credit
5.02 Disposal Account	3,000	1.1.02 Bal b/d	3,000

Inflow/Debit	CASH		Outflow/Credit
1.1.02 Bal b/d	90,800	4.02 Wind-farm Purchase	50,000
3.02 Asset Disposal Account (Generator)	18,000	etc......	
5.02 Asset Disposal A/c (4WD Vehicle)	10,000		
etc......		Bal c/d (to TB)	....

Inflow/Debit	ASSET DISPOSAL: GENERATOR		Outflow/Credit
3.02 Cost of Asset	20,000	3.02 Sale Proceeds	18,000
		3.02 Accum Dep'n	4,000
3.02 Profit on Disposal (to TB)	2,000		
	22,000		22,000

Inflow/Debit	FIXED ASSET COST: WIND-FARM		Outflow/Credit
4.02 Cash	50,000	12.02 Bal c/d (to TB)	100,000
4.02 Creditors	50,000		
	100,000		100,000

Inflow/Debit	CREDITORS		Outflow/Credit
12.02 Bal C/d (to TB)	50,000	4.02 Wind-farm Purchase	50,000

Inflow/Debit	FIXED ASSET DISPOSAL: 4WD VEHICLE		Outflow/Credit
5.02 Cost	16,000	5.02 Accum Dep'n	3,000
		5.02 Proceeds of sale	10,000
		Loss on disposal (to TB)	3,000
	16,000		16,000

Inflow/Debit	FIXED ASSETS COST: VEHICLES		Outflow/Credit
5.02 Cash	13,000	12.02 Bal c/d (to TB)	30,000
5.02	17,000		
	30,000		30,000

THE EXTENDED TRIAL BALANCE FOR YOTHU YINDI LTD AT END OF 2002 (EXTRACT)

EXTENDED TRIAL BALANCE at 31 DECEMBER 2002								
Account	Trial balance		Adjustments		Profit and loss		Balance sheet	
	Dr	Cr	Dr	Cr	Dr	Cr	Dr	Cr
Cash	xxxxx						xxxxx	
Disposal (4WD)	3,000				3,000			
Disposal (Generator)		2,000				1,000		
Creditors		50,000						50,000
Fixed assets:								
Wind-farm	100,000						100,000	
Vehicles	30,000						30,000	
Dep'n charge:								
Wind-farm			5,000					
Vehicle 1			2,000					
Vehicle 2			3,000		10,000			
Accum dep'n:								
Wind-farm				5,000				5,000
Vehicle 1				2,000				2,000
Vehicle 2				3,000				3,000
etc......								
TOTALS	xxxxx	xxxxx	10,000	10,000				

EXTRACT FROM THE FINANCIAL STATEMENTS FOR YOTHU YINDI LTD 2002

Including the depreciation of fixed assets

YOTHU YINDI LTD: PROFIT AND LOSS ACCOUNT		
FOR THE YEAR ENDING 31 DECEMBER 2002 (Extract – all figures are in dollars)		
SALES	xxx,xxx	
less PURCHASES (or cost of goods sold)		(xxx,xxx)
GROSS OR TRADING PROFIT		xxx,xxx
EXPENSES:		
Depreciation for the year	10,000	
Profit on Disposal	(2,000)	
Loss on Disposal	3,000	(xxx,xxx)
etc......		
NET PROFIT FOR THE PERIOD		xx,xxx

YOTHU YINDI LTD BALANCE SHEET				
AS AT 31 DECEMBER 2002 (all figures are in dollars)				
FIXED ASSETS:	Cost	Acc Dep'n	NBV	
Wind-farm	100,000	5,000	95,000	
Vehicle 1	13,000	2,000	3,000	
Vehicle 2	17,000	3,000	14,000	112,000
CURRENT ASSETS:				
Trade Debtors			xxxxxx	
Prepayments			xxxxxx	
Cash			xxxxxxx	
CURRENT LIABILITIES:				
Creditor (Fixed Asset)			50,000	
Trade Creditors			xxx,xxx	
Sundry Creditors			xx,xxx	
Accruals & Provisions			xxx	
			xxxxxx	
				xxx,xxx
NET ASSETS				$xxx,xxx
REPRESENTED BY:				
Share Capital				xxxxx
Profit and Loss Account:	brought forward		97,700	xxxxxx
	for the year		xx,xxx	
SHAREHOLDERS'/OWNERS' FUNDS				$xxx,xxx

Stock allocation, valuation and the cost of sales **10**

Learning objectives

After studying this chapter you should be able to:

- explain what stock or inventory is and how it arises;
- demonstrate the essential relationship between stock and cost of sales;
- understand the difference between opening and closing stock;
- explain what a stocktake is and why it is important;
- define FIFO, LIFO and AVCO, explain the differences and give a brief explanation of the reasons for using each one;
- undertake simple valuations of stock on FIFO, LIFO and AVCO bases;
- explain what is meant by the lower of cost or NRV rule;
- demonstrate the lower of cost or NRV rule in a simple example;
- explain and apply a stock provision;
- explain what happens to stock in a manufacturing organization;
- recognise the relationship between the management accounting system and the financial accounting system for the valuation of manufacturing stock;
- construct a trading account and a simple manufacturing account;
- undertake the basic bookkeeping for stock;
- undertake simple end-of-period adjustments on stock;
- demonstrate how these items are represented in the trial balance, the profit and loss account and balance sheet of the focal organization.

10.1 INTRODUCTION

10.1.1 Chapter design and links to previous chapters

This chapter introduces the third of the major end-of-period adjustments you need to know about in order to construct a basic set of financial statements. It is one of the most important in accounting and is concerned with how the accountants in the focal organization treat **stock** (or **inventory** as it is more usually known in North America) and the related **cost of sales** or **cost of goods sold**. Once again, this adjustment arises because of the *periodicity* principle (dividing the economic events up into specific accounting periods) and the *accrual* principle (matching and allocating those economic events to the appropriate periods). We have already seen the end-of-period adjustments we have to make for accruals, prepayments and general provisions (Chapter 8) and for depreciation of fixed assets (Chapter 9). You are perhaps beginning to see that it is the end-of-period adjustments – the 'accounting' – rather than the recording of the transactions – the 'bookkeeping' – which causes most of the difficulty in putting together the financial statements. As with the previous adjustments, if you can keep a fairly clear picture in your mind as to (i) what is actually happening in the focal organization and (ii) what the accounting process is trying to achieve, then you should not have any great difficulties.

The chapter is organized as follows. The following subsections explain what stock is and how it arises before going on to explain the relationship between stock and cost of sales. Section 10.2 introduces stock valuation methods for the less complicated case of retail stock. The section then proceeds to introduce the 'lower of cost or net realizable value rule' and to demonstrate how the material we have covered up until this point is shown in a basic set of financial statements. Section 10.3 looks at the more complicated situation which arises with manufacturing organizations and introduces the trading account and the manufacturing account. Section 10.4 provides an illustration of all these issues and provides a step-by-step approach to the bookkeeping and accounting necessary to handle stock and cost of sales in financial statements. There then follows the usual summary and conclusions.

10.1.2 What is stock/inventory?

You have already met stock (or inventory if you prefer).[1] In Chapter 7, stock was identified as one of the current assets and, in Figure 7.4, Game Girl Ages Enterprises actually had a small amount of stock in the form of unsold games. We also met stock (although we did not call it this) in Chapter 5 when Bird Industries had some wood and bird seed left over at the end of the accounting period.

So we actually know quite a bit about stock: it is a current asset; it is especially important to recognize its existence at the end of the accounting period (hence it is an end-of-period adjustment); and it relates to unsold things which the focal organization owns. But let's start at the beginning.

Stock arrives in the focal organization as **purchases**. We know that purchases, broadly, can come in four forms:

i   physical things like machinery, land, buildings, etc., which will last more than one accounting period. These we called fixed assets and we saw how to deal with these in Chapter 9. We do not treat these as 'stock';

ii   non-physical things like know-how, patents, research and development, etc., which will last for more than one accounting period. We called these intangible assets and we do not treat these as stock either;

iii   goods which we buy: (a) in order to resell (often called 'trading purchases'), (b) in order to use to make something else (sometimes called 'manufacturing purchases') or (c) in order to use in a general way during the everyday life of the organization (frequently called 'consumables'). All of these goods will pass into **stock**. They will be drawn upon during the accounting period and, if there are any left at the end of an accounting period, the amount we have left will be part of the organisation's **closing stock**;

iv   services we buy, like the services of employees, consultants or advertising agencies, which will also be consumed by the organization in the process of generating its outputs (or sales in a business). These purchases might also form part of the stock – but how this happens is a bit complex and so we will ignore it for the time being and come back to it later in the chapter (in section 10.3).

10.1.3 A simple example introducing cost of sales

Let us just concentrate on the goods which the focal organization purchases in category (iii) above and let us look at the simplest of all cases – goods purchased for resale. Let us imagine that you start with 1,000 pesetas and you buy ten cans of beans for resale. (You have no other business assets including no **opening stock**.) You pay 100 pesetas per can in cash. Your bookkeeping is simple: [Debit purchases 1,000 pesetas: Credit cash 1,000 pesetas]. During the week you sell eight cans of beans at 200 pesetas each for cash. Your bookkeeping for this is [Debit cash 1,600 pesetas: Credit sales 1,600 pesetas). At the end of the week you draw up your financial statements. How do these transactions show in those statements? You have sales of 1,600 pesetas, you have cash of 600 pesetas, and you have two cans of beans. What do you do with the cans of beans (you are not allowed to eat them) and what do you do with the purchases figure of 1,000 pesetas? One step at a time. You have two cans of beans which cost you 100 pesetas each. You have a **closing stock at cost** of 200 pesetas. That is, 200 pesetas' worth of your purchases are still inside the operations subsystem of the focal organization and are available to you for future use – they are a current asset called 'stock'. What about the rest of your purchases – the other 800 pesetas? Well, they have gone. They (the eight cans of beans) left the focal organization when you sold them. Therefore, the 800 pesetas must be the cost of making those sales or your **cost of sales** for the period.

So, what has happened here? Purchases have arrived in the focal organization in the usual way. During the accounting period some have left the organization as sales. Some have remained in the focal organization. At the end of the accounting period we must split our purchases figure up to represent the purchases which have left the organization as part of sales (the **cost of sales** for the period) and those which have remained in the organization at the end of the accounting period (the **closing stock**).

The bookkeeping is shown in Figure 10.1. *Do note* that for simplicity we have simply opened two new accounts for **stock** and for **cost of sales**. Check the numbers through and ensure that you can see where everything has come from and gone to.

Inflow/Debit		CASH		Outflow/Credit	
Opening cash balance etc...			Monday:	Beans purchases:	1,000
During the week: Sales:	1,600				

Inflow/Debit		TRADE PURCHASES		Outflow/Credit	
Monday: 10 tins of beans, cash	1,000		Saturday:	2 tins (stock)	200
			Saturday:	8 tins (sold)	800

Inflow/Debit	SALES		Outflow/Credit	
		During the week: 8 tins cash		1,600

plus two new accounts:

Inflow/Debit		STOCK/INVENTORY	Outflow/Credit
Saturday: 2 tins of beans	200		

Inflow/Debit		COST OF SALES	Outflow/Credit
Saturday: 8 tins of beans	800		

Figure 10.1 Basic T-accounts for buying and selling beans

All that has happened in Figure 10.1 is that, on Saturday, at the end of the trading week, we have looked to see how many tins of beans we have left (we will come to call this a **stocktake**) and have then gone back to our purchases account and split those purchases up into two types of things – things left over (in this case 'stock') and things used up (in this case 'cost of sales'). We have then cleared out the purchases account to reflect this.

You could now take these figure to the trial balance or, because we have no other end-of-period adjustments in this simple example, you could take them directly to the profit and loss account and balance sheet. Extracts from these would like something like Figure 10.2.

BEAN TRADING LTD: PROFIT AND LOSS ACCOUNT FOR THE WEEK ENDING ... 2001
(figures in pesetas)

SALES		1,600
less Cost of Goods Sold		(800)
GROSS OR TRADING PROFIT		800
EXPENSES:		
Listed by category	X,XXX	
......	X,XXX	
......	X,XXX	
	XX,XXX	
Sub-Total of Expenses		(XXX,XXX)
NET PROFIT FOR THE PERIOD		XXX,XXX

BEAN TRADING LTD: BALANCE SHEET AT ... 2001
(figures in pesetas)

FIXED ASSETS		XXX,XXX
CURRENT ASSETS:		
Stock	200	
Trade Debtors	XX,XXX	
Prepayments	XX,XXX	
Cash	600	
	XXX,XXX	
CURRENT LIABILITIES:		
Trade Creditors	XX,XXX	
Sundry Creditors	XX,XXX	
Accruals & Provisions	XX,XXX	
	XX,XXX	
NET CURRENT ASSETS		XXX,XXX
NET ASSETS		**XXX,XXX**
REPRESENTED BY:		
Share Capital		XX,XX
Profit and Loss Account		XXX,XXX
SHAREHOLDERS'/OWNERS' FUNDS		**XXX,XXX**

Figure 10.2 How ten tins of beans appear in the financial statements

10.1.4 Summarizing the basic relationship between stock and cost of sales

Hopefully, you find this all very straightforward. If so, good! This splitting of the purchases is *the* essential issue when accounting for stock and cost of sales. All the rest (and there is a lot more) is simply adding (rather a lot of) whistles and bells to this basic story. But maybe you find the ideas a bit confusing? After all, up until this chapter we had kept the purchases and the sales apart and here we are running them together. Well, think of your flow diagram for the organization.

Inputs (purchases) enter the operational subsystem. The purchases are split into (basically) three categories. Some go off to the fixed and intangibles assets, some go into service accounts (like wages) and others are trade purchases. These trade purchases sit around for a bit and then they leave as outputs (sales). However, not all of them leave – some are left behind as stock. This process is summarized in Figure 10.3.

The stock which is left over at the end of the accounting period (the **closing stock**) is then available at the start of the next accounting period as **opening stock**. (This is just a continuation of the process we have already seen in which the closing balance sheet represents the opening balances for the next accounting period.)

The rest of this chapter will be refining this basic picture. We need to think rather more carefully about the nature of stock and how we treat it. Not all organizations have stock as simple as our ten tins of beans and the more complex the stock situation the more complex the bookkeeping and accounting. Also, we want to have a look in more detail at how we might put these end-of-period adjustments through either the initial trial balance or through a set of T-accounts. It won't be obvious yet, but accounting for stock is one of the most important areas that companies use to 'smooth' their income. That is, because of the very close link between the stock in the balance sheet and the cost of sales figures, changes in the value of stock can have a large effect on the profit and loss account. How much discretion does management have in determining these two figures – and therefore the reported profit or loss figure? This is an issue on which we have to be especially clear.

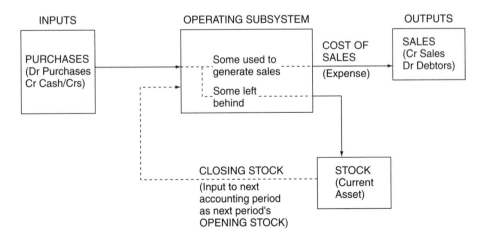

Figure 10.3 A simple stock cycle

10.2 THE VALUATION OF STOCK AND INVENTORY: THE SIMPLE CASE

In this section we will concentrate upon the 'simple' type of stock – that is, goods purchased for retail. This is the simplest situation – for example, a shop, store or wholesaler – where trade purchases are resold without the focal organization doing anything to them (except perhaps displaying them well or putting a variety of items together for customers to look at), the goods come in as purchases and leave as sales. In the following sections we will then turn to look at more complex situations arising with, for example, manufacturing companies.

10.2.1 The stocktake

At the end of every accounting period the focal organization needs to know how much stock it has. There are three main reasons for this:

i   It needs an accurate estimate of the stock for the purposes of constructing its financial statements – that is, for estimating closing stock.
ii It needs to know about the condition of the stock at the end of the year because some of the stock may be deteriorating, or may have been damaged or stolen, for example. A physical, annual (or more frequent) inspection should do this.
iii It needs to know how accurate its own stock accounting records have been during the accounting period. These records are important as a basis for assessing whether particular lines are moving faster than others and are used as a basis of ordering further goods. Their accuracy is therefore very important to the success of the company. Alternatively, in a small concern, there may not be any stock accounting records. Regular stocktakes will overcome this lack of information and, perhaps, lead the focal organization to consider installing a stock records system.

The annual physical stocktake can be a major event. It will usually involve closing the shop, store or warehouse so that all the staff can concentrate on a systematic physical count of all the goods on the premises. Imagine the situation for a major supermarket or retail store. There are many different types and brands of goods on the shelves, on the counters, in the storeroom at the back of the premises or in a warehouse where back-up stock is held. This must all be counted and the results collated so that the focal organization knows what stock it has and where it is located. In the process, the staff will make assessments about the condition and security of the goods and materials and these assessments will then be recorded as well.

Then the office staff will compare the results of the stocktake with the stock records (if they have them) or with an estimate from the accounting records about how much should be still in stock – (purchases less sales of each item). Discrepancies will be investigated and then a final schedule containing the details of all stock, its condition and how quickly or slowly it is moving (its turnover) will be produced. This will then form the basis for the development (if necessary) of the accounting information system with regard to the stock. It will certainly form the basis of the accountants' estimate of the stock figure to appear in the balance sheet.

10.2.2 Costing the stock

So now the accountant has a list of all the stock owned by the company at the accounting date (usually the year-end). They can also now retrieve the prices paid for this stock, item by item. If the focal organization does not keep its accounting records in a computerized form this can be a long-winded process. If the accounting records are not very detailed – or mistakes have been made – it can be necessary to go back to the individual invoices and record, by hand, each of the prices paid for the purchases that are now included in stock. Although this may be a very long-winded process, it is basically a simple one. Or at least it would be if everything behaved in the way we have described it here. Life, as we are always telling you, is, sadly, never that simple.

There are two problems our accountant needs to consider before they can cost the stock. They need to consider how they are going to deal with slow-moving or obsolete stock items (which we will deal with in section (10.2.3) below) and they need to consider *how* they are going to cost the stock. We will deal with this latter point now.

'Hang on!', you might be saying, 'I thought you had just said that we cost stock by taking the physical quantity from the stocktake and multiplying it, item by item, by the price we paid for that item of purchases now included in the stock.' Well, indeed we do, but, unfortunately, 'the price we paid' rarely stays steady over a whole year. Consider the data shown in Figure 10.4.

Look carefully through Figure 10.4. We have kept things a little easier by having no opening stock for each item. Also, we can ignore the sales price for the time being (that comes into play in the next subsection).

The basic question we have to answer is 'What value should we place on stock?'. Now, the question is not quite as simple as it looks because the prices of the purchases have been changing over the period. In general the prices paid by Ridiculous for its purchases have risen over the period. However, this need not be the case. Technological developments or special offers from suppliers might bring the cost to the company down. The question is not so simple because if we look at item 2 ('Sing-along with The Clash'), the company sold none of these until the final quarter of the year. At the end of the year the company has five of these remaining – but which five? Before you leap to a conclusion (which may seem obvious, but wait a minute), there are three main methods of costing stock. These are known as the **first-in, first-out (FIFO)**, **last-in, first-out (LIFO)**[2] and **average cost (AVCO)** methods of stock valuation.

EXTRACT FROM RIDICULOUS RECORDS LIMITED STOCK REPORT: 31 December 2004								
TITLE OF RECORD	Opening stock	Purchases in year			Sales in year			Closing stock
		Date	Number	Cost per item (£)	Date	Number	Price per item (£)	
1. 'The Iron Maiden Mozart Collection: Volume II'	0	2 January	10	2.00	March	8	3.00	
		4 April	10	2.50	June	10	3.00	
		8 April	5	2.50	Sept.	5	3.50	
		7 Sept.	20	2.80	Dec.	15	3.50	
		11 Nov.	5	3.00				12
2. 'Sing-along with The Clash'	0	2 January	10	2.00	March	0	3.00	
		7 Sept.	10	2.00	June	0	3.00	
		11 Nov.	10	.50	Sept.	0	3.50	
					Dec.	25	1.00	5
3. 'St Paul's Cathedral Choir Sing the Sex Pistols: Volume VI'	0	2 January	40	4.50	March	35	3.00	
		4 April	20	4.50	June	0	4.00	
		11 Nov.	5	5.00	Sept.	0	4.00	
					Dec.	20	4.50	10

Figure 10.4 Extract from Ridiculous Record Limited stock reports

Ridiculous Records Ltd has just completed its stocktake for the year ended 31 December 2004. It is the company's first year in business. The company carries over 1,000 different records, tapes and CDs and it is concerned about how to record its stock (and cost of goods sold) in the financial statements for the year-end. The company extracts the information presented here from its accounting records (which now agree with the stocktake) and asks for your advice. (Please ignore the company's bizarre purchasing policy, its strange pricing structure and the seasonal nature of these sales – which are recorded here quarterly.)

(a) First-in, first-out (FIFO)

The 'common sense' answer to the question of which five of item 2 are remaining at the year-end is that the company sold the oldest records first and, therefore, the stock of five consists of the most recent purchases. This is, in fact, the most common choice for stock-valuation. FIFO works on the principle that the oldest stock is sold first. (That is, the first item taken into stock is the first item out when a sale is made. Thus the stock at the end of the accounting period comprises the most recently purchased items.) Therefore, to cost stock you just work back through the purchases. For item 2 this is simple. The last ten items purchased cost 50p each, there are five left, so each of these cost 50p. The value of stock on item 2 is £2.50.

So, what about item 1 ('The Iron Maiden Mozart Collection')? We have 12 items left in stock at the year end. Working on a FIFO basis these must be the last items we bought. But the last purchase we made was only for five items at £3.00 each. We need 12 items, so we go back to the next purchase. This was for 20 items at £2.80 each. So the stock of item 1 comprises, on a FIFO basis, the five items at £3.00 each (£15.00) plus seven items (the 12 in stock less the five we have just costed) at £2.80 each (£19.60). So the stock of item 1, on a FIFO basis, is £34.60.

You do item 3 (St Paul's Cathedral Choir) and if you do not get £47.50 go back and check your sums. If that doesn't work, check the endnote.[3]

Thus, on the FIFO basis, these three items from Ridiculous Records' stocktake are valued at £84.60 (that is, £2.50 + £34.60 + £47.50). And this helps us determine the cost of sales. That is (look back to Figure 10.3 if you have problems), total purchases for these three lines was £468.50 (if this gives you problems see the endnote.[4]) At the end of the year this must be split into those purchases which have left the focal organization (as sales) and those which are remaining as stock. We have just calculated the FIFO stock valuation of £84.60. We know the purchases figure is £468.50. So the FIFO cost of sales must be £383.90 (that is, £468.50 – £84.60). (And we stress that is the *FIFO* cost of sales for reasons which will become apparent in a minute.)

If FIFO *is* the 'common-sense' approach to stock valuation, why do we need other methods? The problem that can arise with FIFO is that, in times of inflation, it *overstates* stock and *understates* cost of sales. That is, cost of sales comprises the oldest items (and therefore the lowest costs) and the stock comprises the newest items (and therefore the highest costs). We may therefore be showing our assets (in this case stock) in their best light and our expenses at their lowest (in this case cost of sales). This may, in certain circumstances, be in contravention of the *prudence* or *conservatism* principle we discussed earlier. (The full implications of this will become apparent in Chapter 16.) Suffice it to say for now, that although some countries permit (and indeed encourage) the use of FIFO (the UK is one such country) other countries (for example, the USA) positively disallow the method for reasons of prudence. In its place, the USA requires LIFO.

(b) Last-in, first-out (LIFO)

LIFO takes the opposite point of view to FIFO. In this case it is assumed that the most recent entries to stock are those which are sold first. (This is not always unrealistic, of course. If one is not careful new stock can be placed on the shelves in front of old stock, new nuts and bolts can be piled into bins on top of old ones. And so on.) If Ridiculous Records valued their stock on LIFO they would value the stock of item 1 at £25.00, the stock of item 2 at £10.00, and the stock of item 3 at £45.00. The stock of these three items would be £80.00. Thus the *LIFO* cost of sales would be £388.50. (Check these figures and if it is not clear turn to the endnote.)[5]

The differences are not great in this case, between LIFO and FIFO, but imagine if inflation (or other price changes) were more extreme and remember that Ridiculous Records has 1,000 lines of stock. The differences can easily become quite significant.

Finally, we have the method of stock valuation which most countries permit and, it has to be said, is perhaps the easiest to operate. That is, the average cost method of stock valuation.

(c) Average cost (AVCO)

The average cost method is something of a compromise. In effect, the average cost of stock says 'let us steer between these two extremes'. It is relatively simple to calculate. The total value of purchases of each item are summed and this total is divided by the number of items purchased. This gives an average unit cost per item of stock (and, of course, the same unit average cost of sales). In the case of Ridiculous Records, the average cost of item 1 is £2.57 per item (£128.50 ÷ 50 items), the average unit cost of item 2 is £1.50 (£45.00 ÷ 30 items), and the average unit cost of item 3 is £4.538 (£295.00 ÷ 65). Thus average cost stock is valued at £83.72 (£30.84 + £7.50 + £45.38) and the average cost of sales is £384.78 (that is £468.50 − £83.72). These results are summarized in Figure 10.5.

There are two final things to notice about the numbers in Figure 10.5. First, the *sum* of the cost of sales and the stock under each method is identical. This *must* be so because all we are doing is allocating purchases between stock and cost of sales. Second, you will notice that for items 1 and 3, for which prices rose during the period, the stock valuation

	METHOD OF STOCK VALUATION		
	FIFO (Sales from the oldest items: Stock consists of the newest items)	AVERAGE COST (Sales and stock are drawn evenly over the year)	LIFO (Sales are drawn from the newest items: stock consists of the oldest items)
Stock Valuation: Item 1 Item 2 Item 3	£34.60 £2.50 £47.50	£30.84 £7.50 £45.38	£25.00 £10.00 £45.00
Stock Total:	£84.60	£83.72	£80.00
Cost of Sales: Item 1 Item 2 Item 3	£93.90 £42.50 £247.50	£97.66 £37.50 £249.62	£103.50 £35.00 £250.00
Cost of Sales Total	£383.90	£384.78	£388.50
TOTAL OF STOCK AND COST OF SALES (i.e Purchases for the period)	£468.50	£468.50	£468.50

Figure 10.5 A summary of LIFO, FIFO and average cost stock valuation for Ridiculous Records Limited

method produces the lowest figures for the LIFO stock, the next lowest for average cost and the highest stock figure for FIFO. The opposite is true for the cost of sales figures for these two items. In the case of cost of sales, FIFO produces the lowest cost of sales whilst LIFO produces the highest cost of sales figure. *This is not true* for item 2. This is because the purchase price of item 2 fell during the period. These points will always hold true. In times of inflation LIFO will produce higher cost of sales figures and lower stock figures than FIFO. In times of deflation (or other causes of price decline) the results from FIFO and LIFO will be the other way around.

A lot more *could* be said about valuation methods for stock but this is quite enough for this stage in your studies. So now, with this under your belt, we can turn to look at the second element of valuing stock – what happens to slow-moving or obsolete stock?

10.2.3 The lower of cost or net realizable value rule and provisions for slow-moving, damaged or obsolete stock

Having physically identified all our stock and then costed it using the focal organization's policy on stock valuation, we now have to stand back and have a bit of a think about the numbers we have calculated. The problem that we have to consider is one with which you are becoming increasingly familiar. That is, what are the figures for *stock* and *cost of sales* supposed to *mean*? Are they just bookkeeping entries for the sake of tidiness – i.e they are the proportion of the costs of purchases which have yet to leave the organization? Or are the figures supposed to tell us something about the financial condition of the focal organization – i.e. they are an 'accurate' measure of the profit for the period and an indication of what the organization has available for sale in future accounting periods as a source of future profits? We have already noted that different countries lay down different rules on whether or not stock should be valued by FIFO or LIFO. This tells us that there *is* some confusion over the accounting profession's views on what 'signal' these numbers should be sending.

These questions *can* get very complicated indeed. (We will look at some of the issues in Chapter 16.) How far can we go without getting too complicated? The easiest way to do this is to look at the standard procedures that accountants undertake – and leave the worry over *why* they do this and what they *should do* to later. So try and remember that what follows is really rather too simple and, more especially, that it is also rather arbitrary – it wouldn't win any prizes in a logical consistency test.

Having identified the cost of stock the accountant has to undertake two further principal investigations. These are both concerned with the 'saleability' of the items contained in the stock figure and involve two steps:

i identification of stock which is damaged, obsolete or slow-moving;
ii examination of what needs to be done (if anything) by the focal organization to make some of the stock saleable.

The two are closely related and fall under the **lower of cost** or **net realizable value** rule. That is, the figure for stock must include each item at the cost of that item (much like we did for Ridiculous Records) *unless* there are grounds for believing that the focal organization will be unable to sell the item at a resale price greater than the cost. That is, the item's **realizable value** (what you could sell it for) might be less than what you paid for it (the figure currently shown in stock). To illustrate, think back to the tins of beans example. We had a stock of two tins of beans which had cost 100 pesetas each.

We valued stock at 200 pesetas. Imagine the situation if one of the tins were damaged so badly that no one in their right mind would buy it and we had to throw it away (sale value of zero pesetas) and the other tin had lost its label so that anyone buying it was taking a gamble and might only pay you 50 pesetas to take that gamble. The *realizable value* of these two tins of beans is, therefore, 50 pesetas, whereas the cost (shown in stock) is 200 pesetas. The cost is clearly higher than the realizable value. The rule says we must show stock at the lower of these two figures. Therefore stock must be shown at 50 pesetas, *not* 200 pesetas.

Such a situation may arise for many reasons. Some of the more common include:

i   damage to stock items (as happened to the tins of beans) which means that customers will not pay a full price – or any price – for the item;
ii obsolete stock items which, for example, have been superseded by a newer product. For example, Ridiculous Records may well find that its stock of vinyl records has become obsolete as more people own CD players. The result of this is that the focal organization may be unable to sell the products or can only sell them by, for example, heavy discounting on the price or incurring extra advertising costs to reach specialist markets;
iii slow-moving stock may be a problem for the focal organization because it may be unsure that it can ever completely sell its stock of an item which is taking up useful space and tying up the cash of the business. It may decide to scrap or discount these items;
iv technological change may mean that newer items can be purchased for less than the older items cost. This happened some years ago with pocket calculators which were fairly expensive at first but came down in price very fast. The older ones had cost the business more than the current market price for the new ones. Competitors may thus be able to sell their stock at a cheaper price, meaning that the focal organization has to 'take a loss' on its stock;
v   other changes may mean that the organization will have to incur extra costs to sell an item – perhaps advertising, or perhaps some extra work to clean up or change an item or, perhaps, additional transport costs to get an item to a new market. In this case the sale price may still be the same but the organization will have to incur additional costs in order to achieve that sale price. Thus the *net* realizable value is reduced – by the amount of the extra costs. If, as often happens, these extra costs are greater than the difference between the sale price of the item and what it originally cost the focal organisation, then the *net realizable value* (the NRV) will be below the cost.

In each of these situations the accountant will have to adjust the stock cost downwards. As suggested above, this will be done in two stages: (1) testing to see which is lower – the cost or the NRV – and if the NRV is lower than the cost, the NRV must be the amount shown in the accounts for that item of stock; and (2) where the cost is lower than the NRV (which will be the case for most resale stock) the accountant will make judgements as to whether or not the cost needs to be reduced to allow for any of the possible problems we have discussed above.

The adjustments that the accountant makes will take the form of a *provision – in the interests of prudence*. This will be an estimate of the amount of the stock value which must be *written off* in order to achieve the desired value for stock. The bookkeeping will be fairly straightforward: first [Credit stock] (to reduce it by the amount judged appropriate), and second [Debit provisions] to produce an expense to be taken to the profit and loss account. *For reasons of convention, the cost of sales figure is not affected by this transaction.*

Let us have a quick look back at Ridiculous Records in order to see how all of this might work. (Refer to Figures 10.4 and 10.5.) Let us stick to Ridiculous Records' FIFO calculations and let us imagine that we discover the following:

1. Ten of the covers on item 1 ('The Iron Maiden Mozart Collection') have been damaged. Replacement covers would cost 60p each. The shop estimates that the records with the damaged covers will sell for £3.00 each.

2. The shop is naturally concerned about the sales patterns on item 2 ('Sing-along with The Clash'). They estimate that they are not going to sell any more until next Christmas – and then only at reduced price. They decide to give the records away as a sales promotion.

3. Item 3 ('St Pauls Cathedral Choir') has caused some problems. Obviously the record is also seasonal and the shop has just heard that Volume VII is being pressed at the moment. Furthermore, the shop could not help but notice that they are selling the item for less than they pay for it. They believe that they should be able to sell all ten items in stock by keeping the price down at £4.50.

> **Hint**
>
> Once again you will gain more from what follows if you take a pen and paper (or a spreadsheet in your personal laptop if you prefer) and try the calculations for yourself before looking at the answers we suggest. The value of this will be to help you clarify your own thinking and this will be especially helpful if you spend time trying to assess why differences (if any) have arisen.

How should Ridiculous Records undertake the adjustments? Take each item, one by one:

1. Item 1 had a FIFO valuation of £34.60 comprising five items at £3.00 cost and seven items at £2.80 cost. Assuming that we do not know exactly *which* of the 12 need the new covers we may as well assume it is the oldest of the FIFO stock. The current price for the record is £3.50. The NRV for 10 of these is *either* £3.50 less 60p for each new cover or £3.00 each (what they would sell for with a damaged cover). That is, the NRV for the stock is 10 items at £2.90 *or* £3.00 and two items at £3.50. The NRV for all 12 items is therefore £37.00 as this is the higher. This is higher than the FIFO cost so the lower of cost or NRV rule is satisfied by the *existing* FIFO stock valuation. So should the shop do any accounting adjustments for this item? The answer is probably 'no'. (However, *it could* prudently adjust the cost of stock upwards to allow for the new covers. See the discussion on this issue in section 10.4.6.) So we can leave item 1.

2. Item 2 has a FIFO stock value of £2.50 and comprises five items at 50p each. The shop decides to give these away and so the NRV is £0. The shop must show the stock at £0 and a provision of £2.50 must be made by crediting the stock account and debiting the provisions account – in the T-accounts, in the extended trial balance or directly through the profit and loss account and balance sheet. (We will explore the bookkeeping processes in section 10.4.)

3. Item 3 has a FIFO stock value of £47.50 comprising five items at £5.00 and five items at £4.50. The shop estimates that the NRV of this stock is £45.00 – 10 items sold at £4.50. (As the shop's accountant or auditor you might want to question whether they are being just a little optimistic in their estimations of sales of this item and its price.)

So the NRV is below the cost of the stock. Stock must be shown as £45.00 and a provision must be made (again) for £2.50 (the repeat of £2.50 is a coincidence). Again the provision can be created in the T-accounts, in the extended trial balance or directly through the profit and loss account and balance sheet.

One way of showing the effect of this in the profit and loss account and balance sheet is given in Figure 10.6.

The figures shown in Figure 10.6 are just those for the three items we know about. The sales are taken from Figure 10.4. These figures show a trading *loss*. This is not surprising because both items 2 and 3 are being sold for less than the cost of the purchase. Clearly Ridiculous Records has a pricing problem and, as a result, the accountant might want to look more carefully at the stock valuation and provisions for all the stock of the company. This is the sort of evidence one is seeking when making prudent judgements about the value of stock.

RIDICULOUS RECORDS LTD: PROFIT AND LOSS ACCOUNT FOR THE YEAR ENDING 31 December 2004 (figures in £s)		
SALES		344.00
less Cost of Goods Sold		(383.90)
GROSS OR TRADING PROFIT/(LOSS)		(39.90)
EXPENSES:		
STOCK PROVISION	5.00	
	X,XXX.00	
	X,XXX.00	
	XX,XXX.00	
Sub-Total of Expenses		(XXX,XXX)
NET PROFIT FOR THE PERIOD		XXX,XXX

RIDICULOUS RECORDS LTD: BALANCE SHEET AS AT 31 December 2004 (figures in £s)		
FIXED ASSETS		XXX,XXX
CURRENT ASSETS:		
Stock	84.60	
Provision	(5.00)	
Trade Debtors	XX,XXX.00	
Prepayments	XX,XXX.00	
Cash	XX,XXX.00	
	XXX,XXX.00	
CURRENT LIABILITIES:		
Trade Creditors	XX,XXX	
Sundry Creditors	XX,XXX	
Accruals & Provisions	XX,XXX	
	XX,XXX	
NET CURRENT ASSETS		XXX,XXX
NET ASSETS		**XXX,XXX**
REPRESENTED BY:		
Share Capital		XX,XX
Profit and Loss Account		XXX,XXX
SHAREHOLDERS'/OWNERS' FUNDS		**XXX,XXX**

Figure 10.6 Ridiculous Records: how some of its stock appears in the financial statements

Armed with the three valuation approaches – FIFO, LIFO and average cost – and some understanding of the lower of cost or NRV rule plus why additional provisions for stock might be made, we can now turn to look at more complex sorts of stock.

10.3 THE VALUATION OF STOCK AND INVENTORY: THE MORE COMPLEX CASES

So far, we have only considered stock which was purchased and sold without any transformation of the items occurring within the operations subsystem. This would usually be the case for a service organization or a retail organization like Ridiculous Records. What happens in, for example, a manufacturing organization?

10.3.1 Raw materials, work-in-progress and finished goods

The accounting tries to follow the actual manufacturing processes that occur. So, for example, purchases arrive at the focal organization in the normal way. For simplicity, we will call these in a manufacturing organization, the **raw materials**. These raw materials sit in the stock room and are then taken to the first (perhaps of many) manufacturing process which will combine raw materials, together with labour, some machine time perhaps, and other inputs. At this stage the stock is known as **work-in-progress**. The manufacturing and finishing processes continue adding further inputs to the work-in-process until it becomes a **finished good** ready for sale. The finished goods may be stored or despatched immediately to various sites ready for sale. The general process is shown in Figure 10.7.

You can see from Figure 10.7 that stock comprises three different sets of things – raw materials, work-in-progress and finished goods. You can also see that cost of sales is derived from the costs incurred in producing the finished goods. The raw materials follow

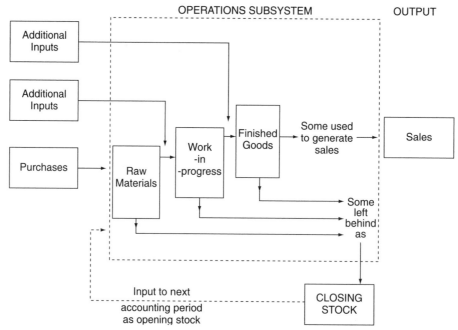

Figure 10.7 A slightly more complex stock cycle

the rules we examined above. The raw material stock value will be the FIFO, LIFO or AVCO adjusted for provisions and NRV. The other elements of stock and of cost of sales will be much more complex.

How the focal organization sets about establishing what these figures should be depends upon how the organization is itself organized as well as how it runs its *costing and management accounting system*. Let us see if we can explain what is happening with the simple example we looked at in Chapter 5 – Bird Industries. One of the things that company did was to make bird houses. The raw materials involved were nice and simple – wood (and a few nails and things). The raw materials of wood were valued at cost as we would expect. When the pieces of wood are taken from the storage area to be worked on, they become work-in-progress and already they 'cost' more than just the cost of the wood. While the wood is sitting in the storage area it is costing money in terms of the cost of the storage area and the electricity necessary to keep the wood at a particular temperature so it doesn't warp. So the raw materials attract (or 'suck in') costs. Once the wood becomes work-in-progress it starts to 'suck in' additional inputs. The cost of the employee fetching the wood, the machines used to cut and shape the wood, the costs of the employees who do the work, the costs of the nails and glue and paint and preservative. The finished bird houses go off to another storage area, perhaps have a label put on them and perhaps are packed for shipment. These are further costs and the longer the finished bird houses sit there the more costs they attract in terms of the costs of the storage area in addition to the cost of the labels and the packaging. The bird houses are then perhaps shipped off and 'suck in' the costs of the transportation. So the finished good, ready for resale, has sucked in a lot of different costs as it has passed from a raw material to a finished good.

At the year end, there will be some raw materials left over, some part-finished birdhouses and some finished goods. Each of these must be costed separately. This is not easy. It is a job for the *costing and management accounting system*. So it is not something we will want to explain in any detail here. In essence, the costing and management accounting system tracks each of these costs as they are 'sucked in' to the product so that, at any point, the accountant can make a reasonably reliable estimate of the costs which are included in the different elements of stock. Depending on how the company operates, this may mean that many of the inputs which we have been treating as expenses must be split between **direct costs** and **indirect costs** (or *overheads*). The direct costs are those which are 'sucked in' to the products as they progress. So a piece of stock may have some of the wages costs, and some of the electricity costs and some of the depreciation charge embedded into it. For accuracy's sake, the accountant would then ensure that their accounting system allocated costs in such a way that the expenses were allocated between production and 'other expenses' (being the overheads). The management accountant could then tell us, when acting as the financial accountant, what the costs of the various elements of stock and cost of sales were.

One can easily see that the more complex the product, the more complex the costing and management accounting system will have to be in order to track different raw materials through different processes, adding in different inputs as the processes develop and identifying all the additional bits and pieces that go to make up the finished product. This is something to be left for your studies of management accounting and costing and for your later studies in financial accounting. For now, however, do not take the stock and cost of sales figures for granted. Different companies use different methods to do this costing and include more or less of the different direct costs. Thus the figures shown for stock and the cost of sales for two companies, which were identical in every way, could be significantly different in any one accounting period. This can become important when we are trying to *interpret* financial statements. We will return to this in Chapter 15.

These points outline the general case. But it can all get rather complicated. How does the financial accountant ensure that they have tracked all appropriate costs when they are constructing financial statements for (say) a manufacturing organization? In practice, it depends a lot on the costing and other accounting systems which the focal organization operates. However, we can get a general idea of what happens if we look at some of the ways in which the profit and loss account can be 'broken down' into more detail. This is what the next subsection is concerned with.

10.3.2 The trading and manufacturing accounts

There is no legal requirement to operate either a trading or a manufacturing account and so, as with many of the whistles and bells of bookkeeping practice, it is simply a matter of choice and convenience on the part of the focal organization. The terms '*trading account*' and '*manufacturing account*' simply refer to the top part of the profit and loss account when prepared in more detail than we have, so far, concerned ourselves with. You should be quite familiar with the layout of what we have called, so far, the profit and loss account. (If you are not, please look back to Figure 10.6 and commit this to memory.)

The top part of this profit and loss account contains the sales, cost of goods sold and gross or trading profit. You may often see this referred to as a *trading account* because, as we saw with Ridiculous Records, this is the place that the buying and selling – the trading – goes on. It is sometimes laid out as shown in Figure 10.8.

There is nothing magical about Figure 10.8 but it deserves a few moments' explanation. So far, in the examples we have looked at, we have simply split the purchases figure into two – the amount left in the organization (stock) and the amount that has left the organization (as cost of sales). In our examples, so far, there has not been an *opening stock* figure. If there had been, this would simply have represented unused purchases from earlier accounting periods. We would add these to this period's purchases and then split *that* figure. Figure 10.8 does this the long way. The trading account here recognizes that there are some unused purchases (opening stock) from earlier accounting periods, adds on the purchases for this accounting period, and then takes off the purchases which have stayed behind in the focal organization at the end of the accounting period (the closing stock).

Whether we do this operation through the T-accounts, through the extended trial balance or through the profit and loss account and balance sheet itself makes no difference to the principle. We are simply trying to track the movement of purchases as they relate to (a) what is left in the organization (stock) and (b) what has left the organization (cost of sales).

SALES		XXX,XXX
Opening Stock	X,XXX	
Add Purchases	XX,XXX	
	XX,XXX	
Less Closing Stock	(X,XXX)	
COST OF SALES	XX,XXX	(XX,XXX)
GROSS OR TRADING PROFIT/(LOSS)		XXX,XXX

Figure 10.8 Pro-forma trading account

We will have a careful look in section 10.4 at the bookkeeping and accounting that is involved with these matters – so do not worry about this at the moment. Also, do not worry about terminology too much. We will continue to use the term 'profit and loss account' to include the trading account – whichever way you decide to identify cost of sales and the closing stock. As long as you have the principles clear in your mind it really does not matter which way you decide to do it or even what you call it.

If, however, the focal organization is a manufacturing organization, then its closing stock comprises raw materials, work-in-progress and finished goods. Also, its cost of goods sold is derived from the costs of the finished goods. So it becomes essential to find some way of separating these things out. This is often the job of the *manufacturing account*.

The key question when constructing a manufacturing account is what are the *direct costs* and what are the *indirect costs*? The direct costs are those which apply directly to the processes that turn raw materials into finished products. For many organizations this can be a relatively simple matter because the manufacturing part (or parts) of the company is on a separate site with its own accounting system. For our purposes, at this stage in your studies, you don't have to get too excited by this problem – we will try and keep it simple.

One way of showing the manufacturing account is provided in Figure 10.9. The manufacturing account (and the trading account which follows it) attempt to record the three stages of stock in a logical way which reflects the manner in which the items of raw material flow through work-in-progress (WIP) to finished goods, sucking in costs as they go. So we start with raw materials. The first part of the manufacturing account deals with movements in raw materials (starting with our opening stock, adding our purchases and then subtracting our closing stock). The resultant figure (presuming our management accountant has done his or her job correctly) *must* be the 'cost of raw materials consumed' – i.e. the costs of raw materials which have flowed into WIP. (Note, this is what flowed into WIP, *not* flowed into sales or anything.) Dwell on this for a moment to make sure it makes complete sense to you.

Then the manufacturing account turns its attention to WIP. This comprises all the direct costs of manufacture plus the opening WIP less the closing WIP. This produces the costs which have been sucked into WIP in the process of making the finished products. This must be added to the costs of raw materials sucked into WIP. (Notice that the way we laid out the pro-forma, we didn't show the raw materials going directly to the WIP. We could have done so if we had thought that would have been more helpful.) Note that any raw materials which have gone to WIP but which have not been used will now be captured in WIP closing stock. So, the two figures added together *must* be the cost of producing finished goods.

This figure is then taken down to the trading account. In the form we have shown in Figure 10.9 we have assumed that the focal organization has *both* manufactured goods and retail stocks. So, these are shown separately. The manufactured goods are shown first and the cost of sales of manufactured goods comprises the opening stock of finished goods, plus the manufacturing cost we have just worked out in the manufacturing account, less the closing stock of finished goods. This gives us a trading profit for manufactured goods. Then the trading account deals with any other (e.g. retail) sales and cost of sales in the same way in order to produce the overall gross profit of the organization.

These things are not set in stone and, often, you can change the layout to get a manufacturing and trading account which suits you or the focal organization you are working for.

Let us now turn and have a look at the practicalities of putting this all together in a worked example.

MANUFACTURING FOR XY LTD AT 31 DECEMBER 200X		
Opening stock of raw materials		
Add Purchases of raw materials		
Less Closing stock of raw materials		
COST OF RAW MATERIALS CONSUMED		
Direct Costs:		
(e.g.)		
Direct wages		
Direct heat and power		
… etc.		
Plus Opening stock of WIP		
Less Closing stock of WIP		
MANUFACTURING COST OF FINISHED GOODS IN THIS PERIOD		

TRADING ACCOUNT FOR XY LTD AT 31 DECEMBER 200X	
Sales of Finished Goods	xxx
Opening stock of finished goods	
Plus Manufacturing cost of finished goods	
Less Closing stock of finished goods	
Cost of sales of finished goods	(xx)
TRADING PROFIT ON FINISHED GOODS	
Sales of other goods and services	
Opening stock of other goods and services	
Plus Purchases of other goods and services	
Less Closing stock of other goods/services	
Cost of sales of other goods and services	
TRADING PROFIT ON OTHER GOODS AND SERVICES	
GROSS PROFIT FOR THE PERIOD:	

Figure 10.9 A pro-forma illustration of a manufacturing and trading account

10.4 AN ILLUSTRATION OF STOCK END-OF-PERIOD ADJUSTMENTS

Once again let us use Yothu Yindi Ltd, the much-abused company from earlier chapters, to illustrate some of the accounting and bookkeeping things we have to do with stock or inventory. You will recall from Chapter 9 that being novice accountants we completely missed the fact that the company had fixed assets in 2000. Well, things haven't got much better. Let us imagine that when we put the financial statements together for 2001 we completely missed the existence of stock! Look back to the figure in Appendix 9A and look at the profit and loss account and balance sheet. There is a purchases/cost of goods sold figure (in the profit and loss account[6] – of course) but (in the balance sheet – of course) no stock. Let us imagine that we incorrectly treated all purchases as cost of goods sold when, in fact, $50,000 of this should have been treated as stock. This would give us the situation shown in Figure 10.10.

YOTHU YINDI LTD: PROFIT AND LOSS ACCOUNT
FOR THE YEAR ENDING 31 DECEMBER 2001 (all figures in dollars)

SALES		500,000
less PURCHASES (or cost of goods sold)		(162,000)
GROSS OR TRADING PROFIT		338,000
EXPENSES:		
Depreciation for the year	5,000	
Rent	120,000	
Rates	24,000	
Telephone	12,000	
Wages	24,000	
Electricity	4,800	
Gas	2,400	(192,200)
NET PROFIT FOR THE PERIOD		145,800

YOTHU YINDI LTD: BALANCE SHEET
AS AT 31 DECEMBER 2001 (all figures in dollars)

	Cost	Acc Dep'n	NBV	
FIXED ASSETS:				
Wind-powered Generator	20,000	4,000	16,000	
4-wheel drive vehicle	16,000	3,000	13,000	29,000
CURRENT ASSETS:				
Stock			50,000	
Trade Debtors			30,000	
Prepayments:			28,000	
Cash			90,800	
			198,800	
CURRENT LIABILITIES:				
Trade Creditors			35,000	
Sundry Creditors			2,000	
Accruals & Provisions			3,100	
			40,100	
				158,700
NET ASSETS				$187,700
REPRESENTED BY:				
Share Capital				40,000
Profit and Loss Account:	brought forward		1,900	
	for the year		145,800	147,700
SHAREHOLDERS'/OWNERS' FUNDS				$187,700

Figure 10.10 The new financial statements for Yothu Yindi Ltd 2001

Just have a quick check through and see that Figure 10.10 is OK. We have decided to identify cost of sales as overstated by $50,000. Therefore cost of sales must be reduced. This increases the profit for the period by $50,000. The current assets have therefore been increased by $50,000 (we have $50,000 worth of stock – and stock is a current asset, remember) and we have already found that profit has increased by $50,000 so the profit at the bottom of the balance sheet also needs to be increased. Our new balance sheet now balances again. (Please do check that you are happy about this before moving on.)

So, in order to illustrate the accounting and bookkeeping issues with stock, we need some new information about Yothu Yindi for the year 2002. This is given in Figure 10.11.

1. You discover that their sales figure comprises sales of their consultancy services plus sales of books, campaigning materials and ethnic artefacts.

2. The closing stock for 2001 comprises books and campaigning materials ($15,000), some basic materials that the company has acquired to make its own ethnic artefacts – principally boomerangs and didgeridoos – (cost of $10,000) and some finished artefacts which were bought ready-made ($25,000).

3. The company is going to start a small manufacturing project in a small outhouse it will rent behind the current office. It is going to try and charge all *direct* costs to the manufacturing process.

4. During the year 2002 the company records the following transactions for the manufacturing process:
   a buys tools, lathes and equipment for $10,000 with an expected useful life of five years and zero scrap value (use straight-line depreciation);
   b direct manufacturing wages $12,000; rent of the outhouse $15,000; heat and power $4,000; purchases of raw materials $70,000; other direct costs $20,000;
   c sales of artefacts during the year: $165,000;
   d at the end of 2002 the company's management accountant estimates that the stock of raw materials should be costed at $35,000, the work-in-progress at $22,000 and the finished goods at $78,000.

5. Sales of the books and consultancy services are $300,000 and associated direct purchases are $190,000. The closing stock of books etc. is costed at $40,000 at the end of 2002 on a FIFO basis.

6. The books are not selling well and a proportion of them, currently having cost the company $10,000, are only expected to fetch $5,000.

7. $3,000 worth of raw materials have been warped through being unprotected during the rains. They are worth an estimated $500 as firewood. Complaints from customers have resulted in the company having to add safety warning to its boomerangs and instructional leaflets to its didgeridoos. This will involve a cost of $400 in order to be able to sell the finished goods held in stock at the end of 2002.

Figure 10.11 Some information about Yothu Yindi Ltd for 2002

10.4.1 Gathering the information

The first step is always to familiarize yourself with what is going on. (This is as true in practice as it is in the classroom.) Remember that one period's closing stock is the next period's opening stock. Therefore Yothu Yindi will start 2002 with some trading stock (the books and campaigning materials), some raw materials and some finished goods. You know from your previous reading that this probably means there is going to be some work-in-progress at some stage so we may as well start with an account for work-in-progress as well – even though this is zero at the start of the new accounting period. (The question doesn't tell us anything about valuation and related matters for 2001 so we just take the balance sheet figures as given at this stage.) Now make sure you have read through the information in Figure 10.11. If you have done so, you should be able to spot that the information comes in what can be thought of as four categories. There is the opening balances information (items 1 and 2 in Figure 10.11), information about the transactions during the year (items 3, 4(a), 4(b) and 4(c) in Figure 10.11), information concerning the end of the year and the closing off of the books (items 4(d) and 5) and, finally, the end-of-period adjustment information (items 6 and 7).[7]

10.4.2 Opening balances

The company has conveniently organized itself so that separate accounting records can be maintained for the manufacturing and the other parts of the business. We keep our books in the same way. So bring down the opening balances for the different accounts in which we are interested at this stage (making sure you try it before looking at Figure 10.12!) and you should have something which looks like Figure 10.12.

Figure 10.12 is simply the opening balances on the relevant accounts – separated between manufacturing and 'other' accounts. (We could have opened accounts for each and every element of the balance sheet – and indeed would do so if we were doing a full bookkeeping exercise. We are just illustrating the stock and cost of sales issues here.)

Please note, in the simple examples we have looked at previously we did not bother with stock accounts. We just kept a purchases account and then split up the purchases in the extended trial balance at the end of the period. *If* we had had opening stock in these simple examples we could have:

- used the opening stock as the opening figure on the purchases account;
- opened a stock account and left it alone and put all the purchases through a purchases account, bringing the stock and purchases together at the end of the period – either in a trading account or through the T-accounts;
- put all our purchases through the stock account.

As with all bookkeeping, what you choose to do depends on the complexity of the focal organization, what is most convenient and what is simplest. *If in doubt*, open extra accounts for everything and wait until the end of period to bring them together. However, the most important thing to remember is that 'stock' is left-over 'purchases'. They are essentially the same transactions and therefore each transaction during the opening of the accounts and during the accounting period cannot go to *both* purchases and stock – this would be double counting. Transactions go to *either* purchases or stock – not both. Only at the end of the period might we wish to move things between the stock and purchases accounts. This should become more obvious as the example develops.

10.4.3 Entering the transactions

We have now dealt with Yothu Yindi's opening balances. The next stage is to put the accounting period's transactions through. For simplicity, assume that wages are paid in cash, all sales are debtor sales and all other payments are made through creditors – but do

MANUFACTURING ACCOUNTS

Inflow/Debit	Raw materials	Outflow/Credit
Balance b/d	10,000	

Inflow/Debit	Work-in-progress	Outflow/Credit
Balance b/d		

Inflow/Debit	Finished goods	Outflow/Credit
Balance b/d	25,000	

NON-MANUFACTURING ACCOUNTS

Inflow/Debit	Trading stock	Outflow/Credit
Balance b/d	15,000	

Figure 10.12 The opening stock T-accounts for Yothu Yindi Ltd 2002

not bother with the cash, debtors or creditors account at this stage. Try it for yourself and then – only then – turn to Figure 10.13 and check that your attempt looks something like it.

In Figure 10.13 we have all the accounts relating to stock and cost of sales and have recorded all the transactions (inputs and outputs) for the period. Note that we have

MANUFACTURING ACCOUNTS

Inflow/Debit	Raw materials	Outflow/Credit
Balance b/d	10,000	

Inflow/Debit	Work-in-progress	Outflow/Credit
Balance b/d	0	

Inflow/Debit	Finished goods	Outflow/Credit
Balance b/d	25,000	

Inflow/Debit	Rent of 'factory'	Outflow/Credit
Creditors	15,000	

Inflow/Debit	Manufacturing wages	Outflow/Credit
Cash	12,000	

Inflow/Debit	Manufacturing heat and power	Outflow/Credit
Creditors	4,000	

Inflow/Debit	Raw material purchases	Outflow/Credit
Creditors	70,000	

Inflow/Debit	Other direct costs	Outflow/Credit
Creditors	20,000	

Inflow/Debit	Manufacturing fixed assets (cost)	Outflow/Credit
Creditors	10,000	

Inflow/Debit	Manufacturing depreciation for the period	Outflow/Credit

Inflow/Debit	Accumulated manufacturing depreciation	Outflow/Credit

NON-MANUFACTURING ACCOUNTS

Inflow/Debit	Trading stock	Outflow/Credit
Balance b/d	15,000	

Inflow/Debit	Sales: Artefacts	Outflow/Credit
	Debtors	165,000

Inflow/Debit	Sales: Others	Outflow/Credit
	Debtors	300,000

Inflow/Debit	Other purchases	Outflow/Credit
Creditors	190,000	

Figure 10.13 The stock T-accounts for Yothu Yindi Ltd 2002

included both the sales accounts in the non-manufacturing accounts. It doesn't matter really, but what we called the 'non-manufacturing accounts' will be the basis of the trading account and the profit and loss account and balance sheet. Put things where you are happiest!

Now comes the interesting bit. What to do with the end of period adjustments? You know from section 10.3 that we have two major options. Put everything through a manufacturing account or do all of the double-entry to produce information for a trading account. The answers are the same, it is simply a matter of which is easier, which is convenient and what information the focal organization requires. We will do both, starting with the double-entry approach.

10.4.4 Double-entry for end-of-period stock

Now, the trick here is to keep a really close eye on what is actually happening. In effect, make sure that you have a mental picture of bits of wood and boomerangs and stuff as they move from process to process. *Do it step by step.*

The first step is to enter the closing balances. You know these as they were given in the question information. *How* you know these is another question. The management accountant must have a 'hot' costing system that has successfully (we hope) assessed the costs which are residing in the different categories of stock. This will have been achieved by a (a) stocktake for each category of stock, (b) the relatively simple assessment of the costs incurred for raw materials and trading stock, and then (c) some method of recovering costs to assess the costs of work-in-progress and finished goods. You will study these processes in your management accounting lectures. For now let us simply be grateful that Yothu Yindi's management accountant seems to know what they are doing. So, enter the closing balances in the appropriate accounts.

Each of these steps is shown in Figure 10.14 – but please try and do them yourself before looking at the answer.

The second step is to look at the raw materials. We started with $10,000 of raw materials and finished with $35,000. Presuming this is not magic, what happened? Well, the focal organization bought some raw materials. So, move the balance of the purchases of raw materials to the stock of raw materials account. This closes off the purchases account and shows that inputs to raw materials were $80,000. We know the closing balance is $35,000, so there must have been an outflow from this account of $45,000. Where did it go to? Think about it. Where do raw materials go? They go to be processed – or manufactured. They become work-in-progress. So the raw material movement is to the work-in-progress (WIP) account. Do this now, and you should end up with an additional input to the WIP account of $45,000.

The next stage is to look at WIP and the way in which it 'sucks in' the other direct costs.

The whole point about direct costs is that they go 'directly' to the manufacturing process.[8] Yothu Yindi have, very kindly, identified what the direct costs are, and these are shown in the 'manufacturing accounts'. Each of these costs is 'sucked in' to the manufacturing process as goods are processed. We therefore need to take all the direct costs to the WIP account. There is only one problem here and that is the 'direct' fixed assets. We need to do the bookkeeping for these as the *depreciation* is the period cost – not the cost of the fixed asset. (You remember this from Chapter 9.) So, do the bookkeeping for the depreciation and then take all the direct costs to the WIP account. (If you have problems with the depreciation see endnotes.[9])

This should give you a WIP account with an opening balance of $0, additional direct costs of $98,000 and a closing balance of $22,000. To make the WIP account balance, we need an outflow from this account of $76,000. What is this? Where does it go? Think about it. What is the output from WIP? It must be finished goods. So the outflow from the WIP account must be an input (of $76,000 in this case) to the finished goods account.

That leaves a balance on the finished goods account of $23,000 which must be the cost of goods sold. (We have already been told what the stock figure is – the left-behind amount – so the only thing the other figure can be is the amount that has gone out of the organization as sales.)

This just leaves, on the manufacturing accounts, the fixed asset account and the accumulated depreciation account which will be taken off to the trial balance (or directly to the balance sheet) in the normal way.

Now do the same thing for the non-manufacturing stock and purchases and you should get a cost of sales for trading stock of $165,000. The sales accounts will, again, be taken off to the trial balance (or directly to the profit and loss account if we prefer) in the normal way.

Putting all this together should produce Figure 10.14. Work carefully through Figure 10.14 and ensure you can follow everything. Then go on and check that you can understand the trial

MANUFACTURING ACCOUNTS

Inflow/Debit	Raw materials		Outflow/Credit
Balance b/d	10,000	WIP	45,000
Raw material purchases	70,000	Balance c/d (to TB)	35,000
	80,000		80,000

Inflow/Debit	Work-in-progress		Outflow/Credit
Balance b/d	0	Finished goods	76,000
Raw materials	45,000		
Rent	15,000		
Wages	12,000		
Heat and power	4,000		
Other direct costs	20,000		
Depreciation	2,000	Balance c/d (to TB)	22,000
	98,000		98,000

Inflow/Debit	Finished goods		Outflow/Credit
Balance b/d	25,000	Cost of sales	23,000
WIP	76,000	Balance c/d (to TB)	78,000
	101,000		101,000

Inflow/Debit	Rent of 'factory'		Outflow/Credit
Creditors	15,000	WIP	15,000

Inflow/Debit	Manufacturing wages		Outflow/Credit
Cash	12,000	WIP	12,000

Inflow/Debit	Manufacturing heat and power		Outflow/Credit
Creditors	4,000	WIP	4,000

Inflow/Debit	Raw material purchases		Outflow/Credit
Creditors	70,000	Raw material stock	70,000

Inflow/Debit	Other direct costs		Outflow/Credit
Creditors	20,000	WIP	20,000

Inflow/Debit	Manufacturing fixed assets (cost)		Outflow/Credit
Creditors	10,000	Balance c/d (to TB)	10,000

Inflow/Debit	Manufacturing depreciation for the period		Outflow/Credit
Accumulated depreciation	2,000	WIP	2,000

Inflow/Debit	Accumulated manufacturing depreciation		Outflow/Credit
Balance c/d (to TB)	2,000	Depreciation for year	2,000

NON-MANUFACTURING ACCOUNTS

Inflow/Debit	Trading stock		Outflow/Credit
Balance b/d	15,000	Cost of sales	165,000
Purchases	190,000	Balance c/d (to TB)	40,000
	205,000		205,000

Inflow/Debit	Sales: Artefacts		Outflow/Credit
To Trading Account (to TB)	165,000	Debtors	165,000

Inflow/Debit	Sales: Others		Outflow/Credit
To Trading Account (to TB)	300,000	Debtors	300,000

Inflow/Debit	Other purchases		Outflow/Credit
Creditors	190,000	To trading stock	190,000

EXTRACT FROM THE EXTENDED TRIAL BALANCE FOR YOTHU YINDI LTD AT END OF 2002

	EXTENDED TRIAL BALANCE at 31 DECEMBER 2002							
Account	Trial balance		Adjustments		Profit & loss		Balance sheet	
	Dr	Cr	Dr	Cr	Dr	Cr	Dr	Cr
Stock: raw mats	35,000						45,000	
Stock: WIP	22,000						22,000	
Stock: Finish Goods	78,000						78,000	
Stock: Trading	40,000						40,000	
Cost of sales: Artefact	23,000				23,000			
Cost of sales: Trading	165,000				165,000			
Manuf Fixed Assets	10,000						10,000	
Manuf Acc. Depn.		2,000						2,000
Sales: Artefacts		165,000				165,000		
Sales: Trading		300,000				300,000		
...								
... ...								
TOTALS								

Figure 10.14 The stock T-accounts for Yothu Yindi Ltd 2002

balance shown at the end of the figure. (It doesn't balance, of course, because we have not done all the bookkeeping for all the other accounts.)

Now please take some time to think about what has happened here. It is the flows of costs and income that are important. There are many ways in which we could have done the bookkeeping and accounting above. This is only one way. Whichever way you choose to do the bookkeeping you should keep it simple and feel comfortable with it. It should also, on this information, produce the same answer! You can see, for example, that doing all these adjustments through the trial balance would have got very messy indeed and, probably, we would have made mistakes. The use of the T-accounts to do the adjustments is therefore good news when we have a complex situation.

We will now do the same thing only directly through a manufacturing account.

10.4.5 The manufacturing account

Technically, the manufacturing account is easier because we simply close off all accounts and take them directly through to the manufacturing account without bothering to do all this double-entry. However, it is our view that it is easier to lose sight of what is actually happening using a manufacturing account. Nevertheless, once again, the choice is yours.

To produce the manufacturing account, we go back to Figure 10.13. Then we simply 'dump' all the costs from the manufacturing accounts into the manufacturing account proper. You met the form of the manufacturing account in the previous section. So try it for yourself – remembering to do the bookkeeping for the depreciation first. The result should look something like Figure 10.15.

Note that we have skipped the trial balance stage doing it this way. That is simply for convenience. We could have taken all the balances from the manufacturing accounts to the trial balance and *then* produced the manufacturing account. To really keep things consistent we might have wanted to put an extra two columns in our extended trial balance to represent the manufacturing account. It is all a matter of convenience.

You should now have a reasonable grasp of how to treat the more complex manufacturing stock but, before we leave this section, you may recall that Yothu Yindi had some end-of-period adjustments for their stocks. We will deal with that now.

10.4.6 Cost versus net realizable value

In Figure 10.11 there were matters identified as needing our attention. Some raw materials had to be scrapped and some of the finished products needed additional costs to make them saleable. In the first case we are told that the condition of the raw materials is such that they cannot be used and the cost is below its NRV. In the second case we will have to examine the situation to see what we need to do – whether, in fact, the cost is below the NRV and what, if anything, we should do. As usual, take it a step at a time.

The first case is simple. The raw materials cannot be used for manufacturing, so they have to be removed from the raw material stock. They are, however, not useless, as we can sell them as firewood. The best place to do this is in the extended trial balance. This is what it is good at.[10] The cost of this raw material was $3,000 (we are told) and its NRV is $500. Therefore we must reduce raw material stock by $2,500 and create a stock provision (write-off) of $2,500 in the profit and loss account. This is shown in the extended trial balance in Figure 10.16.

The second case is a bit more complicated. First, look at the trading account in Figure 10.15. It is obvious from this that the manufactured artefacts are selling for considerably more than it costs to make them. The 'mark-up' is enormous. (We will look at this again in Chapter 15.) The sum of $400 is not large enough to take the NRV of products down below the 'costs of manufacturing finished products'. Therefore, on the cost versus NRV rule, we do not need to do anything. Should we, however, on the grounds of 'accuracy' or 'prudence' take account of the fact that some of our finished goods are not yet finished – they need further expenditure? Well, strictly speaking we should be prudent and *recognize an expenditure or potential expenditure as soon as it arises*. Thus we should create a

MANUFACTURING ACCOUNT		
Opening stock of raw materials	10,000	
Add Purchases of raw materials	70,000	
Less Closing stock of raw materials	(35,000)	
	☞ ☞	
COST OF RAW MATERIALS CONSUMED		45,000
Direct Costs:		
Rent	15,000	
Wages	12,000	
Heat and power	4,000	
Other direct costs	20,000	
Depreciation	2,000	
	53,000	
Plus Opening stock of WIP	0	
Less Closing stock of WIP	22,000	
	☞ ☞	31,000
MANUFACTURING COST OF FINISHED GOODS IN THIS PERIOD		$76,000

TRADING ACCOUNT		
Sales of finished goods		165,000
Opening stock of finished goods	25,000	
Plus Manufacturing cost of finished goods	76,000	
Less Closing stock of finished goods	(78,000)	
Cost of sales of finished goods		(23,000)
TRADING PROFIT ON FINISHED GOODS		142,000
Sales of other goods and services		300,000
Opening stock of other goods and services	15,000	
Plus Purchases of other goods and services	190,000	
Less Closing stock of other goods/services	(40,000)	
Cost of sales of other goods and services		(165,000)
TRADING PROFIT ON OTHER GOODS AND SERVICES		135,000
GROSS PROFIT FOR THE PERIOD:		275,000
...rest of the profit and loss account follows here		

Figure 10.15 Manufacturing and trading accounts for Yothu Yindi Ltd 2002

provision of $400 which would be shown on the profit and loss account as a 'provision for stock improvement' – or something like that – and, to complete the double-entry, show a provision in current liabilities as representing the liability to spend this money in the next accounting period. This is what we have done in Figure 10.16.

And with this we complete our bookkeeping for the stock issues in Yothu Yindi for 2002. However, in practice we might think that doing all that bookkeeping for a measly $400 was hardly worth the effort. Indeed, accountants often decide that something is too

EXTENDED TRIAL BALANCE at 31 DECEMBER 2002								
Account	Trial balance		Adjustments		Profit & loss		Balance sheet	
	Dr	Cr	Dr	Cr	Dr	Cr	Dr	Cr
Stock: raw mats	35,000			2,500			32,500	
Stock: WIP	22,000						22,000	
Stock: Finish Goods	78,000						78,000	
Stock: Trading	40,000						40,000	
Cost of sales: Artefact	23,000				23,000			
Cost of sales: Trading	165,000				165,000			
Manuf Fixed Assets	10,000						10,000	
Manuf Depn for Year	2,000				2,000			
Manuf Acc. Depn.		2,000						2,000
Sales: Artefacts		165,000				165,000		
Sales: Trading		300,000				300,000		
Stock damage provision				2,500		2,500		
Stock correction provision			400	400	400			400
etc. ...								
TOTALS								

Figure 10.16 Extract from the extended trial balance for Yothu Yindi Ltd at the end of 2002

small to bother with. The classic examples arise with fixed assets. For example, a Sellotape dispenser might last for ten years but only cost a few dollars or pounds. All the bookkeeping necessary to maintain a separate fixed asset account for it and depreciate it at the end of every year as well as calculate profit or loss on disposal would be so excessive given the item's value that accountants ignore it and treat it as an expense. This is called following the *doctrine of materiality*.

Materiality is an important concept in accounting practice and is broadly defined as meaning that if any item is too small to make a reader of the information presented in a set of financial statements change their opinion of the company, then the item is *immaterial*. Accountants often operate an *x*% of turnover or a *y*% of profit rule for guidance. In our present case, $400 is significantly less than 1 per cent of closing stock, turnover or gross profit and so is probably immaterial. In practical terms, this adjustment could have been ignored.

SUMMARY

The material we have met in this chapter probably represents the first of the potentially difficult and important *accounting* areas that create the most work for the practising accountant. In the simple situations – typically small retail operations – identifying stock, separating the costs of sales and putting through the appropriate provisions really looks quite straightforward. The situation rapidly becomes more complicated as the organization and its stock situation become more complex. The trick in these situations is to (a) keep a clear mind, (b) follow through the processes step by step *and* (c) try to keep a picture in your mind of the actual physical flows which the accounting numbers are attempting to represent. Stock and cost of sales are frequently very important determinants of the overall picture presented by a set of financial statements. (We look at this in more detail in Chapter 15.) It should be fairly obvious that if we can increase our stock valuation in one year, we can automatically increase our profit for the same period – *mutatis mutandis*. Stock is, as a result, one area of the financial statements that senior management may look at to keep the company's trend of annual reported profits looking 'steady'. This is known as 'income smoothing' and is probably a fairly widespread practice.

The reason for making special mention of it is that as accountants we tend to love the technical detail of (say) the bookkeeping and accounting for stock and, as a result, can easily lose sight of the larger, more important issues. An overly technical affection for parts of accounting can lead to a situation in which an accountant is unable to 'see the wood for the trees'. This is always something to guard against.

Key terms and concepts

The following key terms and concepts have featured in this chapter. You should ensure that you understand and can explain each one. Page references to definitions appear in the index in bold type.

- Average cost (AVCO)
- Changing prices
- Closing stock
- Cost of sales/cost of goods sold
- Direct costs
- Finished goods (account)
- First-in, first-out (FIFO)
- Gross profit
- Income smoothing
- Indirect costs (overheads)
- Inventory
- Last-in, first-out (LIFO)
- The lower of cost and NRV rule
- Manufacturing account
- Manufacturing cost of finished goods
- Materiality
- Net realizable value (NRV)
- Provisions for damaged or obsolete stock
- Raw materials (account)
- Stock
- Stocktake
- Trading account
- Trading profit
- Work-in-progress (WIP) (account)

FURTHER READING

Probably the three most important elements to your further reading on this topic are: (a) doing worked examples (such as those to be found in the Workbook that accompanies this text); (b) cross-referencing the material in this chapter with the work you will do in Chapters 15 and 16 which look at interpreting financial statements and the issues that arise from a period of inflation and/or changing prices; and (c) doing some careful study of your management accounting textbook to see the connections between the accounting numbers we have used here and the costing processes outlined in a good management accounting textbook.

NOTES

1. The term 'stock' is used in North America to mean more or less the same thing as accountants in the UK, Australia and New Zealand (for example) mean by 'shares'. Hence, 'inventory' is the less confusing term. By convention (and habit) we have tended to use 'stock' in this book.

2. You probably know a few of your fellow students who work on the LIFO principle in lectures. When you start training in practice you can expect to be called 'LIFO' if you are frequently late and leave early.

3. The stock for item 3 consists of 5 @ £5.00 (£25.00) plus 5 @ £4.50 (£22.50) which equals £47.50. If this still doesn't make sense work back through the numbers and if that doesn't help, ask for assistance.

4. Purchases of item were 10 @ £2.00 + 10 @ £2.50 + 5 @ £2.50 + so on … Total purchases of item 1 come to £128.50. The same process for item 2 should produce a figure of £45.00 and for item 3 should produce a figure of £295. Total = £468.50.

5. Item 1 has 12 items in stock, so, as the last items in were the first ones to be sold, we value stock by considering the oldest items first. Ten items cost £2.00 each and the next 2 items cost £2.50 each. Thus item 1 is £25.00. The oldest elements of item 2 were £2.00 each and there were 10 of these, so we just take 5 @ £2.00. Thus, £10.00. Item 3 consists of 10 items in stock. We bought 40 items at £4.50 each, so this is the price of the stock. Ten items @ £4.50 is £45. Total purchases were still £468.50, total LIFO stock is £80, so LIFO cost of sales is (£468.50 – £80) £388.50.

6. Or 'trading account' if you were paying attention earlier in the chapter and want to be pedantic.

7. You might like to think about how Yothu Yindi Ltd know all this. Yes! We know we made it up, but in practice how would the company actually know this sort of information? Some of the answer is in Chapter 6. Some you will have to think about for yourself.

8. The assessment of what are 'direct costs' is nowhere near as simple as we have shown it here. Organizations have different systems for recording, allocating *and defining* what they treat as 'direct costs' and allocating other costs to the manufacturing (and other) processes. There will usually be a degree of arbitrariness to the process. Be aware for now that establishing the 'true cost' of anything is frequently very difficult and sometimes impossible.

9. If you have a problem with the depreciation, remember the rules from Chapter 9. Keep the *cost* and the depreciation separate. So, estimate the straight-line depreciation which is $10,000 spread over five years – hence $2,000 per accounting period. This results in an expense (debit/inflow) to the depreciation account for the year account and 'negative asset' (credit/outflow) in the accumulated depreciation account.

10. Now, it would be possible (and, perhaps more 'accurate') to transfer this damaged raw material to trading stock as we will no longer be using it for manufacture, but we might as well keep it simple.

Bad and doubtful debts (and another look at provisions) 11

Learning objectives

After studying this chapter you should be able to:

- define bad debts and doubtful debts;
- explain the actual and accounting differences between them;
- execute simple examples of the bookkeeping for bad debts;
- execute simple examples of the bookkeeping for doubtful debts;
- explain the nature of provisions in some detail;
- explain, in simple terms, why accounting numbers are frequently uncertain;
- be able to distinguish between bookkeeping and the accounting decisions which drive the bookkeeping;
- refute the contention that bookkeeping and accounting are precise 'sciences'.

11.1 INTRODUCTION

11.1.1 Chapter design and links to previous chapters

We have seen how to record transactions as they arise during a focal organization's accounting period and how to summarize them in an initial trial balance. We have then examined the unusual bits and pieces that must be put through the accounting records to prepare the accounting information ready for the construction of a set of financial statements. These *end-of-period adjustments* could either be put through the extended trial balance or through the accounting records (the T-accounts) before they were closed off. The choice as to which way we put through the adjustments was really a matter of convenience. Generally speaking, however, the more involved the adjustment, the more desirable it proved to put the adjustment through the accounting records – not least so that we did not lose sight of what we were trying to do.

We have now looked at end-of-period adjustments for: accruals and prepayments; depreciation and purchases and sales of fixed assets; and, in the last chapter, stock or inventory. This chapter examines the last of these principal adjustments – how to account for **bad** and/or **doubtful debts**. (In the USA these are often called, rather charmingly, 'delinquent receivables'.)

Compared with the other adjustments we have considered, bad and doubtful debts are fairly straightforward. As with many of the accounting adjustments we have been considering, you will find that keeping a mental picture of what is actually happening *beneath* the bookkeeping helps enormously. Keeping such a mental picture is a great deal easier with bad and doubtful debts than it was for the flows of costs involved in accounting for stock (or inventory). Because of this (relative) simplicity we will therefore use this chapter to have another look at – a sort of revision of – the whole question of *provisions*. Doubtful debts (in particular) involve the use of provisions – as did accruals, depreciation and stock. So it may be useful to rethink this peculiarly accounting-related concept and rehearse the bookkeeping and accounting implications of them.

The chapter is organized as follows. The following subsection explains what bad and doubtful debts are. Section 11.2 introduces the bookkeeping and accounting for bad and doubtful debts. It does this by first examining the accounting for bad debts and the accounting for doubtful debts separately and then, in section 11.2.3, accounting for them together to reinforce your confidence in the bookkeeping processes. Section 11.3 re-examines the nature of – and the bookkeeping for – provisions and explains the essential uncertainty inherent in accounting numbers. The chapter closes with the usual summary, key words and further reading.

11.1.2 What are bad and doubtful debts?

Recall, for a moment, how debts arise. A focal organization makes sales. These are, principally, of two kinds: cash sales [Credit sales: Debit cash] and credit sales [Credit sales: Debit debtors]. Cash sales are nice and straightforward: we record them and, on the whole, we can probably forget about them from an accounting point of view. The sales will find their way onto the profit and loss account and the cash will find its way onto the balance sheet in due course.[1] Problems *can* arise with credit sales. That is, these are only *real* sales if they produce cash at some future date (otherwise the focal organization is just giving away its goods or services – these are 'donations'!). Most of our credit sales – our debtors – will turn into cash. But a few debtors will end up not paying us – or not paying the full amount they owe. This is the concern behind the adjustments for bad and doubtful debts.

There are many reasons why a debtor may not pay the focal organization and these may arise because of accounting errors, delivery errors, problems with the product, legal problems or problems with the customer. That is, the focal organization may have incorrectly recorded a sale – perhaps no sale took place or the wrong customer is allocated the sale. Perhaps the goods were incorrectly addressed or incorrectly delivered and so the customer never received them. In these cases the focal organization, when it finds out about them, should put through a journal entry reversing the sale (remember this from Chapter 6). These situations need not worry us from a bad and doubtful debts point of view. The other sources of problems may be less clear and in these cases we may need to use the accounting for bad and doubtful debts.

In essence, bad and doubtful debts arise when the focal organization has recorded what it considers to be a 'good debt' – the goods have been delivered, as requested by a customer and the goods were in good order – but the customer cannot, will not or might not pay the debt which we (the focal organization) believe to be due.

A **bad debt** is one which the focal organization, with good reason, is virtually certain is not going to be paid. The customer may have fled the country, may turn out to be hiding behind a fictitious company name or may be bankrupt, for example. In each case, the sale has been made in good faith but now the focal organization reckons that no cash (or not all the cash) will be forthcoming. The debt (or part of the debt) has 'gone bad'. *Therefore*, bad debts refer to specific debts with specific customers. *Bad debts are specific.*

Use of the term **doubtful debt**, on the other hand, refers to a *general* concern that some, unspecified proportion of, current debts may turn bad in the next accounting period. The focal organization may have noted, for example, that, on average, 5 per cent of debts with university lecturers tend to go bad each year whilst 25 per cent of its debts with university students tend not to be paid. In such circumstances, the focal organization might think it *prudent* to make a *general provision for doubtful debts*. Unlike bad debts, *doubtful debts are general.*

There are many ways in which an accounting system might deal with these issues. There is no legal requirement about how they are treated (although taxation authorities tend to have fairly strong views about them). So, in the next section we will look first at bad debts and then at doubtful debts. We will keep them separate at first. Only then will we look briefly at how they can be run together if one feels so inclined.

11.2 ACCOUNTING FOR BAD AND DOUBTFUL DEBTS

11.2.1 Accounting for bad debts

Because bad debts are specific, they are quite straightforward. Information about a bad debt may arise at any time during an accounting period. (For example, we might receive a letter from Mr X's solicitors informing us that his company, sadly, has gone into liquidation as a consequence of his having invested heavily in ozone-depleting chemicals for which demand is now zero. He owes many millions of pounds and the solicitors are duty-bound to inform us that we have a greater chance of finding a pot of gold at the end of the rainbow than we have of getting any money out of Mr X. This is now a bad debt.) The accounting adjustments necessary for the bad debt may be put through at the time that the information arises or at the end of the accounting period. It really makes very little difference.

How does the focal organization reflect the information that a debt has gone bad? As with all bookkeeping for accounting adjustments, we have to find two aspects of the event to keep the double-entry alive. A debt will have been recorded in the debtors ledger when it arose. The first thing that must be done is to cancel or remove that debt. So stage 1 is [Credit debtors] to remove these bad debts from the debtors ledger. Now, the resultant debits have to go somewhere. But where? Well, what has effectively happened is that (depending on your point of view) either the sales figure which will be shown in the profit and loss account is overstated by the amount of the bad debts (they were not 'real' sales at all) or the focal organization has an additional expense for the period in the form of debts it has to write off. For reasons of convenience and convention, *the bad debts are written off to the profit and loss account*. We do this via a *bad debts account*. So the second stage is [Debit bad debts] to record the amount of the expense which must be written off in this accounting period. At the end of the accounting period the numbers which will go to the financial statements (via the trial balance) will be a reduced figure for debtors (on the balance sheet) and a figure for a bad debts account to be written off in the profit and loss account.

Consider the following example.

Ridiculous Records (from Chapter 10) made sales during 2004 of £100,000. Of these sales £20,000 were credit sales. By the end of the accounting period, the company had received £10,000 of cash for those debts. Of the remainder, the company has received information about the following debts:

(a) Mr D. Jay, the DJ, owes £400 for CDs he has purchased. He is currently in residence in Paraguay and, apparently, has no intention of returning;
(b) the Cacophonic Chorale Appreciation Society owes £600 and has apparently gone into receivership. It is unlikely to be able to pay any of its debts;
(c) the local university students' union owes £1,200 and has, we have heard, had a major financial scandal. The university's accountancy students are active in trying to sort the mess out and estimate that the union will be able to pay 75% of all its ordinary debts (of which Ridiculous Records is one).

Show how this would be reflected in an extract from Ridiculous Records' books and indicate the appropriate financial numbers which would appear in the financial statements.

Before turning to the proposed solution in Figure 11.1, try it out yourself on a bit of paper. How would you set about showing these things in the books and financial statements?

Figure 11.1 shows one way of dealing with these matters in the books of Ridiculous Records. The numbers which would go to the financial statements are also straightforward. The bad debts account would be shown as an expense in the profit and loss account – showing the account being written off. The debtors figure would emerge from the debtors control account (which you may remember from Chapter 6 sums all the individual debtors accounts). This would be, for Ridiculous Records, the total amount of outstanding debtors (the question gives you enough information to work out that this will be £10,000) less those which have been written off (i.e. £1,300), so the figure shown in the balance sheet will be £8,700. In effect what we have done here is to move £1,300 from assets (on the balance sheet) to expenses (on the profit and loss account). The resultant financial statements show us as bearing an expense of £1,300 whilst showing a figure for debtors

DEBTORS LEDGER		
Inflow/Debit	**Mr D.Jay the DJ**	**Outflow/Credit**
Credit sales	400	Bad debts account	400

Inflow/Debit	**The Cacophonic Chorale Appreciation Society**	**Outflow/Credit**
Credit sales	600	Bad debts account	600

Inflow/Debit	**Unseen University Students Union**	**Outflow/Credit**
Credit sales	1,200	Bad debts account	300
		Balance c/d (TB or balance sheet)	900
	1,200		1,200

OTHER LEDGERS		
Inflow/Debit	**Bad Debts Account**	**Outflow/Credit**
Mr D. Jay the DJ	400		
Cacophonic Chorale	600		
Unseen University	300	Balance c/d (to TB or P&L a/c)	1,300
	1,300		1,300

Figure 11.1 Extract from Ridiculous Records Books for 2004

which is lower by the amount of the written-off debts of £1,300. The process seems straightforward and the answer seems sort of OK (doesn't it?).

And that is, more or less, all there is to bad debts. However, we will return to them in a later section.

11.2.2 Accounting for doubtful debts

Sadly, doubtful debts are not quite as simple. Remember that doubtful debts relate to a general situation – not individual and specific debts. How does this work?

Most organizations will have some system of credit control: that is, some process for keeping an eye on debtors, chasing up those that are not paying on time and, perhaps, passing long-term outstanding debts to credit factors and debt collection agencies.[2] The more sophisticated the credit control system, the more likely the focal organization is to *categorize* debts. The simplest way of doing this is to *age* debts, because the older the debt, the more likely it is to be a problem. But an organization may discover (for example) that its international debts are more likely to be a problem or that people called Maxwell are traditionally unreliable, or whatever. This process will lead the organization to identify where debts are *likely* to go bad – as opposed to those that they *know* have gone bad. Typically, the focal organization will therefore (in the interests of prudence) *estimate* what proportion of *current* debts are likely to go bad in future accounting periods and *provide* for this proportion.

This proportion is a *provision* because the exact incidence of the bad debts cannot be known in advance. The provision will therefore be an estimate. It will be created (via the profit and loss account) in the first year of the provision's existence and then, in subsequent years, the provision will be adjusted up or down in line with company policy. Thus as long as the company has a provision it will appear on the balance sheet (either as a current liability or, more usually, as a deduction from debtors – a sort of negative current asset) and *except in the year in which it is created* (when the whole amount of the provision is charged to the profit and loss account) the profit and loss account will just show the *change* in the provision for the present accounting period. (This is the kind of puzzling activity that provisions entail and one of the reasons we will come back to them later in this chapter.)

Let us return to the example of Ridiculous Records.

Ridiculous Records has decided that, in addition to accounting for their bad debts, they will make a provision for doubtful debts based on a proportion of their current debts. For 2004 the company decides to make a provision for doubtful debts of 5 per cent of good debts outstanding at the year end. All other matters remain as they were earlier in the chapter.

How should the company account for this decision and how will this reflect in the financial statements?

Once again, pull out a piece of paper and have a go yourself before turning to the suggestion in Figure 11.2.

All that we have done in Figure 11.2 is to add in two new accounts, one for the charge for the year and one for the provision. (This should sound a bit like things we have done already – such as depreciation charge for the year and accumulated depreciation.) We have then taken the agreed percentage (5 per cent in this case) of the *good* debts (which we know from earlier on is £8,700) and (a) made a charge of the result to one account and (b) set up the provision in the other. This has maintained our double entry. What we have *not* done is reduce the individual debtors accounts. Why not? Well, the whole point about the doubtful debts is that we do not know *which* accounts we are providing for – it is a general

DEBTORS LEDGER

Inflow/Debit	Mr D. Jay the DJ		Outflow/Credit
Credit sales	400	Bad debts account	400

Inflow/Debit	The Cacophonic Chorale Appreciation Society		Outflow/Credit
Credit sales	600	Bad debts account	600

Inflow/Debit	Unseen University Students Union		Outflow/Credit
Credit sales	1,200	Bad debts account	300
		Balance c/d (TB or balance sheet)	900
	1,200		1,200

OTHER LEDGERS

Inflow/Debit	Bad debts		Outflow/Credit
Mr D. Jay the DJ	400		
Cacophonic Chorale	600		
Unseen University	300	Balance c/d (to TB or P&L a/c)	1,300
	1,300		1,300

Inflow/Debit	Doubtful debts		Outflow/Credit
Provision for doubtful debts	435	To TB (or profit and loss account)	435

Inflow/Debit	Provision for doubtful debts		Outflow/Credit
	(Provision to be maintained at 5% of good debts)		
Balance c/d (to TB or balance sheet)	435	Doubtful debts charge for the year	435

Figure 11.2 Extract from Ridiculous Records Books for 2004

provision – and so we cannot reduce individual debtors accounts. What we will do is take the charge to the profit and loss account for the accounting period and then show the provision as a reduction of debtors in the balance sheet. Figure 11.3 shows how we might show the doubtful debts *and* the bad debts in the financial statements of Ridiculous Records for 2004.

Figure 11.3 shouldn't cause you any problems. If it does, however, work back through the foregoing material until it all seems to fit comfortably.

And that is, *basically,* all there is to do on doubtful debts. So, just to reinforce these issues, we will have a brief look at what happens when bad and doubtful debts are accounted for together and do a second year of Ridiculous Records to see how the provisions work.

11.2.3 Accounting for bad and doubtful debts – together

If you are still awake at this point you may well be asking why we might want to bother accounting for bad and doubtful debts together. This is certainly a fascinating question and one which is guaranteed to enthral potential sexual partners at any social gathering you attend. In essence, there is no necessity to put them together and it is certainly more straightforward to keep them apart. However, for the provision for doubtful debts, as for all provisions, there is the basic question 'What is it for?'. (This is an important question which should never be far from your mind and which can be applied successfully to a great deal of what passes for current accounting orthodoxy.) A provision is, implicitly, serving

RIDICULOUS RECORDS LTD: PROFIT & LOSS ACCOUNT		
FOR THE YEAR ENDING 31 December 2004		
SALES		100,000
less Cost of Goods Sold		(XXX,XXX)
GROSS OR TRADING PROFIT		XXX,XXX
EXPENSES:		
Bad debts for the year	1,300	
Provision for doubtful debts	435	
......	X,XXX	
......	X,XXX	
	XX,XXX	
Sub-Total of Expenses		(XXX,XXX)
NET PROFIT FOR THE PERIOD		XXX,XXX

RIDICULOUS RECORDS LTD: BALANCE SHEET AS AT 31 December 2004		
FIXED ASSETS		XXX,XXX
CURRENT ASSETS:		
Stock/Inventory		XXX,XXX
Trade Debtors	8,700	
Less prov'n for doubtful debts	(435)	8,265
Prepayments:		XX,XXX
Cash		XX,XXX
		XXX,XXX
CURRENT LIABILITIES:		
Trade Creditors		XX,XXX
Sundry Creditors		XX,XXX
Accruals & Provisions		XX,XXX
		XX,XXX
NET CURRENT ASSETS		XXX,XXX
NET ASSETS		**XXX,XXX**
REPRESENTED BY:		
Share Capital		XX,XX
Profit and Loss Account		XXX,XXX
SHAREHOLDERS'/OWNERS' FUNDS		**XXX,XXX**

Figure 11.3 Extract from Ridiculous Records profit and loss account and balance sheet for 2004

two functions. First, it is adjusting the financial statement figures in an attempt to reflect some appropriate economic situation through our accounting. In the case of doubtful debts the economic situation is the probable 'delinquency' of some of the focal organization's current debtors. After the year end, the provision is 'left over' and sits around in the books of the focal organization until it is adjusted when the next year's financial statements are put together. Why is it there? Well, in one sense it is there to 'catch' further 'delinquent' debts as they fall bad. So we might want to argue that debts that go bad in the accounting period have already been provided for through the doubtful debts provision. One wouldn't want to get too committed to this idea, but it has a sort of logic and it is the reasoning we will apply in this section. To do that we need some information. We will now look at

Ridiculous Records for 2005 and do the bookkeeping and accounting for bad and doubtful debts together.

Ridiculous Records shows a sales figure for 2005 of £150,000. Of these £100,000 are cash sales, the rest are sales on credit. By the end of the year, the company has received £8,400 of the amounts owing on the 2004 debts and has received £30,000 against credit sales incurred in 2005. The company has decided that the one further outstanding debt for 2004 (for a total of £300) has gone bad. It also decides that two other debts incurred in 2005 (for a total of £900) should be treated as bad. Further, Ridiculous Records has improved its credit control system and has decided to maintain a provision for doubtful debts based on 20 per cent of apparently good debts over 6 months old, 10 per cent of apparently good debts between 3 and 6 months old and 5 per cent of apparently good debts less than 3 months old. Having taken account of the bad debts, the debtors ageing schedule shows £2,000 of debts to be older than 6 months and £7,000 of debts to be between 3 and 6 months old.

Illustrate how Ridiculous Records will reflect this in their bookkeeping records and show the figures that will, as a result, appear in the financial statements at the end of 2005 relating to debtors.

Yet again, have a real go yourself, trying to work out how to go about this, before you look at the suggestion. If you take the matter systematically and follow the suggestions we discussed earlier it should, with a bit of luck, fall out and look something like Figure 11.4.

Take Figure 11.4 step by step. The first thing to do (always) is to bring down the appropriate balance sheet figures. These are, for Ridiculous Records, the debtors figure and the provision for doubtful debts. We open these accounts with these figures (£8,700 and £435 respectively – check back to Figure 11.3 if you are in any doubt). Next, we do the double-entry for the transactions we know about during the year. These are the sales and the cash received from debtors. (We haven't bothered to open a cash account for this question.) The credit sales figure goes to the debtors account (this *is* obvious – isn't it?) and the cash received from debtors in 2005 go as credits to this account. Now comes the funny bit.

Inflow/Debit	SALES		Outflow/Credit
		Cash	100,000
		Debtors	50,000
	150,000		150,000

Inflow/Debit	TRADE DEBTORS		Outflow/Credit
Balance b/d	8,700	Cash for 2004 debtors	8,400
Sales	50,000	Cash for 2005 debtors	30,000
		Bad debt for 2004	300
		Bad debts for 2005	900
		Balance c/d (to TB or balance sheet)	19,100
	58,700		58,700

Inflow/Debit	PROVISION FOR BAD AND DOUBTFUL DEBTS		Outflow/Credit
Trade Debtors (Bad debt for 2004)	300	Balance b/d	435
Trade Debtors (Bad debts for 2005)	900	To profit and loss account (being	
Provision for DD to be c/d (balance sheet)	1,605	bad debts plus change in provision)	2,370
	2,805		2,805

Figure 11.4 Extract from the T-accounts for Ridiculous Records Ltd 2005

We are treating bad and doubtful debts together – but this does not mean they are the same. What it means is that we only need to open the one account. This has already been opened for us by the balance brought down of the doubtful debts provision. So now we write off the bad debts. (We haven't opened specific debtors accounts. In practice we would but we are just using a debtors control account to illustrate the points.) First, we write off the 2004 debt, and then we write off the bad debts for 2005. (Hopefully, you do appreciate that the previously identified 2004 bad debts are all dead and gone and, as a result of going through last year's profit and loss account, are of no interest whatsoever to us in this year. Do try and remember that the profit and loss account is the 'getting rid of things account' and the numbers in it disappear into the great accounting black hole called profit (or loss) never more to be seen again.)

So far, so good. Most of the detail in the question has been accounted for and we have just gone one step at a time. This is always the best plan if you want to avoid getting confused.

We now have only two bits left to worry about. First, we need to calculate the provision for doubtful debts needed for 2005. You know the (apparently) good debts figure (£20,000 less the bad debts written off from this year's debts – i.e. £19,100). You also know the old debts and the medium debts because the question told you. So you can work out the amount of less-than-three-months-old debts. This should give you £10,100. Now work out the percentages of each that the question requires of you and you should get a total of £1,605 (being £400 + £700 + £505). This is the amount you want to show in the balance sheet as the provision for doubtful debts.

The last bit is the clever bit if you keep your cool. The provision for doubtful debts which you calculated must be *one of* the balancing figures for the provision for doubtful debts account. (After all it *is* the balance carried down on doubtful debts. It must be – you just worked it out.) But this does not allow the provision for doubtful debts account to balance. The remaining balancing figure *must* be the amount you have to write off to the profit and loss account. This is an arithmetic result and must produce £2,370.

In order to make sure that this is the right answer (and to clear some opacity for those of you who are still frowning) let us find out what the figure of £2,370 comprises. We *know* (because we worked it out) that we want a provision on the balance sheet of £1,605. We *know* (because it was on last year's balance sheet) that the existing provision is £435. *Therefore*, we *must* need a charge to the profit and loss account of the difference (£1,170) in order to bring the provision up to the level we want.[3] So that accounts for the £1,170. Yes, but we charged more than this to the profit and loss account. What was the difference? Well, we had to get rid of the bad debts. These were £900 from this year and £300 from last year but written off this year. If we add £1,200 to £1,170 we get, eureka, £2,370 – the figure we wrote off. (You are right. It probably *is* magic.)

Like so much that we have done with basic bookkeeping and accounting, there are different ways to do the same thing. In this case we would still have come out with the same answer if we had kept the bad and the doubtful debts apart. *It is not the bookkeeping techniques themselves which determine the accounting numbers but the choices made about how and when to apply the techniques and the assumptions made about the figures which go into the techniques.* So, in the case of doubtful debts it is the *accounting decisions* to construct a provision and the organizational policy about the size of the provision that determine the answer. The bookkeeping techniques, *in themselves*, can be thought of as relatively neutral. Similarly with, for example, the depreciation provisions it was not how we did the bookkeeping – through the T-accounts or through the trial balance

– that affected the results. The resultant depreciation was effectively determined by the *accounting decisions* to have a depreciation provision, the estimated useful life of the asset, its scrap value and the method of depreciation – not by the bookkeeping as such.

We have now looked at all you really need to know at this stage about bad and doubtful debts and, over the last few chapters, the principal things you need to know – *at this stage* – about other areas of end of period adjustments. But these adjustments do raise some difficult issues – not just in the bookkeeping but in the accounting which underlies them. So, it makes some sense to rehearse some of these issues as they arise with provisions. And this is what we will do for the rest of this chapter.

11.3 PROVISIONS REVISITED AND THE 'ACCOUNTING DECISIONS'

11.3.1 The uncertainty of accounting numbers

We first met the nature of provisions in Chapter 7. We subsequently met – and did the bookkeeping for – provisions in Chapter 8 (accruals), Chapter 9 (depreciation), Chapter 10 (stock) and this chapter (doubtful debts). Provisions represent one of the most important end-of-period adjustments. They do not represent the only end-of-period adjustments and neither are these groups of provisions the only ones which are involved in constructing a set of financial statements.

The central problem that conventional financial accounting faces is that, after the initial trial balance has summarized all the *actual* accounting transactions of the accounting period, the accountant has to adjust the resultant numbers for a range of accounting events which either have taken place (but have not yet involved cash movements) or which might have taken place and/or might take place in the future. As a result, there are virtually no items in a set of financial statements that can be stated with certainty because many items depend on the occurrence of some future (unknown) event. We have seen the impact of some of these future events – events which may include the disposal of a fixed asset, the sale of inventory, an invoice for goods or services received or the non-payment of debt. Other future events might involve such matters as payments in foreign currency (will we get as much in our currency as we expect?), actual costs arising from a need to repair or replace faulty goods, costs arising from legal cases where the focal organization has been found negligent or whether or not expenditure on research and development will generate useful future products. There are a whole vast range of future events which influence accounting numbers. As a result, most accounting numbers are essentially uncertain and, therefore, contestable. This means that *any* profit (for example) is a (hopefully best) guess at the point in time at which the financial statements are assembled. It is this sort of uncertainty, together with a range of other disputed aspects of accounting numbers which lead to the difficulties inherent in end-of-period adjustments. We have looked at only a few of these here and have generally asserted that you should choose this or that method to deal with the item. To avoid some of the inevitable dispute that arises from choices over which accounting method to use, worldwide the professional accountancy bodies have issued **accounting standards** to guide these choices. We will look at these in slightly more detail in Chapter 14. But, for now, you should be clear in your mind about the inevitable uncertainty of accounting numbers and the central importance of accounting decisions about those numbers.

Provisions is one area where we make such accounting decisions. So, let us return and examine them a little more closely.

11.3.2 The nature of provisions

All the provisions we have examined have a number of characteristics in common.

Their *accounting* characteristics are that they arise from uncertainty about the future and we deal with this uncertainty by making informed estimates of the sorts of figures which this year's accounting statements might realistically contain. We do this guided by the principles of *matching* and *prudence*. Each of the provisions we have looked at arise because we wish to reflect an event which either has occurred (e.g. use of a machine or purchase of an un-invoiced delivery of goods), might have occurred (a decision by a debtor not to pay us or a decline in the market for some of our goods in inventory), or which might occur in the future (customers complaining about shoddy products or our inability to sell some goods). In each case we created a provision for the amount in question.

The *bookkeeping* characteristics of provision involved the *creation of the provision*, changes in the provision from year to year, and what we did with the provisions we had created. In the first year of a provision, the charge to the profit and loss account and the amount of the provision were identical – because we were creating the provision through the profit and loss account. (This must definitionally be the case.) In each subsequent accounting period changes were made to that provision and the *amount of the change* was the figure to be put through the profit and loss account. So, for example, if we increased the provision then the amount of the increase was put through the profit and loss account [Debit] and added to the provision in the balance sheet [Credit]. But whether we could do this in such a simple way depended upon what the focal organization did with the provision during the accounting period. We need to have another (very brief) look at this.

When we looked at fixed assets, we created a *provision for depreciation*. The charge for that year's depreciation went to the profit and loss account and this amount was added to the accumulated depreciation provision which showed as a diminution in the NBV of the fixed asset in the balance sheet. Each year the provision grew to reflect an estimate of the usage of the fixed asset and a diminution in the amount of the fixed asset left for use by the focal organization. The provision remained in the books of the focal organization as a permanent reduction in the diminution of the NBV until we came to dispose of the asset. At that point the fixed asset *and* the accumulated depreciation of that asset had to be removed from the books. We did this via a disposal of fixed asset account. So we were only interested in the provision for as long as the item to which the provision related (the fixed asset) remained in the books. In this way we attempted to *match* the income earned by the focal organization with help from the fixed asset with an estimate of the costs incurred in generating that income. This was also a *prudent* thing to do because we were attempting to recognize a cost we had almost certainly incurred but whose exact amount we were unsure about.

This process of accounting for depreciation also has one other dimension that you might like to think about. There is a sense in which the balance sheet is supposed to reflect the financial value of the organization. The fixed assets are an important part of that value. By depreciating we are taking the value of the balance sheet and using it up through the profit and loss account. What is left on the balance might be thought of as the value left over. This is, however, a very dubious piece of reasoning and is central to many of the arguments about accounting. Strictly speaking, the balance sheet is a bookkeeping convenience and shows the *unexpired costs* remaining in the focal organization. As a result, to infer that the balance sheet *actually* shows anything related to the *financial value of the organization* is not strictly correct. And yet, you will find that interpretation of the financial statements –

and the balance sheet in particular – suggests that the balance sheet indicates something of the organization's value. We will touch upon this again in Chapters 15 and 16. The issue must be approached with great care.

Whilst the provisions that we created for depreciation related to items which stayed in the organization for some time, the provisions we created for accruals, for example, related to things we expected to 'expire' quite quickly. We have seen how, at the accounting date, we had to estimate provisions for accruals on such matters as electricity we had used but not been invoiced for or goods received but not yet invoiced. These were estimates which we expected to turn into specific accounting transactions very soon in the next accounting period. There were several ways in which we might deal with these provisions – although each way produces the same answer. In every case we would bring down the provision – which would be sitting on the balance sheet under current liabilities (or as a negative current asset) – to open the books for the new accounting period. The provision could be brought down to one of two places. Either we brought it down and opened an account for 'accruals' or we brought it down to open an account which related to the 'subject of the accrual'. So, in this latter case we might bring down the accrual to the account called 'electricity'. In the former case we would *reverse the accrual* when the invoice (or whatever) went through to finalize the accounting transaction – e.g. [Debit accruals/provisions: Credit electricity]. In the latter case we could happily ignore it as the accounting transactions working through the double-entry bookkeeping system would naturally take account of the opening amounts owing. *The important thing to note* is that in each case, the provision disappeared very soon after the year-end. At the next year-end we started again and recalculated the provision necessary for the end of the new accounting period. We did not need to increase or decrease the existing the provision – because it no longer existed. This was nice and straightforward.

The final group of provisions we looked at – for doubtful debts and for stock – were a sort of hybrid provision from a bookkeeping point of view. In both cases we could use the provision (which would be brought down from the balance sheet at the start of the accounting period in the usual way) in one of two ways. The provision could be used to 'catch' subsequent accounting events – the actual disposal of obsolete or damaged stock or a debt actually turning bad – and so, in effect, use up the provision during the subsequent accounting period. In this case, the focal organization had to recreate a new provision at the end of the new accounting period. The alternative is to let the provision sit there for the accounting period and just adjust it for the amount of change needed at the new year end. The effect on the profit and loss account and balance sheet is identical in each case. The only difference is in how the bookkeeping operated and in how *you* think about what the provision was doing during the accounting period.

Once you have the basic bookkeeping techniques outlined in this and the previous chapters, you will be doing yourself a favour (in the long term, at least) if you can think your way through the behaviour of provisions. They illustrate a number of points. Perhaps the first is just how clever the bookkeeping system is in capturing complicated accounting movements in a few simple bookkeeping entries. The second is that unless particular accounting transactions are covered by detailed requirements in company law or accounting standards, there are many ways in which they may be treated. This leads to the third observation that accounting numbers are highly uncertain. Do not let the sophistication and elegance of the bookkeeping algorithms blind you to this essential guesswork in accounting figures. Finally, you should be able to see that bookkeeping and accounting are trying to capture a set of dynamic flows through the focal organization.

Organizations and their transactions are enormously complicated. Bookkeeping and accounting frequently are too simple to capture all aspects of what is going on – especially if we only follow accounting procedures. It is, therefore, so very important to try and think what economic reality (if any) lies behind the accounting transaction and then try and capture this as best one can in the bookkeeping procedures. Accounting is, essentially, an especially elegant *simplification of a complex world*. This elegance does not mean that the simplification is entirely useful or accurate. The role and status of accountants derives not from their ability to do the algorithms – we can get computers to do this – but from their ability to understand the complexities of organizational life and translate this into a basic medium such as financial numbers. It is a failure to always appreciate this distinction that tends to distinguish the 'good' accountant from the 'bad' accountant – and if you read the press (as you should be doing) you will be aware that there are far too many examples of 'bad' accounting.

SUMMARY

The bookkeeping for bad and doubtful debts arises from the matching and prudence concepts. Bad debts are those which relate to debtors who are unlikely to pay the focal organization what they owe. These are written off through the profit and loss account as an expense of the accounting period. They are *not* used to reduce the sales figure – although this is more for convention and convenience than for any especially good logical reason. Doubtful debts are more complicated and arise from a prudent concern by the focal organization to recognize that debts may not be paid. They are general in nature and are accounted for by the creation of a provision. In the year in which the provision is created the whole amount is written off through the profit and loss account and the provision appears as a current liability or negative current asset in the balance sheet. Subsequent adjustments to this provision are made by writing the amount of the adjustment through the profit and loss account and adding or subtracting this adjustment from the provision shown in the balance sheet.

Provisions are tricky items but are central to the principles of conventional bookkeeping and accounting. They emphasise the essential uncertainty of accounting numbers, in that provisions reflect estimates of future events. The outcome of these future events cannot be known at the balance sheet date. The accountants' task is to attempt to make provisions that reflect, as accurately as possible, the 'economic reality' (if such exists) of the actual events underlying the accounting decisions. This is true, not just for provisions, but for the greater proportion of figures which appear in financial statements. Accounting is not, and under present conventions cannot be, an accurate 'science'. Accounting, as presently practised is more of an 'art' or a 'craft' and the simple technical elegance (and cleverness) of the bookkeeping procedures should never blind us to this essentially judgemental nature of accounting.

FURTHER READING

There are three areas in which you may wish to look at further reading. The first relates to the technical bookkeeping elements of bad and doubtful debts – as well as the bookkeeping for provisions. Your best source of information on this is the workbook which accompanies this text. Other introductory textbooks also deal with these issues (in more or less detail) but will often deal with them in slightly different ways. Such books are well worth

---

Key terms and concepts

The following key terms and concepts have featured in this chapter. You should ensure that you understand and can explain each one. Page references to definitions appear in the index in bold type.

- Accounting decisions
- Adjusting provisions
- Ageing debts
- Bad debts
- Bad debts account
- Creating provisions
- Credit control
- Doubtful debts
- Doubtful debts account
- The nature of the accounting craft

- Neutrality of bookkeeping versus judgement in accounting
- Provision for doubtful debts
- Provisions
- Reversing accruals
- Uncertainty of accounting numbers
- Unexpired costs and valuation
- Writing off to the profit and loss account

---

examining, but do so with care in order to avoid confusing yourself too much. The second issue relates to the accounting reasoning behind provisions and, indeed, behind the accounting principles themselves. Any introductory textbook on accounting theory will give you some guidance on this. Finally, you might want to think about the nature of accounting. The nicest article on this is Hines (1988) which we warmly recommend will repay your serious attention. You will find a lot of articles which look at this sort of issue but you may find them too complex for you at this stage. If you can find a copy of Hird (1983), this should entertain you and you may well find the opening chapters of Tinker (1985), Lehman (1992) and Neimark (1992) usefully stimulating.

NOTES

1. The only issue that might arise would be the warranty provision. That is, there may be costs which the focal organization should have incurred (say on the reliability of the product) which we are concerned may now arise in the future. We may make a warranty provision – but this does directly influence the reported sales figure. We will have another look at this later in this chapter.

2. Incidentally, the costs incurred by the focal organization's debt collection agency would also need to be accounted for – perhaps through a particular mechanism or through the doubtful debts system. You will be pleased to know that we won't worry about this here!

3. Think about it. There is a provision of £435 sitting around. We want a provision of £1,605 for next year. We therefore have to increase the provision by £1,170. How do we do this? There is only one way – through the profit and loss account. We do *this* by putting through a charge for that amount. OK? Go back and go through it all again if it is still giving you a headache. If that doesn't work, ask for advice.

From the trial balance to the financial statements: ownership claims, profit, appropriations and social reality

12

Learning objectives

After studying this chapter you should be able to:

- explain the importance of ownership claims;
- briefly explain how taxation of profits is treated;
- define the elements of the ownership claim;
- explain the basic ownership claim in a sole trader;
- explain the basic ownership claim in a company;
- distinguish between ordinary and preference shares in a company;
- distinguish between authorized and issued share capital;
- briefly explain what a share premium account is;
- distinguish between expenses and distributions/appropriations;
- demonstrate the use(s) of the appropriation account;
- draw up a drawings account;
- explain and demonstrate why and how profit is very unlikely to be an accurate figure;
- explain why financial statements can be considered to be a social construction of reality.

12.1 INTRODUCTION

12.1.1 Chapter design and links to previous chapters

The last few chapters have been relatively straightforward in focusing on some of the principal adjustments we need to make to get from our bookkeeping and initial trial balance to a final trial balance and financial statements. This chapter completes this part of the journey and focuses, particularly, on **ownership claims**. The whole area of ownership claims is complex but, as we shall see, is central to the accounting process. Some might even argue, with considerable justification, that conventional financial accounting exists principally because of these ownership claims. They therefore deserve especial attention. We *have* met ownership claims before. We examined different sorts of organizations in Chapter 3 and saw that whilst the different organizational types had different legal structures they also had different ownership structures. In Chapter 4 we introduced – albeit briefly – the ownership transactions and, especially, those which are needed to start an organization. (The owners putting money into an organization is usually the very first thing that happens – as far as the accountant is concerned – to create an *accounting entity*.) Finally, we saw in Chapter 7 how ownership claims were a special category of *liability* – however counterintuitive this might seem. With this basic knowledge, you were able to handle the very simple ownership situations which arose in the Yothu Yindi examples in the preceding chapters (see, for example, Figure 10.10 as an illustration). In this chapter we will look at these things in more detail.[1]

But, once again, we will not jump straight into the deep end. The rest of this section will rehearse – and briefly expand upon – the trial balance categorization that has been so important in the preceding chapters. This will allow us to put ownership claims in perspective. Section 12.2 is a long section which will examine ownership claims in quite some detail. (We will, however, leave out *partnership ownership* claims as these are dealt with in detail in Chapter 13.) Section 12.3 will examine the published form of the profit and loss account and balance sheet. Section 12.4 starts to think about the nature of financial statements and, in particular, about the implications of our estimates of profits and the way in which we accountants help to construct 'social reality'. The chapter rounds off with the usual conclusions and further reading.

12.1.2 Revisiting trial balance categorization

It should all be pretty straight in your mind by now but let us just quickly recapitulate where we have got to. A defined set of *transactions* are captured by the *accounting information system* and recorded (via books of prime entry) in the *accounting records* via the T-accounts (or, more usually, their equivalent in the computer ledger system). These transactions (the basic ones were specified in Figure 4.10) are debited and credited to various accounts which, broadly speaking, reflect the different sorts of *revenues, expenses, assets and liabilities* that seem important to that organization. We summarize these transactions at the end of each accounting period (week, month or year, for example) into an *initial trial balance*. At a very simple level, each of these transactions represents some kind of economic event which involves cash in this accounting period, in earlier accounting periods or in future accounting periods. But, because of the periodicity and accrual conventions, there will be a number of additional events which will require a series of *end-of-period adjustments* to make the accounting records 'more realistic'. These adjustments (for such things as stock, bad and doubtful debts, depreciation and accruals and prepayments – but see also Chapter 14) can either be made through the accounting records (the T-accounts, journals and/or computer files) or through the extended trial balance to produce the *final trial balance*.

This final trial balance is the basis of the financial statements. Each item in the final trial balance is taken to its appropriate place in the profit and loss account and balance sheet: revenues and expenses going to the profit and loss account and assets and liabilities to the balance sheet. The difference between the revenues and expenses shown in the profit and loss account is treated as *profit or loss for the accounting period*. To keep the double-entry intact, this amount is also taken to the balance sheet. In this way we maintain the accounting equations we examined formally in Chapter 7.

This all looks fairly straightforward but we frequently will have difficulty actually defining some of our bits and pieces as assets, liabilities, expenses and revenues. For example, we saw that depreciation was all about deciding how much of a fixed asset should stay on the balance sheet (as the asset) and how much should be taken away to the profit and loss account as 'used up' in that period (as an expense). We saw that some of our expenses (accruals) needed to be increased and this simultaneously increased our liabilities (via creditors and accruals). We also saw, in Chapter 7, that it is not always easy to know what are or are not assets. For example many intangible 'assets' (like reputations, experience of staff and so on) are excluded from the assets on the balance sheet whilst others (like goodwill and research and development, for example) are included. This goes further still: some things which clearly are by definition 'assets' (for example, Sellotape dispensers, computer floppy disks, tools and utensils) may be considered too small ('immaterial') to be worth bothering with as assets and so will be treated as expenses. Finally, there will probably be potential liabilities in a company which it has not yet recognized (or wishes to ignore). For example, the potential costs of repairing environmental damage to (say) land owned by the company will produce, in time, a large liability that may very well not be recognised currently and thus not included in the balance sheet. There are very many examples of these and related difficulties. (Some are considered in Chapter 14 and some of the potential social and environmental 'assets and liabilities' are very briefly considered in Chapter 17.)

The point of all this is that (a) categorizing items as assets, liabilities, revenues and expenses is frequently far from simple; and (b) there will be potential elements that, strictly speaking, should be included – usually under the prudence concept – which are missing from the financial statements. Therefore, once again, we see that, at best, financial statements are an approximation of some economic situation for the organization – they can never be entirely accurate.

You should also be able to see by now that issues of categorization affect both the profit and loss account and balance sheet. Many, if not all, end-of-period adjustments involve moving numbers between categories and this, in turn, either affects both statements directly or affects the profit or loss which itself influences both statements. Profit is the residual figure left over when we do our accounting processes. It is also, however, an important number – not just in terms of whether or not the company has been 'successful' (see later) – *but it is the calculated amount which the company has 'earned' for its owners in this accounting period.* Whilst we have been learning how to keep accounting records and do double-entry bookkeeping for a number of useful reasons (e.g. to help the organization track its cash flows, to keep an eye on what is owed to other organizations, etc.), easily the most dominant reason for going the extra step, doing the end-of-period adjustments and compiling the financial statements is to represent the state of the owners' interest in the business. This is greatly influenced by the profit figure we end up calculating. Therefore, as we mentioned earlier, it is probably correct to say that the whole of the *financial accounting* (as opposed to the bookkeeping) in a commercial organization is driven by the financial interest of the owners. Their ownership claims are therefore, in conventional accounting, the most important thing we have to worry about. There are, of course, the rather larger questions of: (i) whether it is right and proper for owners' rights to dominate all other interests; (ii) whether accounting and the accounting profession are correct in addressing owners' interests to the virtual exclusion of all else; and (iii) what should happen when the ownership of a focal organization is not entirely clear (in, for example, non-commercial organizations or where shareholdings are so diffuse no real control is exercised by the owners). These are major issues which your later studies may well address. All we can do, at this stage, is raise the questions in your mind. We will return and touch upon them again in Chapters 14, 17 and 18.

This seems a good point at which to talk a little more about taxation (which could be thought of as a sort of 'ownership claim by society') and, in particular, its effect on profits.

12.1.3 Taxation

Taxation is a complex area. (For more detail, see further reading at the end of the chapter.) The one aspect that we should know a little more about at this stage is the **taxation of business profits**. Whilst tax is clearly an expense of the business, it is *not* treated with the other expenses in the profit and loss account but is shown separately in what we see below is usually called an **appropriation account**. This is because taxation of business profits is calculated on the basis of the *adjusted* net profit. As a result, it is therefore essential to distinguish between net profit *before* tax (NPBT) and net profit *after* tax (NPAT). Figure 12.1 shows this.

Never make the mistake of assuming that NPAT is some particular proportion of NPBT, because although taxation is charged as a percentage of *taxable* profit, in many countries *accounting* profit is not the same as taxable profit. Many rules govern the calculation of taxable profit and these may differ from the rules and conventions employed in calculating accounting profit.[2] (For example, we charge depreciation in calculating accounting profit, but for UK *taxable* profit, depreciation is not allowed. Instead, something called *capital allowances* is included. The provision for doubtful debts is also not allowed against tax, whereas bad debts are. And so on.) The calculation of this taxable profit, the resultant tax which is due to the taxation authorities (which will usually then appear as a creditor, a current liability in the balance sheet), the dates on which the tax must be paid and how the organization may plan its tax affairs are all matters which are part of the traditional role of accountants. However, on the grounds that a little knowledge is a dangerous thing, we will leave it there. You will meet much more detail in the later stages of your accounting studies and so must hold your enthusiasm in check until then.

We are now in a position to look at ownership claims in more detail.

12.2 OWNERSHIP CLAIMS

As we saw in Chapter 3, organizations come in all shapes and sizes. We have not given a great deal of attention to non-commercial organizations because the accounting and financial reporting issues have, historically, been less complex in these organizations. We will return to have a brief look at this issue towards the end of this chapter. Amongst the commercial organizations we have tended to concentrate on sole traders and companies. We shall continue to do so in this chapter. (We will look at partnerships in some detail in Chapter 13 and then concentrate more or less exclusively thereafter on companies.) Commercial organizations are distinguished by (*inter alia*) how they are owned and whether or not they *can* make profits. In conventional commercial accounting, profits *are* what the owners have earned – no owners, no profit; no profit, no owners.

The ownership claim in a commercial organization comprises four main elements:

Profit & Loss Account for Year Ended February 200X	
Revenue	XX,XXX
Expenses	(X,XXX)
Profit for the year before tax (NPBT)	8,000
Less taxation	(1,000)
Profit for the year after tax (NPAT)	7,000

Figure 12.1 Taxation in a company's financial statement

i   capital injected into the organization;

ii   this year's earning (profit or loss) attributable to the owners and transfers to reserves;

iii   the amount that the organization has passed to its owner(s) via, for example, 'drawings' or 'dividends' – this requires that we know a little about 'appropriation accounts';

iv   earnings from previous years which have not been passed on to the owners (which should enable us to take an overview of the relationship between the profit and loss account and balance sheet and ownership claims).

It will be necessary to keep these four elements clear in your mind. Although they are closely related they are all treated (in accounting as well as in law) in slightly different ways.

12.2.1 Capital injections to the focal organization

A commercial accounting entity needs an owner and an injection of *capital* to bring it into existence. In a sole trader, as we saw, there would be just one such owner (the *sole trader*), for a company there must be at least two such owners (or, more accurately, *shareholders*). How much capital they inject to create the business does not matter – it can be $1 or £1 million, the basic event is fundamentally the same in both accounting terms (credit capital, debit (probably) cash) and in broad legal terms – the owners own (that is, they have voting rights over) their organization. But what *does* matter is the form of organization we are talking about and, in the case of a company, what *sort* of ownership claim has arisen.

The sole trader has complete control over their business and, in the unlikely event that the sole trader is not also the senior employee of the organization, has ultimate power over who is employed and decisions that are taken – if, indeed the sole trader wishes this. The sole trader can put additional capital into the business and, within reason, can take money out of the business (*'drawings'* as they are called in this case) whenever the mood takes them. (We look at this again below in subsection 12.2.3.) The sole trader's situation is, therefore, relatively straightforward when it comes to accounting for the ownership claims.[3]

The situation for a company is a great deal more complex and covered, in virtually all countries, by extensive Companies Acts or their equivalent. The Companies Acts (which we will examine in a little more detail in Chapter 14) will lay down the minimum requirements necessary to bring a company into existence. These minima will probably include a requirement for legal documents outlining the purposes of the company and details of the relationship between the shareholders (owners). These will probably be called the **Memorandum and Articles of Association**. In addition, the Companies Acts will specify who can act as *directors* and how they are to be elected and retired. (The directors are the people who will run the company. They will be legally, if not factually, different from the owners.[4]) The Companies Acts will also lay down the requirement to produce financial accounts (see Chapter 14) and details of what sort of ownership claims can be established.

The basic form of the ownership claim in a company is the **share** or **stock**[5] (both of which are also sometimes referred to as **equity**). These are shares in the ownership of the company. A company may, at the time of its creation, decide to have as few as two shares or many millions of shares.[6] As long as there are at least two **shareholders** it really does not matter (in accounting terms at least) how these shares are distributed amongst those shareholders – even if one owns 999,999 shares and the other just 1 share. The shares may be of two principal types: ordinary shares and preference shares.[7]

An **ordinary share** is, as its name suggests, the most basic kind of share. Each share held gives the holder a part-ownership claim on the company and a vote at meetings of shareholders. (Such meetings must normally be at least once a year and they will vote on such matters as the appointment and remuneration of directors, approving the financial statements and agreeing the level of **dividends** – see below. We will look at some of these issues again in Chapter 14.) In addition to the voting rights, the important things about ordinary shares are that:

i   the shares will carry a *face* value (e.g. they might be £1 shares) which is the *nominal amount* that the shareholders inject to the business at its creation. The amount that a shareholder paid for the share and the value at which the share is traded (e.g. in a stock market) may very well bear little or no relationship to this face, or nominal, value but will, rather, reflect the worth of the company at the time of the purchase or sale of the share. It is these amounts – the face value and, in some cases, the actual amounts that shareholders paid which we need to account for;

ii   the shares will carry a *variable* dividend, see subsection 12.2.3 below; and,

iii in the event of a liquidation of the company, the ordinary shareholders will only receive what is left after *all* other claims on the company have been satisfied. In cases where the company has gone into liquidation because it is not making sufficient money to keep trading, the ordinary shareholders may receive very little indeed. Ordinary shares are, therefore, *risky* in that whilst a shareholder may 'make' a lot of money on holding a share they can also lose all that money; but,

iv   because most companies enjoy *limited liability* this means that if the debts of the business exceed the value of the business at liquidation, the shareholders are only liable for the value of their capital which remains unpaid at the date of liquidation (see later for the distinction between paid and unpaid capital). Their personal assets cannot be reclaimed to cover the debts of the company. In a sole trader or partnership (with *unlimited liability*) the personal assets of the owners *can* be called upon to pay off the debts of the business.

A **preference share** still gives the owner an ownership share in the company and, usually, also carries a voting right at company meetings and the nominal and traded values of the share are, like ordinary shares, likely to be different. However, a preference share is less risky both in terms of *upside* risk – the chance to 'make' a lot of money – and in *downside* risk – the chance of losing all one's investment. This is because a preference share will usually:

i   carry a *fixed dividend* so that the amount that is paid to them every year is likely to be the same;

ii   in the event of a liquidation, the preference shareholders are reimbursed *before* the ordinary shareholders – they are *preferred*;

iii as a company may not wish (or be unable) to pay a dividend every year, the ordinary shareholders may simply have to go without that year's dividend. For a preference shareholder, that year's dividend is paid before the ordinary shareholders' dividend. If the company is unable to afford a dividend at all this year, the preference shareholders' dividend will usually be *cumulative* – that is, this year's dividend is still owed to the preference (but not the ordinary) shareholders and must be paid at some future date.

Let us turn now to the accounting. At the creation of the company a certain amount of *authorized share capital* will be established. This relates to the total number of shares that the company can issue. It may very well choose not to issue all of these at the point of creation but wait and issue shares later when it needs more cash. So, at any one point in time, the company's *issued share capital* and its authorized share capital may not be the same. The authorized share capital will usually be established as a number of shares of some nominal value: for example, 1 million £1 ordinary shares, or (say) 10,000 $5 ordinary shares and 10,000 $10 preference shares. This (£1 million or $150,000) is the nominal value of the share capital and is shown as the *authorized share capital* in the balance sheet. If, and only if, the company issues *all* of these shares, then the issued and authorized share capital would be the same. The company can issue as few or as many shares as it wishes. For each issue, we would debit cash and credit share capital with the appropriate amount. *This* is the amount which appears as *issued share capital* on the balance sheet.

If you turn back to Yothu Yindi Ltd (see, for example, Figure 8.5 for the 2000 financial statements or Figure 10.10 for the 2001 financial statements) you will see that, at the bottom of the balance sheet is a section headed up 'Represented by'. This shows share capital of $40,000. As we do not have any additional information, we can assume that Yothu Yindi Ltd was created with (for the sake of argument) 40,000 $1 shares issued at their nominal value. We can also assume, because it doesn't say (although, strictly speaking, in a real company, it would have to state this), that these are ordinary shares. We can, thus, construct the basic financial statements for Yothu Yindi Ltd for 2002 on this assumption (and drawing from the figures we calculated for stock, fixed assets and depreciation in earlier chapters – the remaining figures you will take on trust as these you have not seen before).

For the moment, the bit we are concerned with is shown at the bottom of the balance sheet where you can see the issued ordinary share capital of the company of $40,000. (You may also note that the company has recorded a loss for 2002, but we will return to that later.) This is, presumably, the amount injected by Yothu Yindi's owners at the creation of the company.

YOTHU YINDI LTD: PROFIT AND LOSS ACCOUNT FOR THE YEAR ENDING 31 DECEMBER 2002 (all figures in dollars)		
SALES		465,000
less COST OF GOODS SOLD		(188,000)
GROSS OR TRADING PROFIT		277,000
EXPENSES:		
Depreciation for the year	12,000	
Profit on disposal	(1,000)	
Loss on disposal	3,000	
Stock provisions	2,900	
Bad and doubtful debts	25,000	
Rent	140,000	
Wages	40,000	
Heat and light	7,400	
Telephone	13,400	
Rates	30,000	
Other expenses	42,000	
		(314,700)
NET LOSS FOR THE PERIOD		(37,700)

YOTHU YINDI LTD: BALANCE SHEET				
AS AT 31 DECEMBER 2002 (all figures in dollars)				
FIXED ASSETS:	**Cost**	**Acc Dep'n**	**NBV**	
Manufacturing plant	10,000	2,000	8,000	
Wind-farm	100,000	5,000	95,000	
Vehicle 1	13,000	2,000	3,000	
Vehicle 2	17,000	3,000	14,000	120,000
CURRENT ASSETS:				
Stocks			172,100	
Trade Debtors			32,000	
Prepayments			26,000	
Cash			(150,600)	
			79,500	
CURRENT LIABILITIES:				
Creditor (Fixed Asset)			50,000	
Trade Creditors			42,000	
Sundry Creditors			2,100	
Accruals & Provisions			4,700	
			98,800	
				(19,300)
NET ASSETS				$100,700
REPRESENTED BY:				
Issued Ordinary Share Capital				40,000
Profit and Loss Account: brought forward			98,400	
for the year			(37,000)	60,700
SHAREHOLDERS'/OWNERS' FUNDS				$100,700

Figure 12.2 The financial statements for Yothu Yindi Ltd 2002

Now, let us assume that the balance sheet is not quite correct. Let us assume that on 30 December the company successfully issued $10,000 of $5 preference shares.[8] This would produce an additional issued share capital of $50,000. Now, further assume that when the share issue was announced, there was such a demand for the shares that the company was able to issue them *at a premium*. That is, potential shareholders were willing to pay more for the shares than the face value of $5. We will assume that everybody paid $6 for each $5 preference share. As a result, the company gains $50,000 of issued share capital and $10,000 of *share premium*. This additional $10,000 share premium generates $10,000 of cash in addition to the basic $50,000 from the issue. Both amounts (the total $60,000) are now part of the shareholders' funds and must be shown as such. However, for reasons normally laid down in the Companies Acts (and we *always* do what the law tells us, don't we?) we must keep the share capital and the share premium separate. So whilst we debit cash with $60,000, we credit share capital with $50,000 and credit share premium account with $10,000. If this is what actually happened then the balance sheet of the company at the end of 2002 should look like Figure 12.3.

In Figure 12.3 you can see the additional share capital shown in shareholders' funds along with the share premium account. The balance sheet balances because the cash received for the issue has been taken into the cash account and so reduces the overdraft.

Whilst it will get a great deal more complicated in your later studies of financial accounting, this is sufficient for us at this stage. The initial and later injections of capital

YOTHU YINDI LTD: BALANCE SHEET			
AS AT 31 DECEMBER 2002 (all figures in dollars)			

FIXED ASSETS:	Cost	Acc Dep'n	NBV	
Manufacturing plant	10,000	2,000	8,000	
Wind-farm	100,000	5,000	95,000	
Vehicle 1	13,000	2,000	3,000	
Vehicle 2	17,000	3,000	14,000	120,000
CURRENT ASSETS:				
Stocks			172,100	
Trade Debtors			32,000	
Prepayments			26,000	
Cash			(90,600)	
			139,500	
CURRENT LIABILITIES:				
Creditor (Fixed Asset)			50,000	
Trade Creditors			42,000	
Sundry Creditors			2,100	
Accruals & Provisions			4,700	
			98,800	
				40,700
NET ASSETS				$160,700
REPRESENTED BY:				
Issued Ordinary Share Capital				40,000
Issued 5% Preference Share Capital				50,000
Share Premium				10,000
Profit and Loss Account:	brought forward		98,400	
	for the year		(37,700)	60,700
SHAREHOLDERS'/OWNERS' FUNDS				$160,700

Figure 12.3 Balance sheet at 31 December 2002

from the owners are *basically* straightforward – at least in simple companies or sole trader organizations.[9] So now we can turn and have a look at the other elements of the ownership claims, starting with the profit (or loss) recorded in the current accounting period.

12.2.2 This years' earnings (profit or loss) and their allocation

Whilst the profit and loss account will help any reader of the financial statements to better understand the organization's financial activities during an accounting period its principal purpose is to calculate the profit or loss earned in that accounting period. This profit or loss is, at its simplest, the amount that has been earned for the shareholders – or proprietor(s) – in the current accounting period. As you may have realized by now, this is not a *real* amount – in the sense of a pile of used cash. (The relationship between profit and cash is re-examined in Chapter 15.) It is an *estimate* of the amount by which the company is 'better or worse off' as a result of its trading activities during the period. This is an *abstract* figure with no real physical reality. And this abstract nature of profit (or loss) is one of the most difficult ideas to come to terms with in accounting. (We will return to it later in this chapter and in Chapter 15.) The simplest way to think of it is that we, the accountants, have calculated a number following a set of accounting procedures and this, resultant, number will be treated *as if* it represented some real sense of better-offness or worse-offness.

Perhaps you might think of this as an increase or decrease in the organization's 'store of wealth' (but see Chapters 16, 17 and 18).

As the central purpose of financial accounting is to provide a set of statements for the owners of the business, it should come as no surprise to learn that, basically speaking, this profit or loss is the shareholders' profit or loss. This is what the company has earned for its owners and, again at the risk of over-simplification, what the company now owes to those owners. *This* is why the ownership claim is always a liability – it is owed by the company to the shareholders.

The question then arises, what does the company *do* with this profit or loss? We saw in our earlier examples (and in Figures 12.2 and 12.3) that we take it from the profit and loss account and put it on to the balance sheet. But this is only a part of the story. Oh, that life were this simple!

The organization – or more particularly the directors of the company or the proprietor of the sole trader – will have to make a series of decisions about what to do with this 'increased (or decreased) store of wealth'. Two major factors will affect these decisions.

First, the profit or loss has been earned on the assumption that the organization will continue in much its present form, that it will not grow and that it is unlikely to be faced by any nasty surprises in the next few years.[10] Let us think about this. The profit and loss account was derived after we had paid all expenses and recognized all revenues earned in this period. We calculated some depreciation that, in effect, stored away an amount to permit the present fixed assets to be replaced.[11] That is, the profit or loss was calculated after we had made such provisions as were necessary to *maintain the capital of the organization*. This principle of *capital maintenance* is very important in conventional accounting practice. In essence, the central 'store of wealth' of the organization must not be diminished. The profit or loss is calculated after we have provided in such a way as to maintain this level of a 'store of wealth'. But, most organizations do not want to stay level. For various reasons (many of them unfathomable – see Chapter 17), organizations are assumed to want to grow. How will they do this? A central factor in that growth is likely to be a need to increase the *productive capacity* of the organization – increase stocks, increase sales representatives, increase fixed assets and so on. So the directors or proprietor may very well decide that they need to *retain profit* to fuel this expansion. So the first decision that the organization makes is how much of the current year's profit must be *retained* for this expansion.

Similarly, if the organization has any sense, it will try and look forward and see if there are any nasty surprises that might emerge. Now, the organization has already stored away *provisions* for those things that it more or less knows are likely to happen (debts not being paid, fixed assets wearing out, customers complaining about the quality of a product or service). It may very well look beyond this and think: should we keep some 'wealth' back in case, for example, we get a chance to take over a competitor? we have to fight off a takeover bid? our fixed assets cost more to replace or we wish to expand or update them? our bank suddenly wants our loans back or our debentures need redeeming? we may want to issue more shares? a change in law requires us to significantly upgrade our environmental performance? and so on.

So, if the organization decides to do either of these things – provide for expansion (what is usually called *organic growth*) or retain some profit for possible future events – the organization will make a **transfer to reserves**. That is, some (if not all), of the current year's profit will be *allocated* to particular reserves and this part of the shareholders' 'increase in the store of wealth' will be retained in the business.[12]

The second – but clearly related – decision the directors will take is how much of the organization's (remaining) current store of wealth should be paid out to the owners. The obvious conclusion is that, following the decision that the company will retain a certain amount for *reserves* it will pay the rest out to the owner(s). In the case of an organization recording a loss, the organization *can* actually pay out to the shareholders from the *retained profits from earlier accounting periods*. So here we see yet another reason why an organization might wish to retain profits in 'good' years to pay out to shareholders in 'bad' years.

So we can now look at *how* this payout process works.

12.2.3 Making payments to the owners

We are considering in this chapter two basic types of organizations – the sole trader and the company. (Partnerships are dealt with in Chapter 13.) As we have already seen, one of the major differences between these two types of organization, from the accountant's point of view, is the formality and legality of the rules governing the company versus the simplicity and convenience of the sole trader. This is especially notable when we look at ownership claims.

One of the major differences between companies' and sole traders' treatment of ownership claims relates to the detail, care and formality we must exercise with companies. We *do* need to think formally and carefully about the distribution of profits and transfers to reserves in the company. In the sole trader, we have far less to worry about. We shall, therefore, look at how the sole trader makes payments to its owner first before looking at some of the detail we need to know about companies.

(a) Distributions to the sole trader: drawings

You will recall (we hope) that although the sole trader is treated as a separate *accounting entity* from the owner, it is not treated as a separate *legal entity*. The consequence of this is that even if the owner works for the business they cannot pay themself a salary or wage as such. *Anything* which the owner takes out of the business is *not treated as an expense* but as a *distribution of profit*. These distributions of profit are called, in the sole trader's case, **drawings**. So, if, say, the owner decides to pay themself a weekly 'wage', take home a few elements of stock for their own consumption, uses cash out of the till for personal expenditures and pays themself a bonus out of the profits at the end of the accounting period, *these are all drawings*.

Drawings are fairly easy to deal with from an accounting point (although in practice, the hardest part is working out what the owner *has* taken out of the business and what to charge for this). There are three basic elements. *First*, open a drawings account and take to this anything which the owner takes out of the business. (Thus, for example, if the owner takes some stock for their private use [debit drawings: credit stock]. If the owner takes a 'wage', [debit drawings: credit cash]. And so on.) *Second*, the drawings account is balanced off at the end of the year (just like all other accounts) and taken to the trial balance where it is shown as an 'appropriation' or 'distribution' of profit – that is, as deduction from the profit for the year. *Third*, the profit for the year, together with the profit and loss account brought forward (see below) and the drawings for the year are then shown under 'proprietor's funds' in the balance sheet. The result, the profit and loss account, might look something like Figure 12.4.

The proprietor in this example has taken total drawings of £10,000. We have shown this in the **appropriation account**. That is, we have identified a section of the profit and loss account which does not record expenses and revenues but rather shows how the profit (or loss) we have calculated is to be split up – appropriated. In this case, the situation is simple, of the £21,000 of profit, £10,000 has been distributed to the owner whilst £11,000 has been retained in the business and will show on the balance sheet (under the 'represented by' section) as an addition to owners claims on the business. (Note that we have ignored taxation – a convenient convention common in introductory courses you will be pleased to learn. *But* you should note that the appropriation account was on net profit before taxation (NPBT) *not* net profit after taxation (NPAT). This is because of the differing tax rules that apply to sole traders as opposed to companies. The same applied to partnerships as to sole traders). The situation in a *partnership* would be very similar except that a separate record would be kept of *each* partner's drawings *and*, in order to prevent chaos, there would be some agreement amongst the partners about how much each could take, when and in what form (see Chapter 13).

(b) Distributions to the shareholder: dividends

In a *company* the situation is more complex. The distribution of profit (if any) normally takes place through *dividends* which the directors of the company (who are a special type of employee of the company and may also be shareholders themselves – see Chapter 14) decide upon each year. Of course, you will remember that *preference* shares carry a fixed rate of dividend and over these the directors have less discretion (although they can recommend that the dividend not be paid in a particular year). But on the *ordinary* shares the directors can pay anything between zero and the total amount of the available profits. The appropriation account of a company might therefore look like Figure 12.5.

In Figure 12.5 we have again taken the profit (but this time after taxation) and shown how the company has allocated it: £1,060 is to be paid out in dividends to the owners whilst the bulk of the profit for the year – £19,940 in this case – is to be retained in the business and taken to the balance sheet as an addition to shareholders' funds.

Net profit before tax		21,000
Proprietor's weekly cash drawings	8,000	
Goods for own use	1,000	
Personal use of business car	1,000	(10,000)
Profit retained in the business		£11,000

Figure 12.4 Appropriation account of a sole trader

Net profit after taxation		21,000
1,000 6 per cent £1 Preference shares: proposed dividend	60	
10,000 £1 Ordinary shares: proposed dividend	1,000	1,600
Profit retained in the business		£19,940

Figure 12.5 Example of a basic company appropriation account

(c) Transfers to reserves

But, inevitably, this is only part of the story. As we mentioned above, this 'retained profit' may well be allocated to different *reserves*. Some of these reserves will be *specific* reserves for particularly identified items, and some will be *general* reserves for non-itemized uses in the business. The appropriation account will, quite probably, also show appropriations to reserves. It might well look something like Figure 12.6.

In Figure 12.6 we see that the company has decided to allocate some of its retained profit to a specific reserve for fixed asset replacement and some to a general reserve. The balance will remain in an account called 'profit and loss account carried forward'. This also will remain as part of shareholders' funds on the balance sheet. However, before we look at that, we need to spend a moment examining the one thing which is still missing – the undistributed amounts from previous years. And with *that* under our belt we can consider what happens on the balance sheet to all these bits and pieces of ownership claims.

12.2.4 Earnings from previous years

So far, all we have considered has been the profit or loss from the present accounting period. At this point, it is common for many students to get confused – so we have given this bit its own section. Whilst we have been messing about with the profit and loss account for this accounting period, what, if anything, has been happening to the balance sheet? On the balance sheet might be several relevant items:

- an amount for the owners' (issued share) capital: this is not a problem and it only changes when there is a change in the capital structure of the organization;
- amounts for specific and general reserves created in previous accounting periods: we do not need to worry much about these – our allocations from this year's accounting period will simply be added to them;
- an existing 'profit and loss account carried forward' or 'retained' which was the unappropriated profit from previous years' profit and loss accounts: this is the one that causes problems.

Students frequently get mixed up over this. There are four elements to the 'profit and loss account'. There is (a) the amount of profit or loss earned in this accounting period and represented in the profit and loss account for this accounting period. This profit (or loss) is then allocated and distributed through the appropriation account. (b) This results in an amount of this year's profit and loss account being unallocated. *Then*, (c) the profit and

Net profit for the year before tax		30,000
Less taxation		(9,000)
Net profit for the year *after* tax		21,000
1,000 6 per cent £1 Preference shares: proposed dividend	60	
10,000 £1 ordinary shares proposed dividend 10 per cent	1,000	1,060
		19,940
Transfer to general reserve	5,000	
Transfer to fixed asset replacement reserve	5,000	10,000
Retained profit carried forward		£9,940

Figure. 12.6 A fuller company appropriation account

loss account brought forward from previous years is *added* (or subtracted if a loss) to the unallocated profit or loss for the current year and (d) the total represents profit and loss account carried forward. (This fourth element will appear on the current balance sheet and be the balance brought forward on *next* year's appropriation account.) It pays to keep these different elements clear in your mind so as to avoid confusion. As long as you remember that the balance sheet carries the total of previous years' profits or losses which have not been allocated and that we add (or subtract) *this* unallocated profit or loss, you shouldn't go too far wrong.

This amount of unallocated profit or loss account is important – not just from an ownership claim point of view but also from a basic accounting and legal point of view. That is, the company may, if it wishes and the circumstances are appropriate, pay a dividend even when it has made a loss. The company will use previous years' unallocated profits to pay this year's dividend. So, in fact, the order in which things happen in the appropriation account does not matter too much. Figure 12.7 gives an idea of what the whole thing might look like when we have a brought-forward figure.

Figure 12.7 now shows the profit and loss account brought forward from the previous year's balance sheet along with the amount of accumulated profit and loss account which will be shown on this year's balance sheet.

We can now put this all together in Figure 12.8. This figure is the financial statements of Yothu Yindi (which are shown in Figures 12.2 and 12.3) with all the appropriations shown on the profit and loss account and the resultant balances taken to the balance sheet.

Figure 12.8 will repay some careful attention. Looking first at the profit and loss appropriation account we see the charge for taxation and we can also note that there are no transfers being made to reserves. We can then notice a *proposed* preference dividend and, just below this, a reference to an *interim dividend* and a statement that no *final dividend* is proposed. You will recall that directors can only *propose* dividends – they have to be approved by the shareholders at the annual general meeting. However, it is not uncommon for directors to pay an *interim* dividend some time during the year – perhaps following particularly strong financial results after a six-month trading period. This interim dividend will normally be 'topped up' after the end of the accounting period by a *final dividend* which the shareholders will approve, together with (the directors hope) retrospective approval of the interim dividend.

Still with the profit and loss account, we can then see the brought-forward profit and loss account (you will not be able to trace this to previous figures in Yothu Yindi's accounts –

Net profit for the year before tax		30,000
Less taxation		(9,000)
Net profit for the year *after* tax		21,000
1,000 6 per cent £1 Preference shares: proposed dividend	60	
10,000 £1 ordinary shares proposed dividend	1,000	1,060
		19,940
Transfer to general reserve	5,000	
Transfer to fixed asset replacement reserve	5,000	10,000
Retained profit brought forward		9,000
Retained profit carried forward		£18,940

Figure 12.7 A full company appropriation account

YOTHU YINDI LTD: PROFIT AND LOSS ACCOUNT
FOR THE YEAR ENDING 31 DECEMBER 2002 (all figures are in dollars)

SALES		465,000
less **COST OF GOODS SOLD**		(188,000)
GROSS OR TRADING PROFIT		277,000
EXPENSES:		
Depreciation for the year	12,000	
Profit on Disposal	(1,000)	
Loss on Disposal	3,000	
Stock provisions	2,900	
Bad and doubtful debts	25,000	
Rent	140,000	
Wages	40,000	
Heat and light	7,400	
Telephone	13,400	
Rates	30,000	
Other expenses	42,000	
		(314,700)
NET LOSS FOR THE PERIOD – before taxation		(37,700)
APPROPRIATION ACCOUNT		
Taxation for the period		(2,500)
Net Loss After Taxation		(40,200)
Preference Dividend proposed		(2,500)
Ordinary Dividend (Interim dividend paid, no Final dividend proposed)		(2,000)
Loss for the year retained		(44,700)
Profit and Loss Account brought forward		98,400
Profit and Loss Account carried forward		$53,700

YOTHU YINDI LTD: BALANCE SHEET
AS AT 31 DECEMBER 2002 (all figures in dollars)

	Cost	Acc Dep'n	NBV	
FIXED ASSETS:				
Manufacturing plant	10,000	2,000	8,000	
Wind-farm	100,000	5,000	95,000	
Vehicle 1	13,000	2,000	3,000	
Vehicle 2	17,000	3,000	14,000	120,000
CURRENT ASSETS:				
Stocks			172,100	
Trade Debtors			32,000	
Prepayments			26,000	
Cash			(92,600)	
			137,500	
CURRENT LIABILITIES:				
Creditor (Fixed Asset)			50,000	
Trade Creditors			42,000	
Sundry Creditors			7,100	
Accruals & Provisions			4,700	
			103,800	
				33,700
NET ASSETS				$153,700
REPRESENTED BY:				
Issued Ordinary Share Capital				40,000
Issued 5% Preference Share Capital				50,000
Share Premium				10,000
Profit and Loss Account: Carried forward			53,700	53,700
SHAREHOLDERS'/OWNERS' FUNDS				$153,700

Figure 12.8 The financial statements for Yothu Yindi Ltd 2002

do not worry about this). This is the unallocated profit from previous accounting periods. It wipes out this year's loss but shareholders' funds will have diminished as a result of this year's activities. The resultant profit and loss account carried forward is then taken back to the balance sheet.

Now, there is one final little accounting twist here that you should not forget. You will recall that we said that the final ordinary dividend (of zero) and the preference dividend (of $2,500) were *proposed*. This means that they have not been paid (the interim dividend will have been paid earlier). This means that there is a current liability somewhere – the company owes the shareholders for the amount of the dividends which it has not yet paid. These must be shown as a current liability and we have shown them under sundry creditors. Look back at Figure 12.8 and (comparing it with Figure 12.3) find the amount relating to this creditor. If you do this correctly, you should find a puzzling amount – that sundry creditors rises by $5,000 but the dividends proposed are only $2,500. Any ideas what the other amount is? It must be the taxation which is shown in the profit and loss account. There is no way that this could have been paid before the end of the accounting period as the taxation figure is estimated on the basis of the accounting profit – which we cannot calculate until the year-end. Therefore, sundry creditors also include $2,500 for a taxation creditor.

With this, you should be able to make sense of all the movements that have led to the financial statements of Yothu Yindi shown in Figure 12.8.

12.3 THE PUBLISHED PROFIT AND LOSS ACCOUNT AND BALANCE SHEET

By this stage in your studies, we presume you are so used to the idea of reaching for a set of financial statements to see what your own chosen companies do with the items we are discussing, that you will have automatically been checking what we have been saying in this chapter with actual published accounts. If this is so, then the following central lessons should have emerged from the preceding sections of this chapter:

i   In understanding how to do the accounting for items related to ownership claims, it is first necessary to know the ownership structure of the organization and to understand what the different elements and terms actually refer to.

ii   What happens on the profit and loss account, and especially in the appropriation account, will be reflected in the balance sheet – emphasizing the interdependent nature of the two statements. The first (the profit and loss account) shows the ownership claim earned this year, how it was earned and what is to be done with it, whilst the second statement (the balance sheet) shows the components of the ownership claim at a point in time and the assets and liabilities that go to make up that ownership claim.

iii When studying an actual set of financial statements you will often have to consult the *Notes to the Accounts* to find the sort of detail we have been discussing here.

iv   The basic bookkeeping on these issues is really quite straightforward. At least it is if (a) you stick to the relatively simple examples we have seen so far and (b) you understand what is actually going on with ownership claims.

To round off your knowledge of ownership claims from companies we suggest that you have a good look at your library of financial statements. (As you already know?) financial accounts are accompanied by extensive notes over several pages which would provide more detail on the numbers on the 'face' of the financial accounts. We will further develop our understanding of the financial accounts of companies in Chapter 14. At this stage of your studies, however, you should now be in a position to give a coherent explanation of what each item in the profit and loss account and balance sheet actually means and to provide a detailed explanation of the bookkeeping and accounting adjustments that were necessary to derive the numbers and bring them to the financial statements.

12.4 STARTING TO THINK ABOUT FINANCIAL STATEMENTS

We haven't entirely finished our introductory studies of how to construct financial statements. We will still need to look at the special issues that relate to partnerships (Chapter 13), the regulations governing company financial statements (Chapter 14), and some of the additional statements that appear with the profit and loss account and balance sheet (Chapters 15 and 17). We are, however, on the home stretch. So now seems a useful time to take a bit of a step back and have an initial think about what we have been working so hard to achieve. (We will extend this thinking in Chapters 15, 16, 17 and 18.) This section of the chapter is therefore going to address three separate issues: how reliable are these profit and loss accounts and balance sheets that we are constructing? how 'real' are they? and what about non-commercial organizations? We deal with each of these in turn.

12.4.1 How accurate is the profit figure?

Perhaps the best way to illustrate the issues is to use the Yothu Yindi profit and loss account and balance sheet in Figure 12.8. Those financial statements show a loss for the period of $37,700. How much discretion did we use to reach that figure? Or, to put it another way, keeping strictly within the parameters that we have met within the chapters of this book, what is the worst loss Yothu Yindi could record for the year? And what is the least worst (or best) position that they could record?

If you are confused, just stop and think. How many of the numbers contained in Figure 12.8 were amounts over which we did not have to make assumptions or make estimates? How many of them are what you might be able to think of as 'hard numbers'? The sales figure may well be a reasonably 'hard number'. The cash seems fairly uncontentious and the fixed-assets cost figures are equally reliable. The rest, though, can all, to some degree or other, be adjusted upwards or downwards by reference to all the *estimates* and *assumptions* which we made when compiling the financial statements. Figure 12.9 attempts to illustrate the principle behind this.

All we have done in Figure 12.9 is to take a few of the accounting numbers we calculated for Yothu Yindi and examined what degree of discretion we had in calculating each number. The amounts shown in Figure 12.9 are very broad-brush estimates because we do not have all the data on 2002's accounting activities which we would realistically need to make firmer estimates. However, you should be able to work through Figure 12.9 and, drawing from Chapters 8, 9, 10 and 11, appreciate why we might be able to vary the profit/loss figure in the way we have. Figure 12.9 suggests that we could, within accounting conventions, vary the loss figure by $25,900 or by well over 30 per cent in either direction. This is important because it emphasizes that the profit figure and the accounting numbers which underlie it are *estimates* – in an ideal world they are *best estimates* of some mid-point between excessive pessimism and excessive optimism.

So, the question remains, how reliable an estimate is the profit/loss reported in any single accounting period? The simple answer is that we can never be absolutely certain.

Accounting item	Current position	Most optimistic accounting	Most pessimistic accounting
Cost of sales	$(188,000)	FIFO is the most 'optimistic' method and is already used. No change here	Change to LIFO – estimate increase cost of sales by (say) $8,000
Depreciation	$(12,000)	Increase estimate of assets' terminal values and the life of the assets. Change method of depreciation. Estimate decrease in depreciation charge for the year by (say) $3,000	Shorten life of assets and re-examine depreciation method. Estimate increase in depreciation charge by (say) $1,000
Profit/loss on disposal	$(2,000)	To have affected these we would have had to make adjustments in earlier years. Not possible for 2002	
Stock provision	$(2,900)	Be less pessimistic about the condition of stock and obsolescence. Estimate stock provision should be reduced by (say) $1,000	Be more prudent. Right off ALL damaged stock. Increase provision by $500
Bad & doubtful debts	$(25,000)	This figure is far too pessimistic. Estimate add back of (say) $10,000	This figure is very pessimistic already
Telephone accrual	$(13,400)	We had to estimate the calls made. Reduce the estimate by (say) $100	We had to estimate the calls made. Increase the estimate by (say) $100
Heat and light	$(7,400)	Reduce estimate by (say) $100	Increase estimate by (say) $100
Warranty provision	$0	–	Add a warranty provision on goods and services sold (say) $1,000
Interest on loan	$0	–	There appears to be no provision for interest on the overdraft. Add this plus (say) additional interest necessary to finance the loan to pay off the fixed asset creditor. Estimate (say) $1,000
Overall profit/(loss)	$(37,700)	$(23,500)	$(49,400)

Figure 12.9 Yothu Yindi best and worse scenarios

However, in a small and simple organization like Yothu Yindi we can probably be fairly comfortable that the estimate is not that outrageous. This is because most of the accounting estimates will turn into real cash numbers at some stage. That is, at some stage the company will sell the fixed asset, at some stage debts will or will not be paid, and so on. This means that, generally speaking, accounting profit figures – especially in smaller organizations – are really quite accurate taken over a period of a few years. If you look back to Figure 12.9 you should be able to see that each of the pessimistic and optimistic estimates we made *must* reverse themselves in some accounting future period.

> **Hint**
>
> If this is not obvious to you, make it a point of principle to try and understand this as your accounting studies progress. If you can systematically explain why and how this statement is correct then you have *really* understood the mechanisms of basic conventional accounting and bookkeeping.

However, for more complex organizations – such as, for example, transnational companies – the opportunities and necessity for estimation and assumption are very much greater. So the 'margin for error' is that much greater. Furthermore, as the rate at which these estimations and assumptions arise in the normal practices of the company is so much higher (for example, fixed assets being bought and sold all over the world all the time) one can only assume that the 'margins for error' balance out over time. One can never be certain, however, so *profit/loss must always be an estimate*.

If you can really appreciate this central point you will be well on the way to having a good understanding of accounting practice. The accounting professions around the world do recognize this – although rarely so explicitly – and have issued guidelines so that these areas of discretion are, at least, dealt with consistently. We will examine some of these guidelines in Chapter 14.

12.4.2 Financial accounting constructs social reality?

It should be apparent from the foregoing that accounting, however well-intentioned, cannot tell *the* truth. What it will do, at best, is tell *a* truth. Does this matter? Well, we shall re-examine this question in Chapter 18 but for now we can use the idea of the **construction of social reality** to try and get across the idea that accounting in general and financial statements in particular may be exceptionally important in all sorts of ways which we tend to ignore.

The best way to understand the concept of 'social reality' is to contrast it with 'physical reality'. If all human beings simultaneously went on holiday to Mars what would be left behind? There would be trees and animals and buildings and machines and flowers and water. There would be elements of physical reality[13] which, we can assume, are entirely independent of human perception and activity. However, there are other things which would cease to exist – the law, institutions, companies and accounting, for example, are all examples of 'social reality'. They are real enough but only because humans constantly create them and, having done so, take them for granted in a way which *makes them real*. They are only 'real' because humans accept them as real. They have no independent reality.

Accounting is one such social reality. That is fairly obvious, it is only numbers on a page or in computer files. Accountants and those who use accounting make it into 'information' and 'useful' and 'real'. But accounting is more than this – it probably helps to create 'social reality'. Perhaps the best example is the idea of 'success'. What is a successful company? We suspect that almost everybody would answer along the lines of 'one which is making a profit', 'one which is growing', 'one which is economically viable'. So 'success' is a social concept dependent upon profit, growth and economic viability. What are profit, growth and economic viability? They are, in turn, social constructs. And how do we know when we have a growing organization? a profitable organization? an economically viable organization? When the accounting says so! We have already seen that accounting attempts to tell part of a truth. That partial truth is crucial to assessing whether a company is successful. If a company is pronounced 'successful', investors and suppliers and customers will treat it as successful and, as a result, it will probably be successful. If, on the other hand, the accountants pronounce a company 'unsuccessful' the directors and financial investors and other stakeholders will treat the company as not successful and, in all probability, it will be become unsuccessful. Accounting, therefore, exists in a world of self-fulfilling prophecies. We, as accountants, largely define success, and others, responding to that definition, react accordingly.

This is a big responsibility for the accounting profession. But, as if this were not enough, the extent of accounting's creation of social reality goes a great deal further than this. You will recall that accounting is strictly limited to the four characteristics. Anything that lies outside these four characteristics is 'not accounting'. Therefore happiness, well-being, the natural environment, justice, love, community, family, etc., all lie outside accounting. That would be fine as long everybody remembered this and acted as though accounting were only a teeny-weeny part of human activity. They do not. Economics and accounting are increasingly treated as the only important part of human existence. This is both nonsense and exceptionally dangerous. To illustrate, a 'successful' (as defined by accounting) company can be killing people, poisoning streams, breaking up communities, polluting the atmosphere, cheating the public and so on. But it is still 'successful'! That should worry us a bit. Equally, an 'unsuccessful' company (as defined by accounting) could be supporting a local community, providing good-quality employment, redistributing wealth, developing human and environmentally sensitive technologies. But it would still be 'unsuccessful'! That should also worry us a bit.

So, accounting paints a particular picture of the world – a picture which is becoming more and more ubiquitous, a picture which is an approximation of a very restricted range of all possible pictures. Society reacts to this picture and, increasingly, treats this approximate partial picture as the *only* picture of activity. (This is probably best illustrated by public sector experiences around the globe where accounting values of a narrow form of 'efficiency' and 'economy' have increasingly driven out other social and environmental values and, as a result, changed – probably for the worse – the nature of public sector activity.)

Thus, accounting is *not* a neutral nor necessarily *objective* activity. It reflects and, to an increasing extent, creates the social reality in which we all live. Accounting is becoming more and more important as a means of constructing our world and to fail to recognize this allows other social and environmental factors to be pushed to one side.

These are complex matters. We have only touched upon them, superficially, here. (We will look at them in a little more detail in Chapter 17.) But this perspective offers one of the more challenging and interesting visions of accounting and its role in society – a vision which you will (we hope) pick up and develop in the later stages of your studies of accounting and finance.

12.4.3 Profit and social reality in the non-commercial sector?

So, if profit is only an estimate of something in the commercial sector and it, together with the rest of the financial statements, helps construct the social reality of organizations, how does this apply – if at all – in the *non*-commercial sector. We have already touched upon this briefly in Chapter 3. There we saw that 'profit' is not really a useful notion in a non-profit organization like a charity or a local government department. This is because the organization is not attempting to generate a financial surplus for its owners (perhaps society, perhaps trustees, perhaps donors). Rather, it is receiving funds so that it can deliver a service which its 'owners' deem appropriate. In more basic accounting terms, a commercial organization generates income through its operational subsystem outputs (typically sales). 'Profit' is then the difference between this income and the costs of generating the outputs. A non-commercial organization attempts to generate income so that it can produce operational subsystem outputs. If it had any 'surplus' it would simply increase the outputs it produced and, thus, soak up that surplus. The rationale is thus completely different.

There have been, it must be noted, increasing attempts to force non-commercial organizations into commercial ways of doing things – a kind of 'back-door' privatization

– of schools, universities, hospitals and so on. This is a strictly political action. What placing commercial pressures on non-commercial organizations achieves is a steady down-grading of the values and achievements of a non-commercial organization – a denial, if you like, of its principal purpose(s). Such pressures may be done in the name of 'efficiency', but this is usually a misnomer meaning 'cheapness' against some artificial measurement of output and an artificially determined price. The imposition of commercial values – through commercial accounting principles – actually *changes* the nature of the organization. It raises the, previously low, importance granted to financial information and places an increased emphasis on accounting and financial statements – thus constructing a social reality which suggests that an organization which was previously perceived as being a (successful?) non-commercial one may now be perceived as (usually) a not very successful commercial organization. A rugby ball is a *not* a funny-shaped soccer ball – it is a different type of ball. A non-commercial organization is *not* a funny sort of commercial organization – it is different – even if we still try and apply commercial accounting to it. In time, of course, accounting is so influential an activity, that the non-commercial organization's values will disappear, to be entirely replaced by pseudo-commercial values defined by the accounting systems. That is a political choice that says that the original values of the organization were not desirable. This is the worst kind of dishonesty hiding an extreme and deeply offensive political ideology within the apparently neutral workings of an 'unbiased' (!) accounting system. It is, however, an extremely good illustration of the powerful role that accounting can play in transforming organizations and, by implication, shows you that conventional accounting will nearly always reflect a right-wing, market-dominated, money-is-the-only-thing-that-matters ideology. As accountants, we have an important duty to recognize this powerful consequence of our activities.

At a more detailed and practical level there are some significantly different elements in the conventional accounting systems practised in commercial and non-commercial organizations. Partly, these are a reflection of the different ways in which the two types of organizations were first established – and the purposes they were intended to achieve. Recall – we have mentioned this already – that the essential differences arise because (a) the ownership structure is more subtle in non-commercial organizations; (b) there is not the direct link between operations subsystems outflows (sales in a commercial organization, services provided in the non-commercial organization) and funds subsystems inflows (sales income or donations income, for example); and (c) most conventional accounting has been derived to meet the perceived needs of the commercial sector organization – not the non-commercial organization. There is a very wide range of types of accounting entities in the public sector and their accounting and finance practices will differ quite considerably. You will deal with these matters in more depth later in your studies – we do not have the space to explore these differences more thoroughly here. Just remember, in basic principles, all organizations *do* conform to our flow diagrams but the organizations will differ in detail as well as in form due to different histories, needs, objectives and controls. (For more detail see the further reading suggestions below.)

SUMMARY

Whilst bookkeeping and general financial control can be desirable in almost any organizational setting, the central thing which drives most conventional commercial *accounting* (as opposed to *bookkeeping*) – and distinguishes accounting in the commercial and non-commercial sectors – is the notion of profit. Profit is some estimate of how much better off (or worse off) an organization's owners are after an accounting period's transactions. It is driven by the basic assumption that the central purpose of financial accounting is to provide an accounting to the owners of the business. If the profit and the rest of the *ownership claims* are so central to accounting practice, we must therefore expect to have to learn quite a bit about them. We have introduced them in this chapter, shown how the ownership claim is constructed in the sole trader and the company and indicated how owners can get money out of the business via drawings (the sole trader) or dividends (the company). (We will look at partnerships in the next chapter.)

This ownership orientation is not always clearly obvious in financial statements. Neither is the fact that the statements are both an *estimate* – as opposed to entirely accurate – and a partial and carefully narrow picture of the organization at a particular moment in time. For these reasons, we should recognize that financial statements have an essential and inevitable bias. This may be no bad thing, you might say. Perhaps so, as long as everyone is aware of this. But accounting has one especially peculiar characteristic: namely, it is probably one of the most important and influential activities in modern society and yet most people think of it as dull, boring and, although important, nothing to get terribly excited about. This a very successful deception. As a result, accounting in general and financial statements in particular have an enormous potential influence on the way we see the world and the way the world is organized. It helps to construct all of our social realities. This case is especially clear in non-commercial organizations[14] where the application of commercial ideology is, to a significant degree, inappropriate and which slowly but surely, changes the nature of the organization. Accounting is a very powerful and influential activity.

Key terms and concepts

The following key terms and concepts have featured in this chapter. You should ensure that you understand and can explain each one. Page references to definitions appear in the index in bold type.

- Appropriation account
- Business taxation
- Capital
- Capital maintenance
- Dividends paid and proposed
- Drawings
- Expenses versus appropriations/distributions
- Non-commercial organizations
- Ordinary shares
- Ownership claims

- Preference shares
- Profit and loss account brought forward
- Profit and loss account carried forward
- Profit as an estimate
- Profit for the period
- Retained profit
- Share premium
- Social reality
- Transfers to reserves

FURTHER READING

The most useful additional reading you can be doing at this stage is a combination of regular reference to published financial statements and regular reading of one of the professional accountancy journals. This will help you become familiar with many of the issues discussed here. For further reading on the central issues of ownership claims you could consult any introductory accounting textbook, but do not get too involved as you will be studying more advanced material on these topics later in your studies. For further stimulation on the 'social reality' issue we very strongly recommend you spend some time with Ruth Hines's 1988 article 'Financial accounting: in communicating reality, we construct reality'. If you try and avoid getting too involved in all the footnotes in this article you should get a lot of interesting insights from this unique and clever piece of writing. There are many good introductions to public sector accounting. One you might look at is Jones and Pendlebury (2000) – *Public Sector Accounting*. Taxation is a matter which quickly gets very complicated and you will spend time with it later in your studies. A brief look at either an introductory accounting text or any introductory business taxation text may be valuable.

NOTES

1. There is certainly an argument to say that you would have benefited from examining ownership claims in much more detail earlier on in the book. In our experience, issues related to ownership are complex and can be confusing but are absolutely crucial. Rather then feed you uncritical material which you could learn, perhaps not very well, we find it more productive to wait until you have developed a somewhat more sophisticated understanding of accounting and bookkeeping before we turn to examine crucial issues of this sort. If you have been puzzled by ownership claims up to now, we apologize but hope you found the wait worthwhile!

2. We will again touch upon this issue of the extent to which accounting rules and taxation rules differ in business financial statements in Chapter 14 when we talk a little about some of the differences between countries' approaches to accounting.

3. You will not have forgotten (will you?) that a sole trader is exposed to *unlimited* liability as the law makes no distinction between the individual who is the sole trader and the sole trader's business.

4. Only in a company must you keep the *roles* that individuals play so completely separate. An individual might be an employee of a company and a shareholder. Only in the case of a company can the salary paid to the employee who is also an owner be treated as an expense. In all other commercial organizations such a payment would be a distribution of profit. This is related to the *legal entity* issues of a company. It also has practical implications as, in many large companies, very many employees may also be shareholders and the ensuing bookkeeping would be horrendous if the two roles could not be treated separately.

5. *Not* to be confused with 'inventory' in this context.

6. The company may, subsequently, change its mind and arrange for there to a greater or lesser number of shares. This is a more complex matter which will be dealt with in your company law studies.

7. There is a wide variety of possible types of shares, many of which are variations on these two basic types. Ordinary and preference shares are the most common – as a quick look at some of the published financial statements you have will show you.

8. You might well be a bit sceptical as to whether or not this company could successfully issue such a share issue when it is running at a loss. This is not so outrageous and, if the company is viewed as an 'ethical' organization, it may well attract 'goodwill' funds to support it. We look at this again in Chapter 17 .

9. Do please be careful about shares which are traded but which are not new issues of shares. When you read (as you should be doing) about share prices rising and falling on, especially, stock markets, this does not *directly* affect the company. One shareholder (or, more usually, gambling investor) has decided to sell their shares to someone else. This does not involve the company. Only when a new issue of shares (including other things like rights issues and stock splits which you will hear about in due course) is made by the company do we need to bring the accounting

system into action. Whilst who actually owns the organization may be a very important factor (e.g. in the case of a hostile takeover) it does *not* directly influence the accounting numbers.

10. This is related to the 'going concern' convention that we met in Chapter 7.

11. *Remember from Chapter 9* that depreciation is *first* a bookkeeping process designed to recognize the costs of fixed assets used up this period as an application of the accrual concept but, *second*, this process, in effect, removed from our profit or loss an amount of wealth which could be used to, in effect, replace current fixed assets. This is confusing, we know, and will look at it again in Chapter 16.

12. The shareholders/proprietor(s) will, if the organization's decision is correct, still receive this 'wealth' but, perhaps, not immediately. The organization may pay the amount out (possibly an increased amount) at some future stage or the overall value of the business may rise, thus increasing the value of the shares of the business.

13. We are ignoring, for the sake of clarity, the philosophical arguments about the nature of reality and its existence or otherwise independent of human perception.

14. Even that language is biased – might it not be more humane to refer to all businesses as 'not-for-charity' organizations or 'non-social' organizations? Would that change how we think, perhaps?

Partnerships 13

Learning objectives

After studying this chapter you should be able to:

- explain the principal characteristics of a partnership;
- outline the main elements you would expect to find in a partnership agreement;
- outline the principal bookkeeping implications that arise in a partnership;
- explain the functions of the partners' capital account and a current account;
- calculate the allocation of profit or loss attributable to the partners;
- calculate the 'interest' and 'salary' due to a partner and show the bookkeeping entries;
- explain in detail the distinction between the accounting entity and the owners of that entity;
- explain and illustrate how a partnership might deal with a joining or leaving partner;
- further explain and illustrate how accounting constructs social reality;
- explain and illustrate why a developed accounting system may not always be beneficial to an organization.

13.1 INTRODUCTION

13.1.1 Chapter design and links to previous chapters

Chapter 12 examined the accounting issues that arise with ownership claims in sole traders and companies and looked briefly at how non-commercial organizations differ in this respect and how the accounting might begin to reflect this difference. In most capitalist countries (but see Chapter 14) the *basic* bookkeeping and accounting, it would seem, only needs to differ to the extent that it is necessary to reflect a different legal and ownership structure.[1] For the sole trader we had to account for the injections of capital, the surplus earnings retained in the business and the withdrawals (the drawings) from the business made by the proprietor. In the company, this was made more formal and we saw that the company's legal existence was maintained distinct from the legal existence of the owners. They are separate legal entities. We then briefly examined the different elements of the ownership claims that arise in companies – the share capital, the reserves and retained profit and loss account and dividends. All of these are matters that will be studied in greater depth in your further studies of accounting and finance.

There are many other organizational forms. (We saw some of these in Chapter 3.) There are many different types of non-commercial organizations (which we have not had the space to examine in any detail here) as well as many other forms of commercial entities – different types of companies, groups of companies, joint ventures and so on. One particular form of commercial organization which deserves our attention at this stage is the **partnership**. The reason we find it useful to consider partnerships at this stage are two-fold. First, the partnership form of organization is an especially useful one and, if you proceed to qualify as a professional accountant, the chances are that you will work within such an organization for at least some part of your career. The second reason is an educational one. Ownership claims are not an especially easy issue to get your mind around. The ownership claims in a partnership are really quite complicated. So, if you can understand partnership ownership claims, you should have little difficulty with ownership claims in general in other organizational forms. (The corollary of this is that if you struggle to make sense of partnership ownership claims, then you have received a useful signal that you do not have a complete grasp of the matters arising with accounting for ownership claims.)

This chapter is organized as follows. The following subsection provides some more detail on the legal and organizational issues that arise in partnerships. Section 13.2 then looks at the accounting for the ownership claims and, in particular, at how to construct **partners' capital and current accounts**. These are certainly the most important aspects of accounting for partnership and you must understand them. Section 13.3 then looks, briefly, at some of the other issues that arise with partnerships and, in particular, provides some brief insights into how we might deal with **partners joining and leaving** the organization. Section 13.4 briefly attempts to clarify the *construction of social reality* issues from Chapter 12 by using the accounting example from section 13.2. There are the usual conclusions and further reading at the end of the chapter.

13.1.2 The nature of partnerships

The basic elements of the partnership were introduced in Chapter 3, subsection 3.3.1(b). They arise when two or more individuals (or other legal entities) join together for the purposes of trade. In essence, they are best thought of as somewhat more formal than sole traders but subject to rather less detailed formality than companies. Each **partner** will, generally speaking, introduce an amount of *capital* and, in return, share a proportion of the profits and losses of the business. The essential accounting aspects of partnership concern the relationships between the partners and their duties, responsibilities and rights. In straightforward partnership organizations this will relate to the amounts of capital they must introduce, what share of the profits and losses they take, and the form in which each partner can draw money from the business. Later, we will briefly examine how partnerships may deal with partners who wish to leave or new partners who wish to join.

Two central characteristics of most general partnerships are that:

- the partners are *jointly and severally liable*; and,
- the partners are subject to *unlimited liability*.

This means that if one partner binds the business to a deal which (for example) makes a massive loss, then all the partners must share in that loss. Further, if the assets of the business are insufficient to cover the losses of the business (in, for example, a liquidation of the partnership), the personal assets of the individual partners can be drawn upon to cover the business's debts.[2] This, you will recall, is the meaning of unlimited liability.[3]

Each country will have different basic law governing the relationships between the partners. This will normally be under some form of Partnership Act which will lay down regulations on a variety of different factors. Alternatively, partners may establish the partnership by creating a *Partnership Deed* which, whilst it will not necessarily remove the partnership entirely from the law may well overrule the Acts on most important issues. A Partnership Deed will normally cover:

- the amounts (and forms) of capital to be introduced by each partner;
- the partners' shares in the profits and losses (which will be assumed to be equal in the absence of any ruling in the Deed);
- the rate of interest, if any, which will be charged on partners' capital – bearing in mind that 'interest' in this context will be an appropriation of profit, *not* an expense (assumed to be zero unless the Deed says otherwise);
- the salaries, if any, to be paid to partners – bearing in mind that 'salary' in this context will be an appropriation of profit, *not* an expense (it will be assumed that no salaries are paid unless the Deed says otherwise);
- issues to do with the internal management of the partnership – this may cover, for example, loans made by partners to the business and the interest on these (assumed to be 5% unless the Deed specifies otherwise).

From the accounting point of view, the most important matters we need to address are the **partners' capital and current accounts**. These will be covered in the next section.

13.2 PARTNERSHIP CAPITAL AND CURRENT ACCOUNTS

13.2.1 Introduction

The bookkeeping for the capital and current accounts is really fairly straightforward as long as (a) you are systematic, (b) you maintain a very clear picture in your mind about the central issues of what does, and what does not, relate to the owners' (*as* owners) interactions with the business, *and* (c) you keep a very clear distinction in your mind between what happens in capital accounts and what happens in current accounts.

Whilst there may well be many instances in partnership where a partner has a relationship with the business in some capacity other than as a partner – as a customer, as a supplier, as a lender of money, etc. – these can confuse the issue and, so, for simplicity's sake, we will concentrate on the partners' interacting with business only as owners. Therefore we shall assume here that *all* a partner's transactions with the business are ownership claim transactions and will, as a result, involve some increase or decrease in the ownership claim of that partner – an increase or decrease in the amount owed by the partnership to the partner. *All* of these transactions will go through *either* the capital account or the current account.

The **capital account** records the partners' initial injections of capital, any further injections of capital and any removal of capital from the business (for example, if a partner leaves the partnership). There are unlikely to that many transactions being passed through the capital account in the normal course of business.

The **current account** records all of the partners' other transactions with the partnership. These include appropriations of profit or loss, drawings, interest and salaries (if any). There are likely to be frequent entries to the current account in the normal course of business, especially at the end of accounting periods.

13.2.2 The capital account

The initial bookkeeping for the capital account is simple – it pretty much follows the principles of the sole trader's capital account. The first decision to make is a somewhat trivial one – whether to have separate capital accounts or show all the partners' capital accounts together with separate columns for each partner. We will use this latter choice. (Your computer software may well make this choice for you anyway.)

Having decided on the physical format, then the bookkeeping for the initial injection is as you might expect: debit cash (or in whatever other form the capital is introduced) and credit the capital account with the amount of the initial capital.

To illustrate, let us suppose that Fender, Gibson and Marshall go into partnership as the Shredders Partnership on 1 January 2000. Fender introduces $1,000 capital, Gibson introduces $2,000 and Marshall introduces $3,000. All the capital is introduced as cash. We would show the $6,000 as a debit to the cash book (an inflow of funds to the funds subsystem) and the credits would go to the capital account (outflow of information from the decision and control subsystem). Assuming that there were no further transactions on the capital account during 2000, the account would look like Figure 13.1.

The capital account shows the three partners and provides them with columns on both debit and credit sides. The total account summarizes the whole capital of the business but each column shows the individual partners' share of the total capital. These individual amounts (the balances carried down in Figure 13.1) would be shown on the balance sheet as the business's capital in the 'Represented by' section of the balance sheet. At any point in time, the capital account shows – subject to valuation issues (see below) – the amount of capital which is due to the owners.

Just to force home the point let us pretend that during 2000, Marshall ran into personal financial difficulties and needed to withdraw $1,000 of his capital from the business. His partners agreed to let him, and Fender agreed to put in an extra $1,000 to compensate the business. Let us assume that this does not affect the Partnership Deed. The capital account would then look like Figure 13.2.

In Figure 13.2 we can see that Marshall has received $1,000 in cash (credit cash, debit capital) whilst Fender has put in an extra $1,000 in cash (debit cash, credit capital). The balances brought down still total $6,000 but the partners now have equal amounts of capital in the business – each has capital of $2,000.

THE SHREDDERS PARTNERSHIP – CAPITAL ACCOUNT AT 31.12.2000							
	Fender	Gibson	Marshall		Fender	Gibson	Marshall
				1.1.00 Cash	1,000	2,000	3,000
31.12.00 Bal c/d	1,000	2,000	3,000				
	$1,000	$2,000	$3,000		$1,000	$2,000	$3,000

Figure 13.1 An illustration of a partnership capital account

THE SHREDDERS PARTNERSHIP – CAPITAL ACCOUNT AT 31.12.2000							
	Fender	Gibson	Marshall		Fender	Gibson	Marshall
				1.1.00 Cash	1,000	2,000	3,000
30.6.00 Cash			1,000	30.6.00 Cash	1,000		
31.12.00 Bal c/d	2,000	2,000	2,000				
	$2,000	$2,000	$3,000		$2,000	$2,000	$3,000

Figure 13.2 An illustration of a partnership capital account

This should be pretty clear by now, so let us have a look at partners' current accounts.

13.2.3 The current account

The current account is constructed in exactly the same way as the capital account – either separate accounts or a columnar approach as we saw in Figures 13.1 and 13.2. The current account records all the transactions (apart from capital transactions) that take place between the partners and the business and, indeed, if desired, between the partners themselves. In essence, the current account should show how much the partner can legitimately take out of the business, how much they have taken out of the business in the way of, for example, drawings, and what the partner has earned – 'on their own account' – during the accounting period.[4]

To illustrate, let us return to Shredders and remain with the *initial* capital situation as represented in the first figure – Figure 13.1. We will now assume that the partners charge the business with 5 per cent interest on their capital balance at the end of the accounting period and that Fender is to be credited with a 'salary' of $2,500 (which he has not been actually paid yet). Fender has also taken out drawings during the year of $1,750. The profit for 2000 was $6,400 (before charging interest and the partners' salary) and, under the Partnership Deed, is to be shared in the same ratio as the partners' capital accounts at the end of the current accounting period.[5] All payments and calculations are to be undertaken at the end of the accounting period. (We will ignore any transfers to reserves or other such nuisances.) The partners' current accounts would look like Figure 13.3.

Now, do not panic! There is a lot happening in Figure 13.3 but if you remember what we said above – 'be systematic' – you can sort all of this out, step by step. *Before going any further*, can we check if we have the 'right answer'? Well, yes we can. Being owners, the partners can only earn profits from the business and, inversely, all of the profit belongs to the partners. The current account in Figure 13.3 allocates the profit of $6,400 to the partners. If you look at the credit side of the account in Figure 13.3 and total up what each has received ($3,150, $1,300, $1,950) this will come to $6,400. So, overall, the answer is 'right'. What about the detail? One step at a time.

First, what is the profit figure? It is $6,400 and has to be allocated between the partners. *But*, before it can be allocated to the partners there are other allocations that have to be made – the interest and the salary. *Now*, these *could* be made *after* allocating the profit to the partners but that would get really messy. So, as a general rule: *make the specified allocations to the partners before allocating the partners' share of profits or losses.*

So, second, we calculate the interest due on the capital. This is 5 per cent on each of the partners' capital outstanding at the end of the current accounting period. (That is, 5 per cent of Fender's $1,000 = $50 and so on.) Then we enter it into the account: [Debit profit and

THE SHREDDERS PARTNERSHIP – CURRENT ACCOUNT AT 31.12.2000							
	Fender	Gibson	Marshall		Fender	Gibson	Marshall
30.6.00 Drawings/cash	1,750			31.12.00 Interest	50	100	150
				Salary	2,500		
				Profit	600	1,200	1,800
31.12.00 Bal c/d	1,400	1,300	1,950				
	$3,150	$1,300	$1,950		$3,150	$1,300	$1,950

Figure 13.3 An illustration of a partnership current account

loss account (*remember, we are talking about owners so we are allocating profit, not charging expenses*): Credit current account].

Then, third, we 'pay' the salary. Remember again, because the partner is an owner and the business and the partner are not separate legal entities, this is just a way of allocating one partner a particular share of the profits. It frequently arises with junior partners, partners who bring something special to the partnership – other than capital – or partners who do the lion's share of the management of the business whilst the others are, perhaps, 'sleeping partners'. So [Debit profit and loss account: Credit current account].

Fourth, we allocate what profit is left. How much is this? (You should get the answer $3,600, being $6,400 less the interest of $300 and the salary of $2,500.) This amount must be allocated in the proportions in which the partners own capital in the business (in our case, at the end of the current accounting period). That is, Fender 1: Gibson 2: Marshall 3. So we divide the figure of remaining profit ($3,600) by 6 (being 1 + 2 + 3, the partners' shares) to get $600 per share. Fender gets 1 share, Gibson gets 2 and Marshall gets 3. These also go into the current account. [Debit profit and loss account: Credit current account].

We now know how much each partner earned in the accounting period and, all other things being equal, how much each partner is entitled to take out of the business. *But*, Fender has already taken some of his share out of the business in drawings. We must also show this in the current account. This we have also done in Figure 13.3 [Credit cash: Debit current account].

So, at the end of this accounting period the business ends up owing the partners: $1,400 to Fender, $1,300 to Gibson and $1,950 to Marshall – in addition to their capital account amounts. Subject to any restrictions placed on the partners (in the Partnership Deed) on withdrawing cash from the business, the partners could now withdraw their current account balances and go for a wild binge for a day or two.

Now, whilst the transactions that may go through the current account may get more complicated, they will not change much in principle. These basic elements of allocating the profit (or loss) for the period to the partners and recording their drawings throughout the year more or less captures the main elements you will need.

To reinforce this and to revise some of your bookkeeping, we now turn and work through a more detailed example of partnership accounting.

13.2.4 Introducing the Jeopardy Partnership

The basic information about the Partnership and its activities in its first year of operation (2009) are shown in Figure 13.4.

Read through the material carefully. This will also serve as a very useful refresher on your incomplete records, bookkeeping and financial statements.

Now pull out a piece of paper and a pencil (or turn to your spreadsheet if you prefer) and start the question. If you proceed with care you should be able to produce a capital and current account which looks something like Figure 13.5.

When you have made your own attempt at the Jeopardy question, compare your answer with Figure 13.5 and work through it, isolating any differences. *These may not necessarily be wrong – they may have arisen from different interpretations. Do not be afraid of interpreting questions.* (The rest of the bookkeeping plus the financial statements are included in the appendix to this chapter.)

The data given for the Jeopardy Partnership are fairly complex and there are a good number of transactions to take through the partners' current and capital accounts. We will

You have been appointed as accountant to the Jeopardy Partnership. The Partnership have kept fairly detailed records – although nothing you would recognize as 'accounting records' and have asked you to produce a set of accounts for the Partnership for 2009.

Your learned the following:

1. The Partnership is a local rock band. The founding members (DH, PM, JY & RG) met in late 2008 and decided to form the Partnership (the group) on 1 January 2009.

2. They agreed to put up their own equipment as capital and to take individual responsibility for maintaining it. Additions to capital were to be treated as capital. Maintenance of equipment was to be treated as current expenditure.

3. They further agreed that all income from the band would be retained to fund the recording of an album sometime in the future. Each member would contribute equally to the costs of hiring rehearsal rooms and they would bear their own transport and incidental costs.

4. Initial capital was valued as:
   DH £1,000
   PM £2,500 (including £1,500 of PA equipment used by all the band)
   JY £800
   RG £1,500 (including £400 of PA equipment used by all the band)
   Equipment is to be depreciated on a straight-line basis over 10 years. To keep matters simple only the balance of equipment at the end of the year is to be depreciated.

5. The group keep a diary from which you learn the following details about rehearsals in 2009. The band rehearsed at four places in 2009 —
   i   The Man in the Moon public house: 12 times at a cost of £10 per night.
   ii   The Castle Hotel: 29 times at £15 per night.
   iii The Brewery House Hotel: 3 times at no cost.
   iv   The Lodge: 38 times at no cost although RG paid a £25 non-refundable deposit for the key.

6. During the year the diary showed that the following changes in capital occurred:
   DH sold all his equipment for £600 and paid a further £1,000 for new equipment.
   PM bought further PA equipment for £450. Sold his personal equipment (costed originally at £1,000) for £750 and paid a further £700 for replacement equipment.
   JY sold his existing drumkit for £600 and paid a further £1400 for a replacement kit.
   RG bought a further £100 of equipment.
   [NB: Any profits or loss on disposal of equipment should be taken to Capital A/c]

7. During 2009 the members incurred the following incidental expenditure:
   DH Strings £50, Repairs £40.
   PM Strings £24, Repairs £50.
   JY Sticks £17.
   RG Strings £75, Maintenance £40.
   [These costs are considered to have arisen equally between rehearsals and gigs]

8. A schedule of gigs is collated from the diary and shows that £760 was earned from 13 gigs. In addition the band performed their first two gigs for free and did two charity performances (at no charge) during the year. The diary also shows that the band spent £25 on three newspaper advertisements on 21 May, 30 June and 8 September (looking for other musicians), settled up with Julie by paying her the £50 mentioned below and made two payments of £10 each to Lyn during the year – all of which was paid out of the group's cash from the gigs.

9. On doing a bank reconciliation you discover that the band has earned £6 of interest on its banked earnings during the year. You also discover two invoices – one for posters and cards for £37 paid by PM and one for newspaper adverts for singers for £29 which has not yet been paid.

10. The group also allow £5 for petrol costs for each gig.

11. The band had additional members (none of whom contribute to day-to-day costs) during the year.
    i   Julie (a singer) joined in February 2009. She brought no capital, incurred no costs and left in September 2009. The band gave her £50 as a token of her earnings with the band.
    ii   Stephanie (a keyboard player) joined in June 2009 with capital of £500 and left in November 2009. She attended 12 rehearsals and played at 5 gigs incurring her own transport costs. She took her capital out but no further financial arrangement was agreed. It was informally agreed that she should have a T-shirt and tape when available.
    iii Lyn (a singer) joined in November 2009 bringing no capital and incurring no costs. The group allow her £10 from gig receipts on those nights when she would have been working.

You are required to:

1. Write up the group cashbook, the partners' current and capital accounts and such other accounts as you find useful.

2. Produce a profit and loss account and balance sheet for the year ended 31 December 2009.

Figure 13.4 Introducing the Jeopardy Partnership

> **Hint**
>
> *You really should work through this under your own steam and ensure that you can make sense of the material.* The key points are:
> a   Be very systematic and take one thing at a time.
> b   Start by opening up a cashbook and the current and capital accounts as suggested. (You will need space for five people in the capital account and six people in the current account. You are advised not to open accounts for Julie.)
> c   Open such other accounts as you need, as you go along, so as to ensure that you do not lose sight of any transactions, movements or agreements.

JEOPARDY PARTNERSHIP CAPITAL ACCOUNTS (2009)
(all figures are in pounds)

	DH	PM	JY	RG	Steph		DH	PM	JY	RG	Steph
Sale of equipment	600	750	600			Initial equipment	1,000	2,500	800	1,500	500
Loss on sale	400	250	200			PA equipment		450			
Resignation (Steph)					500	New equipment	1,600	1,450	2,000	100	
	1,000	1,000	800	–	500		2,600	4,400	2,800	1,600	500
Balance c/d	1,600	3,400	2,000	1,600	–						
	2,600	4,400	2,800	1,600	500		2,600	4,400	2,800	1,600	500

JEOPARDY PARTNERSHIP CURRENT ACCOUNTS (2009)

	DH	PM	JY	RG	Steph	Lyn		DH	PM	JY	RG	Steph	Lyn
							Hire costs	139	139	138	139		
							Petrol costs	410	410	410	410	60	
							Lodge				25		
							Rehearsal costs	45	37	9	57		
							Gig costs	45	37	8	58		
							Publicity		37				
Resignation (Steph) (Creditors)					85		Petrol gigs	85	85	85	85	25	
Lyn (Cash)						10							
Lyn Cash						10							
	–	–	–	–	85	20		724	745	650	774	85	–
Loss for year		762	762	762	–	128							
Bal c/d				12			Bal c/d	38	17	112	–	–	148
	762	762	762	774	85	148		762	762	762	774	85	148

Figure 13.5 Jeopardy Partnership capital accounts 2009

only concentrate on those transactions which go through the partners' accounts – you should be able to work out the remaining transactions on your own.

i   The first partners, transaction is item 4 in Figure 13.4 – the initial injection of capital. This goes – predictably (?) – to the partners' capital account. The debit goes to the fixed asset account because the partners provided their capital as equipment rather than as cash.

ii   Item 5 in Figure 13.4 gives us a total of rehearsal payments of £555 plus the £25 paid by RG as a deposit. These are not amounts which are paid by the accounting entity (the Jeopardy Partnership) itself, but are paid by the partners on behalf of the Partnership. Thus, although they are expenses of the business (debit rehearsal costs), the credit has to be treated as amounts of money which the accounting entity *owes to the partners*. So we show this in the partners' current accounts. The £555 is borne equally by the partners and appear as credits ('hire costs') in their current accounts.

iii The 82 rehearsals also incur £5 per partner per rehearsal for petrol costs and are treated in the same way as the hire costs.

iv Item 6 reflects changes in both the fixed assets of the band and in the partners' capitals. This is an eccentric and awkward set of transactions. The purchase by PM of an additional £450 of equipment is straightforward – debit fixed assets and credit capital account. The others are less obvious. Think carefully about what is actually happening and then think how the accounting transactions might reflect this. Starting with DH, he has, at the end of his buying and selling, increased his capital in the partnership (his fixed assets) to £1,600. This will be his closing capital figure. How did he get there? His old capital (£1,000) was taken out of the Partnership and new capital of £1,600 was introduced. So, as long as the capital account showed the removal of the £1,000 and the introduction of the £1,600, the capital account will reflect the situation. But what happened to the fixed assets which are the other side of his capital? There again, we have to remove the £1,000 of fixed assets and re-introduce the new £1,600 of fixed assets. This side of the transaction we could have kept really simple and ignored the profit or loss on disposal. This is because the profit or loss on disposal is not something which the partnership is going to bear directly – the loss is borne by the partner and so the Partnership could ignore it. (That is, it is the owner who is buying and selling the assets as part of his capital, it is not the partnership that is doing the buying and selling – see below.) *But*, the diminution in the market value of the fixed assets which DH discovers when he sells his fixed assets has, presumably, arisen, at least in part, as a result of the equipment's use for the Partnership. Although DH is not going to be recompensed for this diminution in value, it may be useful for the accounting to recognize what has actually happened so that the partnership has the information for future reference. (We return to this issue below.) So, in this case we have recognized the loss on disposal suffered by the partners which, although the losses do not change the basic financial situation of the Partnership, do tell us something about unrecognized costs suffered by the partners. The same principles are then applied to each of the partner capital transactions.

Hint

This is *very* complicated and requires very careful thinking about the difference between the accounting entity and the owners. Because there is no Partnership Agreement which carefully specifies how all the transactions between the Partnership and the partners should be treated, the distinction between the accounting entity and the owners is blurred. This may often happen in practice in small organizations and it means that there may be several different ways in which the organization might account for some transactions. What we have shown here is only one way in which to recognize what has happened.

---

v Item 7 gives us further information about costs incurred by the partners on behalf of the Partnership. These are treated in the same way as the hire costs above because they reflect costs incurred by the Partnership *but* paid for by the partners. Thus, the

Partnership has not paid the costs (i.e. they do not go through the Partnership cash book) but the Partnership owes these amounts to the partners.

vi   Items 9 and 10 are similarly treated.

vii   Item 11 needs some care. Here we have a series of new partners joining and leaving the Partnership. If this were a strictly commercial accounting entity, we would want to, in effect, wind up the Partnership whenever a partner change occurred and then value the goodwill that the new partner would have to purchase or that a leaving partner would expect to be paid for. (We look at this in more detail in section 13.3 below.) You can see from the text in Figure 13.4 that the existing partners have chosen to do this on a much more casual basis and – if all the individuals involved are happy about it – this is a much simpler way of proceeding.

(a) Julie's joining the Partnership has no implications. Her leaving does. But rather than open a detailed current account for her (she has no capital), the £50 is treated as a one-off, *ad hoc* payment for reason of simplicity.

(b) Stephanie is more complicated because she brings capital into the band. The capital account has to reflect this. Similarly, she bears expenses which must, as with the other partners, be reflected in her current account. When she decides to leave, the Partnership owes her (i) the costs she has incurred in the band on behalf of the Partnership (shown in her current account) plus (ii) any goodwill payment that the band might make to her. As the information in Figure 13.4 does not specify the details of the goodwill element, the answer we have provided assumes that the Partnership still owes her the amount outstanding on her current account.[6] The goodwill payment (of a T-shirt and a tape of the band's recordings) has no financial number attached to it at the moment. Therefore we cannot account for it without making a wild guess – we do not know (and the band did not know at this point) what the costs incurred in recording a tape and printing T-shirts would be. We have therefore ignored it for now. *This is not good accounting but does keep life simpler.*

(c) Lyn has no capital so does not need a capital account. She needs a current account and this must show that she is making *drawings* of £10 on certain gig nights. This is shown in the current account.

viii The final item in the current accounts is the allocation of the loss. This cannot be undertaken until the profit and loss account has been constructed. So the current account stays uncompleted whilst the rest of the bookkeeping for the year is undertaken. Once the profit and loss account is complete the loss can be allocated to the different members of the Partnership. As the partners share the profits and losses equally, the loss has been allocated to them on the basis of the time they have spent with the band. The initial partners have been with the band for 12 months whilst Lyn has only been with the Partnership for 2 months. So the loss is allocated on the basis of 50ths (12 + 12 + 12 + 12 + 2 = 50) and then taken to the appropriate current accounts. These can then be balanced off and brought, with the capital accounts to the balance sheet.

The foregoing, although complicated, should be reasonably sensible as long as you (a) remember to take one item at a time and try and reflect what has actually happened and (b) remember that this is not a fully commercial organization with a full and detailed Partnership agreement nor a complete separation of the owners from the accounting entity. As a result, some of the transactions have to be put through on a 'best guess' basis and you have to think to yourself 'does this reasonably reflect what I understand to be the actual situation?'. With one exception, the material in Figure 13.5 and in Appendix 13 does this.

The exception is the depreciation and, by implication, the use of the partners' equipment for the Partnership's activities. Had this been a strictly commercial organization then the Partnership would have bought the equipment off the partners and would, therefore, own the equipment. The Partnership and not the partners would then have undertaken the sales and purchases of new equipment, borne the depreciation on the fixed assets and borne the profits or losses on disposal of fixed assets. However, the Partnership would not have had enough cash to undertake all the required transactions and so would have had to negotiate either a bank overdraft or loans with partners to inject further cash. This would have been a great deal more formal and, although the individual bookkeeping transactions would have been more straightforward, the overall accounting for the Partnership would have been more complex still. Given that the band is primarily interested in making music, this did not seem like a good plan. Hence the simpler – but definitely more sloppy – approach we have taken here. This raises one or two lessons which we might reflect upon. Some of these are considered in the next subsection and a major one – the construction of social reality issue – is dealt with in section 13.4

13.2.5 Some lessons from Jeopardy

The Jeopardy Partnership is not an easy accounting entity for which to produce accounting records. This should interest you – not least because it is obvious that Jeopardy must be one of the simplest partnerships that one could imagine. The problem arises then, not with the overall complexity of the organization itself, but with the formality and complexity of the ownership claims. In Jeopardy, the ownership claims were very informal but fairly complex. The result was a somewhat messy piece of accounting. This raises further issues.

One of the critical factors in accounting is the very careful separation of the accounting entity from the owners. This is very artificial but an absolute prerequisite to allow conventional accounting to operate normally. If you can sort out, to your own satisfaction, the ownership and entity issues in Jeopardy you can be reasonably confident that you have a fairly well-developed grasp of this important – but artificial – distinction.

One final point worth mentioning also relates to the ownership claims in Jeopardy. The partners in Jeopardy were given no credit for the amount of capital they had injected. It would not be uncommon for the Partnership to pay each partner a notional interest payment so that the overall allocation of the profit (or loss) reflected the fact that different partners had introduced different amounts of capital to the business. Similarly, the depreciation charge was shown as a charge to – an expense of – the business. We have already identified that the Jeopardy Partnership raises a question as to whether or not the Partnership or the partners own the fixed assets. If the Partnership owns the fixed assets it is right and proper that the Partnership should bear the depreciation as an expense – which is what we have done in the answer. However, the partners have undertaken the purchases and sales of their 'own' equipment and borne the associated losses. Given this is the situation, can the depreciation be used to compensate the partners for the diminution of the value of their ownership claims? That *is* a tricky question upon which you might well enjoy dwelling. It is the sort of issue which will arise later in your studies. For now, we just hope we have shown you how important the entity/ownership distinction is and what a central role this basic assumption plays in conventional accounting practice.

13.3 FURTHER PARTNERSHIP ISSUES

13.3.1 Introduction

Accounting for partnerships is a favourite subject in professional accountancy examinations and is a subject which can rapidly get really quite complicated quite quickly. If you have followed, understood and (even perhaps?) enjoyed the material so far, then you have a good initial grasp of partnerships. We do not want to confuse you by engaging in too much esoteric detail at this stage. We do, however, need to take matters just a little further.

Partnerships are funny things when anything happens to change the essential nature of the collaborative venture – most particularly, when a partner joins or leaves. We saw partners joining and leaving in the Jeopardy example and dealt with it in a fairly straightforward way in the interests of simplicity. We could do this because, in essence, Jeopardy was not a commercial organization and so many of the issues that would arise in a fully commercial business, were simply not important. (We re-examine this assertion in section 13.4 below.) In a fully commercial organization we would have to take matters rather more seriously and be a lot more precise in our dealings. This is what we need to look at – albeit briefly – in this section.

The introduction of a new partner or the resignation of an old partner simply does not arise with a sole trader or in a company. In the case of a sole trader one simply sells the business as a whole. In the case of a company one simply sells one's shares and the organization carries on regardless.[7] In a partnership, any change in the partners who make up the partnership effectively dissolves the old partnership. So, in order to let partners leave and new ones join, we need to know a little about 'dissolving organizations'. This can be an enormous subject in its own right – liquidations, bankruptcies and dissolutions are complex specialist areas and all too common. We can only touch briefly upon it here. We will look, briefly, at the nature of **goodwill** in a partnership – as this is the central issue with joining and leaving partners. Finally, we have a look at how to deal with entering and leaving partners.

13.3.2 Dissolving a partnership

In a partnership dissolution, the basic aim of the bookkeeping is to end up with only the remaining partners' capital and current accounts, a cash account and a new account, the **realization account**. If the partnership were sold as a going-concern business (not beyond the bounds of possibility) this would be a fairly simple matter. Usually this is not the case, however. So, *all the assets except the cash* are transferred to the realization account: [Credit asset account: Debit realization account]. All the expenses of realization go through the realization account: [Credit cash: Debit realization account]. The assets are sold: [Debit cash: Credit realization account]. All the partnership liabilities should now be paid off, closing off the liability accounts and crediting cash – any shortfall credited to the realization account. At this point, the books of the business should be fairly clear and now the realization account is cleared out to the partners' capital account – in the ratio laid down in the Partnership Deed or as specified in the appropriate Partnership Act. The balances on the partners' current accounts are also brought to the capital account. At this point we should only have left a capital account and a cashbook – which, arithmetically, should be identical! Any surplus or shortfall is then shared between the partners as agreed or as the law recommends. (Remembering that any shortfall either relating to other liabilities or between the partners must be met by the partners from any private resources they are fortunate enough to own.)

This, apparently slightly tedious but essentially simple bookkeeping process, can no more than summarize likely situations. If the partnership is winding up due to major trading losses it is likely that the process will be long, protracted and complicated and will owe as much to law as to accounting. On the other hand, in the event that the partnership has been dissolved simply to admit a new partner or to allow an old partner to leave, this process is immensely cumbersome – and might well lead to a business having to stop trading every time partners joined or left. This is not good business practice! So, simpler mechanisms are devised to deal with joining and leaving partners. The key factor in this is the valuation of *partnership goodwill*.

13.3.3 Partnership goodwill

We discussed goodwill briefly in Chapter 7, section 7.4.3, where we gave a very cursory glance at *intangible fixed assets*. **Goodwill** is a subject on which much has been written. It is a complex issue but, in essence, the goodwill of the business is the difference between (a) value of the business as a whole (i.e. what an individual would – or does – pay to buy the business) and (b) the existing book value of the net assets (i.e. basically the fixed assets plus the current assets less the liabilities). Goodwill may often be the most important asset a business possesses and may derive from the well-known name and reputation of the business, its products and patents, its production processes, its skilled workforce, its customer base and so on.

When a partner leaves a partnership they will normally want to take from the business what they are owed. This will only partly be represented by the balances on the partners' capital and current accounts. There will also be the *goodwill* of the business which the partner has (hopefully) helped to create. The leaving partner is due a proportion of that goodwill and, in effect, the continuing partners must buy it from them.

Similarly, when a new partner joins they will earn profits which, in part at least, are probably due to the hard work of the existing partners over the preceding years in building up this goodwill. The new partner will have to inject capital into the business *and* buy their share of the goodwill pertaining at that moment in time from the existing (or a leaving) partner.

Goodwill, therefore, is the central issue in assessing the amount that a leaving partner is due or a joining partner must buy.

There are an infinite number of ways in which we might set about valuing the goodwill of the partnership. One basis would be to find some way of getting an overall value for the business. This is unlikely to be an easy option. (It is relatively easy in quoted companies where the quoted share price gives a guide to the business's value, but is very unlikely to be possible in a partnership.) Much more usual in valuing any unquoted business is to make an estimate based on the level of earnings (profits) of the business. A frequently used 'rule of thumb' is to take three times the average profits for the last three years. The goodwill of the business is then estimated as the difference between this figure and the book value of net assets. This gives, at least, a broad-brush appreciation of the business's earning capacity. This basically crude 'rule of thumb' can be extensively modified.

What we are trying to establish is what are the 'above-normal returns' which the business is earning – what economists sometimes call 'super profits'. That is, if you took the amount of money tied up in the business and invested in an 'average business' or in some other safe investment what rate of return would it earn for you? Are the present earnings of the partnership greater than this? If so, then there is your goodwill element.

More formally, then, to value goodwill of a partnership, one may very well take the following steps:

i   define what is a 'normal annual rate or return';
ii   assess the business 'above-normal rate of return' (its annual profits in excess of this normal return) for a number of years, say 3, 4 or 5 years;
iii perhaps discount back these super-earnings figures;[8]
iv   'value' the business by use of some suitable equation based on annuity rates that will allow you to effectively identify a capitalized value for the super-earnings the business is earning.

As we said, we can get ever so sophisticated and complicated in the valuation of a business but it is essentially a matter of instinct, luck and professional judgement. But, by some means or other, one needs to establish this *goodwill* value so that leaving partners can be recompensed and joining partners can 'buy in' to an existing success story.

When we have valued the goodwill, then the bookkeeping to effect the change of partners can take place.

13.3.4 The basic elements of the bookkeeping for a leaving or joining partner

At the risk of becoming repetitive, there are a large number of different methods that can be used to effect the transactions for a joining or leaving partner. The differences principally arise because a partnership can make two basic choices in the way in which it handles the joining or leaving partner:

i   The partnership has to decide whether or not it wants to have an asset called 'goodwill' on its balance sheet or not. Whilst most businesses do have some goodwill, accountants are generally unhappy about showing it on the balance sheet – primarily because it is intangible, difficult to value and the exigencies of *prudence* suggest that one should not really recognize such assets until they can be turned into cash. Whether goodwill stays on the balance sheet of the partnership or is removed affects the bookkeeping.
ii   The second decision the partnership has to make is whether or not they want cash to change hands for the goodwill. They may well have to pay some cash out to a leaving partner for *their* share of goodwill but will the partners expect either to be paid personally or to take cash from the business on the arrival of a new partner?

We will try to illustrate these issues using the Shredders Partnership. Figures 13.1 and 13.3 represented the Shredders Partnership at the end of 2000. Let us imagine that at the end of December Gibson decides to leave and a new partner, Gretsch, decides to join. He will bring in $2,000 capital. The partnership has only been in existence for one year so goodwill is not a major issue. The existing partners agree to value goodwill at $12,000. How much can Gibson take from the business? How much should Gretsch be charged for the goodwill?

This is a basically simple situation and we can deal with the bookkeeping in a very straightforward manner.

i   Open a goodwill account. Debit the goodwill account with $12,000 and think about where to put the credit. This is a 'new asset' and it is owned by the existing owners. So it should be shared between them in their agreed ratios – you may recall that the partners (in our examples) share everything in the ratio of their capital accounts.

ii Credit the existing partners' capital accounts with the goodwill – Fender $2,000, Gibson $4,000, Marshall $6000.

iii We now have an estimate of Gibson's share of the business. It comprises his current account (which we know from Figure 13.3 is $1,300) plus his capital account (which comprises the original $2,000 plus the $4,000 of goodwill).

iv Now the simplest thing to do – remembering that this is the most straightforward situation – is for Gretsch to buy Gibson's share directly from him by paying him, directly, $6,000. (This is the capital of $2,000 and the goodwill of $4,000. The current account belongs to Gibson himself and will be taken by Gibson directly from the business – say in cash.)

v Then, because of the accountants' desire to be prudent, the partnership will probably be advised to remove the goodwill account. This is done by reversing the original entries, writing off the goodwill against the partners' capital accounts.

This process is shown in Figures 13.6 and 13.7

THE SHREDDERS PARTNERSHIP – CAPITAL ACCOUNT AT 31.12.2000							
	Fender	Gibson	Marshall		Fender	Gibson	Marshall
				1.1.00 Cash	1,000	2,000	3,000
Retiral of partner		6,000		Balance at y/e	1,000	2,000	3,000
				Goodwill a/c	2,000	4,000	6,000
31.12.00 Bal c/d	3,000		9,000				
	$3,000	$6,000	$9,000		$3,000	$6,000	$9,000

THE SHREDDERS PARTNERSHIP – CURRENT ACCOUNT AT 31.12.2000							
	Fender	Gibson	Marshall		Fender	Gibson	Marshall
30.6.00				31.12.00			
Drawings/cash	1,750			Interest	50	100	150
				Salary	2,500		
				Profit	600	1,200	1,800
Retiral of partner		1,300					
31.12.00 Bal c/d	1,400		1,950				
	$3,150	$1,300	$1,950		$3,150	$1,300	$1,950

Figure 13.6 An illustration of a partner leaving

THE SHREDDERS PARTNERSHIP – CAPITAL ACCOUNT AT 1.1.2001							
	Fender	Gretsch	Marshall		Fender	Gretsch	Marshall
1.1.01				1.1.01			
Write off				Bal b/d	3,000		9,000
goodwill	2,000	4,000	6,000	New partner		6,000	
1.1.01 Bal c/d	1,000	2,000	3,000				
	$3,000	$6,000	$9,000		$3,000	$6,000	$9,000

THE SHREDDERS PARTNERSHIP – CURRENT ACCOUNT AT 1.1.2001							
	Fender	Gretsch	Marshall		Fender	Gretsch	Marshall
				31.12.01			
				Bal b/d	1,400		1,950
1.1.01 Bal c/d	1,400	0	1,950				
	$1,400	$0	$1,950		$1,400	$0	$1,950

Figure 13.7 An illustration of a partner joining

Again, for simplicity, we have taken the leaving and joining partners separately. In Figure 13.6 the goodwill account is created and credited to the existing partners' capital accounts. Gibson then takes out his share (this could either be a credit to cash or a credit direct to Gretsch – see below). The balances on the capital accounts carried down thus relate only to the two remaining partners. The current accounts are as previously except that Gibson removes the balance on his current account (probably in cash) and the balances carried down relate only to the remaining partners.

In Figure 13.7 Fender's and Marshall's capital accounts are shown with their balances brought down and Gretsch introduces his capital. Then the goodwill account is written off to remove it from the books. No action is taken on the current accounts.

Now, this is simplest of all possible arrangements and, because of this simplicity, it may seem that the creation and removal of the goodwill account is more trouble than it is worth. But many other possibilities may arise. Most typically, a joining partner may not simply buy the share of the outgoing partner and/or the old partners may take the opportunity of a change in the partnership to change their capital and profit-sharing arrangements. In these cases, the step-by-step approach becomes more important so that at no stage does one lose sight of what is happening and how the shares of the partners are being renegotiated. You may very well find yourself needing to study the more complex partnership arrangements later in your accounting courses. Our view is that this is quite sufficient at an introductory stage to grasp the essential elements of a partnership arrangement and, thereby, to clarify your own thinking on the issues that can arise in more intricate ownership claims. What we do not wish to do is burden you with so much excessive detail that you lose sight of the central issues. So, with the exception of further questions in the workbook which accompanies this text, we think that this is quite enough detail on partnerships for now.

So to complete this chapter we want to return to some of the issues we raised in Chapter 12 when we began to think about what financial accounting was actually achieving.

13.4 THINKING ABOUT FINANCIAL ACCOUNTING – AGAIN

This chapter and Chapter 12 have concentrated almost exclusively on the ownership claims in commercial organizations. This is highly appropriate because conventional capitalist accounting (what we have been studying so far) has two principal *raisons d'être*: (i) to keep financial records for managing and controlling the organization and (ii) to assess the amount due to the owners after each accounting period. In broad terms these, in fact, are the purposes behind, respectively, bookkeeping and accounting. Thus, a major purpose – and certainly a major effect – of conventional accounting is to focus attention on the financial aspects of an organization and to make the owners' financial claims the centrepiece of that focus. This may be a perfectly proper and useful thing to do in many circumstances, but look back to the Jeopardy Partnership and *think* about what we did to that 'organization'.

First of all, we can tell you that Jeopardy was a real rock band of moderate local success. It comprised a group of people who became good friends and who enjoyed playing music. It seemed that many others apparently enjoyed listening to them. The members of the band were blithely indifferent to the financial aspects of the group, with the exception of Lyn who, being unemployed, needed any extra cash she could find. Each of the other members had employment and sources of income far in excess of anything a local rock band could afford them – unless they achieved major international success. This was both fairly unlikely and, indeed, something in which the band had no interest. Why are we telling you all this? To make a series of important points about accounting. First, the group had absolutely no interest in their financial accounts.[9] They served only two (intentional) purposes: they provided evidence to the tax authorities that the group was a 'hobby' not a 'business';[10] and provided material with which to illustrate a simple semi-commercial partnership for students! So, it is possible for an 'organization' not to bother with financial accounting. (This is not an option for companies by the way.[11]) For small, generally 'social' rather than 'economic', organizations it may very well be in the interests of the organization to ignore financial accounting. We turn to this in a moment.

You now have two pictures of Jeopardy – the one painted by the financial information given earlier and the social picture we have just painted above. If you had been to a pub to listen to the band you would have had yet another picture of the 'organization'. The accounting picture certainly did not dominate the band members (but see below). We doubt very much whether audiences sat in the pub thinking things like 'bet they're making a profit', 'love that last debit and credit solo', 'I wonder who writes their songs and does their accounts'. So which is the 'true' picture? In a sense they all have elements of 'truth' but what is more important is that when faced with a financial accounting picture of an organization we, as accountants, set out to treat an organization as an 'economic' entity when a more sensible reaction might be, not 'I wonder if they made a profit?', but rather 'I wonder if they enjoy themselves?'. The financial accounting *constructs a social reality* of an organization, making it appear to be dominated by its economic factors. In such circumstances, the economic factors *can come to dominate it.*

This is what, in fact, happened with the Jeopardy Partnership. When they saw the financial accounts, they began to be concerned about (a) whether the band was being equitable between its partners (it wasn't) and (b) why they were not making more money. That is, the band began to think of itself *as* an economic entity. In some cases this can be a very good discipline, in some cases it is not. To illustrate, it is quite clear that different members of Jeopardy put in different amounts of capital but did not get appropriate financial returns from doing so. The band began to argue because it was *made explicit* that PM was subsidizing the band and other members were (financially) free-riding. This is economically unfair. The band began to fall apart. There were two solutions. First, the accountant's solution would be to draw up a partnership agreement, pay interest on capital and increase the sophistication of the accounting. That is, the accountant's solution is to make the organization *more* economic by giving it *more accounting*. The other solution – the one the band adopted – was to stop doing the accounting altogether, forget about the economics and get on with enjoying themselves. After all, the group was a set of friends who, like all friends, operate on the principle of 'each according to their needs, from each according to their abilities'. This is not something that accounting can recognize. So they got rid of the accounting and went on to enjoy their music and their regional success for some years.

What was happening here? Accounting was imposing an economic rationality on a situation which did not need it. So much so that the imposition of accounting actually started to destroy the other aspects of the organization. The accountant's solution was to add more of the thing which had caused the problem – increase the dose of accounting. This would have destroyed the friendships and social aspects of the band.

This is a true story, folks! But you may think it pretty irrelevant to an understanding of accounting. The principle is not irrelevant. First, there are very many small organizations – many, many more than large organizations – and whilst the discipline of financial accounting and control will often be essential to the well-being and survival of these small organizations, there will often be a social price to be paid. Second, it has been shown, most persuasively, that the increased application of accounting to non-commercial organizations and especially public sector organizations slowly but inexorably destroys the essential nature of those organizations.[12] Finally, if you can at least see the basic principle we are trying to communicate – that accounting is never neutral, is often positive, but can also be very negative – then you should be able to see that there *must* be negative consequences to accounting development. Whether these are greater or smaller than the undoubted benefits that come from increased accounting development is a matter for your own opinion – and later studies.

SUMMARY

Partnerships are a particular form of organization which reflects a particular ownership structure. Less formal and detailed than a company and more formal than the simple sole trader, partnerships raise a number of difficult but interesting issues. These issues are only different from the accounting in other organizational forms to the extent that the accounting transactions affect the owners and their claims. We used a somewhat simple but informal example to illustrate the importance of the distinction between the accounting entity and the ownership claims. The unique accounting issues that arise in the partnership are: the capital and current accounts which are used to record the owners' ownership claims and changes therein over the accounting period; the allocation of profits and losses to the partners – including notional interest and notional salaries; and the calculations of goodwill when a partner joins or leaves the partnership. The educational value of learning about partnerships lies in the less than perfectly clear distinctions that arise between the entity and the ownership claims.

Key terms and concepts

The following key terms and concepts have featured in this chapter. You should ensure that you understand and can explain each one. Page references to definitions appear in the index in bold type.

- Accounting entity versus owners
- Allocation of profit or loss
- Creating social reality
- Dissolving a partnership
- Joining and leaving partners
- Jointly and severally liable
- Partners' capital accounts
- Partners' current account
- Partners' drawings
- Partners' interest and salary
- Partners' ownership claims
- Partnership
- Partnership deed or agreement
- Partnership goodwill
- Unlimited liability

FURTHER READING

In addition to the examples in the workbook, the basic technical material we have covered in this chapter is also considered in some other introductory textbooks which you could consult if you need further help on these matters. On the more reflective issues we have discussed, read again the excellent article by Hines (1988).

NOTES

1. This is, perhaps, an oversimplification. You should not imagine that accounting is an uncontentious activity. Accounting could be virtually anything we wanted it to be and it is increasingly obvious that accounting could usefully be varied to better reflect the organizational and societal context in which it operates. However, conventional capitalist accounting is increasingly ubiquitous and is exercised in nations which are not capitalist and which do not operate on European or Anglo-Saxon principles. The export of a particular form of conventional accounting – that which we are studying in this text – might therefore be imposed inappropriately on societies as a form of imperialism. This, again, is a complex matter to which your future studies of accounting (we hope) will give attention.

2. There is an old apocryphal story which illustrates this. Partner A, arriving at work one morning discovers that his partner, Partner B, has committed the partnership to a series of massive debts about which Partner A knew nothing. Partner B has left a note and fled the country. Partner A is devastated and returns home, relieved that, at least, he has left the family home in the name of his wife and, as a result, it cannot be called upon to satisfy the losses of the business. Upon reaching home, Partner A discovers with whom Partner B has fled the country!

3. There are other sorts of partnerships (as there are other types of companies). Some partnerships may be established as limited partnership under appropriate elements of the Partnership Acts. This tends not to be common in practice.

4. It may not be uncommon for a partnership to transfer some or all of the balance outstanding on a partner's current account to his/her capital account at the end of each accounting period. We will ignore this practice here.

5. Perhaps a more common arrangement on this issue is to charge interest (and make other allocations – see below) on the basis of the balances on the partners' capital accounts at the end of the *preceding* accounting period. The assumption in such cases is that *that* is the amount of capital available to the partnership during the *current* accounting period. For simplicity (and because it is the first year of the partnership) we have chosen to allocate on the basis of the balances on the partners' capital accounts at the end of the current accounting period.

6. Please note that the data in the question suggest that Stephanie, on leaving, has removed her equipment from the partnership and *this* comprises her total capital account. The partnership is, therefore, assumed *not* to owe her anything further on the capital account – except for any goodwill. (Some of the issues arising from this approach to the capital of the partnership are apparent in the buying and selling of fixed assets which we dealt with above.)

7. It is not quite this simple, as your future studies will demonstrate. The principle is sufficient for now, however.

8. Note: you should have met discounting in your finance, economics or statistics course by now. If you haven't, you will shortly. Discounting in this context means adjusting future streams of money downwards to recognize that money in the future is worth less to you than money now.

9. This is not the same as saying they had no interest in the cash side of the business. The cash was very carefully accounted for in a bank account. Its importance for the band lay in the fact that the cash would eventually be used to record an album of music. The band was very interested in the cash balance, but had no interest in its financial statements, capital or current accounts. This is not so unusual and illustrates that accounting can serve very different functions in very different circumstances.

10. This is a complicated issue but basically arises from the concern of taxation authorities that they want your income if then can get it but they do not want to recognize your losses if they can possible help it.

11. Keeping no accounting records is not a realistic option for any organization which will be approached by the taxation authorities for an assessed amount of tax. Neither is it a realistic option for an organization which will need a loan from a bank. Furthermore, companies, as we shall see in Chapter 14, are *legally* required to keep appropriate accounting records as part of the privilege of limited liability.

12 You are no longer a student, you are clients' agents and you are not receiving an education but a product which has been carefully costed. Your department is a profit centre which will increasingly be forced to reduce and cancel tutorials and lectures because they are uneconomic. The principles of scholarship, understanding and development of civilized educated people cannot survive in the tightly constrained accounting-led world that public sector education (and hospitals and schools and charities and housing departments and …) is becoming. Inappropriate accounting can be a very damaging exercise!

APPENDIX 13: FULL T-ACCOUNTS AND FINANCIAL STATEMENTS FOR THE JEOPARDY PARTNERSHIP

Jeopardy Partnership Accounts (2009)

Inflow/debit	Cashbook		Outflow/credit
Gigs	760	Advert	10
Interest	6	Advert	10
		Advert	5
		Resignation (Julie)	50
		Lyn (Current A/c)	10
		Lyn (Current A/c)	10
		Bal c/d	671
	£766		£766

Inflow/debit	Publicity costs		Outflow/credit
Posters: PM Current	37	P & L A/c	91
Advert accruals	29		
Advert (cash)	10		
Advert (cash)	10		
Advert (cash)	5		
	£91		£91

Inflow/debit	Fixed assets (equipment)		Outflow/credit
DH capital	1,000	Disposal	1,000
PM capital	2,500	Disposal	1,000
JY capital	800	Disposal	800
RG capital	1,500	Steph resignation	500
PM capital	450		
PM capital	1,450		
DH capital	1,600		
JY capital	2,000		
RG capital	100		
Steph capital	500	Balance c/d	8,600
	£11,900		£11,900

Inflow/debit	Equipment disposal a/c		Outflow/credit
DH	1,000	DH cash	600
		& loss on disposal	400
PM	1,000	PM cash	750
		& loss on disposal	250
JY	800	JY cash	600
		& loss on disposal	200
	£2,800		£2,800

Inflow/debit	Gig costs		Outflow/credit
DH current a/c	45	P & L a/c	513
PM current a/c	37		
JY current a/c	9		
RG current a/c	57		
Petrol costs – current a/cs	340		
Petrol costs – Steph	25		
	£513		£513

Inflow/debit	Rehearsal costs		Outflow/credit
Man in the Moon	120	P & L a/c	2,428
Castle Hotel	435		
Lodge (RG)	25		
Petrol costs (82x5x4)	1,640		
Petrol costs – Steph	60		
DH current a/c	45		
PM current a/c	37		
JY current a/c	8		
RG current a/c	58		
	£2,428		£2,428

Inflow/debit	Partner resignation a/c		Outflow/credit
Julie payout	£50	P & L a/c	£50

Inflow/debit	Sales (gigs)		Outflow/credit
P & L a/c	£760	Cash	£760

Inflow/debit	Depreciation for the year		Outflow/credit
Acc Depn	£860	P & L a/c	£860

Inflow/debit	Accumulated depreciation		Outflow/credit
Bal c/d	£860	2009 Depn	£860

Inflow/debit	Sundry creditors		Outflow/credit
Bal c/d	114	Advert accrual	29
		Steph current a/c	85
	£114		£114

Inflow/debit	Interest		Outflow/credit
P & L a/c	£6	Cash	£6

Jeopardy Partnership P & L A/c for year ended 31/12/09

Income:		
Sales/Gigs	760	
Interest	6	766
Expenditure:		
Depreciation	860	
Publicity	91	
Gig costs	513	
Rehearsal costs	2,428	(3,892)
Loss for the year		(3,126)
Partner resignation		(5)
		(3,176)
Appropriation Account		
DH (12/50)	762	
PM (12/50)	762	
JY (12/50)	762	
RH (12/50)	762	
Lyn (2/50)	128	(3,176)

Jeopardy Partnership Balance Sheet as at 31/12/09

Fixed assets:			
Equipment		8,600	
Accumulated Depreciation		(860)	7,740
Current assets:			
Cash		671	
Current liabilities:			
Sundry creditors		114	
Net current assets			557
			£8,297
Represented by:			
Capital accounts:	DH	1,600	
	PM	3,400	
	JY	2,000	
	RG	1,600	8,600
Current accounts:	DH	(38)	
	PM	(17)	
	JY	(112)	
	RG	12	
	Lyn	(148)	303
			£8,297

Accounting regulation and company accounts 14

Learning objectives

After studying this chapter you should be able to:

- understand the basic principles of the regulatory framework of financial reporting;

- recognize both the international nature of accounting regulation and be able to illustrate the rapidly changing nature of accounting regulation;

- understand the role of the accounting profession in the regulation of financial reporting through the auditor and the accounting standards-setting bodies;

- understand the basic principles of company law;

- explain the role of the statutory auditor;

- read intelligently a simple set of financial statements published by a company;

- take each item in those financial statements and explain the accounting and accounting information systems processes by which it has reached the profit and loss account and balance sheet;

- appreciate the rudiments of the regulation of financial accounting and reporting as it applies to organizations other than companies.

14.1 INTRODUCTION

14.1.1 Chapter design and links to previous chapters

Law, and other sources of relevant regulations, will always be amongst the major influences in the focal organization's substantial environment. These regulations (including such accounting-related regulations as Companies Acts and accounting standards – see below) govern not only the formation and very existence of the organization but also lay down rules covering the activities of the organization. These rules are one of the many sources of information inputs to the decision and control subsystem and compliance with them is the price the organization pays for the privileges it enjoys (e.g. limited liability in the case of companies). The regulations will usually lay down that the maintenance of the decision and control subsystem will be the responsibility of the senior management (e.g. the directors of the company). It is their responsibility to ensure that the rules are complied with.

From the accountant's point to view, the main concern is that the decision and control subsystem must maintain sufficient accounting records of the inputs and outputs of the three organizational subsystems in order to enable the decision and control subsystem to produce the periodic financial statements. These financial statements are an output of the decision and control subsystem and are crucial input to certain of the finance-providing organizational systems in the focal organization's substantial environment. This information output, together with certain outputs of the funds subsystem (e.g. payments of dividends and interest and repayments of capital) are required of the focal organization as a condition of the inputs to the funds subsystem from the finance-providing organizations.

You now know that financial accounting has basically three closely related functions:

i   the capture and recording of transactions and the keeping of the financial records (bookkeeping);

ii   the accounting decisions that allow the focal organization to transform the initial trial balance into a set of financial statements (accounting decisions); and

iii the adjustment and amendment of these financial statements – more formally, the communication and presentation of information for external participants (financial reporting).

Bookkeeping involves a great deal of detail. In the creation of this detail and in the creation of the financial statement from the trial balance, the accounting activity relies on a wide range of additional information which is not explicitly shown in either the records or the accounts themselves. (We are referring here to, for example, information on asset lives, market conditions, wastage in production, etc.) The financial statements are only a financial summary of all this information, carefully aggregated, which is then communicated to the external participants. If the external participants were only to receive the financial accounts with no additional supporting information they would hear a most partial story about the focal organization.

Now, if there were no external participants requiring information then every organization could treat any accounting transaction as it suited the managers of that organization. Some might, for example, choose not to depreciate fixed assets, others might choose to account entirely on a cash rather than accrual basis. In a general sense this would not matter as the managers of the focal organization could, in principle at least, always obtain extra information when it was needed and they would be familiar with the 'accounting policies' employed by their organization. However, for the external participant who receives only a summary of the records (the financial statements), knows little or nothing of the 'accounting policies' adopted by the focal organization, and perhaps is not in a position to request further information should he/she want it, the financial reporting process is likely to mean very little indeed.

Largely as a result of this situation we find that there are 'rules' governing financial reporting. These help to establish *to whom* the focal organization should account and perhaps more pertinently:

i   *how* to account for the tricky items; and

ii   *what* information should be contained in financial statements.

These two functions of the rules are usually referred to as, respectively, the '*treatment*' of accounting information and the '*disclosure*' of accounting information.

The major 'rules' derive from two principal sources – law and the accounting profession. This is shown in Figure 14.1 which is an attempt to demonstrate the general way in which these two sources would appear to influence the form and content of the focal organization's financial statements.

The accountant's preparation of the financial statements (on behalf of the senior managers of the focal organization) will be influenced by his/her training, by formal

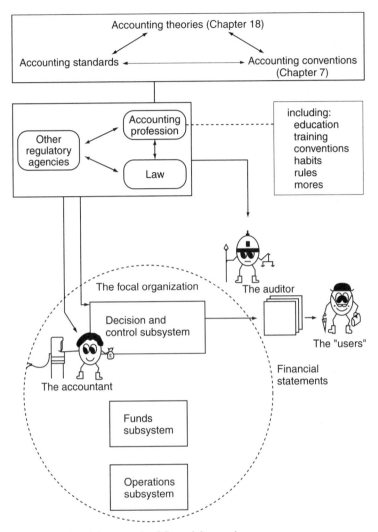

Figure 14.1 The institutional framework of financial reporting

directives from influential bodies (typically the accounting profession and the government) and by what the organization thinks it can get away with. There is also, therefore, an 'anticipatory' influence upon the financial statements in the form of the auditor who is required to check to see whether the financial statements do comply with all extant rules.

14.1.2 Design of the chapter

This chapter is designed to provide you with an introduction and overview of the complex world of accounting regulation. The next section introduces the elements of the accounting regulation process and attempts to give you an insight into both the rapidly changing nature of accounting regulation and the importance of the international dimension. Section 14.3 concentrates on company law and the format of company accounts. This section provides a general outline of what you can expect to find in a Companies Act: its impact on the structure of the organization, the responsibilities of the directors and the requirements to produce financial statements. This section also provides an illustration from a set of UK published company accounts before proceeding to examine the important role of the auditor. Section 14.4 looks at the role of the professional accountancy bodies in regulating financial accounting standards. It briefly explains the process of setting standards and identifies the sorts of areas on which you can expect to find accounting standards (as they are known), before concentrating on just one area of accounting regulation – the disclosure of accounting policies. Section 14.5 briefly considers other forms of accounting regulation and the regulation of non-company organizations. The chapter concludes with a summary, key terms and a guide to further reading.

14.2 AN OVERVIEW OF THE REGULATION OF FINANCIAL ACCOUNTING

14.2.1 Introduction

Financial accounting and the production of financial statements can serve many purposes and have many unforeseen effects (as we have noted in previous chapters – see also Chapter 17). But its central *raison d'être* lies in its legally required status as the principal means by which the managers of an organization (typically, the directors of a company) discharge their duty of accountability to the owners (and financial stakeholders) of that organization (typically the shareholders and other financiers). Companies are becoming more complex, they are changing more rapidly and they frequently span the globe as transnational corporations (TNCs). A basic accounting system which works for a rock band or a manufacturer of ethnic artefacts is unlikely to bear more than a passing resemblance to the accounting system of a major TNC. The basic bookkeeping will look much the same but the sheer volume of transactions, the variety of financial and economic situations in which the organization finds itself and the vast array of clients, customers, shareholders and financial markets in which it operates will raise a plethora of unusual and complex matters to which the accounting system will have to respond.

On top of this, you will be aware that the biggest accounting firms are major TNCs themselves and, with the growth of regional economic units (such as the European Union and other similar units in America, the Pacific Rim and elsewhere throughout the world) it becomes more and more difficult to think of business, finance or accounting on a national basis. (We return to this below.) Furthermore, and perhaps most importantly, you will hear more and more about the internationalization of financial markets with the result that an Australian company may be wholly owned by a company in the USA which is in turn owned by shareholders in many different countries. Many of these shareholders may be individuals but many will be investment and pension funds and other companies and governments. Suddenly the world is a great deal more complex. Add to this the exponential growth in the rate of economic and financial change and you have a maelstrom of near-chaos which the accounting system has to try and record.

In order to try and impose a little order on this chaos we will simplify the situation somewhat in the following sections. In addition, as we have mentioned on a number of occasions, because companies tend to be the organizational form with the most detailed regulations, we will concentrate upon these for the bulk of this chapter.

14.2.2 The basic institutional framework of accounting regulation

Figure 14.1 identified the groups of institutions which govern the production, content and communication of financial statements. As the role of accounting theories in accounting regulation is frequently opaque we will largely ignore these until we get to Chapter 18. That leaves us with *accounting conventions*, *law*, *the accounting profession* and *other regulatory agencies*. This last group comprises *two* separate elements: national or local agencies and international agencies. Figure 14.2 summarizes these influences and their functions.

Accounting conventions were covered in some detail in Chapter 7. (You should, by now, be easily familiar with these but do check back if they are still causing problems.) These conventions provide the basic assumptions about what conventional accounting is all about. They get refined – or even changed – over time (we will see one example of this in Chapter 16), and are often codified in company law and/or in accounting standards. *Company law* is probably the most important influence on financial statements, however. This also changes over time but, most importantly, lays the requirement that companies *must* produce financial statements. A great deal of what we study in financial accounting derives, in the first place, from this unique requirement that organizations must produce regular statements about their activities. We will, therefore, examine the accounting implications of company law in section 14.3. (Other aspects of company law will be dealt with in other courses you will study.) **Accounting standards** have grown dramatically – in number, complexity and importance – in recent decades. They are typically determined by the accounting profession of the country – or by a body on which the accounting

THE PRINCIPAL SOURCES OF REGULATION ON COMPANY FINANCIAL STATEMENTS		
SOURCE OF INFLUENCE	**PURPOSE AND COVERAGE**	**EXAMPLES**
Accounting conventions	Historically derived procedures and accepted norms of accounting behaviour. Usually derived *ad hoc* rather than coherently	Prudence, accrual, consistency, going concern, financial measurement, etc. Sometimes are subsequently formally established in law or accounting standards
Company law	Rules governing the nature, structure and management of a company. Lays down requirements for financial statements and (often basic) rules on accounting treatment and disclosure. Includes rules on auditors	UK Companies Acts; Belgian Company Law and Royal Decrees; French Accounting Acts and Decrees
National accounting standards	Provides additional detail on the treatment and disclosure of specific issues in financial statements. Normally set by the accounting profession or, at least, greatly influenced by it	USA's Statements of Financial Accounting Standards (SFAS) established by the Financial Accounting Standards Board (FASB) covering matters as diverse as depreciation and goodwill. Each country will have an equivalent of FASB and SFAS
Stock exchange	Additional rules relating to companies which are – or wish to be – quoted on the national stock exchange	The USA's Stock Exchange Commission (SEC); UK's Stock Exchange 'Yellow Book'. Will, for example, cover matters relating to new issues of shares (e.g. prospectuses and the national accounting standard which should be adhered to)
International regulation	Typically attempts to provide more consistency and coherence between different accounting practices in different countries	The European Union's Accounting Directives on, for example, Consolidation of Accounts; The International Accounting Standards Committee (IASC) – see text

Figure 14.2 Sources of generally accepted accounting principles (GAAP)

profession has a great deal of influence. Accounting standards tend to deal with (a) detailed issues of *accounting treatment* and *accounting disclosure* not covered by company law and (b) with new issues – such as the effects of inflation or intangible assets – which arise from time to time and cause concern in the financial community. Most (so-called) developed countries have their own standard-setting procedures. These vary somewhat from country to country but there is an increasing effort to harmonize accounting standards at the global level (see below). These professional pronouncements are examined in section 14.4.

As a country's economic development becomes more complex it is usual to see the development of a **stock exchange** where, amongst other things, company shares can be bought and sold. Only a small minority of companies are *quoted* on stock exchanges but these tend to be the largest companies in a nation and will tend to include most international 'household name' companies. The stock exchange will typically lay down additional rules on accounting and disclosure for those companies which wish to be quoted. These are briefly considered in section 14.5. Finally, there are the *international attempts to regulate accounting and financial reporting*. This is having an increasing influence on the preparation of financial statements. It is this we now turn to before looking in detail at the other areas of regulation.

14.2.3 The rapidly changing world of accounting regulation

As we have seen, accounting, especially for companies, is becoming more complex – almost by the day. In the developed countries accounting regulation is having to keep pace with an ever-changing corporate and financial world and, even in the (so-called) lesser developed and emerging nations accounting regulation is becoming more important. There was a time within living memory when Companies Acts were produced only occasionally. Now a new Companies Act with new requirements for financial accounting can be produced, in some cases, every two or three years. Whereas, not long ago, an accountancy profession might be content with issuing occasional guidelines on contentious and/or difficult issues it now is faced with an escalating need for more and more complex and stringent accounting regulation on an increasing number of issues. In addition, stock exchanges and transnational bodies are producing ever-increasing volumes of guidance on a wider and more complex set of issues pertaining to financial accounting.

The regulation of financial accounting has become a major growth industry. The only certainty that would seem to remain, is that whatever you learn today at this stage in your studies, is highly likely to be out of date, obsolete or incorrect by the time you qualify in practice.

So you (and we) face a difficult but interesting problem. How to give you a good 'feel' for the increasingly complex world of accounting regulation without burdening you with rapidly outdated and parochial detail? Some of this is down to you as a student. We have, from time to time throughout this book, recommended that you subscribe to a professional accountancy journal. This is one very important way in which you can keep informed of the way in which your future profession is developing. Within this chapter, however, we will attempt to concentrate on the key elements of accounting regulation that are fairly consistent and likely to remain so. This should give you a sufficient basis on which to understand the changes that you read about in your professional journal and let you 'sharpen up' your specific knowledge about the country-specific structure of accounting regulation, the industry-specific developments, the structure and the regulation set by the accounting body you intend to join. In addition, it should give you a basis from which to begin to understand new, emerging specific issues to do with (say) financial instruments, environmental liabilities, intangible assets, increases in disclosure and control and so on – issues which will be examined in more detail later in your studies and professional development.

14.2.4 The international perspective

Whilst the overview given by Figure 14.1 is broadly accurate it does hide the importance of the international dimensions of accounting regulation. There are two major 'international dimensions' reflecting (i) differences between countries and (ii) the increasing emphasis on harmonization of international accounting rules. We need to say a few words about these, bearing in mind the basic structure we introduced above – that is, accounting regulation comprises *national laws, local accounting standards, stock exchange and other requirements* plus *international regulations where appropriate*.

(a) Differences in approaches to accounting between countries

Virtually all countries have some sort of Companies Act or acts. We will look at the likely contents of such Acts in section 14.3 below. For now, however, it is useful to recognize that Companies Acts do vary between nations and there are two *principal* ways in which they vary. The first major way they vary is a *conceptual* as well as a *legal* difference. That is, many countries are unwilling to tolerate a variety of practice and a flexibility in accounting procedures. (You saw some of the implications of this in Chapter 12.) So a much more rigorous and detailed *plan comptable général* or *accounting plan* is laid down which gives very specific guidance on how each and every accounting transaction is to be treated. Although there are variations in both the approach and detail, Germany and France plus countries which have been influenced by these countries (for example, Poland, Greece and Algeria) are those where this approach is most notable. Its principal objective is to identify a *correctness* and *precision* to the financial accounting system. This contrasts sharply with the Anglo-American influence where there is a greater concern with the *overall view* conveyed by the financial statements. In such countries as the UK, the USA, Canada, Australia, New Zealand and the Netherlands, we are more likely to observe financial accounting following broad principles established with a higher degree of flexibility in the accounting treatment of individual elements. (There are, however, still considerable differences within this, or indeed any, broad approach.) As a result, in these countries the accounting profession has been historically more influential and active in the decisions over emerging contentions over accounting treatments. However, such differences are tending to narrow as a result of international regulation (see below).

The second major area of difference is frequently related to the first. This is the extent to which the published financial statements (the financial statements you are reading in the company annual reports you are collecting) are also used as the basis for *taxation*. Generally speaking, the national taxation authorities do not want a lot of flexibility in the calculations upon which they will base a company's tax assessment. In the UK, for example, this is overcome by having *two sets* of financial statements – one for publication under the Companies Acts and one upon which the revenue authorities can base their tax assessment. The first set are based on **generally accepted accounting principles** (referred to as **GAAP** – the combination of law, accounting standards and locally accepted accounting practices) whilst the second are based on strict regulations agreed with the taxation authorities. Other countries (to a lesser and lesser extent because of the difficulties of giving a sensible financial view of the company by following strict taxation rules), prefer to have a single set of financial statements that will serve both purposes.

These two principles – *(i) correctness and accuracy* versus *a 'true and fair view'* (see below) and *(ii) taxation accounts* versus *financial statements for investors* – present enormous problems when it comes to trying to pull together accounting on the international stage.

(b) Differences in detailed treatment and disclosure between countries

The next problem that arises is to do with the principles that different countries adopt in their more detailed regulations. A transnational corporation (hereafter, TNC, which is a very large group of companies with common ownership and with operations across several countries), for example, might be required to use a LIFO method of inventory valuation in one country but a FIFO basis in another. Some countries will permit some things to be capitalized (do you remember that this means to 'make into an asset rather than record as an expense'?), which other countries will not. Countries differ in their concerns over things like intangible assets and some countries, most notably the USA, have relatively detailed regulations over all manner of accounting issues with which other countries have not yet concerned themselves.

The result of all this is that an exactly identical company can report massively different profit (or loss) figures in different countries. This raises problems for international investors who have difficulty making sensible comparisons between (say) a Greek company and a New Zealand company.[1] It also raises problems for the TNCs which find they have to account for similar transactions in different ways in different countries and, similarly, for the international firms of accountants that have to audit (see below) similar transactions treated in significantly different ways.[2]

There have been two major consequences to these areas of difference. The first is that some countries require companies to provide a schedule explaining and reconciling the differences between accounting numbers calculated in different countries. (If any of your financial statements relates to a TNC you may see just such a document included at the back of the Annual Report.) The second major consequence has been the attempts to *harmonize* accounting practices between countries.

(c) Harmonizing and reconciling country differences

Two major illustrations of this 'bringing together' of different financial statements will suffice. Probably the most important is that of the International Accounting Standards Committee (IASC). Based in London, this body represents accountancy professions around the world and produces **accounting standards** which it hopes will be acceptable – and thus adopted – by nations around the world. The IASC is dominated by the Anglo-American countries and so it is an attempt to bring nations into line with this broad approach to accounting regulation. Generally speaking, national accounting standards are supposed to fall into line with International Accounting Standards (IAS). The Committee has had some success in harmonizing accounting practice and its approach has had one major consequence. That is, smaller nations which have no well-developed accountancy profession – or, at least, no major accounting standard-setting process – are encouraged to adopt IAS as their own national accounting standards. For better or worse, this brings an increasing number of nations into line with (principally) Anglo-American ways of thinking about and doing financial accounting.[3] The Committee has produced standards on a whole raft of accounting treatment and disclosure issues including: stocks and inventory; depreciation; gains and losses on foreign currency transactions; and goodwill; as well as a requirement that companies should disclose accounting policies it has used in compiling its financial statements.

The second illustration of international harmonization relates to the European Union (EU) which has been attempting for many years to formalize accounting regulations for all its member states. Its principal mechanism for moving nation states in this direction is the *accounting directive*. These directives are issued from time to time to deal with, often major, aspects of accounting practice in the different countries. After long debate (and dispute) the EU will issue a directive concerning (for example) the treatment of groups of companies in financial statements and each of the nation states will attempt (it is hoped) to introduce the directive into its own accounting regulations in order to bring its accounting practices more into line with the rest of the community. The EU has had varying degrees of success here, and whilst there has certainly been an increase in the areas of agreement, one of the major consequences has been a greater awareness of the different European accounting traditions throughout the Union.

It is also important to note that as this book was being written the EU has proposed that by 2005 all member states should have adopted IAS. Proposals about how to do this politically and technically difficult task are likely to emerge in the accounting press as your studies proceed. Here is yet another reason to read the accounting press in order to keep up to date with the development of accounting practice!

With this background, we can now turn and have a somewhat more detailed look at the sorts of things with which accounting regulations will be concerned.

14.3 INTRODUCTION TO COMPANY LAW AND THE FORMAT OF COMPANY ACCOUNTS

You are very likely to be currently studying (or will study in the near future) company law in some depth. In this section we will restrict ourselves to an overview of the major accounting elements that you will find in most company law. Whilst we will keep things very general, there will be an inevitable, if slight, bias towards UK law. *Whatever* country you are based in you should ensure that have a copy of the latest Companies Acts which you can consult as we progress through this section. Figure 14.3 indicates some of the matters that you can expect to find covered in company law.

i	Definition and types of company.
ii	How companies are to be formed.
iii	The types of shares that a company may issue and the rules governing their issuance.
iv	The rights and duties of directors.
v	Accounting principles and the format of company accounts.
vi	The records that companies must keep and 'file'.
vii	The audit of company accounts.

Figure 14.3 Some issues likely to be covered by a Companies Act

In the following subsection we will first have a brief look at the legislation governing the company as an organization before moving on to look at the requirements governing the profit and loss account and balance sheet.

14.3.1 Organizational requirements of company law

As you now know, a company is a legally defined entity, distinct from those who own it (the **shareholders**) and from those with the responsibility for running and managing it (the **directors**). As we saw in Chapter 12, the ownership claims of a company are represented by shares (often called equity), and there must be a minimum of two shareholders, although there is no legal maximum. You will also recall that it is legally possible for the shareholders, the directors and the employees to be the same people but (with minor exceptions) a Companies Act will not recognize this. The company, its owners and managers are separate organizational systems in the eyes of the law.

For our purposes we need to distinguish between **private companies** ('Ltd' in the UK for example) and **public companies** ('plc' in the UK for example). The principal distinguishing characteristics are usually that a *public company*: must be of a certain minimum size (as measured by the size of its share capital, which usually has to exceed a certain minimum before it could be a public company); its shares are freely transferable (i.e. they may be quoted and traded on the stock exchange); and the rules governing its share capital are rather onerous. On the other hand, a *private company* is cheaper and easier to form but its shares cannot be freely traded.

In addition, you will remember that most companies, both public *and* private, enjoy what is called **limited liability**. This means that the liability of the owners is limited to the amount of their investment in the company. Thus, crudely speaking, if the debts of a company exceed its ability to pay (thus forcing the company into liquidation) the shareholders stand to lose the whole of their investment plus any amounts they still owe on the shares, *but no more*. In contrast, the sole trade, or the partners of a partnership, can be required to make good *personally* any deficit of their businesses. This will not normally happen with the owners of a company. The very great number of additional rules (not least relating to accounting) with which limited companies (both public and private) have to comply can be considered to be the cost of the privilege of limited liability.

14.3.2 Accounting requirements of company law

From the accounting point of view, the most important requirement of the Companies Acts will usually relate to the duty of the directors of the company to prepare annually a set of financial statements. These financial statements will probably be required to meet certain criteria. In the UK, amongst the most important of these criteria are (a) that the statements show a *true and fair view* of the company and (b) they must be audited and (c) presented to the shareholders at the annual general meeting. (The 'true and fair view' and auditing requirements are touched upon in section 14.3.7 below.) It will usually be laid down in the law that the accounts must be made available to all shareholders and debenture holders and they must be 'filed' in some public place – such as with a registrar of companies.[4]

A Companies Act will also usually outline what is required in a set of company financial statements. This typically comprises:

● the company's balance sheet

- the company's profit and loss account
- notes to the accounts and supplementary statements
- the directors' report
- the auditors' report
- the group accounts (where appropriate). (**NB** Whilst group accounts will be touched upon here and there, their serious study lies beyond the scope of this book.)

We will deal with these in the following subsections.

14.3.3 The profit and loss account, balance sheet and additional information

The profit and loss account and the balance sheet contain the bulk of the publicly available financial information about a company. We should note that as a company is usually required to disclose quite a lot of information about its financial position and activities for the year, these two financial statements could become confusing in their detail. It is therefore more common for the profit and loss account and balance sheet to contain only the bare bones which are fleshed out by what are called the **notes to the accounts**. (Consult your own library of company financial statements where you will observe, typically, several pages of these notes giving more detail on a whole range of accounting matters. See, also, below.)

The Act is then likely to go on to establish the detailed information it expects in a set of financial statements and the categories of information that a company must provide. The *balance sheet* will normally show the following principal categories:

- fixed assets
- current assets
- current liabilities
- long-term loans
- owners' claims

and will very probably specify the subcategories of information it requires within these broad headings as well as any additional accounting information required. The requirements governing the *profit and loss account* will similarly outline the basic categories of information with which you are now familiar:

- turnover, i.e., for example, revenue from sales or fee income
- cost of sales
- gross profit
- other expenses and income
- tax on the profits
- net profit after tax
- amount available for reserves and dividends (detail on such movements will normally be shown in the notes to the accounts)

plus other additional items such as *extraordinary items* or *group and/or associated companies*. (We have met neither of these yet.)

In addition, the Companies Act may very well lay down requirements for *additional information* which is required to be presented with the profit and loss account and balance sheet. We have already briefly mentioned the *notes to the accounts* which can normally be expected to cover such matters as:

- a statement of the policies used in preparation of the financial statements (e.g. the rates of depreciation and the method of stock valuation)
- purchases and sales of fixed assets
- information about employees and their remuneration
- information about directors and their remuneration
- movements on reserves and dividends
- additional data about elements in the profit and loss account and balance sheet.

Finally, it is not uncommon for company law (or other elements of the regulatory framework – see below) to require *additional information or supplementary financial statements*. You will no doubt study these as they apply to your own situation as your studies progress. Suffice it say for now, that the most common of these supplementary statements is one which attempts to explain the cash movements and/or liquidity of the company. Such statements, often called a *cash flow statement* will be dealt with in some detail in Chapter 15.

So, although company law varies greatly from country to country (and changes over time) we can usually expect it to provide a fairly detailed framework within which companies are required to formulate the basic accounting information which will form the basis of their financial statements. But before going on to look at other aspects of company law – especially that related to the directors' report and to the auditor – experience tells us that we should take just a brief moment out to explain where this all fits in relation to the earlier chapters.

14.3.4 Disclosure as opposed to accounting

Throughout this book, so far, we have taken a sort of 'bottom-up' approach. That is, we started with an accounting entity, identified and captured its accounting transactions, recorded them and then summarized them in an initial trial balance. At each stage we were building towards a set of financial statements. To make the final step, we took the initial trial balance and put through a series of end-of-period adjustments which provided us with the numbers which were then used to construct our profit and loss account and balance sheet. We had to take a series of decisions along the way – how to depreciate fixed assets, how to value stock, and so on. This chapter is principally about the sources which influenced those decisions. We are now in the process of introducing the framework within which we were (implicitly) working in the earlier chapters.

We are thus working, now, in a sort of 'top-down' way. We are now looking at what the final outcome of the process should be – the regulated financial statements – and this will enable us to look back at each of the stages we have been through in the first 13 chapters.

This framework, as we have now seen, determines: that the financial statements must be produced; who they are for; how individual items should be *treated*; and, finally, what information should be *disclosed* in the financial statements. That is, not all the information in all the categories we used in our bookkeeping and end-of-period adjustments will necessarily appear in the published financial statements. The company may very well have a very detailed final trial balance but, because of the rules governing financial reporting, it will simplify this information, aggregating it into specific categories. So, there is actually less information (and certainly less detail) contained in a profit and loss account and balance sheet than will normally be contained in the final trial balance. Thus as well as learning about *accounting treatment decisions* we have to learn about *disclosure decisions*.

Disclosure will govern *how* the company *shows* the information, *what* information it has to show and what *additional information* a company annual report should contain.

Why this should be the case, why a company does not simply publish all the detailed information it used when doing the accounting and producing the final trial balance, is something we will look at briefly in Chapter 18. The situation is a great deal more systematic in countries which follow the *plan comptable général* we discussed above. In countries which follow the Anglo-American model of financial reporting, students have to keep in mind the treatment *and* the disclosure rules whilst assembling financial statements. This inevitably causes confusion. However, take heart. More experience with practice will, eventually, make all this seem second nature to you.

14.3.5 A brief review of a set of published financial statements

The best way to illustrate what we have covered so far is to examine an actual set of reported financial statements. If you have been following our advice and referring to financial statements as you have gone along, this section will only be revision. Figure 14.4 shows the profit and loss account and balance sheet from a medium-sized UK company from 1999. It is an example of a relatively straightforward profit and loss account and balance sheet and is shown for illustration only – it must not be treated as an up-to-date *pro-forma* to guide you in an understanding of current accounting regulations. In addition, we shall only examine its main features, rather than all the detail it contains.

The immediate things to notice are that the profit and loss account and balance sheet specify the dates at which the financial statements have been drawn up – the *accounting dates* at the end of the *accounting periods*. You will notice that the company has also reported the previous accounting period's figures. This is normal. You will also note that the balance sheet is signed by two of the directors, emphasizing that it is the directors' duty to prepare and report these financial statements. In addition, the date at which these statements were signed is noted. This is a couple of months after the year end – it takes some time to finalize the accounts and to have them audited.

The profit and loss account should look fairly familiar to you. It lays out the principal categories of financial information with which we have been working throughout the book. Against each item is a *note* number where further data on this item – in accordance with the regulatory framework – are shown. Two matters are briefly worth drawing your attention to. First, all the expenses of the business are aggregated under the heading 'costs'. This differs from what we have been doing to date. This profit and loss account does not list all the categories with which we were concerned when doing the bookkeeping – heating and lighting, wages, depreciation, etc. are all lumped together in the one figure (the notes to the accounts provide a little more detail on *some* of these costs). The second issue to bring to your attention is the special column in the accounts for exceptional items. You have not met these yet and we will touch upon them briefly in subsection 14.4.2(a).

The balance sheet similarly has the major categories with which you are familiar and also shows the *comparative figures* for the previous accounting period. You will notice that creditors are split between 'amounts falling due within one year' (short-term liabilities like trade creditors) and 'amounts falling due after more than one year' (longer-term liabilities). Also, the company has not used the phrase 'represented by' to cover the shareholders' funds but has simply referred to them as 'capital and reserves'. Such relatively minor details may well be covered by the extant company law and one of the less enviable jobs of the accountant is to monitor yearly developments in how the company's financial statements should be laid out.

You should now be in a position to make reasonable sense of the central financial statements of a simple company – and, indeed, to make reasonable headway with more complex companies. We now turn and look at some of the other information contained in a company's annual report which we, as accountants, must know about.

14.3.6 Directors and the directors' report

The directors are the legal managers of the company. They are appointed by the shareholders as the 'trustees' of the company's resources and are accountable to the shareholders for their stewardship. The financial statements are the principal means by which the directors discharge this accountability – the means by which they tell the shareholders what they have done with their funds. In the process of managing the organization's resources, the directors must also ensure that company law is complied with in its entirety. This means that as well as fulfilling the responsibility to prepare, present and file the annual financial statement, the directors will probably be also required to (*inter alia*):

Group profit and loss account
For the Year ended 31 December 1999

	Notes	1999 £m Before Exceptional Items	1999 £m Exceptional Items	1999 £m Total	1998 £m Before Exceptional Items	1998 £m Exceptional Items	1998 £m Total As restated
Turnover							
Baird Brands – ongoing		311.3		311.3	316.2		316.2
Baird Brands – acquisitions		22.6		22.6	–		–
		333.9		333.9	316.2		316.2
Baird Clothing – to be discontinued		163.7		163.7	214.3		214.3
	2	497.6		497.6	530.5		530.5
Costs	3,4	(482.6)	(3.2)	(485.8)	(499.4)	(4.6)	(504.0)
Operating profit/(loss)							
Baird Brands – ongoing		20.8	(3.2)	17.6	24.2	(1.2)	23.0
Baird Brands – acquisitions		1.7	–	1.7	–	–	–
		22.5	(3.2)	19.3	24.2	(1.2)	23.0
Baird Clothing – to be discontinued		(7.5)	–	(7.5)	6.9	(3.4)	3.5
		15.0	(3.2)	11.8	31.1	(4.6)	26.5
Loss on termination of Baird Clothing operations							
Costs of closing Baird Clothing Division	4	–	(70.2)	(70.2)	–	–	–
Goodwill previously charged to reserves	4	–	(33.3)	(33.3)	–	–	–
		–	(103.5)	(103.5)	–	–	–
(Loss)/profit on ordinary activities before interest	2	15.0	(106.7)	(91.7)	31.1	(4.6)	26.5
Interest	5	(1.8)	–	(1.8)	(0.6)	–	(0.6)
(Loss)/profit on ordinary activities before taxation	5	13.2	(106.7)	(93.5)	30.5	(4.6)	25.9
Taxation	7	(4.0)	18.0	14.0	(9.5)	1.4	(8.1)
(Loss)/profit attributable to ordinary shareholders		9.2	(88.7)	(79.5)	21.0	(3.2)	17.8
Dividends	8			(6.1)			(12.3)
Retained (loss)/profit for the year	19			(85.6)			5.5
Earnings/(loss) per share – basic and diluted	9	7.9p		(68.1)p	18.0p		15.2p

→

Balance sheets
As at 31 December 1999

	Notes	Group 1999 £m	Group 1998 £m As restated	Company 1999 £m	Company 1998 £m
Fixed assets					
Intangible assets	10	8.5	–	–	–
Tangible assets	11	39.0	57.3	–	2.2
Investments	12	12.0	12.3	101.3	165.8
		59.5	69.6	101.3	168.0
Current assets					
Stocks	13	104.8	114.2	–	–
Debtors	14	58.1	50.7	25.2	54.3
Short term deposits		8.9	7.9	–	–
Cash at bank and in hand		7.1	9.3	9.4	–
		178.9	182.1	34.6	54.3
Creditors: amounts falling due within one year	15	(122.0)	(104.0)	(5.7)	(42.4)
Net current assets		56.9	78.1	28.9	11.9
Total assets less current liabilities		116.4	147.7	130.2	179.9
Creditors: amounts falling due after more than one year					
Other creditors	15	(3.7)	(2.5)	(26.6)	(30.0)
Provisions for liabilities and charges	16	(27.2)	(5.4)	–	–
		(30.9)	(7.9)	(26.6)	(30.0)
		85.5	139.8	103.6	149.9
Capital and reserves					
Called up share capital	18	58.6	58.6	58.6	58.6
Share premium account	19	32.2	32.2	32.2	32.2
Revaluation reserve	19	12.8	12.8	–	–
Merger reserve	19	–	–	–	37.8
Profit and loss account	19	(18.1)	36.2	12.8	21.3
		85.5	139.8	103.6	149.9

Signed on behalf of the Board
Sir David Cooksey
B M Hynes
28 February 2000

Extracted from the accounts of William Baird plc for the year ended 31 December 1999

Figure 14.4 A published profit and loss account and balance sheet.

i   arrange for an *annual general meeting* of the shareholders;
ii   keep proper *accounting records* and the other *statutory registers*;
iii make the appropriate *annual returns*;
iv   ensure that the activities of the company do not contravene any *provisions of the Companies Act*, such as the rules governing the distribution of profits or the issuance of shares; and
v   ensure that the company remains within the terms of its *memorandum and articles of association*.

These terms require a little explanation. Company law usually requires that every company must hold an **annual general meeting** (AGM). Notice of this meeting must usually be provided to all shareholders so that they (basically) may exercise their right to vote on such matters as the appointment, removal and remuneration of directors and the appointment and removal of auditors (see below), and (again generally speaking) for the shareholders to receive, question and accept or reject the financial accounts. The principle behind the AGM is to ensure democratic control of the company by the shareholders. However, shareholders rarely attend AGMs and they tend to pass their rights to vote to the directors via a proxy. Thus, whilst legally the shareholders control the company and such important matters as appointing the auditors (see below), it frequently transpires in practice that through the trust (warranted or misplaced), laziness, ignorance, indifference or perhaps infirmity of shareholders, the directors have effective control of the company.

Company law will also usually require that the *accounting records* must be sufficient to show the financial position of the company at any time and to enable the directors to ensure that the annual financial statements comply with the law. In the UK, for example, these accounting records must include what amounts to:

- a detailed cashbook/cash account;
- a record of the company's assets and liabilities;
- a record of sales and purchases;
- a record of stock and annual stock counts.

The directors' responsibility to maintain the *statutory registers* extends to including the requirement that they must also be available for *public* inspection. They also have the annual responsibility of filing the *statutory returns* with a registrar of companies (or equivalent). These are filed with the financial statements and are available for inspection by the public. The whole process is intended to ensure that we should all be able to find out a substantial amount of information about companies should we wish. (The records to which this relates are shown in Figure 14.5.)

Finally, for our present purposes, the directors also have the duty of maintaining and abiding by the **Memorandum and Articles of Association**. These documents, which are drawn up when the company is formed, are, in effect, the company's constitution. They lay

---

Statutory registers:

(i)   the names and addresses of the members;

(ii) the number of shares held by each member;

(iii) the names, addresses and *occupations* of the directors and the company secretary(ies);

(iv) the register of charges;

(v)   the directors' interests in (i.e. holdings of, directly or indirectly) the shares and debentures of the company;

(vi) the minute book (of board meetings mainly, and which is *not* available for public inspection).

Statutory returns:

(i)   changes in shareholders during the year;

(ii) transfers of shares and details of share capital;

(iii) address of the company's registered office;

(iv) all charges (i.e. secured debentures and mortgages);

(v)   details of the directors and the company secretary.

Figure 14.5 Statutory records maintained by UK directors

down the rules governing the company's relationships with the 'outside world' (the Memorandum) and those which govern the internal relationships of the participants (the Articles). Probably the most important part of the Memorandum is the *objects clause* which sets out the intentions of the company in terms of what activities the company (and thus the board of directors) is allowed to undertake. Actions by the company outside this objects clause are known as *ultra vires*, i.e. beyond the legitimate right of the company (directors) to undertake. The articles cover, *inter alia*, the rules governing the rights of the shareholders towards each other, the rules about shares and how much the company can borrow.

The critical importance placed on the role of the directors by company law is emphasized by a typical requirement that every company must include within its financial statements a **directors' report**. Although the directors' report may also include a 'review of operations' (usually a review of achievements of the company and its products which tends to emphasise the public relations role – and value – of the financial statements), Figure 14.6 indicates the sorts of things that might be covered in a UK company report. (The directors' report is an area which varies considerable from country to country.)

This list not only indicates the range of the directors' responsibilities but also gives some indication of the growth in information required of a company – in the UK much of it is non-financial and related to employees. Such matters concern accountants both in their role as general reporting agents (see Chapter 18) and, more prosaically, because the directors' report falls within the scope of the duties of the *auditor*. These are covered in the next section.

(i) A review of the business for the year.

(ii) The recommended dividend for the year.

(iii) The proposed transfer to reserves.

(iv) The names of the directors.

(v) The principal activities of the company.

(vi) Significant changes in fixed assets in the year.

(vii) An indication of the difference between the market value and the book value of the company's land and buildings.

(viii) Details of any important events that have occurred since the year-end.

(ix) An indication of likely future developments.

(x) An indication of research and development activities.

(xi) Directors' interests in shares and debentures.

(xii) Political and charitable donations by the company.

(xiii) Details of any transactions in which the company has purchased or assisted in purchasing its own shares.

(xiv) Details of the employment of disabled persons.

(xv) Details of total employees and information on the extent to which effort is made to involve the employees in the activities of the company.

(xvi) Details of the employees' health, safety and welfare at work.

Figure 14.6 The contents of a UK company directors' report

14.3.7 The auditor and the company

When we talk of the **auditor**, we are usually referring to a firm of accountants. Within that firm, there will probably be one partner who will eventually *sign off* the financial statements each accounting period on behalf of the partnership, but the work will have mainly been done by the trainees and junior members of the firm.

Auditors provides the critical link in the information chain between the company and the directors on the one hand and the shareholders and other readers of financial statements on the other. The directors, as we now know, must provide an account of their actions (the financial statements) to the shareholders. If the information contained in these statements is to be more reliable than (say) advertising, then somebody must *attest* to its correspondence with the actual events it purports to describe. This is the task of the auditor.

The **statutory audit**[5] is an *independent* attestation that the financial statement show (for example in the UK) a 'true and fair view' and comply with the current Companies Act(s). The auditor *does not prepare* the financial accounts – that is the duty of the directors. The auditor simply *expresses an opinion* upon them.

The auditor must normally be a member of one or more of the professional bodies of accountants which are specified in the country's company law as authorised to undertake such audits. (Refer to the Companies Acts in your own country to establish which these are.) The law will also, usually, specify that the auditor *must not* be an officer or servant of the company, be in the employ or a partner of anyone who is an officer or servant of the company, or be a body corporate (typically a company).

The law will usually further provide that the auditor shall be appointed by the shareholders at *each* AGM where his or her remuneration is fixed. He or she will usually be permitted to attend and speak at the AGM and particular provisions are typically laid down by the law for the auditor to contest his or her removal by the directors.

The auditor must provide an *auditor's report to the members*, the contents of which are usually governed by a combination of sections of the Companies Act(s) and pronouncements from the professional accountancy bodies. Figure 14.7 illustrates what such a report might look like. You should also consult your own library of financial statements for other examples. Let us briefly examine this report, point by point.

The auditor's report is addressed to the 'members' (that is, the shareholders) of Bunzl plc. It specifies what has been audited (the financial statements – i.e. the profit and loss account, the balance sheet and the cash flow statement) and makes this doubly clear by giving the page numbers on which these statements (and the notes relating to these statements) may be found in the annual report and accounts package.

In the first paragraph, the report emphasizes that financial statement preparation is the responsibility of the directors and that the auditor's responsibility is to express an opinion on these statements. This statement (and several others in the report) is made to make sure that readers of the audit report know how the company–auditors relationship operates. There is often confusion in the minds of 'laypeople' about the function of the audit report and the role of the auditors (this will be covered later in your studies) – hence this seemingly self-evident statement (it was self-evident to you?).

The next paragraph explains, briefly, what the auditors are going to state an opinion on. This, they hope, makes the *scope* of the audit report clear to readers.

The third paragraph refers to the 'combined code' – this relates to a set of standards regarding corporate governance. This part of the auditor's report is fairly recent. The relevance of this observation is to reinforce in your minds the fact that as accountancy

---

Auditors' report

To the members of Bunzl plc
We have audited the financial statements on pages 4 to 27.

Respective responsibilities of directors and auditors
The directors are responsible for preparing the annual report and accounts. As described above, this includes responsibility for preparing the financial statements in accordance with applicable United Kingdom law and accounting standards. Our responsibilities, as independent auditors, are established in the United Kingdom by statute, the Auditing Practices Board, the Listing Rules of the London Stock Exchange and by our profession's ethical guidance.

We report to you our opinion as to whether the financial statements give a true and fair view and are properly prepared in accordance with the Companies Act 1985. We also report to you if, in our opinion, the Directors' Report is not consistent with the financial statements, if the Company has not kept proper accounting records, if we have not received all the information and explanations we require for our audit or if information specified by law or the Listing Rules regarding directors' remuneration and transactions with the Group is not disclosed.

We review whether the statements on pages 2 and 3 reflect the Company's compliance with the seven provisions of the Combined Code specified for our review by the London Stock Exchange, and we report if it does not. We are not required to consider whether the Board's statements on internal control cover all risks and controls, or form an opinion on the effectiveness of the Group's corporate governance procedures or its risk and control procedures.

We read the other information contained in the annual report and accounts, including the corporate governance statement, and consider whether it is consistent with the audited financial statements. We consider the implications for our report if we become aware of any apparent misstatements or material inconsistencies with the financial statements.

Basis of audit opinion
We conducted our audit in accordance with Auditing Standards issued by the Auditing Practices Board. An audit includes examination, on a test basis, of evidence relevant to the amounts and disclosures in the financial statements. It also includes an assessment of the significant estimates and judgements made by the directors in the preparation of the financial statements and of whether the accounting policies are appropriate to the Group's circumstances, consistently applied and adequately disclosed.

We planned and performed our audit so as to obtain all the information and explanations which we considered necessary in order to provide us with sufficient evidence to give reasonable assurance that the financial statements are free from material misstatement, whether caused by fraud or other irregularity or error. In forming our opinion we also evaluated the overall adequacy of the presentation of information in the financial statements.

Opinion
In our opinion the financial statements give a true and fair view of the state of affairs of the Company and the Group as at 31 December 1999 and of the profit of the Group for the year then ended and have been properly prepared in accordance with the Companies Act 1985.

KPMG Audit Plc
Chartered Accountants
Registered Auditor
London
28 February 2000

Extracted from the accounts of Bunzl plc for the year ended 31 December 1999

Figure 14.7 A sample audit report

practice changes over time, so you too will need to keep up to date with these changes. You should expect to add to and amend your accounting knowledge over time. The issue of corporate governance is one which you will cover in more detail later in your degree course.

The fourth paragraph notes that the auditor has read other information contained in the annual report package (outside of the pages they specify that they have audited) and that this information does not contradict the financial statements. What this does not imply, however, is that the information outside of the pages specified are 'true and fair' in the same way as the financial accounts are.

The next two paragraphs give the 'basis of the audit opinion' which provides information about the standards used by the auditors (as specified by the Audit Practices Board) and a very general outline of how they conducted the audit. This paragraph makes reference to *generally accepted auditing* standards which are issued in many countries to guide auditors as to best practice in auditing.

Finally, the auditors express their opinion. In this case (because the report is for a UK company) the auditors express an opinion as to whether the accounts show a *true and fair view*. If, for example, the audit report had been for a US company the opinion would be based on whether the financial statements *present fairly* the underlying economic activity of the company and that they are in accordance with GAAP (which will usually include all of the elements we spoke about in Figure 14.2 above). Both 'true and fair view' and 'present fairly' are general terms and are not tightly defined, but they probably mean something like 'the accounts are a reasonable representation of the economic events underlying the accounting entity'. You will examine this issue in more detail later in your studies.

The auditors then sign and date the report.

Such a process should allow the shareholders (and other readers of the financial statements) to treat the information presented in those statements as reasonably reliable. That is, that the directors are, more or less, telling the truth (in so far as this is possible with accounting information) and are acting lawfully and competently. How reliable and useful such opinions are is a question which you should ask yourself. If you are reading the professional accountancy press you will be aware of an increasing questioning of the auditors' reliability and independence. This is a major issue you will also study in more depth later in your course.

This brings us to the end of our brief look at company law. We now turn to look at the activities of the accounting professions themselves in regulating company reporting.

14.4 PRONOUNCEMENTS BY THE PROFESSIONAL ACCOUNTANCY BODIES

14.4.1 Background to accounting standards

Company law, incorporating and developing the accounting conventions as it does, provides the main structure for financial accounting and reporting by companies. Yet, despite the steady development and refinement of the accounting requirements of company law over the years, there still remain conflicts and disagreements over how to account properly for particular activities and over what information should be shown in the financial statements of companies. Professional pronouncements represent a major influence in the development of company law as well as a significant attempt both to systematize financial reporting and to solve outstanding conflicts and disagreements.

Accounting standards is a broad term covering a range of authoritative pronouncements from the professional accountancy bodies. They tend to be more important in the regulatory framework in the Anglo-American countries where areas of difference in accounting practices and an emphasis on self-regulation by the profession are more accepted. The USA, Canada, the UK, Australia and New Zealand, for example, all have an extensive code of accounting standards formulated by their indigenous accounting bodies. You will come across references to, for example, Statements of Financial Accounting Standards (SFAS) and Opinions in the USA, and Statements of Standard

Accounting Practice (SSAPs), Statements of Recommended Accounting Practice (SORPs) and Financial Reporting Standards (FRS) in the UK. Each has different authority but all are presumed to represent elements of 'best practice' in accounting when they are issued. Most standards are issued after wide consultation with interested parties (including governments, the stock exchange, directors of companies and so on) and usually pass through an *exposure draft* stage when these interested parties are invited to comment on the potential standard. Increasingly, there is concern that the accountancy bodies do not have the authority (or independence) to be the sole arbiter of these important standards and so there has been a general trend towards providing government backing to the standard-setting process. To give you a flavour of the background to the accounting standards issue, Figure 14.8 provides a brief outline of the UK experience of formal accounting standard-setting.

In the UK, attempts by the accounting profession to purportedly systematize financial reporting by companies really date back to 1942. Between 1942 and 1969, the Institute of Chartered Accountants of England and Wales (ICAEW) issued *49 Recommendations on Accounting Principles* which were non-mandatory suggestions (cajolery if you like) as to how accountants might perhaps best deal with problem issues. By the late 1960s these *Recommendations* were increasingly recognized as insufficient and growing public discontent with the unreliability of the published financial statements of companies became too serious to ignore.

The issues which are usually assumed to have brought matters to a head were a series of financial 'scandals' during the later years of the 1960s.

(i)   A company called Rolls Razor Ltd collapsed in 1964 shortly after publishing a set of financial statements that failed to indicate that anything was wrong.

(ii) In 1967, GEC (now plc) was making a takeover bid for a company called AEI. AEI published a statement forecasting *profits* of £10m which GEC, after the takeover, announced should have been, in their view, a *loss* of £4.5m. The difference, they said, consisted of £5m of 'fact' and £9.5m of 'judgement'. The use of accounting principles was at the centre of the subsequent row.

(iii) The same problem arose in the Leasco-Pergamon takeover discussions. In 1968, a profit of £1.5m was reported by Pergamon and this figure was certified by a large firm of auditors. A subsequent audit by another large firm of auditors certified a £600,000 loss! (The takeover did not proceed.)

(iv) Finally, as if to rub salt into the wounds, Rolls-Royce Ltd went into liquidation in the early 1970s, leaving a great number of shareholders holding shares of negligible value and a set of financial statements that appeared to show a healthy company.

The response by the accounting profession and, in particular, by the ICAEW, was to create, in 1969, a new body – the Accounting Standards Steering Committee (later to be known as the **Accounting Standards Committee (ASC)** and later still the **Accounting Standards Board (ASB)**). The ICAEW issued a *Statement of Intent on Accounting Standards* in the 1970s which laid out their intentions to formulate and publish Accounting Standards which would:

(i)   narrow the areas of difference and variety of accounting practices;

(ii) require the disclosure, in financial statements, of the accounting bases employed in their construction;

(iii) require that departures from applicable accounting standards be disclosed and explained.

During the 1970s and 1980s the ASC issued over 20 SSAPs supported by over 40 (often contradictory) exposure drafts. In 1990, as result of increasing concern over the lack of coherence of the standards and their lack of legal status, the ASC was replaced by the Accounting Standards Board which was answerable to a government-appointed Financial Reporting Council. The ASB issued Financial Reporting Exposure Drafts (FREDs) and Financial Reporting Standards (FRSs) which slowly but surely replaced the SSAPs. Whilst the FRSs were perhaps more theoretically coherent they did not remove the conflict over accounting standards. If anything, the disagreements over the regulation of financial reporting between accountants, auditors, company directors and the users of financial statements have increased. In essence, the conflict arises from a lack of clarity over the central purpose of financial reporting and the role that accounting regulation should play. This is pretty fundamental but it is a conflict that the accounting professions seem unable to resolve.

Figure 14.8 A review of early UK experience with accounting standards

14.4.2 The subject coverage of accounting standards

We have already given a fair indication of the sorts of issues which give rise – in the profession's mind – to the need for an accounting standard. Figure 14.9 provides a further list of some of the topics on which accounting standards have been issued.

Whilst each standard will vary from country to country (and through time – see below), they will all follow broadly the same structure. That is, each standard will discuss why the need for guidance on this issue has arisen and what alternatives there are (or at least a selection of those alternatives) for both the treatment and the disclosure relating to this item. The relative merits and demerits of each (as perceived by the professional accountancy body) will be reviewed and then the standard will state its preferred method of treatment of this item in company accounts (e.g. LIFO or FIFO for stock or inventory; straight-line or reducing-balance depreciation; whether research and development expenditure should be treated as an expense of the period or carried forward as an asset to be matched against the income from the future periods in which the benefits from the innovation are generated). The standard will also suggest what disclosure, if any, should be made by companies on this issue.

Most of the issues shown in Figure 14.9 are ones upon which you will spend considerable time later in your studies. Two of the issues are ones on which we concentrated in earlier chapters of the book – depreciation and the valuation of inventory. (You may also notice that issues on which we spent time – accruals and prepayments and bad and doubtful debts are not covered by standards – presumably because they have not arisen as publicly contentious issues.) In addition, we will spend time on funds and/or cash flow in Chapter 15, and, in Chapter 16, we will briefly review the issues associated with accounting for changing prices and inflation. So, by the time we reach the end of this book you will have some knowledge of some of the issues arising with accounting standards.

- disclosure of accounting policies
- mergers, acquisitions and goodwill
- groups of companies
- exceptional and extraordinary items
- stock and inventory
- depreciation (including that on land and building and on properties held for resale)
- inflation and changing prices
- taxation
- research and development expenditure
- treatment of foreign currency transactions
- contingencies and contingent liabilities
- leases and hire purchase contracts
- pension fund contributions
- statements of funds or cash flow
- specialist topics for particular industries (e.g. oil and gas accounting or charities)
- changes in accounting figures as a result of changing policies or new information
- financial investments/assets

Figure 14.9 An illustrative list of some topics covered by accounting standards

There are, however, two issues on which we should just spend a moment or two at this stage – those relating to exceptional and extraordinary items and those relating to the disclosure of accounting policies.

(a) Exceptional and extraordinary items

Exceptional and/or extraordinary items crop up frequently in accounting and, although the terminology used for them changes – as do the views on how they should be treated – they are important enough to deserve a moment's attention here. Whilst there *is* some confusion over the *precise* purpose of the profit and loss account and balance sheet (see Chapter 18), there is a widely held view that the profit should distinguish between the organization's *normal* and *abnormal* activities. Let us suppose that buying and selling goods are the organization's normal activities on which it makes profits and losses. But every now and then, along will come an abnormal event – a factory may burn down, the company's main supplier may be in a country which is suddenly war-torn, there may be a major strike by the workforce or there may be a drastic change in government policy which affects the company. These are not really part of the *normal operating profits and losses* of the entity and to include them within normal profits and losses might be to send a misleading signal to the readers of the financial statements. Therefore, in one way or another, it is usual for financial statements to *separately identify and disclose* the financial implications of these *abnormal events*. These events may be called *exceptional* or *extraordinary* events, they may have a different name, and their definition will frequently vary through time and across countries, but the central principle will remain – they are issues outside the normal business of the company. (You will find exceptional items in Figure 14.4 which arise from costs incurred in reorganization and restructuring of the business.)

(b) Disclosure of accounting policies

In virtually all cases where accounting standards have been issued, there will be at least one standard which lays down and codifies the basic principles on which financial accounting statements are constructed. For example, in the UK the (then) Accounting Standards Steering Committee first issued SSAP2 *Disclosure of Accounting Policies* in 1971. This specified that there were four fundamental accounting concepts which financial statements must follow. These were the *going concern concept,* the *consistency concept*, the *accruals concept and matching principle* and the *prudence or conservatism principle*. (You will recall we met each of these in Chapter 7.) The standard then went on to require that companies disclose the detail of the accounting policies they have adopted in the compilation of their financial statements. An example from a British company is shown in Figure 14.10.[6]

Each standard-setting body has issued something similar to the UK SSAP2 but, as time has gone on and financial accounting has become more complicated, it has been found that this simple statement of principles is insufficient to guide the production of accounting standards. Indeed, increasingly, accounting standards are found to be inconsistent, to be insufficiently flexible to deal with new changes and/or not to be prescriptive enough to keep company accounts comparable. To a disturbing degree, accounting standard-setting bodies have to withdraw standards and issue new ones. Often the treatment and disclosure required in the first standard is completely different from that required in the subsequent standard. This sort of thing doesn't have to go on for long before accounting regulation and

Notes to the accounts

1 Accounting policies

The accounts have been prepared in compliance with applicable accounting standards and under the historical cost convention, modified by the revaluation of certain fixed assets.

Adoption of FRS12 and prior year adjustments

As a result of the introduction of FRS12 – "Provisions, Contingent Liabilities and Contingent Assets", a full review of the actual and potential liabilities of the Group was carried out following which a prior year adjustment of £1.7 million was made mainly in respect of onerous property contracts. The profit and loss account and the balance sheet prior year comparatives have been restated to recognise the change in accounting policy. The impact on the profit and loss account for 1998 and 1999 is not material.

Financial instruments

In this year's accounts, the Group has adopted FRS13 – "Derivatives and Other Financial Instruments: Disclosures".

The Group uses financial instruments, in particular forward currency contracts and currency swaps, to manage the financial risks associated with the Group's underlying business activities and the financing of those activities. The Group does not undertake any trading activity in financial instruments.

A discussion of how the Group manages its financial risks in included in the Financial Review on pages 16 and 17. The Group has taken advantage of the exemption available for short term debtors and creditors.

Basis of consolidation

The Group accounts include those of the Company and its subsidiary undertakings prepared to 31 December. The Group profit and loss account includes the results of subsidiary undertakings acquired from the effective date of acquisition. No profit and loss account is presented for the Company as permitted by S230(3) of the Companies Act 1985.

Goodwill

Goodwill arising on acquisitions prior to 31 December 1998 was set off directly against reserves. Goodwill previously eliminated against reserves was not reinstated on implementation of FRS10. Goodwill arising on acquisitions from 1 January 1999 has been capitalised, classified as an asset on the balance sheet and amortised on a straight line basis over its useful economic life. If a subsidiary or business is subsequently sold or closed, any goodwill arising on acquisition that was written off directly to reserves, or that has not been amortised through the profit and loss account, is taken into account in determining the profit or loss on sale or closure.

Fixed asset investments

Fixed asset investments are initially recorded at cost. The investments, other than own shares, are subsequently carried at directors' valuation with any revaluation surplus being taken to the revaluation reserve.

Turnover

Group turnover represents sales of goods and services, excluding value added tax, by Group undertakings to outside customers.

Taxation

The taxation charge is based on the profit for the year and includes deferred taxation provided on the liability method for those timing differences which are expected to reverse in the future without being replaced, calculated at the rate at which it is anticipated the timing differences will reverse.

Depreciation

Depreciation is not provided on freehold land. Provision for depreciation of other tangible fixed assets is made by allocating the cost or valuation of each asset over its anticipated life on a straight line basis. Depreciation is calculated as follows:

	% per annum
Freehold buildings	2 to 5
Leasehold properties	over the terms of leases
Plant and equipment	10 to 33

The carrying values of tangible fixed assets are reviewed for impairment when events or changes in circumstances indicate the carrying value may not be recoverable.

Stocks

Stocks are valued at the lower of cost, including an appropriate proportion of production overheads based on the normal level of activity, and net realisable value. Net realisable value is based on estimated selling price less further costs to be incurred to completion and disposal.

Operating Leases

Rentals paid under operating leases, with the exception of onerous leases, are charged to the profit and loss account on a straight line basis over the term of the lease.

Foreign currencies

Transactions in foreign currencies are recorded at the rate ruling at the date of the transaction or at the contracted rate if the transaction is covered by a forward exchange contract. Monetary assets and liabilities in foreign currencies are retranslated at the rate of exchange ruling at the balance sheet date or, if appropriate, at the forward exchange control rate. Resulting exchange gains and losses are taken to the profit and loss account.

In the Group accounts, the balance sheets of overseas subsidiary undertaking are translated at the rate of exchange ruling at the balance sheet date. Trading results are translated at the average rate of exchange for the year. The exchange differences resulting from the retranslation of the balance sheets of overseas subsidiary undertakings at closing rates, together with differences between the trading results translated at average rates and at closing rates, are dealt with in reserves.

Pensions

The Group operates a number of defined benefit pension schemes which generally require contributions to be made to separately administered funds. Contributions are charged to the profit and loss account so as to spread the cost over the employees' working lives. The regular cost is attributed to individual years using the projected unit credit method. Variations in pension cost identified as a result of actuarial valuations are amortised over the expected working lives of employees. Differences between the amounts funded and amounts charged to profit and loss account are shown in creditors or prepayments in the balance sheet.

The Group also operates a defined contribution scheme. Contributions are charged to the profit and loss account as they become payable in accordance with the rules of the scheme.

Extracted from the accounts of William Baird plc for the year ended 31 December 1999

Figure 14.10 Disclosure of accounting policies

the reporting in financial statements become something of a mess. This has led to more of the accounting bodies searching for what is known as *a conceptual framework for accounting* – a sort of theoretical code within which to set accounting standards. For reasons too complex to go into at this stage (but see Chapter 18 and Figure 14.11 for a brief introduction), this search for the *holy grail of accounting* has been largely an expensive failure. This need not necessarily be the case but it illustrates one point quite clearly – current accounting practice and current accounting standards are *never right*! There is *no* absolute 'right way' to do accounting – each accounting standard is a political choice made, one hopes, in the best interests of the affected parties in the light of the best information available at the time. (This is a rather optimistic view of what actually happens.) Figure 14.11 offers a brief review of some of these problems.

The disclosure of accounting policies is an important standard because it tries – at least – to clarify the accounting decisions that companies should make and to require information on those accounting decisions that companies *do* make. The disclosure of accounting policies will thus, as you can see in Figure 14.10, cover the choices that a company has made on many different aspects of the preparation of the financial statements – areas which are themselves almost certainly covered by other accounting standards. Subject to this statement and the disclosure of accounting policies in the financial statements, a reader of the financial statements can reasonably presume that a company has

The first problem – how to choose the best rules – is frequently identified as a problem which arises from the lack of a conceptual framework, i.e. a comprehensive theoretical structure which identifies the purposes and parameters of financial statements. This, it had been hoped in some quarters, would lead to accounting and accounting standards being less contentious and more consistent (unlike the present situation). No such framework exists despite laudable attempts in the UK, the USA and Canada. The problem is one of complex social choice involving conflict of views about the objectives of financial reporting, about who has rights to information, about what effects financial reporting has and thus which effects are 'good' and which are 'bad', and so on. (These matters are explored further in Chapter 18.)

The second problem – of obtaining agreement on the rules – follows from the first. Setting accounting standards (and also enacting law) is recognized as a complex political process the whole world over. Put crudely, if information is 'power' then reporting information moves power from one group to another. This might please the second group (e.g. shareholders) but is unlikely to meet the whole-hearted approval of the first (e.g. directors) – hence the argument.

As if this were not enough, just because rules exist does not mean that anybody will comply with them. In fact there is evidence to suggest that companies and auditors are a bit haphazard about ensuring that published financial statements are in compliance with all existing rules and, oddly, you might think, the professional bodies seem largely unconcerned with ensuring that their pronouncements are complied with (i.e. with 'policing the standards' – see, for example, Gray and Hope 1982).

The result of all this is that despite the plethora of rules from the law and the profession's attempts at self-regulation, whilst company reporting is much more systematic than 25 or 30 years ago, one could hardly call it coherent – or necessarily reliable. A hundred well-meaning and substantially honest accountants could still produce you 100 different profit/loss figures for the same company and all of them would be within the rules.

Figure 14.11 Some problems with regulating financial reporting

followed the 'best practice' laid down in all the other accounting standards as they apply to that company.

You will be studying this area and other aspects of accounting standards as your course progresses. You should also check in your professional accountancy magazine and follow the discussions about accounting standards and, in particular, the reports about old standards which are being withdrawn and the new standards which are being introduced. As we said much earlier in this chapter, accounting regulation is a growing and complex area – and if you wish to fully embrace your chosen profession you will need to stay abreast of all these developments.

14.5 OTHER REGULATIONS AND THE REGULATION OF NON-COMPANY ORGANIZATIONS

You have now seen enough to know that the regulation of company financial reporting is a complex matter. In addition to the broad principles we have outlined here, there will be the detail of the accounting regulation system in the specific country in which you are studying. In the USA this will be an immensely detailed and copious volume of regulation, in the UK, Australia and New Zealand, there is a middling amount of such detailed regulation whereas in some (so-called) developing or emerging nations the amount of detailed regulation will either be small or will comprise, more or less, the International Accounting Standards – perhaps adjusted for local conditions. In addition, each company has to be aware of such international regulation as affects it and, perhaps more importantly, to be conscious of the stock exchange requirements in the appropriate countries. One can easily imagine the complexity of the financial reporting process for a TNC which reports in 15 different countries!

Other, non-company, organizations do not generally speaking have their financial reporting so heavily regulated. The one exception here, perhaps, are the *banks* which are coming under ever-increasing scrutiny and which, whilst not automatically covered by company reporting regulations, are finding an increasing volume of financial accounting regulation heading in their direction. We have already mentioned sole traders and partnerships and recognized that they have a much lower burden placed on them in terms of accounting regulation but they too are assumed, under normal circumstances, to comply with accounting standards where appropriate. Non-commercial organizations – such as local government, charities, clubs, universities and so on, have historically had little direct regulation of the detail of their reporting practices but here again there is a trend towards increasing the regulation of these bodies' financial statements and, to a noticeable degree, they are also expected to comply with an increasing number of accounting standards – albeit ones suitably amended to reflect the differing circumstances of the non-commercial sector.

Thus, one can see an inexorable trend towards increasing regulation of financial reporting and, as a result, an increasing complexity of the financial statements. Whether this actually improves the situation and helps accounting better achieve its objectives (whatever they are – see Chapter 18) is a moot question. It all means, however, that even if all this increased regulation does not make society any better off, it *does* mean that your studying is more complex and there is more work for accountants to do. It is not immediately obvious that is an especially good thing.

SUMMARY

In the preceding 13 chapters, we met accounting regulation in a somewhat *ad hoc* manner. We identified areas where accounting decisions had to made – notably the end-of-period adjustments – and decided upon one or other approach in our construction of the appropriate financial statements. In this chapter we set about codifying those accounting decisions by recognizing the accounting regulatory regime within which all financial accounting and reporting takes place.

External reporting by organizations would, most likely, be a fairly random and haphazard phenomenon were it not governed by some sort of rules and regulations. Financial accounting by organizations, we have discovered, is governed by four broad categories of rules:

- convention
- law
- professional pronouncement
- other factors.

Both financial accounting and the rules governing its practice are, we also discovered, at their most developed when considered in the context of the company. (This goes some way towards explaining why the company has tended to dominate in this book and in many accounting textbooks is virtually the *only* form of organization to receive any attention.)

A constant problem with the study of financial accounting is the vast amount of institutional regulative material that one has to consider. The main danger is that one can easily lose sight of the wood because of the trees. That is, for example, arguing about whether a Companies Act treatment or the accounting standards treatment of overheads in stock is 'correct', is all very well for the prospective accountant but one should not lose sight of the rather more crucial questions such as whether or not it is 'correct' to be producing profit and loss accounts and balance sheets for shareholders in the first place.

Baxter (1982) warned of this with respect to accounting standards. There are so many of them that a course which just concentrated on the output of the accounting standard-setting body would be quite demanding enough. However, such a course could induce premature paralysis of the thinking organ because it could all too easily accept that what the accounting standards body issues *is* accounting and, by corollary, what the profession does not pronounce upon is not accounting. Had such a situation existed in Britain, for example, it might have led to the ridiculous situation that few financial accounting courses before 1973 would have considered 'inflation accounting', few before 1977 would have considered the issues of foreign currency, few before 1980 would have considered pension costs or leases and very few financial accounting courses would have considered either non-commercial organizations or social and environmental issues until very recently. Ridiculous, of course! Unfortunately, this is what actually seems to have happened. Hence our continual hectoring – accounting is too important to be left to accountants.

Nevertheless, we do need to know something of the rules and regulations governing the practice of financial accounting and this we have considered in this chapter. The rules are frequently clever, often contradictory, usually *ad hoc* and they are never right – they cannot be, can they? We concentrated upon the company. Company law lays down rules for (*inter alia*):

- the very existence of the organization
- the directors and their responsibilities
- the financial statements
- the auditors.

These are refined and developed by the accounting standards laid down, ostensibly, by the national and international accounting professions. Despite differences in ownership and objectives much of company accounting practice has become accepted, for better or for worse, as 'best accounting practice' for the non-commercial organization.

Key terms and concepts

The following key terms and concepts have featured in this chapter. You should ensure that you understand and can explain each one. Page references to definitions appear in the index in bold type.

- Accounting conventions
- Accounting regulation
- Accounting standard-setting body
- Accounting standards
- Accounts for taxation
- The audit report
- Company law
- Conceptual framework
- Directors
- The directors' report
- Disclosure of accounting policies
- EU accounting directives
- Exposure drafts
- Harmonization
- IASC
- The institutional framework for accounting regulation
- International Accounting Standards

- International differences
- Limited liability
- Memorandum and Articles of Association
- Non-company regulation
- Notes to the accounts
- *Plan comptable général*
- Private versus public companies company regulation
- Profit and loss account and balance sheet
- The statutory auditor
- Stock exchange regulation
- Treatment versus disclosure
- True and fair view

FURTHER READING

The most useful additional reading for this chapter is regular and careful reading of your professional accounting magazine. This will help you fill in the details of the material here and give you greater insight into the importance – and difficulty – of the whole area of accounting regulation. In addition you will have noticed a few references in the text at various points – follow these up if the topics to which they refer interest you. Your tutors can guide you to additional readings that relate to your own country. In the UK, useful material is provided in Carsberg and Hope's *Current Issues in Accounting* and in Taylor and Turley (1986). In addition, Roberts *et al.* (1998, and more current editions) provides an excellent guide to international accounting, whilst the issues arising with TNCs are examined with great care in Bailey *et al.* (1994a, b).

NOTES

1. It is not entirely clear why the accountancy profession should be greatly troubled by this problem, however.
2. One should, however, note that TNCs will frequently find these differences useful in that they can move transactions around between countries to exploit accounting differences to the benefit of their shareholders and management. Trying to control TNCs is becoming one of the biggest single issues the global economy faces and there is no sign, at present, of there being the will or the capacity to address this crucial issue sensibly. (See, for example, Bailey *et al.* 1994a, b).
3. There is a fairly widely held view that this constitutes a rather subtle form of economic imperialism by the 'developed' western capitalist nations – another issue which makes accounting so fascinating to study. But, again, a matter for later in your studies.
4. That is, in the UK, for example, the financial statements must be sent to Companies House in Cardiff, where the staff of the Registrar of Companies will file them and where they are available for inspection by the public – which includes you by the way!
5. The term 'audit' is used in many different contexts. You will come across internal audits, management audits, efficiency audits, social audits, environmental audits and so on. 'Audit' in the present context refers specifically to this independent attestation of financial statements.
6. There is one matter mentioned in Figure 14.10 which we have not yet met. You will note the reference under 'Basis of Preparation' to 'this historical cost convention'. The meaning of this will be explained in Chapter 16.

Part IV
Beyond the Profit and Loss Account and Balance Sheet

Reading the financial statements and the annual report: cash flow analysis and interpreting financial numbers

15

Learning objectives

After studying this chapter you should be able to:

- define liquidity and explain its importance;
- explain why the profit/loss of an organization does not indicate its liquidity;
- describe a cash budget and explain its function;
- construct a simple cash flow statement from information provided to you;
- reconcile profit/loss and cash flow;
- derive an approximate cash flow statement from two sets of financial statements;
- explain the difference between a cash flow and a funds flow statement;
- explain briefly why a cash flow statement is considered to be 'useful';
- explain the role of the annual report and financial statements in understanding an organization's economic position;
- briefly describe what additional information is necessary to make sense of an organization's annual report;
- make an initial reading of an organization's annual report;
- explain the role of ratio analysis;
- calculate and interpret the principal financial ratios of a company;
- make a reasonable assessment of a company's economic position;
- explain the limitations of ratio analysis.

15.1 INTRODUCTION

15.1.1 Chapter design and links to previous chapters

You will recall that in Chapter 14 we started to change our perspective. We started to move away from examining the detail of the bookkeeping system and the construction of the profit and loss account and balance sheet to looking in more detail at the finished product – the financial statements themselves. We continue that process in this chapter and begin to look at how we might begin to read the story that a set of financial statements tells us. The financial statements are, after all, supposed to provide information about the economic operations of an organization. The profit or loss figure gives us some important information but it does not – neither should it purport to – give us the whole story. To gain a better picture of the enterprise's economic performance we need to be able to read and *interpret* the data provided by the bookkeeping and accounting system.

Now, reading and interpreting information produced by an organization is a complex process on which you will spend more time as your studies progress. We are going to begin the process by examining two major elements: *the relationship between profit/loss and cash* (and other measures of *liquidity*) and *the interpretation of financial statements* (along with other information presented in an organization's annual report). We shall, once again, be concentrating on companies and their published information. As we have said many times, we shall be doing this because companies tend to have the more detailed – and perhaps, better developed – reporting systems. In addition, the interpretation of company information is an important and growing business. However, much of what we say in this chapter can be successfully applied – with care – to the information produced by other organizations.

The chapter is organized as follows. The next subsection offers a brief examination of the usefulness of financial statements. The main elements of the chapter begin by examining company liquidity and cash flow in section 15.2 which looks at the nature of liquidity, management cash budgets, and the differences between cash flow and profits/losses. Section 15.3 then examines the cash flow statement in some detail. Section 15.4 introduces the idea of 'reading the financial statements' and helps you to place the financial statements in the context of a company annual report and a wider panorama of background information about the organization. Section 15.5 comprises a detailed examination of ratio analysis. The chapter concludes with the usual summary, key terms and further reading.

15.1.2 Users of financial statements

You may recall that, right back at the start of the book, we identified *four characteristics* which helped us define conventional financial accounting. These were:

- an accounting entity;
- a concentration on economic events;
- events which could be financial described;
- an assumption that the information would be useful to (usually) financial participants in the organization.

Now is a good time to say a bit more about the last of these characteristics. Accounting has little – if any – intrinsic value. Its value lies in the role which the information produced by the accountants serves. This might be helping managers keep a track of what they owe and what is owed to them (creditors and debtors), managing cash flow (the cash book) or providing basic data on which management may make assessments of the costs of products or make choices between competing alternative investments (a role usually attributed to management accounting). For these, and other, reasons, management will normally consider it sensible to have some form of financial accounting system. But left to their own devices, it is unlikely that management would generally want to produce a full set of financial statements every 12 months. They generally speaking only do so because the companies acts (and probably the taxation authorities) require them to do so.

The objectives of the taxation authorities are fairly clear in that they see the financial statements as a basis for the regular collection of taxation income. Why the Companies

Acts should require financial statements is somewhat less clear. Certainly there is a view within most companies acts that the owners and the other financial participants (for example lenders and other creditors) have a right to – and deserve – some information about the financial health of the company. As a result, there is a widely held belief that a major purpose of financial statements is *to provide information which is useful to financial participants*.[1] Therefore, accountants will normally assume that, underlying all the accounting end-of-period adjustments and the regulations governing financial reporting which we have been examining in the preceding chapters, is a rationale that encourages them to make this information as useful as possible for shareholders, lenders and creditors.[2]

This, inevitably, leads to a question about what sorts of information the financial participants will find useful. This is a *most* complex question which we will briefly examine in Chapter 18. For now, we can keep matters simple by assuming that the financial participants want to know things like:

- Is this a financially sound company?
- Is it financially successful?
- Is it performing as well as its competitors?
- Can it pay its debts?
- Can it pay me a dividend?

And so on. It is these sorts of questions that this chapter will help you answer.

Now, it is obviously the case that the profit and loss account and balance sheet have already provided you with some of this information. Certainly the profit or loss figure gives you *some* kind of guide to the economic success or failure of the company. But this single number alone cannot give you a full picture. To gain that fuller picture you will need to 'read' the rest of the profit and loss account and balance sheet and the other information which accompanies it.

Such a reading of the accounts will often start with questions about cash and liquidity. It is with this that we begin.

15.2 COMPANY LIQUIDITY AND CASH FLOW

15.2.1 Introduction

We have already met some of the issues that arise, in an organization, with cash and liquidity. We examined the importance of cash in Chapter 2 and undertook a bank reconciliation in Chapter 6. Cash is essential to *any* organization. It must generate enough cash to pay its wages and bills for goods and services – or else it is very unlikely to remain as an organization. This is the same for a charity as it is for a transnational corporation. And yet, the profit and loss account and balance sheet do not, in themselves, tell you a great deal about the company's cash or liquidity situation. Indeed, you will frequently come across tales of companies which are recording profits but have had to go into liquidation because they were unable to pay their bills. So, as well as being profitable, a company must also be 'liquid'.[3]

Liquidity refers, at its simplest, to the ability of an organization to pay its bills. It will normally use cash to pay bills but the maintenance of liquidity does not relate *only* to cash. An organization may have many '*near-cash*' assets – like investments, shareholdings and amounts which it is owed – which can be turned into cash (liquidated) in a very short time.

As long as these 'near-cash' assets can be liquidated in time to produce the cash needed – to pay interest, pay creditors, pay wages, taxation or whatever – the company can be thought of as 'liquid'. So the important factor is not *just* the cash situation of the organization but its liquidity or cash plus near-cash.[4]

15.2.2 Management and liquidity: a brief word

Now, the management of any organization will, if it has any sense, keep a very close eye on the organization's liquidity. Whilst the cash book will give it *some* information on the subject it will not be enough to help the management plan and control the cash flow. Any good management will wish to ensure that there is enough cash or near-cash to pay bills as they fall due. However, in purely economic terms, it is also bad management to hold *too much* cash because this cash – in petty cash or in bank account – is not 'working for' the organization and it could be either on deposit earning interest or, more productively still, invested in productive activity for the organization. Thus management will want to maintain a sensible balance between these two extremes. (And, as we shall see later, the shareholders will, similarly, want to see that the management are maintaining a sensible – but not too high – balance of liquidity.) In order to achieve this, the management will maintain a *cash budget* which will attempt to forecast the inflows and outflows of cash and near-cash in the forthcoming months and, even, years. The cash budget will be a constantly updated document which will show projected receipts (from, for example, sales, dividends and interest) and projected payments (to, for example, employees, creditors, banks and taxation authorities). It will look something like Figure 15.1.

The cash budget itself is not a particularly difficult document to prepare in technical terms. The difficulty arises in trying to guess when cash will come in – given that, for example, debtors do not necessarily always pay on time. So, a sensible cash budget will allow for lags in both receipts and payments.

The clever bit with cash budgeting comes when the projected receipts and payments do not match. If the organization projects that it will have too much cash, it has to make a sensible decision about what to do with it. If the organization is likely to be short of cash, from where will it acquire the shortfall? This opens a fascinating – and increasingly sophisticated – area of accounting and finance frequently known as *working capital management* and *treasurership*. Working capital is, crudely speaking, the current assets less the current liabilities of the organization. As you will recall from Chapter 10, these assets and liabilities represent a kind of cycle in which purchases (through creditors) are turned into things for resale (through stock) which are, in turn, transformed into sales (debtors) and thus cash. Cash is then employed to pay the creditors. And so on. Managing the working capital cycle will, it is hoped, ensure that there is a steady and productive flow through the cycle. Treasurership involves ensuring that any surplus liquid funds are sensibly employed – perhaps in a bank deposit, perhaps lent shortterm to the money markets or perhaps held in some form of financial derivatives like options or swaps. It also involves assessing the best ways to finance shortfalls in the organization's cash needs – a bank overdraft or loan, a new issue of share capital or some more sophisticated financial instrument.[5]

You can perhaps see that the economic heart of an organization comprises two elements – the 'real economy' of the organization (that is, what it does for a living – making guitars, doing people's tax returns, hauling goods, etc.) and the 'financial economy' of the organization (that is, how these activities are financed and how surplus funds are employed). (This distinction between the 'real economy' – more usually referred to as

DEL AMITRI LTD: CASH BUDGET FOR THE FIRST 6 MONTHS OF 200X						
	January	February	March	April	May	June
RECEIPTS						
Cash sales	40,000	40,000	40,000	50,000	50,000	30,000
Debtors	120,000	110,000	100,000	160,000	180,000	160,000
Loans			500,000			
Share issue				1,000,000		
Investment income	20,000				15,000	
Sales of fixed assets		43,000				
TOTAL RECEIPTS	180,000	193,000	640,000	1,210,000	245,000	190,000
PAYMENTS						
Materials for cash	20,000	20,000	15,000	25,000	10,000	10,000
Trade creditors	140,000	120,000	120,000	100,000	80,000	140,000
Wages and salaries	22,000	22,000	22,000	22,000	25,000	29,000
Taxation	500	5,000	500	500	600	600
Sundry cash payments	1,000	1,000	500	1,200	1,200	1,200
Sundry creditors	800	500	1,000	1,000	600	500
Interest paid	500	600	500	20,000	20,000	20,000
Dividends paid	1,500					2,500
Purchase of fixed assets				480,000	800,000	
TOTAL PAYMENTS	186,300	169,100	159,500	649,700	937,400	203,800
Opening cash balance	(40,000)	(46,300)	(22,400)	458,100	1,018,400	326,000
Surplus/(deficit) for the month	(6,300)	23,900	480,500	560,300	(692,400)	(13,800)
Closing cash balance	(46,300)	(22,400)	458,100	1,018,400	326,000	312,200

Notes:
- The cash budget shows when the cash is expected to be actually received or paid.
- The surplus (deficit) is the difference between cash receipts and cash payments for that month.
- The opening balance of cash in any one month is the closing balance from the previous month.
- Although this looks like an increasingly cash-healthy company, there is a potential major problem with its cash management. This is the sort of issue we will examine below.

Figure 15.1 Illustration of a cash budget

'operating activities' – and the 'financial economy' – more usually split between 'investing' and 'financing activities' is an important one to which we will return in due course.) Increasingly an accounting and finance professional needs to know a fair amount about these issues but – you may be pleased to know – we will leave them for other aspects of your studies in management accounting and financial management where the matters will be fully explored.

For now, we want to turn back to the domain of financial accounting and, whilst the management's concern with liquidity and funds management is far from irrelevant, we will take a slightly different perspective on the issues. This is because financial accounting is primarily concerned with preparing information for external participants – not with managing the organization *per se*. So what do the shareholders and other financial participants need with respect to assessing the liquidity of the focal organization?

We will answer this question in two stages. First, we shall look at the increasing importance of the *cash flow* and *funds statement* which companies typically report alongside the profit and loss account and balance sheet. Then, when we turn to look at the wider *interpretation of financial statements* we will try and assess the basic liquidity of the organization using these financial statements.

15.2.3 The difference between cash and profit/loss

An organization can report healthy looking profits and still go into liquidation due to a lack of cash. A company can be reporting bad losses but, with judicious management of a healthy cash surplus 'buy' its way out of trouble. Anybody with a financial interest in the organization – most obviously the shareholders and creditors, but also banks and employees – would really want to know whether the signals of economic health or illness they were receiving from the profit or loss figure were *real* signs of a well-run company or of one in terminal decline. Were they going to receive a dividend? Is their investment likely to decline in the future? Were they going to receive their wages? And so on. So how is it that the signal sent by the profit/loss figure can be in conflict with that sent by the cash figure? How does this happen?

There is an irony here that we hope does not depress you too much. In Chapter 2 we examined the importance of cash. Cash is something everybody understands. We have then spent the last 12 chapters, in effect, adjusting those cash transactions to produce a profit and loss account and balance sheet. Is it the case that we should not have bothered and that the cash is the important thing? Well, 'no', the cash is important and so is the profit and loss account and balance sheet. The difficult thing is understanding the difference between the two. That is, can we easily work out why a change in the cash during the year is not the same as a change in the profit or loss during the year? The difference between cash and profit/loss is simply a question of *timing differences* – what we have called *accruals*. In a situation of no inflation (see Chapter 16) the difference between the cash of a business at the very beginning of its life and the cash at the very end of its life (plus any cash given to the owners as drawings or dividends less any inputs of loans or share issues) would be (to all intents and purposes) equal to the total profits or losses of the organization over its whole life. If a business is in existence for 100 years this is a bit long to wait to find out how it is performing. Hence, it is argued, we need annual statements.

The way in which the cash flows into and out of the business are different from the way that the profits or losses flow into and out of the business – the *timing* is different. Some of these differences are illustrated in Figure 15.2.

Spend some time with Figure 15.2 and make sure you can see what is happening. This figure could be extended for everything we have looked in the last few chapters – all the accruals and bad debts, the stock and cost of sales, the debtors and the creditors, the depreciation and the provisions, etc., are all items where the cash impact is likely to be different in any one accounting period from the expense/revenue implications in that same accounting period. This is all because of the accrual concept.

So there *are* very significant differences between the cash figure and the profit and loss account. These differences are important, not just to the management of the enterprise, but also to the financial participants in the organization – most especially the shareholders. The external financial participants thus need some information which bridges this gap. This is the purpose of the **cash flow statement**.

15.3 THE CASH FLOW STATEMENT

15.3.1 Introduction

Before we go any further, we really must try and tidy up the terminology used in this area. It really is quite confusing. *Cash* is alright, isn't it? We know what that is – coins, notes, instant available money in the banking system. But it is not that simple! There are a whole

THE TIMING OF CASH FLOWS AND THE TIMING OF FLOWS OF INCOME AND EXPENDITURE		
Economic activity	**The cash flow**	**The flow of income or expenditure**
Purchase of Fixed Assets	Payment almost immediate subject to credit terms giving by the vendor of the land, building, etc. Cash outflow in Year 1	Annual depreciation over the expected useful life of the asset. Smaller expense outflow in subsequent years
Sale of Fixed Assets	Receipt recognized almost immediately subject to credit granted to purchaser	Not recognized but a calculation of profit or loss on sale is recognized
Trade Sales	Receipt recognized immediately on a cash sale. Credit sale recognized when debtors pay	Recognized at point of sale
Trade Purchases	Payment recognized when made	Purchase recognized at point of purchase and taken to stock. Only taken to the profit and loss account as cost of sales when used
Wages and Salaries	Recognized when they are actually paid – usually one week or month after they are incurred	Recognized when they are incurred (may be included in stock figures as part of manufacturing stock)
Loans from (e.g.) the bank.	Recognized when received. Interest recognized when paid	Not recognized in the profit and loss account. Interest recognized when due – not when paid
Issue of Share Capital	Recognized when the cash is received. Dividends recognized when actually paid	Not recognized in the profit and loss account. Dividends recognized at the year end – not when they are actually paid
Provisions and Reserves	Not recognized until they become actual expenses – this may be a year or many years in the future	Recognized immediately they are created

Figure 15.2 The difference in timing between cash flows and profit/loss flows (i.e. income and expenditure)

range of things which can be thought of as *cash equivalents* in that they are virtually cash – short-term deposits and investments, bearer bonds, and so on. Or would you rather think of this as *near-cash* along with (say) gold, and cash in transit perhaps? What we have here is a spectrum of liquidity from currency/cash-in-hand, at one end, to – what? – at the other. The other end of the liquidity spectrum might most usefully be thought of as *working capital*. That is, the debtors, creditors, inventory, cash and near-cash in net current assets are all part of the process that will turn into cash and, in a well-managed organization, will turn into cash fairly quickly. Working capital is therefore an indicator of the short-to-medium-term liquidity of the organization. (We will see this later when we look at ratio analysis.)

All of these versions of cash/liquidity are referred to by the accounting profession, from time to time, as *funds*. The term 'funds' can be used to mean cash, cash equivalents, near-cash or working capital – or any combination of these.[6] So, you have to tread carefully around these words – what exactly is meant by them? Although it will be reasonably obvious what is meant in particular contexts, it *is* important to be careful when we are talking about *cash flow statements* and/or *funds flow statements*.

At the risk of over-simplification, a **cash flow statement** is an attempt to show how the cash (and/or cash equivalent and/or near-cash) balance of an organization has changed during an accounting period. It can take two forms: (i) a *direct-method* cash flow statement which is, in effect, a restatement and aggregation of the cash book of the organization; and

(ii) an *indirect-method* cash flow statement which seeks to reconcile the change in cash (and/or cash equivalent and/or near-cash) balance with the profit or loss earned during the accounting period. The first shows *actual expenditures and revenues* which, when aggregated, produce the final cash balance shown in the closing balance sheet. The second shows how the *combination* of the profit/loss, balance sheet movements and actual cash revenues and expenditures have resulted in the change in cash balance shown on the closing balance sheet. We will illustrate this difference in a moment.[7]

A *funds flow statement* is principally (although not always) designed to explain changes in the working capital of the organization by reference to the *combination* of the change in the profit/loss, balance sheet movements and actual cash revenues and expenditures. The funds flow statement will normally, therefore, be based only on the indirect method.

So, a simple summary of the differences between the two statements would be that the funds flow statement is designed to explain working capital movements by the indirect method whilst the cash flow statement seeks to explain changes in the cash balance by *either* the direct *or the* indirect method. What does all this mean? We will look at the two approaches to producing the cash flow statement. The indirect approach to producing a cash flow statement can be very easily amended to produce the (less useful) funds flow statement should you wish to do so.

15.3.2 A simple cash flow statement

The simplest way to give shareholders a view of the cash situation in an organization would be to simply publish the cash book. This, of course, would be immensely clumsy – just imagine how massive the 'cash book' of the Ford Motor Company or Samsung actually must be. Also, there will be information in the cash book which organizations will simply not want others to know about – information which might be useful to competitors or sensitive information like how much the managing director actually spends on entertaining. So companies may well publish a *summary* of the cash book. (This is the *direct* method we referred to above.) Accounting standards-setting bodies (see Chapter 14) may very well provide guidance on how this is done. Figure 15.3 provides one example of how this might look.[8]

This is the simplest way of providing shareholders with cash information. It splits inflows and outflows of cash into three categories: operating activities, investing activities and financing activities (which we mentioned earlier) and shows where the cash has come from (often referred to as *sources* in this context) and where it has gone to (sometimes referred to as *applications* in this context). The operating activities section shows the cash received from sales and other sources and then the cash expended on expenses of the business. The investing activities section shows what the company has done about the infrastructure of the organization – mainly its fixed assets. Finally, the section on financing activities shows what the company has done to finance its activities (noting that dividends are the price of acquiring share capital from shareholders). The very bottom of the statement then shows the cash (and, in this case, the cash equivalents) figure at the start and end of the accounting period. If the company has done its sums properly the difference between starting and ending cash should be explained by the inflows and outflows shown in the main cash flow statement.

So, what we have here is, in effect, a cash reconciliation which shows how the cash figure reported in the last accounting period's balance sheet has increased and decreased to produce the cash figure shown in this period's balance sheet. It certainly goes some way

```
┌─────────────────────────────────────────────────────────────────────────┐
│              Cash Flow Statement Tindersticks Ltd for the year ended 31 December 200X
│                            (all figures are in pounds)
│
│  Operating activities:
│         Cash received from customers                           285
│         Interest and dividends received                         25
│         Cash payments to suppliers                            (190)
│         Cash paid to and on behalf of employees                (85)
│         Interest paid                                          (10)
│         Payments to Customs and Excise on operating activities (15)
│         Corporate tax paid                                      (8)
│         Charitable donations                                    (5)
│
│  Cash flow from operating activities                                       (3)
│
│  Investing activities:
│         Purchase of shares in ABC Ltd (trade investment)      (15)
│         Purchase of fixed assets                              (72)
│         Sale of patent                                          5
│         Sale of plant and machinery                            15
│         Received from Customs and Excise on investing activities 8
│
│  Cash flow from investing activities                                      (59)
│
│  Financing activities:
│         Increase in short-term borrowings                      40
│         Mortgage of property                                   25
│         Payment of dividend                                    (5)
│
│  Cash flow from financing activities                                       60
│
│  Net decrease in cash and cash equivalents                                 (2)
│  Cash and cash equivalents 1.1.200X                                        26
│  Cash and cash equivalents at 31.12.200X                                   24
└─────────────────────────────────────────────────────────────────────────┘
```

Figure 15.3 Example of a cash flow statement: restating the cashbook

towards providing an external party with a better idea of what is happening in the organization. (We will re-examine the question of what is actually *useful* later in this chapter and in Chapter 18.)

The alternative approach is the *indirect* method which attempt to provide the potentially more useful information on the relationship between these cash movements and the movement on profit and loss. For us to produce such a statement requires more effort.

15.3.3 The reconciliation of profit/loss and cash movement

If there is one thing which causes students puzzlement it is the way in which profit/loss and cash movements are reconciled. We will try and do this in two ways: first by playing around with the arithmetic of the profit and loss account and balance sheet, and second by following a more conventional approach which you are more likely to see in a published set of company accounts. We will work through an example to see how it all works.

Figure 15.4 shows the profit and loss account and balance sheet of a company in its first year of existence. Life is simpler if we start by looking at an organization's first year of trading. This is because its previous balance sheet doesn't exist – there was no company – so all the 'brought-forward figures' are zero. You will see why this helps us in a moment.

MIDNIGHT OIL LTD
TRADING, PROFIT AND LOSS A/C
FOR THE SIX MONTHS ENDED 30 JUNE 2007
(all figures are in dollars)

Sales		123,000
Cost of Sales		
Material	57,400	
Wages	24,600	82,000
Gross profit		41,000
Selling and distribution costs	3,600	
Administration costs	7,700	
Depreciation	600	11,900
Net profit		$29,100

BALANCE SHEET
AS AT 30 JUNE 2007

	Cost	Depn	NBV
Fixed Assets:			
Building	30,000	–	30,000
Equipment	12,000	600	11,400
	42,000	600	41,400
Current Assets:			
Inventory	24,000		
Debtors	45,000	69,000	
Less Current Liabilities:			
Trade creditors	14,000		
Sundry creditors	2,500		
Bank overdraft	14,800	31,300	37,700
			$79,100
Represented by:			
Share capital			50,000
Net profit			29,100
			$79,100

Figure 15.4 Midnight Oil Ltd: financial statement for the six months ended 30.6.2007

Midnight Oil Ltd (in Figure 15.4) has finished its accounting period (of six months, just for a change) with an overdraft of $14,800. (You can see this on the balance sheet can't you?) What has happened to the cash in this accounting period? At the very start of the accounting period the company had no cash (the company did not exist). At the end of the accounting period it had an overdraft of $14,800. The overall cash flow of the company in this accounting period is a *negative* flow of $14,800. How did this come about? After all, it had a change in profit during the year of +$29,100. Why the difference?

Let us start answering this by using our 'playing about with the arithmetic' method. Despite all our efforts and the general importance of a profit and loss account and balance sheet they are just exercises in arithmetic – just a lot of additions and subtractions of debits and credits. This means that if we move things around in the profit and loss account and balance sheet, as long as we keep the arithmetic right, it will still make some sort of sense. Can we move things around so that the arithmetic, rather than showing the profit as 'the answer' in the profit and loss account and the shareholders' funds as the 'answer' in the balance sheet, shows the cash figure as 'the answer'? It is a matter of elementary algebra and so the answer is 'yes'. Start with the balance sheet and *pretend* that debits are '+' and credits are '−' and rearrange the balance sheet to produce the answer of $14,800 cash. Try it now and then check you answer against Figure 15.5.

Now, don't get excited about Figure 15.5. It is *only* arithmetic and all it shows is that all the debit balances (excluding cash) of the company *less* all the credit balances (excluding cash) of the company equal the cash situation of the company. This *must* be (arithmetically) true.

Now, what *is* interesting from Figure 15.5 is that if we recall that the opening balances of the organization were all zero (before the company came into existence) then each of the numbers in Figure 15.5 represents the *change* in those balances during the accounting period. That is the *increase* in the assets during the period, less the *increase* in the liabilities during the period has resulted in a *decrease* in the cash situation.

Here is the tricky bit. Whilst the *combination of changes* has resulted in the *change in cash*, the **individual** items have probably not changed the cash situation as suggested. Let's have a look at this.

Figure 15.5 tells us that the company spent money (had applications of funds – which will comprise cash and creditors) in the areas of:

● new buildings
● new equipment
● build-up of inventory
● and the financing of the debtors who owed the company money.

(This must be so because at the start of the accounting period everything was zero.) The company was able to *apply* funds only because it had a series of *sources* of funds. These sources were:

● finance from trade creditors to whom the company owes money;
● finance from sundry creditors to whom the company owes money;

MIDNIGHT OIL: BALANCE SHEET AS AT 31.6.2008	
DEBITS	**BALANCE SHEET AMOUNTS**
Buildings	30,000
Equipment	11,400
Inventory	24,000
Debtors	45,000
Total Balance Sheet Debits excluding cash	**$110,400**
CREDITS	
Trade Creditors	14,000
Sundry Creditors	2,500
Share Capital	50,000
Retained Profit	29,100
Total Balance Sheet Credits excluding cash	**$95,600**
Balance Sheet cash (overdraft)	**$14,800**

Figure 15.5 A cash-oriented rearrangement of the balance sheet

- finance from shareholders;
- finance generated from earnings (the profit figure – this is an important number we will return to in a moment).

The net result of these sources and applications was a net decrease in cash of $14,800.

Now, we *know* (from Figure 15.2) that these items are very unlikely to have had the direct equivalent effect on cash that this suggests. We do not know if the building or equipment or inventory have actually been paid for. We know that there are many items in the profit figure which are not cash equivalent. **This does not matter**. It is arithmetically true that the *combination* of these changes resulted in the cash change and, it has to be said, the changes in the balance sheet balances gives a strong indication of the broad way in which the cash change arose. Are you still with us so far?

Now, if we rearrange Figure 15.5 just a little further we can reconcile the cash change with the profit change. Move the profit figure up to the top of Figure 15.5 and – *hey, presto* – we have a basic reconciliation. Look at Figure 15.6.

Figure 15.6 shows us that the increase in profit during the accounting period (because we started with zero profit) is different from the increase in the cash *because* of a *combination* of changes in the sources and applications of funds during that accounting period. That is, the increase in profit ($29,100) less the increase in applications ($110,400) plus the increase in sources excluding profit ($66,500) produced a change in cash of $14,800. The changes in the sources and the applications – *when taken in combination, not individually* – explain the change in the cash amount.

This needs some thinking about – but *do not* think too hard. The individual amounts are *not* especially meaningful but the combination of them is.[9] This is an arithmetic exercise. And just to make sure, see if you can talk yourself through another accounting period of Midnight Oil. Let us say that at the end of the second six months of 2008, Midnight Oil's balance sheet has the following balances:

- the original cost of the buildings and equipment are the same although the equipment has been further depreciated by $600 for the period;
- inventory has risen to $32,000;

MIDNIGHT OIL: BALANCE SHEET AS AT 31.6.2008		
RETAINED PROFIT		29,100
DEBITS	**BALANCE SHEET AMOUNTS**	
Buildings	30,000	
Equipment	11,400	
Inventory	24,000	
Debtors	45,000	
Total Balance Sheet Debits excluding cash		$110,400
CREDITS		
Trade Creditors	14,000	
Sundry Creditors	2,500	
Share Capital	50,000	
Total Balance Sheet Credits excluding cash & profit		$66,500
Balance Sheet cash (overdraft)		$14,800

Figure 15.6 A reconciliation of profit and cash by a cash orientation of the balance sheet

- debtors have fallen to $34,000;
- trade creditors have risen to $28,000;
- sundry creditors have risen to $5,600;
- share capital is unchanged;
- retained profit is shown as $42,000.

Armed with this information, work out for yourself what the closing balance on the cash account must be and produce a figure (like Figure 15.5) explaining the cash balance. (You should get a cash balance of $18,800 – is it an overdraft or a positive balance?[10])

Now, this is not the whole story, is it? We cannot 'explain' the figures, we *only* explain the *change* in the figures. So, we now have to identify the *changes between the balance sheets*. Try it for yourself. This should produce something which looks like Figure 15.7.

Figure 15.7 – again just an exercise in arithmetic – shows you that the *increase* in the retained profit ($12,900) less the *change* in the applications of funds (*minus* $3,600 – we'll explain why it's minus in a moment) plus the *change* in the sources of funds ($17,100) produces a *change* in cash of $33,600. The applications of funds usually mean outflows but, in this case, the change in the applications is downwards – that is, there has been a *reduction* in the applications. A *reduction in applications* is actually a *source of funds*. Sources of funds are an *addition* to funds (obviously?) and so we *add* this decrease in applications rather than as in the previous case where we subtracted the increase in applications. Stop and think about this for a minute.

First, just concentrate on the arithmetic for a moment. We have two balance sheets. We are interested in trying to explain the *difference* in the cash figure by reference to *changes* in the other items. Arithmetically, the difference column *must* be OK. But what does it mean? If anything?

If our applications of funds *decrease* between two periods, then less of our cash is going out on applications than it was before. Midnight Oil are, for example, waiting for less cash from their debtors. The reduction in the period's cash is itself reduced. If you receive $5 every week and normally spend $4 of it, you will normally have $1 left at the end of each week. If you only spend $3 one week, you will be left with $2. You are still spending your

MIDNIGHT OIL: BALANCE SHEETS AS AT 31.6.2008 & 2009			
	31.6.08	31.12.08	Difference
RETAINED PROFIT	29,100	42,000	12,900
DEBITS			
Buildings	30,000	30,000	0
Equipment	11,400	10,800	(600)
Inventory	24,000	32,000	8,000
Debtors	45,000	34,000	(11,000)
Total Balance Sheet Debits excluding cash	$110,400	106,800	(3,600)
CREDITS			
Trade Creditors	14,000	28,000	14,000
Sundry Creditors	2,500	5,600	3,100
Share Capital	50,000	50,000	0
Total Balance Sheet Credits excluding cash & profit	$66,500	83,600	17,100
Balance Sheet cash balance/(overdraft)	$(14,800)	$18,800	$33,600

Figure 15.7 A reconciliation of profit and cash by a cash orientation of the balance sheet

cash but the cash amount left at the end has risen. Your applications have decreased and so your cash balance rises.

This means that, when doing a profit/cash reconciliation you must recognize that a decrease in an application is actually a source. Similarly, if your sources of cash decrease, this is, in effect an application when trying to explain the change in your cash position. Is this clear? If not, think about it and then work carefully through the example again. Some of the major forms of sources and applications are summarized in Figure 15.8.

There should now be only one item from the above examples which is bothering you. You have every right to be puzzled by the way *depreciation* seems to have been treated. That is, in Figure 15.7, the decrease in the fixed assets figure was shown as a source of funds. This decrease in the fixed assets figure was entirely due to the depreciation recorded on the assets in the accounting period. How can this be a source of funds – after all, depreciation is a book adjustment and has absolutely no impact on cash whatsoever? This is true! It is not really a source or an application of funds. But, for the sake of the arithmetic, it had to be included somewhere. We now have to confess that this is the wrong place to put it – but it kept the arithmetic correct.

Depreciation has to be taken out of our sources and our applications because it doesn't belong there. The only sources and applications we want to recognize for fixed assets are purchases and sales of fixed assets – not depreciation of them. But depreciation *has* to go somewhere. Now think. What is odd about depreciation? Well, it is one of the very few items which appear on both the profit and loss account and balance sheet. It has already been deducted from the income to arrive at the profit figure. We are using the profit figure here as an indicator of a source of funds (generated through the operating activities of the company). Depreciation does not involve any movement of funds – so we get rid of it! To do this *we add it back to the profit figure*. This actually makes some sense because not only do we thus remove the figure (correctly) from sources and applications but we actually improve the profit figure as an indicator of funds generated. The profit figure is thus adjusted for 'items not involving the movement of funds' – generally speaking this means depreciation.

Figures 15.6 and 15.7 are, to all intents and purposes, cash flow statements by the indirect method. We have arrived at these by a fairly circuitous route. If the principles are clear in your mind, can we now produce such a cash flow statement by a more direct route?

Balance sheet item	If it INCREASES in the accounting period it is a(n) ...	If it DECREASES in the accounting period it is a(n) ...
Retained Profit	Source	Application
Fixed Assets	Application	Source
Stock/Inventory	Application	Source
Debtors	Application	Source
Creditors	Source	Application
Loans	Source	Application
Share Capital	Source	Application
Debit Balances	Application	Source
Credit Balances	Source	Application

Figure 15.8 A summary of the sources and applications of liquid and near-liquid funds

15.3.4 Constructing a cash flow statement

If you have followed and understood the foregoing – admittedly tortuous – process you should have no difficulty constructing a simple cash flow statement. Indeed, a very basic statement would be no different from Figure 15.7 except that depreciation would be shown differently. Really, it is the content which matters – not the format – but Figure 15.9 illustrates one suggestion of how such a statement might look in practice.[11]

Figure 15.9 shows us that we start with operating profit and add back the depreciation. Then adjust for increases and decreases in debtors, creditors and stock (the working capital management items we talked about earlier). Next comes the investing activities which most typically will comprise movements in fixed assets and shares. In the final section financing issues are itemized. At the bottom, once again, the difference is reconciled with opening and closing cash balances. That, really, is all there is to it. And just to confirm that, Figure 15.10 is taken from a set of financial statements published by a medium-sized UK company in the late 1990s. Although the layout is a little different, you should be able to trace and explain all of these figures.

There is, however, one major difference between the process we undertook with the changes in the balance sheets and the illustrations in Figures 15.9 and 15.10. A number of the figures in the published cash flow statements are actually taken from the accounting records of the enterprise – not from the balance sheet. The increases/decreases in debtors, creditors and inventory, the operating profit and the depreciation charge are all taken from the profit and loss account and balance sheet. The other figures are, however, the *actual* amounts paid and received by the company in the accounting period. You will recall that

---

Cash Flow Statement Tindersticks Ltd for the year ended 31 December 200X (all figures are in pounds)

Operating Activities:

Profit before tax and before extraordinary items	100	
Depreciation charged	10	
Increase in debtors	(15)	
Increase in creditors	5	
Increase in stock	(90)	
Effect of other deferrals & accruals of operating cash flows	(5)	
Corporation tax paid	(8)	
Cash flow from operating activities		(3)
Investing Activities:		
Purchase of shares in ABC Ltd (trade investment)	(15)	
Purchase of fixed assets	(72)	
Sale of patent	5	
Sale of plant and machinery	15	
Received from Customs and Excise on investing activities	8	
Cash flow from investing activities		(59)
Financing Activities:		
Increase in short-term borrowings	40	
Mortgage of property	25	
Payment of dividend	(5)	
Cash flow from financing activities		60
Net decrease in cash and cash equivalents		(2)
Cash and cash equivalents at 1.1.200X		26
Cash and cash equivalents 31.12.200X		24

Figure 15.9 Example of a cash flow statement reconciling profit and cash

Group cash flow statement

For the Year ended 31 December 1999

	Notes	1999 £m	1999 £m	1998 £m	1998 £m
Net cash inflow from operating activities	22		12.4		17.8
Returns on investments and servicing of finance					
Interest received		0.7		0.7	
Interest paid		(2.3)		(1.2)	
			(1.6)		(0.5)
Taxation paid			(3.2)		(9.0)
Capital expenditure and financial investment					
Purchase of tangible fixed assets		(12.7)		(17.7)	
Sale of tangible fixed assets		1.7		4.2	
Purchase of own shares by employee benefit trust		–		(0.5)	
			(11.0)		(14.0)
Acquisitions			(14.4)		–
Equity dividends paid			(17.0)		(12.0)
Net cash outflow before use of liquid resources and financing			(34.8)		(17.7)
Management of liquid resources					
Short term deposits			(1.1)		23.7
Financing					
Issue of ordinary share capital		–		1.6	
Repayment of loan notes		–		(0.8)	
Repayment of bank loans		(8.7)		–	
Increase in bank loans		41.9		–	
			33.2		0.8
(Decrease)/Increase in cash			(2.7)		6.8
Reconciliation of net cash flow to movement in net (debt)/funds					
(Decrease)/increase in cash			(2.7)		6.8
Movement in short term deposits			1.1		(23.7)
Repayment of debt			8.7		0.8
Increase in bank loans			(41.9)		–
Change in net funds resulting from cash flows			(34.8)		(16.1)
Exchange rate differences			(0.1)		–
Acquisition of subsidiary undertakings			(8.7)		–
Movement in net funds			(43.6)		(16.1)
Net funds at beginning of year			15.6		31.7
Net (debt)/funds at end of year			(28.0)		15.6

22 Notes to the statement of cash flows

a Reconciliation of operating profit to net cash inflow from operating activities

	1999 £m	1998 £m
Operating profit after exceptional items	11.8	26.5
Exceptional items	3.2	4.6
Operating profit before exceptional items	15.0	31.1
Depreciation charge	7.5	8.0
Amortisation of goodwill	0.3	–
Movement in stocks	14.9	(0.8)
Movement in debtors	0.8	3.9
Movement in creditors	(13.6)	(20.2)
Movement in provisions	(1.4)	–
	23.5	22.0
Net cash outflow from exceptional items – operating	(2.0)	(4.2)
– non-operating	(9.1)	–
Net cash inflow from operating activities	12.4	17.8

b Analysis of net funds/(debt)

	At 1 January 1999	Cash Flow	Acquisitions	Exchange Movement	At 31 December 1999
Cash in hand and at bank	9.3	(2.1)	–	(0.1)	7.1
Overdrafts	(0.7)	(0.6)	–	0.1	(1.2)
	8.6	(2.7)	–	–	5.9
Deposits	7.9	1.1	–	(0.1)	8.9
Loan notes	(0.9)	–	–	–	(0.9)
Bank loans	–	(33.2)	(8.7)	–	(41.9)
Net funds/(debt)	15.6	(34.8)	(8.7)	(0.1)	(28.0)

Extracted from the accounts of William Baird plc for year ended 31 December 1999.

Figure 15.10 Example of a cash flow statement

The cash flow statement:

- seeks to explain the actual change in the cash (and/or cash equivalent and/or near-cash) in an organization during an accounting period;
- it achieves this either by:

  i showing which *specific* changes actually produced the change in cash (direct); or

  ii showing a combination of balance sheet and actual cash movements (indirect);

- and it emphasizes actual movements of cash;
- and thus provides additional information not otherwise available from the financial statements.

The funds flow statement:

- seeks to explain the change in working capital or some other measure of relatively liquid funds during an accounting period;
- it achieves this by means of a *combination* of changes in other balance sheet items without specifying which balance sheet changes produced (say) changes in cash or changes in creditors;
- it reports changes between balance sheets;
- and thus reports no new information which could not be derived from the basic financial statements.

Figure 15.11 Main differences between cash flow and funds flow statements

we had to make assumptions, when working from the balance sheet, that, for example, purchases of fixed assets and repayments of loans, were actually paid in the accounting period. From a standard profit and loss account and balance sheet you simply cannot tell for certain whether this is so – although one can make a reasonably educated guess. A published cash flow statement therefore does provide a little additional information to the external participants about the liquidity of the organization and herein lies the basic difference between the cash flow statement and the funds flow statements we discussed earlier. This is summarized in Figure 15.11.

So why is the cash flow statement thought to be a good idea? This is something which we should now have a brief look at.

15.3.5 The usefulness of a cash flow statement

The usefulness of the cash flow statement lies in the ways it differs from, particularly, the profit and loss account. That is:

- it is more objective – cash movements actually happen whereas most elements in a profit and loss account are estimates;
- users generally feel happier with cash and are more likely to understand such a statement;
- by comparing these statements over time there is a better chance (especially when read with the profit and loss account and balance sheet) of spotting when something is beginning to go wrong (e.g. payments from debtors are slowing down, stocks are increasing but sales are not, interest payments are getting out of hand or fixed assets are not being replaced);
- and most importantly, the statement should improve estimates of the company's solvency.

But do not accept these advantages without critical thought. The cash flow statement still provides no guarantee of the company's liquidity and the most useful information for shareholders – the company's own cash budget (see Figure 15.1) – is still not available to the external participants. To make any kind of sense of the cash flow statement it really has to be carefully read along with all the other information which is available to the shareholder (see section 15.4 below) – and even then, really important signals can so easily be missed or the shareholders misled.

One of the most important things one can learn from this area, though, is to recognize that the purpose of financial statements – as currently produced – is *not* to fully satisfy the information wants of the shareholders. There is no question that it is *cash flow forecasts or projections* which are just about *the* most helpful thing that a shareholder can receive. Companies do not – and will not – produce these documents for external participants. Therefore, the widely mooted statement that financial statements are intended to satisfy shareholders' wants should be treated with some scepticism. At least it is a statement that needs to be heavily qualified. This is something the accounting professions of the world seem reluctant to do!

Finally, we will return to these sorts of questions in Chapter 18 but let us just leave you with the thought – why should accountants and the accounting profession be concerned with what shareholders want? Is there any good professional reason for this? We think not but we will have another look at this later.

15.4 READING THE FINANCIAL STATEMENTS

15.4.1 Introduction

We have already seen that we can derive a fair amount of information about a company from its profit and loss figure plus its cash flow statement. But this is only a small part of the overall information we will use if we are to try and make any sensible assessment of an organization's economic health and economic performance. Pick up one of your company's annual reports and have a look through it. You will see that there is a lot more in the annual report than a simple set of numbers. You should find:

- a chairman's statement which will highlight major successes and failures of the accounting period and tell you (usually) why things will be better next year;

- some kind of operating review which will review the financial and economic activities of the organization and will (for example) discuss 'difficult' markets and new products;
- profit and loss account, balance sheet and cash flow statement;
- the notes to the accounts;
- the auditors' report;
- the directors' report;
- other information including (for example) legal details of the company, its subsidiary companies and, perhaps, some explanation of differences in local and international accounting treatments.

When you want to 'read' an annual report you will, therefore, normally treat the data in three sections:

- background and market information;
- chairman's statement, directors' report and other information;
- the financial statements.

We will have a brief look at the first two of these and then go back to the financial statements in some detail in section 15.5.

15.4.2 Background and market information

One of the biggest mistakes that new accountants make when reading an annual report is to assume that all the information they want is contained in that one document. Before making any real sense of the data in the annual report it is essential to know something about the organization in which you are interested, the industry in which it operates, general economic conditions and so on. So, for example, if the company you are examining is making a loss and all other companies in that industry are making a profit you might well be concerned. If all companies in that industry were making a loss, then the problem would appear to lie with the industry, not the specific company. You need to know the specific circumstances of your company and its competitors. If your company's main trade is in holiday villas in Ruritania and Ruritania has just declared war on all its immediate neighbours, this will probably not be good for business. If your company specializes in waste disposal through incineration and incineration has just been made illegal, this is unlikely to be good for business. If you are in the drugs industry and your major competitor has beaten you to the latest vaccine for AIDS, this will not be good for your business. And so on.

So, making sense of an annual report requires:

i an understanding of general economic conditions in the countries in which the company operates and from which it buys and sells;
ii an understanding of the industry and current industry conditions;
iii an awareness of any factors which may specifically affect the company you are studying.

Only then will the information in the annual report make any realistic sense.

15.4.3 Chairman's statement, directors' report and other information

Another of the big mistakes that new accountants make when studying and interpreting financial statements is to ignore the information which is reported alongside the actual financial statements themselves. The chairman's statement is the most widely read part of the annual report and, whilst you would be well advised to read it with a degree of scepticism, it will usually contain important information. The same is true of the other information in the annual report. Here you may be warned that the company has sold off its subsidiaries in the USA, is fighting off a takeover bid from a French company, is facing the retirement of the senior directors who have led the company since its inception, or the company has major new innovations about to come to the market. You will also learn a little about the trading conditions that the company is facing in its different areas of business or in different parts of the globe. All this will highlight key areas for you to examine when trying to infer an overall economic picture of the company.

In addition, in the light of Chapter 14, you may find international comparison information about the way in which the accounts have been compiled and, in relation to matters we will discuss in Chapter 17, you will probably find information about the company's social and environmental performance during the accounting period and you may find that this influences your perceptions of the organization.

So, having learnt something about the company and its economic environment, the second stage in interpreting an annual report is to actually read the document before you and identify issues which the directors and chairman raise in their discussions of the year and their tentative projections about the coming accounting periods. Only *then* can we turn to the financial statements themselves.

15.4.4 An initial review of the financial statements

Finally, we can turn to the financial statements themselves and start to investigate the detail of the economic story of the company. We now know a fair amount about the financial statements. You can turn to any annual report and, for example, find whether the profit has risen or not, whether the company's capital employed has risen and if so why, and what the liquidity situation looks like. The more time you spend, the more you will realize how complex these accounts are. There is a lot of data contained here. Having satisfied your initial curiosity about the broad indicators of profit and growth you can settle down and begin to find out what is actually in the accounts. We will now consider a few important stages that you should go through first.

> **Hint**
>
> At the risk of the most tedious repetition which we hope is no longer necessary, you should be consulting your library of financial statements at this point and checking out what we say against the accounts/annual reports that you have to hand. If spoilt for choice, stick with the company which you feel you know best and with whose financial statements and annual report you have become particularly familiar.

(a) The auditors' report

First, check the auditors' report. If you are a shareholder of the company you have paid a lot of money for this report – it makes sense to see what it says. In 99 times out of 100 the report will more or less follow the standard form we outlined in Chapter 14. The importance of the auditors' report is that if it *does* follow the standard format you have every right to assume that the numbers contained in the financial statements are reasonable and fairly reliable. (Please note, you have every right to make this assumption but you would be naive if you trusted accounting numbers and auditors' words without questioning them at least a little.) If the auditors' report *does not* follow the standard form (that is, the report is, to use the jargon, '*qualified*'), then you must read it most carefully because it will tell you important things about the financial statements. Perhaps the auditors were unable to collect all the information they needed to reach their opinion or perhaps the company is very shaky and can only survive if it receives further bank funding. In either case, the auditors' report should tell you this and you should, not surprisingly, treat the financial statements with appropriate caution as a result.

(b) The accounting policies

As we mentioned in Chapter 14, accounting standard-setting bodies have given a lot of attention to the issue of determining how companies should treat items in the financial statements, what information should be disclosed and, most particularly, the disclosure of the accounting policies used by the company. So, the next stage might well be to try and make use of this information. A read through the accounting policies shown in the accounts will give you a clue about the sorts of tricky items that the company has had to account for and what approach it has taken. It makes sense to ensure that we can understand each of these policies and that they appear to accord with our understanding of (what is thought of as) current best practice. If some items have been treated in odd ways (the auditors' report really should have mentioned this) then we will have to be more careful when looking at the numbers in the financial statements. As an extreme (and unlikely) example, just to illustrate the point, imagine that you are looking at a company which does not depreciate any of its land and buildings but all other companies in the industry *do* depreciate land and buildings. This may well mean we may have to treat the figures for land and buildings with some care and, more likely, we will have to be very careful when comparing our company's performance with that of other companies in the industry.

(c) The notes to the accounts

Next we might turn to the notes to the accounts in order to, for example, see what issues are explained there, to familiarize ourselves with the information which is available and to 'get a feel' for the direction in which the figures are moving. You might want to ask yourself questions about the company such as: Are the fixed assets wearing out and not being replaced? Have the directors given themselves a nice fat pay increase? Is turnover rising in all areas of the business? Are there any unusual items in the data on provisions and other liabilities? What has the company done about (for example) the major court case they have just lost on polluting the local river? And so on. By asking yourself these questions (which you should be able to make reasonable answers to) you will begin to focus in on the detail of the economic data you have in front of you.

(d) Interpreting the numbers

So, having done all this, you are now in a position to try and see what, if anything, the numbers actually mean. There are a number of, increasingly sophisticated, ways of doing this. The most commonly used is something called **ratio analysis**. This is important enough to warrant its own section.

15.5 RATIO ANALYSIS

15.5.1 An overview

If you have been following the issues we have been discussing in this chapter with an actual annual report there should be a major and disturbing question in your mind. This should go something like 'What does it all mean???'. So retained profit is (say) £400 million – so what? You have no basis on which to say whether this should be £400, £4 million, or £4 billion. So the company has assets of (say) £9.5 billion. That's quite a lot of fixed assets if you are a corner shop. Is it a lot if you are an international motor manufacturer?

The easiest way to make the numbers more accessible is to turn them into ratios, proportions or percentages. To illustrate, if two students each save £2 per week this might be quite interesting as it tells us that these students appear to be prudent individuals. If they also spend £10 each on entertaining every week then we, again, learn a little about them. If, however, we also learn that one of the students (Sonic) has an income of £20 per week and the other (Knuckles) has an income of £1,000 per week we learn a great deal more (and not just about the inequities of the distribution of income!). Sonic saves 10% of her income and spends 50% on entertaining. Knuckles, on the other hand, saves only 0.2% of her income and spends only 1% on entertaining. That is, we have combined different attributes of the students' financial records with each other (that is, spending with income, saving with income) and then compared the two students. From this we can learn a great deal more. This is because the raw numbers are now *given a context*.

This is where the problems with your company accounts come from – they have no context. So, the best way to go about understanding company financial reporting numbers is to give them a context by (a) combining numbers – usually in the form of ratios; (b) looking at any trends through time in these numbers; and then (c) comparing different companies and/or single companies with the industry to which they belong. This is known as **ratio analysis**.

Broadly speaking, ratios can be conveniently categorized into five groups. These are:

i   *profitability ratios* which, as their name suggests, are concerned with the examination of profit (or loss) and its sources;
ii *activity ratios* which are broadly concerned with assessing the efficiency with which the organization has employed its resources;
iii *liquidity ratios* which complement our earlier analysis of the organization's cash and funds flow;
iv *gearing ratios* which look at the *capital structure* of the organization and, in particular, any implications for the owners arising from the company's borrowings;
v   *market ratios* which examine how a company's performance looks in the light of its share performance including its share prices (if it is a quoted company).

Each of these groups of ratios seeks to provide information on different aspects of the organization's economic performance. Taken together, they should provide a fairly detailed analysis of how the company is faring. We will examine each in turn and illustrate its calculation and interpretation with a simple example. Figure 15.12 provides you with three years' data for Saturn Ltd. Figure 15.13 summarizes how the ratios are calculated and what the ratios look like for this company.

Saturn plc
Condensed profit and loss accounts
For the years ended 31 December

	2005 £000	2006 £000	2007 £000
Sales: Cash	1,000	1,000	1,100
Credit	1,000	1,200	1,100
	2,000	2,200	2,200
Cost of sales	1,000	1,050	1,200
Gross profit	1,000	1,150	1,000
Expenses*	400	750	750
Net profit	600	400	250
Taxation	200	100	50
	400	300	200
Dividends payable	200	200	200
	200	100	–
Retained profit b/fwd	100	300	400
Retained profit c/fwd	£300	£400	£400
*The expenses figure includes the following:	£000	£000	£000
Depreciation: Plant	100	150	160
Motor vehicles	50	70	80
Loss on disposal: Plant	–	130**	–
Motor vehicles	–	–	160**
Interest of debentures	40	50	70
Other expenses	210	350	280
	£400	£750	£750

** Written down value of plant sold £300
    Written down value of motor vehicle sold £350

Saturn plc
Condensed balance sheets
As at 31 December

	2005 £000	£000	£000	2006 £000	£000	£000	2007 £000	£000	£000
Fixed assets (net):									
Plant & Equipment			800			1,000			1,100
Motor Vehicles			300			400			450
			1,100			1,400			1,550
Current assets:									
Inventory		400			500			600	
Debtors		200			300			400	
Bank		150			50			–	
		750			850			1,000	
Less Current Liabilities									
Creditors	300			400			500		
Taxation	200			100			50		
Dividend	200			200			200		
Bank	–	700		–	700		50	800	
Net Current assets			50			150			200
Capital employed			£1,150			£1,550			£1,750
Represented by:									
10% debentures			400			500			700
Share Capital (£1 shares)		450			650			650	
Retained profit		300	750		400	1,050		400	1,050
			£1,150			£1,550			£1,750

Cash flow statement for Saturn plc				
	2006			2007
Operating Activities:				
Profit before tax	400		250	
Depreciation	220		240	
Loss on disposal of fixed assets	130		160	
Increase in debtors	(100)		(100)	
Increase in creditors	100		100	
Increase in stock	(100)		(100)	
Tax paid	(200)	450	(100)	450
Investing Activities:				
Purchase of fixed assets	(820)		(740)	
Sales of fixed assets	170	(650)	190	(550)
Financing Activities:				
Issue of shares	200			
Issue of debentures	100		200	
Dividend paid	(200)	100	(200)	0
Increase/(Decrease) in cash		(100)		(100)
Cash balance at 1.1.2006/2007		150		50
Cash balance at end of period		50		(50)

Figure 15.12 Financial statements for Saturn plc

15.5.2 Profitability ratios

Profitability ratios are usually of two basic types:

- ones which relate profits/losses to sales;
- those which provide a relationship between profits/losses and the asset base from which they are generated.

Figure 15.13 highlights a number of ratios. The first three are profitability ratios – two which relate profit/loss to sales and one which relates profits/losses to the asset base. The actual formulae for calculating these three ratios are contained in the first column of Figure 15.13 (as is the case for all the ratios to be discussed). Thus, to avoid repetition, we will, throughout this section, simply describe the ratios rather than reiterate how each is specifically calculated. The **gross margin** and **net profit ratios** both relate different measures of profit to sales.

(a) Gross margin ratio

Often called the *gross profit ratio*, this ratio is concerned with the profitability of trading activities. It reflects the percentage gross profit generated through selling goods and services. In normal circumstances it is assumed that this ratio figure should be reasonably constant over time if the organization's pricing policy and command over the market are both consistent and buoyant. It is thus a primary indicator of trading performance.

(b) Net profit ratio

This ratio relates net profit to sales revenue. The net profit figure, of course, is the resulting amount after all expenses have been deducted (but before deducting taxation and

	Formula	2005	2006	2007
Profitability				
Gross margin	$\dfrac{\text{Gross profit}}{\text{Sales}} \times 100$	$\dfrac{1{,}000}{2{,}000} \times 100 = 50\%$	$\dfrac{1{,}150}{2{,}000} \times 100 = 52.27\%$	$\dfrac{1{,}000}{2{,}200} \times 100 = 45.5\%$
Net profit	Earnings before interest and tax (EBIT) $\dfrac{\text{EBIT}}{\text{Sales}} \times 100$	$\dfrac{640}{2{,}000} \times 100 = 32\%$	$\dfrac{450}{2{,}200} \times 100 = 20.45\%$	$\dfrac{320}{2{,}200} \times 100 = 14.54\%$
Return on capital employed (ROCE)	$\dfrac{\text{EBIT}}{\text{Capital employed}} \times 100$	$\dfrac{640}{1{,}150} \times 100 = 55.65\%$	$\dfrac{450}{1{,}550} \times 100 = 29.03\%$	$\dfrac{320}{1{,}750} \times 100 = 18.28\%$
Activity				
Inventory turnover	$\dfrac{\text{Ave stock}}{\text{Cost of sales}} \times 52 \text{ (weeks)}$	$\dfrac{400}{1{,}000} \times 52 = 20.8 \text{ weeks}$	$\dfrac{450}{1{,}050} \times 52 = 22.3 \text{ weeks}$	$\dfrac{550}{1{,}200} \times 52 = 23.8 \text{ weeks}$
Debtor's collection period	$\dfrac{\text{Debtors} \times 365}{\text{Credit sales}}$	$\dfrac{200 \times 365}{1{,}000} = 73 \text{ days}$	$\dfrac{300 \times 365}{1{,}200} = 91.25 \text{ days}$	$\dfrac{400 \times 365}{1{,}100} = 132.72 \text{ days}$
Sales to capital employed	$\dfrac{\text{Sales}}{\text{Capital employed}}$	$\dfrac{2{,}000}{1{,}150} = 1.74$	$\dfrac{2{,}200}{1{,}550} = 1.42$	$\dfrac{2{,}200}{1{,}750} = 1.26$
Liquidity				
Current ratio	$\dfrac{\text{Current assets (CA)}}{\text{Current liabilities (CL)}}$	$\dfrac{750}{700} = 1.07$	$\dfrac{850}{700} = 1.21$	$\dfrac{1{,}000}{800} = 1.25$
Acid test	$\dfrac{\text{CA–Stock}}{\text{CL}}$	$\dfrac{350}{700} = 0.5$	$\dfrac{350}{700} = 0.5$	$\dfrac{400}{800} = 0.5$
Gearing				
Basic gearing	$\dfrac{\text{Long-term debt (LTD)}}{\text{LTD + Equity}}$	$\dfrac{400}{1{,}150} = 1{:}3$	$\dfrac{500}{1{,}500} = 1{:}3$	$\dfrac{700}{1{,}750} = 1{:}2.5$
Debt to equity	$\dfrac{\text{LTD}}{\text{Equity}}$	$\dfrac{400}{750} = 1{:}2$	$\dfrac{500}{1{,}050} = 1{:}2$	$\dfrac{700}{1{,}050} = 1.25$
Percentage claims against the business	$\dfrac{\text{LTD = CL}}{\text{Fixed assets + CA}} \times 100$	$\dfrac{1{,}100}{1{,}850} \times 100 = 59.46\%$	$\dfrac{1{,}200}{2{,}250} \times 100 = 53.33\%$	$\dfrac{1{,}500}{2{,}550} \times 100 = 58.82\%$
Times interest earned	$\dfrac{\text{EBIT}}{\text{Interest}}$	$\dfrac{640}{40} = 16 \text{ times}$	$\dfrac{450}{50} = 9 \text{ times}$	$\dfrac{320}{70} = 4.57 \text{ times}$
Market ratios				
Note: Share price		£7	£6	£4
Dividend yield	$\dfrac{\text{Dividend rate (\%)} \times \text{nominal value of the shares}}{\text{Market price of shares}}$	$\dfrac{200}{450} \times 100 \times \dfrac{1}{7} = 6.35\%$	$\dfrac{200}{650} \times 100 \times \dfrac{1}{6} = 5.13\%$	$\dfrac{200}{650} \times 100 \times \dfrac{1}{4} = 7.69\%$
Dividend coverage	$\dfrac{\text{Earnings after interest and taxes (EAIT)}}{\text{Dividend payable}}$	$\dfrac{400}{200} = 2$	$\dfrac{300}{200} = 1.5$	$\dfrac{200}{200} = 1$
Earnings per share (EPS)	$\dfrac{\text{EAIT}}{\text{No. of ordinary shares issued}}$	$\dfrac{400}{450} = 88.89\text{p per share}$	$\dfrac{300}{650} = 46.15\text{p per share}$	$\dfrac{200}{650} = 30.77\text{p per share}$
Earnings yield	$\dfrac{\text{EPS} \times 100}{\text{Market price of shares}}$	$\dfrac{88.89}{700} \times 100 = 12.70\%$	$\dfrac{46.15}{600} \times 100 = 7.69\%$	$\dfrac{30.77}{400} \times 100 = 7.69\%$
Price earnings (PE)	$\dfrac{\text{Market price of shares}}{\text{EPS}}$	$\dfrac{700}{88.89} = 7.87$	$\dfrac{600}{46.15} = 13$	$\dfrac{400}{30.77} = 13$
Value of the company	PE × EAIT or Market price of shares × No. of ordinary shares in issue	7.87 × 400,000 = £3.15m 7 × 450,000 = £3.15m	13 × 300,000 = £3.9m 6 × 650,000 = £3.9m	13 × 200,000 = £2.6m 4 × 650,000 = £2.6m

Figure 15.13 Saturn plc: selected profitability, activity and liquidity ratios

dividends) and it may well be the case that varying cost structures in particular organizations will lead to marked variations in the ratios over time.

(c) Return on capital employed (ROCE) ratio

This is the most common of the ratios. It relates profit to the resources used (*capital employed* as it is called) in generating that profit. It is, as its name suggests, an attempt to measure the percentage profitability of the capital employed even though, as we know, the asset base used will contain a collection of different items (e.g. buildings, equipment, inventory, debtors, creditors, cash, etc., all at different values), thus giving a somewhat dubious view about what constitutes the capital employed. The ROCE ratio is normally considered to be the most important indicator of a company's profitability and one which is very closely related to other ratios as we will see.

(d) Comments on the profitability ratios for Saturn plc

If we turn to the specific figures with regard to Saturn plc (Figure 15.12) for these three ratios (contained in the last three columns of Figure 15.13) we can make the following comments on Saturn's profitability. *First*, the trading margin, as indicated by the gross margin ratio, appears to be rather variable and has declined rather disturbingly in 2007. Whether this marks the start of a downward trend is difficult to know and certainly should not be assumed, but it is something to watch when the ratios are calculated for forthcoming years. *Second*, both the net return on sales, as depicted by the net profit ratio and the ROCE (return on capital employed) ratio indicate that there is declining profitability in terms of sales and asset usage.

To a certain extent the declining profitability may be explained by the high changes in the asset base which have occurred in 2006 and 2007[12] which are yet to be made fully operational. Even though this may be a plausible explanation for the decline in the ROCE ratio, it does not explain the decline in the trading margin. Clearly, other expenses are increasing. But even here, as Figure 15.12 indicates, the problem of the revamping of the fixed assets has had an effect on this issue since large losses on disposal have been incurred which naturally increase the charges against profit.

15.5.3 Activity ratios

Activity ratios are intended to measure different aspects of the efficiency of resource utilization of the focal organization. Although there are quite a number of alternative ratios which we can use to expose this information, the primary ones are the **inventory turnover**, **debtors' collection period** and **sales to capital employed ratios**, the detail of which are contained in Figure 15.13.

(a) Inventory turnover ratio

This ratio attempts to show the number of times the average inventory is turned over or completely sold and replaced in the trading process. The more often inventory is turned over the lower will be the storage, financing and deterioration costs, making the trading process seemingly more efficient. However, drawing conclusions about what is an optimal, and hence efficient, inventory turnover rate must always be set in the context of the business of the organization. This might be done by, for example, a comparison of norms with other organizations in the same industry. The ratio we used here requires you to have a cost of sales figure. If you did not have this figure then it is possible to substitute the turnover figure for the cost of sales figure. If you do this then the ratio becomes a rather crude measure of stock turnover. This is because the ratio is calculated by comparing inventory which is *cost-based* with sales whose value is determined by *market prices*. Nevertheless, over time, it does supply some relative measure, at a very basic level, of declining or increasing trading activity of the organization. You should use cost of sales whenever you can.

(b) Debtors' collection period ratio

This ratio measures the amount of time it takes to realise in cash the amount owing from debtors. Revenues are the short-term financial lifeblood of all commercial organizations and the *actual receipt* of the amount – rather than the *promises* - from debtors is what really counts. Thus the control of debtors is of paramount importance, and in periods when the time taken to collect debts is increasing there is a clear need for control due to the potential liquidity crisis this could create.

(c) Sales to capital employed ratio

This ratio measures the ability of the capital employed base to generate sales. It is related to the ROCE ratio which sees profit as a return on the asset base but, in this case, it attempts to draw from this ratio the efficiency with which the assets are being used rather than provide a measure of the relative level of return generated. In fact, the ROCE ratio is often calculated by combining the sales to capital employed ratio with the net profit ratio:

$$\frac{EBIT}{Sales} \times \frac{Sales}{Capital\ employed} = ROCE$$

This, of course, can be reduced to:

$$\frac{EBIT}{Capital\ employed} = ROCE$$

as before. (Recall that EBIT means earnings before interest and taxation.)

(d) Comments on the activity ratios of Saturn plc

Once again these ratios for Saturn plc are contained in the last three columns of Figure 15.13. A number of things are clear from these figures. First, the number of days for the inventory to turn over has been increasing over the three-year period. Second, the collection of debts has been taking considerably longer; and, third, the capacity of the asset base to generate sales has also been declining.

All these ratios suggest a decline in efficiency of Saturn plc over time which certainly requires some explanation. The decline in the productivity of the asset base may be explainable, as in the case of the ROCE ratio, by the point that the replacement and expansion of the fixed assets has not as yet started to pay off in terms of increased output. However, this kindly interpretation should be checked before it is accepted, and it certainly does not apply to the declining situation with regard to inventory and debtors.

15.5.4 Liquidity ratios

Liquidity ratios are intended to give some indication of the focal organization's ability to meet immediate financial obligations and thus avoid the possibility of a liquidity crisis. Two ratios which predominate in trying to assess this issue are the current ratio and the acid test ratio. Both ratios are closely related and have a close relationship with our earlier examination of liquidity – through a cash flow or funds flow statement. Because of this, the cash flow statements (in Figure 15.12) can play a particularly valuable part in interpreting these ratios.

(a) Current ratio

This ratio presents a general picture of the liquidity of the organization by relating the total current assets to current liabilities figures. This makes the clear assumption that all the different elements which make up current assets are convertible into cash receipts in the short-to-medium term. Thus, for instance, cash, debtors and inventory are all assumed to be in a state where they could be turned into cash in the relatively immediate future. This may well be a dubious assumption!

What the appropriate level for this ratio may be is uncertain. A commercial rule of thumb suggests that the current ratio should be something less than 2 (say about 1.7 or 1.8) but the justification for this is unclear. However, it can be argued that high scores on this ratio are not very beneficial to the organization since it indicates that there may well be problems in the area of usage or turnover of current assets (e.g. unnecessary build-up of inventory or debtors).

(b) Acid test ratio

This ratio attempts to be a little more discerning about the current assets and current liabilities being compared. It does not assume that all current assets are immediately convertible into cash. As a result, the acid test ratio excludes inventory from the current assets (because it will take time to pass through the operations subsystem and be turned into products or services for sale). The remaining current asset amounts are then compared with the current liabilities to obtain a measure of liquidity.

Because this is much closer to a measure of the immediate liquidity of the focal organization it is normally assumed to be imperative that the acid test ratio should at least equal unity, even though current commercial wisdom seems to argue for something less (e.g. 0.7). Once again it is difficult to justify beyond dispute that the ratio should be 1 or 0.7 or any other figure, and it is important that you do not make hard and fast rules about these norms.

Although there are other ratios for measuring the liquidity of any organization the two ratios outlined above supply some general insights which help to explain the liquidity position of commercial organizations. However, it is important to complement this information with insights which can be provided through the cash flow statements. These help to explain the reasons for any deterioration or improvement in the above ratios over time. They are, therefore, a very valuable source of additional information.

(c) Comments on the liquidity of Saturn plc

If we turn to look at the calculated figures for Saturn plc in Figure 15.13 we can make a number of observations. First, the current ratio has been slowly increasing over the three years, which, on the surface, may appear welcome. However, all is not well. The cash flow statement in Figure 15.12 suggests that inventory increases, together with decreases in taxation and the declining cash balance might be a cause for concern. This suggestion is reinforced by the inventory turnover and debtors' collection period ratios, both of which are declining. The inference is that inventory and debtors are not necessarily in an optimal state or optimally managed. Equally, whilst the increase in creditors and decline in the bank balance are not particularly drastic changes on their own, when they are occurring with a declining profit position and possibly deteriorating inventory and badly managed debtors then they do become somewhat disturbing changes.

Second, the acid test ratio is at a consistent but perilous level throughout the three years. Since this ratio deducts the inventory from the current assets it leaves, in 2007, only the debtors as the numerator. Yet the debtors are seemingly not as well controlled as they should be judging by the debtors' collection period ratio which suggests a potentially doubly perilous position for Saturn plc. Thus the 'near-cash' assets which do remain to meet the liabilities may prove to be bad debts given the delays in collection which are apparent.

A more general perusal of the cash flow statements in Figure 15.12 indicates why there is so little change in the above ratios, how this stability has been achieved and at what cost. What emerges from these statements is that the funds from operations have not been enough both to maintain the dividend level as well as fundamentally restructure the asset base of the company. As a result, heavy long-term borrowing has been undertaken to cover the shortfall between the net cost of restructuring and the net funds generated from operations after taxation and dividends. This action, while maintaining stability in terms of liquidity, increases the longer-term debts of the company, which in turn affects the *gearing* of the organization, as we will see below.

15.5.5 Profitability, activity and liquidity ratios – their interconnection

Before moving on to look at the gearing ratios it is worth stopping and exploring some of the interconnections between the three sets of ratios already discussed. The three sets of ratios measure different things, yet they are interconnected very largely because a profitable commercial organization must have reasonable levels of activity occurring as well as having adequate levels of liquidity in order to maintain a profit over time.

To demonstrate this point it is usual to see these three sets of ratios in the context of a pyramid with the top point being the important return on capital employed (ROCE). This ratio is, as we have seen, built up from profit and capital employed which in turn are derived from sales less expenses in the former case and fixed assets, current assets and current liabilities in the latter case. These, in turn, can be further subdivided. This forms the pyramid effect and each of the defined variables is used in different ways in the ratios for profitability, activity and liquidity.

A typical pyramid for Saturn plc following this logic is contained in Figure 15.14 which traces the actual breakdown of the ROCE ratio of Saturn plc for 2005 – the elements of which form the numerators and denominators in all the ratios contained in the first column of Figure 15.13.

Of course, the pyramid can get ever more refined right down to, say, specific production processes and the actual credit management procedures, with highly detailed ratios relating the various factors involved. Yet, in terms of the external analysis of financial statements this process becomes impossible since the information is not available to the external reader of financial statements. But at least the pyramid approach helps to put the various detailed ratios in a context and relate them one to another as well as indicating the levels which are missing from the analysis.

15.5.6 Gearing ratios

Gearing ratios are addressed to assessing the financial implications surrounding a commercial organization's capital structure (the relationship between equity and long-term loans). The two general classes of long-term capital – long-term loans and equity claims – have different rights over the resources of the organization. Equity claims possess unique

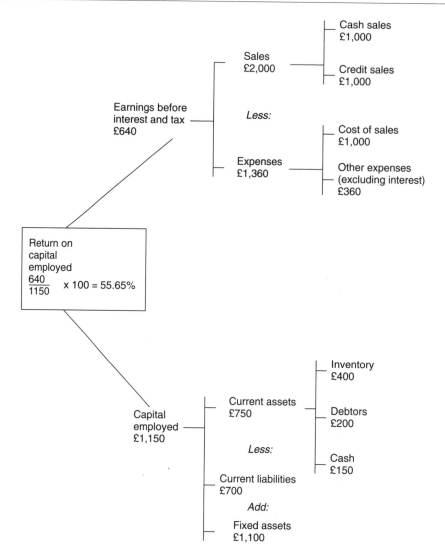

Figure 15.14 Saturn plc: the ROCE pyramid and the relationship between profitability, activity and liquidity ratios for 2005 (in £000s)

ownership rights but must suffer the good with the bad times with no fixed guarantee that a regular dividend will be paid (although in the case of preference shares the case is a little more complex – see Chapter 12). On the other hand, long-term loans have a right to be paid regular and agreed interest but lenders' capital rights to the organisation's resources are restricted to the amount of the loan originally made. The different combinations of these two types of financing (the *capital structure* in other words) can have a marked effect on the vulnerability of the organization in terms of its long-term survival and growth.

There are a number of different ratios to measure this gearing effect, although usually they are divided into two different sets:

- the first looks at the basic relationship between the two categories of long-term claimants and draws certain conclusions from these. There are normally two ratios used in this context: the *basic gearing* and *debt-to-equity* ratios.
- the second set of ratios attempts to assess the potential financial vulnerability of the capital structure adopted. Two typical ratios used in this respect are the *percentage-claims-against-business* and the *times-interest-earned* ratios.

Figure 15.13 again indicates how these ratios are calculated.

(a) Basic gearing and debt-to-equity ratios

These ratios are related to one another. What they measure and the interpretations of these measures can best be illustrated through a further numerical example, the data for which are contained in Figure 15.15.

Figure 15.16 shows the effects of the alternative capital structures for Woodstock Supplies plc from which three points need to be highlighted:

i   To note the effect on the two gearing ratios using the alternative capital structures. Under capital structure A both ratios indicate that this company has high gearing (i.e. 1:1.1 and 10:1 respectively). On the other hand, using capital structure B, Woodstock would become a company with low gearing (i.e. 1:11 and 1:10 respectively).

ii The effects on the potential returns to equity claimants need to be noted. With capital structure A the returns per share are greater but do not occur in the first year, whereas, with B, returns are always possible but they are constantly in a reduced form in that there are more shares over which profits must be spread.

iii It is important to note the effect on the viability of the company. Basically capital structure A requires that profits of at least £1,000 must always be made (to cover the loan interest) whereas B sets the profit threshold at only £100, being the amount to cover loan interest. This, needless to say, indicates something about the riskiness to the investor of the different capital structures of the focal organization.

Woodstock Supplies plc needs £11,000 to start business and is considering the following sources of finance:

Capital structure A:	
Equity: 1,000 £1 Shares	1,000
Long-term loan: £10,000 10% Debentures	10,000
	£11,000
Capital structure B:	
Equity: 10,000 £1 Shares	10,000
Long-term loan: £1,000 10% Debentures	1,000
	£11,000

The estimated net profit before interest, taxation and dividends for the first three years is as follows:

2001	£1,000
2002	£2,000
2003	£3,000

Draw out the implications of each of the capital structures using the basic gearing and debt to equity ratios

Figure 15.15 Woodstock Supplies plc: alternative capital structures

Capital structure A		2001	2002	2003
		£	£	£
Profit		1,000	2,000	3,000
Interest		1,000	1,000	1,000
Profit for distribution		–	£1,000	£2,000
Profit per share		–	£1	£2

Basic gearing: $\dfrac{10,000}{11,000} = 1{:}1.1$ Debt to equity: $\dfrac{10,000}{1,000} = 10{:}1$

Capital structure B		#2001	2002	2003
		£	£	£
Profit		1,000	2,000	3,000
Interest		100	100	100
Profit for distribution		£900	£1,900	£2,900
Profit per share		0.09p	0.19p	0.29p

Basic gearing: $\dfrac{1,000}{11,000} = 1{:}11$ Debt to equity: $\dfrac{1,000}{10,000} = 1{:}10$

Figure 15.16 Woodstock Supplies plc: effect of gearing changes

These three observations can be combined to supply something of a more general picture of the implications of these two ratios:

- High basic gearing and debt-to-equity ratios indicate a capital structure which is more risky at lower levels of profit but one which can supply a greater return to equity shareholders.
- Low basic gearing and debt-to-equity ratios, on the other hand, indicate a capital structure which is less risky at lower profit levels but one which will not supply particularly beneficial returns to the shareholders.

(b) Percentage-claims-against-business and times-interest-earned ratios

The second set of ratios which attempt to assess the financial vulnerability (or long-term solvency as it is often referred to) of the capital structure looks at these issues from a 'capital' and 'income' perspective. The percentage-claims-against-business and the times-interest-earned-ratios are typical examples.

The percentage-claims-against-business ratio looks at the amount of assets which are claimable by short- or long-term liability claimants. This ratio expresses something about the 'capital' aspect of the financial vulnerability picture.

The times-interest-earned ratio compares the interest payable on the loan outstanding with the earnings before interest and tax, and thus measures the financial vulnerability of the capital structure from a more 'income'-type perspective.

(c) Comments on the gearing ratios of Saturn plc

The last three columns of the top part of Figure 15.13 show the calculated gearing ratios for Saturn plc. The basic gearing and debt-to-equity ratios indicate that Saturn plc was reasonably highly geared in 2005 and has become increasingly so as the years have progressed. This situation, of course, indicates a potential risk problem at lower levels of profit but with the possibility of greater returns to equity holders if profits increase. However, as we know, profits are declining which means that there may be problems in future years over coverage of the growing interest charges. This is certainly borne out by the times-interest-earned ratio for Saturn plc which demonstrates a declining level of coverage of the interest payable. Finally the percentage claims against the business ratio indicates a very slight decline over the years but is still consistently running at over 50 per cent of the asset base claimable by short- and long-term liability claimants. This figure assumes that the assets which form the denominator of the equation can actually realise the amount stated if they had to be sold, which may be a little overoptimistic judging by the heavy losses already incurred through the disposal of fixed assets in 2006 and 2007.

15.5.7 Stock market ratios

The final set of ratios refers only to those commercial organizations whose equity shares have a market value due to their being traded on the stock market (i.e. those denoted as plcs in the UK).

Although there are many different ratios which can be calculated once an organization's shares are listed on the stock market the most common ones are the first five listed at the bottom of Figure 15.13. The sixth and final one listed in Figure 15.13 is a derived measure of the value of the commercial organization which arises from some of the insights provided by the five main market ratios.

(a) Dividend yield ratio

This ratio is an attempt to measure the dividend paid to a shareholder as a percentage of the market value of a share at a particular point in time. The idea behind this is that the listed value of a share has an actual cash-equivalent value which could be invested in an alternative shareholding at a particular rate of return. The dividend yield ratio provides the actual return currently being earned which can be compared with any alternative investment possibility to see whether a switch would be a sensible financial proposition.

(b) Dividend coverage ratio

The dividend coverage ratio provides some insight into the organization's ability to sustain the payment of the dividend given the current level of earnings (after interest and taxes have been paid).

(c) Earnings-per-share (EPS) ratio

The earnings-per-share ratio is a popular way of assessing the value of shares: it relates earnings after interest and tax (whether these are distributed or not) to the number of issued ordinary shares. The result is a rather crude depiction of the earnings which have been generated during the period in question through one ordinary share (i.e. the earnings 'owned' by that share though not necessarily distributed). All manner of complications can surround the calculation of this ratio when, for example, extraordinary income is involved, or when taxation is deferred. (These and other complications have led accounting standard setting bodies to produce guidance to standardize the handling of these difficulties.)

(d) Earnings yield ratio

The earnings yield ratio is very similar to the dividend yield ratio except that in this case all earnings after interest and tax are used rather than the actual dividends paid. This helps to obtain a somewhat fuller picture of the real yield of the share even if it is not actually received in the period under review.

(e) Price earnings (PE) ratio

The price earnings ratio provides what financial analysts call a 'capitalization factor' which can be applied to current levels of earnings to assess the longer-term earning potential of the company. It basically relates earnings per share to the current market value of a share to indicate, rather crudely, the estimated number of years it is anticipated (by the market) that these earnings, at this level, will continue. It is undoubtedly only a crude measure of this earning potential since it simply maintains that a share value contains so many 'bundles' of current earnings without any thought about how valid this really is.

(f) Value of company

The price earnings ratio and the market value of the shares form a basis for an attempt to provide a value of company figure. There are two ways to do this (as the formulae at the bottom of Figure 15.13 indicate): either we can multiply the price earnings ratio by current earnings or we can simply take the market price of a share times the number of shares in issue. Both of these calculations come to the same answer, subject to minor rounding errors, and both are meant to indicate the value the stock market places on the company, as a whole.

(g) Comments on the stock market ratios of Saturn plc

The final three columns of Figure 15.13 calculate these ratios with regard to Saturn plc for the three years from 2005 to 2007. Each ratio shows something of a general decline in the market's expectations of this company which, at a more general level, is clearly visible in the declining share valuation: £7 at the end of 2005 and £6 and £4 respectively at the ends of the following two years. The dividend yield, dividend cover and the earnings yield ratios provide an interesting picture of Saturn plc's desperate attempt to keep up a stable dividend policy whilst finding it increasingly difficult to do so, with the final result that both the dividend and earnings yields come together in 2007 at a rather low level. In addition, the earnings per share has steadily declined over the three-year period and, although the price earnings ratio has increased between 2005 and 2006, it is now stabilizing on a very much reduced earnings expectation. Investment analysts would interpret the price earnings ratio as indicating that the market believes that the company does have at least 13 more years of life even if at a somewhat reduced level of earning! How accurate this interpretation is depends on many factors which are not encompassed in the figures used – this registers again the problems and dangers involved in using ratios for predictive purposes. Finally, even though the value of Saturn plc increased in 2006, due probably to the expectations raised through the major restructuring, the market was increasingly disillusioned with the possibility and, as a result, the value dropped quite substantially in 2007.

15.5.8 A concluding comment

Although it would be wrong to read too much into all these ratios (either in the abstract or specifically with regard to Saturn plc) it is clear that they do, at least, provide a vehicle for drawing out additional information about any commercial organization from the traditional financial statements. It is very easy to fall into the trap of believing that ratios can provide some exhaustive insights as well as form a basis for predicting the future. In fact we could, on the evidence before us, conclude that Saturn plc is a very sick company indeed and predict that it may well be involved in either liquidation or takeover proceedings very shortly. We make these, often wild, generalizations because of the natural tendency to look at ratios over more than one year, specify trends in these data and then assume that the trends will continue into the future. Yet it would be wrong to assume that the life of any commercial organization, like Saturn plc, is so clearly determined.

Given this important caveat, on a more positive note the ratios should always be looked at together and in the context of industry averages if they are to provide meaningful, if limited, insights into commercial organizations. Although throughout this section we have been looking at individual ratios, when it comes to making any overall judgement about the organization it is important to look at the ratios as a whole. We have already seen how the profitability, activity and liquidity ratios are intertwined. You should also be able to see that the gearing ratios and the market ratios are similarly interwoven. Equally it is important always to look at these ratios in the context of the industry of which the particular organization is part (e.g. the food, steel, brewery industries, etc.). Average industry ratios are available in most countries through government or stock exchange figures or through one of the growing number of statistical services available to industrial companies. Although comparisons are always difficult it is important that if they are undertaken they relate like with like, which is more probable with organizations that are involved in the same type of business and trying to capture the same market.

SUMMARY

This chapter has attempted to give you an overview of how to try and make sense of a set of financial statements. We did this by a systematic examination of what we can infer from the annual report about the underlying organizational economic well-being. (Other aspects of its well-being will be looked at in Chapter 17.) This involved, in effect, four stages:

i   understanding the organization and its business;
ii knowing something about other organizations in the same line of business and the macro-economic conditions under which the organization operates;
iii examination of the liquidity and cash flow position of the organization as a complementary source of information taken with the profit and loss account and balance sheet;
iv systematic calculation and (careful) interpretation of the accounting ratios of the organization.

The first, third and fourth of these could be largely derived from the organization's published annual report. With practice you should now be able to make reasonable sense of an organization's reported information. Do not, however, assume that a few ratios will yield up the economic secrets of an organization. If it were that simple (a) we wouldn't need accountants; and (b) everybody would make sensible investment decisions. So, whatever you do, do not oversimplify this difficult and complex area.

Key terms and concepts

The following key terms and concepts have featured in this chapter. You should ensure that you understand and can explain each one. Page references to definitions appear in the index in bold type.

- Activity ratios
- Cash budget
- Cash flow
- The cash flow statement
- The difference between cash flow and profit/loss
- The difference between funds flow and cash flow
- The funds flow statement
- Gearing ratios
- The importance of background information
- Integrating the different sources of information about an organization
- Liquidity
- Liquidity ratios
- Market ratios
- Profitability ratios
- Ratio analysis
- Reading the annual report
- Reading the financial statements
- Sources and applications of funds
- Usefulness of financial statements
- Working capital cycle

FURTHER READING

The most useful reading you can do for this section is to spend serious time with the annual reports of organizations. The time spent reviewing, trying to interpret and make sense of these documents will stand you in excellent stead later on. One particularly useful idea is to try and get hold of the annual reports of a company which has gone into liquidation or which has been involved in a major financial scandal – but get the annual reports from *before* the event. Could you have spotted it? Similarly, you should get into the habit of reading the investment analysts' reports in a good quality newspaper and try and follow the reasoning that the analysts follow. Just get used to the idea that the financial statements are a coded story, coded by accountants (i.e. you) and which now has to be decoded by you. You *should* be able to do it! For more conventional reading matter, make sure you have the professional pronouncements of your own standard-setting body and see what they have to say on these sorts of things. Further, you will find that most basic or intermediate financial accounting textbooks will provide you with another view on these matters.

NOTES

1. This is probably a reasonable assumption as far as it goes. We will, however, look at this assumed purpose of financial statements in more detail in Chapters 18 and 17.
2. Information produced by accountants is *not* in the form most useful to users but accountants conventionally persist in maintaining this assumption. Don't ask us to explain this contradiction because we haven't a clue why this myth persists. However, as we are trying to show how conventional accounting works we will stick with conventional explanations – however bizarre – for the time being.
3. These matters, and those that follow, will overlap with your studies of financial management.

4. Terminology can be a real problem in this area. We will re-examine what we mean by these words in section 15.3.

5. Again, these are matters you will examine in some depth in your financial management studies.

6. We are therefore widening the term from the sense in which we used it in the 'funds subsystem' of the organizational flow model. You will notice that we use the term 'funds' in a number of places in this chapter. We were careful not to define it. This is because, historically, the cash flow statement in many countries was actually a *funds flow statement* concerned not with explaining the movements in cash but the movements in *working capital*. The problem was that there are many definitions of both 'funds' and 'working capital' and the statements that were published by companies as 'funds flow statements' were frequently unintelligible. However, you should be able to see that:

    (a) it would be relatively easily to change the way in which we did our arithmetic and come up with an explanation of movements in (for example) net current assets or something; and,

    (b) knowing something about the way in which debtors, creditors, stock and cash were interacting would actually be fairly helpful to the external participant trying to read the financial statements.

    In the end, it was recognized by the accounting professions that cash flow statements were simpler, more straightforward and more helpful than funds flow statements. In addition, if external readers of financial statements wanted information on working capital management there were probably better ways of getting it. This is one of the major things that 'reading the financial statements' and 'ratio analysis' are all about.

7. *Please note* that the cash flow statement which we are discussing here must not be confused with cash flow projections and forecasts. The cash flow statement is a *historic* document whereas forecasts are predictive documents. The prediction of future cash movements is an issue of major importance in accounting theory and will be touched upon in Chapter 18.

8. This example is adapted from the discussions by the UK's Accounting Standards Committee (as it was then known) in the lead-up to the removal of the funds flow statement (previously required under SSAP10) and its replacement by the more 'user-friendly' cash flow statement.

9. With a bit of luck it will have dawned on you that, for example, the fixed assets will have involved *either* an outflow of cash *or* an outflow of information relating to creditors. The same with inventory – we have either paid cash (an outflow from the cashbook) or we still owe for it – in which case it has affected creditors. The share capital will either have been an inflow of cash or else we are still owed for it – so it will be in debtors. *This* is why it is the combination of the figures that produces the cash change. The figures individually actually produce a change in working capital, which we touch upon again below.

10. It is a positive balance. At the end of the second six months Midnight Oil has a cash surplus.

11. This again is adapted as referred to in note 8.

12. You can see this from the balance sheets and if you prepared a cash flow or even a funds flow statement this would also become apparent.

16 Accounting for changing prices: an introduction

Learning objectives

After studying this chapter you should be able to:

- explain the nature of inflation and changing prices;

- demonstrate the impact of changing prices on accounting numbers and financial statements;

- explain the different principal ways in which financial accounting attempts to reflect in financial statements the effects of changing prices;

- adjust historic cost figures to reflect the different principal approaches to asset valuation;

- adjust financial statements to reflect the different principal concepts of capital maintenance;

- discuss the history of accounting for changing prices in the UK;

- briefly outline some of the major further refinements necessary to produce financial statements that reflect the different major approaches to accounting for changing prices.

16.1 INTRODUCTION

This chapter introduces what has probably been one of the most widely discussed issues in accounting in recent decades – the so-called 'inflation accounting debate'. This is the most *technically* difficult area you will meet in your introductory studies of financial accounting. That technical difficulty should not blind you to the fact that many of the problems raised by the subject are, in practice, social and political in nature, as well as economic.

16.1.1 Chapter design and links to previous chapters

In Chapters 3 to 14 we examined the construction of traditional or conventional financial statements. In Chapter 15 we saw how we could use these financial statements to develop further information about the focal organization. In this chapter we go a significant stage further and consider how we might reconstruct a focal organization's financial statements when faced with the problem of changing prices.

All the financial statements we have examined so far have been built upon what is known as the **historic cost convention**. In a period of changing prices this convention can cause serious problems. We will therefore examine ways in which we can either adjust the traditional historic-cost financial statements to take account of this problem or else employ some other basis upon which to construct financial statements.

This chapter is divided into six sections. In the rest of this section (section 16.1) we provide an introduction to the nature of inflation and changing prices and indicate the effect that this has upon the profit of the focal organization. Section 16.2 examines *how* these price changes affect accounting numbers through a simple worked example. Section 16.3 introduces different concepts of asset valuation. Section 16.4 introduces the concept of capital maintenance and the different approaches to it. Section 16.5 briefly outlines the part of the history of the (UK) profession's attempts to deal with these issues. Section 16.6 provides the very briefest of introductions to some of the technical refinements that have been suggested in an attempt to enable financial statements to reflect the effects of changing prices. The chapter summary is rather longer than usual in that is also provides a short review of some other possible approaches to the problems faced by traditional financial accounting and thus provides an taster for Chapter 18.

16.1.2 Background

Nobody has ever suggested that the traditional form of financial statements is perfect but organizations, and those associated with them, have found that they can, generally speaking, 'live with them'; that is, until inflation and/or changing prices became a semi-permanent feature of economic life. Then these financial statements rapidly become more and more misleading. For example, assets bought at different times, when different prices are ruling, are added together in the balance sheet and the resulting aggregate figure for (say) fixed assets means ... what? Perhaps more importantly, in times of changing prices/inflation, neither the owners, the managers nor anyone else *really* knows how well or how badly the organization is performing in financial terms. For a variety of reasons, the already dubious 'profit' figure becomes increasingly misleading to the point where organizations with apparently healthy financial statements can face liquidation. This was exactly the situation, for example, throughout the mid and late 1970s in the UK (and, indeed, elsewhere) and many organizations were having to resort to simple cash accounts (statements of receipts and payments) plus cash forecasts in order to keep themselves informed about the state of their activities in an attempt to keep themselves solvent.

Before we go on to examine some of the effects that inflation and changing prices can have on financial statements we need to lay a little groundwork. In particular, we need to know what we mean by 'inflation and changing prices' and we also need to know something about what we mean by 'profit' or, as it is more usually termed in this context, 'income'.

16.1.3 The nature of changing prices

Paraphrasing Scapens (1981), inflation and changing prices involve a change in the relationship between money on the one hand and goods or services on the other. From the start, it is absolutely essential to remember that:

- accounting seeks to describe economic events in some way or other;
- those economic events, be they related to goods, services, transactions, actions of labour or whatever, can *stay exactly the same* but the description of them will *change* if the relationship between money and those events changes.

Consider something you have to hand – say a Biro. As long as we do not physically interfere with that Biro it remains a Biro no matter how we describe it. As an accountant, you could describe it at 27p (say, what you paid for it), at 15p (say, what one of your colleagues is willing to pay to buy it from you), at 31p (say what it will cost you to replace it because prices have gone up), and so on. It is still a Biro, the same Biro, although there are a great number of different ways to attach a financial figure to it. (These three values have formal names that will be useful later on: 27p is the Biro's *historic cost*, 15p is its *realizable value*, and 31p is its *replacement cost*.)

There are two broad ways in which the relationship between money and the goods (or whatever) can change. These are by *general price changes* or by *specific and/or relative price changes*. Our Biro above was subject to a specific price change. That is not (for our purposes anyway) 'inflation', although that specific price rise (i.e. from 27p to 31p) might be the result of inflation. Inflation is a general rice in prices and in the UK, for example, we measure this by indices, the most common of which is the retail price index (RPI). When you hear on the news that inflation has been (say) 5 per cent for the first quarter of 200X, this means that the RPI (or an equivalent measure in other countries) has risen by 5 per cent in this period. The RPI is an attempt to measure the general effects of inflation on the individual's purchasing power. It consists of a weighted bundle of goods (bread, electricity, nappy pins, etc.) whose prices are constantly checked. Differences in price changes are thus averaged out to give an indication of the general level of inflation.

If inflation has run at 5 per cent since you bought your Biro to the time you read this and try and value it, then if the Biro kept exactly in tune with general inflation we would expect to pay today 28.35p to replace it (i.e. $27p \times 105/100 = 28.35p$). As we would have to pay 31p in this example, than the specific price rise has been greater than the general level of price rises in the economy. Why that should be will not concern us here. Rather, our obsessive interest in your Biro is to illustrate a crucial point. Your Biro could be valued, as we saw, on the basis of three different approaches. Now, there is also a fourth approach to assigning value that is of interest to us. The 27p you have tied up in your Biro represents a certain amount of *purchasing power*. The 27p you spent some time ago is *now*, because of general inflation, the equivalent of 28.35p – you would need this latter figure to release the equivalent purchasing power that is tied up in (represented by) your Biro. So we have a fourth valuation method. (This one is known as *current purchasing power*.)

Inflation refers to general price-level rises, but there are also specific price rises. The specific price rises may occur for all sorts of reasons. These may be because, for example, a change in technology has reduced the cost of the item. Equally a specific price change may be the result of a *relative price change* – the rarity value of Biros or a technical breakthrough that allows word processors to be sold for 21p each will influence the *relative* price of your asset.

16.1.4 The focal organization's income

As we will see in the rest of the chapter, one of the major reasons we all get so worked up about these different ways of valuing things is because we want to know our (commercial) focal organization's income. So, what do we mean by 'profit' or 'income'? Well, that is one of accounting's most difficult questions. The usual way to approach solving this difficulty is to draw from the definition given by Hicks (1946). He had a great number of useful things to say about 'income', but for our purposes we shall keep it simple and define **income** as:

the maximum an individual can consume in any period without leaving himself/herself any worse off than he/she was at the start of the period.

In terms of a company or other commercial organization, this would mean the amount the owners could take out of the business *without leaving it any worse off at the end of the year* than it was at the beginning. The problem, as we shall see, is what do we exactly mean by 'worse off' and, just as tricky, how do we measure it? As we shall see in the next section, during times of changing prices the traditional financial statements we have been studying in this book produce misleading answers. (That is, even more misleading than usual!) The values in the traditional balance sheet are very likely to become less and less meaningful in a period of changing prices and, therefore, it is highly probable that comparing balance sheets at the beginning and end of an accounting period will produce dubious information. Similarly, because of the inextricable link between balance sheet values and the figures in the profit and loss account this latter account will produce a net profit which is unlikely to satisfy Hick's definition in a time of changing prices.

The usual way to start to try and solve this is with something called *economic value*. We will not be going into great detail about this here, but it is useful to have the basic idea in mind. Very crudely, the economic value of a thing (in our case, typically either an asset or an organization) is the sum of the future income it will generate, suitably adjusted for what is called the *time-value of money. Discounting*, as this is known, is the process of adjusting to allow for the fact that funds that are due in ten years' time are not as valuable as funds now in hand – which would you rather have; £1 now or £1 in 20 years' time?[1] We hope you would rather have the £1 now! The result of all this is that, in theory at least, we can measure our income in any one accounting period by calculating the difference between:

i   the sum of our future income streams at the beginning of the year, and
ii   the sum of our future income streams at the end of the year.

If everything you are ever going to earn into infinity, when discounted back to now, produced a greater total sum at the end of the year than it did at the beginning of the year, then you made an *economic income* in that year and that is the figure you can spend without being any worse off! Easy, isn't it?

As you might imagine, the practical problems of trying to do this are rather horrendous and so it remains largely a good idea in theory. (For more detail, see Lewis and Pendrill 1996: Chapters 15–18). We will not be saying very much more detail about it.

The issue of accounting for changing prices/inflation is very difficult and we are trying to approach it at a simple level. The whole idea is one of trying to describe sets of economic events in circumstances when (for our purposes at least) those economic events are fixed and unchanging. It is the medium we use to describe them that keeps changing (try painting a picture of the Mona Lisa when someone keeps slightly altering the colours on your palette without telling you). In order to keep yourself oriented you should hang on to two points:

i   The accounting profession has really only come up with three broad approaches to the problems raised by accounting for changing prices/inflation.[2] These are:
     –   the 'traditional' approach we have been considering in Chapters 3 to 15 of this book (known as *historic cost accounting*);

-   an approach which concentrates on the effects of *general* changes in prices – i.e. inflation (known as *current purchasing power accounting*); and
-   an approach which concentrates on *specific* prices and the *current values* of the assets and other items in the financial statements – the replacement cost and the realizable value of your Biro (this is known as *current cost accounting*).

ii   These three basic approaches are principally distinguished by two elements – how they treat *asset valuation* and how they treat *capital maintenance*.

We will now look at a specific example to illustrate these general points.

16.2 THE EFFECT OF CHANGING PRICES ON FINANCIAL STATEMENTS: A WORKED EXAMPLE

In this section we examine the effects of changing prices with the help of a very simple example – Slowhand Ltd. The initial data relating to Slowhand Ltd are given in Figure 16.1. Figures 16.2 and 16.4 later show different ways in which the financial statements might be prepared to reflect the effects of changing prices. Sections 16.3 and 16.4 further develop the Slowhand example. To do this, it is necessary to complicate the data somewhat. Figure 16.6 (in section 16.3) presents the more complex data for Slowhand Ltd upon which the later developments are based.

Figure 16.2 shows Slowhand's financial statements on the principles we have examined throughout the earlier chapters of the book. As long as all prices have stayed constant throughout the year then Slowhand Ltd is £70 better off at the end of the year than it was at the beginning. Paraphrasing Hicks's terminology, £70 could be withdrawn from the business without leaving it (and/or its owners) any worse off than it was at the beginning of the accounting period.

However, the £70 is not and cannot be the measure of the business's 'better-offness' if for example:

i   for £80, Slowhand Ltd can buy less material than it could a year earlier (in this case the business after the withdrawal of £70 is worse off as it has not retained its production potential);

ii   the assets (the machine) are worth less than £20 (ignoring the depreciation) (in this case the 'worth' of the business indicated by the balance sheet is *overstated* and the withdrawal of £70 has left the business *worse off* – or *mutatis mutandis* if it is 'worth' more than £20);

iii the £120 of share capital will not buy as much at the end of the year as it bought at the beginning of the year (in this case the £70 is *not* a measure of their 'better-offness' – its 'worth' will have been eroded to some degree).

(i)   On 1 January 200X Mr Clapton started up his own business to manufacture 'slowhands' – a specialist labour-intensive product. Slowhand Ltd was formed with £120 share capital.

(ii)   On 2 January, Mr Clapton purchased a machine for £20 and materials (just enough to make eight slowhands) for £80.

(iii) He spent all year working on the slowhands and sold all eight on 31 December 200X for £150 cash. (By a technological miracle convenient for this question, there was no need to depreciate the machine. There are no additional inputs required and Mr Clapton provides the only labour input for which he receives no wages.)

Figure 16.1 The initial simple data for Slowhand Ltd

```
                            SLOWHAND LTD
                    Balance Sheet at 1 January 200X

                                                           £
Cash                                                      120

Represented by:
Share capital                                             120


                    Balance Sheet at 2 January 200X

                                                           £
Fixed assets                                              20
Stock                                                     80
Cash                                                      20
                                                         120


            Profit and Loss Account for the year to 31 December 200X
                                                           £
Sales                                                    150
Less Cost of sales                                       (80)
Profit                                                    70


                    Balance Sheet at 31 December 200X

                                                           £
Fixed assets                                              20
Stock                                                      –
Cash                                                     170
                                                         190


                        Represented by:

Share Capital                                            120
Profit and loss account                                   70
                                                         190
```

Figure 16.2 Slowhand Ltd balance sheet

These three possibilities are not uncommon in fairly stable situations but in times of changing prices and/or inflation they are likely to be the norm. Let us now introduce some changing prices and inflation as given in Figure 16.3 and see the effect that this has on Mr Clapton.

Although this situation is deliberately exaggerated the combined effect of these changes is very typical of the situation facing all organizations in recent years. If you look at the financial statements of Slowhand Ltd in Figure 16.2 bearing in mind these changing prices, you will see that they now make no real sense. In particular, the financial statements *are not comparing like with like*. Look at the profit and loss account. Here we are subtracting the

---

(i)   There was general inflation of 10% during the year – that is, the Retail Price Index rose by 10% in the period.

(ii) An identical machine to that owned by Slowhand could be bought new for £30 on 31 December 200X. Slowhand's own machine could be *sold* for net proceeds of £25 on 31 December 200X.

(iii) To replace the stock of materials with an identical amount and quality would cost, at 31 December 200X, £90.

(iv) The sales price of slowhands has risen during the year – eight slowhands would have generated a sales revenue of only £130 if sold at the *beginning* of 200X.

Figure 16.3 Price change data for the initial Slowhand example

material for eight slowhands at January 'values' from eight slowhands at December 'values' – rather like subtracting drachmas from deutschmarks to get … what? The balance sheet consists of a machine at January 'values' plus 'profit' that itself is the result of mismatching January and December 'values'. The result is that the profit and loss account does not tell us what 'better-offness' is available and the balance sheet does not tell us what the business is 'worth'. (The situation would be much worse in a practical example because there would be all sorts of fixed assets, all purchased at different times and facing different price changes, *and then added together;* the same would be true of stock and so on.)

The financial statements we prepared for Slowhand Ltd were prepared under the historic cost convention. Each item went into the accounting records and thus into the financial statements at its cash-equivalent value *at the time the transaction was made* (hence 'historic'). However, in times of changing prices/inflation the financial statements produced under this convention – **historic cost accounting** (or HCA) – are virtually meaningless and so a variety of different approaches have been suggested to overcome the problem. It is not at all certain that any of these suggested alternatives make an enormous amount of sense either, but they represent perhaps the best attempts to date to deal with a significant problem. Let us rework some of Slowhand Ltd's figures and see what alternatives we can come up with.

All of the figures in Slowhand's HCA financial statements have been affected in some way or other by the changing prices/inflation. First, let us see what would have happened if there had been *no* changes at all. Well, the sales income would not have been as high had the price of slowhands not risen. As we saw above (in Figure 16.3), eight slowhands would have sold for £130 if there had been no inflation, and so profit would have been £50, not £70. But there *was* inflation and the business *did* receive £70. Thus, from this perspective a profit of £50 was earned from the activities of the organization (what is called the *operating profit*) and £20 was gained through the luck or foresight of having bought materials when they were cheaper in money terms. (This is known as the *holding gain or revaluation surplus*.)

However, *this* approach is impractical because few situations are as simple as Slowhand's – had the business been going for several years, how far back would one have to go to get everything on the same terms, even if 'on the same terms' were a realistic possibility? Therefore, it is much the preferred approach to bring the calculations *forward* (rather than going back as we did here) and express the figures in some form of current terms of 'values'.

One way of doing this is to recognize the *specific* price changes that have occurred. We know that the price of material for the slowhands has risen and that if we do not recognize this, then the business will only be able to replace its stock for future production by impoverishing itself. (That is, if Slowhand Ltd were to distribute £70 and then had to spend £90 (as opposed to £80) on new materials for next year the organization would be £10 worse off than it was on 2 January 200X. If this process carried on for three years the company would be insolvent.) We could record this by entering the cost of sales at its **replacement cost** (RC), i.e. at the figure that will not persuade the business to distribute funds that it needs to maintain what is known as its *operating capacity*. (The operating capacity of the organisation is its ability to continue operating at the existing level – to continue producing the same range and quantity of goods and services.) Thus the cost of sales would be £90, not £80, and the profit would then be shown as £60, not £70 (or £50). This is referred to as the **cost of sales adjustment** *(COSA)*. We would also put in the machine at its replacement cost for consistency and in order to show the 'worth' of the business more accurately. The financial statements are shown in the first half of Figure 16.4.

The accounts do not balance now. The £20 difference consists of a £10 holding gain on the machine (i.e. simply by owning the machine the *money* 'worth' of the business has risen)

```
                          SLOWHAND LTD
   Simple RC Profit and Loss Account for the year to 31 December 200X
                       (all figures in pounds)

   Sales                                                    150
   Less Replacement cost of sales                          (90)
   Replacement cost 'profit'                                 60

           Simple RC Balance Sheet at 31 December 200X

   Fixed assets (at replacement cost)                        30
   Stock                                                      –
   Cash                                                     170
                                                            200

   Represented by:
   Share capital                                            120
   Profit and loss account                                   60
                                                            180


   Simple CPP Profit and Loss Account for the year to 31 December 200X

   Sales                                                    150
   Less CPP cost of sales                                   (88)
   CPP 'profit'                                              62

           Simple CPP Balance Sheet at 31 December 200X

   Fixed assets                                              22
   Stock                                                      –
   Cash                                                     170
                                                            192

   Represented by:
   Share capital                                            132
   Profit and loss account                                   62
                                                            194
```

Figure 16.4 Slowhand's RC and CPP financial statements based on the initial example

and the £10 which has been effectively 'put aside' for replacement of stock. These have to be introduced somewhere to make the statement balance. We will examine the question of where when we look at the major recommended approaches in later sections of this chapter (although both might best be shown as some sort of reserve alongside profit).

So we now have a number of alternative 'profits':

i   historic cost profit of £70;
ii   a sort of 'opening values' profit of £50 (plus the £20 holding gain – thus £70); and,
iii a replacement cost profit of £60 (plus £10 holding gain on the machine and £10 'put aside' for replacement of stock – thus £80).

And that is far from the end of the story. You might wish to argue that the 'replacement cost' of the assets does not show the 'true worth' of them and they should be shown at what they could be sold for. That is, the machine should be in the balance sheet at £25 – its *realizable value*. This produces a holding gain on the machine of £5, not £10, which gives yet another perspective on 'profit'.

The last of the major ways in which we might adjust Slowhand Ltd's financial statements for the effects of changing places/inflation is to recalculate the whole set of figures to show the effect that the change in the RPI has had on the accounts. This process involves restating all the figures in '31 December 200X pounds' (i.e. not what the *actual pounds* put into the business are worth in terms of what they will buy, but the number of '31 December 200X pounds' needed to describe the economic events that the business has undertaken *and* leave the business no worse off – from this perspective). This is known as **general purchasing power** *or* **current purchasing power** *(CPP)* accounting. As the rate of inflation prevailing during the period was 10 per cent, we might therefore update the cost of sales figure (£80 + (£80 × 10%)) and the figure for the machine (£20 + (£20 × 10%)) *and* the ownership equity (£120 + (£120 × 10%)), thus getting everything into '31 December 200X pounds'. (NB: The sales figure is already in '31 December pounds' because the sales took place on the last day of the year.) This is a very simple approach and it would produce financial statements of the form shown in the lower half of Figure 16.4.

Once again the balance sheet doesn't balance, except that this time the reason is rather more complex, although simple arithmetic will show you how the £2 is constituted. (Assets rise by £2 on the fixed assets and the liabilities and claims rise by £4. The £4 rise consists of a £12 rise on share capital and a reduction of £8 on 'profit' because the cost of sales rose. Net effect is £2.)

Each of these different approaches to trying to adjust Slowhand's financial statements for the effects of changing prices/inflation can be (and must be) much refined and any number of variants and hybrids can be derived. But we have quite enough 'profits' for the moment. What we have done for Slowhand Ltd can be summarized under four categories of approaches to accounting for changing prices/inflation:

i **historic cost accounting** *(HCA)* – all figures at the cash-equivalent value reigning at the time of the transaction which created the item;

ii **replacement cost accounting** *(RCA)* – basically all assets are entered in the financial statements at the cash-equivalent value of what it would cost the organization to replace them;

iii **realizable value accounting** *(RVA)* – basically all assets are entered at the net proceeds that could be generated by their sale – their 'closing down sale' price;

iv **current purchasing power accounting** *(CPP)* – all figures in the financial statements are restated (via the RPI) in terms of how many current pounds are now necessary to buy, at the balance sheet date, the same amount as they would have bought when the item first entered the focal organization's records.

It is not uncommon to express the different approaches in terms of (to introduce a little further jargon) *entry values* and *exit values* to distinguish between those approaches which depend upon valuation as the item enters the focal organization and those which depend upon valuation as it leaves. This is shown in Figure 16.5 and allows us to perhaps put economic value in some context (see section 16.1).

You will also notice that CPP does not appear in Figure 16.5. This emphasizes the fact that CPP stands rather out on a limb in accounting for changing prices in that CPP seeks to adjust for general price-level changes rather than seeking some reflection of the values intrinsically tied up in the organization.

Space prevents much more being said about either economic value or the realizable value approach. In the following sections we will concentrate on the two methods that have most exercised the accounting profession in the UK and abroad – replacement cost accounting and current purchasing power accounting. But before going into detail on these it is necessary to explore two concepts which are central to our discussion and which have implicitly underlain everything in this section – the concepts of asset valuation and capital maintenance.

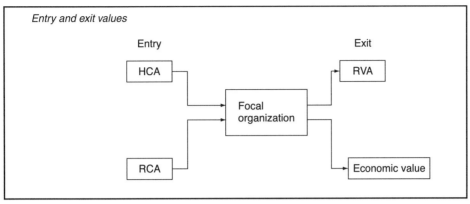

Figure 16.5 Entry and exit values

16.3 METHODS OF ASSET VALUATION (AND EXPENSE DETERMINATION)

The first of the two major distinguishing features of any approach to accounting for changing prices/inflation is the way in which assets are valued in the financial statements.

There are three broad approaches to asset valuation in financial statements:

i *Historic cost (HCA)*. Items enter the financial statements at their cash-equivalent value at the time that they first entered the organizational subsystems – usually the double-entry bookkeeping system. This is the basis we employed in Chapters 3 to 15 above.

ii *Current (or general) purchasing power (CPP)*. All items are brought into the financial statements in the *same* monetary units in order to reflect the effect of general price-level changes on the items in the statements.

iii *Current cost (or current value)*. Items are brought into the financial statements at figures which reflect *specific* price changes. The current cost or current value approach has two main sub-approaches reflecting how specific price changes have influenced what it would cost the organization to replace the item (replacement cost – usually RCA) or what the organization would receive if it were to sell the item (realizable value – RVA).

> **Hint**
>
> The similarity of the names used here to describe asset valuation methods and the names used (at the end of section 16.2) to describe the approaches to accounting for changing prices is not coincidence. The methods of accounting tend to take their name from the asset valuation method used.

As the valuation we place on assets (for example, fixed assets and stock) will determine many of the expenses of the organization for the accounting period (for example, depreciation and cost of sales) then it follows that many of the details of the profit and loss account will largely 'fall out' from our treatment of assets. Other profit and loss account items (such as wages, for example) are normally assumed to be paid continuously and so automatically reflect changing prices.

It is conventional – and extremely convenient – when considering approaches to accounting for changing prices/inflation to divide the main balance sheet items into three categories. These three categories are slightly, but importantly, different from the categories that have been used earlier. Now, instead of talking of assets, claims and 'distributions' we are going to talk of:

i   *capital* (ownership claims);
ii *non-monetary assets* (i.e. those whose worth is dependent upon their contribution to the outputs from the focal organization's operations subsystem, e.g. fixed assets and inventory); and
iii *monetary items* (i.e. those whose worth is fixed in monetary terms, e.g. cash, overdrafts, debtors, creditors, loans and debentures).

The profit and loss account is treated in different ways and so is not explicitly noted in this list.

These three categories help us simplify the process of tracing the effects that different approaches to accounting for changing prices will have on our financial statements. First, we can forget about capital (i.e. ownership claims) for the moment, as this will come under our discussion of approaches to capital maintenance in the following section (16.4). Depending on the approach we adopt, monetary items will either be ignored (that is, treated as they were under HCA) or adjusted by a fairly tricky mechanism – see section 16.6. It is upon the *non-monetary assets* that the main influences of the different valuation bases centre and it is with these that we will therefore begin our analysis.

Let us now go back and complicate Mr Clapton's life slightly in order to show that this 'asset-valuation' part of the basic adjustment of financial statements for the effect of changing prices is really fairly straightforward (see Figure 16.6, which is a development of Figure 16.1).

This will now give him an opening balance sheet as shown in Figure 16.7(a). (*Remember that if there are no price changes of any sort then financial statements prepared under HCA, RCA and CPP will look identical.* Therefore, if we make the reasonable assumption that there have been no price changes during the 24 hours from the time Mr Clapton bought the assets to the time he made up his balance sheet then the first balance sheet in Figure 16.7 is an HCA, RCA and CPP statement.)

Mr Clapton's HCA financial statements at the end of December 200X are shown in Figure 16.7(b). They are based on the assumptions, for the sake of illustration, that the building is *not* depreciated and that the machine is depreciated on the straight line method over five years.

(i)   Mr Clapton now has £220 to start his business (in Figure 16.1, Mr Clapton put £120 into the start of the business).

(ii) He now buys a building for £100, the machine for £20 and stock, now, of £100. (In the initial data he bought a machine for £20 and stock for £80.)

(iii) All other conditions remain the same except that we will remove the technological miracle and require that the machine be depreciated over 5 years.

NB: If you are finding the lack of realism in this example starting to jar, simply mentally adjust all the figures into hundreds of thousands of pounds.

Figure 16.6 More complex data for Slowhand Ltd

Slowhand Ltd HCA, CPP and RCA financial statements based on the more complex data:
(a) Balance sheet at 2 January 200X;
(b) HCA financial statements at 31 December 200X;
(c) CPP financial statements at 31 December 200X;
(d) RCA financial statements at 31 December 200X.

a

SLOWHAND LTD
Balance Sheet at 2 January 200X
(all figures are in pounds)

Fixed assets – building	100
machine	20
Stock	100
Cash	–
	220
Represented by:	
Share capital	220
Profit and loss account	–
	220

(b)   HCA Profit and Loss Account for the year to 31 December 200X

Sales	150
Less Cost of sales	(80)
	70
Less Depreciation	(4)
'Profit'	66

HCA Balance Sheet at 31 December 200X

Fixed assets – building		100
machine	20	
Less Depreciation	(4)	16
Stock		20
Cash		150
		286
Represented by:		
Share capital		220
Profit and loss account		66
		286

(c)   CPP Profit and Loss Account for the year to 31 December 200X

Sales	150
Less Cost of sales	(88)
	62
Less Depreciation	(4.40)
'Profit'	57.60

CPP Balance Sheet at 31 December 200X

Fixed assets – building		110
machine	22	
Less Depreciation	(4.40)	17.60
Stock		22.00
Cash		150.00
		299.60
Represented by:		
Share capital		220
Profit and loss account		57.60
		277.60

(d)   RCA Profit and Loss Account for the year to 31 December 200X

Sales	150
Less Cost of sales	(90)
	60
Less Depreciation	(6)
	54

RCA Balance Sheet at 31 December 200X

Fixed assets – building		120
machine	30	
Less Depreciation	(6)	24.00
Cash		22.50
		150.00
		316.50
Represented by:		
Share capital		220.00
Profit & loss account		54.00
		274.00

Figure 16.7 Slowhand Ltd HCA, CPP and RCA financial statements

If all the other conditions hold then we will have six items which will need adjustment if we are to try and show the effects of changing prices on Mr Clapton's financial statements. These are:

i   the building;
ii   depreciation on the building (if we deem such depreciation necessary);
iii the machine (as before);
iv   depreciation on the machine;
v   cost of sales (as before);
vi   stock (i.e. £80 used and £20 'left over').

We have already seen how to recalculate cost of sales (COSA) and the machine for both the CPP and the RCA methods of adjusting for price changes/inflation, but we must still do something with the other items. The building is straightforward – we would either subject it to the change in the RPI (or some other index) or assess its replacement cost. The CPP method would require us to put the building into the financial statements at £110 (£100 plus 10 per cent in this case). For RCA financial statements we might ask a professional valuer, for example, to assess the building's replacement cost; let us suppose the figure is £120 for the sake of illustration. (Incidentally, for the machine we would have, perhaps, had to consult suppliers' price-lists or something similar in order to ascertain the replacement cost.) The stock remaining at the year end will be reassessed in exactly the same way as was cost of sales. That is, £22 under CPP approach to asset valuation or, under RCA, £22.50 (i.e. the cost of stock, we know from our initial example, went up from £80 to £90 so the £20 will similarly have risen by 12.5 per cent (90/80 × 100) to £22.50).

The depreciation is a bit tricky though. To keep things simple, the depreciation (which you will remember is intended to spread the asset's cover over its useful life) is calculated on the basis of the *revised* asset 'value' – whether it be CPP or RCA. Thus, for the machine, we will enter a depreciation change under the CPP approach of £4.40 (£22 – the inflation adjusted cost – spread evenly over 5 years) and under the RCA approach of £6 (£30 – the replacement cost – spread evenly over 5 years). Our financial statements under these different approaches to asset valuation are shown in Figure 16.7(c) and (d).

Once again the balance sheets do not balance because, of course, we have not done the double-entry for these adjustments. How we get the balance sheets to balance depends principally on what sort of capital maintenance concept we employ (see section 16.4), but it also depends to a lesser extent on how the monetary items are treated. This last point will be dealt with in section 16.6.

Before moving on to look at capital maintenance, we should perhaps say a few words about the above calculations. Under the different approaches or conventions, Mr Clapton's accounts show profits of:

i £66 HCA
ii £57.60 CPP, and
iii £54 RCA.

The first point to make is that there is absolutely no reason why asset valuation using RCA should necessarily produce profits lower than those based on CPP asset valuation. It will in some cases, but not in others. This will depend on the types of assets held, the rate of inflation and so on. The second point to remember is that despite the difference in the figures, Mr Clapton is in exactly the same physical and cash position in each case. The underlying reality that the figures purport to describe is entirely unchanged – only the description of that reality has been altered.

Finally, remember that none of these is the right figure – no such figure exists. Each approach to asset valuation in accounting for the effect of changing prices/inflation (and there are more than the three we have looked at) is primarily a reaction to the weaknesses of HCA. Each then attempts to recalculate the basic figures from the focal organization's accounting system in a way which will better reflect one perspective on the organisation. Thus, differing approaches to accounting for changing prices are not only not 'right' but are, on the whole, incomparable as each has a different objective in mind and a different set of operating assumptions.

16.4 CONCEPTS OF CAPITAL MAINTENANCE

16.4.1 Introduction

Having selected our method of valuing assets (HCA, RCA or CPP), we must next select which concept of capital maintenance to apply. The capital maintenance concept determines how much of the period's income (the 'profit') we must set aside in order to maintain the opening capital of the organization. That is, you will remember that we said 'income' was the amount the organization could distribute without becoming 'worse off' – the concept of capital maintenance determines what we mean by 'worse-offness'.

Capital maintenance will usually be defined in one of three ways – in terms of:

- money capital;
- general purchasing power;
- operating capacity.

(a) Money capital

This is the simplest of the three definitions and is the traditional concept of capital maintenance. It simply requires that the organization maintain the money amount of the opening capital intact (i.e. the stated amount that the owners have injected into the organization). In practical terms, therefore, all that is required is that the business refrain from distributing (in the form of dividends for example) more than is contained in the profit and loss account.[3]

(b) General purchasing power

This definition of capital maintenance requires that the general purchasing power of the owners' capital be maintained. Thus, sufficient must be put aside each year to ensure that the owners' initial capital will buy the same (in general purchasing power terms) at the end of the accounting period as it did at the beginning of the period. This approach to capital maintenance adopts a *proprietary view* of the organization and its capital. That is, it sees the problem from the point of view of the owners (the proprietors) and seeks to ensure that the worth of their ownership is not diminished.

(c) Operating capacity

This definition takes an *entity view* of the problem. From this perspective sufficient must be allocated from the year's operations and 'put aside' in order to maintain the organization's ability to deliver the same range, quality, etc. of goods and services year after year.

Now, of course, the majority of organizations will seek to increase the capital of the organization (however measured) from year to year. What these capital maintenance concepts do is to try and identify the minimum that is required in order to leave neither the organization nor the owners any worse off.

We now have three asset valuation bases and three capital maintenance concepts which, at our simple level of analysis, give us nine possible combinations. (There are of course many more possible variants.) In fact, of the nine only five are commonly used and these are listed in Figure 16.8.

Thus, although the asset valuation methods and the capital maintenance concepts need not necessarily coincide in theory, they may often do so in practice. Let us now have a look and see how these different concepts apply to Mr Clapton.

16.4.2 Historic cost with money capital

First, we had the HCA financial statements (see Figure 16.7(b)). Assets were valued at their historic cost and, without being explicit about it, we maintained the organization's money capital. That is, the £220 introduced into the business was Mr Clapton's money capital and as long as this was not touched and/or taken out of the business (i.e. the organization did not distribute more than the £66 HCA profit we calculated), its money capital was maintained.

Asset Valuation Method	Capital Maintenance Concept
Historic Cost	Used with monetary capital maintenance
CPP	Used with general purchasing-power capital maintenance
Replacement Cost	Used with monetary capital maintenance
Replacement Cost	Used with operating-capacity capital maintenance
Replacement Cost	Used with general purchasing-power capital maintenance

Figure 16.8 Common combinations of asset valuation and capital maintenance methods

16.4.3 CPP with general purchasing-power capital

Mr Clapton's CPP balance sheet before adjustment to the reserves was shown in Figure 16.7(c). The problem, from the general purchasing-power perspective of capital maintenance is that Mr Clapton's share capital will not now buy as much as it would at the beginning of the accounting period because of inflation. We must thus provide a capital maintenance reserve equivalent to this loss of general purchasing power. You will remember that the rate of inflation in our example was 10 per cent and so we must provide an amount of £22 (10 per cent of £220). The second half of the balance sheet as it should now appear is shown in Figure 16.9(a) and the balance sheet now balances. (It is rarely this easy as we will normally have to adjust for what is called the gain or loss on holding monetary items, none of which Mr Clapton held during the year – see section 16.6 below.)

a) CPP with general purchasing-power capital:		
Represented by:		
Share capital		220.00
Capital maintenance reserve		22.00
Profit and loss account		57.60
		299.60
b) Calculation of total RCA holding gains:		
Building	20	
Machine (NBV)	8	
Closing stock	2.50	30.50
Plus the 'extra' profit 'put aside':		
'Extra' depreciation	2	
'Extra' cost of sales	10	12.00
Total holding gains		42.50
c) RCA with money capital maintenance		
Represented by:		
Share capital		220.00
Profit and loss account		54.00
Holding gains		42.50
		316.50
d) RCA with general purchasing-power capital maintenance		
Represented by:		
Share capital		220.00
Capital maintenance reserve		22.00
		242.00
Profit and loss account	54	
Holding gains	20.50	74.50
		316.50
e) RCA with operating-capacity capital maintenance		
Represented by:		
Share capital		220.00
Capital maintenance reserve		42.50
		262.50
Profit and loss account		54.00
		316.50

Figure 16.9 Effects of different capital maintenance concepts on the balance sheet of Slowhand Ltd

What has happened, in effect, is that the increase in the values attributed to the assets as a result of general inflationary rises can be counted as some sort of gain to the organization. This consists of £10 on the building, £1.60 on the net book value of the machine and £2 on the stock, totalling £13.60. We have also put aside some additional profit – £8 on the cost of sales (which we have not actually spent) and 40p worth of extra depreciation, totalling £22. In a simple-minded world these gains would be classified as 'profits' and added to our £57.60 to show a 'profit' of £79.60. However, some of this profit must be retained in the business to cover the diminution of Mr Clapton's capital. It just so happens in this case (because there are no monetary assets held throughout the year) that this is also £22.

16.4.4 Replacement cost with differing capital maintenance concepts

Finally, we produced a set of financial statements for Mr Clapton based on replacement cost asset valuation. (The balance sheet was shown in Figure 16.7(d).) In this case, the balance sheet does not balance because of the *holding gains* that the organization has enjoyed. These have been introduced into the asset values, but the double-entry has not been completed for them. The constitution of the holding gains (£42.50) is shown in Figure 16.9(b). This £42.50 is, again, some sort of gain to the organization and could, similarly, in a simple-minded world be added to the profit figure. If we did this the bottom part of the balance sheet would look as shown in Figure 16.9(c). And once again the balance sheet balances.

How we treat these holding gains is determined by the capital maintenance concept we wish to employ:

i   If we employ a *money capital* concept of capital maintenance then all the holding gains are treated as income and are, in effect, added to the profit figure and are therefore available for distribution. Thus capital is maintained in money terms – it remains at £220. (This is the case in Figure 16.9(c).)

ii If we employ a *general purchasing-power* concept of capital maintenance then we must allocate some of the holding gains to enhance the owners' capital in order to maintain its purchasing power. Thus, £22 (10% – the rate of inflation ruling in our example – of the opening capital, £220) must be put aside as a capital maintenance reserve. In this case the second part of the balance sheet will look as shown in Figure 16.9(d).

iii If we employ an *operating-capacity* concept of capital maintenance, then all the holding gains are treated as an addition to capital maintenance (as all the 'gains' are necessary to maintain the fabric of the organization's ability to deliver goods and services). Figure 16.9(e) shows how the bottom part of Mr Clapton's balance sheet will look in this case.

The basic figures are the same in each case – the capital maintenance concept has simply determined how much of the calculated profit (under the RCA asset valuation method) should be allocated to the capital of the organization and how much of it can be treated as income.

Although by no means complete, we now have the major components of the more popular approaches to accounting for changing prices. In the next section we will review these in the light of the professional debate on the subject of accounting for changing prices before moving on (in section 16.6) to take a brief look at the some of the adjustments which are necessary to apply the methods in practice.

16.5 ACCOUNTING FOR CHANGING PRICES AND THE ACCOUNTING PROFESSION

We now have five bases for traditional financial statements:

i   Historic cost accounting, with a money capital maintenance reserve. (These were shown for Slowhand in Figure 16.7(b).)

ii Current purchasing-power accounting with a general purchasing-power capital maintenance reserve. (See Figure 16.7(c) and 16.9(a).)

iii Replacement-cost accounting with a money capital maintenance reserve. (See Figure 16.7(d) and 16.9(c).)

iv Replacement-cost accounting with a general purchasing-power capital maintenance reserve. (See Figure 16.7(d) and 16.9(d).)

v   Replacement-cost accounting with an operating-capacity capital maintenance reserve. (See Figures 16.7(d) and 16.9(e).)

This excludes the various refinements that we might make to these bases, and it also excludes other bases such as realizable value, continuously contemporary accounting and cash flow accounting (see the summary to this chapter). Therefore the range of choice facing accountants trying to decide on the 'best' method of accounting for changing prices is fairly daunting. This choice is all the more fundamental because, as Whittington (1981a) argues, before trying to choose a method of preparing financial statements we must decide whether we wish to take an 'entity' view (the owner looking into the organization) or a 'proprietorship' view (the organization looking out), and we must decide what purpose the information in the financial statements is supposed to serve. These are contentious and difficult issues to which there can be no unique solution (for more details see Chapter 18). Whittington goes on to argue that we must recognize that each method has its own strengths and that a case can be made for reporting different accounting bases to different users with different purposes in mind.

Such difficulties illustrate that central to accounting – and accounting regulation in particular – is the difficulty in deciding exactly what financial statements are for and what they are supposed to show. The 'inflation accounting debate' was less about how to cope with the inflationary effects on financial numbers than about what accounting was actually supposed to be doing. Figure 16.10 summarizes some of the major stages in the UK's inflation accounting debate.

There are important lessons to be learnt from the experience of the accounting profession in the UK (and other countries) as it attempted to 'solve' how best to account in a period of rapidly changing prices. *First*, it illustrates the very difficult problems which face standard-setting bodies. The UK accounting profession proposed two completely different approaches to the issue within a space of 2½ years (PSSAP 7 to ED 18) and then proposed a further four variations on one of these themes, and still came to no agreement. This amply attests to the fundamental disarray in which the conceptual foundations of accounting and the accounting profession find themselves. If the profession cannot agree on such basic issues as the purpose of financial statements, then it should come as no surprise that disagreement over accounting policy will be the rule rather than the exception. *Second*, this experience illustrates that accounting policy is a matter of agreement rather than a matter of fact. As a result, the whole debate about accounting, its nature and its policy (e.g. any particular accounting standard) is just as likely to be the result of some powerful individual's preference (because it suits them or the organization they represent) as it is the result of argument about 'best' accounting or the social role of

In the UK, inflation, as measured by the RPI, did not fall below 8% during the 1970s, and rose as high as 25% in 1975. This undermined any usefulness of HCA. The UK accounting profession responded as follows:

- In 1973 the Accounting Standards Committee (ASC) issued Exposure Draft (ED) 8 which recommended a form of CPP with a general purchasing-power capital-maintenance reserve.

- In 1974, the ASC issued Provisional Statement of Standard Accounting Practice (SSAP) 7 which enacted the provisions of ED 8. This is the only time that the ASC had issued a provisional standard.

- In 1975, the Sandilands Committee (a government committee) recommended current cost accounting (CCA) – a variant on our RCA with a general purchasing-power capital-maintenance reserve.

- In 1976, the ASC published ED 18 which recommended a very detailed version of Sandiland's CCA. ED18 was a disaster – the UK accounting profession rebelled and rejected the recommendation and its complexity.

- In 1977 the ASC published the Hyde Guidelines. This simple version of CCA required HCA to be subject to three relatively simple adjustments. This brought CCA closer to operating-capacity capital maintenance.

- In 1979, the ASC issued ED 24. This developed the Hyde Guidelines, produced a variant of CCA with operating-capacity capital maintenance plus some adjustment for the changing purchasing power of the owners' equity. In 1980, ED 24 (more or less) became SSAP 16.

- SSAP 16 had a moderately bumpy ride and was withdrawn in 1985.

Figure 16.10 The UK's experience with inflation accounting

financial statements and the accounting profession. (We briefly return to these matters in Chapters 18 and 19.) *Third*, the debate over accounting for changing prices has left the accounting profession with a somewhat tattered image and self-esteem. Business, government and the general public were not impressed by the profession's inability to come up with a solution to such a seemingly simple problem. After all, accountants have not gone out of their way to inform the public that financial statements (under any convention) contain a fair amount of guesswork and choice and are a long way from being the 'factual' statements they are often believed to be. The 'inflation' accounting debate raised the spectre of possible government intervention in the determination of the rules for financial reporting and regulation of the accounting profession.

16.6 SOME FURTHER REFINEMENTS

Simply for the sake of completeness, it is useful to recognize at this point that whilst the basic approaches to accounting for changing prices involves (a) adjustments to maintain capital, and (b) adjustments to the valuation of assets (including the cost of sales adjustment), the actual application of the methods we have mentioned involved rather more technical detail to 'make them work'. It would be inappropriate to do more than touch upon them at this stage in your studies but you should have, at least, a general awareness of what this involves. *Please note*, what follows is no more than a slight taste of the issues which, if you were to study them in detail, rapidly get very complicated indeed. At this stage, simply try and grasp the *general* principles that are involved.

Before the approaches to accounting for changing prices can be made operational – even at a simple level – it is necessary to deal with the following issues:

i   adjustments for monetary items;

ii   backlog depreciation;

iii realized versus unrealized holding gains;

iv the gearing adjustment.

This section provides a very brief introduction to these issues.

16.6.1 Adjustment for monetary items

The adjustment for monetary items arises in the application of both CPP and RCA. Under CPP the concern is with attempting to identify the *gain or loss on holding monetary items* and under RCA the concern is with something called the *monetary working capital adjustment*.

The gain or loss on holding monetary items attempts to reflect the fact that, in times of inflation, one loses from holding cash as opposed to other assets. That is, if you could hold £10 in cash or £10 worth of gold, you would choose the gold because the inflation would mean that, at the end of the year, its value in pounds would mean that it would buy more than 10 pound coins. The holding of cash in times of inflation results in a loss of purchasing power.

The same effect occurs for items which are defined in monetary terms – the monetary assets and liabilities. These include debtors, bank balances, creditors, loans, overdrafts and debentures. If an organization holds, say, a debtor of £20 and a creditor of £30 for one year when inflation is running at 10 per cent, that organization will effectively lose £2 on the debtor and gain £3 on the creditor. This is because, at the beginning of the year, it delivered £20 worth and received £30 worth of goods or services. When these amounts are paid in cash, the cash is worth less than it was at the time the debts were incurred. £20 and £30 in year-end pounds are worth less than £20 and £30 in start-of-year pounds. In this particular example, the organization makes a net gain on holding monetary items of £1. This is more usually stated as the gain from holding net monetary liabilities. Should our organisation have had more debtors than creditors over the period there would have been a loss on holding net monetary assets.

The RCA monetary working capital adjustment (MWCA) is an altogether more complicated and disputed issue. Put simply, the monetary working capital adjustment is an attempt to adjust the financial statements in order to reflect the impact of changing prices on the working capital or the organization. In particular (remembering what RCA is all about), it is an attempt to demonstrate what effect these changing prices have had on the organization's needs for finance to maintain working capital.

For a variety of reasons (that we need not examine here), the MWCA concentrates on trade debtors and trade creditors. What we are trying to establish is whether we need to 'put aside' more of our income (i.e. increase our capital maintenance reserve) in order to finance the net debtors, or whether we can release some income because we have net creditors and these are helping to finance us. Remember, at its simplest level, it costs us to have debtors (they, in effect have got our money), and it pays us to have creditors (we, in effect, have got their money). So what we have to do is find out how the price changes have affected our net position. To do this we work out how much of the change in total net trade debtors or net trade creditors is a result of volume changes, and how much is due to price changes. If there are more creditors than debtors *and the* price changes on debtors and creditors have arisen equally (not entirely unlikely in inflationary times), this will be in the organization's favour – the creditors are helping to finance the debtors. This is then a source of RCA income and so will be credited to the RCA profit and loss account and the debit can be taken to the RCA reserves which are starting to build up on the balance sheet. (It will thus reduce the RCA reserves – because it is a debit – reflecting the fact that we can reduce our capital maintenance reserve by this amount.)

16.6.2 Backlog depreciation

Backlog depreciation arises because under the different asset valuation approaches to accounting for changing prices we based the depreciation for the accounting period on the revalued asset. If we perform this exercise for more than one accounting period we meet a slight problem. This is simply a matter of arithmetic. Although we are basing each accounting period's depreciation on the revalued (adjusted asset value) figure the effect of each subsequent year's revaluation and depreciation is to leave the asset under-depreciated with respect to earlier years. To prevent this cumulative shortfall getting worse and worse and thus failing to spread the revalued figure over the anticipated life of the asset, a calculation is made each year of backlog depreciation.

In practice we do not have this difficulty with CPP because of the arithmetic whereby each figure is adjusted for the RPI in that year. So in practice the problem of backlog depreciation only arises with RCA, in which case the depreciation for the accounting period is calculated as the usual percentage of the gross RC value and then we calculate the backlog depreciation and add it to the *accumulated* depreciation figure.

16.6.3 Realized versus unrealized holding gains

The third issue is the separation of holding gains into realized and unrealized. So far we have not made this distinction although this runs counter to the prudence or conservatism convention that we met in Chapter 7. This stated that the accountant should not recognize income until it is certain and/or realised. (Because of the way in which CPP financial statements are created, it is not really appropriate to talk about CPP holding gains. Therefore, to all intents and purposes the separation of holding gains is once again an RCA matter only.)

In our earlier examples we have treated *all* holding gains as direct accretions to profit or capital (depending on the capital maintenance reserve concept employed). A realized holding gain (RHG) arises most typically on the sale of the organization's goods or services when the gain from holding stock or inventory which is transformed into an output from the operations subsystem is realised in the sale price (i.e. the *potential* gain existing in the stock is made real – is transformed into cash). If you think back to Mr Clapton, in section 16.2, you will note that his HCA profit consisted in part of operating profit and in part of holding gains which were realized at the time of sale. The other 'gains' that we identified as arising on his building and machine and on the stock he still had in hand, remained *unrealized* at the accounting date. These gains were still potential gains whose 'reality' had yet to be established for certain. The unrealized holding gains (UHG) are thus probable, not certain, gains.

There are no hard and fast rules on how to treat these different elements of holding gains but the general view is that UHG should *not* be available for distribution and therefore should not be counted as income for the period. They should, rather, be taken to reserves. The RHG, on the other hand, will be treated as distributable – depending on the approach to capital maintenance adopted.

16.6.4 The gearing adjustment

The gearing adjustment, because of the way that the capital maintenance reserve is calculated under CPP, can be taken as applying only to RCA. The problem that the gearing adjustment seeks to solve is as follows. It is unusual to find an organization entirely funded by ownership capital. Most have some debt (debentures, loan stock or overdraft) and virtually all organizations are partially funded by their trade creditors. (That is, if you do not pay for what you receive immediately with cash, your creditor is, in effect, allowing you a short, interest-free loan to the value of the goods or services for which you owe.) This means that in order to maintain the operating capacity of the organization intact it may not be necessary to 'put aside' all the holding gains as some of them are – *and will be in the future* – financed, not by the organization or its owners, but by the creditors. The gearing adjustment is, rather like the MWCA, a transfer out of the RCA reserves to the profit and loss account in order to pass on to the owners some of the benefits which accrue to the organization from borrowing in times of rising prices.

This completes our very brief (and superficial) review of the additional adjustments that might be undertaken to produce financial statements which will (hopefully) reflect the effect of changing prices on the focal organization.

We will now, in the final section of this chapter, provide a summary of all these machinations and a brief evaluation of the attempts to date to deal with these undoubtedly difficult problems.

16.7 A REVIEW, SUMMARY AND SOME CONCLUDING REMARKS ON ACCOUNTING FOR CHANGING PRICES

By now you will have seen that accounting for changing prices is a very complex subject involving difficult technical issues. These technical issues cannot be uniquely resolved because the social, political and conceptual issues which underlie the whole accounting activity are themselves unresolved. The main points that we covered in this chapter are as follows:

- No matter what we do to the accounting numbers (the financial statements) by way of various adjustments the first and foremost thing to remember is that the *economic reality* which underlies the numbers has not changed.
- There are broadly two types of changes in the relationship between the events and the money we use to describe them. There are those that arise from *general* price level changes (i.e. inflation), and those that arise from *specific* (or *relative*) price changes.
- This gave us three broad groups of asset valuation approaches – *historic cost, current purchasing power* and *current cost* or *values*. HCA does not recognize the changing relationship between the economic events and the money used to describe them. CPP recognizes only *general* price-level changes, i.e. inflation. Current cost or values recognizes *specific* prices changes in various ways.
- There is a variety of different approaches to current cost or current values accounting. We only studied the *replacement cost* approach. (More about these alternatives in a moment.)
- The next problem was something called *capital maintenance*. The Hicksian definition of *income* has been used to suggest that income was the amount that the organization could consume (i.e. distribute) within a given period without leaving itself any worse off. The question was, how do we define 'worse off'? Three definitions predominate, all stated in terms of the capital of the organization – *money capital, general purchasing*

power capital and *operating capacity*. Under the last two of these different capital maintenance concepts the organization must allocate a proportion of the income of the accounting period to a capital maintenance reserve fund, thus keeping within the organization sufficient funds to maintain the capital (however defined).

● Finally, we looked at a number of adjustments which were necessary to refine the different approaches and make them operational. For the CPP/general purchasing power approach we required just one adjustment – that to calculate the *gain/loss on holding monetary items*. This adjustment attempted to reflect the fact that, in times of inflation, one *loses* from holding cash and debtors, and, by corollary, one effectively *gains* from holding creditors and *not* holding cash. The current cost approach required four adjustments. (Whilst we only looked at the RCA variant, the same principle applies to the other current cost/current values approaches.) These four adjustments were:

i   *the monetary working capital adjustment (MWCA)*. This adjustment attempted to reflect the effect that holding assets and liabilities defined in money terms has on the organization's need to provide finance for working capital;

ii *backlog depreciation*, to adjust for the fact that an annual revaluation of depreciated assets will leave those assets effectively under-depreciated because of the arithmetic effect of the way the annual depreciation charge is calculated;

iii *holding gains*, which we separated into *realized* and *unrealized* in order to distinguish which parts of income were 'real' and which were only 'potential income'. How we treated each depended upon our capital maintenance concept;

iv *the gearing adjustment*, which attempted to reflect (in a way not entirely dissimilar from the MWCA) the way in which the holding of trade and loan creditors means that part of our organization's activities are financed by those creditors and thus less is required to be allocated from the income of the accounting period to maintain capital.

It is well recognized that, particularly, the MWCA and the gearing adjustment are difficult matters to grasp. As we have stressed throughout, our intention here was to give a basic introduction to these matters – the detail of these things is more appropriately developed later in your studies. What we *have* discussed can be summarized as in Figure 16.11.

There *are* other approaches to the problems raised by accounting for changing prices which, for reasons of simplicity, we have avoided in this chapter. One such alternative is the

A summary of approaches and adjustments				
Name of accounting method	**Basis of asset valuation**	**Basis of capital maintenance**	**Additional adjustments necessary**	**Area of financial statements affected**
HCA	Historic cost	Money	–	–
CPP (proprietary)	Current purchasing power	General purchasing power	Loss/gain on holding monetary items	Trade debtors and trade creditors
CCA (entity)	Replacement cost (for example)	Money GPP Operating capacity	MWCA Backlog deprec'n Holding gains Gearing	Trade debtors and creditors Depreciation Assets Borrowing

Figure 16.11 A summary of Chapter 16

development of *cash flow accounting* (to be distinguished from cash flow statements in Chapter 15), which comes in many forms, from the simplest (something like receipts and payments accounts) through to sophisticated attempts to include estimates of future cash flows to be generated by the segments of the organization. Other approaches which, in effect, involve variations on the adjustments and concepts we have reviewed above, include something called *value to the business* (or, more colourfully, *deprival value),* an approach pioneered in Australia by Chambers (1966) called *continuously contemporary accounting* (or CoCoa), and an approach pioneered by Grinyer (1985) geared towards the evaluation of managers called *Earned Economic Income* (EEI). Each of *these* approaches, as with the more widely attempted methods we have discussed above has its adherents, its strengths and its weaknesses. This sheer diversity of approaches to what – on the surface at least – looks like a fairly straightforward problem has produced some real benefits from this professional confusion. *First* of all, as we stated earlier, the debate has emphasized the fact that financial statements cannot be an unequivocal statement of anything. Such education is valuable. *Second*, the debate has brought to the forefront of our attention the concept of operating capacity which is clearly central to the management and control of any organization. *Third*, and following from this, the discussion explicitly raises the question of whether the financial statements are *only* for the shareholders or whether other parties have a legitimate right to the information contained therein. (See the discussion in Chapter 17.)

It is the operating capacity question that drew the techniques of accounting for changing prices into the sphere of interest of non-commercial organizations. Whilst we have not examined the appropriateness of what we have said to these organizations, there has been effort from time to time to apply these concepts to the larger and more capital-intensive utilities and public-sector service organizations. Of course, some of our discussion is irrelevant to non-commercial organizations as they are rarely in a position to define their 'owners'. The concept of operating capacity has, however, provided a most useful addition to management thinking in these organizations.

You can see that it does not take much in the way of complications before both the preparer of the financial statements and the reader will begin to wonder what the statements really mean. The relationship between the things being described and the description becomes more convoluted and abstruse to the point where many will simply lose sight of it altogether. It is probably for this reason that research evidence about the usefulness of either CPP or CCA financial statements has been, at best, mixed. It is far from clear that the 'experts' who use financial statements in their everyday life (e.g. bankers, financial analysts, auditors) have found that either CPP or CCA financial statements have made their job any easier or have, in fact, helped them do their job any better. The lack of any clear evidence that transforming financial statements to allow for the effects of changing prices is useful, has heartened those who have opposed all the machinations, and has been rather disheartening for those who have given so much of their professional life to their development.

Apart from the fact that research is always likely to be unclear when it comes to testing people's beliefs and opinions, the questions which are raised by accounting for changing prices are quite fundamental to an understanding of the subject of 'traditional' accounting. Even if we could establish the *purpose* of accounting (see Chapter 18) and even if we restrict 'accounting' to the financial inputs and outputs discussed in Chapters 3 to 15 (but see Chapter 17), then, as we can now see, there are still many demanding technical *and* social issues to be resolved in our attempts to provide financial descriptions of organizations' economic activities and the organizations' 'worth', 'value' and/or 'income' at any point in time. Much of your further study of accounting will be addressed to issues such as these.

Key terms and concepts

Here is a list of the key terms and concepts which have featured in this chapter. You should make sure that you understand and can define each one of them. Page references to definitions in the text appear in bold in the index.

- Adjustment for monetary items
- Asset valuation
- Backlog depreciation
- Capital maintenance
- Cost of sales adjustment
- Current cost
- Current purchasing power
- Current value
- Economic value
- Entity view
- Entry and exit values
- Gearing adjustment
- General purchasing power
- Historic cost
- Holding gain
- Income
- Inflation
- Monetary items
- Monetary working capital adjustment
- Operating capacity
- Operating profit
- Price changes
- Proprietary view
- Realizable value
- Replacement cost

FURTHER READING

There is no shortage of literature on the issues we have raised in this chapter. For additional reading, we particularly recommend Whittington (1981b) and Hope (1984). For more advanced material, the books by Scapens (1981) and Lewis and Pendrill (1996) are a more useful place to start.

There are two very useful articles which deal with these issues as well: Coombes and Eddey (1986) demonstrate a novel way of seeing the relationship between capital maintenance and asset valuation, and Shalchi and Smith (1985) provide a slightly more advanced review of the issues and the research findings in this area. Further readings by Whittington (1981b) and Whittington and Tweedie (1984) also make interesting and stimulating reading.

NOTES

1. You should be aware, however, that discounting means treating the future as though it were less important than the present. This may be OK in a purely financial sense but in a social or environmental sense it is very dangerous indeed. A great deal of the environmental crisis can be traced to a tendency, in the past, to treat the future (and the resultant pollution, soil erosion or drought, for example) as less important than the (then) present. Even simple techniques are not without their price! We return to this in Chapter 17.

2. There are others such as continuously contemporary accounting and earned economic income. They have not, at the time of writing, been very widely embraced although, for some, they are more attractive methods. You will (perhaps) meet these later in your studies.

3. This is an essential element of basic accounting procedure and principles. We have been doing this throughout the earlier chapters but have not, up until now, made the principle explicit. The principle is typically enshrined in a country's Companies Acts.

Expanding the reporting function: social and environmental accounting and reporting

17

Learning objectives

After studying this chapter you should be able to:

- describe how social and environmental accounting and reporting differ from conventional financial accounting and reporting;

- describe the types of non-financial information contained in companies' reports;

- briefly outline the function of the value-added statement;

- describe the activities which fall within the scope of social accounting and reporting;

- describe the activities which fall within the scope of environmental accounting and reporting;

- briefly explain the idea of sustainable development;

- debate the arguments for and against social and environmental accounting and reporting.

17.1 INTRODUCTION

Up until now we have generally concentrated upon those issues which fall within the traditional orthodoxy of accounting. The aim of this chapter is to question this traditional accounting model and introduce a number of the ways in which the orthodoxy is being challenged. We are thus breaking out from the four characteristics of conventional accounting and the eight types of financial transactions that we introduced in earlier chapters. This, we hope, will encourage you to question further the role, purpose and effect of the accounting activity.

17.1.1 Background

The 'traditional accounting model', as we have seen, is defined by four characteristics: *an accounting entity, economic events, financial description,* and *an assumed set of users (typically financial participants) who will find the accounting information useful.* A fairly obvious question which should come to mind is 'Why is accounting restricted in this way?'. It is probable that we have to maintain some sort of assumption about an accounting entity – because without something to account *for* it is pretty difficult to undertake any kind of accounting. So the *accounting entity* characteristic is a fairly logical and practical one. But what about the other characteristics? Why do we restrict ourselves to only economic events? Why are we only concerned with financial description? Why do only certain users have rights to accounting information?

Once you ask these questions, you should be able to see that there is an enormous range of possible accountings of which conventional financial accounting is only one, small subset. That is, we can account for the *social* or *environmental* consequences of the events we have provided a financial account of. We can also account for events *other than* those we have so far sought to account for. We can account for various events in different ways using *descriptive* or *quantified* data rather than financial data. We can account to groups other than the financial participants. For example, we may provide information to *employees, local and international communities*; *customers*; *other interest groups*; and *society as a whole*. This wider set of possible users of information about an organization are usually called **stakeholders**: that is, they are individuals and groups who are affected by and who affect the organization. The traditional users of financial accounts – shareholders – are also stakeholders but are just one group of many.

Relaxing the 'rules' as to what events to account for, how we may account for events and to whom we provide accounts results in an enormously wide range of possible approaches to accounting. This area of accounting is called **social and environmental accounting and reporting (SEAR)**.[1] The purpose of this chapter is to introduce you to some of the universe of all possible accountings and to demonstrate to you that conventional financial accounting is a small subset of all possible accounts.

Viewed in this way, we can see that the traditional financial accounting model maintains a very restricted perspective on organizational activity – one which implies that the financial story of the organization is the most important one and the only one in which the various external participants are interested. Taken to extremes this might imply that managers, loan creditors and shareholders are uninterested in (say) product or service quality, consumer satisfaction, the welfare of the human beings who work in the organization, the members of the local community affected by the noise, pollution, advertising, etc., *except insofar as these issues might influence the financial position of the focal organization.* This is a very narrow view.

A parallel implication of the traditional financial accounting model is that accounting *per se* is an isolated, neutral and amoral activity and that accounting is an activity the actions of which have only *financial* implications. This is, quite simply, untrue. Accounting has many social and environmental effects and it behoves anyone who takes the study of accounting seriously to consider these. This is what we start to do in this chapter.

17.1.2 Chapter design and links to previous chapters

Part III of the text examined the construction of financial statements which were firmly bonded to the eight types of financial transactions introduced in Chapter 4 as the basis of the traditional financial accounting activity. Chapter 15 and, to a greater extent, Chapter 16 began to loosen those bonds. Chapter 17 completes the process and thus sets the scene for Chapter 18 in which we begin a process (which will continue through your accounting studies) in which the foundations of financial accounting and reporting are thoroughly re-examined.

The chapter is organized as follows. Section 17.2 introduces the range of 'non-financial' information reported to shareholders in the Annual Report. This includes a brief consideration of something known as the *value-added statement*. Section 17.3 then attempts to introduce activities which fall under the banner of social accounting and reporting while section 17.4 moves to introduce environmental accounting and reporting as well as briefly considering the concept of sustainable development. Finally, we will review some of the implications that these developments (and some of the issues we raised with the traditional accounting model) have for our understanding of the accounting activity and the accounting profession. This provides a 'taster' for Chapters 18 and 19.

Hint

Please note, in Chapter 14 we emphasized that company reporting both varied from country to country and was rapidly changing. This is perhaps even more true for SEAR than it is for conventional financial accounting. The following is, therefore, a fairly broad-brush overview of social and environmental accounting and reporting (SEAR) with an (inevitable) UK bias. You should be referring to your library of annual reports and your professional accountancy magazines for more pertinent depth and illustrations. See also Gray *et al.* (1996) for a wider, more international, perspective.

17.2 DISCLOSURES IN COMPANY ANNUAL REPORTS

17.2.1 Introduction

Shareholders are certainly the main focus of company reporting and accounting. It is principally for them that so much law and so many accounting standards and guidelines exist (see Chapters 12 and 14). The history of company law can be seen as one of a steady increase in the information provided by companies (e.g. the notes to the accounts, Chapter 14; the cash flow statement, Chapter 15; the attempts – albeit spasmodic – to introduce supplementary accounts using different accounting bases, Chapter 16) to enable the shareholders to protect their investment.

Some of the information provided in the full document in which the organization's financial statements appear (usually called the *annual report and accounts* for shareholders) has, however, moved away from information which is clearly and directly related to the shareholders' financial involvement in the organization. There has been an increase in the emphasis placed on information about a number of issues arising from company activities. This information is briefly summarized in Figure 17.1.

You should take this opportunity to read through the annual report and accounts of the company/ies which you have in your reports library and see if you can identify the information noted in the mandatory column. In addition, you may like to take a note of the other information you identify while reading your reports and see how it fits within Figure 17.1.

The categories of information outlined in Figure 17.1, whilst they have *some* financial implications are not obviously essential to the shareholders' financial management of their investment. In part, at least, this information is probably intended for those who maintain a longer-term interest in and involvement with the organization (see subsection 17.3.4 for a more extended discussion of this). However, as the information appears in the annual report and accounts to *shareholders* we should first examine it as though it were intended primarily for the owners of the business. The rest of this section will examine items from Figure 17.1 which will not be covered under with social or environmental accounting and reporting. Primarily this is the value-added statement and disclosures which were suggested in *The Corporate Report* (which fall under the heading of voluntary additional financial and general information).

Type of information	Required to be disclosed in the Annual Report and Accounts (by, for example, the Companies Act 1985)	Voluntary disclosures found in the Annual Report and Accounts
Purely economic information	Financial statements and notes	Additional trend data Value-added statement
Additional financial and general information	Innovations Future prospects	Statement of money exchanges with government Statement of transactions in foreign currencies Analysis of the business Statements about strategy
Corporate governance	Compliance with the 'combined code' (if listed on the London Stock Exchange)	Other corporate governance information
Information about employees	Employee numbers, categories of employment and remuneration Analysis of employees receiving more than £30,000 per annum Policy on employment, training and career development of disabled employees Policy on consultation with employees and their representatives Details of total salary, social security and pension costs	Health and safety record Training undertaken Redundancies Other employee reporting Employment practices in South Africa (during the apartheid regime)
Other social information	Political and charitable donations	Community activities/impact information Sustainability information
Other environmental information		Environmental information/reporting

Figure 17.1 Some examples of mandatory and voluntary disclosure in UK company annual reports since the mid-1970s.

17.2.2 The value-added statement

In the majority of countries there is no statutory or professional requirement to produce value-added statements (VAS). It is thus an example of voluntary disclosure, and, as a result, subject to variations in fashion. Further, it has remained more or less a big-company phenomenon.[2] The VAS is (rather like the cash flow statement) effectively a rearrangement of existing financial information, most (if not all) of which can be gleaned from the existing financial statements. On the face of it, therefore, the VAS might seem to belong in Chapter 15. The reason for considering the VAS at this stage, however, is that any significance it might have lies in what it implies, rather than in the information it actually presents.

The principal prompt to companies producing VAS in the UK came from *The Corporate Report* (see also next section) in 1975 which argued:

> The simplest and most immediate way of putting profit into proper perspective vis-a-vis the whole enterprise as a collective effort by capital, management and employees is by presentation of value-added (that is, sales income less materials and services purchased). Value added is the wealth the reporting entity has been able to create by its own and employees' efforts. This statement

would show how the value-added has been used to pay those contributing to
its creation.

(*Paragraph 6.7*)

This quotation gives the general outline of how to construct this essentially simple statement. The statement would normally be in two sections: (a) the calculation of value-added, and (b) its distribution.

Value-added is usually defined as: *(Turnover minus Materials and services purchased).* To turnover might be added any other revenue that the organization received. The materials and services purchased is effectively all the cost of sales and operating expenses but with the payments for wages and salaries and related taxation, pensions and social security, depreciation and loan interest taken out.

The reason for these exclusions is quite simple – the second part of the VAS treats these as *distributions of value-added* rather than as expenses. Thus, rather than showing (as the profit and loss account does) only dividends, business taxation and reserves as distributions, the VAS 'moves' all those items which are either payments to employees, the government (taxation) and loan creditors, or 'distributions' to the business (i.e. retained within the business for the future) down 'below the line' and shows them as distributions ranking alongside those to the shareholders.

The best way to show this is by way of an example. Milburn New Zealand Ltd – a non-European company by way of a change – provide a VAS in their 1992 *annual report and accounts.* This is reproduced in Figure 17.2. Figure 17.2 is a particularly simple example. What the organization earned less what it spent on services and materials from outside the organization produced the value-added figure of $61.8 million. The second part of the statement shows that this was 'distributed':

- 31% to employees in take-home pay and pension contributions;
- 15% (10% plus 5%) to the government by way of income tax, corporation tax and social security contributions;
- 26% (10% plus 16%) to the providers of finance; and
- 28% was retained in the business.

As you can see from Figure 17.2 the VAS is simply a reorganization of figures from the profit and loss account.

The VAS has its fair share of controversy because:

- it places emphasis on the *collective* contribution of the different groups to the well-being of the organization, thus de-emphasizing the importance of the shareholders as the *raison d'être* of business activity. In this sense the statement is a fairly radical step for a capitalist country;
- it focuses attention on the ability of the company to create wealth and contribute to the national economy;
- it is claimed that value-added is less susceptible to the vagaries of accounting measurement than is the case with the conventional profit and loss account;
- Bougen (1983) says it might be seen as not only a clearer and more understandable way of communicating the performance of the entity but it might also be more 'neutral' – in that in its de-emphasis of the rights of capital it is less pejorative and less likely to alienate the employees.

These are attractive advantages, but the VAS has its limitations. The most important of these is the concern that the VAS, despite its apparent openness, is really only a smoke-screen to

Consolidated
Value Added
Statement
As at 31 December 1992

The following statement shows the distribution of disposable income which has been created (value-added) through the use of the group's resources.

		1992		1991	
		$000	%	$000	%
Group Revenue	Turnover	128,290	–	128,402	–
	Other income	6,273	–	4,198	–
		134,563	–	132,600	–
	Less:				
	Cost of goods and services purchased	72,705	–	70,754	–
	Value added by the group	61,858	100	61,846	100
Value-added was distributed as follows					
Earnings or Employees	(i) Salaries, wages and superannuation subsidies	19,003	31	19,059	31
	(ii) PAYE tax paid on employees' behalf to Government	6,275	10	5,887	10
Income Tax payments to Government		3,153	5	3,891	6
Providers of Capital	Dividends and subvention payments	5,983	10	4,633	7
	Interest	9,927	16	11,394	18
Provision for the	Depreciation of fixed assets	13,772	22	14,014	23
Future of the Group	Retained earnings	3,745	6	2,968	5
		61,858	100	61,846	100

Figure 17.2 Illustration of a published value-added statement

persuade the employees to the point of view of capital. This concern is based on a number of points.

First, the amounts for reinvestment in the business (see the Milburn example in Figure 17.2) are legally funds due to the shareholders and, it is suggested, should be shown as part of *their* distributions. Second, the treatment of redundancy payments as a distribution to employees, rather than as an expense of the business, has attracted criticism. Third, whilst directors, managers and the 'workforce' are all technically employees, the usual failure to split the figure has been thought to produce figures which imply a higher return to the 'blue-collar' workforce than is in fact the case. Other criticisms have included the way in which depreciation is treated as a 'distribution' rather than as an expense of the business in order to maintain physical operating capital. This treatment, it is said, is misleading. In addition the range of presentations and the potential scope for management to alter the presentation to suit themselves, plus normally the exclusion of the VAS from the auditors' report (this is *not* the case with Milburn), have all attracted criticism as to the reliability and usefulness of the VAS. Nevertheless, the VAS remains one of the more interesting developments upon the traditional financial accounting model despite an observable and distinct decline in significance in the UK since 1979 (Burchell *et al.* 1985; Gray *et al.* 1995).

17.2.3 *The Corporate Report*

Companies also occasionally disclose information (apart from the social, employee and environmental information – see below), over and above that required by law or accounting standards. Examples of the sort of additional information which shareholders might find useful were proposed in *The Corporate Report* (Accounting Standards Committee (ASC) 1975) – probably the most progressive document published by the UK accounting profession. *The Corporate Report* recommended, amongst other things, that business organizations should publish:

- a statement of money exchanges with government;
- a statement of transactions in foreign currencies;
- a statement of future prospects;
- a statement of corporate objectives.

Bougen (1982)[3] found that very few companies produce this type of information: a little over 1 per cent of his sample of 300 companies produced the money exchanges statement, 1 per cent gave the foreign currencies statement, although a further 4 per cent gave *some* information on this (accounting standards had some impact on this). No more than 4 per cent gave statements of future prospects and only 2 per cent gave information on corporate objectives.

Despite the apparent lack of success of the attempt to encourage companies to develop fuller disclosure, company reports do, however, abound with very general information. Most large company reports contain (usually in their *Review of Operations* or the *Operating and Financial Review*), reviews of their products, new developments, Queen's Awards for this and knighthoods for that, bar charts of progress and many photographs of the organization's activities. Whether this is really 'information' or 'advertising' is difficult to determine.[4]

17.3 SOCIAL ACCOUNTING AND REPORTING

17.3.1 Introduction

Social accounting and reporting covers a wide array of activities. The main volume of disclosure in this area and the most long-standing practice of social accounting relates to information about or provided to *employees* and *employees' representatives* such as unions. As we have already seen with the VAS, the relationship between organizations and their employees is a very important one and as a result there is much information disclosed around this relationship. In addition to employee-related information, this section will also briefly review what are considered the other main elements of social accounting. We shall briefly introduce *social reporting*, *social auditing* and also the idea of a *silent social account*. Finally, we will discuss the advent of the *ethical investor* – a move which has created some demand for SEAR. The idea of an ethical investor also challenges some of the ideas we may have about the role of a shareholder in the life of an organization.

17.3.2 Employee reporting

There are three elements to employee reporting: information provided *about* employees, information provided *to* employees and information provided for collective bargaining.

Most large-company reports will contain a wide range of data about employees, including such matters as: numbers employed; training and racial and sexual equality; remuneration of employees and directors and provisions for the health and safety of the workplace. Some of this data is required in the UK by the Companies Act (see Figure 17.1) while the rest is voluntary.

Some companies take a systematic approach to providing this information and produce what is called an *employment report*. This report, in effect, draws this information together in one place and (usually) enhances it with further details on, for example, age distribution, length of service and accident statistics. The *employment report* may be an integral part of the annual report and accounts or may be produced as a separate document. Such reports are not common, although, as with most areas of (what amounts to) voluntary disclosure, their popularity waxes and wanes in response to fashions in reporting. So, for example, in the UK employment reports were most popular in the 1970s. The 1980s saw an unsurprising emphasis on redundancies, whilst the late 1980s and early- to mid-1990s saw a small but noticeable increase in attention given to racial and sexual equality and to the health and safety of employees. This contrasts with the USA, where broad employment reporting generally receives less emphasis, and continental Europe where health and safety matters have traditionally been of greater importance. (Consult your library of annual reports for examples.)

One further area of employment information that deserves a brief mention is *information about practices in South Africa*. This was not a legal requirement but, in the UK, was encouraged by a recommendation from the Department of Trade. This suggested that companies should publicize, through their annual report and accounts, that information about the employment practices of companies operating in South Africa with respect to black employees *was* publicly available. Not all companies gave this information and, with the demise of apartheid in South Africa, the perceived importance of the disclosure has fallen away.[5] Another important point to draw from this subtype of employee reporting is the fact that changes in political regimes and politics in general will have an impact upon reporting practices. As a result, SEAR is a continually changing activity.

In contrast to accounting *for employees*, information provided *by companies to their employees* is usually thought of as falling into two distinct categories. The first is information which is communicated directly to the individual employees – through perhaps an *employee report, the house magazine* or statutory information to employees about, for example, *toxic hazards in the workplace*. This communication with individual employees is to be distinguished from information communicated to employees' representatives (e.g. trade unions) – often for the purposes of collective bargaining. We will maintain this distinction here.

Although the owners of a business are considered to be the primary organizational participants, there is a growing trend to consider the employee group as the second-ranking group of stakeholders in the organization. One justification for this is:

> Just as the shareholder has financial capital tied up in the firm, contingent upon its future performance, so has the employee 'human capital' dependent for its realisation on the same source and subject to equivalent, if not greater, risk.
>
> *(Maunders 1981:7)*

Gray *et al.* (1987) take this further when they say:

> There is of course also a strong moral case to be made out for treating employees as primary stakeholders in that they are undoubtedly the people most immediately affected by corporate decisions, not only in the workplace but also as members of the community within which the firm operates.

Thus, the argument goes, if the shareholder has a right to an extensive amount of financial information to manage his or her investment, does not the employee have similar rights?

Attitudes to this question vary enormously from country to country – but the outcome is, as you might expect, that in the developed capitalist countries the interests of the shareholder and other financial participants continue to dominate to a considerable degree. However, employee information rights have developed – but only slowly. For example, apart from a brief period in the 1970s, UK legislation requiring information to be disclosed to employees has been very thin on the ground. In addition to the information that employees might glean from the *annual report and accounts* (to which they have no *statutory* right), and the information provided to employee representatives for the purposes of collective bargaining (which the bulk of the employees may never see), the only legislative requirement is that contained in the Health and Safety at Work Act 1974. This requires that employees be kept informed about the hazards they may face in the workplace (for example, through the handling of toxic substances).

This position contrasts with that in France where, from 1977, companies have been required to produce a *bilan social* (social balance sheet). This document must include information on:

- numbers employed;
- wages and fringe benefits;
- health and safety conditions;
- other working conditions;
- education and training;
- industrial relations;
- other matters relating to the quality of working life.

The significance of the *bilan social* lies not so much in the information it contains as in the fact that it has statutory standing. In the UK, as in continental Europe, reporting to employees remains a largely voluntary exercise by organizations[6] and the accounting profession continues to be reluctant to get closely involved with the issue.

So, why, therefore, might employees be expected to want/need/use corporate information? Generally, it seems that employees find information most useful to assess:

- job security: forecasts of company and divisional performance and information on the workforce (see also below for information for collective bargaining);
- company performance;
- wealth sharing: particularly the distribution of the value-added (see also the VAS at section 17.2.2).

This contrasts with a continuing tendency for companies, when they *do* issue information to employees, to emphasize the jolly, much-simplified reports that more normally pass as 'information for employees'. Employees are likely to be interested in employment information and the VAS. But, as we have also seen, the employees have no statutory right to information appearing in the *annual report,* however relevant it might seem.

The area of collective bargaining is the one major area of information for employees which *is* governed by legislation in the UK (see Gray *et al.* 1987, 1996). The UK requires that trade unions should receive any information:

- without which they would be materially impeded in collective bargaining, and/or
- which it is 'good industrial relations practice' to disclose.

This is constrained by the organization's right to withhold any information which would be very expensive to collect and/or which could cause substantial injury to the employer's business. This, unsurprisingly, places significant limitations on the information received by the employees' representatives. It should also be noted that information provided to the trade union does not necessarily mean that the employees are also party to it. *Neither does* any of the above mean that trade union officials (and employees in general) will necessarily understand the information, particularly the financial information. A quite surprising number of shareholders and financial analysts do not understand financial statements, so, *a priori,* there is no reason why general employees and trade union officials with no financial training should do so. (After all, few accountants understand engineering specifications.)

Whilst the increase in the willingness of organizations to communicate information (financial or otherwise) to employees and their representatives constitutes a small but definite move in the direction of a little more democracy in the UK and elsewhere, many commentators do see the questions of the provision of information to employees as less to do with the growth towards the 'partnership of labour, management and capital' ideal (purportedly envisaged by the proponents of the VAS, for example, see Burchell *et al.* 1985) and more to do with the conflict between labour and capital. The employers are the ones with the information which they can choose to hand out if it suits them, and the capital providers have the full legislative backing of a substantial body of law to ensure *their* information rights. Labour, on the other hand, have few rights relative to their involvement with the organization and must continually strive for greater information, greater control, and (depending on the strength of one's political persuasion) seek to overthrow the dominance of the capital system. (Accountants, as the servants of capital, will surely be the first up against the wall when the revolution comes!)

17.3.3 Social reporting, the social audit and silent social accounts

Social reporting is usually considered to include employee- and employment-related information, but given that this set of information is governed by some law and contains fairly well-established practices we dealt with it separately from other social reporting. As a result, what is left to introduce here is non-employment-related social accounting. Here, as noted elsewhere, practice is variable because there are no set legal requirements in this area and also because as issues wax and wane in popularity so do social accounting and reporting practices.

Social reporting is at once an old and a new area of activity. While the early phase of activity in this area occurred in the 1960s and 1970s, we shall concentrate on socially reporting activities which have developed in the late 1990s (but see Gray *et al.* 1996 for a historical overview).

> **Hint**
>
> For the company reports you have, we suggest that you visit the web site of the organization and ascertain if they produce a social report, an environmental report, a sustainable development report or any combination or variation of the above. Whether or not the organization has any such reports may be difficult to ascertain from the annual report itself. If this is the case, the web *may* provide a better source of information (this general principle does not hold for all organizations!). If you can identify that there are additional reports for the organization(s) you are interested in then you should ask the company to send you a copy. Reading some social and environmental reports will help you make sense of the information contained in this chapter.

Social reports purport to gather together elements of the social performance of an organization. This performance will usually relate to the actions and impact of the organization with respect to:

- employees (see section 17.3.2 above);
- customer safety, satisfaction and special services offered to some customers (such as the elderly or those with specific physical disabilities);
- the local community within which the organization operates (such as how the organization deals with the disruption it causes to the local area – for example, the impact of an airport);
- the nature and effectiveness of charitable activities;
- interactions with other countries (for example, how a large transnational interacts with the governments of countries within which it operates – especially given that the company may be larger than the country itself).

These reports are usually available to employees, special-interest groups and society in general (if you know they exist!). They may or may not be 'audited' in some way. The volume of reports of this nature has increased since the mid-1990s.

Social audit (confusingly this term is sometimes used by companies to describe their social reports) differs from social reporting in one crucial way. With a social audit the collection and reporting of social information about an organization is conducted by an organization *outside* and *independent* of the focal organization. As a result a social audit is less likely to be as 'self-serving' as some social reports and is likely to be seen to be a more credible piece of information (the social audit, however, will not be neutral – remember our discussion of the way financial reporting creates a particular picture of an organization? – the same general point applies to social and environmental reporting).

Once again, the practice of social audit has a relatively long history. The *Council on Economic Priorities* in the USA is one of the longest-established and best-known organizations to conduct social audits, whilst, in the UK, organizations such as *Social Audit Ltd, New Consumer, Counter Information Services* and *The New Economics Foundation* have all (in their very different ways) demonstrated how accountability can be forced upon reluctant organizations. Social Audit Ltd, for example, sought to publish information (on companies such as Tube Investments and Avon Rubber Company) that gives a *balancing view* of organizational activity. Their overriding concern was with democracy, which, they maintain, cannot exist without the accountability of organizations. This requires that society be informed of the organization's social performance. Counter Information Services, by way of contrast, was a Marxist collective dedicated to discrediting the capitalist system. Believing 'the system' (that is, the capitalist mode of production) to be inherently in conflict with true human development, the collective sought to hasten its eventual downfall through the collection and provision of information about the 'bad side' of organizations (they did not purport to provide a balanced view). A further contrast is provided by the UK's experience with the *local authority social audits*. Some local authorities, concerned by the drastic local effects arising from companies' closing down plants and thus faced with a declining economic infrastructure, rising unemployment and associated social problems, sought to collect information to show the effects of plant closure in order either to attempt to persuade government to do something or to try and persuade companies to change their closure decisions.

The final element in our discussion of social reporting is the **silent social report**. This refers to the practice of gathering together from the annual reports of, mainly, large companies all the social and environmental data they produce. This information can then be collated into one report which in effect could recreate a sort of 'social and environmental report'. For a typical UK company this would be a document of between four and eight pages. The idea is that such a practice would enable social reports to be produced for organizations that presently do not have them. Interestingly, the 'picture' of an organization which can be gained from putting all their social and environmental accounting information in one place is different from the impression gained when all the data are spread about the annual report. An illustration of a UK company's recreated social and environmental report can be found in Gray (1997). In addition, you could have a go at creating such an account yourself by photocopying and 'cutting and pasting' from your own annual report and accounts.

17.3.4 Ethical investment

An **ethical investor** (either an individual or an investment fund) is one that seeks to invest in companies in a way which has regard for more than just the financial performance of the investment. The most common way to invest ethically is to buy 'units' in an ethical fund which can be purchased from any number of investment houses. Ethical funds were established to produce a commercial return for investors *but* investors were able to express their ethical preferences *vis-à-vis* where their funds were invested. As a result, one fund might emphasize high environmental performance whilst another might be exercised by the treatment of employees and communities in developing countries. Yet another may avoid investing in the arms industry or in firms which conduct experiments on animals. Despite being a relatively new phenomenon, these funds are increasingly well understood and they continue to grow. This suggests that investors/shareholders *can* be persuaded to invest on social and environmental grounds as well as on financial grounds.

Of direct relevance to us here has been the finding that 'ethical investors' suffer one important deficit – they cannot obtain the social and environmental information they need to make informed judgements about the companies in which they wish to invest! Here is another example of accounting failing to satisfy the information needs of users – this time financial participants. (For more detail see, for example, Harte *et al.* 1991; Perks *et al.* 1992.) As a result, social reporting (and environmental reporting if the fund is concerned about such matters) is likely to help the ethical investor make judgements about the 'soundness' of particular companies.

This seems a good place to for us to further discuss the nature and role of shareholders in organizations. You may well have tended to think about shareholders as individuals who have invested their money in a company and who have a long-term interest in the performance of that company. This is a reasonable assumption to make but one which is not altogether accurate. Many of those individuals and institutions (such as pension funds and insurance companies) who own shares do *not* do so because they are interested in the particular company, but rather because they have a need to earn some return on their money. Shareholders of this type, therefore, are not so much interested in the company itself as they are interested in earning a return on their funds to satisfy their own financial needs. As a result, these shareholders (which we may call investors) have less loyalty to a particular company. If that company performs badly financially they are likely to sell their shares and buy those of another company which offers a better return. If the company treats its employees poorly the investor is not that interested, as long as this does not impact on financial performance. If the company is performing well but holding those shares is no longer in the investor's interest then it will sell those shares. If the investor can see an opportunity to make money from selling shares then it will do so. Clearly, the attitude you have about owning the shares of a company will affect how interested you are in the social and environmental performance of that company. So the shareholding/investing world is more complicated than first appears. The tendency for investors to be only interested in the short-term financial gain which can be obtained by holding shares is something which will come up again in your future studies.

17.4 ENVIRONMENTAL ACCOUNTING AND REPORTING

17.4.1 Introduction and overview

Like social accounting, environmental accounting and reporting encompasses a wide array of activities. Some of these activities relate to how an organization organizes its operations (such as having an environmental policy and environmental plans) and the role of accounting in controlling its operations (such as how environmental factors affect project selections and environmental costing). These activities are properly covered under the guise of management, management accounting and financial management so we shall not focus on them here. Rather, our attention will be focused on (a) environmental reporting and the related (but actually quite distinct) activity of (b) accounting for sustainable development.

17.4.2 Environmental reporting

Environmental reporting is very similar in nature to social reporting. Indeed, environmental reporting is usually viewed as a subset of the broader area of social reporting. We believe, however, that it warrants separate noting, primarily because of its present widespread popularity in the UK and throughout much of the developed world. We would have expected that you would have come across reference to environmental reports and environmental reporting from your reading of companies' reports as well as the financial and accountancy press. The UK, in particular, has high levels of environmental reporting by large corporations. You should be able to obtain some environmental reports using the web, as indicated in the hint under section 17.3.3 above.

In broad terms, environmental reporting will provide discussion (and hopefully data) on one or more of the following topics

- amounts of raw materials extracted for production;
- levels of emissions to air, water and land;
- amounts of energy used;
- levels of wastes produced;
- accidental spills of toxic hazards;
- fines incurred for breaching environmental laws.

Environmental reporting is a little more systematic than social reporting, primarily because of the existence of a large number of guides to best practice in this area. In addition, since 1991 one of the UK professional accounting bodies (the Association of Chartered Certified Accountants) has sponsored an environmental reporting award scheme. There are similar schemes in a number of countries in mainland Europe, for Europe as a whole, as well as Australasia and Canada. To give a taste of what one could expect from environmental reporting, a summarized version of the award criteria is outlined in Figure 17.3.

Further information of environmental accounting and reporting can be gleaned from the further reading given at the end of this chapter. In addition, you may well have the opportunity to study this topic further in your future studies.

17.4.3 Accounting for sustainable development

Before we can bring our discussion of SEAR to a close one final area should be considered: that of the issues which arise should organizations seek to pursue sustainable development. Like all the areas we have introduced in this chapter, accounting for sustainable development is a large and complex area of study in itself. What we aim to provide you with here is a taster of the issues arising in this area.

Sustainable development is defined as

> development which meets the needs of the present without compromising the ability of future generations to meet their own needs.
>
> *(World Commission on Environment and Development 1987: 8)*

The need for sustainable development arises from the current perception that development (that is, broadly speaking how we conduct ourselves in an economic sense) is not sustainable and that there are significant adverse impacts arising from our economic activities. These adverse impacts are usually categorized into environmental impacts (that is, development is damaging the environment – this includes the hole in the ozone layer and

Characteristic of environmental report to be judged	Examples of elements sought in the reports
Completeness, in terms of ... • Conveying a complete view of the organization's operations and environmental impact • Scope of report clearly specified (and closely linked with the definition of the accounting entity)	• Key (direct and indirect) environmental impacts • Environmental policy, targets and performance indicators • Consideration of produce impact 'from cradle to the grave' • Report audience identified
Credibility, in terms of ... • Internal credibility – assurance that the organization has information systems in place to produce information on its environmental impact • External credibility – external assurance or verification that the environmental report is credible	• Environmental management systems • Staff allocated responsibility for environmental affairs • Data on activities and environmental impact • Internal audit procedures • Accreditation or certification with various environmental management schemes • Use of 'best practice' forms of reporting • Third-party verification statement
Communication, in terms of ... • How well the report communicates to target audience	• Layout and appearance • Understandability, length and use of technical terms • Use of internet to aid reporting • Use of graphs, illustrations and photos

Figure 17.3 Environmental reporting award criteria

global warming) and social impacts (that is, the costs and benefits of development are not fairly distributed). The world governments (to a greater or lesser extent) have agreed that all development should be sustainable. What this means in practice, however, is not very clear – although the available evidence suggests that our current ways of 'doing things' is certainly *not* sustainable.

Increasingly, large companies have started to recognize the importance of sustainable development and are moving towards providing reports on how their activities have an impact upon the goal of sustainable development. Indeed, reports labelled 'sustainable development' appear to be superseding social and environmental reporting. A term you may also see used in this context is that of a company's 'triple bottom line'. This phrase derives from a book by John Elkington (1997) and refers to three elements of a company's impact on sustainable development: economic, environmental and social.

There are many elements to evaluating how an organization impacts upon the goal of sustainable development. For example, one may look at the *ecological footprint* of an organization or a country (that is, how much materials and energy are required by corporate or state activities – this gives some idea as to the scale of activities); the efficiency with which resources are used by an organization (this is usually termed *eco-efficiency*); the social impacts arising from activities (such as whether 'fair' wages have been paid for work undertaken – this is sometimes considered under the label of *eco-justice*); and the way in which economic values have been ascribed to various transactions (especially cross-border transactions and whether wealth generated in one country is remitted to another country through, for example, transfer pricing arrangements). Sustainable development, and accounting for sustainable development, is an extremely complex area but one which we anticipate will grow in importance in the future.

17.5 THE PROS AND CONTRAS OF SEAR

There can be few areas of accounting over which there has been as much disagreement as SEAR. Apart from the efforts of those organizations undertaking the social audits and the efforts of a few of the larger companies, SEAR remains something of a peripheral activity. This is primarily because of disagreement over whether or not SEAR is (a) desirable and/or (b) necessary.

Views on these two issues vary considerably. At one extreme, Milton Friedman argues:

> there is one and only one social responsibility of business – to use its resources and engage in activities designed to increase its profit, as long as it stays within the rules of the game, which is to say, engages in open and free competition without deception and fraud ... Few trends could so thoroughly undermine the very foundations of our free society as the acceptance by corporate officials of a social responsibility other than to make as much money for their shareholders as possible.
>
> *(Friedman 1962: 133)*

At the other extreme are commentators who might see organizations and organizational power as inconsistent with the well-being of society, destroying landscapes, manipulating consumers' resources and effectively determining society's future. Between these two extremes lies the bulk of opinion on the question of what (if any) responsibilities an organization owes to its host society. There are powerful arguments for all positions and one's agreement or disagreement is essentially dependent upon one's preconceptions and political and social preferences.

Views on the nature of the responsibilities determine the necessity or otherwise to report. Voluntary organizational SEAR will naturally tend to be self-serving. Until there is some sort of statutory requirement upon organizations to report the extent of compliance with the 'rules of the game' SEAR will remain self-serving and society will remain ignorant of whether or not its laws are being adhered to.

SUMMARY

In this chapter we have stepped substantially outside the simple orthodoxy of traditional financial statements bonded to the four characteristics and the eight types of financial transactions, and examined some of the ways in which information for a wider accountability might be developed. We have examined this information in two broad (but overlapping) categories as: (a) the developments in information available to shareholders and (b) the developments in information for employees and other groups in society.

One of our major arguments was that in accounting there is a tendency to consider the shareholder (and the investor) above all other individuals but, important though this group may be, they are not the only ones with legitimate and reasonable interests in organizations and in information about organizations. When we move outside the traditional orthodoxy of financial accounting a whole vista of possibilities opens up. We have tried to show in this chapter how some of these possibilities might be expressed in practice and have, in addition, argued that a study of accounting without a consideration of these wider issues leaves one with a very partial and misleading view of the subject and fails to recognize much of its potential.

We now, by way of conclusion, turn to the final theme we mentioned at the beginning of this chapter: the impacts of the accounting activity upon the substantial environment. If we are to view accounting as a purely financial activity, concerned only with the restricted organizational perspective we referred to at the beginning of this chapter, then much of the information expansion we have described in the previous sections is, at best, marginal and, at worst, irrelevant. Such a perspective would find a lot of support amongst practising accountants. Yet, in a changing world, there is a substantial minority of accountants who recognize that the growing requirements for information for the shareholder, the employee and society constitute an essential feature of a profession that must respond to the needs of society if it is not to be overtaken by events and find itself with a diminished role. In part, the relevance of issues such as information expansion depend on what we see as the purpose of accounting.

We use the word 'accountant' to encompass many different people and functions. The word implies both *functional* and *professional* elements. There is a danger that if we simply view the accountant as a functional actor we focus exclusively on what an accountant *does* and ignore what an accountant *should* or *could* do.

A professional perspective would suggest that it is the duty of accountants to identify their role in society and then seek means of fulfilling that role as best they can. This takes the 'accountant' out from the very real commercial exigencies of day-to-day activities and examines what they *should* be doing. If we consider the accountant's role as the preparation of information for the purposes of controlling the focal organization and discharging its accountability (and this, we must emphasize, is only one view, and one far from uncontentious – see Chapter 18), then a concern with the shareholder rather than the investor, a recognition of employees as importantly placed participants, and a desire to devise ways of aiding the focal organization discharge its informational responsibilities to the host society (if only with respect to law) become so much more understandable.

And, professional accounting bodies around the world have not entirely eschewed this concern. The ASC's *Corporate Report* in 1975 demonstrated such a concern. Professional accountancy bodies in the UK, the USA, Australia, Canada, New Zealand and continental Europe have all commissioned studies into such matters as environmental accounting, employee and employment reporting, VASs and accounting for sustainable development. None of these studies, however, has resulted in binding requirements on the profession's members. This may arise because SEAR requires, at times, radical departure from conventional accounting principles and, as such, is unlikely to win sufficient widespread support amongst such an essentially conservative and reactionary group of folk as accountants.

Similarly, accounting and accountants have significant influence on society. Perhaps most contentiously, the insistence on seeing the *investor* as the principal focus of accounting policy may be said to have influenced significantly the information which companies produce and which in turn may be seen as encouraging the owners of a business to 'play the market' rather than concentrating on getting their company back in order. It has been suggested that the accountant's role as the servant of capital has been a major factor in encouraging the continuing consideration of the investor as the major (if not only) participant. That the accounting profession has yet to fully recognize the existence of, let alone the needs of, the 'ethical investor' is simply quite sad.

There are many examples of occasions where accounting might have significant influences on society, not least those which relate to decisions taken in the 'short-term interests of capital'. The accounting activity *does* have economic and redistributional effects, and there exists the very real possibility that this seemingly straightforward, unmoralistic, non-political, wholly neutral profession of accounting may in fact be none of these things. (This is explored further in Chapter 18.) Do politics and society have nothing to do with accounting? Quite the opposite! Accounting dull, dry and boring? Not at all!

These themes are explored more substantially in Chapters 18 and 19 when we turn to re-examine carefully much that we have covered in the book and reconsider the foundations of this subject of accounting.

Key terms and concepts

Here is a list of the key terms and concepts which have featured in this chapter. You should make sure that you understand and can define each one of them. Page references to definitions in the text appear in bold in the index.

- Collective bargaining
- Corporate social reporting
- Disclosure of information
- Employee report
- Employment report
- Environmental report
- Ethical investment
- Investors' rights to information
- Shareholder
- Silent social account
- Social audit
- Social and environmental accounting and reporting
- Social report
- Stakeholders
- Sustainable development
- Value-added statement
- Voluntary disclosure

FURTHER READING

Most of the material in this chapter is covered in much greater depth in Gray *et al.* (1996). The environmental issues are given particular attention in Owen (1992) and Gray and Bebbington (2001). We would recommend these as your principal sources of further reading. More detailed and up-to-date information on social and environmental accounting from around the world is given in the Centre for Social and Environmental Accounting Research's newsletter *Social and Environmental Accounting* which can be recommended for accessible articles. The centre itself can be found on that web at www.gla.ac.uk/departments/accounting and look for the button for centres of research excellence. In addition, as before, keep on taking the medicine of annual reports and your national profession's magazine – these will be your best sources of detailed and practical information.

NOTES

1. Social and environmental accounting is not formalized in the way conventional financial accounting is – as we shall see. There are therefore many definitions and terms used to describe the phenomenon. 'Social accounting', 'social and environmental accounting', 'corporate social reporting' and 'social responsibility accounting' are amongst the more popular phrases used to mean the same thing.
2. For example, Bougen (1983) found that 38 of the UK's largest listed companies produced VAS. See also Burchell *et al.* (1985) and Gray *et al.* (1995) for more information.
3. The research is now quite old and the absence of any more recent surveys of this sort can be taken as a reasonable indication that these areas of disclosure (in the UK at least) have declined to virtually zero over the last 20 years.
4. Make up your own mind by looking through some annual reports.

5. A review of annual reports of larger international companies from, say, the 1980s will produce examples of this. One of the notable examples in the UK was BP plc's *BP in South Africa Social Report 1986* but many large companies – see, for example, RTZ and BOC – also produced such reports.

6. However, continental Europe, through the European Union (EU) has been developing employee rights and many countries have adopted *two-tier* boards of directors whereby employee representatives sit on a second-tier decision-making board.

18 Thinking about accounting: theoretical perspectives on financial accounting and reporting

Learning objectives

After studying this chapter you should be able to:

- articulate the nature of the financial accounting problem;

- explain why this problem is so difficult to resolve;

- describe the different approaches to solving the financial accounting problem and explain their differences;

- discuss some ways in which such differences might be resolved.

18.1 INTRODUCTION

18.1.1 Chapter design and links to previous chapters

We have travelled a long way in this book already. There is still a long way to go in your accounting studies but just one more giant step is needed to round off this introductory journey we embarked upon 17 chapters ago. This final step involves examining and attempting to clarify, more systematically, the nature of financial accounting. The first 15 chapters of the book have assumed that there is but one way to produce financial accounting information – through the construction of trading and profit and loss accounts and balance sheets. Chapters 15 and 16 maintained this basic belief while expanding the number of statements and questioning the valuation base used in these statements. Chapter 17, on the other hand, prepared the way for the contents of this chapter by showing that different organizations in the substantial environment of any focal organization may well require different types of accounting information to satisfy what turned out to be a rather ill-defined set of information needs or wants. We now need to extend the direction in which Chapter 17 took us by looking at alternative general designs for the financial accounting function. These will include, as one of the alternatives, the model that has dominated this book so far.

Of necessity, the contents of this chapter will be pitched at a more theoretical and abstract level than the contents of previous chapters. So far we have concentrated, for most of the time, on a detailed consideration of how to construct this or that accounting statement. This detail is, of course, vitally important to the financial accounting function. In the end the output from conventional financial accounting will usually be a report of some sort from a particular focal organization to the users situated in its substantial environment. But immersion in this detail inevitably leads to an inability to stand back and

(a) look *more widely* at what is occurring in conventional accounting practice or (b) think about fundamentally different alternatives to conventional practice. In this chapter we attempt to help you to reflect on some of the alternative approaches that are available. Our concern in this chapter is not with detailed financial accounting reports but rather with alternative fundamental approaches and how they compare one with another.

The specific concerns of this chapter can be divided into three parts. In the latter part of this section we clarify the nature of the financial accounting problem and the broad solutions which have been advanced. In the process we show where the approaches already discussed in this book fit into this schema.

In sections 18.2 to 18.4 the postulated alternatives are explored in a little more depth: in section 18.2 we look at the *data-oriented approach*, in section 18.3 the *decision usefulness approach* is explored and in section 18.4 the *organizational resource approach* is analysed.

Section 18.5 explores some ways in which we might go about deciding which of these mutually exclusive approaches should be the guiding theoretical basis for financial accounting practice.

18.1.2 An overview of different approaches

We need to start our exploration by reminding ourselves what really is the essence of the problem of financial accounting. Figure 6.2 presented in diagrammatic form the basic nature of the financial accounting problem. Financial accounting is primarily concerned with gathering data from the focal organization and moulding them into particular information statements which are then dispatched into the substantial environment. In the first 15 chapters of this book we have assumed that what is reported through the financial accounting system is traceable to the eight financial transactions summarized in Figure 4.10. Even the contents of Chapter 16 did not move very far away from this data set although the values it placed on, primarily, the assets and claims did differ. However, in Chapter 17, we suggested an alternative data set to the eight basic categories of financial transaction, and alternative accounting statements. Put another way, what was recorded concerning movements in the three subsystems when using the thinking from Chapter 17 was not restricted to those flows derived from the four characteristics or generated through the eight types of financial transactions.

In Chapter 17 some possible new sets of records and resulting statements were suggested, determined partially by the varying needs, wants or rights of certain users in the environment. But less than total guidance was provided on how one goes about deciding what these users really want, need or should have in terms of information. This can only really be answered if we work at a rather higher theoretical plane to decide on the alternative basic approaches. This would then supply a clearer direction on what to record and send out as financial accounting information. It is these issues which are our concern in this chapter.

Chapter 17, however, has indicated the importance of the users (which in our systems terminology can be called *recipient organizations*) in helping to resolve which information should be supplied. If we are to make progress then we need to develop the contents of Figure 6.2 using the insights we have already gained about the nature of the recipient organizations in the substantial environment of any focal organization. There are three possible destinations for the financial accounting information flows from any focal organization. The outputs from the focal organization's financial accounting system will form an input into the decision and control subsystem of:

- finance-receiving organizations;
- finance-providing organizations;
- some other organizations which are not tied directly to the focal organization by the finance they receive or supply.

These are three general types of recipient organization.

This way of presenting the problem of financial accounting emphasizes the need to define the output first. This then helps to clarify the inputs necessary to produce this output. More formally we can define the financial accounting problem as:

> A specification of the nature of the information which should be supplied by focal organizations to the various recipient organizations (situated in the substantial environment) which will, in turn, specify the required data about past, present or future actions and activities (of the focal organizations' subsystems) needed to satisfy these requirements.

In a nutshell the financial accounting problem is the reporting problem of: what to report, to whom, in what form and from what data.

You will notice that this definition opens up the possibility that the information supplied may well involve some predictions about what will happen in the future. So far we have assumed, to a considerable extent, that the information supplied to recipient organizations can only include measures of events and activities which *have* occurred.[1] But this does not have to be so.

Although it is difficult ever to be exhaustive about the range of theoretical solutions for the financial accounting problem, it is possible to look at a range of the more popular proposed solutions. A fairly wide-ranging selection can be derived from three academic papers: the American Accounting Association's *Statement on Accounting Theory and Theory Acceptance (SATTA) (1977),* Laughlin and Puxty (1981) and Davis *et al.* (1982). We will look briefly at the contents of all three and then draw from these surveys what appears to be a common set of fundamental solutions to the financial accounting problem.

(a) Statement of Accounting Theory and Theory Acceptance (SATTA)

SATTA is an important study by a committee of the American Accounting Association (AAA) which is a prestigious body of academics and practitioners based in America. *SATTA* was an attempt to summarize financial accounting thinking up to 1977. What the *SATTA* study found was that, in the financial accounting literature, there were three basic *approaches* which it called: (i) the *classical ('true income' and inductive) models,* (ii) the *decision usefulness* approach; and (iii) the *information economics* model.

The literature categorized by *SATTA* as 'classical models' is that which is principally concerned with identifying 'best' measures of the income and wealth of the focal organization. The literature categorized as focusing on 'decision usefulness' is concerned with supplying information which is more directly useful for decision-making wants or needs. The literature *SATTA* categorized under the 'information economics' umbrella sees accounting information as a type of organizational (albeit economic) resource which is demanded and supplied in much the same way as other economic goods and services. Each of these three approaches produces different solutions to the financial accounting problem.

(b) Laughlin and Puxty

Building on the *SATTA* classification Laughlin and Puxty (1981) also saw three approaches to financial accounting. The three approaches were actually quite similar to *SATTA's* model but with important differences – particularly with regard to the labels used to describe them. The first, which they termed the *'weak decision usefulness'* approach, encompassed the literature in *SATTA's* 'classical models', but they extended the category to include *accountability* measures. In both cases there is an *assumption* about what users (recipient organizations) find useful for decision-making (hence the label 'weak'). The second category, which they termed *'strong decision usefulness'*, was almost identical to *SATTA's* 'decision usefulness', including as it did all literature which sees the function of financial accounting as being to satisfy the specific information needs and wants for the decision-making of recipient organizations. These needs or wants, however, are identified through research rather than simply assumed (hence the label 'strong'). The third and final set of literature they termed the *'organization control'* approach. Here information is seen as an organizational resource which can be used, by the focal organization, as a type of tool to control its environment.[2] Although the literature in this area encompasses *SATTA's* 'information economics' category it also gives greater emphasis to the position of the focal organization in the decision concerning information supply.

(c) Davis, Menon and Morgan

Davis, Menon and Morgan (1982) use the concept of 'images' to classify financial accounting. Images in financial accounting are general impressions that define (i) what we see to be the *nature* of the financial accounting problem and (ii) the consequent solution to that problem. Davis *et al.* (p. 309) maintain that:

> Four principal images have shaped the development of financial accounting. They are those which treat accounting as a historic record, as a descriptor of current economic reality, as an information system and as a commodity.

The literature they see as reflecting the image of a 'historic record' encompasses much of the contents of the first 15 chapters of this book plus some of Chapter 17. That is, the historic record encompasses the processes involved in recording economic transactions and rearranging these into financial statements (including the cash flow statement) and some of the other accountability statements discussed in the previous chapter. Those seeing the financial accounting function as a descriptor of 'current economic reality' are primarily those who see the information flow as containing information about important economic phenomena – usually income and wealth. The basis for this is not historic events but economic theory. The 'information system' image sees the financial accounting flow as a relationship between a transmitter (the focal organization) and a receiver (the recipient organizations) of information intended to satisfy the latter's information needs or wants. Finally, the 'commodity' image describes those who see financial accounting information as a type of organizational resource which can be demanded and supplied and is susceptible to all the rules which govern market behaviour.

(d) Common themes

All three schemata have clear overlaps – which may be both reassuring and surprising. It is reassuring since it does indicate that three different sets of writers have arrived at largely similar classifications of the financial accounting literature. However, perhaps it should not really be so surprising that this commonality should emerge since all three were working from the same sources of literature and the same broad set of ideas.

There appear to be common themes which dominate these classifications. These themes and how they relate are outlined in Figure 18.1. Each approach gives a different emphasis to the fundamental nature of the financial accounting information, as summarized in the figure.

The **data-oriented approach** concentrates on 'best measures' as the basis for the solution to the financial accounting problem. This approach may entail: seeking measures of income and wealth, identifying a specification of (accounting) events of interest, or deriving some other measures to satisfy a clearly defined accountability concern. The **decision usefulness approach** maintains that the information supplied through financial accounting should be primarily addressed to the specific information wants or needs of particular recipient organizations. The **organizational resource approach** sees financial accounting information as an organizational resource which can either be used as a control tool or as an economic commodity which is open to negotiation as to nature and amount.

The three alternatives are distinguishable in terms of what the various proponents can actually say about the contents of the information flow in particular organizations. Those working under the data-oriented approach maintain that it should be possible to specify the information content for *all* organizations. Under the decision usefulness approach the information content may well vary across organizations since the users' (the recipient organizations') needs or wants are variable. In a similar manner, under the organizational resource approach the information content will also vary across organizations as a result of the interplay between the intentions of the supplier of information and the needs or wants of the recipient organizations.

The information actually supplied by each of these different approaches may, on occasions, coincide. This is to be expected. The point about the differences is that they each register a fundamentally different attitude by the supplier concerning the *purpose* for which the information is supplied. These different purposes interpret the nature of the financial accounting problem in a different manner which in turn suggests a need for alternative data and information statements.

In the following three sections we will look at each of these basic approaches in a little more depth.

18.2 DATA-ORIENTED APPROACH

The data-oriented approach is built on the primary assumptions that (a) financial accounting should provide accurate measures of particular phenomena, (it should tell either 'the truth' or 'a truth'); (b) the supply of the information is deemed to be the *right*

Basic common approach	*SATTA* (1977)	Laughlin and Puxty (1981)	Davis *et al.* (1982)
Data-oriented	Classical models	Weak decision usefulness	Historical record and current economic reality
Decision usefulness	Decision usefulness	Strong decision usefulness	Information system
Organizational resource	Information economics	Organizational control	Commodity

Figure 18.1 Commonalities in classification schemes of financial accounting

of the receivers; and (c) the resultant information is assumed to be 'useful' to those receiving these data.

The basic nature of this approach can be summarized as in Figure 18.2 (drawing from the schema developed in Figure 6.2). This starts with some general *assumption* about the information needs of *all* recipient organizations in the substantial environment of any focal organization. This general set of needs is, in large measure, assumed by all those who adopt this way of thinking but are rarely clearly articulated. From this assumed set of needs a data set is derived and communicated to the recipient organizations.

18.2.1 Traditional income and wealth measures

The traditional financial accounting model discussed in the first 15 chapters of this book is the dominant expression of this basic model. It starts from the assumption that some

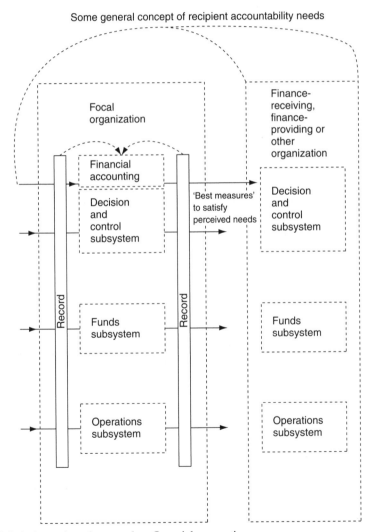

Figure 18.2 A data-oriented approach to financial accounting

form of **income** and **wealth measures** are important to satisfy the assumed needs of all potential users but that the source of these measures emanates from the eight types of financial transactions expressed in and through accounting profit and financial position measures discussed in earlier chapters.

This modelling, of course, starts from a defined data set to derive these measures of profit and financial position. The other data-oriented approaches which we have looked at in Chapter 16 start from a more clearly defined view about the nature of these concepts and mould the appropriate data to this understanding. Most of these latter approaches, as we have already seen, rely on a definition of income and wealth following the work of Hicks (1946) who defined income as the maximum which can be consumed by a person (or organization) in a particular period without depleting the wealth that existed at the start of the period. This income measure shifts the concern to the difference between alternative measures of wealth at two points in time. It is this which supplies the necessary information required rather than some manipulation of eight different types of financial transactions which have occurred.

18.2.2 Alternatives to income and wealth measures

Adopting either historic cost values or any of the other alternative valuation bases discussed in Chapter 16 results in different income figures, but which of them constitutes the 'best' measures for reporting purposes under this data-oriented approach? It is over this question that there are fundamental disagreements. Four key strategies have been suggested in answer to this question. First, that we should find a way to rationalize and decide upon either multiple measures or a particular measure of income and wealth. Second, that we should abandon trying to measure income and wealth and instead supply measures of 'cash flows' only. Third, that we should abandon trying to measure income and wealth but rather supply a databank of 'events' (which will include the financial transactions, but more besides). Fourth, and somewhat related to the third strategy, that we should abandon trying to measure income and wealth *per se* but rather supply a databank of events which are related to some concept of 'accountability'.

We will look at each of these below.

(a) Rationalizing income and wealth measures

For those who call for some way to rationalize the different measures of income and wealth there is little agreement as to how to conduct this process. Some (e.g. Mattessich 1971) maintain that the whole range of income and wealth measures should be reported to allow the user to decide on relevance. Others (which include a very large majority of those writing in this area) maintain that this thinking is an abrogation of responsibility and that a clear and coherent choice should be made for one of the approaches (e.g. Parker, *et al.* 1986). In this connection, both in academic and professional circles, there appears to be a trend towards some variant of replacement cost accounting (see Chapter 16). Others, whilst agreeing with the need for choice, maintain that this should be undertaken on the basis of the 'predictive ability' of the resulting income measures (e.g. Beaver *et al.* 1968). The rationale underlying the latter way of thinking is some appeal to a general concept of information use – basically that financial accounting information is likely to be used for undefined decisions, decisions need predictions, therefore whichever measure of income has the greatest ability to predict future income levels must be the 'best'.

(b) Cash flow accounting

Second, there are those who maintain that the whole concern with income and wealth measures is too myopic a view of 'best measures' and argue that instead measures of periodic cash flows should be reported. Those who hold this view (e.g. Lawson 1978; Lee 1978) maintain that we should record only the cash movements (payments and receipts) for the period under investigation. The reasons for this, according to these proponents, centre on the importance of these flows to any understanding of the activities of the focal organization. In addition, cash flows may be an important indicator of future actions and activities. Cash flows are deemed to be more informative than the highly aggregated measures of income and wealth (recall the material we discussed in Chapter 15).

(c) Events accounting

Third, there are those who maintain that even measures of cash flows do not go far enough in satisfying the criteria of 'best' measures and advance the importance of communicating a wide range of economic 'events' in the financial statements (e.g. Sorter 1969; Johnson 1970; Lieberman and Whiston 1975). The logic behind this approach (known as *events accounting*) is that the proponents are less and less convinced that one can realistically assume a certain set of information needs but, rather than go and find out directly what these needs are (as in the decision usefulness approach), they suggest that we should report disaggregated events (which may include cash flows but will often go beyond these to other actions and activities of the focal organization) and let the users take what they want from this data set.

(d) Accountability measures

Accountability measures are the final strategy we will consider. These, building to an extent on eventist thinking, define the nature of the information supplied in the context of an accountability relationship. The focal organization is seen as an entity which is entrusted with certain responsibilities and needs to account to some 'principal' (e.g. society) as to the discharge of these responsibilities (e.g. Gray *et al.* 1996). In many ways this broad-based concern does not comfortably fit into any of the three-way classification we are using in this chapter, yet it can be argued that its appropriate home is under this data-oriented umbrella. This is because the principal's accountability needs are taken as given and defined and do not need to be discovered as they would under the decision usefulness approach. Equally it is assumed that the focal organization is a compliant supplier of information rather than a possible manipulator of the data as would occur under the organizational resource approach. This leaves the dominant concern with a specification of the best measures to satisfy a defined, and to a certain extent unchanging, accountability concern. This is, of course, the dominant concern of the data-oriented approach more generally.

(e) A concluding comment

Perhaps we could conclude this discussion by returning to our case of Mr Brain with whom this book started, in order to amplify the different interpretations given to this data-oriented approach. Mr Brain is like any other organization under the data-oriented approach. He, like all focal organizations, should supply either measures of income and wealth (following the rules we have formulated in Chapters 3 to 12 or those contained in Chapter 16), or measures of cash flows or events, or defined measures of an accountability nature. Any of these variants would be a legitimate expression of the data-oriented approach applicable not only to Mr Brain but to all focal organizations.

18.3 DECISION USEFULNESS APPROACH

18.3.1 Decision-makers and decision models

Under the decision usefulness approach the purpose of financial accounting information is to satisfy the information needs (i.e. what is required according to some criteria) or wants (i.e. what the recipients require according to their personal wishes) of users. These needs and wants are determined by the users' (recipient organizations') decision-making – since it is in this context that information is necessary to help reduce the inevitable uncertainty which surrounds every action. Information needs or wants, however, are not *assumed* to be of a certain type as is the case in the data-oriented approach. The decision usefulness approach can only pronounce on information needs or wants after these have been discovered through research with regard to the recipient.

The decision usefulness approach is normally recognized as having two different thrusts:

i   The first, which is often called a *decision-makers* emphasis (e.g. Sterling 1972; AAA, 1977), maintains that the decision-makers (recipient organizations) know best what information they want and that the financial accounting function should satisfy these desires.

ii The second, called a *decision models* emphasis, maintains that the accountants (or the preparers) know what the decision-makers really need (related to the objectives they wish to achieve through the focal organization), and it is this need which should guide the contents of financial accounting flows.

We can present the basic nature of these variants of the decision usefulness approach as in Figure 18.3.

Some of the dynamics and interrelationships of these two different emphases are presented in diagrammatic form in Figure 18.4. From the perspective of the decision-makers variant the only part of this figure which is of importance is the top left-hand circle. This is because in the case of the decision-makers emphasis the only real concern is to discover what information the decision-makers say they want and then to supply this. (One largely ignores how they use this information.[3])

In the case of the decision models emphasis the 'ideal' prediction and decision model needs to be specified. From this the necessary information inputs are derived.

The ability of this 'ideal' prediction and decision model actually to influence the users' decision mechanism depends on many factors, two of which are particularly important to note at present:

i   The first concerns the distance between the ideal and actual prediction and decision models of users – marked as a dashed-line connection between the two in Figure 18.4.

ii The second centres on the ability to educate users to use the 'ideal' prediction and decision models.

The outcome of these two factors will have implications not only for whether the 'ideal' forms the background basis for decision-making, but also as to whether the financial

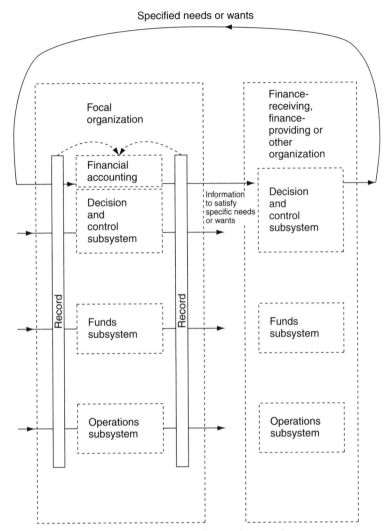

Figure 18.3 The decision usefulness approach to financial accounting

accounting information supplied through the decision models approach will actually be used – hence the question mark over the connection between the 'ideal' model and the actual decision mechanism used in Figure 18.4.

A great deal of work has been undertaken in both of these broad areas concerned with decision usefulness and in the following discussion we will look at some of the main strands of this research. In an introductory textbook we can only give the flavour of this work, which will be expanded in your later courses.

18.3.2 Research into the decision-makers emphasis

With regard to the decision-makers emphasis the only way to discover information wants is to go and ask the recipient organizations and draw from these observations insights which will provide the basis for the contents of the financial accounting reports. In this

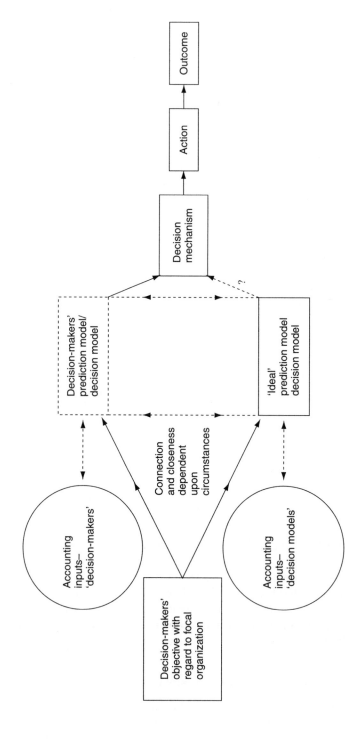

Figure 18.4 Relationship between the decision-makers and decision models variants of the decision usefulness approach

connection there have been two basic approaches to this discovery which are referred to as **behavioural accounting research** (**BAR** hereafter) and **security price research** (**SPR** hereafter). These research endeavours are connected as Figure 18.5 indicates. BAR explores the relationship between present or proposed accounting information in the context of the information wants of users (recipient organizations) either as individuals or groups. SPR, on the other hand, explores the relationship between accounting information and the 'wants' of the stock market (a sort of collective recipient organization) which sets the share prices for those companies whose capital is traded in this market. The determination of stock market prices is complex, yet they are generated by the actions of individuals, groups, companies, etc. However, the connection between these people, and consequently their wants as users (explored through BAR) and the market prices they create through the capital market, remains an 'unresearched link'.

The work coming under the umbrella of BAR is a blend of disconnected studies exploring the basic relationship between the users and their information wants. An attempt to provide a comprehensive classification of research findings coming under this categorization was made by Dyckman *et al.* (1975b) who saw the BAR literature falling into four broad areas:

i   The first set of studies explores the adequacy of financial statement disclosure according to the general views of various individuals and groups (e.g. Buzby, 1974).

ii   The second set of studies explores the usefulness of financial statement data for specific decision problems. These studies are rather more specific than the first set, looking at wants in the context of particular decision problems, primarily investment and disinvestment decisions in company share capital (e.g. Chandra 1974).

iii The third set of studies attempts to measure the attitudes and preferences of various individuals and groups to particular present or proposed reporting practices (e.g. Copeland *et al.* 1973).

iv   The fourth and final set attempts to explore some of the causal roots which lie behind certain preferences for information. This literature explores how individuals and groups make judgements about what is 'material' in terms of information content (e.g. Boatsman and Robertson 1974), and how information is processed in decision-making

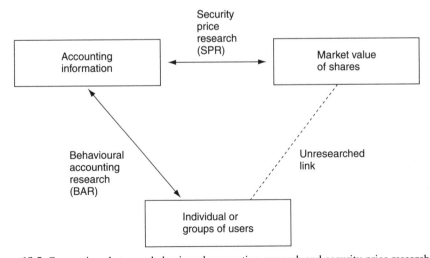

Figure 18.5 Connections between behavioural accounting research and security price research

(referred to in the literature as human information processing (HIP) – see Snowball 1980, for a reasonably comprehensive summary of this work).

The work coming under SPR draws out the financial accounting implications which come from the efficient markets hypothesis. This hypothesis maintains, in its semi-strong form, that the stock market instantaneously and without bias compounds into an organization's share price all relevant publicly available information (including accounting information). As many authors have indicated, this hypothesis provides a mechanism to evaluate the information content of accounting information. In general terms the rationale is simply that if any form of accounting information is published then its actual information value can be judged by whether there is a movement in the share price as a result. If there is, then the information has *information value* to the market, or, more specifically, to those who make the market (or in other words it satisfies the information wants of these users). There has been a great deal of work exploring the ramifications of this view but for the purposes of this book we do not need to go into the detailed content of these studies.[4]

It is difficult to draw any coherent pattern from BAR and SPR concerning the nature of the information wants of users. Part of the reason for this could be the youthfulness of the research to date and the seeming inability of researchers to build on the insights of others. Another reason could be that 'wants' do differ and do change over time, thus making any general picture of these an unattainable hope. Certainly at the moment those who propound the merits of this type of approach for the financial accounting function cannot predict the desirability of certain types of information to individuals, to groups or to the market. In fact, using SPR research, the desirability of information can only ever be assessed after its declaration (i.e. by its effect on the movements in share prices).

18.3.3 Research into the decision models emphasis

The above problems are significant but they fade into insignificance for those who propound the merits of a decision models emphasis. According to those taking this view the concern for assessing information *wants* is of secondary importance to the more important concern with ascertaining information *needs*. The proponents of the decision model approach are concerned with assessing the nature of efficient and effective decision-making processes and clarifying the information needs of these processes. This involves dividing up the decision process into the elements contained in Figure 18.4 and then refining the contents.

A not atypical development of these processes can be found in the Report of the Committee on Accounting Theory Construction and Verification (AAA 1971). The main elements involved (in a somewhat adapted and simplified form) are contained in Figure 18.6. They maintain that any decision is guided by a decision model which, in turn, is serviced by a prediction model which draws its data from an accounting system. There are three key predictions which are important for any decision model to be activated, and it is supplying the data for these three elements which becomes the important function of the accounting system (see Figure 18.6). It is thus the information which forms the contents of these inputs to prediction models which, following the logic of the decision models interpretation to the financial accounting function, becomes the information flow.

Each recipient organization will have different objectives and different prediction and decision models for these purposes. As a result, different information flows will be needed. However, the overarching view is that it is possible to generalize about the information

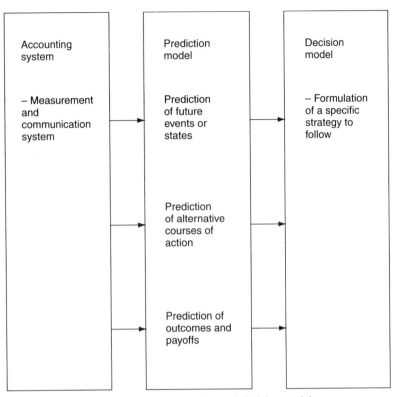

Figure 18.6 The position of accounting in prediction and decision models

needs of particular *groups* of users (e.g. shareholders or employees). Some work has been undertaken with regard to employees in this context (e.g. Maunders and Foley 1974; Foley and Maunders 1977; Cooper and Essex 1977), but the dominant concern in the literature has been with investors. *SATTA* (AAA 1977: 10–17) summarizes investors' decision models as needing measures of the likely cash flows to them and the financial and other events which generate these flows. This then becomes the information which should be supplied via the financial accounting function.

18.3.4 A concluding comment

In general, then, the decision usefulness approach to the financial accounting function is geared to providing, in one way or another, information which users want or need. The resulting information flows are more specialist and selective than those arising from the data-oriented approach. Instead of producing comprehensive and complex attempts at measuring, say, the income and wealth of the focal organization for some assumed and unclear purpose, the contents of the decision useful information flow is determined by either what the particular users want in terms of information or what they are perceived to need.

If we return to our case of Mr Brain, his financial accounting information under a decision usefulness approach would have to look to the needs or wants of his recipient organizations. He would have to find out what his parents and creditors really want in the way of information or what they need in terms of the objectives they wish to achieve through their involvement with him (as a focal organization), and supply this.

18.4 ORGANIZATIONAL RESOURCE APPROACH

The organizational resource approach to the financial accounting function shifts the emphasis for determining the information to be supplied from the needs of the receiver to that of the supplier. It is neither the assumed needs or wants nor the researched needs or wants of recipient organizations which predominate in determining the financial accounting information content under the organizational resource approach. These are not ignored, but the supply of information to satisfy these requirements is severely influenced by the needs and wants of the focal organization itself. The basic nature of the organizational resource approach can be depicted as in Figure 18.7.

There are two different variants of the organizational resource approach – one heavily reliant on economic theory and the concern with the supply of and demand for information, and the other on a broader theoretical base concerned with the control of the focal organization. We will look at each of these in turn.

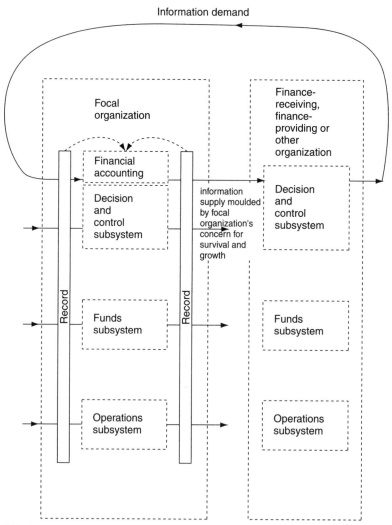

Figure 18.7 The organizational resource approach to financial accounting

18.4.1 The supply and demand model

This version of the organizational resource approach is built around the basic market economic model of supply and demand – only applied to information. Information will be supplied providing there is a demand for it. This is refined by a redefinition of the relationship between the recipient organizations which demand the information and the focal organization which supplies it. The former are deemed to be **principals** and the latter **agents**. These relationships are always set in the context of the transference of resources (invariably funds) primarily by what we have called finance-providing organizations to the focal organization for the purpose of increasing the value of the principal's wealth. In these situations the finance-providing organizations, which transfer the resources, are deemed to be principals (e.g. shareholders) and the (receiving) focal organization which uses these resources and has greater information as to their use is seen to be an agent.

Using this framework it is taken that agents should act in the interests of the principals but that for various reasons this may not always occur. All individuals (or organizations, in our terminology) are assumed under this approach to be resourceful and wealth-maximizing, which may result in the agent (the focal organization) not always working in the complete interests of the principal (the finance-providing organization). The economics literature calls this the 'moral hazard problem' since there is a legal expectation that the agent should work in the interests of the principal, but because of the basic assumptions which are deemed to govern economic behaviour there is a doubt as to whether this will happen automatically. In this situation the principal is assumed to want to monitor the actions of the agent but at minimum cost, while the agent will not want to be monitored too formally and so will provide information about what actions they (the agent) are taking. (For more details see Beaver 1981.)

This logic, according to those who argue for this interpretation, provides the basis for understanding the nature of the contents of the financial accounting flow. The actual information demands of the finance-providing organizations (the principals) form the background for the focal organization's decision as to what to supply. But this decision is always assumed to be heavily influenced by (a) the demands of the principal and (b) what the agent actually wants to declare. This in turn must be carefully balanced to prevent the agent's appearing to be deceptive.

The overall view is that the focal organization (or more specifically, the managers of this organization), to some extent, manipulates and uses its legally contracted agency position for seemingly selfish ends. This view is built on a particular understanding about organizations and the people who constitute them which is not shared by those adopting the second (organizational control) interpretation of financial accounting as an organizational resource.

18.4.2 The organization control model

The **organization control** model is based on the assumption that the focal organization, and the individuals who manage it, are – or rather should be – the focus for all the varying and conflicting interests of the individuals and groups (depicted as recipient organizations in our terminology) situated in the focal organization's substantial environment. Management in this context is involved in a complex balancing act of different interests, with the function of financial accounting being a potential source of influence on the behaviour and/or demands of these organizations when their expectations are out of line with current possibilities.

This approach to financial accounting has been propounded for a number of years by Laughlin and Puxty (e.g. 1981, 1983; Puxty and Laughlin 1983) but its roots can be more obviously found in the literature of organization theory, sociology and systems theory. The most systematic general schema is provided by Schoderbek *et al.* (1980) with what they call 'mismatch signals'. The concern is to specify what the focal organization would like to see with regard to certain aspects of the recipient organizations (which they call 'X'), a discovery of the actual state with regard to the same variables (which they call 'Y'), the ascertainment of the resulting mismatch signal (i.e. X–Y), and the formulation of information strategies to reduce these differences.

This general model can be reinterpreted into our accounting focus. Here various actual measures of the recipient organizations are discovered (the 'Y' measures, such as a willingness to lend, say, $10m to the focal organization at 20 per cent interest), these are compared with some perceived 'ideal' measures (variables 'X', such as the possibility of the focal organization's paying 10 per cent interest on loans needed of, say, $12m), resulting in different mismatches which particular information strategies (e.g. some bargaining strategy with the potential lender) attempt to resolve. These information flows form the essential content of the financial accounting reports adopting this interpretation. Thus, based on this thinking, the information acts as a way to influence the behaviour and/or aspirations of any particular recipient organization where this is out of line with that which is deemed to be feasible or appropriate given the demands of all recipient organizations involved with the focal organization.

The nature of X and Y and the information strategy one follows is extremely complex but these issues are not important at this stage. What is important to appreciate, however, is that this thinking provides yet another alternative basis for the nature of the financial accounting function, as does the one based on the economic laws of supply and demand and agency theory more generally.

18.4.3 A concluding comment

If we return to our case of Mr Brain: his financial accounting information under an organizational resource approach would be based on a mixture of the needs or wants of both himself and the various recipient organizations (parents, etc.). Invariably any financial accounting information Mr Brain supplied would be moulded by a strong concern to demonstrate his worthiness so as to ensure that cheques from his parents continue to arrive!

18.5 AN EVALUATION OF THE ALTERNATIVES

What should be clear to you by now is that there is more than one possible alternative approach to determining the contents of the financial accounting reports supplied by any focal organization. We have discussed three different approaches to this problem but even within each of these we have highlighted a number of variants.

Many of these various alternatives are mutually exclusive, which suggests that there needs to be some mechanism for attempting to decide which of the suggestions should actually guide the choice of the contents of the financial accounting reports. To suggest any form of evaluation is fraught with all sorts of problems.

This is inevitable since all the alternatives advanced in the accounting literature have their own advocates along with very genuinely held reasons for their respective support.

However, one possible way to advance towards an evaluation is to divide the interested parties on these accounting issues into broad sets of people and see what their overarching viewpoints are, and then find some mechanism for arbitrating on the differences which emerge. The logic of this comes from the realization that insights are not self-evidently true but must find their support in the communities which need to adopt and use them.

For our purposes we can divide up our financial accounting world into three groups of people:

(i) the **academics** who propound ideas about financial accounting;
(ii) the standard-setting bodies who propose and, through standards, attempt to ensure compliance with various alternatives (the **standard-setters** hereafter);
(iii) those in the focal organization who produce the accounts in question (the **producers** hereafter).

The users of financial accounting information (the recipient organizations) are excluded from the parties under consideration not because they are unimportant but rather because their needs are explicitly and implicitly accounted for in the attitudes of the three groups we have highlighted.

There are all sorts of factions and disagreements inside these broad communities but it is still possible to say something about the basic tenor of the thinking of all three so as to highlight some key issues of substance which give meaning to each.

18.5.1 Academics, standard-setters and producers: their views

In the main the academics would appear to be predominantly of the opinion that some variant of the decision usefulness approach should dominate the financial accounting function. In different guises over the last 50 or so years the literature on financial accounting has been dominated by the view that decision usefulness should guide the contents of the financial accounting flow. This awareness led Staubus to make the rather bold claim that:

> Decision usefulness is now widely accepted as the appropriate objective of accounting.
>
> (*Staubus 1977: 33*)

This may well be a majority view amongst academics (it certainly is not a unanimous view). It is not, however, even a predominant view amongst either standard setters or producers.

The standard-setters, although making moves towards the decision usefulness approach, still appear to be locked into the more traditional aspects of the data-oriented approach. At least one might infer this judging by the standards that are being produced. Admittedly there have been many attempts in the UK, Canada, Australia, New Zealand, the USA and the International Accounting Standards Committee to adopt a decision usefulness approach[5] but the results – in terms of actual impact on accounting standards – would appear to be minimal. All the standards are built around different problem areas concerning the traditional approach to measuring income and wealth as we saw in Chapter 14 – a data-oriented approach in other words. Even the worldwide experiments with inflation accounting (see Chapter 16) have been simply different facets of the data-oriented approach.

On the other hand, it can be argued that the producers have adopted a more organizational resource approach to the issue. A flavour of this can be picked up from the response of some US practitioners (producers) to a survey on their attitudes to the dominant objective of the conceptual framework programme (namely that 'the basic objective of financial statements is to provide information useful for making economic decisions'). Malcolm Marshall, the chairman of the Financial Accounting Standards Board (FASB), notes with some amazement:

> I am sure you will be astounded to learn that only 37 percent of our respondents were able to recommend the adoption of this objective.
>
> *(Armstrong 1977: 77)*

What is apparent from this is that there is a different philosophy operating in the minds of those who are working in organizations.

The nature of this philosophy was partially explored by Laughlin and Puxty (1983). Their study analysed how companies responded to standards not in terms of their implicit merit to supply either more accurate or useful information or to bolster the wealth of the managers (as Watts and Zimmerman (1978) suggest in a similar study) but rather whether these standards had implications for the survival of the organization. This analysis was used to demonstrate that the management of focal organizations view financial accounting information from an organizational resource perspective, even though they are often prevented from expressing this due to the constraints which both the law and the profession (the standard-setters) create around the financial accounting behaviour of these organizations.

In general, then, all three communities of the accounting profession appear to take different views about the function of financial accounting for both commercial and non-commercial organizations.

i   The academics, in the main, argue for a decision usefulness approach.
ii   The standard-setters take a fundamentally data-oriented approach to the problem while leaning towards a decision usefulness approach.
iii The producers, on the other hand, adopt a more organizational resource approach to the issues.

These 'worldviews' are undoubtedly not the only lines of thought in these three communities, but they are dominant and so they could be seen as moulding the respective financial accounting pronouncements (from particularly the academics and setters) for both commercial and non-commercial organizations.

18.5.2 A unified view?

Faced with these differences one has to ask whether it is possible to obtain a unified view for the total accounting community. There are at least three possible strategies which could be adopted to help formulate this common view.

First, we could look towards the intersection of views among the groups. However, using this strategy, as Figure 18.8 indicates, could well result in the producers' views remaining largely ignored since it is highly likely that strategies will be adopted which fit the larger overlap of acceptability between academics and standard-setters.

Second, and to an extent building on the above, we could legitimately concentrate on this decision usefulness/data orientation overlap on the grounds that, in the end, it is the responsibility of the academics and standard-setters to lead on the matters of accounting practice and the producers to react through compliance with these suggestions.

Third, that we evolve some way to evaluate the three basic approaches (data-oriented, decision usefulness and organizational resource) according to some 'higher' criteria and

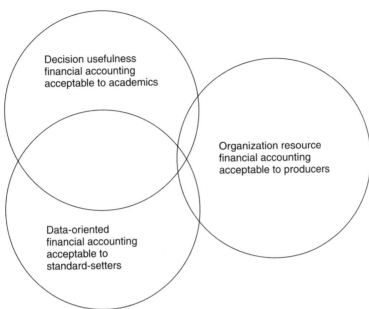

Decision usefulness
financial accounting
acceptable to academics

Organization resource
financial accounting
acceptable to producers

Data-oriented
financial accounting
acceptable to
standard-setters

Figure 18.8 Attitudes about financial accounting of academics, standards-setters and producers: tracing the interconnections

then, adopting this 'worldview', persuade the communities which do not currently hold these beliefs to adopt an alternative viewpoint.

Some of the work which adopts this third perspective has been started by Laughlin and Puxty (1981, 1983 and Puxty and Laughlin 1983). In these studies they attempt to evaluate the three accounting approaches according to a social welfare function which is deemed to encompass the 'higher' criteria which should be used to judge the merits of alternative financial accounting approaches. A social welfare function has also been used by others to evaluate financial accounting alternatives (e.g. American Accounting Association 1975; FASB 1977). The conclusions from these studies are rudimentary, at best, suggesting that much work is still to be done before an alternative emerges which is universally accepted as being socially the 'best'.

SUMMARY

In this chapter we have attempted three things. First, we refined our understanding about the problem of financial accounting for any and all focal organizations. In this connection we have not discriminated between commercial and non-commercial focal organizations since we have pitched the discussion at a much higher level of abstraction which encompasses both. We concluded that the problem of financial accounting could be seen in terms of the information flow between a focal organization's decision and control subsystem and some recipient organization's decision and control subsystem.

Second, we have attempted to clarify the alternative general solutions which have been advanced in the accounting literature. These solutions are clustered into three 'worldviews' which we have entitled the 'data-oriented approach', the 'decision usefulness approach' and the 'organizational resource approach'. In addition we highlighted a number of different variants of these ways of thinking, providing different interpretations of their overarching viewpoints. So, following the data-oriented approach, we have shown how this can be expressed in terms of the more traditional measures of income and wealth from the cash or near cash transactions of any organization as well as other, somewhat less restrictive, measures of income and wealth. Equally we have shown that this data-oriented approach can also find its expression through measures of cash flows or more general events of interest or in terms of measures of accountability. In the decision usefulness approach we have also indicated variants in terms of supplying either the information wants or needs of recipient organizations. In the organizational resource approach we have shown how the contents of the financial accounting information flow can be determined under the rules of supply and demand set in the context of a principal–agent relationship. Alternatively the financial accounting information flow could be seen as a channel through which the focal organization, as a focus for the needs of all recipient organizations, attempts to influence the behaviour of the recipient organizations in certain circumstances.

Third, we attempted an evaluation of these different basic approaches on the grounds that they are difficult to amalgamate. To start the evaluation we divided up the community of financial accounting into academics, standard-setters and producers to ascertain their respective allegiances to the different approaches and discovered a matching of:

- academics with the decision usefulness approach;
- standard-setters with the data-oriented approach;
- producers with the organizational resource approach.

From these insights we suggested that a process of evaluating these allegiances from a higher social welfare perspective might aid our endeavours to discover the 'best' alternative for financial accounting.

The issues we have been introducing in this chapter are extremely important for the future of financial accounting, with the resolution of the differences at a very basic level being a priority. We will return to this theme in the final chapter, where we also present a summary of the contents of the whole book.

Key terms and concepts

Here is a list of the key terms and concepts which we have featured in this chapter. You should make sure that you understand and can define each one of them. Page references to definitions in the text appear in bold in the index.

- Academics
- Accountability measures
- Agents
- Behavioural accounting research (BAR)
- Cash flow accounting
- Data-oriented approach
- Decision-makers variant
- Decision models variant
- Decision usefulness approach
- Events accounting
- Income and wealth measures
- Organization control
- Organizational resource approach
- Principals
- Producers
- Recipient organization
- Security price research (SPR)
- Standard-setters

FURTHER READING

Any of the references cited in this chapter will provide a more than adequate source for further reading. However, at this stage in your studies it is important that you obtain something of a clear overview of the alternative financial accounting approaches which have been put forward in the literature. In this context we would advise you to read in depth: AAA (1977), Chapter 2; Davis *et al.* (1982: 307–318); and Laughlin and Puxty (1981: 44–61 and 74–80), which provide a basis for this overview.

NOTES

1. You will recall, however, that the end-of-period adjustments involve estimates of *future* events. It is these future events which will indicate what actual past events have occurred – how much of a machine has been used, what proportion of debtors are good, and so on.
2. Rather than assuming that the organization permits the environment to control it!
3. Yet, given the assumption that decision-making processes are rational activities, it is possible to trace the implicit decision elements which use this information. This will be the decision-makers prediction and decision model which is intended to propose certain strategies to achieve some defined objectives which will lead to an actual action.
4. The interested reader is referred to the texts by Dyckman *et al.* (1975a), Beaver (1981) and Hines (1984) for more details about these studies.
5. If you are reading your professional accountancy magazine you could hardly fail to have spotted references to these various attempts over the years.

Part V

Where Have We Been?
Where Do We Go Next?

Where have we been? Where do we go next? 19

Learning objectives

After studying this chapter you should be able to:

- leap tall buildings in a single bound;
- juggle with live hand-grenades;
- wrestle dragons with your bare hands;
- turn lead into gold;
- make the perfect cup of tea;
- pass your introductory examinations;
- move on to further and more advanced studies of accounting and finance.

19.1 LOOKING BACK OVER THE COURSE

19.1.1 Introduction

Some months ago, the probability is that you knew little or no accounting. If you are reading this, you have probably now completed your introductory course in financial accounting and are in the process of revising for examinations. You now have a substantial basic knowledge about the subject. This brief chapter is designed to help you sharpen up that revision and use what you have learned as a productive basis for further studies in accounting and finance.

As you have now discovered, accounting is a difficult subject to study. It comprises equal parts of *learning*, *doing* and *thinking*. These are different intellectual skills and the challenge of an accounting education is being equally proficient in all areas – not easy. More particularly, in the last 18 chapters:

- you have *learnt* about what accounting is;
- you have *learnt* about a series of techniques that make up the core of financial accounting;
- you have *learnt* a range of material about the context and professional structure of accounting;
- you have then had to *comprehend* this material – trying to *understand* the reasoning behind it;
- this then provided a basis for you to *apply* the material to questions and situations – to *identify* accounting transactions, *create* a set of accounting records (bookkeeping), and *construct* a range of financial statements;

- if you have sufficiently grasped these *application and comprehension* skills you are then in a position to begin to *analyse* what you have done and to begin the wider process of *reflecting* on conventional accounting, identifying its (many) strengths and weakness and considering *other possibilities*;
- to do this well requires a fairly high level of abstract thinking as you begin to see the connection between the detailed mechanics of accounting and the social, environmental and political implications of those mechanics.

It's no wonder that financial accounting is a difficult subject! This is a very demanding range of intellectual skills to be acquired in a relatively short space of time. It is hard enough *doing* these complicated accounting mechanics without having to also *think about* and *reflect upon* them. The structure of the book and the way in which we articulated the different stages in the accounting process were all designed to help you, as much as possible, achieve this demanding balance: an accountant who can only *do* but cannot *think about what they do* is just as bad an accountant as one who can *theorize about* accounting but cannot *handle the mechanics*.

The rest of this sections will revise the structure of accounting and the way we approached in this book – subsection 19.1.2 – and then subsection 19.1.3 will offer a few hints about revising the material. Section 19.2 will look forward to your future studies in accounting. Finally, section 19.3 will return to the opening theme of Chapter 1 and briefly discuss some issues of accounting and education.

19.1.2 The structure of financial accounting

We have tried to inculcate a particular approach to conceiving of financial accounting. This had the following stages:

Context

- We introduced a model of an organization (the accounting entity).
- We then introduced the characteristics which define the way conventional accounting looks at the organization.

Bookkeeping

- This permitted us to identify a set of flows into and out of the organization – the debits and credits.
- These debits and credits centred around eight basic transaction types.
- We used double-entry to produce the basic accounting records (the T- accounts) from these transactions/flows.
- These were summarized at the end of the accounting period into an initial trial balance.

Accounting

- These initial balances had to be adjusted to bring them in line with accounting conventions.
- We put the end-of-period adjustments through, either the extended trial balance or directly through the T-accounts.
- These adjustments are governed by conventions, company law and accounting standards.

- This produced a final trial balance which provided the basis for the construction of the financial statements.

Reporting

- The financial statements comprised a profit and loss account and balance sheet, a cash flow statement (which we reached by a more circuitous route), and notes to the accounts.
- The form of these is governed by company law and accounting standards.
- The financial statements form part of the annual report which is intended primarily for financial participants in the focal organization.

Developing the financial statements

- More could be done with these statements to provide different or perhaps better information.
- We could construct cash flow or funds flow statements.
- We could attempt to adjust the financial statements for the effects of changing prices or inflation.
- We could analyse the financial statements using ratios to help us 'see inside' the picture given by the organization.

Thinking about it – taking it further

- Nobody is going to try and argue (whilst sober) that conventional financial accounting is a coherent and logical system.
- Attempts have been made to explain financial accounting through a series of accounting theories.
- They have been partly successful but the theories are very important as yardsticks against which we might decide to either evaluate current accounting or try and set up a new and better system of financial accounting.
- One way of doing this was to ask why conventional accounting operates as it does. We could expand accounting – and thereby recognize many of its limitations – by developing social and environmental accounting.
- The organizational model, the four characteristics and the eight transactions – with which we started the book and which gave you a (relatively) coherent basis for your bookkeeping – can now give you a basis upon which to think about these difficult but important accounting theory issues.

It is our view that the more you work through this basic scenario, the easier you will find it to put all the elements into their proper place. Once that happens, linking the 'doing' of accounting with the 'thinking about' accounting becomes easier, more productive and a great deal more fun.

Speaking of fun, what about revising?

19.1.3 Revising financial accounting

A 'good student' is one who reads and thinks before lectures, returns from lectures and revises the lecture notes, reads further and makes notes on that, thinking as they go. For such a student, studying will become fun and revision will be a very exciting opportunity (we are not being sarcastic, honest!) to pull together all the material and begin to see how the wider picture works. Such a student will experience the immense creative satisfaction of suddenly seeing what the lecturer or the textbook has being going on about for the last few months. A new vision forms in the mind which affects how you see both your subject and the world in general. And *that* is what we call *education*.

However, we are experienced lecturers and know that whilst a few of you will have followed the above path, most of you will have not. Indeed a sad few may even have got to the point of revision without having opened the book yet. (If you are reading this the probability is that you are not one of these educational black holes.) So how to go about revising this material if you are a 'normal student'?

First, reread section 19.1.2 above and get the schema of financial accounting really clear in your head. This is your 'mental map' of financial accounting.

Second, the job you now have is to (a) find out how much of the map is missing and (b) fill in the those missing details.

Third, you start back at Chapter 1 and work through the text and the workbook. 'But this will take ages!', you cry. If you are beginning to make real progress in financial accounting this will only take a few *intensive* days. (Note 1 gives you some idea what is meant by 'intensive' and offers few hints on study technique.[1]) If it does take ages – say two or three intensive weeks – this is because you do not know and/or understand the material and *need* that time to make sense of the material.

Fourth, work and rework the numerical examples until they are clear and virtually second nature – but *don't* ignore them.

Fifth, think about what you are doing and why. Take every opportunity to discuss – argue even – about the issues with colleagues from your course and from other courses. The more you discuss these issues, the more you will identify what you do and do not understand and you will become more articulate and thoughtful about your subject.

Sixth, if this doesn't work, go off and do something easy like a degree in rocket science.

Presuming you pass you examinations and proceed with your accounting studies, what can you expect?

19.2 LOOKING FORWARD

This book has tried to give you a basis for *deep learning* about accounting. That is, it has tried to change the way you see the world in a manner which will stay with you throughout your studies. Not all of accounting can be learnt in this way. Courses which you will take in future years will span a very wide range: from the detailed application of complex accounting rules in advanced financial accounting to the complex and sophisticated but very precisely constrained world of financial management; from the intensely practical courses – perhaps like auditing and accounting information systems – to the very reflective and political courses – perhaps like accounting policy and regulation, accounting theory and social and environmental accounting. Different courses will be taught in different ways. Different teachers will emphasise different intellectual skills. Some of you will love the detailed algorithms of advanced financial accounting or finance but hate the uncertainty and political introspection of accounting theory, for example. Some of you will have the opposite experience.

We have tried to give you a balanced view so that you can acquire a real proficiency in financial accounting techniques whilst being able to think about those techniques in a reasonably sophisticated way. If you have the good fortune to be studying at a university offering a 'good degree' in accounting, you will experience this range of approaches and the balance we have sought in this book will be reflected in the range of courses you do.

You now have enough material to advance – in terms of both knowledge and intellectual development – to more advanced courses and, we hope, to enjoy them. But we would like to finish where we started – talking about the nature of education and the accounting profession.

19.3 EDUCATION AND THE ACCOUNTING PROFESSION

One of the most reliable conclusions from research into education is that a student's intellectual and moral maturity grows and develops as they get older and as their years of education increase. This is a sort of educational law: that [Years + Education] = [Greater intellectual and moral maturity]. This seems to hold for most countries, most people and most degrees. That is, *except for accounting and business studies degrees where the intellectual and moral maturity actually appear to decline!* (For more detail see Gray *et al.* 1994.) This is not the sort of absolute 'scientific' conclusion like 'the earth goes round the sun' or 'apples fall off apple trees' but there is sufficient evidence to make us, as professional accountants, somewhat worried that accounting education is *not* encouraging the right sort of development in you. This is why we have spent so long in this book chatting to you – or, if you prefer, giving you little sermons – about how important it is to think about accounting and not just treat it as a set of complex plumbing techniques for exceptionally bright and well-paid people who find accounting boring and who assume that accounting has really nothing to do with their political and social beliefs about the world.

It requires hard work to think this through and to retain a wider vision about the astonishing and all-embracing importance of accounting whilst you are trying to wrestle with the advanced, complex and very important techniques of your later studies. The startling irony that perplexes us is that very many accountants and accounting students consider *accountants* to be very important but really consider *accounting* to be very unimportant. Please spend some time thinking about this – it is the other way around. It is not easy, but with intellectual effort you should be able to see that there is a very direct link between:

i   issues you have studied with us and will study in future courses (for example, financial accounting treatment of goodwill, research and development, environmental liabilities; management accounting treatment of performance appraisal, investment appraisal and costing systems; financial management's treatment of investor motivation and stock market behaviour; the overarching role of profit and costs); and

ii issues which affect you and the world around you. Examples which affect you directly include your funding for university, class sizes, the amount of time lecturers have to spend with you, your employment prospects. Less direct effects we discussed in Chapter 1 include decline or improvement of social and public sector infrastructure; environmental degradation; inequalities of income; unemployment; economic well-being of economic units; the power of TNCs.

It may all seem a little far-fetched at this stage but work at it. The results are astonishing. Enjoy your studies, really put some mental muscle into them. The world needs good, thoughtful accountants.

Good luck and best wishes.

NOTES

1. An 'intensive day' involves 9 or 10 hours of solid work excluding lunch breaks, coffee breaks, breaks to scratch yourself or breaks to watch the spider climbing up the wall. You should work in 45–60-minute bursts, stopping every 45 minutes or so, stretching, making a drink or walking around for 5 minutes. Then back to work. Take notes all the time so that (i) you learn more quickly and (ii) you can monitor whether you *are* working or day-dreaming whilst staring at a page.

References

Accounting Standards (formerly Steering) Committee (1975) *The Corporate Report*, ICAEW

Allen, K. (1991) In pursuit of professional dominance: Australian accounting 1953–1985. *Accounting Auditing and Accountability Journal* 3(1), 51–67

American Accounting Association (1966) *A Statement of Basic Accounting Theory*, American Account Association, Saratosa, Florida

American Accounting Association (1971) Report of the committee on accounting theory construction and verification. *The Accounting Review (Supplement)* 46, 50–79

American Accounting Association (1975) Report of the committee on concepts and standards for external financial reports. *The Accounting Review (Supplement)* 50, 41–49

American Accounting Association (1977) *Statement on Accounting Theory and Theory Acceptance*, AAA, Sarasota, Florida

Anthony, R.N. and Young, J. (1984) *Management Control in Non-profit Organizations*, Irwin, Homewood, Illinois

Armstrong, M.B. and Vincent, J.I. (1988) Public accounting: a profession at the crossroads. *Accounting Horizons* (March), 94–98

Armstrong, M.S. (1977) Statements in quotes: the politics of establishing accounting standards. *Journal of Accountancy* (February), 76–79

Bailey, D., Harte, G. and Sugden, R. (1994a) *Making Transnationals Accountable: A Significant Step for Britain*, Routledge, London

Bailey, D., Harte, G. and Sugden, R. (1994b) *Transnationals and Governments: Recent Policies in Japan, France, Germany, the United States and Britain*, Routledge, London

Baxter, W.T. (1982) Accounting standards – boon or curse? *Accounting and Business Research* 3–10

Beaver, W.H. (1981) *Financial Reporting: An Accounting Revolution*, Prentice Hall, Englewood Cliffs, NJ

Beaver, W.H., Kennelly, W.J. and Voss, W.M. (1968) Predictive ability as a criterion for the evaluation of accounting data. *The Accounting Review* 43(4), 675–83

Boatsman, J.R. and Robertson, J.C. (1974) Policy capture on selected materiality judgements. *The Accounting Review* 49(2), 342–352

Boom, B.S., Englehart, M.B., Furst, E.J., Hill, W.H. and Krathwohn D.R. (1956), *Taxonomy of educational objectives. The classification of educational goals. Handbook I: Cognitive domain*, Longmans Green, New York

Bougen, P. (1982) Additional dimensions of corporate reporting in *Financial Reporting 1982/83* (eds D.J. Tonkin and L.C.L. Skerratt), ICAEW, London, pp. 827–51

Bougen, P. (1983) Valued added, in *Financial Reporting 1983/84* (eds D.J. Tonkin and L.C.L. Skerratt) ICAEW, London, pp.151–163

Broadbent, J., Laughlin, R. and Read, S. (1991) Recent financial and administrative changes in the NHS: a critical theory analysis. *Critical Perspectives on Accounting* 2(1), 1–30

Burchell, S., Clubb, C. and Hopwood, A. (1985) Accounting in its social context: towards a history of value added in the United Kingdom. *Accounting, Organizations and Society* 10(4), 381–413

Buzby, S.L. (1974) Selected items of information and their disclosure in annual reports. *The Accounting Review* 49(1), 423–435

Carsberg, B. and Hope, T. (1984) *Current Issues in Accounting*, Philip Allen, Oxford

Chambers, R.J. (1966) *Accounting, Evaluation and Economic Behavior*, Prentice Hall, Englewoods Cliffs, NJ

Chandra, G. (1974) A study of the consensus on disclosure among public accountants and security analysts. *The Accounting Review* 49(4), 733–742

Coombes, R.J. and Eddy, P.H. (1986) Accounting income: the relationship between capital maintenance and asset measurement. *Issues in Accounting Education* 1(1), 112–122

Cooper, D.J. and Essex, S.R. (1977) Accounting information and employee decision making. *Accounting, Organizations and Society* 2(3), 201–217

Copeland, R.M., Francia, A.J. and Stawser, R.H. (1973) Students and subjects in behavioural business research. *The Accounting Review* 48(2), 365–374

Cowton, C. (1989) Note: Differences that are multiples of nine. *British Accounting Review* 21(4), 377–80.

Davis, S.W., Menon, K. and Morgan, G. (1982) The images that have shaped accounting theory. *Accounting, Organizations and Society* 7(4), 307–318

Donald, A. (1979) *Management Information Systems*, Pergamon, Oxford

Dyckman, T.R., Downes, D.H. and Magee, R.P. (1975a) *Efficient Capital Markets and Accounting*, Prentice Hall, Englewoods Cliffs, NJ

Dyckman, T.R., Gibbins, M. and Swieringa, R.J. (1975b) Experimental and survey research in financial accounting, in *The Impact of Accounting Research on Practice and Disclosure* (eds A.R. Abdel-Khalik and T.F. Keller), Duke University Press, Durham, NC, pp. 48–60

Elkington, J. (1997) *Cannibals with Forks: the Triple Bottom Line of 21st Century Business,* Capstone, Oxford

Financial Accounting Standards Board (1977) *Objectives of Financial Reporting and Elements of Financial Statements of Business Enterprises* (Exposure Draft), FASB, New York

Foley, B.J. and Maunders, K.T. (1977) *Accounting Information Disclosure and Collective Bargaining*, Macmillan, London

Friedman, M. (1962) *Capitalism and Freedom*, University of Chicago Press, Chicago

Gray, R.H. (1997) The silent practice of social accounting and corporate social reporting in companies, in *Building Corporate Accountability* (eds S. Zadek, R. Evans and P. Pruzan), Earthscan, London

Gray, R.H. and Bebbington, K.J. (2001) *Accounting for the Environment*, Sage, London

Gray, R.H. and Hope, A.J.B. (1982) Disclosure: where the auditors are failing. *Accountancy* 93(1072), 19–20

Gray, R.H., Bebbington, K.J. and McPhail, K. (1994) Teaching ethics and the ethics of accounting teaching: educating for immorality and a case for social and environmental accounting education. *Accounting Education* 3(1), 51–75

Gray, R.H., Kouhy, R. and Lavers, S. (1995) Corporate social and environmental reporting: a review of the literature and a longitudinal study of UK disclosure. *Accounting, Auditing and Accountability Journal* 8(2), 47–77

Gray, R.H., Owen, D.L. and Adams, C. (1996) *Accounting and Accountability: Social and Environmental Accounting in a Changing World*, Prentice Hall, London

Gray, R.H., Owen, D.L. and Maunders, K.T. (1987) *Corporate Social Reporting: Accounting and Accountability*, Prentice Hall, Hemel Hemstead

Greenwood, E. (1957) Attributes of a profession. *Social Work* (July), 44–55

Grinyer, J.R. (1985) Earned economic income: a theory for matching. *Abacus* 21(2), 130–140

Harte, G. and Owen, D. (1991) Environmental disclosure in the annual reports of British companies: a research note. *Accounting, Auditing and Accountability Journal* 4(3), 51–61

Hicks, J.R. (1946) *Value and Capital*, Oxford University Press, Oxford

Hines, R.D. (1984) The implications of stock market reaction (non-reaction) for financial accounting standard setting. *Accounting and Business Research* 15(57), 3–14

Hines, R.D. (1988) Financial accounting: in communicating reality, we construct reality. *Accounting, Organizations and Society* 13(3), 251–261

Hird, C. (1983) *Challenging the Figures*, Pluto Press, London

Hope, A.J.B. (1984) Accounting and changing prices, in *Current Issues in Accounting* (eds B. Carsberg and T. Hope), Philip Allen, Oxford, pp. 67–83

Johnson, O. (1970) Towards an 'events' theory of accounting. *The Accounting Review* 45(4), 641–653

Jones, R. and Pendlebury, M. (2000) *Public Sector Accounting*, Pitman, London

Kast, F.E. and Rosenweig, J.E. (1974) *Organization and Management: A Systems Approach*, McGraw-Hill, Kograkusha

Laughlin, R.C. and Puxty, A.G. (1981) The decision-usefulness criterion: wrong cart, wrong horse. *British Accounting Review* 13(1), 43–87

Laughlin, R.C. and Puxty, A.G. (1983) Accounting regulation: an alternative perspective. *Journal of Business Finance and Accounting* 10(3), 451–479

Lawson, G.H. (1978) The rationale of cash flow accounting, in *Trends in Management and Financial Accounting*, *Vol. 1* (ed. C. van Dam), Martinus Nijhoff, Amsterdam, pp. 85–104

Lee, T.A. (1978) The cash flow alternative for corporate financial reporting, in *Trends in Management and Financial Accounting, Vol. 1* (ed. C. van Dam), Martinus Nijhoff, Amsterdam, pp. 85–104

Lehman, C. (1988) Accounting ethics: surviving survival of the fittest. *Advances in Public Interest Accounting* 3, 37–157

Lehman, C. (1992) *Accounting's Changing Role in Social Conflict,* Paul Chapman, London

Lewis, C. and Pendrill, D. (1996) *Advanced Financial Accounting*, Pitman, London

Lieberman, A.Z. and Whiston, A.B. (1975) A structuring of an event accounting information system. *The Accounting Review* 50(2), 246–258

Lowe, A.E. (1972) The finance director's role in the formulation and implementation of strategy. *Journal of Business Finance* 4(4), 58–63

Lowe, A.E. and McInnes, J.M. (1971) Control of socio-economic organisations. *Journal of Management Studies* 8(2), 213–227

Mattessich, R. (1971) *Accounting and Analytical Methods*, Scholars Book Co., Houston, Texas

Maunders, K.T. (1981) Social reporting and the employment report, in *Financial Reporting 1981–1982* (eds D.J. Tonkin and L.C.L. Skerratt), ICAEW, London, pp. 217–227

Maunders, K.T. and Foley, B.J. (1974) Accounting information and collective bargaining. *Journal of Business Finance and Accounting* 1(1), 109–127

Millerson, G.L. (1964) *The Qualifying Association*, Routledge & Kegan Paul, London

Neimark, M.K. (1992) *The Hidden Dimensions of Annual Reports*, Markus Wiener, New York

Owen, D.L. (1992) *Green Reporting: The Challenge of the Nineties*, Chapman & Hall, London

Parker, H.G., Harcourt G.C. and Whittington, G. (1986) *Readings in the Concept and Measurement of Income*, Philip Allen, Oxford

Perks, R.W. (1993) *Accounting and Society*, Chapman & Hall, London

Perks, R.W, Rawlinson, D. and Ingram, L. (1992), An exploration of ethical investment in the UK. *British Accounting Review* 24(1), 43–65.

Puxty, A.G. and Laughlin, R.C. (1983) A rational reconstruction of the decision usefulness criterion. *Journal of Business Finance and Accounting* 10(4), pp. 543–60

Roberts, C., Weetman, P. and Gordon, P. (1998) *International Financial Accounting: A Comparative Approach*, Pitman, London

Scapens, R. (1981) *Accounting in an Inflationary Environment,* Macmillan, London

Schoderbek, C.G., Schoderbek, P.P. and Kefalas, G.G. (1980) *Management Systems: Conceptual Considerations*, Business Publications, Dallas, Texas

Shalchi, H. and Smith, C.H. (1985) Research on accounting for changing prices: theory, evidence and implications. *Quarterly Review of Economics and Business* 25(4), 5–37

Sikka, P., Willmott, H.C. and Lowe, E.A. (1989) Guardians of knowledge and the public interest: evidence and issue of accountability in the UK accountancy profession. *Accounting, Auditing and Accountability Journal* 2(2), 47–71

Snowball, D. (1980) On the integration of accounting research on human information processing. *Accounting and Business Research* 10(39), 307–318

Sorter, G.H. (1969) An events approach to basic accounting theory. *The Accounting Review* 44(1), 12–19

Staubus, C.J. (1977) *Making Accounting Decisions*, Scholars Book Co., Houston, Texas

Sterling R. (1972) Decision-orientated financial accounting. *Accounting and Business Research*, Summer, 1972, pp.198–208

Taylor, P. and Turley, S. (1986) *The Regulation of Accounting*, Basil Blackwell, Oxford

Tinker, A.M. (1985) *Paper Prophets: A Social Critique of Accounting*, Holt Sanders, Eastbourne

Tinker, A.M. (1992) The retreating intellectual. *Pass Magazine* (February), p. 8

Wallis, R.W. (1970) *Accounting: A Modern Approach*, McGraw-Hill, London.

Watts, R. and Zimmerman, J. (1978) Towards a positive theory of the determination of accounting standards. *Accounting Review*, pp.112–134

Whittington, G. (1981a) *Inflation Accounting: All the Answers*, Deloitte, Haskins and Sells Lecture, UC Cardiff

Whittington, G. (1981b) The British contribution to income theory, in *Essays in British Accounting Research* (eds M. Bromich and A. Hopwood), Pitman, London

Whittington, G. and Tweedie, D. (1984) *The Debate on Inflation Accounting*, Cambridge University Press, Cambridge

Willmott, H (1990) Serving the public interest? A critical analysis of a professional claim, in *Critical Accounts* (eds D. Cooper and T. Hopper), Macmillan, Basingstoke, pp. 315–331

World Commission on Environment and Development. (1987), *Our Common Future (The Brundtland Report)*, Oxford University Press, Oxford

Zeff, S.A. (1987) Does the CPA belong to a profession? *Accounting Horizons* (June)

Index

academics   427–9
accountability measures   35–6, 413, 417
accountants   36–7, 298–9
    self regulation   16
accounting **8, 52**
    background   3–6
    characteristics   9–11, 33–4
    conventions   132, 137–42, **138**
    dates   309
    decisions   14, 246–9, 308–9
    entity   **9**, 41, 60, 86, 261, 283, 285
    equations   132–6
    four characteristics   9–11
    harmonisation and reconciliations   304–5
    history of   6–7
    inappropriate   290–2, 294
    information   35–7
    negative effects   290–2, 294
    notes   266–7, 307–8, 320, 349
    period   31, 87, 96, 309
    plan   303
    policies   109, 319–22, 349
    procedures manual   116
    process   109–10
    reference period   142
    records   108, 110, 311, 312
    rules and regulations   301–2
    social reality   269–71, 273, 290–2
    sustainable development   **404**–5
    transactions   12, 72–3, 78
    treatment and disclosure   308–9
accounting information system (AIS)   108,
        149, 156–7
    process   109–12
    accounting profession   16, 39, 298–9,
        383–4
    education and training   17–18, 437–8
Accounting Standards Board   39, 317
Accounting Standards Committee   317

accounts
    balancing off   96–9
    chart/index   116–18
    closing off   96
    code   116
    illustrated   93–6
    notes to   266–7, 307–8, 320, 349
accrual convention **139**-40
accruals   149, 157–8, 159
    illustrated   161–6
    invoice   158
    reversing   248
    sundry   158
acid test ratio   356
activity
    normal/abnormal   319
    ratios   354–5
agents   425
American Accounting Association   8, 412
amortization   180, 200
annual
    general meeting **311**-12
    returns   311
appropriation account   254, 261–2
    illustrated   263–5
arithmetic method   101
Articles of Association   311, 312–13
assets   102, **132**, 144–6
    current **144–5**
    disposal   197–8
    fixed **144**
    intangible   145–6
    non-monetary   376
    valuation   370, 375–9
audit   109, **325**
    internal/external   121–2
    statutory   121, 314–16
auditor   314–16
    report   314–15, 348

average cost (AVCO)   213, **215**-16

bad debts   149, **238**–9
   accounting   239–41
   written off   239
balance brought forward   111, 119
balance sheet   31, **130**, 266–7, 307–8
   cash-orientated   339–41
   illustrated   169, 171, 173
   published   309–16
balancing figure   26, 96–9
bank
   correcting errors   123
   reconciliations   122–6
   regulation   323
   statement   122
behavioural accounting research (BAR)
   421–2
Bilan Social   399–400
Blooms taxonomy of learning   18
Bookkeeping   4, 6–7, 51, 84
   basic transactions   73–8
   for depreciation   187–93
   illustrated   55–8, 71–2, 84–93
   for jointing/leaving partners   288–90
   process   103
   records   112–13
   single entry matrix   104–5
books of prime entry *see* day books/journals
brands   145
business finance *see* financial management

capital   73, 77
   account   77, **277**, 278–9
   allowances   254
   expenditure   143
   injection of   77, 255–9
   maintenance   260, 370, 379–82
   structure   358, 359–360
cash   22–**3**, 334, 334–5
   application   **336**, 342
   budget   332–3
   equivalents   335
   near   23, 331
   petty   26, 30
   purchases   73–5
   sales   75
   sources   **336**, 342
   vs. profit   334
cash flow accounting   389, 417
cash flow statement   308, 334–6
   constructing   343–5

illustrated   343–5
(in) direct method   335, 336
reconciliation   337–42
simple   336–7
usefulness   346
vs. funds flow statement   345
cash-in-hand   26, 28–30
cashbook   23–6, **25**, 118
   columnar   27–8
   correcting errors   123–5
   developments from   31–3
   illustrated   23–8
   petty   26, 30
   receipts and payments   25–6
   reconciliation   122–6
   summary of   38
central government   46
chairman's statement   347–8
charities   46
   regulation   323
chart of accounts   109, 116–18
claims *see* liabilities and claims
classical model   412–13
closing balance   118–19
collective bargaining   400
commercial organizations   **46**, 78–81
commodity image   413
Companies Acts   16, 302, 305
   variations between nations   303–4
company   **45**, 225–7, 273–4
   annual report disclosures   393–7
company law   305–16
   accounting requirements   306–7
   organizational requirements   306
conceptual framework   321
conservatism principle *see* prudence
   (conservatism) principle
consistency convention   141
consolidation accounts   138
continuously contemporary accounting
   (CoCoa)   389
control account   120
conventional (traditional) accounting
   core/advanced techniques of
      four characteristics   9–11
conventions
   accounting   137–42
   conflict between   141
copyright   145
The Corporate Report (1975)   393, 394, 397
corporate social reporting *see* social and
   environmental accounting and reporting

cost of sales adjustment (COSA)   372
cost(s)
    direct **221**
    indirect **221**
    of sales/goods   209–11
    true   236
    unexpired   247
    verses NRV   216–17, 232–4
Council on Economic Priorities   402
Counter Information Services   402
creditors   75
    ledger   118
    sundry   158
credits   **53**–4
cross cast   27
currencies   34
    foreign   321, 324
current account   **277**, 279–80
current cost (value)   370
current economic reality   413
current (general) purchasing power (CPP)
        370, 374
    capital   380, 381–2
    illustrated   374
current ratio   356
cut-off   142

data   109
    capturing   112–14
    control processes   111
data orientated approach   414–18
Davis *et al.*,   413
day books/journals   111
    illustrated   114–16
    purchases   114–15
    sales   114–15
debits   **53**–4
debtors   76–7
    collection ratio   355
    control account   120
    ledger   118
debts
    ageing   244
    bad   149, **238**–9, 239–41, 242–6
    doubtful   149, 238–**9**, 241–2, 242–6
decision and control subsystem   50
decision makers research   **418**–22
decision models research   **418**, 422–3
decision usefulness   412, 414, 418–23
    makers and models   418–23
    strong   413
    weak   413

depreciation   149, 180–1, 186
    arbitrariness   201–2
    backlog   386
    bookkeeping for   187–91
    calculation of   181–6
    charge for the year   187
    and fixed assets   193–7
    illustrated   187–91, 191–6
    on land and buildings   200
    and non-Anglo Americans   202
    policy on   181
    reducing balance   181, 183–5, 186
    for replacement   200–1
    straight line   181, 182–3, 186
    sum of digits   185
    for taxation   202
deprival value   389
directors   306, **310**
    report   310–13, 347–8
disclosure
    of accounting policies   319–22
    of information   298
discounting   369
disposal of asset
    account   197–8
    illustrated   199
    profit and loss on   197–8
dividends   87, 262
    cumulative   256
    final   264
    fixed   256
    interim   264
    proposed   264, 266
    variable   256
double-entry   53–4, 57
    bookkeeping   55–8, 96–9
    for end of period stock   299–32
doubtful debts   149, 238-**9**, 242–6
    accounting   241–2
    provisions for   241–2
drawings   **261**–2
duality   53

earned economic income (EEI)   389
earnings
    allocation   259–61
    from previous years   263–6
    per share (EPS)   361
    price (PE)   362
    yield   362
eco/ecological
    efficiency   405

footprint 405
justice 405
economic
events 9–10
value 369
education and training 17–18
deep/shallow learning **18**
effectiveness 36
efficiency 36
employee/employment reporting 398–400
end of period adjustments 102, 118, 148–9, 156–7
entity convention 138
entry value 374–5
environment
general 49
substantial 47, 49–50
environmental
accounting and reporting 403–5
reporting award schemes 404–5
equity 255
estimated
scrap value **181**
useful life **181**
ethical choice 37
ethical investment 402–3
European Union 301, 305
events accounting 416, 417
exceptional/extraordinary items **319**
exit value 374–5
expense determination *see* assets, valuation
expenses 102, **132**, 143–4
extended trial balance 102, 131
illustrated 136–7
exploration costs 145

financial
description 10
management **15**–6
record keeping 23
financial accounting 12–3
alternative approaches 303–4
data oriented 414–18
decision usefulness 418–23
organizational resource 424–6
problem 412
regulation 300–5
structure 13–15, 436–7
Financial Reporting Council 317
Financial Reporting Exposure Drafts (FRED's) 317
Financial Reporting Standards (FRS) 39, 317

financial statements 109, 129–32
illustrated 167–9, 169–71
reading 309–10
supplementary 308
true and fair view 149, 304, 306
usefulness 331
users of 330–1
financial transactions 12
eight types **72–3**
in practice 73–8
finished goods **220**
first in/first out (FIFO) 213–**14**
fixed assets 149
depreciation 193–7
disposal 197–9
illustrated 199
focal organization **9**, 50
illustrated 65–71
funds 23
subsystem 50
funds flow statement 336

gearing adjustment 387
gearing ratios 357–61
basic 359–60
debt to equity 359–60
percentage claims against the business 360
times interest earned 360
GEC 317
general
environment **49**
journal 118–19
general purchasing power *see* current (general) purchasing power
generally accepted accounting principles (GAAP) 301, **303**, 316
going concern convention 138–9
goodwill 145
in partnerships 287–8
grants, paid and received 76, 77–8

harmonization 304–5
Health and Safety at Work Act (1974) 399
Historical Cost Accounting (HCA) 369, 374
with money capital 380
historical record 413
holding gains
realized vs. unrealized 386
Human Information Processing (HIP) 422

ICAEW 317

imprest system   30
income   368–**9**
    in advance   160–1
    smoothing   211
income and wealth measures
    alternatives to   416–18
    rationizing   416
    traditional   415–16
indebtedness   87
independent attestation   121
inflation
    accounting   324
    debate   383–4
    valuation of assets   375–9
information
    additional   307
    for collective bargaining   400
    for control   35
    for decisions   35
    economics   412
    employee   398–400
    inputs/outputs   51
    market   347
    needs and wants   422
    supply   35, 36–7
    system   413
initial trial balance   96
    categorization   102
    illustrated   99–101
inputs   13
interest account   87
internal control *see* system of internal control
International Accounting Standards Committee
    (IASC)   304
International Accounting Standards (IAS)   304
international perspective   300
    differences between countries   303–5
    harmonization and reconciliation   304–5
inventory *see* stock
inventory turn over ratio   354
investments   75–6
investors
    financial statements   304
    ethical   402–3

Joint Stock Companies Act (1844)   6
journals *see* day books/journals

last in/first out (LIFO)   213, **214**-15
Laughlin and Puxty   413
law *see also* regulations
learning *see* education and training

Leasco-Pergamon takeover   317
leases   324
ledgers   118
    creditors   118
    debtors   118
    nominal   118
legal entity   261
level of resolution   60
liabilities   102
    of partnerships   276–7
    (un)limited   276–7
liabilities and claims   **132**, 146, 147
    current   146, 147
    long term   146, 147
licences   145
limited liability   45, 306
liquidity   **331**–4, 367
    ratios   355–7
    spectrum   335
loans   75–6, **77**
    interest   87
    principal   87
local government   46
    regulation   232
logging   59
lower of cost   216–20

management accounting system   **15**–16,   111,
    221
manufacturing account   **222**–4
    illustrated   224–34
matching convention   139–40, 180
materiality   234
Memorandum of Association   255, 311,
    312–13
    objects clause   313
monetary items   385
monetary working capital adjustment (MWCA)
    385–6
money
    capital   379–80
    measurement convention   138
    time value   385
moral hazard problem   425

nationalized industry   45
net book value (NBV)   **182**
net realizable value (NRV)   216–17, 232–4
New Consumer   402
New Economics Foundation   402
non-commercial organizations   44, 78–81
    profit and social reality   270–1

regulation   322–3

objectives   36, 42
operating
    capacity   380
    financial review   397
operation subsystem   50
organizational flows   50–2, 71–2
    illustrated   54–5, 65–71
organizational resource   424–6
    control   413, 425–6
    supply and demand   425
organizational system(s)   47–50
    open/closed   47
    subsystems   47, 50–1
organization(s)   41–**2**
    commercial   43–4, 45–6
    non commercial   44, 46–7
    types of   42–4
outputs   13
overheads   170, 22
ownership   87
ownership claims   102, 254–66
    capital   255–9
    four elements   254–5

participants   87
partnership   45
    capital account   **277**, 278–9
    current account   **277**, 279–80
    deed/agreement   277
    dissolving   286–7
    goodwill   287–8
    illustrated   280–5
    interest and salary   279
    joining and leaving   288–90
    nature of   276–7
    regulation   277
    subject to unlimited liability   276
patents   145
payments in advance see prepayments
pensions   324
periodicity convention   142
petty cashbook see cash
Plan Comptable Generale   303
position statement see balance sheet
post balance sheet events   142
predictive ability   416
prepayments   149, 158–60
    illustrated   161–6
price changes
    accounting for   370–9, 380–2

effect of   370–5
general   368
nature of   367–8
specific (relative)   368
valuation of assets   375–9
principals   425
private
    company   306
    sector   43
processes   13
producers   427–9
profit
    arbitrariness   267–9
    estimate   267–9
    gross   170
    net   170
    net after tax   254
    net before tax   254
    normal/abnormal activities   319
    retained   260
    and social reality   270–1
    super   288
    taxable   254
    trading   170
    vs. cash   334
profit and loss account   31, **130**, 307–8
    illustrated   169–70, 173, 266–7
profitability ratios   352–4
    gross margin   352
    net profit   352–3
    return on capital employed (ROCE)   353–4
proprietorship view   383
provisions   102, 144, **146**–8
    characteristics   247–9
    for doubtful debts   241–2
    general   161
    warranty   147–8
prudence (conservatism) convention   140
public
    company   **306**
    interest   16
    sector   43
purchase(s)   208–9
    ledger   118
purchasing power   368

ratio analysis   350–62
    activity   354–5
    gearing   357–61
    illustrated   351–62
    interconnections   357
    liquidity   355–7

profitability   352–4
    stock market   361–2
raw materials   **220**
realisation account   286
realizable value   139, 216–17
    accounting   374
    see also net realizable value (NRV)
reconciliations   109
    bank, see bank
    other   120
record of transactions   96
record keeping   23
    capturing   112–14
    controlling   119–26
    incomplete   113
    legal requirements   311–12
    organizing   114–19
registrar of companies   306
replacement cost accounting (RCA)   374
replacement cost (RC)
    with differing capital maintenance concepts
        382
research and development   145
reserves   102, 149
    transfer to   260, 263–6
Retail Price Index (RPI)   368
revaluation surplus   372
revenues   102, **132**, 143
    expenditure   143
risk   360
Rolls Razor Ltd   317
Rolls Royce Ltd   317

sales
    capital employed ratio   355
    trade   143
security price research (SPR)   421–2
self-checking reconciliation systems   121
share capital
    authorized   257
    issued   257
share premium   258
shareholders   306
shares
    nominal (face) value   **256**
    ordinary   **256**
    preference   **256**
Social Audit Ltd   402
social audits   **401**–2
    silent   402
social and environmental accounting and
    reporting (SEAR)   392

pros and cons   406
social reality constructs   **269**–71, 273, 290–2
social welfare   8
software development costs   145
sole traders   45
source documents   111
    illustrated   112–14
South Africa   398
spreadsheet   104–5
stakeholders   392
standards
    accounting   246, 301
    background to   316–17
    changing prices   383–4
    setters   427–9
    subject coverage   318–22
Statement on Accounting Theory and Theory
    Acceptance   412
Statements of Financial Accounting Standards
    (SFAS) and Opinions   316
Statements of Recommended Accounting
    Practice (SORPs)   317
Statements of Standard Accounting Practices
    (SSAPs)   317
statutory
    audit   **121**, 314–16
    registers   312
    returns   312
stock   149, **208**–9
    closing   211
    complex valuation   220–4
    costing   212–16
    damaged   216–20
    illustrated   209–11, 213–16, 218–20
    opening   211
    simple valuation   212–20
    turnover ratio   354
stock exchange   302
stock market ratios   362–2
    dividend coverage   361
    dividend yield   361
    earnings per share (EPS)   361
    earnings yield   362
    price earnings (PE)   362
    value of the company   362
stocktake   210, 212
substantial environment   47, 48, **49**–50
suspense/error account   120, 121
sustainable development   **404**–5
system **47**
    of internal control (SIC)   109, 120
    organizational   47–50

T-accounts
    illustrated   93–9
taxation   76, 254, 303
trade unions   400
trademarks   145
trading account **222**–4
    illustrated   224–34
traditional accounting *see* conventional
    accounting
training *see* education and training
transnational corporations (TNCs)   **300**, 325
treasureship   332
trial balance
    categorization of   252–3
    illustrated   99–101

triple bottom line   405
true and fair view   149, 304, 306

ultra vires   313
unit of account   23, 34
unlimited liability of partnerships   276
users of information   10–11, 13

value added statement (VAS)   394–7
value to the business   389
voluntary disclosure   394

work in progress   **220**
working capital   335
    management   332